FIFTH EDITION

Introduction to the Counseling Profession

David Capuzzi
Pennsylvania State University
Professor Emeritus, Portland State University

Douglas R. Gross
Professor Emeritus, Arizona State University

Columbus, Ohio
Upper Saddle River, New Jersey

Library of Congress Cataloging-in-Publication Data

Introduction to the counseling profession / David Capuzzi, Douglas R. Gross, co-editors.— 5th ed.
    p. cm.
Includes bibliographical references and index.
    ISBN-13: 978-0-205-59177-0
    ISBN-10:   0-205-59177-9
1. Counseling—Vocational guidance. I. Capuzzi, David. II. Gross, Douglas R.
BF636.64.I58 2008
158'.3—dc22   2007050318

Vice President and Executive Publisher: *Jeffery W. Johnston*
Acquisitions Editor: *Meredith D. Fossel*
Director of Marketing: *Quinn Perkson*
Editorial Assistant: *Maren Vigilante*
Marketing Manager: *Kris Ellis-Levy*
Production Editor: *Mary Beth Finch*
Editorial Production Service: *TexTech International*
Electronic Composition: *TexTech International*
Composition Buyer: *Linda Cox*
Manufacturing Buyer: *Linda Morris*
Cover Administrator: *Joel Gendron*

This book was set in Janson by TexTech. It was printed and bound by R. R. Donnelley. The cover was printed by Phoenix Color.

Pearson Education Ltd.
Pearson Education Singapore Pte. Ltd.
Pearson Education Canada, Ltd.
Pearson Education—Japan

Pearson Education Australia Pty. Limited
Pearson Education North Asia Ltd.
Pearson Educación de Mexico, S.A. de C.V.
Pearson Education Malaysia Pte. Ltd.

Merrill
is an imprint of

www.pearsonhighered.com

10 9 8 7 6 5 4 3 2 1
ISBN 13: 978-0-205-59177-0
ISBN 10:   0-205-59177-9

CONTENTS

iii

16 **Counseling in Mental Health and Private Practice Settings   421**

Jane E. Rheineck

PREFACE

The profession of counseling is best described as one through which counselors interact with clients to assist them in learning about and dealing with themselves and their environment and the roles and responsibilities inherent in the interactive process. Individuals exploring counseling as a career choice need to be aware of the personal, professional, and societal demands that are placed on the professional counselor. The role of the professional counselor calls for individuals who are skilled and knowledgeable in the process and theory that undergird the profession, who are able and willing to reach deeper levels of self-understanding, and who are able to integrate this skill, knowledge, and self-understanding to provide the effective counseling interaction to which clients are entitled. Individuals attempting to decide whether this career choice is right for them will find the information in this book helpful in the decision-making process.

This book is unique in both format and content. The contributed-chapter format insures that readers are getting state-of-the-art information from experts in their respective fields. The comprehensive content provides readers with coverage of topics not often addressed in introductory text books. Examples of these include chapters devoted to counseling from a rehabilitation perspective, brief therapies, and to client diagnosis and assessment (including an introduction to the *DSM-IV-TR*). A unique introductory chapter offers a comprehensive look at the historical foundations of counseling as a profession, and another explores the legal considerations in counseling. A section of four chapters looks at counseling special populations. In addition, this fifth edition continues to include useful chapters on research and writing in counseling and technology and counseling.

This book is designed for students who are taking a preliminary course in the counseling field and who are trying to determine if they are well matched to the profession of counseling; it provides an orientation to the profession and can be used by CACREP-accredited and CACREP-equivalent programs to help meet the professional orientation standard. This book presents a comprehensive overview of the major aspects of counseling as a profession and provides its reader with insight into the myriad issues that surround not only the process of counseling and its many populations but also the personal dynamics of the counselor that have an impact upon this process. We know that one textbook cannot adequately address all the factors that make up this complex profession. We have, however, attempted to provide our readers with a broad perspective on the profession of counseling.

What's New in This Edition

To ensure that readers will have the most current and authoritative information, we have commissioned new chapters on a variety of topics. New authors bring fresh perspectives and different backgrounds to five chapters in this edition. These include chapters on helping relationships, spirituality counseling, school counseling, counseling in mental health and private practice settings, and counseling gay, lesbian, bisexual, and transgender clients. More discussion of the implications of counseling with diverse populations, additional case studies, and Web resources for each chapter also add freshness and dimension to this new edition.

How This Book Is Organized

The format for this coedited and coauthored text is based upon the contributions of authors selected for their expertise in various areas of counseling. With few exceptions, each chapter contains information specific to a topic and uses case examples to demonstrate the various concepts within the chapter. The text is divided into four sections:

- Part One: Counseling Foundations
- Part Two: Counseling Skills
- Part Three: Counseling in Specific Settings
- Part Four: Counseling Special Populations.

Part One, Counseling Foundations (Chapters 1 through 6), begins by exploring the philosophical and historical perspectives that serve as the foundation of the counseling profession and then builds on this foundation, with current information regarding legislation, professional associations, certification, licensure, accreditation, and current issues and trends related to counseling in chapters entitled the Helping Relationship, Counseling People of Color, Ethics and the Beginning Counselor: Being Ethical Right from the Start, Research and Writing in Counseling, and Technology and Counseling.

Part Two, Counseling Skills (Chapters 7 through 14), introduces the skills counselors must acquire through a combination of education, supervision, and practice. These chapters are titled Individual Counseling: Traditional Approaches, Individual Counseling: Brief Approaches, Group Counseling, An Introduction to Career Counseling, Counseling and Spirituality, Creative Approaches to Counseling, Counseling Uses of Tests, and Diagnosis in Counseling. All of these chapters provide overviews and introduce readers to roles that cut across a variety of work settings.

Part Three, Counseling in Specific Settings (Chapters 15 and 16), looks at counseling in contexts that many, perhaps most, counselors eventually work in: schools, and mental health and private practice settings. These chapters, Professional School Counseling and Counseling in Mental Health and Private Practice Settings, highlight specific processes and procedures that have applications to these diverse settings.

Part Four, Counseling Special Populations (Chapters 17 through 20), covers the wide spectrum of clients who present for the services of the counselor. Included in this section are special approaches for dealing with older adults; couples and families; lesbian, gay, bisexual, transgendered, and questioning clients; and clients with disabilities. Each chapter has not only a discussion of the needs of these populations but also specialized approaches and techniques that have been found to be effective with these groups.

The editors and contributors have made every attempt to provide readers with current information in each of the twenty areas of focus. It is our hope that *Introduction to the Counseling Profession* (5th ed.) will provide the neophyte with the foundation needed to make a decision regarding future study in the professional arena of counseling.

Supplementary Resources

In addition to this book itself, both students and instructors have access to robust supports for learning and instruction.

- For instructors, a **Test Bank** is available for download from the Pearson Instructor's Resource Center. To access this resource, visit www.pearsonhighered.com and click on Instructor Support.
- For students, Pearson's unique *MyHelpingLab* (www.myhelpinglab.com) is a comprehensive resource for the helping professions, including videos, case studies, and extensive research help. This book can be packaged with access to *MyHelpingLab* at no additional cost, or students may purchase access at www.myhelpinglab.com.

Acknowledgments

We would like to thank the authors who contributed their time, expertise, and experience to the development of this textbook for the beginning professional. We are grateful to the reviewers who provided suggestions for this new edition, including Charlotte Daughhetee, Sally Murphy, Stephen Haberman, Johnette McCracken, and Salene Cowher. Our families have provided support to make our writing and editing efforts possible. We appreciate the efforts of the editorial and production staffs at Allyn & Bacon, including Virginia Lanigan, Ginny Blanford, Matthew Buchholz, Mary Beth Finch, and Douglas Korb.

David Capuzzi
Douglas R. Gross

CONTRIBUTORS

Meet the Editors

David Capuzzi, PhD, NCC, LPC, is an affiliate professor of Counselor Education, Counseling Psychology, and Rehabilitation Services at Pennsylvania State University. He is professor emeritus at Portland State University. From 2004 to 2007, he served as scholar in residence at Johns Hopkins University. He is past president of the American Counseling Association (ACA), formerly the American Association for Counseling and Development.

From 1980 to 1984, Dr. Capuzzi was editor of *The School Counselor*. He has written textbook chapters and monographs on the topic of preventing adolescent suicide and is coeditor and author, with Dr. Larry Golden, of *Helping Families Help Children: Family Interventions with School Related Problems* (1986) and *Preventing Adolescent Suicide* (1988). In 1989, 1996, 2000, 2004, and 2008 he coauthored and edited *Youth at Risk: A Prevention Resource for Counselors, Teachers, and Parents*; in 1991, 1997, 2001, 2005, and 2008, *Introduction to the Counseling Profession*; in 1992, 1998, 2002, and 2006, *Introduction to Group Work*; and in 1995, 1999, 2003, and 2007, *Counseling and Psychotherapy: Theories and Interventions*, with Douglas R. Gross. He also wrote *Approaches to Group Work: A Handbook for Practitioners* (2003), and *Sexuality Issues in Counseling* (coauthored and edited with Larry Burlew), and *Suicide Across the Life Span* (2004). He recently coedited *Career Counseling: Foundations, Perspectives, and Applications* (2006) and *Foundations of Addictions Counseling* (2008) with Mark D. Stauffer. He has also authored or coauthored articles in a number of ACA-related journals.

A frequent speaker and keynoter at professional conferences and institutes, Dr. Capuzzi has also consulted with school districts and community agencies interested in initiating prevention and intervention strategies for adolescents at risk for suicide. He has facilitated the development of suicide prevention, crisis management, and postvention programs in communities throughout the United States; provides training on the topics of youth at risk and grief and loss; and serves as an invited adjunct faculty member at other universities as time permits. He is the first recipient of ACA's Kitty Cole Human Rights Award and also a recipient of the Leona Tyler Award in Oregon.

Douglas R. Gross, PhD, NCC, is a professor emeritus at Arizona State University, Tempe, where he served as a faculty member in counselor education for 29 years. His professional work history includes public school teaching, counseling, and administration. He is currently retired and living in Michigan. He has been president of the Arizona Counselors Association, president of the Western Association for Counselor Education and Supervision, chairperson of the Western Regional Branch Assembly of the ACA, president of the Association for Humanistic Education and Development, and treasurer and parliamentarian of the ACA.

Dr. Gross has contributed chapters to seven textbooks: *Counseling and Psychotherapy: Theories and Interventions* (1995, 1999, 2003, 2007), *Youth at Risk: A Resource Guide for Counselors, Teachers, and Parents* (1989, 1996, 2000, 2004, 2008), *Foundations of Mental Health Counseling* (1986, 1996), *Counseling: Theory, Process and Practice* (1977), *The Counselor's Handbook* (1974), *Introduction to the Counseling Profession* (1991, 1997, 2001, 2005, 2008), and *Introduction to Group Work* (1992, 1998, 2002, 2006). His research has appeared in the *Journal of Counseling Psychology, Journal of Counseling and Development, Association for Counselor Education and Supervision Journal, Journal of Educational Research, Counseling and Human Development, Arizona Counselors Journal, Texas Counseling Journal*, and *AMACH Journal*.

For the past 15 years, Dr. Gross has provided national training in bereavement, grief, and loss.

Meet the Authors

Christina L. Aranda, BA, is a doctoral student in the Counseling Psychology program at the University of Oregon. She received her BA in psychology with a specialization in health and development from Stanford University in 2003. She has served as a group home counselor for adolescents in the foster care system and as a behavior therapist for children with autism. Her research and clinical interests include stress and coping for families with children with disabilities.

Malachy Bishop, PhD, is a certified rehabilitation counselor and an associate professor of Rehabilitation Counseling in the Department of Special Education and Rehabilitation Counseling at the University of Kentucky. He completed his doctoral study in rehabilitation psychology at the University of Wisconsin–Madison. He has worked in a range of professional settings serving persons with disabilities as a rehabilitation counselor and rehabilitation psychologist. His research interests include quality of life, adaptation to chronic illness and disability, and the psychological and social aspects of chronic neurological conditions. Dr. Bishop has made more than 30 presentations at national and international professional and consumer conferences. He has coauthored one book and written several book chapters and more than 35 journal articles.

Teresa M. Christensen, PhD, is a licensed professional counselor in Virginia and a licensed professional counselor and board approved supervisor in Louisiana. She is also a nationally certified counselor, a certified school counselor in Idaho and Louisiana, and a registered play therapist-supervisor who has counseled children, adolescents, and families for more than 15 years. In 2006, Dr. Christensen moved from New Orleans to Norfolk, Virginia. She is currently an associate professor of Counselor Education at Old Dominion University and works part-time at a private practice where she offers play therapy and counseling to children, adolescents, and families. Prior to moving to Virginia, she was an associate professor of Counselor Education at the University of New Orleans and the director of School Counseling for the UNO Charter School Initiative. Dr. Christensen has received several awards, most recently the Best Group Research Article of the Year in an ACA Journal 2006 Award. She serves on the Executive Board for the Association for Play Therapy and has served on several editorial boards for professional journals, including *Counselor Education and Supervision*, the *Journal for Specialists in Group Work*, and the *Journal of School Counseling*. She is actively involved in state and national organizations, including the American Counseling Association, the Association for Counselor Education and Supervision, the American School Counseling Association, the Association for Specialists in Group Work, and the Association for Play Therapy.

Tamara Davis, EdD, EdS, is an associate professor of Psychology at Marymount University in Arlington, Virginia. With almost 20 years of experience in education, she teaches primarily graduate school counseling courses in Marymount's CACREP-accredited program. Prior to working in higher education, Dr. Davis was an elementary and high school counselor for 9 years in Manassas, Virginia. She has been president of the Virginia Association for Counselor Education and Supervision and president of the Virginia School Counselor Association. Dr. Davis has made presentations locally, regionally, and nationally on school counseling topics. Her publications include the book *Exploring School Counseling: Professional Practices & Perspectives* (2005), a student resource manual for a textbook on theories of counseling, and several book chapters and articles. Dr. Davis has been selected as the 2007 American School Counselor Association Counselor Educator of the Year.

Jessica M. Diaz, MA, is a doctoral student in the Counselor Education Program at the University of Maryland. Ms. Diaz received her master of arts degree in Rehabilitation Counseling at the University of Maryland. Her research interests include issues in multicultural counseling and mentoring relationships in the Latino community. In conjunction with Dr. Courtland Lee, she has made presentations at national conferences on research topics in multicultural counseling and the cross-cultural zones of counseling.

Sarah K. Dixon, MPH, graduated with her master of public health degree specializing in Health Promotion from The George Washington University. She is currently a Counseling Psychology doctoral student at Arizona State University. Her research interests include professional ethics.

Cass Dykeman, PhD, is cochair ad interim and associate professor of Counselor Education at Oregon State University. He is a national certified counselor, master addictions counselor, and national certified school counselor. Dr. Dykeman received a master's in Counseling from the University of Washington and a doctorate in Counselor Education from the University of Virginia. He served as principal investigator for two federal grants in the area of counseling. In addition, he is the author of numerous books, book chapters, and scholarly journal articles. Dr. Dykeman is past president of both the Washington State Association for Counselor Education and Supervision and the Western Association for Counselor Education and Supervision. He is also past chair of the School Counseling Interest Network of the Association for Counselor

Education and Supervision. His current research interests include addiction counseling and psychopharmacology.

Jeannie Falkner, PhD, MSSW, has more than 25 years of clinical experience in private practice working with individuals, children, adolescents, and groups. Dr. Falkner has presented numerous national and regional workshops on the role of money in group counseling and financial wellness for counselors. Her research interests include integrated health and mental health and resiliency in African American families in the Mississippi Delta. She is currently an assistant professor of Social Work at Delta State University.

Linda H. Foster, PhD, NCC, NCSC, LPC, is a national certified counselor, a licensed professional counselor, and a national certified school counselor. She is a member of the Board of Directors of the National Board for Certified Counselors (2004–2010). She worked with the National Board for Certified Counselors in updating the standards for the National Certified School Counselor credential, in creating the revised National Certified School Counselor Examination, and in serving as NBCC's liaison to the National Board for Professional Testing Standards. She recently joined the faculty at the University of Alabama at Birmingham as an assistant professor and clinical coordinator in the Counselor Education Program, Department of Human Studies.

Harriet Glosoff, PhD, NCC, LPC, ACS, is an associate professor and director of Counselor Education at the University of Virginia. She has a doctorate degree from American University in Counseling and Human Development and a master's degree in Counseling and Student Personnel Services from the University of Maryland. She is a licensed professional counselor (Mississippi), national certified counselor, and a nationally approved clinical supervisor. Her multifaceted professional background includes teaching, counseling supervision, research, and providing counseling services in diverse settings, including community mental health agencies, inpatient and outpatient psychiatric facilities, public schools (kindergarten–higher education), and private practice. She has served as the assistant executive director for the American Counseling Association (ACA) and remains active in the ACA at the national, state, and regional levels. She most recently served as president of the Association for Counselor Education and Supervision (ACES), cochair of the ACA Ethics Committee, and a member of the ACA Code of Ethics Revision Task Force. Her current primary professional and research interests are in the areas of ethical and cultural issues in counseling, supervision, and counseling education; ethical decision-making processes; and spirituality in counseling.

Melinda Haley, PhD, received her doctorate in Counseling Psychology from New Mexico State University in Las Cruces and completed her internship at Texas Women's University in Denton, Texas. She currently works for South Texas Rural Health Services, a nonprofit organization dedicated to providing medical, dental, and mental health services to the poor. Dr. Haley has written numerous book chapters and multimedia presentations on topics as diverse as group psychotherapy and counseling, school counseling, career counseling, counseling theory, single parenting, teen sexuality, technology in counseling, and risks and protective factors associated with suicide. She has extensive applied experience in working with adults, adolescents, inmates, domestic violence offenders, and culturally diverse populations in assessment, diagnosis, treatment planning, crisis management, and intervention. Her planned therapeutic specialties include mood disorders, personality disorders, and multicultural issues in therapy. Dr. Haley's research interests include multicultural issues in counseling, personality development over the lifespan, personality disorders, psychology of criminal and serial offenders, trauma and posttraumatic stress disorder, bias and racism, and social justice issues.

Jeneka Joyce, BA, is a Counseling Psychology student at the University of Oregon. Before pursuing doctoral studies, she served as an AmeriCorps member working collaboratively with teachers to close the achievement gap in high-poverty elementary schools. Her research interests include risk and protective factors for ethnic minority and sexual minority youth, adolescent psychosocial development, and the intersections of race/ethnicity, gender, and sexuality in the workplace.

Courtland C. Lee, PhD, is a professor and director of the Counselor Education Program at the University of Maryland, College Park. He has edited or coedited four books on multicultural counseling and two books on counseling and social justice. He is also the author of three books on counseling African American males. In addition, he has published numerous articles and book chapters on counseling across cultures. Dr. Lee is president of the International Association of Counselling and a past president of the American Counseling Association.

Rolla E. Lewis, EdD, NCC, is an associate professor of Educational Psychology and School Counseling coordinator at California State University, East Bay. His research and scholarship interests include developing an eco-contextual model to guide school counseling education programs and practices, using structured narratives and appreciative inquiry in counseling and supervision, and creating university–community collaborations that place counselors-in-training in service to high-need youth and families. When at Portland State University, he was recognized twice with the Civic Engagement Award for creating programs that build upon local knowledge and community service. Dr. Lewis has published numerous chapters and articles and has developed web-based venues for professional school counselors to share what works best in their learning communities to construct programs that help all students live up to their greatest potential. He was awarded the Oregon Counseling Association's Leona Tyler Award for outstanding contributions to professional counseling.

Benedict T. McWhirter, PhD, is an associate professor of Counseling Psychology at the University of Oregon. He teaches many counseling courses, with emphasis on courses related to working with at-risk youth, helping skills, and counselor supervision theory, models, and practica. His primary research focuses on the factors that contribute to risk and resilience and interventions and outcomes for late adolescents to early adults, including youth who are at risk for problem behavior and college students. He is also interested in ethnic identity as a protective factor and the development of multicultural competencies among counseling professionals. His publications include coauthoring *At Risk Youth: A Comprehensive Response* (4th ed., 2007). For each of the past 12 years, Dr. McWhirter has visited and worked in Penalolen, Chile, a poor community of Santiago, where with his wife, Dr. Ellen Hawley McWhirter, he has conducted pro bono training workshops for couples on conflict resolution, family communication, parenting, and group leadership skills. He was named a Fulbright Scholar to Chile in 2004. He currently continues his international research, service, and teaching activities.

Ellen Hawley McWhirter, PhD, is an associate professor in the Counseling Psychology program at the University of Oregon. Dr. McWhirter is the author of *Counseling for Empowerment* and coauthor of *At-Risk Youth: A Comprehensive Response* (4th ed.). Her scholarship areas include social cognitive factors associated with the career development of adolescents of color and girls, prevention practice for youth at risk, and empowerment in counseling. Her teaching interests include theories of career development and adult practica.

Jennifer J. Miesch, MA, is a doctoral student in the Counseling Psychology program at the University of Oregon. She received her BA from Berea College and her MA in counseling psychology from Lewis & Clark College. Her interests include facilitation of self-efficacy, self-esteem, empowerment, and connectedness for women in career and life transitions.

Rochelle Moss, PhD, is currently an assistant professor in the Counselor, Adult, and Rehabilitation Education Department at the University of Arkansas at Little Rock. She taught previously at Texas A&M–Commerce and the University of Mississippi, was a school counselor for 15 years, and has worked in private practice for 8 years. She also served an internship at a residential treatment center. Dr. Moss holds professional counseling licenses in Texas and Arkansas and has worked extensively with adolescents, young adults, and college athletes, as well as cancer patients and their families. Her research interests include eating disorders, body image, addictive behaviors, and effective strategies for counseling adolescents.

Jane E. Rheineck, PhD, is currently an assistant professor in Counseling, Adult and Higher Education at Northern Illinois University. Dr. Rheineck has worked with children and adolescents as a mental health counselor in inpatient residential treatment, outpatient treatment, and the schools. Her publications and research reflect her work with not only children and adolescents but also other marginalized populations, including people of color and the lesbian and gay community. In addition to Dr. Rheineck's clinical experience, she has given presentations nationally on multicultural and diversity issues in counseling, supervision in counseling, gender issues, sexual identity development and its relationship to career development, and adolescent and college student development.

Sharon E. Robinson Kurpius, PhD, after graduating from Indiana University with her doctorate in Counseling and Educational Inquiry Methodology, joined the Counseling and Counseling Psychology faculty at Arizona State University, where she is now a full professor. She teaches and researches the topic of professional ethics. In addition, she sits on the Ethics Committee for the American Counseling Association.

Linda Seligman, PhD, LPC, was a writer, professor, researcher, and practicing counselor and psychologist. Before her death in December, 2007, she was the author of 14 books, including *Selecting Effective Treatments, Diagnosis and Treatment Planning in Counseling,* and *Theories of Counseling and Psychotherapy.* She also wrote more than 75 professional articles and book chapters. Dr. Seligman was a licensed psychologist and a licensed professional counselor. She had a private practice in Bethesda, Maryland, where she specialized in counseling people with depression and anxiety, as well as people coping with chronic and life-threatening illnesses. Dr. Seligman also was professor emeritus at George Mason University, where she was a full professor, codirector of the doctoral program in Education, and coordinator of the Counseling and Development Program and the Community Agency Counseling Program. She was a faculty member at Walden University and a faculty associate at Johns Hopkins University. Dr. Seligman served as editor of the *Journal of Mental Health Counseling* and president of the Virginia Association of Mental Health Counselors. The American Mental Health Counselors Association selected her as Researcher of the Year. In addition, she served as consultant to many professional organizations, including the American Counseling Association, the American Mental Health Counselors Association, Sage Publications, and the Department of Health and Human Services.

Laura R. Simpson, PhD, earned her doctorate in Counselor Education from the University of Mississippi. An assistant professor of Counselor Education, Dr. Simpson is a licensed professional counselor, national certified counselor, and approved clinical supervisor, with 15 years of experience as a mental health clinician. She has presented research at state, regional, and national conferences and serves on the boards for the Mississippi Counseling Association and the Mississippi Licensed Professional Counselor Association. She has published numerous scholarly writings within professional journals and counseling textbooks. Her primary areas of interest include counselor wellness and secondary trauma, spirituality, crisis response, cultural diversity, and supervision.

Donna Starkey, PhD, earned her doctorate in Counselor Education from the University of Mississippi. An assistant professor of Counselor Education at Delta State University, Dr. Starkey is a licensed professional counselor, national certified counselor, and approved clinical supervisor. In addition to teaching, her professional experiences include providing vocational preparation for individuals with developmental disabilities, working with children and adolescents in residential group home settings, serving as the adult outpatient services coordinator in a community mental health setting, and supervising students in a university counseling center. Her primary areas of interest include self-disclosure research, counselor development, ethics, and supervision.

Mark D. Stauffer, PhD, specialized in couples, marriage, and family counseling during his graduate work in the Counselor Education Program at Portland State University, where he worked as a research assistant before entering the doctoral program in Counselor Education and Supervision at Oregon State University. Dr. Stauffer enjoys scholarly writing and has coedited three textbooks: the 2006 editions of *Introduction to Group Work* and *Career Counseling: Foundations, Perspectives and Applications* and the 2008 *Foundations of Addictions Counseling*. He has worked in the Portland, Oregon, metro area at crisis centers and nonprofit organizations with individuals, couples, and families. He has studied and trained in the Zen tradition and is vitally interested in the use of meditation and mindfulness in the counseling process.

Jason Vasquez, MA, is a doctoral student in the Counseling Psychology program at New Mexico State University in Las Cruces. He has experience in assessment, diagnosis, and outpatient counseling with populations such as high school students, college students, domestic violence offenders, older adults, and ethnically diverse populations. He has extensive teaching experience at the university level in introductory psychology, human development, adolescent development, and gender roles. His professional research interests include identity development, multicultural counseling, sex therapy, and social justice issues.

Ann Vernon, PhD, recently retired from the University of Northern Iowa, where she was a professor and coordinator of the School and Mental Health Counseling programs for 23 years. Dr. Vernon has written numerous books, chapters, and articles, primarily related to counseling children and adolescents. Her specialty is applications of REBT with children and adolescents, and she has published several emotional education curricula (*Thinking, Feeling, Behaving* and *The Passport Program*) and a book on individual counseling interventions, *What Works When with Children and Adolescents*. Currently, Dr. Vernon is a visiting professor at the University of Oradea in Romania, where she teaches school counseling courses. She also regularly conducts REBT workshops in the Netherlands and Australia.

PART ONE

Counseling Foundations

Counseling as a profession has an interesting history and encompasses a number of basic premises and foundational perspectives in which the counselor needs to be educated. This section provides the beginning counseling student with an overview of both the historical context of counseling and the philosophical basis on which the counselor operates. It introduces the counseling student to not only the process of counselor–client interaction, the helping relationship, but also information dealing with diversity issues in counseling and with ethical and legal considerations. It also provides the student with important information on research and writing in counseling, as well as on technology and counseling.

The development of counseling as a distinct profession is outlined in Chapter 1, "The Counseling Profession: Historical Perspectives and Current Issues and Trends." It traces the roots of counseling from the vocational guidance movement at the beginning of the 20th century to the current status of professional associations, legislation, certification, licensure, accreditation, and current issues and trends related to counseling.

Chapter 2, "The Helping Relationship," presents to students the characteristics and qualities that distinguish helping professionals. Essential components of the helping relationship and personal qualities that effective helpers possess are described, as well as basic and advanced skills and concepts pertinent to the development of a safe and productive counseling relationship. These core skills—and the corresponding integration of case study material—provide a foundation for the beginning counselor to both understand the counseling process and become more self-aware about his or her own interpersonal interactions.

Most counselors, regardless of their particular work setting or client population, will need to confront the issue of effective multicultural counseling. Chapter 3, "Counseling People of Color," presents a 21st-century paradigm for responding to the challenges and opportunities in counseling people of color. Demographics, history, race and ethnicity, an exploration of the "cross-cultural zone," ethical considerations, and guidelines for ethnically responsive counseling are discussed to provide the beginning professional with an excellent introduction to the topic.

The relationship between the client and the counselor does not exist in a vacuum; rather, it is ingrained in the personal, legal, and ethical context of our society.

Counselors are often called upon to make decisions regarding clients when the "correct" mode of action may not be immediately clear. There may be two contradictory obligations—for example, the obligation to respect the confidentiality of a client and the obligation to protect that client from self-harm or from harming others. When faced with situations such as this, the counselor cannot rely simply on personal judgment but, instead, needs to act on the basis of the professional guidelines and codes of ethics of the counseling and human development professions. Chapter 4, "Ethics and the Beginning Counselor: Being Ethical Right from the Start," provides an overview of the ethical and legal guidelines on which counselors must base their decisions. It discusses the role of personal values versus professional ethics, the question of counselor competence, clients' rights, confidentiality (including HIPAA and the "Privacy Rule") and informed consent, and the practicalities of dealing with legal issues and client-related litigation. The chapter also reflects the increasing commitment among members of the profession to respect the diversity of our clientele. Such concepts are essential for the beginning counselor to understand and incorporate in gaining a sense of the professional status of the counselor.

Research and writing are major components of the experience of counselor education students in graduate programs all over the country. The fifth chapter in this text, "Research and Writing in Counseling," provides the beginning student with invaluable information about the integration of research, practice, and theory; the definition of research; how to access databases; the differences between and value of both quantitative and qualitative research; guidelines for writing a term paper and developing thesis and dissertation proposals; and the ethics of writing and conducting research. This chapter is critical to the future success of all those working toward the completion of an advanced degree.

The use of technology in counseling and the possibilities for information retrieval presented by the World Wide Web is a topic of growing importance to counselors in all settings. Chapter 6, "Technology and Counseling," overviews information related to technology and its applications to counseling. Cybercounseling and distance counseling, computer-assisted counseling, technology in assessment and diagnosis, technological aids for client interventions, technologically based resources for counselors and clients, using technology for client–therapist referrals, technology in counselor supervision, technology and continuing education units, technology-aided counselor communication, and the paperwork and scheduling applications are all discussed. The content of this chapter underscores the importance of technology to the success of the counseling practitioner; it also addresses positives, negatives, and ethical issues connected with the counseling applications of technology.

1

The Counseling Profession: Historical Perspectives and Current Issues and Trends

HARRIET L. GLOSOFF, PhD
University of Virginia

Historical and Formative Factors

If one assumes that counseling is advising, counselors have existed since people appeared on earth. Mothers, fathers, friends, lovers, clergy, and social leaders all provide such counsel—whether sought after or not. The idea of a professionally trained counselor is relatively new. This idea did not, however, emerge because of the recognition of a "deep need within human development" (Stripling, 1983, p. 206). The counseling profession evolved in response to the demands made by the industrialization and urbanization of the United States. At the turn of the 20th century, America faced a confluence of social and economic problems, such as the proper distribution of a growing workforce, an increasingly educated population, the needs of immigrants, and the preservation of social values as family connections were weakened (Aubrey, 1982; Herr, 1985).

A representative democracy demands an educated citizenry taking responsibility for the government itself. As the new democracy developed, so did the ideal of education for all citizens. Toward the end of the 19th century, the curriculum of schools began to change, and choices among school subjects became available. Help with such choices was necessary. Jessie Davis, one of the pioneers in counseling, declared in his autobiography that he had graduated from school "fairly well prepared to live in the

I would like to extend my gratitude and appreciation to Perry Rockwell Jr., PhD, professor emeritus of Counselor Education at the University of Wisconsin at Platteville. His pioneer work in the historical underpinning of guidance and counseling in the United States formed the bases for the first edition of this chapter. I also would like to thank Scott Barstow, director of public policy for the American Counseling Association, for information on federal legislation enacted since the last edition of this chapter.

Middle Ages" (Davis, 1956, p. 57). His experiences led directly to the establishment of guidance and counseling services in schools. Other factors were providing pressures that made the evolution of professionally training individuals to help people make choices inevitable. The industrial revolution and its attendant job specialization and technologic advances were some of those pressures. There was also an increase in democracy after the Civil War ended in 1865. If the United States had continued to exist as a slave society or a closed class society, there probably would have been little need for the development of counseling services.

The population of the country was on the increase, and the census of 1890 revealed that the frontier was essentially closed. Larger cities were growing increasingly more crowded, and immigrants to the United States and other citizens could no longer move westward without regard for others. "Free" land was all but gone. It became necessary to remain near the cities to work, to live, and to get along with one's neighbors. Providing assistance in the choices necessary to live in the large industrially based cities became necessary.

During the 20th century, the development of professional counseling in the United States was influenced by a variety of factors. The newly developed science of psychology began, and continued, studying the differences among individuals. Instruments for appraising people were in their infancy but were known to pioneers in the field, who noted the need for counseling services. As these tools developed more sophistication, they were adapted and/or adopted by counselors. Other factors contributing to the evolution of counseling included the work of leaders of the early settlement house movement and other social reformers; the mental hygiene movement; the extent to which Americans value personal success; the emphasis placed on the awareness and use of one's talents, interests, and abilities; the ongoing industrialization of the country; the continued growth of career education and career guidance; the development of psychology as a profession; and the rapid changes in all fields due to the increased availability of technology (Shertzer & Stone, 1986).

Pressures from various socioeconomic factors also led to the kaleidoscope we know as counseling today. The history of counseling has continued the thread of individual choice in a society that prizes freedom to choose as an ideal. Like a kaleidoscope, the form, emphasis, and brightness of various aspects of counseling have changed as society changes. This chapter examines the following select facets of that kaleidoscope that have shaped the counseling profession:

- The vocational guidance movement
- The mental health counseling movement
- The development of professional identity
- The influence of federal legislation
- The history of the American Counseling Association
- Credentialing and the "professionalization" of counseling

The chapter concludes with a brief review of current issues and trends in the counseling profession.

Beginnings of the Vocational Guidance Movement

Perhaps the earliest notion of professional counseling in response to societal pressures was that of Lysander S. Richards. In 1881, Richards published a slim volume titled *Vocophy*. He considered vocophy to be a "new profession, a system enabling a person to name the calling or vocation one is best suited to follow" (Richards, 1881). His work has been dismissed because there is no documented proof that he actually established the services he advocated. Nevertheless, his ideas foreshadowed what was to come. He called his counselors "vocophers" and urged that they study occupations and the people they counseled.

Richards (1881) included letters from various famous people of the day in his book *Vocophy*. He believed that aspirants to particular occupations should consider what successful people had to say about the qualifications for success in that field. Letters from Grant, Longfellow, Westinghouse, and others, which described the ingredients for success in their occupations, were included in the book.

Later, a series of pamphlets published by the Metropolitan Life Insurance Company in the 1960s and used widely by school counselors asked the question, "Should your child be a ———?" A famous person in a field would describe what was necessary for success in that field. Using successful people to provide career information is a technique employed by counselors today as well.

Richards also seemed advanced for his time regarding his views of women and youth and their work. He said that if a woman could do the work "though at present solely followed by man, there can be no objections, whether normally or religiously considered, to her following it" (Richards, 1881, preface). He deplored the drifting of youth from job to job without consideration of what would be best for them and for society.

Whether Richards influenced those who followed is speculative. Influence is the quicksilver of history. He was active in the literary societies in the Boston area, as was Frank Parsons. Did they meet? Did they debate? Richards's *Vocophy* was in the Harvard Library in the 1890s. In an article published in the later 1890s, Parsons (1894) expressed ideas similar to those of Richards. Brewer (1942) noted that Meyer Bloomfield, a colleague of Parsons at the Breadwinners Institute, mentioned Richards in his Harvard courses, as did Henry C. Metcalf of Tufts and Frank Locke of the YMCA in Boston.

Frank Parsons

Regardless of who influenced whom, the need for counseling about vocational choice seems to have permeated American society of the late 19th and early 20th centuries. There is no question of the credit given to Frank Parsons for leading the way to vocational guidance. Parsons had a long history of concern for economic and political reforms that would benefit people. He published books and articles on a wide variety of topics, including taxation, women's suffrage, and education for all people. Of all his endeavors, Parsons was most interested in social reform and especially in assisting people to make sound occupational choices. Other pioneers in the field credited him with being the first counselor (Davis, 1914; Reed, 1944), and he has often been referred to as the "father of guidance." Parsons alone, of those individuals who had some direct connection with the organization and extension of guidance services, had a definite, well-thought-out, and organized social philosophy, which he articulated often and at length (Rockwell, 1958).

Parsons was one of the many in the late 19th and early 20th centuries who were striving to make the world a better place in which to live. These people saw in the growth of large private fortunes, based on industrial might and the resultant political power, a clear danger to the realization of a more perfect society based on the brotherhood of all humankind. They were humanitarians all, each seeking the good things in life for the individual within society. Parsons found himself in the company of such notables of this movement as Henry D. Lloyd, Edward Bellamy, Phillip Brooks, and Benjamin O. Flower (Rockwell, 1958). Parsons believed it was better to select a vocation scientifically than to drift through a variety of vocations, perhaps never finding one that would be best for the person and, thus, make society better. Meyer Bloomfield, director of the Civic Service House in Boston, asked Parsons to establish such a service within the Civic Service House. Thus, Parsons became director of what was called the Breadwinners Institute from 1905 through 1907 (Brewer, 1942). Parsons developed a plan for individualized counseling and opened the Vocational Bureau of Boston in January 1908. He served as its director and vocational counselor. The primary goal of the bureau was to develop the potential of Boston's growing immigrant population. Although Parsons was but one of many who were seeking social reforms at this time, he was able to secure the support of the leaders of powerful groups in business, labor, education, and politics. His report to the members of the board controlling the Vocational Bureau was the first recorded instance of the use of the term *vocational guidance*. (Brewer, in 1942, published the report as an appendix to his *History*.) Parsons's report emphasized that counseling was not designed to make decisions for counselees. "No attempt is made, of course, to decide FOR [*sic*] the applicant what his calling should be; but the Bureau tries to help him arrive at a wise, well-founded conclusion for himself" (Brewer, 1942, p. 304). According to Williamson (1965), this was consistent with the moral and intellectual atmosphere of that time. He traced the growth of counseling before Parsons's work to the concept of "vocational freedom of choice" (p. 3). He noted that the climate of the late 1800s stimulated practical application of vocational choice or individuals' freedom to pursue choice in personal development.

Parsons also developed a plan for the education of counselors. His plan was outlined in his book *Choosing a Vocation* (1909), published posthumously. Parsons's prescriptions for how counselees should examine themselves and their lives reflected his political and social philosophy (Rockwell, 1958, pp. 74–130).

Early Ties Between Vocational Guidance and School Counseling

Many see educational settings as the first homes to the profession of counseling, especially in terms of vocational guidance. In 1898, at about the same time that Parsons opened the Vocational Bureau, Jesse Davis began advising students about educational and vocational matters (Aubrey, 1982). Jessie B. Davis had been unsure of what he wanted to do with his life throughout his educational career. He was questioned thoroughly by Charles Thurber, one of his professors at Cornell University, and that left a lasting impression on him. He began to use the professor's methods in his work with students at the Central High School in Detroit and attempted to incorporate guidance into the normal educational experience of students. In 1907, Davis became principal of the Grand Rapids, Michigan, Central School and was able to implement his ideas of self-study, occupational study, and examination of self in relation to the chosen occupation throughout the 7th through 12th grades (Brewer, 1942). This was done primarily through essays written in English classes. Essay topics varied from self-examination of values and ideals to the selection of a vocation by the 12th grade. Throughout the topics, social and civic ethics were emphasized (Davis, 1914). Just five years later (1912), Grand Rapids established a citywide guidance department.

Grand Rapids was not the only city in the early 1900s that housed newly developed vocational guidance services. Both Anna Y. Reed in Seattle and Eli Weaver in New York established counseling services based on Social Darwinian concepts (Rockwell, 1958). Similar to Darwin's biological theory of "survival of the fittest," Social Darwinism contends that certain groups in a society become powerful because they have adapted best to the evolving requirements of that society. Reed decided that counseling services were needed for America's youth through her study of newsboys, penal institutions, and charity schools. She emphasized that business people were the most successful and that counseling should be designed to help youth emulate them. She equated morality and business ideals and was much concerned that whatever course of action was taken on any social question should be taken on the basis of social research, of economy, and of how it would be accepted by the business world. Reed urged that schools keep children focused on the potential for making money, which she believed every pupil could understand (Reed, 1916).

The guidance services that Reed developed were similar to those of modern placement agencies that focus on an individual's acceptability to employers. Other programs, she said, "savored too much of a philanthropic or social service proposition and too little of a practical commercial venture" (Reed, 1920, p. 62).

Eli Weaver also believed in working within the framework of the existing society and looked on counseling as a means of keeping the wheels of the machinery well oiled. He was chairman of the Students' Aid Committee of the High School Teachers' Association of New York in 1905. In developing the work of his committee, Weaver concluded that the students were in need of advice and counsel before their entrance into the workaday world. He had no funds or active help from school authorities but was able to secure the volunteer services of teachers to work with young people in New York. By 1910, he was able to report teachers actively attempting to aid boys and girls discover what they could do best and how to secure a job in which their abilities could be used to the fullest advantage (Brewer, 1942; Rockwell, 1958).

Counselors in the school systems of Boston and New York during the 1920s were expected to assist students in making educational and vocational choices. It was during the 1920s that the certification of school counselors began in these two cities.

It was also during that decade that the Strong Vocational Interest Inventory was first published (1928) and used by counselors, setting the stage for future directions in career counseling (Shertzer & Stone, 1986).

The Creation of the National Vocational Guidance Association

The early pioneers in counseling clearly reflected society's need for workers who were skilled and happy in what they did. A distinct influence in early counseling was the vocational education movement. In 1906, the National Society for the Promotion of Industrial Education (NSPIE) was formed. Advocates of vocational counseling served on its board and later on the board of the Vocation Bureau established by Parsons. Ralph Albertson, an employment supervisor at William Filene's Sons Company and confidant of Frank Parsons, became secretary of the board of trustees of the Vocation Bureau (Stephens, 1970). Frank Snedden, a vocational educator from Massachusetts, is given credit for suggesting that a vocational guidance conference separate from the NSPIE be held (Brewer, 1942). Such conferences were held in 1911 and 1912.

At a third national conference in 1913, the National Vocational Guidance Association (NVGA) was formed in Grand Rapids, Michigan (Norris, 1954). Frank Leavitt became the first president and noted the economic, educational, and social demands for guidance and the counseling it entailed. He also felt that it was necessary "for the very preservation of society itself" (Norris, 1954, p. 17). Counseling in regard to career choice remained an integral part of the movement.

Beginnings of the Mental Health Counseling Movement

The economic, educational, and social reform forces that led to the organization of NVGA also led to other movements, which were later incorporated into the kaleidoscope we call counseling today. In the early 1800s, American reformers such as Dorothea Dix advocated for the establishment of institutions that would treat people with emotional disorders in a humane manner. Although these reformers made great strides in accomplishing their goals, following the Civil War there was a rapid decline in the conditions related to the humane treatment of institutionalized individuals (Palmo & Weikel, 1986).

Clifford Beers, who had suffered harsh treatment for mental illness in several psychiatric institutions, published *A Mind That Found Itself*, an autobiography about his experience (Beers, 1908). Publication of this book served as a catalyst for the mental hygiene movement and studies of people with emotional and behavior problems. Early studies of children with emotional problems supported the concept of providing counseling for all children in schools. Beginning at about the same time as vocational guidance, the mental hygiene movement and the field of psychology have had equally strong influences on the development of professional counseling. In 1908, the same year Frank Parsons opened the Vocational Bureau, William Healy, a physician, established the first community psychiatric clinic. The Juvenile Psychopathic Institute was founded to provide services to young people in Chicago who were having problems. The institute used testing, modified psychoanalysis, and involvement of family members. In 1909, leaders of Cook County, Illinois, deciding that counseling services would benefit children, established countywide child guidance clinics. In this same year, the U.S. Congress founded the National Committee on Mental Hygiene.

Early Psychologists

Wilhelm Wundt must be credited with establishing, in the late 1870s in Germany, the first experimental psychology laboratory. One way that Wundt endeavored to study how the mind is structured was by using a form of introspection or asking subjects to use self-reflection and to verbalize what they were experiencing (Belkin, 1988).

In the United States, William James modified Wundt's approach and tried to discover the functions of the mind, rather than focusing primarily on its structure. James believed that individuals function as holistic beings who used thoughts, reasoning, emotions, and behaviors. James and his followers are referred to as "functionalists," and they developed experimental designs to facilitate understanding why human beings' minds function as they do (Belkin, 1988). James's interest in the ideas of "adaptive functioning," "free will," and the conscious functioning of individuals is clearly pertinent to the development of the counseling profession. A scientific approach to social problems had become popular in the late 19th and early 20th centuries. Granville Stanley Hall founded what many consider the first psychology laboratory in the United States in 1883 at Johns Hopkins University, where he focused on collecting data on the mental characteristics of children (Belkin, 1988). His study of the development of children's mental and physical abilities continued under his tenure as president of Clark University, where he emphasized graduate study and research. The scientific approach to social problems was based on the assumption that the answer to a social problem could be discovered through objective research. Many consider G. Stanley Hall the "father of American psychology" (Belkin, 1988, p. 15). Even though his work itself has not endured, in addition to founding one of the first psychology departments, G. Stanley Hall was also the primary person to organize the American Psychological Association (APA), and he bestowed the first doctorates in the field of psychology. Of course, the early behaviorists, such as John Watson and B. F. Skinner, and experimental psychologists, such as Max Wetheimer and Wolfgang Kohler, are also associated with the development of the field of psychology.

David Spence Hill, who organized the first guidance and counseling services in New Orleans, was a graduate of Clark University during the presidency of G. Stanley Hall. As director of research for the New Orleans schools, he discovered a need for guidance while researching whether there was a need for a vocational school in his district (Rockwell, 1958). He concluded that there was a need for such a high school, and he also believed it necessary to assist youth in assessing their abilities and in learning about the opportunities that would best help them use those skills. He was aware of Binet's appraisal work and attempted to use the Binet tasks in helping the students in the New Orleans schools. He realized the need for counseling because of his belief that the education of an individual must be of the highest order. Counseling based on scientific research would help secure the best education for each pupil. If counselors were to help youth know themselves and match their characteristics with qualifications for jobs, some means of measuring individual characteristics was necessary. Counselors relied a great deal on questioning youth about their abilities and their desires, with the implicit assumption that counselees know themselves and can reason about their reported skills and their qualifications for jobs. A counselor's task was to help them in this process by using greater maturity and objective judgment. The development of tests and appraisal instruments lent a scientific air to the process.

During the late 1800s and early 1900s, the testing movement was also taking hold. In the 1890s, James Cattell was the first person in this country to focus on ways to measure intelligence. In 1894, he introduced the first mental abilities test, which was administered to freshmen entering Columbia University (Goldenberg, 1973).

In 1905, the Binet-Simon Test was introduced in France. In 1916, L. M. Terman of Stanford University released a revised version of the Binet-Simon Test he had developed, titled the Stanford-Binet Test. With the release of the Stanford-Binet Test, the term *intelligence quotient* or *IQ* was first used. Although the development of the Stanford-Binet certainly helped spearhead the testing movement in the United States, it was World War I that truly gave flight to the development and use of standardized instruments (Baruth & Robinson, 1987).

Influences of World War I and the Development of Testing

World War I influenced the counseling profession's roots in both the vocational guidance and mental health arenas. The Army, in order to screen personnel, commissioned the development of psychological instruments, including the Army Alpha and Beta IQ tests of intelligence. In the period following World War I, the number and variety of such instruments proliferated, and even though counselors were not the major creators of the instruments, they became users. Counselors began to use standardized instruments as tools for use in military, educational, and clinical settings. These screening tools also supported the development of aptitude and interest tests used by counselors in business and educational settings (Aubrey, 1982). Quantifying a person's intelligence, aptitude, achievement, interest, and personality gave a great deal of credibility to a counselor's judgment about the person (Ginzberg, 1971).

After World War I, psychological testing became pervasive in industrial personnel classification, in education, and in counseling offices. Knowledge about and skill in using standardized tests became part of the education of a counselor. Data derived from appraisal instruments were used to make better judgments about counselees and to advise them about what decision was the wisest to make. Large commercial producers of psychometric devices emerged. The process of developing and marketing tests to industry, education, government, and counselors in private practice became quite sophisticated. Counselors were expected to be experts in selecting and using appropriate instruments from a myriad of those offered. Their use in the counseling process became such that testing and counseling were often considered synonymous.

The practice of using tests in counseling was not without controversy. Criteria for psychometric instruments used in decision making were not published until 1954, with the publication of the American Psychological Association's *Technical Recommendations for Psychological Tests and Diagnostic Techniques* (Stephens, 1954). Publications such as *Testing, Testing, Testing* (Joint Committee on Testing, 1962), *The Educational Decision-Makers* (Cicourel & Kitsuse, 1963), and *The Brain Watchers* (Gross, 1962) are examples of many voices questioning counselors and others' reliance on test data.

Beginnings of Professional Identity

The Great Depression and the Continuation of the Career Guidance Movement
There was continued progress in the development of career counseling during the 1930s. The Great Depression, with its loss of employment for millions of people, demonstrated the need for career counseling to assist adults as well as youth to identify, develop, and learn to market new vocational skills (Ohlsen, 1983). At the University of Minnesota, E. G. Williamson and colleagues modified the work of Frank Parsons and employed it in working with students. Their work is considered by some to be the first theory of career counseling, and it emphasized a directive, counselor-centered approach known as the "Minnesota point of view." Williamson's approach continued to emphasize matching individuals' traits with those of various jobs and dominated counseling during most of the 1930s and 1940s. The publication of the *Dictionary of Occupational Titles* in 1938 provided counselors with a basic resource to match people with occupations for which they were theoretically well suited (Shertzer & Stone, 1986).

The concept that society would be better if individuals and their occupations were matched for greater efficiency and satisfaction continued to shape the vocational guidance movement. There was a plethora of organizations dedicated to this end. In 1934, a number of them met to form the American Council of Guidance and Personnel Associations, or ACGPA (Brewer, 1942, p. 152), including the American College Personnel Association, the National Association of Deans of Women, the National Federation of Bureau of Occupations, the National Vocational Guidance Association, the Personnel Research Foundation, and the Teachers' College Personnel Association. By 1939, the name was changed to the Council of Guidance and Personnel Associations (CGPA), and other groups were added: the Alliance for the Guidance of Rural Youth, the International Association of Altrusa Clubs, the National Federation of Business and Professional Women's Clubs, the Western Personnel Service, the American Association of Collegiate Registrars (withdrew in 1941), the Institute of Women's Professional Relations, the Kiwanis International, and the Association of YMCA Secretaries met with the group from time to time.

Brewer (1942) stated that the October 1938 issue of *Occupations*, the publication of the NVGA, listed 96 organizations interested in furthering vocational guidance among the young people of the nation. Counseling per se was coming to the forefront of concerns within the vocational guidance movement. All groups seemed dedicated to placing "square pegs in square holes" through the use of tests.

During the 1950s, the U.S. government was particularly interested in issues related to vocational guidance or career guidance. In response to the Soviet Union's successful space program (for example, the launching of *Sputnik*), the government became concerned with identifying young people with scientific and mathematical talent. To this end, they passed the National Defense Education Act (NDEA) in 1958.

Some contend that the impact of NDEA goes well beyond funding of vocational guidance programs. Hoyt stated that NDEA "had a greater impact on counselor education than any other single force" (1974, p. 504). NDEA funded the training of guidance counselors at both the elementary and secondary levels, and NDEA training programs were established to produce counselors qualified for public schools (Herr, 1985). Although the legislation established counselor education programs specifically to train professionals to identify bright children and steer them into technical fields, these counselors were also trained in other domains of counseling as well.

Influence of World War II

World War II strongly influenced the confluence of the vocational guidance and mental health movements, along with that of rehabilitation counseling. The U.S. government continued to rely on standardized instruments and classification systems during World War II. The government requested that psychologists and counselors aid in selecting and training specialists for the military and industry (Ohlsen, 1983). Before and during World War II, millions of men and women were tested and assigned to particular duties according to their test scores and their requests. The armed forces stationed counselors and psychologists at many induction and separation centers. Picchioni and Bonk (1983) quote Mitchell Dreese of the adjutant general's office as saying that counseling "is essentially the same whether it be in the home, the church, the school, industry, business or the Army" (p. 54). The process was certainly an extensive use of the scientific approach to counseling. Society, through its representatives in government, had become embroiled in what counseling should be and what it should become. Society has not relinquished that sense of involvement through all the forms, shapes, and colors of the kaleidoscope counseling had become.

The use of standardized tests is not the only reason World War II had a tremendous influence on the counseling profession. Personnel were also needed on the front lines and in aid stations to help soldiers deal with "battle neuroses." This was accomplished through minimum training and what seemed to be an "overnight" credentialing of new medical school graduates and research-oriented clinical psychologists. Even though minimally trained, their interventions resulted in a significant reduction of chronic battle neuroses (Cummings, 1990).

In 1944, the War Department established the Army Separation-Classification and Counseling Program in response to the emotional and vocational needs of returning soldiers. The Veterans Administration (VA) also established counseling centers within their hospitals (Shertzer & Stone, 1986). The VA coined the term *counseling psychology* and established counseling psychology positions and training programs to fill these positions. The National Institute of Mental Health (NIMH) was established just after World War II and established a series of training stipends for graduate programs in professional psychology. NIMH reinforced the VA's standard of the doctorate being the entry level into professional psychology by setting up PhD training stipends. The American Psychological Association (APA) was asked to set standards of training for the new programs in university graduate schools. Although the goal of the VA and NIMH was to train counseling psychologists for the public sector, more and more trained psychologists chose to enter private practice.

In addition, during the 1940s a trend toward working with the psychological problems of "normal people" emerged. In reaction to the Nazi movement and World War II, humanistic psychologists and psychiatrists came from Europe to the United States. Their work gradually influenced the strong quantitative leanings in counseling and contributed to the work of well-known psychologists such as Rollo May, Abraham Maslow, and Carl Rogers.

Carl Rogers and the Continuation of the Mental Health Movement

In reviewing a history of what has happened, it is often difficult to know whether events have shaped a leader of an era or whether a person has influenced events. There seems little doubt that Carl R. Rogers, his ideas, and his disciples affected counseling from its core outward. Rogers's idea was that individuals had the capacity to explore themselves and to make decisions without an authoritative judgment from a counselor. He saw little need to make diagnoses of client problems or to provide information or direction to those he called *clients*. He emphasized the importance of the relationship between the counselor and client. In his system, the client rather than the counselor was the most important factor. Because no advice was given or persuasion used to follow a particular course, Rogers's system became known as *nondirective counseling*. Rogers became interested in the process of counseling and pioneered the electronic recording and filming of counseling sessions, an unheard-of idea at that time. Working in the academic environment of Ohio State University and the University of Chicago, Rogers published his ideas in *Counseling and Psychotherapy: Newer Concepts in Practice* in 1942 and *Client-Centered Therapy* in 1951.

It is not the purpose of this chapter to delineate all the postulates of what became known as *client-centered counseling* and, later, *person-centered counseling*. It is important to note, however, the impact that approach had on counseling has continued to the present day. The rise to prominence of Carl Rogers's theory was the first major challenge to the tenets of the Minnesota point of view. In fact, many programs at counseling conventions debated the issue of client-centered versus trait-factored counseling.

Rogers himself remained within the scientific approach to counseling. His concern was to learn what went on in the counseling process, to learn what worked (for him) and what did not. His was a search for necessary and sufficient conditions under which effective counseling could take place. Whenever research about client-centered counseling was reported by Rogers, it was supported by psychometric data. Certainly one of the effects of Rogers on the profession was to emphasize understanding the counseling process and the need for research. The ensuing debates about the primacy of feeling or rationality as a proper basis of counseling stimulated professional counselors to research their processes and techniques. Theories were refined, and new instruments for determining their efficacy were developed. Counselors in training became as familiar with recording devices as they were with textbooks.

Aubrey (1982) noted that "without doubt, the most profound influence in changing the course and direction of the entire guidance movement in the mid and late 1940s was Carl Rogers" (p. 202). Rogers built on the humanistic and individualistic foundations of the education guidance movement in which he was trained at Columbia University by formulating the nondirective client-centered approach to counseling. He brought a psychologically oriented counseling theory into the guidance movement, thus grounding the counseling profession in the broad disciplines of education and psychology (Weikel & Palmo, 1989).

Federal Legislation and Its Influence on the Counseling Profession

The Great Depression prompted the development of government-sponsored programs that included a counseling component with an emphasis on classification. Both the Civilian Conservation Corps (CCC) and the National Youth Administration (NYA) attempted to help youth find themselves in the occupational scene of the 1930s (Miller, 1971). In 1938, the George-Dean Act had appropriated $14 million for vocational education, and by 1938 the Occupational Information and Guidance Services was established. The federal government became influential in the field of counseling and remains so today.

The following list exemplifies how the federal government has influenced the development of the counseling profession by offering *examples* of governmental actions and legislation. Primary sources of this information include American Counseling Association legislative briefing papers available from the ACA Office of Public Policy and Information, S. Barstow (personal communication, August 25, 2003; May 15 and June 15, 2007), Baruth and Robinson (1987), and Vacc and Loesch (1994). This is not an exhaustive list of all legislation that has influenced professional counseling and counseling services. In addition, many of these acts (e.g., Rehabilitation Act, No Child Left Behind) must be reauthorized on a regular basis. I have noted only major revisions to the original bills enacted, rather than listing each reauthorization.

1917   *The Smith-Hughes Act* created federal grants to support a nationwide vocational education program.

1933   *The Wagner-Peyser Act* established the U.S. Employment Services.

1936   *The George-Dean Act* continued the support established by the Smith-Hughes Act.

1938   The U.S. Office of Education established the Occupational and Information Guidance Services Bureau that, among other things, conducted research on vocational guidance issues. Its publications stressed the need for school counseling.

1944   The Veterans Administration established a nationwide network of guidance services to assist veterans. The services included vocational rehabilitation, counseling, training, and advisement.

1944   The U.S. Employment Service was begun under the influence of the War Manpower Commission. Fifteen hundred offices were established, and employment "counselors" were used.

1946   *The George-Barden Act* provided government support for establishing training programs for counselors. The emphasis was on vocational guidance and established a precedent for funding training for counselors.

1946   The National Institute of Mental Health (NIMH) was established just after World War II, and the National Mental Health Act passed in 1946 authorized funds for research, demonstration, training, and assistance to states in the use of effective methods of prevention, diagnosis, and treatment of people with mental health disorders.

1954   *The Vocational Rehabilitation Act* (VRA) recognized the needs of people with disabilities. The VRA was a revision of earlier vocational rehabilitation acts and was prompted, in part, by the government's attempts to meet the needs of World War II veterans. It mandated the development of counselors who specialized in assisting persons with disabilities and allocated funds for training these counselors.

1955   *The Mental Health Study Act* of 1955 established the Joint Commission on Mental Illness and Health.

1958   As noted previously, the emphasis of the National Defense Education Act (NDEA) was on improving math and science performance in our public schools; counseling in the schools was seen as an important function in helping students explore their abilities, options, and interests in relation to career development. Title V of this act specifically addressed counseling through grants to schools to carry out counseling activities. Title V-D authorized contracts to institutions of higher education to improve the training of counselors in the schools.

1962   *The Manpower Development Training Act* established guidance services to individuals who were underemployed and/or economically disadvantaged.

1963   *The Community Mental Health Centers Act*, an outgrowth of the Mental Health Study Act, is considered by many to be one of the most crucial laws dealing with mental health that has been enacted in the United States. The act mandated the creation of more than 2,000 mental health centers and provided direct counseling services to people in the community as well as outreach and coordination of other services. The Community Mental Health Centers Act also provided opportunities for counselors to be employed outside educational settings.

1964   *The Amendment to the National Defense Education Act* of 1958 continued to affect counseling through the addition of counselors in the public schools, especially elementary schools, aimed at reducing the counselor–student ratio.

1965   *The Elementary and Secondary Education Act* (ESEA) did much to develop and expand the role of the elementary school counseling program and the services provided by the elementary school counselor.

1972   Title IX of the Education Amendments to the 1964 Civil Rights Act mandated that no one be discriminated against or excluded from participating in any federally funded educational program or activity on the basis of sex. It also prohibited sex-biased appraisal and sex-biased appraisal instruments.

1975   *Public Law (P.L.) 94-142*, also known as the Education for All Handicapped Children Act, mandated guidelines for the education of exceptional children in public schools. It declared that all children, regardless of their disabilities, were entitled to an appropriate free public education. Counselors became instrumental in designing, implementing, and evaluating the individualized education plans that were required for each student with special needs.

1976   *P.L. 94-482* extended and revised the Vocational Education Act of 1963 and its 1968 amendments. It directed states to develop and implement programs of vocational education specifically to provide equal education opportunities to both sexes and to overcome sex bias and stereotyping. It also specified that funds must be used in vocational education for individuals who are disadvantaged, had limited English proficiency, and/or had handicapping conditions.

1977   Sections 503 and 504 were added to the civil rights law typically known as the Rehabilitation Act of 1973. Section 503 mandates all employers conducting business with the federal government (meeting specific criteria) to take affirmative action in the recruitment, hiring, advancement, and treatment of qualified persons with disabilities. Section 504 notes that no qualified person (spanning all age ranges) who is disabled may be discriminated against in any federally assisted program.

1977   President Carter established the President's Commission on Mental Health.

1979   *The Veterans' Health Care Amendments* called for the provision of readjustment counseling and related mental health services to Vietnam-era veterans.

1980   *The Mental Health Systems Act* stressed the need for balancing services in both preventive and remedial mental health programs. The act required the development of new services for children, youth, minority populations, older people, and people with chronic mental illness. The act was repealed during the same year it was passed because of the severe federal budget cuts for social programs during the first year of President Reagan's term in office.

1981   *The Older Americans Act* was enacted to improve the quality of life for many individuals who are 60 years old or older by authorizing a comprehensive social services program. The act provides assistance for creation and implementation of services, including counseling.

1984   *The Carl D. Perkins Vocational Education Act* amended the Vocational Education Act of 1963. Its primary purpose was to help the states develop, expand, and improve vocational education programs. The act sought to include previously underserved people, such as those with disabilities, adults in need of training or retraining, and single parents. The legislation indicated that career guidance and counseling functions should be performed by professionally trained counselors. In addition, the entire act was filled with language that showed how important legislators believed counseling and career development services to be.

1990   *The Americans with Disabilities Act* (ADA) prohibited job discrimination against people with disabilities. It also mandated that individuals with disabilities have the same access to goods, services, facilities, and accommodations afforded to all others.

1990   *The Carl D. Perkins Vocational Education Act* was reauthorized, setting directions for state and local agencies to develop vocational and applied education programs. It targeted single parents, displaced homemakers, and single pregnant women and noted that states were to use a certain percentage of their funds to provide basic academic and occupational skills and materials in preparation for vocational education and training to provide these people with marketable skills. In addition, states were required to use funds to promote sex equity by providing programs, services, and comprehensive career guidance, support services, and preparatory services for girls and women.

1994   *The School-to-Work Opportunities Act* set up partnerships among educators, businesses, and employers to facilitate the transition of students who plan on moving directly to the world of work from high school.

1995   *The Elementary School Counseling Demonstration Act* allocated $2 million in grant money for schools to develop comprehensive elementary school counseling programs.

1996   *The Mental Health Insurance Parity Act* (enacted in 1996 and effective January 1, 1998) prevents health plans that cover mental health services from placing unequal caps on the dollar amount covered (either annually or on a lifetime basis) for the provision of mental health services if these same caps are not placed on the coverage of other medical services. Although this act has several limitations, it was a major step toward parity of insurance coverage for mental health services. Some of these limitations include that health plans are not required to provide mental health benefits. Additionally, it does not prohibit health plans from requiring higher deductibles and copayments for mental health services or from placing strict limits on the number of days of treatment covered for mental health conditions. Further, health plans that experience a 1% increase in premiums as a result of the parity provision, as well as businesses with fewer than 50 employees, are exempt from the provision (ACA Office of Public Policy and Information, 1996).

1996   *The Health Insurance Portability and Accountability Act* (HIPAA, P.L. 104-191) included language to promote "administrative simplification" in the administration of health care benefits by establishing national standards for the electronic transmission of health information, for the use and disclosure of personally identifiable health information, and for the security of information. Although the standards do not contain any counselor-specific provisions, they have an impact on all counselors, both as providers of mental health services and as health care consumers.

1997   *The Balanced Budget Act* included provisions that prohibit Medicaid managed care plans from discrimination against providers on the basis of the type of license they hold. This did not extend to fee-for-service plans administered through Medicaid.

1998   *Higher Education Act Amendments* reauthorized higher education programs into law for another 5 years. In addition to dropping student loan interest rates and increasing Pell Grant awards, the act created the Gaining Early Awareness and Readiness for Undergraduate Programs (GEAR-UP), which provides grants for establishing partnerships between colleges, schools, and community organizations. The provisions included payment for counseling services to certain at-risk and low-income students and other elementary, middle, and secondary school students. These services were specified to include counseling on financial aid, college admissions and achievement tests, college application procedures, and efforts to foster parental encouragement of students' interest in college education. In addition, the amendments allow for personal counseling, family counseling, and home visits for students with limited English proficiency. The act also sent a clear message against the use of drugs. It declared that students who are convicted of any state or federal offense for the possession or sale of a controlled substance will not be eligible to receive any grant, loan, or work assistance under the Higher Education bill (ACA Office of Public Policy and Information, 1998a).

1998   *The Health Professions Education Partnerships Act* (HPEPA) is a landmark piece of legislation. It recognizes professional counselors under health professional training programs. Specifically, education programs, counseling students and graduates, and counselor educators are eligible for a wide range of programs operated by the federal Health Resources and Services Administration (HRSA) and the federal Center for Mental Health Service (CMHS) to the same extent as other master's-level mental health professions. Where the term "graduate programs in behavioral and mental health practice" is referenced in these programs, the provisions passed in HPEPA include graduate programs in counseling (ACA Office of Public Policy and Information, 1998b).

1998   *The Workforce Investment Act* (WIA) revamped all job training programs in the country and reauthorized the Rehabilitation Act. According to the ACA Office of Public Policy and Information (1998c), the WIA streamlined requirements for the major federal grant programs that support training and related services for adults, dislocated workers, and disadvantaged youth. Under the WIA, all adults, regardless of income or employment status, became eligible for core services including skills assessments, job search assistance, and information on educational and employment opportunities.

The WIA mandated that states and local governments set up and maintain networks of "one-stop centers" in which consumers are afforded a single point of entry to federal job training and education programs, job market information, unemployment insurance, and other federal and state services and programs. The WIA required that training services for adults be delivered through vouchers. In addition, the programs are to be administered at the state level by a board. These boards, in turn, designate local service areas. The provisions call for existing JTPA (Job Training Partnership Act) service delivery areas with populations greater than 200,000 to be designated as service areas (as long as they met JTPA performance standards during the previous 2 years).

1998   *Reauthorization of the Rehabilitation Act.* As noted, the WIA reauthorized the Rehabilitation Act for another 5 years. The act funds state-administered vocational rehabilitation services for people with disabilities. In addition, the act funds research on rehabilitation and disabilities, training for rehabilitation counselors, independent living centers, advocacy services, and other initiatives that facilitate the employment of individuals with disabilities. The act upheld previous requirements that state agency professionals meet state or national certification or licensure requirements. This means that professional rehabilitation counselors need to hold a master's degree in rehabilitation counseling or a closely related field. The act extended this requirement to private contractors with state agencies. In addition, the act renamed Individualized Written Rehabilitation Plans as Individual Plans for Employment and expanded consumer choice and participation in the these plans (ACA Office of Public Policy and Information, 1998c).

1999   *The Medicare, Medicaid, and SCHIP Balanced Budget Refinement Act* (P.L. 106-554) included a section requiring the Medicare Payment Advisory Commission (MedPAC) to conduct a study on the appropriateness of establishing Medicare coverage of licensed professional counselors and other nonphysician providers, including marriage and family therapists and pastoral counselors. MedPAC issued a weakly written report recommending *against* covering licensed professional counselors, marriage and family therapists, and pastoral counselors in June 2002. Although MedPAC came to a negative conclusion, the language in P.L. 106-554 calling for the report marked the first time that Congress and the president had enacted legislation referencing licensed professional counselors with respect to Medicare.

1999   *The Elementary School Counseling Demonstration Act* was approved as part of the Omnibus Spending Package for fiscal year 2000. The act allocated $20 million for schools to hire *qualified* school counselors for school districts that are awarded 3-year grants by the Department of Education (ACA, 1999a).

1999   *The Work Incentives Improvement Act* (WIIA) may be the most significant federal law enacted for people with disabilities since the Americans with Disabilities Act passed in 1990 (ACA, 1999b). The WIIA removed many of the financial disincentives that prevented millions of people with disabilities from working. For example, it changed outdated rules that end Medicaid and Medicare coverage when people with disabilities enter or reenter the workplace. Among several provisions, the WIIA allowed people to buy into Medicaid when their jobs pay more than low wages but they may not have access to private health insurance. It also allowed people with disabilities to keep their Medicaid coverage even though their medical condition improved as a result of the medical coverage. In addition, it extended Medicare Part A coverage for people on Social Security disability insurance who return to work for another 4 and a half years. This results in a difference between monthly premiums of almost $350 (the cost of purchasing Part A and B coverage) and $45.50.

The WIIA also made major changes in the employment services systems for people with disabilities. People receiving SSI or SSDI benefits were allowed to choose among participating public and private providers of vocational rehabilitation and employment services who were paid a portion of the SSI or SSDI benefits if the person went to work and achieved "substantial earnings" (to be further determined through regulations not yet promulgated at the time this chapter was written).

2001   *Department of Defense Authorization Act* (P.L. 106-398) included language requiring the Tricare Management Authority to conduct a demonstration project allowing mental health counselors to practice independently, without physician referral and supervision. Licensed professional counselors are the only nationally recognized mental health professionals that Tricare requires to operate under physician referral and supervision. The demonstration project was expected to be concluded at the end of 2003, with a report to Congress by the Department of Defense to follow. Physician referral and supervision requirements for both marriage and family therapists and clinical social workers were removed by Congress following similar demonstration projects.

2001   *No Child Left Behind Act* (NCLB, P.L. 107-110) was a massive reauthorization of the federal education programs contained in the Elementary and Secondary Education Act and included language renaming the Elementary School Counseling Demonstration Program as the Elementary and Secondary School Counseling Program (ESSCP). This language both removed the "demonstration" tag from the program and expanded it to secondary schools. Under the NCLB language, the first $40 million appropriated for the program in any year must be devoted to supporting counseling programs and services in elementary schools.

2006   *The Veterans Benefits, Healthcare, and Information Technology Act* (P.L. 109-461) includes language establishing explicit recognition of licensed mental health counselors as health care professionals within the Department of Veterans Affairs (VA) health care programs. In addition to allowing the hiring of licensed professional counselors in clinical and supervisory positions with VA health care facilities, enactment of this provision should lead to the development of a position description for counselors by the Federal Office of Personnel Management, which would be applicable to all federal agencies.

Continuing Development of Professional Identity

History of the American Counseling Association

Vacc and Loesch (1994) noted that one way to understand the evolution of a profession is to study the history of a representative professional organization. The American

Counseling Association (ACA) has a rich history that exemplifies its representation of professional counselors. The philosophical development of the counseling profession can be seen by reviewing the three names by which ACA has been known, along with the times those name changes occurred. From its founding in 1952 until 1983, ACA was known as the American Personnel and Guidance Association (APGA). From 1983 until 1992, it was called the American Association for Counseling and Development (AACD). In 1992, the governing body of the association renamed it the American Counseling Association. For purposes of simplicity, the association will be referred to as ACA regardless of the time reference.

Although its official inception is noted as 1952, ACA can trace its organizational beginnings to the turn of the 20th century with the formation of one of its founding divisions, then the National Vocational Guidance Association. Its roots in vocational guidance, education, and psychology have made for an interesting, rich, and often rocky evolution of counseling as a profession unto itself, even before the founding of ACA. The NVGA had considered changing its name at least five times between 1922 and 1948 to better reflect the concern members had about the total adjustment of their clients (Norris, 1954). Members of the American Council of Guidance and Personnel Associations, a federation of associations, were also considering whether it was wise or efficient to attempt to belong to several organizations doing essentially the same thing. Groups belonging to the federation had the practice of meeting in conventions at the same time and place. By the late 1940s, groups had established their identities in work settings, and members had begun to see commonalities of purpose and function. The name of the federation had changed from the American Council of Guidance and Personnel Associations (ACGPA) to the Council of Guidance and Personnel Associations (CGPA) in 1939, so there was a precedent for a name change.

In 1948 Daniel Feder, as chair of CGPA and president of NVGA, urged forming a national organization to include individuals as well as associations. A committee on unification was appointed to develop a plan for such an organization. Its plan was presented at the 1950 convention and forwarded to the organizations concerned (McDaniels, 1964). Both the NVGA and the American College Personnel Association approved the plan and arranged their constitutions to join the new organization as divisions in 1951. At this time the Personnel and Guidance Association (PGA) was born. The following year, 1952, PGA changed its name to the American Personnel and Guidance Association (APGA) to avoid confusion with the Professional Golfers Association (PGA). APGA is now known as the American Counseling Association (ACA). Table 1.1 presents highlights of the ACA's development since its founding.

Professionalism: A Developmental Perspective

The mission of the American Counseling Association is "to enhance the quality of life in society by promoting the development of professional counselors, advancing the counseling profession, and using the profession and practice of counseling to promote respect for human dignity and diversity" (ACA, 2003). A review of Table 1.1 indicates not only the developmental nature of the ACA but also the evolving diversity of its

TABLE 1.1   Organizational Chronology of the American Counseling Association

Year	Division Name	Event
1951	PGA	The Personnel and Guidance Association was formed.
1952	APGA	American Personnel and Guidance Association became the new name for PGA.

The following divisions became founding partners of APGA:

Year	Division Name	Event
1952	ACPA	American College Personnel Association.
	NVGA	National Vocational Guidance Association.
	SPATE	Student Personnel Association for Teacher Education.
	NAGSCT	National Association of Guidance Supervisors and College Trainers.

The following divisions became part of ACA or changed their names:

Year	Division Name	Event
1953	ASCA	American School Counselors Association became a division.
1958	DRC	ACA added the Division of Rehabilitation Counseling.
1961	ACES	Association for Counselor Education and Supervision replaced the former NAGSCT.
1962	ARCA	American Rehabilitation Counseling Association became the new name for the former DRC.
1965	AMEG	Association for Measurement and Evaluation in Guidance was established.
1966	NECA	National Employment Counselors Association became a division.
1972	ANWIC	Association for Non-White Concerns in Personnel and Guidance was formed.
1973	ASGW	Association for Specialists in Group Work was established.
1974	NCGC	National Catholic Guidance Conference became a division.
	POCA	Public Offender Counselor Association was established.
1975	AHEAD	Association for Humanistic Education and Development replaced the former SPATE.
1977	ARVIC	Association for Religious Values in Counseling replaced what had been known as NCGC.
1978	AMHCA	American Mental Health Counselors Association became a division.
1983	AACD	American Association for Counseling and Development became the new name for what had been called APGA.
1984	AMECD	Association for Measurement and Evaluation in Counseling became the new name for the former AMEG.
	NCDA	National Career Development Association became the new name of the former NVGA.
	AMCD	Association for Multicultural Counseling and Development replaced the former Association for Non-White Concerns in Personnel and Guidance.
1984	MECA	Military Educators and Counselors Association became an organization affiliate of AACD.
1986	AADA	Association for Adult Development and Aging was formed.

1989	IAMFC	International Association of Marriage and Family Counselors was established.
1990	IAAOC	Association of Addiction and Offender Counselors replaced the former POCA.
1991	ACCA	American College Counselors Association was formed to replace ACPA, which was in the process of withdrawing from ACA.
1992	ACPA	American College Personnel Association disaffiliated from ACA.
	AAC	Association for Assessment in Counseling became the new name for AMECD.
1993	ASERVIC	Association for Spiritual, Ethical and Religious Values in Counseling became the new name for ARVIC.
1995	ACEG	Association for Counselors and Educators in Government became the new name for MECA.
1996	AGLBIC	Association of Gay, Lesbian, and Bisexual Issues in Counseling became an organizational affiliate.
1997	AGLBIC	AGLBIC achieved division status.
1998	ACEG	ACEG became a division.
1999	CSJ	Counselors for Social Justice became an organizational affiliate.
	C-AHEAD	AHEAD changed its name to the Counseling Association for Humanistic Education and Development.
2002	CSJ	CSJ became a division.
2004	ACC	Association for Creativity in Counseling became a division.
2003	AACE	AAC changed its name to the Association for Assessment in Counseling and Education.
2007	ALGBTIC	AGLBIC changed its name to the Association for Lesbian, Gay, Bisexual, and Transgender Issues in Counseling.

divisions and its membership. The concept of unification was a common theme in this country in the 1950s (Vacc & Loesch, 1994). This trend may have influenced the four independent founding organizations—NVGA (now NCDA), American College Personnel Association (replaced as an ACA division now by ACCA), the National Association of Guidance and Counselor Trainers (NAGSCT, now ACES), and SPATE (now C-AHEAD)—to come together and work as one federation. The basic format of autonomous divisions working within an umbrella organization has continued to the present time. Divisions have been added as members' interests or counselor work settings changed because of changes in the socioeconomic milieu. Table 1.2 shows the divisional structure of ACA as of June 2007.

Change is very much reflected in the chronological evolution of ACA. For example, the parent organization, APGA, changed its name twice over a 40-year period. Before 1983, APGA began to feel pressures from its membership for a name change that would accurately reflect the purposes and work activities of its members. The terms *guidance* and *personnel* were onerous to some members. In addition to describing the profession better, the term *counseling* was more prestigious and better understood by the public. By 1983, several of the divisions already recognized the terms *counseling* or *counselor* in their titles (ASCA, ARCA, ACES, ARVIC, POCA,

TABLE 1.2   **Divisions of the American Counseling Association as of June 2007**

AACE	Association for Assessment in Counseling and Education**
AADA	Association for Adult Development and Aging***
ACC	Association for Creativity in Counseling
ACCA	American College Counseling Association**
ACEG	Association for Counselors and Educators in Government
ACES	Association for Counselor Education and Supervision
ALGBTIC	Association for Lesbian, Gay, Bisexual, and Transgender Issues in Counseling
AMCD	Association for Multicultural Counseling and Development
AMHCA	American Mental Health Counselors Association**
ARCA	American Rehabilitation Counseling Association**
ASCA	American School Counselors Association**
ASERVIC	Association for Spiritual, Ethical and Religious Values in Counseling
ASGW	Association for Specialists in Group Work
C-AHEAD	Counseling Association for Humanistic Education and Development
CSJ	Counselors for Social Justice
IAAOC	International Association of Addictions and Offenders Counselors***
IAMFC	Internal Association of Marriage and Family Counselors**
NCDA	National Career Development Association*
NECA	National Employment Counseling Association**

*ACA membership is required for professional members only (not required for affiliate, regular student, and/or retired members of these groups).

**ACA membership is not required for members of these groups.

***AADA requires ACA membership for all but "regular" members; IAAOC requires ACA membership for all except retired members.

NECA, and AMHCA). To appease its growing and diverse membership, to have a clearer identity with counseling, and to attract new members in a changing society, APGA became the American Association for Counseling and Development (AACD). Nine years later in 1992, the name was again changed to the American Counseling Association, removing the word *development* from its title.

Such change was not limited to the parent organization. As can be seen in Table 1.1, six divisions (NVGA, SPATE, NAGSCT, ANWIC, POCA, and MECA) changed their names at least once and two divisions (AMEG and NCGC) changed their names twice since they were formed. Such changes not only reflected the changing nature of the work of the divisions and their members but also brought the divisions' names more in line with the name changes that had occurred within the parent organization.

Beginning in 1952 with four divisions, the first new division to join the parent organization was the American School Counselors Association (ASCA) in 1953, which quickly became one of the two largest ACA divisions. After World War II, there was a growing recognition in America that people with disabilities had counseling needs. At the same time that the Veterans Administration was attempting to meet the needs of returning World War II servicemen and women, a number of ACA members were becoming involved in rehabilitation counseling. These factors resulted in the organization of the second new division to join ACA, the American Rehabilitation Counseling Association (ARCA) in 1957 (known as the Division of Rehabilitation Counseling from 1957 to 1962).

Seven years passed before the addition of two new divisions. In 1965, professionals who used psychometric instruments in their settings needed an organization to help them improve the use of such instruments and to communicate among themselves. The Association for Measurement and Evaluation in Guidance (AMEG) was organized to serve this purpose, although not until 1968 was it formally incorporated as an ACA division. The continued interest in vocational counseling at that same time is evident in the formation of the National Employment Counselors Association (NECA) in 1966. NECA members, who came from both the private and public sectors of counseling, had a strong interest on vocational counseling and focused specifically on employment counseling.

The number of divisions in ACA again remained static for seven years, but the 1970s saw the formation and acceptance of several new divisions. There was increasing concern about minority representation with the structure of ACA. That concern, along with the general social consciousness movement in the 1960s and early 1970s, prompted the development of an interest-based division entitled the Association for Non-White Concerns in Personnel and Guidance (ANWIC), which was added in 1972.

In 1973, based on the growing use of groups as a form of counseling intervention, the Association for Specialists in Group Work (ASGW) became the tenth division of ACA. The following year, 1974, the National Catholic Guidance Conference (NCGC) became the 11th division of ACA and brought to the parent association its first division with a strong religious orientation. During the last few decades, the focus of this division changed from that of a Catholic-based organization to a broader examination of spirituality, religious values, and ethical considerations in the field of counseling. This shift in focus is reflected in NCGC changing its name to the Association for Religious Values in Counseling (ARVIC) in 1977 and later (1993) to the Association for Spiritual, Ethical and Religious Values in Counseling (ASERVIC).

In 1974, the Public Offender Counselor Association (POCA) became the 12th division and brought into the organization people involved with juvenile and adult probation and those who worked with or within our prison systems. The creation of POCA is one example of how responsive the counseling profession has been to the complex social problems faced by our society. During the 1980s, the correlation between addictive and criminal behaviors became quite clear. Many POCA members became interested in broadening the focus of POCA, and it became the International Association of Addictions and Offenders Counselors (IAAOC) in 1990.

As the demand for school counselors diminished in the early and mid-1970s, a need for counselors in a variety of community agencies developed, and counselors found themselves in a variety of noneducational work settings. More nonprofit organizations and services such as crisis centers, hotlines, drop-in clinics, shelters for battered women, rape counseling centers, and clinics for runaway youth emerged. More agencies began to be funded by local governments and hire people with master's degrees and experience to run these centers. The profession responded, and in 1978 the American Mental Health Counselors Association (AMHCA) became the 13th division of ACA. Between 1976 and the early 1980s, AMHCA's membership expanded more quickly than probably any other mental health organization's (Weikel, 1985). It became the largest division within ACA and, along with ASCA, remains one of the two largest groups affiliated with ACA.

As noted previously, it was in 1983 that APGA changed its name to the American Association for Counseling and Development (AACD). The change symbolized the evolving professional orientation among the association's members, the fact that these members were being found more and more in noneducational work settings, and the concept that what members "did was counseling, not guidance" (Herr, 1985, p. 395).

In 1986, as a reflection of an increasingly larger aging population and the problems of growing older in a youth-oriented society, the Association for Adult Development and Aging (AADA) became the 14th division of what was now called the American Association for Counseling and Development. The strongest emphasis of AADA has been on gerontological counseling, midlife development, and preretirement planning, but its members have broadened their focus to include the counseling needs of persons across the adult life span.

In 1989, based on the growing emphasis on marriage and family counseling and the fact that many ACA members provided marriage and family counseling, the International Association of Marriage and Family Counselors (IAMFC) became the 15th ACA division.

Later in the 1980s, ACPA members who served a wide variety of student development needs on college campuses became unhappy with the increasing de-emphasis of guidance and personnel issues in ACA and began movement to disaffiliate from ACA. The withdrawal of ACPA in 1992 led to the formation of its successor, the American College Counseling Association, with a more focused emphasis on counseling college students. At this time AACD became the American Counseling Association.

Members of ACA, recognizing the growing numbers of counselors who serve clients dealing with issues associated with their sexual orientation, lobbied for a specialty division that would focus on the needs of these clients and counselors. In April 1996, the Association of Gay, Lesbian, and Bisexual Issues in Counseling (AGLBIC) became an organizational affiliate of ACA. An organizational affiliate was defined before 1998 as an interest group with fewer than 1,000 members. In March 1998, the ACA Governing Council voted to amend the ACA bylaws to require 500 or more members to achieve or maintain division status and, in March 2003, to reduce that number to 400. AGBLIC's membership quickly grew, and it achieved status as a division in 1997. As of June 2007, there were more than 775 members of AGLBIC. The AGLBIC board voted in 2007 to change its name to the Association for Lesbian, Gay, Bisexual, and Transgender Issues in Counseling (ALGBTIC).

In 1998, the Association for Counselors and Educators in Government (ACEG) became a division of ACA. This professional group was originally formed as an organizational affiliate in 1984 under the title of Military Educators and Counselors Association

(MECA). Members of this division have primary professional affiliations to some branch of the military establishment or various levels of government.

Counselors for Social Justice (CSJ) was formed as an organizational affiliate in 1999 to address issues related to social justice, oppression, and human rights within the counseling profession and the community at large. CSJ became an ACA division in 2002.

Finally, in 2004, the Association for Creativity in Counseling (ACC) was established to provide a forum for counselors, counselor educators, and counseling students interested in creative, diverse, and relational approaches to counseling. An additional goal of this division is to "develop, implement, and foster interest in counseling-related charitable, scientific, and educational programs designed to further creativity, diversity, and relatedness in the work and lives of counselors, clients and communities" (ACC, 2007).

The American Counseling Association is much more than a collection of divisions. There is also a geographical regional structure: (1) North Atlantic (Connecticut, Delaware, the District of Columbia, Maine, Maryland, Massachusetts, New Hampshire, New Jersey, New York, Pennsylvania, Rhode Island, Vermont, and the Virgin Islands); (2) Southern (Alabama, Arkansas, Florida, Georgia, Kentucky, Louisiana, Mississippi, North Carolina, South Carolina, Tennessee, Texas, Virginia, and West Virginia); (3) Midwest (Illinois, Indiana, Iowa, Kansas, Michigan, Minnesota, Missouri, Nebraska, North Dakota, Ohio, Oklahoma, South Dakota, and Wisconsin); and (4) Western (Alaska, Arizona, California, Colorado, Hawaii, Idaho, Nevada, Montana, New Mexico, Oregon, Washington, Wyoming, and Utah). Each region, representing ACA state branches, was established to provide leadership training, professional development, and continuing education of branch members following the strategic plan adopted by the association.

Through its ACA Press, the association provides its membership with a plethora of books, scholarly journals, and monographs on topics of interest to counselors. Its workshop and home study program and regional and national conventions provide intensive training opportunities that keep members up-to-date and provide the continuing education units necessary to maintain licensure or certification. Its *Code of Ethics* (ACA, 2005) provides members and the public with both professional direction and guidance. Its legislative arm not only alerts members to current legislation that is either helpful or harmful to counseling but also gives members a voice in policy development at the federal, state, and local levels.

In 2007, with 19 national divisions, 56 state and territorial branches, 4 regional assemblies, a myriad of divisional affiliates in each of the branches, and a membership of approximately 41,000, the American Counseling Association remains the strongest organization representing counselors on the national scene. It is not, however, without problems. ACA developed from a "group of groups" and has been faced with ongoing organizational challenges that stem from the groups continued desire to have independence while working under an umbrella structure. In October 1997, the governing council voted to amend the ACA bylaws so that, effective July 1, 1998, ACA members were no longer required to also belong to a division and division members were no longer required to also belong to ACA. This freedom of choice for members has led to some interesting developments. As of December 1999, 14 of the then 18 divisions (77.8%) opted to require their *professional members* (typically defined as members with a master's degree in counseling) to belong to ACA in addition to their division. As of June 2007, only 12 of the divisions (63.2%) required *professional members* to also join ACA, and 7 divisions (AACE, ACCA, AMHCA, ARCA, ASCA, IAMFC, NECA) (36.8%) did not require ACA membership for any category of division membership. Membership for all groups except for AMHCA and ASCA are processed through ACA. AMHCA and ASCA collect their own fees.

It is difficult to discern how policy makers (e.g., legislators) view the structure of ACA. To date, a "strength in numbers" philosophy has facilitated passage of legislation that has been important to the provision of counseling services and the recognition of professional counselors. It seems that all ACA entities, regardless of whether ACA membership is required, have managed to work together to have a positive influence on the passage of some key pieces of legislation since 1997. It is not clear, however, if ACA's current governing structure is the most effective or efficient way to advance public policy or to serve the "parent organization" and the divisions. Different strategies to reorganize ACA have been reviewed and rejected by its governing council, but this has not yet been resolved. As of June 2007, the members of the governing council were considering new categories and packages of membership (e.g., a reduced rate if individuals join ACA and their state branch, or if they join ACA and at least one division, and so on) that might best serve ACA, ACA divisions, and all members.

Issues related to divisional and ACA membership may certainly be influenced by finances and what counselors can afford to pay for association membership. It may, however, also be indicative of ongoing problems with professional identity. Do members consider themselves professional counselors first and specialists second or the other way around? The struggle of coming from a group of groups appears to remain in issues related to professional identity and to the governance of the profession.

Credentialing and the "Professionalization" of Counseling

The most commonly noted criteria used to evaluate whether an occupation has evolved to the status of a profession include (1) a specialized body of knowledge and theory-driven research, (2) the establishment of a professional society or association, (3) control of training programs, (4) a code of ethics to guide professional behavior, and (5) standards for admitting and policing practitioners (Caplow, 1966; Glosoff, 1993). Given these criteria, no historical perspective of the counseling profession can be considered complete without a discussion of the development of standards related to the preparation and practice of professional counselors.

The counseling profession has met the majority of conditions just noted. There is an evolving body of knowledge and systematic theories and a body of literature to provide a forum for such information. ACA serves as the primary professional association for counselors. There are standards for training programs, professional preparation and ethical behavior (see Chapter 4). Accredited counselor-training programs have been established, and credentials are granted to individuals demonstrating professional competencies (Glosoff, 1993; Remley, 1991). Great progress has been made in establishing licensure and certification regulations, legally validating the profession.

The term *credentialing* was created to represent a broad array of activities pertaining to the establishment of professional training standards and regulations for practice (Bradley, 1991). This term most typically covers three major professional activities: academic program accreditation, certification, and licensure (Loesch, 1984).

Accreditation

Accreditation is one means of providing accountability. The licensed professions in this country began the process of regulation and quality control by developing standards for training programs. One definition of *accreditation* is provided by Altekruse and Wittmer (1991) as follows:

> [a] process by which an association or agency grants public recognition to a school, institute, college, university, or specialized program of study that has met certain established qualifications or standards as determined through initial and periodic evaluations. (p. 53)

The development of standards of preparation for counselors began approximately 40 years ago when a joint committee of the ACES and ASCA, divisions of ACA, began two major studies in 1960. More than 700 counselor educators and supervisors and 2,500 practicing counselors participated in the studies over a 5-year period (Altekruse & Wittmer, 1991). The results facilitated the creation of the "Standards for Counselor Education in the Preparation of Secondary School Counselors," the first set of standards sanctioned for counselor education, in 1964. After a 3-year trial, they were officially adopted by ACES in 1967 (Association for Counselor Education and Supervision, 1967). Shortly thereafter, "Standards for Preparation of Elementary School Counselors" (APGA, 1968) and "Guidelines for Graduate Programs in the Preparation of Student Personnel Workers in Higher Education" (APGA, 1969) were established.

The Council on Rehabilitation Education (CORE), incorporated as a specialized accrediting body with a focus on rehabilitation counseling in 1972, was a forerunner in setting educational standards and graduate program accreditation in counseling (Sweeney, 1991). The leaders responsible for the creation of the Council for Accreditation of Counseling and Related Educational Programs (CACREP) used CORE as a model. Both councils require similar generic counseling curricula (not focused on specialties) and standards. In addition, CORE focuses on rehabilitation counselor education (RCE) curricula while CACREP addresses program area curricula and standards in other specialty areas but does not include specific RCE curricula.

Council on Rehabilitation Education (CORE)

In addition to ARCA, the following four professional organizations were represented on the first CORE board: Council of Rehabilitation Educators (now the National

Council on Rehabilitation Education, NCRE), Council of State Administrators of Vocational Rehabilitation (CSAVR), International Association of Rehabilitation Facilities (now American Rehabilitation Association, ARA), and the National Rehabilitation Counseling Association (NRCA). CORE's current membership has two public members, the chair of the Commission on Standards and Accreditation, and individuals appointed from the following sponsoring organizations: NRCA, ARCA, NCRE, CSAVR, and the National Council of State Agencies for the Blind (NCSAB).

As of June 2007, CORE had accredited 102 master's programs offering a degree in rehabilitation counseling, with 7 programs in "candidacy" status (Marv Kuehn, CORE staff, personal communication, June 13, 2007). Since its creation, CORE has reviewed and revised the standards for the accreditation of master's programs in rehabilitation counselor education on a regular basis. The first major standards revisions in 1981 were followed by revisions in 1988, 1997, and 2004. The most recent revisions in the CORE standards can be reviewed on the CORE Web site (www.core-rehab.org). The 2004 standards present some significant changes from the 1997 standards in the language and format used to describe curricular areas and outcomes required. Based on the 1997 CORE *Manual* (1997), all CORE-accredited programs were expected to include courses in the following areas of study: foundations of rehabilitation counseling, counseling services, case management, vocational and career development, assessment, job development and placement, and research. Effective August 2004, all CORE-accredited programs are expected to address the following 10 curricular areas of study: professional identity; social and cultural diversity issues; human growth and development; employment and career development; counseling and consultation; group work; assessment; research and program evaluation; medical, functional, environmental, and psychosocial aspects of disability; and rehabilitation services and resources (CORE, 2007). Supervised practicum and internship experiences are required under both the 1997 and 2004 standards. These experiences are very similar to the current (2001) CACREP standards.

Council for Accreditation of Counseling and Related Educational Programs (CACREP)

According to Altekruse and Wittmer (1991), ACES developed "Standards for Entry Preparation of Counselors and Other Personnel-Service Specialists" in 1973. This document, which merged earlier guidelines, was officially adopted by the ACA governing body in 1979. At that time, ACES was the only association accrediting body using the standards of training. Not until 1981 did ACA's board of directors adopt a resolution to formally oversee the responsibilities of the ACES National Committee on Accreditation. This led to the establishment of the Council for Accreditation of Counseling and Related Educational Programs (CACREP), which was formed as an independently incorporated accrediting body, separate from ACA but sponsored by ACA and several divisions (CACREP, 1987). Since its inception, CACREP has conducted reviews of its accreditation standards. After the initial flurry of changes to the 1981 standards, CACREP declared a 5-year time period during which only minor changes would be allowed (Altekruse & Wittmer, 1991). There have been three significant revisions made to the 1981 standards adopted by CACREP, in 1988, 1994, and 2001. These revisions are necessary to keep up with the continually evolving field of counseling, and CACREP was in the process of revising the 2001 standards when this book went to press.

In addition to providing for accreditation of doctoral-level programs in counselor education and supervision, the 1994 CACREP standards provided for accreditation of master's degree programs in community counseling, with and without specialization in career counseling or gerontological counseling, marriage and family counseling/therapy, mental health counseling, school counseling, student affairs practice in higher education (with college counseling or professional practice emphases), and doctoral degree programs in counselor education and supervision (CACREP, 1994). The current CACREP standards (CACREP, 2001) accredit doctoral programs in counselor education and supervision and master's degree programs in the following specialty areas; career counseling (separate from community counseling); college counseling (no longer listed as an emphasis area under student affairs); community counseling; gerontological counseling (accredited separately from community counseling); marital, couple, and family counseling/therapy (instead of "marriage and family counseling/therapy"); mental health counseling; school counseling; and student affairs.

As of June 2007, CACREP had 500 accredited programs (Jenny Gunderman, CACREP staff, personal communication, June 13, 2007). Of these 500 programs, 49 are doctoral level, and 451 are master's programs in 208 institutions. The majority of the master's programs are in the areas of school counseling (179) and community counseling (149). In addition, there were 47 accredited mental health counseling programs, 37 accredited in college counseling or student affairs programs (11 accredited under the 2001 standards as "college counseling" programs, 11 in student affairs with an emphasis in college counseling, and 15 in student affairs with an emphasis in professional practice, administrative, or developmental emphases), 29 accredited marriage and family counseling/therapy programs, 8 accredited career counseling programs, and 2 accredited gerontological counseling programs (Jenny Gunderman).

All academic programs accredited by CACREP, regardless of specialty designation, share a common core of curricular requirements. According to the 2001 CACREP *Accreditation Procedures Manual* (CACREP, 2001), all accredited programs must address the following eight curricular areas: professional identity, social and cultural diversity, human growth and development, career development, helping relationships, group work, assessment, and research and program evaluation. Supervised practica and internships also are required across all program areas. In addition to these common core areas, CACREP-accredited programs must also offer specific types of curricular experiences related to the specialty accreditation, such as community counseling, school counseling, and mental health counseling.

As previously noted, CACREP was in the process of revising the 2001 standards at the time this chapter was written. The CACREP board appointed a standards revision committee and released the first draft of the proposed 2008 standards for public comment in October 2005. The second draft was released in May 2006, and CACREP again solicited comments (until December 15, 2006). The third draft was posted on-line from June through November 2007. Members of the Standards Revision Committee held forums at several conferences (e.g., ACA, the 2007 ACES conference, the five regional ACES conferences held in fall 2006, ASCA, AMHCA, and the American Association of State Counseling Boards). The proposed drafts represent a significant shift from knowledge-based to outcome- or performance-based standards. Students will need to demonstrate the ability to implement their knowledge in the core and specialty domains, and programs will need to document these outcomes. Another major proposed change is that new full-time faculty hired after 2013 will be required to have earned a doctoral degree in counselor education (rather than counseling psychology or other related fields) if they have not already taught in counselor education programs. Further major revisions in the drafts include combining the current college counseling and student affairs standards into one college student development and counseling program area and revisions to the community and mental health counseling specialties.

Along with the feedback that the Standards Revision Committee received from individuals and professional groups, two things caused CACREP to extend the timeline for the next standards to 2009. First, CACREP was awarded a grant though the Department of Health Resources and Services Administration (HRSA), a division of the U.S. Department of Health and Human Services, to investigate how to best include training standards related to disasters and emergency response preparedness. Second, at the request of the CACREP Board, the Standards Revision Committee included a draft of standards for the proposed new specialty area of addictions counseling in the third draft of the proposed standards. CACREP staff anticipates having the final standards approved and posted online by mid-August 2008 and available in hardcopy as part of a new manual in January 2009.

Another professional organization that accredits counseling-related programs is the American Association for Marriage and Family Therapy (AAMFT). Along with CACREP, AAMFT accredits counselor education programs that emphasize marriage and family therapy. Unlike CACREP, however, AAMFT also accredits academic programs in departments of social work and home economics, as well as nonacademic programs such as agency-based training programs (Hollis, 2000).

Certification

Certification is one of the most confusing of the credentialing terms (Brown & Srebalus, 1988). It is used in reference to (1) the process of becoming qualified to practice in public schools, (2) state laws passed in the same ways as licensure laws, and (3) recognition bestowed on individuals by their professional peers (such as certified public accountants).

Certification is often referred to as a "title control" process because it grants recognition of competence by a professional group or governmental unit but does not confer authority to the holder to practice a profession (Forrest & Stone, 1991; Loesch, 1984). As befits the confusing nature of the term *certification*, there is one exception to this rule. A designated state agency, most typically a state department of education, certifies school personnel. Professional counselors holding positions as public school counselors must be certified by the state to do so. Therefore, school counselor certification regulations are actually practice acts, because they control who may and may not practice as a school counselor (Loesch, 1984).

Types and Purposes of Certification

Certification in Schools.   As noted, state boards or departments of education, by authority of state legislatures, establish certification standards for teachers, counselors, administrators, and other school personnel. Certification of school counselors first began in Boston and New York in the 1920s, but not until the National Defense Education Act (NDEA) was passed in 1958 did this type of certification take hold nationwide. By 1967 more than 24,000 guidance counselors were trained under NDEA funding. The NDEA also mandated the establishment of criteria that would qualify schools to receive funds for the services of school counselors, which led to the rapid growth of certification (Sweeney, 1991).

National Board Certification.   Many professional groups have initiated credentialing efforts at the national and the state levels to encourage excellence by promoting high standards of training, knowledge, and supervised experience. These standards promulgated by professional organizations may or may not be considered by governmental agencies, such as state departments of education or mental health, in relation to hiring and promotion requirements (Sweeney, 1991).

The first counseling-related national certification addressed the specialty of rehabilitation counseling. During the late 1960s, rehabilitation counselors belonging to the National Rehabilitation Counselors Association and American Rehabilitation Counselors Association (an ACA division) began to work together toward establishing certification for rehabilitation counseling specialists (Forrest & Stone, 1991). Their efforts came to fruition in 1973, when the Commission on Rehabilitation Counselor Certification, known as CRCC, began to certify rehabilitation counselors (Forrest & Stone, 1991; Sweeney, 1991). More than 15,580 rehabilitation counselors were designated as CRCs as of June 2007. Until recently, in addition to the general certification in rehabilitation counseling (CRC), CRCC offered specialty certification in addictions counseling and in clinical supervision. CRCC is no longer accepting new applications for certification in these specialties; however, individuals currently certified in these specialties who meet the continuing education requirements may apply for certification renewal.

CRCC divides the criteria for certification as a CRC into several categories. Depending on the category under which the applicant is seeking certification, requirements include either a minimum of a master's degree in counseling (nonspecified) or a master's degree specifically in rehabilitation counseling. In addition to the requirement of a master's, CRCs are required to have relevant supervised professional experience as a rehabilitation counselor (if the applicant did not graduate from a CORE-accredited program) and successful completion of the CRCC examination (CRCC, 2007). The supervised experience requirement varies, depending on the type of degree earned by the applicant.

As noted, graduates of CORE-accredited programs are not required to have postmaster's employment experience before applying to become a CRC. They do, however, need to complete an internship of 600 clock hours supervised by an on-site

CRC or a faculty member who is a CRC. The internship must have been in rehabilitation counseling. Those who graduate with a master's in rehabilitation counseling from a non-CORE-accredited program must demonstrate the completion of an internship comparable to that in CORE-accredited programs and must have 12 months of acceptable employment experience under the supervision of a CRC (or complete a provisional contract). If applicants have a degree in rehabilitation counseling but do not have 600 hours of internship in rehabilitation counseling, they must have 24 months of acceptable employment experience, including a minimum of 12 months under the supervision of a CRC; if lacking the supervision by a CRC, they must complete a provisional contract (CRCC, 2007).

There also are eligibility criteria for individuals with master's degrees in counseling with an emphasis other than rehabilitation counseling who have had a minimum of one graduate course with a primary focus on theories and techniques of counseling. CRCC staff reviews applicants' transcripts to determine that they have had required courses. The employment requirements vary for these applicants, depending on the number of required courses they have taken. For example, applicants who have had one graduate course in counseling theories and at least one course in assessment, occupational information, medical or psychosocial and cultural aspects of disabilities, and community resources or delivery of rehabilitation services must also have 36 months of acceptable employment experience, including 12 months under the supervision of a CRC. A person who has had a theories and technique course and only one course in medical or psychosocial and cultural aspects of disability and one graduate course in the other three areas previously noted is required to have 48 months of acceptable employment experience with a minimum of 12 months under the supervision of a CRC. Finally, applicants who have had a theories and technique course and only one course in medical or psychosocial and cultural aspects of disabilities must demonstrate 60 months of acceptable employment experience, including a minimum of 12 months under the supervision of a CRC.

CRCC also offers certification to graduates of doctoral programs offering degrees in counseling or rehabilitation counseling. The doctoral transcript must include a minimum of one graduate-level course in theories and techniques of counseling, one graduate-level course on medical or psychosocial and cultural aspects of disabilities, and 600 hours of internship at the doctoral level in a rehabilitation setting supervised by a CRC or 12 months of acceptable employment experience under the supervision of a CRC. In all these situations (master's and doctoral level), if applicants meet the employment criteria but lack supervision by a CRC, they must complete a provisional contract (CRCC, 2007).

In 1979, the National Academy of Certified Clinical Mental Health Counselors (NACCMHC) was the next national counselor certifying body to be established. The NACCMHC merged with the National Board for Certified Counselors (NBCC) in 1992. Basic requirements to become a Certified Clinical Mental Health Counselor (CCMHC) include (1) completion of a minimum of 60 graduate semester hours, (2) graduation with a master's or higher degree from an accredited counselor-preparation program encompassing at least 2 years of postmaster's professional work experience that included a minimum of 3000 client-contact hours and 100 clock hours of individual supervision by a CCMHC or a professional who holds an equivalent credential, (3) submission of an audiotape or videotape of a counseling session, and (4) successful completion of the CCMHC's Mental Health Counselor Examination for Specialization in Clinical Counseling (NBCC, 1995). Weikel and Palmo (1989) noted that the stringent requirements to become a CCMHC may be one reason that there were only slightly more than 1000 National Certified Clinical Mental Health Counselors (NCCMHCs) in 1985.

NBCC is probably the most visible and largest national counselor-certifying body (Sweeney, 1991). As of June 2007, NBCC certified 41,022 National Certified Counselors, or NCCs (NBCC, 2007c). The founding of NBCC offered the public a way to identify professional counselors who meet knowledge and skills criteria set forth by the counseling profession in the general practice of counseling. This was especially important given the paucity of counselor licensure laws at that time. The concept of a general practice of counseling is in line with CACREP's belief that there is a common core of knowledge that is shared by all professional counselors, regardless of any specific area of specialization. It is assumed that all counselors, regardless of their specialty area(s), must have a shared knowledge base and be able to perform some of the same activities (Forrest & Stone, 1991).

To be certified by NBCC as a National Certified Counselor (NCC), applicants who are not licensed by a state as a professional counselor (or equivalent title), must (1) hold a master's degree or higher with major study in counseling, including a minimum of 48 semester hours or 72 quarter hours in graduate coursework; (2) demonstrate that their graduate coursework was from a regionally accredited institution and includes at least one course (carrying at least two semester/three quarter hours) in each of the core curriculum areas delineated in the CACREP accreditation standards; (3) have successfully completed two academic terms of supervised field experience in a counseling setting or 1 year with an additional year of postmaster's supervised experience (1,500 additional hours of counseling experience including 50 extra hours of face-to-face supervision) beyond the required 2 years of postmaster's supervised experience; (4) provide two professional endorsements; and (5) pass the National Counselor Examination (NCE). Counselors who have not graduated from a CACREP-accredited program must also document the completion of a minimum of 3,000 hours of work as a counselor over at least 24 months since the date an advanced degree with a major study in counseling was conferred. In addition, these individuals need to document that they received at least 100 hours of face-to-face counseling supervision over a minimum of 2 years, provided by a supervisor who holds an advanced degree in counseling or a closely related field (social work, psychology, or marriage and family therapy) (NBCC, 2007a).

Once counselors have earned the designation of NCC, they can then qualify for specialty certification as an *Approved Clinical Supervisor* (ACS, through the Center for Credentialing & Education, a corporate affiliate of the National Board for Certified Counselors), National Certified School Counselor (NCSC), Certified Clinical Mental Health Counselor (CCMHC), Masters Addiction Counselor (MAC), and/or National Certified Career Counselor (NCCC). There are currently 2212 NCSCs, 1160 NCMHCs, 667 MACs, 577 NCCCs, and 157 NCGCs (NBCC, 2007c). The NBCC board of directors decided in 1999 to stop taking new applications for the NCGC and the NCCC specialization areas because of the low number of people who had pursued the credential (Schmitt, 1999).

NBCC and CRCC are not, however, the only bodies that certify specialists in counseling and counseling-related specialties. For example, the National Board for Professional Teaching Standards (NBPTS) offers certification in school counseling in addition to teaching. NBCC participated in negotiations with NBPTS for quite some time to arrive at joint standards (similar to the MAC standards adopted by both NBCC and the National Association of Alcoholism and Drug Abuse Counselors). Negotiations apparently broke down, and NBPTS moved forward with plans. One major problem in developing mutually agreed upon standards was that the NBPTS had proposed certifying school counselors who do not hold a master's degree in counseling. This has been a core criterion for all NBCC credentials. As of June 2007, NBPTS has certified 964 school counselors at the early childhood/young adult level (Shannon Fox, director of Knowledge Management, NBPTS, personal communication, June 15, 2007). It is unclear what this may mean for how school counselors perceive themselves in regard to being counselors or educators first and how having national certification offered by both NCCC and NBPTS will influence the public's perceptions of counselors.

School counseling is not the only specialty area in which organizations other than NBCC and CRCC offer certification. In addition to being an ACA division, IAMFC is an affiliate of the National Academy for Certified Family Therapists, which offers five options for certification of family therapists. The option most relevant for professional counselors requires professionals who are already NCCs or licensed as professional counselors to document professional training, supervision, and experience in working with couples and families (Smith, Carlson, Stevens-Smith, & Dennison, 1995). The American Association of Marriage and Family Therapy (AAMFT) also certifies its own members who meet certain criteria and has done so since the 1970s (Everett, 1990). AAFMT's credential is granted to members who have clinical member status. The International Certification Reciprocity Consortium (ICRC), NAADAC, NBCC, and the CRCC (as previously noted) all offer specialty addictions certification. Finally, professionals specializing in the treatment of sexual dysfunction can be certified by the American Association of Sex Educators, Counselors and Therapists. Having multiple certifications offered by different associations in the same specialty areas may prove confusing for both professionals and consumers of mental health services.

Licensure

Brown and Srebalus (1988) define a *license* as "a credential authorized by a state legislature that regulates either the title, practice, or both of an occupational group" (p. 232). Although states enact licensure laws as a means to protect the public from incompetent practitioners, such laws also provide benefits for the profession being regulated. The very fact that a state considers a profession important enough to regulate may lead to an enhanced public image and increased recognition for that profession. Among several types of credentials presented to 1604 professional counselors surveyed, a license as a professional counselor (or similar title) was considered the most important to hold (Glosoff, 1993). Likewise, licensure has often been espoused as the most desirable of the different types of credentials in regard to securing recognition by insurance companies, government and private mental health programs, and consumers; being given preferred status in job hiring; and adding to the qualifications necessary to be seen as an expert witness (Foos, Ottens, & Hills, 1991; Glosoff, 1993; Remley, 1991; Sweeney, 1991; Throckmorton, 1992).

Just as certification can be confusing, so, too, can the concept of licensure. Because licensure laws typically delineate a "scope of practice" connected with the profession, licensing acts are often known as "practice acts" (Shimberg, 1982). States with such laws in place require people to be licensed or to meet criteria for exemption from licensing noted in those laws to engage in specified counseling activities. There are, however, licensing laws that dictate who may identify themselves as "licensed counselors" or use other counseling-related titles but do not regulate people who are not licensed. These laws are typically referred to as "title acts." Sweeney (1991) pointed out that it is essential to examine specific state laws and their accompanying regulations to determine the implications for practice. ACA assists counselors in this process by providing information about licensure requirements in each state and the District of Columbia on its Website (http://www.counseling.org). ACA also typically publishes an annual list of counseling regulatory boards in the November–December issue of the *Journal of Counseling and Development*. In addition to using the resources provided by ACA, I strongly encourage practitioners in those states with counselor licensure laws to ask the regulatory boards if they need a license to practice and what they may and may not call themselves.

Licensure of counseling practitioners, separate from psychologists, can be traced to the early 1970s. Before 1976, no state law defined or regulated the general profession of counseling. This left the profession in a state of legal limbo—although counseling was not expressly forbidden (except where the laws regulating psychology specifically limited activities of professional counselors), it was not legally recognized as a profession, either (Brooks, 1986). At that time, the American Psychological Association began to call for stringent psychology licensure laws that would preclude other professionals from rendering any form of "psychological" services. In Virginia, this resulted in a cease-and-desist order being served to John Weldon, a counselor in private practice in 1972 (Hosie, 1991; Sweeney, 1991). The Virginia State Board of Psychologist Examiners obtained a court order restraining Weldon from rendering private practice services in career counseling (*Weldon v. Virginia State Board of Psychologist Examiners*, 1972). The board claimed that Weldon was in fact practicing psychology, even though he presented himself as providing guidance and counseling services. In October 1972, Weldon was found to be practicing outside the law, but the court also ruled that the Virginia legislature had created the problem by violating his right to practice his chosen profession of counseling. The court proclaimed that personnel and guidance was a profession separate from psychology and should be recognized and regulated as such (Hosie, 1991). In response to the Weldon case, the Virginia legislature passed a bill certifying personnel and guidance counselors for private practice in March 1975 (Swanson, 1988). This law was amended by the Virginia legislature in 1976 and became the first general practice act for professional counselors.

At about the same time, Culbreth Cook, an Ohio counselor, faced a challenge similar to that of Weldon. Cook, well known and respected in his community, was employed at a 2-year college and provided private educational assessment on a part-time basis. Cook's education and training qualified him to offer the assessment services he rendered, but he was arrested on the felony charge of practicing psychology without a license (Hosie, 1991; Swanson, 1988). Carl Swanson, an attorney, counselor educator, and ACA

Licensure Committee cochair testified on Cook's behalf (Sweeney, 1991). The Cleveland Municipal Court judge refused to provide a restraining order against Cook, noting that even attorneys used the tools of psychology (*City of Cleveland, Ohio v. Cook*, 1975).

ACA has focused on licensure since the 1970s. In 1973, the first ACA licensure committee was created by the Southern Association for Counselor Education and Supervision (Hosie, 1991; Sweeney, 1991). The next year ACA published a position statement on counselor licensure and, in 1975, appointed a special licensure commission. The commission distributed an action packet in 1976, including information about counselor licensure, the fourth draft of model state legislation, and strategies to pursue licensing (APGA, 1976).

Model legislation offers a prototype for counselors in states that do not have licensure laws, in states that are in the process of revising their current laws, and where credentialing laws face sunset or legislative review (Glosoff, Benshoff, Hosie, & Maki, 1995). It also facilitates the development of uniform standards for the preparation and practice of professional counselors across the United States.

Since the first model legislation for licensed professional counselors was created, ACA has revisited and amended its model to reflect changes in standards within the profession and experiences in states that have implemented counselor licensure laws. An underlying philosophy of ACA's model legislation is that state licensure laws legalize the general practice of counseling within each state, whereas the credentialing of counseling specialists remains under the purview of professional credentialing organizations such as CRCC and NBCC.

The rate of licensure for counselors during the two decades between the time Virginia passed the first counselor licensure law and the endorsement of ACA's 1994 model legislation is seen by some to be painstakingly slow and by others as quite rapid. Brooks (1986) noted that "legislative successes were distressingly slow in the years following 1974" (p. 253). During the early 1980s, licensure took off when 15 states passed some form of credentialing acts between 1981 and 1986, 14 passed laws between 1987 and 1989; and 7 passed laws between 1990 and 1994 (Glosoff, 1993; Glosoff et al., 1995). Having counseling licensure laws enacted at that rate of progress is exceptional when compared with the 20 years it took the first 18 state psychology laws to be passed (Brooks, 1988). Since 1994, licensure has been achieved in the remainder of all states except California, and a number of states passed amendments that brought existing credentialing laws more into line with ACA's model legislation (for example, changing title acts to practice laws, expanding the scope of practice of professional counselors to include diagnosis and treatment of people with mental disorders, and increasing educational and experience requirements).

Current Issues and Trends in Counseling

Counselors continue to respond to pressures from various socioeconomic factors—some of which led to the kaleidoscope we know as counseling today and others that will shape the future of the profession. These pressures cut across the various specialty areas of counseling and cannot be categorized or delineated as neatly as in a historical review of the profession. To illustrate these pressures, the following areas have been selected: diverse clientele, multicultural counseling and social justice issues, licensure, recognition and reimbursement of professional counselors, and legislation (Health Professions Education Partnerships Act, Medicare and the Federal Employees Benefits Program, Tricare, Veterans Affairs, and Medicaid). Current issues and trends in technology are discussed in Chapter 6; issues and trends in private practice and managed care are discussed in Chapter 16.

Diverse Clientele

Counselors are employed in a wide variety of work settings. They provide services to people who exhibit a full range of functioning from healthy adaptation to pathology—from those seeking assistance with self-exploration to those individuals who are dysfunctional enough to require hospitalization. There is not enough space to comprehensively explore all of those work settings and types of services, but I will attempt to briefly review some of the major trends related to types of clients being served by counselors in a variety of work settings. The types of clients served by professional counselors are as diverse as the work settings in which counselors are employed. Following are a few examples of the types of clients receiving increasing attention from professional counselors.

The frequency of abuse of all kinds in our country is astounding. Today's counselors are increasingly serving individuals who are abused, including very young children, adolescents, adults, and elderly clients—both men and women across all racial, ethnic, and socioeconomic groups. In addition, there has been a greater focus of late on treatment of the abuser. This often involves working with people who have been incarcerated for sexual assault, domestic violence, or pedophilia or those who are on parole. Professional counselors also serve individuals who have been incarcerated for other reasons.

According to the U.S. Department of Justice (Bureau of Justice Statistics, 2005), of the more than 2.1 million individuals incarcerated in state and local facilities in the United States, approximately 16% have a mental illness. It seems that our jails and prisons often are alternatives to mental health facilities for people who are homeless and have mental disorders and that individuals with substance abuse disorders are being incarcerated rather than treated in the community. Mental health services clearly are needed in our jails and prisons. In addition, there are often significant implications for the children and other family members of persons who have been incarcerated. Counselors have been active in providing these services as well as advocating for effective treatment for many years (note the IAAOC was established in 1974).

Another subset of clientele groups receiving increased attention from mental health professionals, including counselors, are people who are HIV positive or have AIDS. There is probably not a community in the country that has gone untouched by the AIDS epidemic. Fear of people with HIV or AIDS may lead them to feel a strong sense of isolation, increasing the already difficult task of living with a life-threatening or terminal illness. Counselors are needed to help ease this difficulty, but many may not have the training needed to specialize in assisting people with chronic and terminal diseases. This is an issue for counselor education programs.

A similar training issue exists in regard to counselors being adequately prepared to provide services to veterans, especially those who have served in combat. As previously discussed, the counseling profession has been strongly influenced by U.S. involvement in wars. Sadly, this continues today. Posttraumatic stress disorder (PTSD) and other mental health effects of combat can be seen in veterans years after they return home. Clawson (2007), testifying before the President's Commission on the Care of Wounded Warriors, noted that approximately one in eight soldiers who fought in Iraq reported symptoms of PTSD and that more than one in three soldiers who served in combat in Iraq, Afghanistan, and other locations later sought help for mental health problems. These numbers may increase as military personnel have been required to serve for longer periods than ever before without significant breaks. Of course, this also has implications for their families and loved ones. In turn, this has implications for counselor education programs.

There also has been a marked increase in counseling services targeted to older individuals. This makes sense, given the "graying of America" shown by the steadily increasing average age of the population. One facet of the aging of baby boomers is the increasingly large numbers of individuals who are ready to retire or have done so already. These individuals may not fall under the purview of gerontological counseling and appear to be an underserved population (Gladding & Ryan, 2001). Given our strong roots in the career development area, this seems to be an excellent market for professional counselors. In addition, a report by the Substance Abuse and Mental Health Services Administration (SAMHSA) indicates that the need for mental health care for older adults with substance abuse or psychiatric disorders is anticipated to increase by 13 to 50% (Bartels, Blow, Borckmann, & Van Citters, 2005). Vacc and Loesch (1994) predicted that in response to the needs of older people, gerontological counseling would continue to grow as an area of specialization for professional counselors. Although this may be true, as I previously noted, professional counselors did not seek certification as gerontological counselors in high enough numbers to warrant NBCC maintaining it as an area of certification. This still seems to be an important marketplace issue for counselors to consider.

I have seen estimates that 4 to 18% of the U.S. population are bisexual, gay, lesbian, or transgendered. This variance indicates the difficulty in obtaining accurate demographic information on sexual orientation. Sexual orientation and gender identification are not easily measured constructs, and individuals who are gay, lesbian, bisexual, or transgendered (GLBT) may be reluctant to identify themselves as such in surveys. Regardless, the results of several studies have strongly indicated that many individuals who are GLBT experience bullying and discrimination in their schools while growing up and in their workplaces as adults. For example, according to the Williams Institute (2007), since the mid-1990s, there have been 15 studies in which 15% to 43% of GLBT respondents experienced discrimination in the workplace (e.g., being fired or denied employment based on their sexual orientation, being verbally or physically abused). In addition, 15% to 57% of people who identified as transgendered reported experiencing employment discrimination. The 2005 National School

Climate Survey conducted by the Gay, Lesbian, and Straight Education Network (GLSEN, 2006) indicated that more than 75% of student participants have heard derogatory remarks and name-calling such as "faggot" or "dyke" frequently in their schools and 37.8% of students experienced physical harassment at school on the basis of sexual orientation. The results of the 2005 study further indicate that having supportive staff makes a difference to students and is correlated with positive indicators such as a greater sense of safety, reports of missing fewer days of school, and a higher incidence of planning to attend college. To assist counselors, ALGBTIC developed "Competencies for Counseling Gay, Lesbian, Bisexual, and Transgendered (GLBT) Clients" (htpp://www.aglbic.org/resources/competencies.html).

Counselors are likely to work with a client (child, adolescent, or adult) who is gay lesbian, bisexual, or transgendered. Although clients may or may not be open about their sexual orientation, and their sexual orientation may or may not be a primary counseling issue, counselors must be prepared to work effectively with individual clients who are GLBT and to advocate for affirmation, respect, and equal opportunity for all individuals, regardless of sexual orientation or gender identity.

People with addictions (such as substance abuse problems, gambling, and sexual addictions) are yet another group being served by increased numbers of professional counselors. These services focus on delivering prevention and remediation of addictive behaviors in community mental health agencies, residential treatment programs, schools, and employee assistance programs (Gladding & Ryan, 2001). The expansion of services in this area can be seen in the numbers of professional organizations offering certification to people who specialize in the delivery of addictions counseling.

Although counselors traditionally have worked with well-functioning individuals, they increasingly have been serving people with severe and chronic mental illness in hospital and community settings. Counselors with both master's and doctoral degrees are expected to provide a variety of assessment and diagnostic services with clients who exhibit a wide range of clinical disorders (Hosie, West, & Mackey, 1993).

Regardless of the functioning level of clients, a "wellness" orientation remains the basis for many counselors' work. Counselors are working with clients who seek to achieve greater physical and mental health by making positive lifestyle choices and are doing so in a variety of settings, such as behavioral medicine clinics, HMOs, community centers, and employee assistance programs (EAPs). In 2000, there were approximately 14,000 EAPs in the United States (Gladding & Ryan, 2001). EAPs emphasize very short-term treatment and referral of employees to help them address problems that may influence their job performance. Counselors working in EAPs typically work on issues such as substance abuse, family concerns, financial problems, stress, and interpersonal difficulties that affect them in their work setting (Hosie & Glosoff, 2001). Counselors may be EAP program administrators or be employed as counselors directly by a corporation and have an office within a company. It is also not unusual for counselors to work on a contractual basis to provide counseling services to workers at a particular business (Hosie & Glosoff).

In addition to EAPs, counselors are being hired in business and industry to assist employees who have been laid off or reassigned as a result of new technology, economic fluctuations, or shifts in services and products. Many counselors also have been hired to provide career counseling with an emphasis on training and retraining, outplacement, and relocation services to those employees (Hosie & Glosoff, 2001).

Many businesses also have focused on the effective use of their employees. Counselors have been hired or contracted to serve as consultants on organizational development and training issues, both of which typically require strong assessment and group process skills. Team building, stress management, preretirement planning, conflict management, and supervision are just a few examples of the types of training counselors provided in business and industry.

Unfortunately, many preventive and wellness-oriented programs have focused more on physical than on mental well-being. As professional counselors continue to make strides in being recognized as qualified providers of services to individuals with diagnosable disorders, it seems that the profession's roots in wellness may be forgotten. There are, however, wellness-based programs in business and health organizations that may be ripe for counselors who choose to market their services to expand wellness programs to include a stronger mental health component.

Multicultural Counseling and Social Justice Issues

One of the most significant trends in relation to professional counselors' clients is that they reflect the diversity of today's society in terms of age, race, ethnicity, gender, and sexual orientation. Sue (1991) wrote, "We are fast becoming a multicultural, multiracial, and multilingual society" (p. 99). He reported that 75% of people entering the labor market at that time were minorities or women. According to D'Andrea and Daniels (2001), the U.S. Bureau of the Census in 1998 indicated that 71% of the total U.S. population are from non-Hispanic, White European backgrounds. They further noted that by 2020, only 64% of the U.S. population is predicted to come from non-Hispanic, White European backgrounds.

These demographic changes have had a notable impact on society in general as well as on the counseling profession. Many leaders in the field consider multiculturalism to be the fourth force in the profession (Pedersen, 1991b). This force calls for reexamining assumptions that are inherent in the delivery of traditional counseling services. The leaders of ACA also realized the importance of addressing the assumptions inherent in the ACA *Code of Ethics* and have regularly reviewed and revised it. In 2002, ACA leaders appointed an ethics revisions task force to review the 1995 code. A key charge assigned to the task force members was to specifically review the 1995 revision of the *Code of Ethics and Standards of Practice* through a culturally sensitive lens. The revised *Code of Ethics* was approved by the ACA Governing Council in the summer of 2005, and one can see that issues related to cultural sensitivity have been infused in the document.

It is more likely than not that counselors will work with clients who have different cultural backgrounds than their own. Although people from all cultures may encounter problems that counselors are trained to address, these problems are experienced within a cultural context that counselors may not understand. The profession must determine the applicability of traditionally taught theories to diverse clientele, as well as explore the effectiveness of *how* services are delivered (for example, 50-minute sessions, in counselors' offices, that focus on intrapsychic phenomena).

Counselors need to develop an increased awareness and understanding of cultural factors if they are to effectively provide services to a pluralistic clientele. In addition, counselor educators must help prepare the next generation of counselors to work from multicultural perspectives. Further, counseling-related research will need to include recognition of cultural differences and ensure that findings adequately reflect the cultural influences of research participants. Pedersen (1991a) asserted that counselors need to "translate the skills, strategies, and techniques of counseling appropriately to many culturally different populations so that the counselor is prepared to match the right approach to each culturally different population" (p. 250). Although Pedersen presented no small challenge, it is clearly one that counselors and counselor educators must accept.

The ACA *Code of Ethics* (2005) requires counselors to develop and maintain cross-cultural effectiveness. Standards related to diversity and cross-cultural counseling are apparent throughout the code. For example, the preamble states that we "recognize diversity and embrace a cross-cultural approach in support of the worth, dignity, potential, and uniqueness of people within their social and cultural contexts." In addition, the majority of introductory statements speak specifically to ethical obligations of counselors to consider cultural contexts related to the standards in the related sections. Many sections of the ACA code speak specifically to diversity, multiculturalism, and advocacy. This is beyond the scope of this chapter, however, and is covered in Chapter 4.

Both CACREP and CORE standards mandate that accredited programs address social and cultural foundations. Kiselica and Ramsey (2001) anticipated that multicultural training will become more infused throughout counselor education curricula and offer some suggestions for ways to do this. One major development was the publication by AMCD of specific competencies associated with counseling clients from diverse populations. The multicultural competencies were adopted by ACA in 2003 and then by several ACA divisions. In addition, several theories of multicultural counseling have been presented in professional literature (Fuertes & Gretchen, 2001). More recently, the concept of the "fourth force" has been expanded by some from multicultural counseling to include diversity, advocacy, and social justice. As discussions about multicultural counseling have moved forward, there has been an increased emphasis on the interrelatedness of cultural competency, advocacy, and social justice. Although it is important to examine social and cultural foundations from a theoretical base, some say that this is not enough. Sue, Bingham, Porché-Burke, and Vasquez (1999), writing about the symbiotic relationship between multiculturalism and social justice, stated,

> Our own stand on this matter, however, is quite clear. Multiculturalism is not only about understanding different perspectives and worldviews but also about social justice. As such it is not value neutral: Multiculturalism stands against beliefs and behaviors that oppress other groups and deny them equal access and opportunity." (p. 1064)

Conversely, others claim that the multicultural competencies and the advocacy competencies (also adopted by ACA in 2003) impose a political agenda of social activism on the counseling profession that extends beyond professional issues and into imposing mandates on the personal lives of counselors (Weinrach & Thomas, 2002).

Although debate about "mandating" advocacy and social justice continues, both have long been emphases in the counseling profession (Kiselica & Robinson, 2001), from the work of Frank Parsons and Clifford Beers to the establishment of AMCD, ALGBTIC, and CSJ as ACA divisions and the adoption by ACA of the Multicultural and Advocacy Competencies. This long-standing tradition, however, has not yet yielded clarity in the profession about how to most effectively have the concepts and practice of multiculturalism, advocacy, and social justice come together to affect the types of changes needed in our organizations and service systems to best serve individuals and groups who have been marginalized (Constantine, Hage, Kindaichi, & Bryant, 2007). In addition to conducting research and including issues of multiculturalism across counselor education curricula, there has been a call for faculty to go further by addressing sociopolitical development and dynamics across courses and incorporate lessons on how counselors can advocate for change in systems as well as for individual clients and the counseling profession.

Licensure

In the 32 years since the passage of the Virginia certification law, 49 states and the District of Columbia have enacted some form of counselor credentialing legislation, leaving only California without licensure for professional counselors (California does license marriage, family, and child counselors). It appears that counseling has made great progress in gaining recognition as a profession. For example, in 1996, 23 (53.5%) of the then 43 counselor credentialing laws regulated both the practice of counseling and the use of related titles ("practice acts"), and 46.5% of the credentialing laws provided protection only in reference to the use of counseling-related titles (Espina, 1999). In June 2007, 45 of the 50 jurisdictions (90%) with counselor credentialing laws were practice acts (ACA, 2007a). The model legislation endorsed by ACA's governing body in 1994 is clearly a practice act and establishes a comprehensive scope of practice for licensed professional counselors (LPCs). This scope of practice represents the broad continuum of services provided by professional counselors in the general practice of professional counseling and across specialty areas (Glosoff et al., 1995). The broadness of the scope is not meant to imply that all LPCs are experts in providing all services. Including a comprehensive scope of practice does, however, legally protect LPCs who are practicing within their scope of expertise. Without this protection, LPCs practicing within their scope of training (for example, career counseling, crisis intervention, or assessment) may find themselves, like John Weldon, legally prevented from rendering the very services for which they have been trained (Glosoff et al., 1995).

The 1994 ACA model legislation for LPCs includes the following requirements for licensure:

1. Completion of a minimum of 60 graduate semester hours in counseling from a regionally accredited institution of higher education, including an earned master's degree in counseling or an earned doctoral degree in counseling. The master's degree must have a minimum of 48 semester hours. Applicants graduating

from programs offering at least 48 graduate semester hours but less than 60 can become licensed upon completing postmaster's course work to meet the 60-hour requirement.

2. Applicants must document that their 60 semester hours consisted of study in each of the following areas: (a) helping relationships, including counseling theory and practice; (b) human growth and development; (c) lifestyle and career development; (d) group dynamics, processes, counseling, and consultation; (e) assessment, appraisal, and testing of individuals; (f) social and cultural foundations, including multicultural issues; (g) principles of etiology, diagnosis, treatment planning, and prevention of mental and emotional disorders and dysfunctional behavior; (h) marriage and/or family counseling therapy; (i) research and evaluation; and (j) professional orientation and ethics.

3. A minimum of 3000 hours of supervised experience in professional counseling performed over a period of not less than 2 years under the supervision of an approved supervisor.

4. Documentation that the 3000 supervised hours included at least 1200 hours of direct counseling with individuals, couples, families, or groups and a minimum of 100 hours spent in direct (face-to-face) supervision with an approved supervisor.

5. Successful completion of a written examination as determined by the counseling regulatory board.

Although a great deal has been achieved in the licensing arena and ACA's model legislation has provided counselors with much guidance in the development of counselor-credentialing laws, the statutes are far from uniform in their scope and requirements. This may be due, in part, to the revisions of ACA's model legislation for licensed professional counselors over the years. Licensure laws passed in the 1980s mirror the education, training, and supervision standards that were endorsed by the profession at that time, whereas those passed recently tend to be more comprehensive in the scope of practice and to impose more stringent requirements than earlier licensure laws.

The state of licensure, however, is confusing to many because the requirements vary from state to state. For example, 19 states and the District of Columbia have one tier of licensure. Other states have tiered licensing, with different scopes of practice and different criteria for eligibility. Twenty-two states have two tiers of licensure (e.g., licensed professional counselor as a "basic license" and licensed clinical counselor as a more "advanced" license), seven states have three tiers, and one state has four tiers of licensure (ACA, 2007a). As of June 2007, education requirements range from a master's degree with no specified number of hours to 60 semester hours including a master's degree, with 44 states and the District of Columbia requiring between 48 and 60 graduate semester hours. Wisconsin requires a minimum of 42, Iowa a minimum of 45, and Georgia, Washington, and West Virginia do not specify the number of credit hours required in their laws but may in their regulations. Some argue that most master's-level professional counselors do not have 60 semester hours, yet 46% of the 1604 ACA members who participated in a 1993 study reported having earned a minimum of 60 graduate semester hours in counseling (Glosoff, 1993). In addition, Hollis (2000) predicted a trend in counselor education programs of increasing the required credit hours for graduation to ensure that their graduates will meet state licensure requirements.

According to ACA (2007a), the majority of states require 3,000 hours or more of postmaster's supervised counseling experience, to be completed in no less than 2 years. For example, 25 states and the District of Columbia require 3000 to 3600 hours of postmaster's supervised counseling experience, 3 states require 4000 to 4500 hours, and 7 states require between 3000 and 4000 hours for the highest level of licensure. Even the titles granted to professional counselors by the regulatory boards vary. "Professional counselor" is the most frequently used title, followed by "mental health counselor," "clinical professional counselor," and "clinical counselor." I believe this lack of uniformity in titles used by state-credentialed counselors has proven to be detrimental to credentialed counselors in their ongoing efforts to gain the same recognition afforded to psychologists and clinical social workers.

Requirements for counselors to continue their education once they are licensed also vary from state to state. According to ACA (2007a), the majority of jurisdictions (45 or 90%) specifically include continuing education credits as a requirement for licensure renewal (not including Nevada, which had not yet written regulations addressing this). The number of continuing education hours required ranged from 10 to 55 every 2 years.

I believe that continuing education requirements for counselors to renew their licenses increased, and will continue to increase, for three reasons. First, most professions require members to stay abreast of current information in their fields after graduation from training programs. Requiring continuing education is one way to inspire confidence in professional counselors, and this will be important in the profession's continuing efforts to gain recognition from legislators, other policy makers, and the public. Next, NBCC and CRCC both require a minimum of 100 clock hours of approved continuing education during each 5-year period. Finally, requiring continuing education to renew licensure supports the professional standards set forth in the 2005 ACA *Code of Ethics*, which specifically directs counselors to maintain their level of competence in the skills they use and to stay reasonably aware of new scientific and professional information.

In addition to lack of uniformity, or maybe because of it, there have been legal challenges regarding what professional counselors can and cannot do as part of their scope of practice. For example, licensed counselors in several states have found themselves embroiled in legal battles over their ability to use standardized assessment instruments. This is ironic, given the strong roots that the counseling profession has in testing and assessment. The challenges are driven by efforts on the part of state psychological associations to proclaim that the use of most tests comes under the sole purview of doctoral-level psychologists. The tests noted by psychologists as requiring a doctorate in psychology to administer and interpret run the gamut from personality tests to psychoeducational and career-related measures.

Counselors will continue to fight for their right to administer and interpret those tests based on their education and training rather than on the name of the degree they earned. Legislation proposed by several state psychological associations may serve to bring together master's- and doctoral-level counselors, social workers, marriage and family therapists, and speech therapists, who may all find themselves unable to legally provide testing services for which they are trained. In response to proposed legislation that seeks to limit the use of tests based solely on degrees or licenses held, the national Fair Access Coalition on Testing (FACT) was created in 1996. FACT represents more than 500,000 counseling and mental health professionals. The organization has taken an active role in challenging proposed and enacted legislation and in defending mental health professionals who are charged with practicing psychology without a license based on their use of standardized instruments for which they have been adequately trained.

This same type of challenge has been put forth as to counselors' abilities to diagnose and treat clients, especially those with mental disorders. These efforts to restrain trade require that counselor licensure laws include language similar to the 1994 ACA model legislation that specifically states that counselors "(c) conduct assessments and diagnoses for the purposes of establishing treatment goals and objectives. . . . Assessment means selecting, administering, scoring and interpreting psychological and educational instruments designed to assess achievements, interests, personal characteristics, disabilities, and mental, emotional and behavioral disorders" (Glosoff et al., 1995, p. 211). According to ACA (2007a), only 34 of 48 states and the District of Columbia (Nevada had not yet passed its licensure law) specifically include both the diagnosis of emotional disorders and the treatment of persons with emotional or mental disorders in the scope of practice of credentialed counselors. This does, however, represent gains made by the counseling profession in this area. In 1999, although the majority of jurisdictions (82.6%) specifically allowed credentialed counselors to treat people with emotional or mental disorders, only 40% specifically included diagnosis in the scope of practice of credentialed counselors (Espina, 1999). As presented earlier, laws passed in the 1980s tend to be less comprehensive in the scope of practice afforded to counselors. Rather than try to enact new laws, some states have attempted to broaden their requirements and scope of practice through changes in regulations.

There is clearly a great deal of variance in licensure laws, often making it difficult for counselors licensed in one state to easily move to another state and become licensed. Many states that have practice licensure laws in place include a provision to obtain licensure through a review of credentials or endorsement. This, however, is often cumbersome and time-consuming and still does not allow counselors to simply take their license with them from state to state. To assist with the portability of credentials, the American Association of State Counseling Boards (AASCB) established the National Credentials Registry (AACSB, 2004). This registry allows licensed counselors, for a fee, to deposit or store information relevant to licensure (e.g., their education, work history, and supervised experience). Once this information is "banked," counselors who want to apply for licensure in another state can ask that AASCB send all information to that licensing board.

Another effort underway that may yield positive results in the long run for licensure portability is the 20/20 Future of Counseling Oversight Committee established by ACA and AASCB. This committee is comprised of representatives from all ACA divisions, and its charge included creating licensure portability by the year 2020. The committee's charge, however, went far beyond this and addressed other issues that have been discussed in this chapter, such as to clearly define the profession of counseling, to examine how to present counseling as one profession rather than as a group of groups, to improve recognition and public perception of counseling, and to expand and promote the research base of the counseling profession.

Recognition and Reimbursement of Professional Counselors

Credentialing has far-reaching ramifications for hiring and reimbursing professional counselors. Contrary to popular belief, credentialing affects the reimbursement of those professionals in settings other than private practice. Administrative rules used by several federal, state, and local agencies specify that only state-licensed practitioners can be employed by these agencies. These same rules often stipulate that only licensed workers can supervise mental health services, and they call specifically for licensed psychologists. In the late 1970s, Alabama eliminated all counselor position titles because of this type of thinking. Many university counseling centers hire only licensed psychologists. These are just a few examples of how credentialing has become strongly related to employment opportunities for counselors, and there is an increasing trend in this direction (Glosoff, 1993).

Reimbursement for services rendered has played a strong part in the licensure movement for all mental health practitioners. A motivating force in the psychological licensing in the late 1960s and early 1970s was to secure third-party reimbursement and to be included in national health insurance (Hosie, 1991). To facilitate these two goals, in 1975 APA established the National Register for Health Service Providers in Psychology as a means of identifying qualified practitioners of psychological services. Since January 1, 1978, to be listed in the National Register, one was required to have obtained a doctoral degree in psychology from a regionally accredited educational institution. Even though it has been argued that proficiency can be developed just as well in a counselor education department as in a psychology department, criteria for inclusion in the National Register clearly does not allow anyone who was trained elsewhere than a psychology department to take the examinations for licensure or certification as psychologists in most states (Rudolph, 1986). This had direct economic consequences for many doctoral-level professional counselors who were previously eligible to be licensed as psychologists.

Legislation

As I previously discussed, legislation has greatly influenced the development of the counseling profession. Counselors have made strides in being recognized as providers of mental health services in many pieces of legislation enacted over the past 10 years. At the same time, the struggle and the need for ongoing advocacy in this area continue. Following are examples of current issues related to some key laws.

Health Professions Education Partnerships Act

Professional counselors are included in some federal legislation and federally funded programs. For example, counselors were successful in their efforts to be recognized as qualified providers under the Health Professions Education Partnerships Act (HPEPA). According to the American Counseling Association Office of Public Policy and Information (1998b), HPEPA revised the Public Health Services Act (PHSA) by including counselors under the definition of mental health professionals. In addition, the HPEPA provisions directly affect counselor education programs in competing for clinical training grants by having graduate programs in counseling included in the HPEPA term "graduate program in behavioral and mental health practice." The act did not include a specific authorization level for any programs. Therefore, the passage of HPEPA does not, in itself, guarantee that counselors will be eligible for any specific program. For example, although HPEPA added "counseling" to the current list of mental health professionals who are eligible for the Center for Mental Health Services (CMHS) clinical traineeship program, at the time HPEPA was enacted, the staff of the CMHS indicated that they did not expect any new clinical traineeships to be granted.

The passage of HPEPA resulted in counselors being included in the National Health Service Corps loan repayment program (ACA Office of Public Policy and Information, 1998b). This program provides financial assistance in repaying student loans in exchange for working in health professions in underserved areas for 2 to 4 years following graduation (e.g., serving in public inpatient mental institutions or federal or state correctional facilities or as members of the faculties of eligible health professions). Other programs authorized by HPEPA provide grants to schools to identify, recruit, select, and financially support people from disadvantaged backgrounds for education and training in health and behavioral and mental health fields, as well as grants to aid in the establishment of centers of excellence in health professions education for underrepresented minority individuals.

Medicare and the Federal Employees Health Benefits Program

As of 2007, counselors were not yet included as recognized providers under Medicare, except when providing services "incident to" the services of a physician or psychologist. This means that professional counselors are not recognized to practice independently, which has indirectly had a negative impact on counselors being included as reimbursable providers of service under other public and private insurance programs. This may change in the near future. During 2004–2007, the Senate twice approved legislation that would establish LPCs as recognized mental health providers who could practice independently. At the time I wrote this chapter, bills were pending in both the House and the Senate that would establish Medicare coverage for licensed professional counselors, as well as make other improvements in Medicare's mental health benefits. Increased support for counselor reimbursement under Medicare in the House of Representatives should increase the chances for enactment of such a provision. Counselor recognition under Medicare, when achieved, should go a long way toward evening the playing field for counselors in the health care provider marketplace.

In addition to advocating for recognition of professional counselors in federal laws, ACA, AMHCA, and members of ACA's state branches also have attempted to change the laws and regulations that have excluded professional counselors as eligible providers of services paid for through Medicare and federal employee health benefit plans (FEHBP). Although FEHBP is regulated by a federal law, group policies are written across the country by various insurers—most often Blue Cross/Blue Shield. At present, these policies are required by law to cover mental health services provided by psychologists and clinical social workers. Although policy makers *may* cover services provided by professional counselors and marriage and family therapists, this coverage is optional rather than mandated.

Because professional counselors are not included as independent Medicare providers in the federal statute, they have been unable to "sign off" on the delivery of mental health services through Medicare. This, in turn, may deter administrators from hiring professional counselors. Many people are not aware that the Medicare policy on the coverage of partial hospitalization services furnished in community mental health centers (CMHCs) allows services to be provided by professionals *other than* physicians and psychologists. This has been used to have CMHCs and other state agencies write regulations and policies to include LPCs as employees. Even so, the law itself needs to be amended to specifically include LPCs *or* do away with the list of providers and include a statement that covered services include "individual and group therapy provided by any licensed mental health professional."

Tricare

Another area for continued advocacy is the current Office of the Civilian Health and Medical Program of the Uniformed Services (known as Tricare) regulations that recognize licensed counselors and Certified Clinical Mental Health Counselors but only if clients are referred by a physician and if the physician provides ongoing supervision of the counseling. These limitations are not placed on services provided by clinical psychologists, clinical social workers, psychiatric nurses, and marriage and family therapists. ACA and AMHCA have been working for several years to enlist congressional support for parity between counselors and other Tricare mental health service providers. The Department of Defense (DoD) Authorization Act (P.L. 106-398), enacted in fiscal year 2001, included language requiring the Tricare Management Authority to conduct a demonstration project allowing mental health counselors to practice independently, without physician referral and supervision. The demonstration project concluded with a report to Congress by the Rand Corporation in May 2005. Physician referral and supervision requirements for both marriage and family therapists and clinical social workers were removed by Congress following similar demonstration projects (Scott Barstow, personal communication, August 25, 2003). Bills in Congress in 2005 and 2006 included LPCs in the DoD authorization law. Although the Rand report was essentially neutral with regard to the inclusion of professional counselors as independent mental health service providers, the Senate viewed the report as an indication that there were more reasons than not to disallow independent practice by counselors, and the bills, unfortunately, were rejected in both years. Receiving recognition by the Tricare Management Authority for professional counselors remains a strong priority.

Veterans Affairs

Public Law 109-461, the Veterans Benefits, Healthcare, and Information Technology Act of 2006, includes language that clearly recognizes LPCs and licensed marriage and family therapists as mental health specialists within all health care programs operated by the Department of Veterans Affairs (VA) (ACA, 2007b). Although it will take time to write regulations to fully implement this law, it will greatly expand the job opportunities for counselors in the VA system. Rehabilitation counselors had long been employed by the VA, but the VA had not, until the enactment of this law, recognized counselors as mental health specialists (ACA). Because of that, counselors have not been paid at the same rate as clinical social workers and were not eligible to be considered for supervisory positions that have been open to social workers and others in the VA. The enactment of P.L. 109-461 should greatly affect counselors not only within the VA but also in all federal programs because the Office of Personnel Management (OPM) will need to create a new occupational classification for mental health counselors, which will be applied to other federally operated programs.

Medicaid

Medicaid, a federal program, is implemented through state regulations. The enactment of the 1997 Balanced Budget Act included provisions that prohibit Medicaid managed care plans from discriminating against providers on the basis of the type of license they hold. The act, however, did not extend to fee-for-service plans regulated through Medicaid, and most states have traditionally used fee-for-service programs. This is changing, however, and many states have moved to managed Medicaid care plans. The battle to include professional counselors as recognized Medicaid providers continues to be fought at the state level.

Most third-party reimbursers have major criteria for acceptance as reimbursable practitioners that include educational degrees and a license that allows the mental health provider to practice independently (Bistline, 1991; E. Bongiovanni, personal communication, April 27, 1993; Throckmorton, 1992). State licensure is also a prerequisite to becoming eligible for third-party reimbursement by insurance companies via any state mandates regulating insurance codes. Research indicates that LPCs do receive reimbursement from some insurance companies in states that do not legally mandate this (Throckmorton, 1992; Zimpfer, 1992). However, without a state mandate, there are no guarantees that LPCs or their clients will be reimbursed for services rendered.

A number of states have legislated mandates, often called "freedom of choice" (FOC) laws, that require reimbursement for services provided by specific professionals, such as LPCs, if these services are covered by a health plan. FOC laws increase consumers' choice of providers, thereby expanding the markets for mental health providers. These laws, however, do not regulate managed care companies, employers that set aside money to pay for the medical claims of their employees, or publicly funded (state or federal) insurance programs. Licensed counselors are included as clinicians and as administrative staff in managed mental health systems (Throckmorton, 1992).

Summary

The roots of counseling are deeply embedded in a variety of disciplines that have come together and created different emphases at various points in time. These emphases have led to the development of counseling specialties, counselors working in a wide variety of settings and offering a broad range of services, and the profession struggling with the formation of an identity.

Counselors in the United States, regardless of work setting or theoretical orientation, are linked by the common belief that a person has the capacity and right to choose directions and activities that are most personally satisfying. Choices must be made within the bounds of social and moral value systems that will not bring harm to self or to others. The counselors who were pioneers and the counselors who work now are dedicated to helping individuals find their way in an increasingly complex society.

Counselors are active in dealing with a great number of social problems that affect the populations with which they work. Society is in turmoil, trying to deal with the use of illegal drugs; changing family structures; the effect of technology on education, occupations, and employment; immigration issues; and complex pluralism, leading to the development of special populations at risk of being inundated by the majority. There is not space here to discuss each issue and the role of counselors in addressing these. Counselors must work to ensure that through their systematic, scientific, and professional efforts, individuals and groups will be served well. The following Web sites provide additional information on chapter topics.

USEFUL WEB SITES

American Counseling Association:
http://www.counseling.org

American Counseling Association Public Policy Information:
http://www.Counseling.org/publicpolicy/

Chi Sigma Iota:
http://www.csi-net.org

National Board for Certified Counselors:
http://www.NBCC.org

Commission on Rehabilitation Counselor Certification:
http://www.crccertification.com

REFERENCES

Altekruse, M., & Wittmer, J. (1991). Accreditation in counselor education. In F. Bradley (Ed.), *Credentialing in counseling* (pp. 53–62). Alexandria, VA: American Association for Counseling and Development.

American Association of State Counseling Boards. (2004). *AASCB portability policy and procedure.* Retrieved October 10, 2004, from http://www.aascb.org/pdfs/AASCB%20Portability%20document1-9-04.pdf

American Counseling Association. (1999a). *Special message: Congress approves $20 million for school counseling as part of Omnibus Spending Package for FY2000.* Retrieved March 20, 1999, from http://www.counseling.org/urgent/special112299a.html

American Counseling Association. (1999b). Special message: WIIA passes house and senate. Clinton to sign bill into law. Retrieved October 22, 1999 from http://www.counseling.org/urgent/special112299a.html

American Counseling Association. (2003). *Mission and vision statements.* Retrieved August 2, 2003, from http://www.counseling.org/site/PageServer?pagename=about_mission

American Counseling Association (ACA). (2005). *Code of ethics*. Alexandria, VA: Author.

American Counseling Association (ACA). (2007a). *ACA licensure requirements for professional counselors*. Alexandria, VA: Author.

American Counseling Association (ACA). (2007b). New Veterans Affairs law recognizing counselors to be implemented. Retrieved June 1, 2007, from http://www.counseling.org/PublicPolicy/PositionPapers.aspx

American Counseling Association Office of Public Policy and Information. (1996). *Briefing paper: Mental Health Insurance Parity Act passed*. Alexandria, VA: Author.

American Counseling Association Office of Public Policy and Information. (1998a). *Briefing paper: Higher education programs updated*. Alexandria, VA: Author.

American Counseling Association Office of Public Policy and Information. (1998b). *Briefing paper: Congress passes bill recognizing counselors under health professional training programs*. Alexandria, VA: Author.

American Counseling Association Office of Public Policy and Information. (1998c). *Briefing paper: Workforce Investment Act signed into law. Legislation revamps job training, reauthorizes the Rehabilitation Act*. Alexandria, VA: Author.

American Personnel and Guidance Association (APGA). (1968). *Standards for preparation of elementary school counselors*. Washington, DC: Author.

American Personnel and Guidance Association (APGA). (1969). *Guidelines for graduate programs in the preparation of student personnel workers in higher education*. Washington, DC: Author.

American Personnel and Guidance Association (APGA). (1976). *Model for state legislation concerning the practice of counseling, 1976, draft no. 4*. Alexandria, VA: Author.

American School Counselor Association. (2005). *The ASCA national model: A framework for school counseling programs*. Herndon, VA: Author.

Association for Counselor Education and Supervision (ACES). (1967). Standards for the preparation of secondary school counselors. *Personnel and Guidance Journal, 46*, 96–106.

Association for Creativity in Counseling (ACC). (2007). *Bylaws of the Association for Creativity in Counseling (2004)*. Retrieved May 5, 2007, from http://www.aca-acc.org/aboutACC.htm

Aubrey, R. F. (1982). A house divided: Guidance and counseling in 20th century America. *Personnel and Guidance Journal, 61*, 198–204.

Barstow, S. (1999). *Counselors unfairly treated by TRICARE/CHAMPUS* (Briefing paper for the American Counseling Association). Alexandria, VA: American Counseling Association.

Bartels, S. J., Blow, F. C., Brockmann, L. M., & Van Citters, A. D. (2005). *Substance abuse and mental health among older Americans: The state of the knowledge and future directions*. Substance Abuse and Mental Health Services Administration. Retrieved February 10, 2006, from http://www.samhsa.gov/aging/SA_MH_%20AmongOlderAdultsfinal102105.pdf

Baruth, L. G., & Robinson, E. H., III. (1987). *An introduction to the counseling profession*. Englewood Cliffs, NJ: Prentice Hall.

Beers, C. W. (1908). *A mind that found itself*. New York: Doubleday.

Belkin, G. S. (1988). *Introduction to counseling* (3rd ed.). Dubuque, IA: Wm. C. Brown.

Bistline, J. (1991, February). Self-insured plans and their impact on the counseling profession. *Advocate*, p. 10.

Bradley, F. (1991). *Credentialing in counseling*. Alexandria, VA: American Association for Counseling and Development.

Brewer, J. M. (1942). *History of vocational guidance*. New York: Harper.

Brooks, D. K. (1986). Credentialing of mental health counselors. In A. J. Palmo & W. J. Weikel (Eds.), *Foundations of mental health counseling* (pp. 243–261). Springfield, IL: Charles C. Thomas.

Brooks, D. K., Jr. (1988). Finishing the job. In R. L. Dingman (Ed.), *Licensure for mental health counselors* (pp. 4–7). Alexandria, VA: American Mental Health Counselors Association.

Brown, D., & Srebalus, D. (1988). *An introduction to the counseling profession*. Englewood Cliffs, NJ: Prentice Hall.

Bureau of Justice Statistics. (2005). *Prison statistics: Summary of findings*. U.S. Department of Justice, Office of Justice Programs. Retrieved March 9, 2007, from www.ojp.usdoj.gov/bjs/prisons.htm

Caplow, T. (1966). The sequence of professionalization. In H. M. Vollmer & D. L. Mills (Eds.), *Professionalization*. Englewood Cliffs, NJ: Prentice Hall.

Cicourel, A. V., & Kitsuse, J. I. (1963). *The educational decision-makers*. Indianapolis, IN: Bobbs-Merrill.

City of Cleveland, Ohio v. Cook, Municipal Court, Criminal Division, No. 75-CRB 11478, August 12, 1975. (Transcript dated August 19, 1975).

Clawson, T. W. (2007). *Written testimony by Dr. Thomas W. Clawson before the President's commission on the care of wounded warriors*. Retrieved June 3, 2007, from http://www.nbcc.org/home/newspage/nbccnews/dr.-thomas-clawson-submits-written-testimony-before-the-presidents-commission

Commission on Rehabilitation Counselor Certification (CRCC). (2007). *CRC Certification guide*. Retrieved May 22, 2007, from http://www.crccertification.com/downloads/10certification/A/Certification_Guide_0507I.htm

Constantine, M. G., Hage, S. M., Kindaichi, M. M., & Bryant, R. M. (2007). Social justice and multicultural issues: Implications for the practice and training of counselors and counseling psychologists. *Journal of Counseling & Development, 85*, 24–29.

Council for Accreditation of Counseling and Related Educational Programs (CACREP). (1987). *Accreditation procedures manual for counseling and related educational programs*. Alexandria, VA: Author.

Council for Accreditation of Counseling and Related Educational Programs (CACREP). (1994). *Accreditation standards and procedures manual*. Alexandria, VA: Author.

Council for Accreditation of Counseling and Related Educational Programs (CACREP). (2001). *Accreditation procedures manual for counseling and related educational programs*. Alexandria, VA: Author.

Council on Rehabilitation Education (CORE). (1997). *Accreditation manual for rehabilitation counselor education programs*. Rolling Meadows, IL: Author.

Council on Rehabilitation Education. (2007). *Accreditation Manual*. Retrieved May 11, 2007, from http://www.core-rehab.org

Cummings, N. A. (1990). The credentialing of professional psychologists and its implication for the other mental health disciplines. *Journal of Counseling and Development, 68*(5), 485–490.

D'Andrea, M., & Daniels, J. (2001). Facing the changing demographic structure of our society. In D. Locke, J. Myers, & E. Herr (Eds.), *The handbook of counseling* (pp. 529–540). Thousand Oaks, CA: Sage.

Davis, J. B. (1914). *Moral and vocational guidance*. Boston: Ginn.

Davis, J. B. (1956). *Saga of a schoolmaster: An autobiography*. Boston: Boston University Press.

Espina, M. (1999). *Licensure chart: Requirements for mental health counselor credentials* (Unpublished paper prepared for members of the American Counseling Association). Alexandria, VA: American Counseling Association.

Everett, C. A. (1990). The field of marital and family therapy. *Journal of Counseling and Development, 68*(5), 498–502.

Foos, J. A., Ottens, A. J., & Hills, L. K. (1991). Managed mental health: A primer for counselors. *Journal of Counseling & Development, 69*(4), 332–336.

Forrest, D. V., & Stone, L. A. (1991). Counselor certification. In F. Bradley (Ed.), *Credentialing in counseling* (pp. 23–52). Alexandria, VA: American Association for Counseling and Development.

Fuertes, J. N., & Gretchen, D. (2001). Emerging theories of multicultural counseling. In J. G. Ponterotto, J. Manuel Casses, L. A. Suzuki, & C. M. Alexander (Eds.), *Handbook of multicultural counseling* (2nd ed.). Thousand Oaks, CA: Sage.

Gay, Lesbian, and Straight Education Network (GLSEN). (2006). GLSEN's 2006 national school climate survey sheds new light on experiences of lesbian, gay, bisexual, and transgender (LGBT) students. Retrieved January 18, 2007, from http://www.aglbic.org/resources/compentencies.html

Ginzberg, E. (1971). *Career guidance*. New York: McGraw-Hill.

Gladding, S. T., & Ryan, M. (2001). Community counseling settings. In D. Locke, J. Myers, & E. Herr (Eds.), *The Handbook of Counseling* (pp. 343–355). Thousand Oaks, CA: Sage.

Glosoff, H. L. (1993). An assessment of the career benefits of state statutory credentials and national board certification as perceived by professional counselors. *Dissertation Abstracts International, 55*(09), 2719. (UMI No. AAC95–03041)

Glosoff, H. L., Benshoff, J. M., Hosie, T. W., & Maki, D. R. (1995). The 1994 ACA model legislation for licensed professional counselors. *Journal of Counseling and Development, 74*(2), 209–220.

Goldenberg, H. (1973). *Contemporary psychology.* Belmore, CA: Wadsworth.

Gross, M. L. (1962). *The brain watchers.* New York: Random House.

Herr, E. (1985). *Why counseling?* Alexandria, VA: American Association for Counseling and Development.

Hollis, J. W. (2000). *Counselor preparation: Programs, personnel, trends* (10th ed.). Muncie, IN: Accelerated Development.

Hosie, T. W. (1991). Historical antecedents and current status of counselor licensure. In F. Bradley (Ed.), *Credentialing in counseling* (pp. 23–52). Alexandria, VA: American Association for Counseling and Development.

Hosie, T. W., & Glosoff, H. L. (2001). Counselor education. In D. Locke, J. Myers, & E. Herr (Eds.), *The Handbook of Counseling* (pp. 393–416). Thousand Oaks, CA: Sage.

Hosie, T. W., West, J. D., & Mackey, J. A. (1993). Employment and roles of mental health counselors in employee assistance programs. *Journal of Counseling and Development, 71,* 355–359.

Hoyt, K. B. (1974). Professional preparation for professional guidance. In E. Herr (Ed.), *Vocational guidance and human development* (pp. 502–527). Boston: Houghton Mifflin.

Joint Committee on Testing. (1962). *Testing, testing, testing.* Washington, DC: American Association of School Administrators.

Kiselica, M., & Ramsey, M. (2001). Multicultural counselor education: Historical perspectives and future directions. In D. Locke, J. Myers, & E. Herr (Eds.), *The Handbook of Counseling* (pp. 433–452). Thousand Oaks, CA: Sage.

Kiselica, M. S., & Robinson, M. (2001). Bringing advocacy counseling to life: The history, issues, and human dramas of social justice work in counseling. *Journal of Counseling & Development, 79,* 387–397.

Loesch, L. C. (1984). Professional credentialing in counseling—1984. *Counseling and Human Development, 17*(2), 1–11.

McDaniels, C. O. (1964). *The history and development of the American Personnel and Guidance Association, 1952–1963.* Unpublished doctoral dissertation, University of Virginia, Charlottesville.

Miller, C. H. (1971). *Foundations of guidance* (2nd ed.). New York: Harper & Row.

National Board for Certified Counselors (NBCC). (1995). *Specialty certification.* Greensboro, NC: Author.

National Board for Certified Counselors (NBCC). (2007a). Eligibility checklist . Retrieved June 1, 2007, from http://www.nbcc.org/checklist2

National Board for Certified Counselors (NBCC). (2007b). The practice of Internet counseling. Retrieved June 1, 2007, from http://www.nbcc.org/webethics2

National Board for Certified Counselors (NBCC). (2007c). Statistics on NCCs. Retrieved June 1, 2007, from http://www.nbcc.org/stats

Norris, W. (1954). *The history and development of the National Vocational Guidance Association.* Unpublished doctoral dissertation. George Washington University, Washington, DC.

Ohlsen, M. M. (1983). *Introduction to counseling.* Itasca, IL: F. E. Peacock.

Palmo, A. J., & Weikel, W. J. (1986). *Foundations of mental health counseling.* Springfield, IL: Charles C. Thomas.

Parsons, F. (1894). The philosophy of mutualism. *The Arena, 9,* 738–815.

Parsons, F. (1909). *Choosing a vocation.* Boston: Houghton-Mifflin.

Pedersen, P. B. (1991a). Concluding comments to the special issue. Special issue: Multiculturalism as a fourth force in counseling. *Journal of Counseling and Development, 70*(1), 250.

Pedersen, P. B. (1991b). Multiculturalism as a generic approach to counseling. Special issue: Multiculturalism as a fourth force in counseling. *Journal of Counseling and Development, 70*(1), 6–12.

Picchioni, A. P., & Bonk, E. C. (1983). *A comprehensive history of guidance in the United States.* Austin, TX: Texas Personnel and Guidance Association.

Reed, A. Y. (1916). *Vocational guidance report 1913–1916.* Seattle, WA: Board of School Directors.

Reed, A. Y. (1920). *Junior wage earners.* New York: Macmillan.

Reed, A. Y. (1944). *Guidance and personnel services in education.* Ithaca, NY: Cornell University Press.

Remley, T. P. (1991). An argument for credentialing. In F. Bradley (Ed.), *Credentialing in counseling* (pp. 23–52). Alexandria, VA: American Association for Counseling and Development.

Richards, L. S. (1881). *Vocophy.* Marlboro, MA: Pratt Brothers.

Rockwell, P. J., Jr. (1958). *Social concepts in the published writings of some pioneers in guidance.* Unpublished doctoral dissertation. University of Wisconsin, Madison.

Rogers, C. R. (1942). *Counseling and psychotherapy: Newer Concepts in Fractice.* Boston: Houghton Mifflin.

Rogers, C. R. (1951). *Client-centered therapy.* Boston: Houghton Mifflin.

Rudolph, J. (1986). Third-party reimbursement and mental health counselors. In A. J. Palmo and W. J. Weikel (Eds.), *Foundations of mental health counseling* (pp. 271–284). Springfield, IL: Charles C. Thomas.

Schmitt, S. (1999). NBCC drops career and gerontology counseling specialties. *Counseling Today, 41*(2), 1, 19.

Shertzer, B., & Stone, S. C. (1986). *Fundamentals of counseling.* Boston: Houghton Mifflin.

Shimberg, B. (1982). *Occupational licensing: A public perspective.* Princeton, NJ: Educational Testing Service.

Smith, R. L., Carlson, J., Stevens-Smith, P., & Dennison, M. (1995). Marriage and family counseling. *Journal of Counseling and Development, 74*(2), 154–157.

Stephens, W. R. (1954). *Technical recommendations for psychological tests and diagnostic techniques.* Washington, DC: American Psychology Association.

Stephens, W. R. (1970). *Social reform and the origins of vocational guidance.* New York: Harper & Row.

Stripling, R. O. (1983). Building on the past—A challenge for the future. In G. R. Walls & L. Benjamin (Eds.), *Shaping counselor education programs in the next five years: An experimental prototype for the counselor of tomorrow* (pp. 205–209). Ann Arbor, MI: ERIC/CAPS.

Sue, D. W. (1991). A model for cultural diversity training. Special issue: Multiculturalism as a fourth force in counseling. *Journal of Counseling and Development, 70,* 99–105.

Sue, D. W., Bingham, R. P., Porché-Burke, L., & Vasquez, M. (1999). The diversification of psychology: A multicultural revolution. *American Psychologist, 54,* 1061–1069.

Swanson, C. (1988). Historical perspective on licensure for counselors. In R. L. Dingman (Ed.), *Licensure for mental health counselors* (pp. 1–3). Alexandria, VA: American Mental Health Counselors Association.

Sweeney, T. J. (1991). Counselor credentialing: Purpose and origin. In F. Bradley (Ed.), *Credentialing in counseling* (pp. 23–52). Alexandria, VA: American Association for Counseling and Development.

Throckmorton, E. W. (1992). Mental health counselors and reimbursement decisions: How do third-party payers of mental health benefits decide which mental health providers to pay? *Dissertation Abstracts International 53*(03). (UMI No. AAC 9230310)

Vacc, N., & Loesch, L. (1994). *A professional orientation to counseling* (2nd ed.). Muncie, IN: Accelerated Development.

Weikel, W. J. (1985). The American Mental Health Counselors Association. *Journal of Counseling and Development, 63*(7), 457–460.

Weikel, W. J., & Palmo, A. J. (1989). The evolution and practice of mental health counseling. *Journal of Mental Health Counseling, 11*(1), 7–25.

Weinrach, S. G., & Thomas, K. R. (2002). A critical analysis of multicultural counseling competencies: Implications for the practice of mental health counseling. *Journal of Mental Health Counseling, 24,* 20–35.

Weldon v. Virginia State Board of Psychologist Examiners. Corporation Court Opinion (Court Order). Newport News, VA: October 4, 1972.

Williamson, E. G. (1965). *Vocational counseling: Some historical, philosophical, and theoretical perspectives.* New York: McGraw-Hill.

Williams Institute (2007). *Bias in the workplace: Consistent evidence of sexual orientation and gender identity discrimination.* Retrieved March 2, 2007, from http://www.law.ucla.edu/williamsinstitute/publications/Bias%20in%20the%20Workplace.pdf

Zimpfer, D. G. (1992, January). *Insurance experience of licensed counselors.* Paper presented at the 1992 National Conference of the Association for Counselor Education and Supervision. San Antonio, TX.

CHAPTER

2

The Helping Relationship

ROCHELLE MOSS, PhD

University of Arkansas, Little Rock

Introduction

Imagine that you are the client, and you are about to walk through the door of the counselor's office for your very first visit. For the past year, you have contemplated going to talk to someone, but fear and anxiety have kept you from seeking help. You have worried that the counselor might judge you or that the counselor might tell people in the community about your problems. You have questioned whether the counselor will truly be able to help you. But finally you have made the decision to obtain help, and with all the courage you can muster, you walk through the door.

What do you hope to find on the other side of the door? What will you need from this trained professional? And how will this person go about helping you get what you need from this experience?

When you place yourself in the position of the client, you can understand the importance most clients place on their decision to seek counseling and the apprehension they often feel about the counseling process. This chapter focuses on the characteristics, knowledge, and skills the counselor needs to build effective counselor–client helping relationships. The first section describes the helping relationship and its importance. The following sections review what research has shown to be the characteristics of effective counselors and the skills needed to help clients move toward positive change. Also, a case study provides examples taken from conversations between the counselor and client; these examples demonstrate specific techniques you might use when working with clients.

What Is the Helping Relationship?

There are many informal helping relationships in our lives in which we seek assistance from friends, family members, or coworkers. These relationships meet the mutual

I would like to express my appreciation to the coauthors who wrote previous versions of this chapter, which appeared in earlier editions of the book: Susan Halverson-Westerberg, PhD, LPC, LMFT, NCC, NCSC, and Russell D. Miars, PhD. Their knowledge and scholarly contributions are reflected in the present version.

needs of those involved. Unlike these relationships, the counselor–client helping relationship is unique in that it is established as a one-way relationship with the purpose of resolving a concern and/or fostering the personal growth of one person—the client. The counselor is designated as the helper and is assumed to have the knowledge and training to assist the client in an intentional and systematic way. Rogers (1961) defined a helping relationship as one "in which at least one of the parties has the intent of promoting the growth, development, maturity, improved functioning and improved coping with life of the other" (p. 39).

The goals of any counselor–client relationship, whether in educational, career, or personal counseling, can be placed into four basic goal areas: changes in behavior and lifestyle, increased awareness or insight and understanding, relief from suffering, or changes in thoughts and self-perceptions (Brammer & MacDonald, 1996). An important aspect of the helping relationship is that it is a process that enables a person to grow in directions that person chooses. It is the counselor's job to make the client aware of possible alternatives and encourage the client to accept responsibility for taking action on one or more of these alternatives.

The helping relationship minimally can be broken down into three phases: relationship building, challenging the client to find ways to change, and facilitating positive client action (Egan, 2007). In the first phase, the goal is to build a foundation of mutual trust that promotes the client's exploration of the presenting issues. In the second phase, the client has a deeper level of awareness and understanding regarding the issues, and the helper then challenges the client to "try on" new ways of thinking, feeling, and behaving. In the final phase, the counselor facilitates client actions that lead toward change and growth in the client's life outside the counseling relationship.

Seligman (2004) suggests that a positive helping relationship has the following characteristics:

- It provides a safe and protective environment for clients.
- It encourages collaboration, with both clients and counselors playing an active role in the counseling process.
- It has mutuality or a feeling of shared warmth, caring, affirmation, and respect.
- Clients can identify with their counselors and perhaps use them as role models.
- Client and counselor have an agreement on goals and procedures; sessions are structured in such a way as to clearly move toward accomplishment of these goals.
- Client and counselor view themselves as engaged in a shared endeavor that seems likely to succeed. (p. 212)

Studies repeatedly show that the quality of the helping relationship is the most important predictor of positive counseling outcomes (Horvarth & Symonds, 1991; Orlinksy, Grawe, & Parks, 1994; Sexton & Whiston, 1994). The contributions of the helping relationship are independent of the theoretical orientation or type of treatment (Norcross, 2001). Specific procedures and techniques have been proven to be much less important than the alliance between counselor and client (Assay & Lambert, 1999).

It is the counselor's responsibility to begin establishing this vital relationship as quickly as possible. Researchers have found several essential elements that make the relationship more favorable for client growth.

Essential Components of a Helping Relationship

Several decades ago, Carl Rogers was instrumental in determining the core conditions necessary for a beneficial relationship in counseling. Rogers (1957) believed that congruence, unconditional positive regard for the individual, and empathic understanding needed to be present for the relationship to be therapeutic.

When describing *congruence*, Rogers (1961) emphasized the importance of being genuine and real in the relationship. He explained that counselors should strive to have congruence between what they are feeling on the inside and what they are outwardly communicating. When a counselor is congruent, interactions with the client are characterized by honesty, transparency, and openness. Rogers believed that "it is only by providing the genuine reality which is in me, that the other person can successfully seek for the reality in him" (p. 33).

When Rogers (1961) explained the condition of having *warm, unconditional positive regard* for the clients, he stressed the importance of accepting the client without evaluation or judgment. He stated that this acceptance "makes for him [the client] a relationship of warmth and safety, and the safety of being liked and prized as a person seems a highly important element in a helping relationship" (p. 33). This attitude of valuing the client and showing positive regard is referred to as nonpossessive warmth by more recent writers (Cormier & Hackney, 2008).

Rogers (1961) described the condition of *empathy* as being necessary for the client to feel the counselor's acceptance. Empathy is often defined as the understanding of the client's experiences and feelings as if they were your own but without losing the "as if" quality (Rogers, 1957; Bozarth, 1997). When a counselor effectively communicates empathy, it assures clients that they are understood; it also can provide a sense of safety and encourage client exploration (Bohart, Elliott, Greenberg, & Watson, 2002). Rogers (1961) described this process:

> It is only as I understand the feelings and thoughts which seem so horrible to you . . . it is only as I see them as you see them, and accept them and you, that you feel free to explore all the hidden nooks and frightening crannies of your inner and often buried experiences. (p. 34)

Rogers's core conditions have proven to be essential in establishing and maintaining effective helping relationships and are now considered to be basic helping skills used in the majority of counseling approaches. Additional elements necessary for a therapeutic relationship include commitment, respect, trust, confidentiality, and benevolent power (Kottler & Shepherd, 2008).

- *Respect* describes the helping attitude that communicates acceptance of the client as a person of worth and dignity (Rogers, 1957). In utilizing this skill, the counselor demonstrates a belief in the client's ability to deal with his or her problems in the presence of a facilitative person. Respectful counselors use communication skills to actualize the power, ability, and skills the client already possesses. In other words, the counselor believes in the client's problem-solving ability. These skills and attitudes are very important in facilitating an effective helping relationship. They communicate a willingness to work with the client and an interest and belief in the client as a person of worth (Cormier, Cormier, & Cormier, 1997).

■ *Trust* is essential in a healthy, productive counseling relationship. Trust can be established by being genuine and by expressing respect and positive regard for the client's individual worth. Trust can be maintained by consistently following ethical standards and always remembering to put the needs of the client first and foremost.

■ *Confidentiality* assures clients that whatever they tell will remain private (within certain limits; see Chapter 4). This promise allows the client to feel safe and promotes telling information that would otherwise remain hidden.

■ The *use of benevolent power* refers to using the interpersonal influence one has as a counselor in a careful manner. According to Strong and Claiborn (1982), counselors are influential because of their perceived levels of expertness, attractiveness, and trustworthiness and must use this power responsibly in facilitating change for the client.

■ *Commitment* to carry out respective responsibilities in the helping relationship is important for both counselors and clients. Counselor responsibilities include delivering specified services and following ethical guidelines; client responsibilities include a commitment toward working on his or her problems and investing energy in the counseling process.

We have examined components of an effective helping relationship; next, we will outline specific counselor characteristics and attitudes that are linked with being an effective and competent helper.

Personal Characteristics of Counselors

Effective counselors have specific personal qualities and are able to convey those qualities to the people they help. Increasing evidence supports the concept that helpers are only as effective as they are self-aware and able to use themselves as vehicles of change (Okun, 2008).

Combs (1986) summarized 13 studies that looked at helpers in a variety of settings. These studies supported the view that there are differences in the beliefs of effective and ineffective person-centered helpers. Effective counselors are interested in and committed to understanding the specialized knowledge of the field and find it personally meaningful. As such, they are challenged to remain current in their knowledge and skills. They like people and have a feeling of oneness with others. Effective counselors use interventions that focus on the individual's perception of self and expand the individual's view of life rather than narrowing it. They are committed to freeing rather than controlling the client and are able to be objectively involved with, rather than alienated from, their clients.

In other studies, effective counselors have been shown to be compassionate and believing of the client's world. In their own lives, they are open to a full range of experiences and feelings, are spontaneous, and have a sense of humor. When interacting

TABLE 2.1   **Checklist of Desirable Counselor Characteristics**

Intelligent	Empathic
Energetic	Optimistic
Caring	Self-confident
Trustworthy	Self-aware
Genuine	Creative
Emotionally stable	Flexible
Resourceful	Hardworking
Unselfish	Insightful
Curious	Nonjudgmental
Good listener	Knowledgeable
Realistic	Ethical
Dependable	Friendly
Hopeful	Sense of humor
Respectful of individual differences	Comfortable with intimacy
Maintains balance in own life	Able to express self clearly

with others, they are able to be involved yet remain somewhat detached (Cormier et al., 1997). In the process of dealing with problems and issues, they help clients clearly see their own worlds while adding a fresh perspective to the issues.

Because counseling is demanding work, effective counselors often display high energy levels (Carkhuff, 1986). Intense focusing with another individual, trying to hear clearly, often needing to tolerate ambiguity (Pietrofesa, Hoffman, Splete, & Pinto, 1978), and taking appropriate risks can put heavy demands on the counselor's physical and emotional energy. Therefore, a challenge to individuals pursuing the counseling profession is to have good self-care strategies (see Brems, 2000).

Examine the checklist of desirable counselor characteristics in Table 2.1. The items have been compiled from numerous resources (Combs, 1986; Gladding, 2007; Rogers, 1957, 1961; Seligman, 2004; Sexton & Whiston, 1994) and are listed in no particular order of importance. Check those you believe you possess, and make note of those you have not yet developed.

In the next section, the fundamental helping skills of counseling are explained, beginning, with microskills and attending skills.

Basic Skills and Concepts

According to Ivey and Ivey (2007), the aim of counseling is personal and social development. They have described a hierarchy of microcounseling skills that define what the counselor does in an interview to achieve specific results. The hierarchy rests on a foundation of attending behaviors and basic listening skills. The list of skills presented here is based on Ivey and Ivey's model, with additional information taken from Cormier and colleagues (1997) and Egan (2007).

Attending Skills

Attending behavior, including eye contact, body language, vocal quality, and verbal tracking, is one of the most powerful communication skills (Ivey & Ivey, 2007). In the counseling relationship, counselors communicate through body language and words that their full attention is on the client's nonverbal and verbal behaviors. Eye contact, facial expressions, and body posture are the physical fundamentals that indicate to others that you are either carefully attending or not attending to them.

Eye Contact.   Good eye contact is not an unwavering stare but an intermittent yet frequent looking into the eyes of the client. It tells others that you are interested in them and what they have to say. It also can signal understanding and provide feedback (Evans, Hearn, Uhlemann, & Ivey, 2008). Effective eye contact occurs more frequently when there is a comfortable distance between counselor and client and when topics being discussed are not too threatening. Cultural differences abound in what is considered appropriate eye contact (Ivey & Ivey, 2007). For example, Anglo-Americans usually have more eye contact when listening and less when talking; the opposite is true of many African Americans. In some cultures, eye contact is avoided when discussing serious topics (Evans et al., 2008). The counselor should first consider cultural differences if eye contact seems strained or awkward in the relationship.

Attentive Body Language.   Body orientation can encourage or discourage interpersonal interactions. In Anglo-American culture, a slight forward body lean and a relaxed, comfortable posture are usually received favorably and indicate interest in the client. Egan (2007) uses the acronym SOLER to describe this attentive body posture: *S*quarely face the client, *O*pen body posture, *L*ean forward slightly, *E*ye contact, and *R*elaxed manner. Facial expressions should fit the material being discussed.

Distance.   The distance between counselor and client also affects communication. There is an optimal "comfort zone" for conversing that is largely controlled by cultural influences. It is about an arm's length in American culture. The counselor must be aware of the level of comfort or discomfort that the client is experiencing with the distance and adjust it if necessary.

Although there are many things counselors can do to convey an interest in their clients, certain mannerisms are distracting. Behaviors such as gum chewing, cigarette smoking, or continual change of body position may seriously affect any interpersonal interaction and convey a lack of counselor interest.

Vocal Tone.   Another aspect of attending behavior is voice tone. A warm, pleasant, caring voice strongly indicates an interest and willingness to listen. The pitch, volume, and rate of speech can convey much of one's feeling toward another person or situation. Scherer (1986) has shown that the use of specific paralinguistic cues can convey either high or low levels of self-confidence. High levels of confidence are conveyed when you speak in a caring voice that is neither hesitant nor rapid and projects inner qualities of warmth, respect, and compassion for the client. These cues of self-confidence can affect client perceptions of counselor expertness, attractiveness, and trustworthiness, as well as associated satisfaction with the counseling relationship (Barak, Shapira, & Fisher, 1988).

Verbal Tracking. Even when the client engages in long, irrelevant discourses, the counselor often needs to remain relaxed and follow the client's topic and logic. The counselor can choose to either attend or ignore certain portions of the client's statements, which is termed *selective attention*. The portions of the client's statements to which a counselor attends depend upon the counselor's theoretical orientation and professional beliefs. Counselors have to be aware of their own patterns of selective attention, for the topics their clients focus on will tend to be partially determined by those topics to which the counselor unconsciously attends.

Silence is another important part of verbal attending behavior. The counselor's ability to remain silent while clients are silent facilitates clients listening to their inner voice (and also may give the counselor time to think of the most effective way to respond). Silence may give the client time to further contemplate or process the issues at hand, and a deeper level of understanding may be the result. Remaining silent is often an excellent tactic to start a reluctant client talking because silence is often perceived as a demanding condition that must be filled with a response. However, the

TABLE 2.2 Helping Skills

Attending Skills	Description
Eye contact	Intermittent yet frequent looking into the eyes of the client
Attentive body language	Having a comfortable, relaxed, open posture
Distance	Awareness of personal space; distance appropriate from client
Verbal tracking	Attending to client's story; may involve selective attention
Active Listening Skills	
Observing nonverbals	Noting physiological changes, facial expressions, body language
Verbal behavior	Noticing key words, topic changes, topic exclusions, incongruities
Minimal encouragers	Head nodding, "um-hmm," interested facial expressions
Paraphrase	Rephrasing the content of the client's message
Summarization	Restating overall meaning from a long period of conversation
Reflection of feelings	Accurately recognizing and communicating the client's emotions
Questions	Using open-ended questions beginning with *what* and *how*
Concreteness	Helping to make feelings, experiences, and behaviors more specific
Advanced Skills	
Advanced Empathy	Communicating a deeper underlying meaning of client's experiences
Self-disclosure	Sharing personal information for specific reasons, such as modeling
Confrontation	Communicating to the client his or her discrepancies or mixed messages
Immediacy	Discussing what is happening in the moment or the "here and now"

meaning of silence is culturally based (Murphy & Dillon, 2008). The challenge for beginning counselors is learning to be comfortable enough with silence to use it effectively.

The following section begins with a case study that gives specific examples of basic helping skills and advanced skills.

Case Study

Melissa is a 16-year-old female who was brought in to counseling after swallowing a bottle of Tylenol. She told her mother what she had done, and her mother rushed her to the hospital, where the emergency staff pumped her stomach. She recovered and was referred for individual counseling.

During the first few sessions, the client explored several significant issues with the counselor. First of all, she emphasized the main issue behind the overdose was that her boyfriend broke up with her. She also said that she was very upset over the fact that a 19-year-old male friend was being deployed to the Middle East in a couple of months. She felt guilty and worried because she had not been on good terms with him and "had been mean to him." Melissa stated that these two stressors were behind her taking the overdose.

In addition, Melissa explained that she has few, if any, true friends. She believes that she does not belong in any group. She is not a "goody-two-shoes," nor is she a "nerd." She also has decided that her old group may have some behaviors that she does not want to get mixed up with, such as drug use. However, she later reveals that she does smoke a little marijuana from time to time.

Melissa's parents are divorced, and she lives with her mother. She is an only child. Melissa said that she wants to have a good relationship with her father and that they try to see each other about once a month. However, she added that if she has anything else to do, she will make an excuse and not see him. Her mother has a very busy work schedule with lots of job responsibilities but seems to pay attention to Melissa when there is a crisis situation.

The Basic Listening Skills

Active listening is an extremely important dimension of counselors' work (Egan, 2007). Counselors need to be sure that they are hearing the client accurately, and clients must know that the counselor has fully heard them, seen their point of view, and felt the world as they experience it. The basic listening skills that facilitate active listening include client observation; noticing client nonverbal behavior; the use of encouraging, paraphrasing, and summarization statements; the reflection of client feelings; and the use of open and closed questions. The outcome of using these basic listening skills in combination is the establishment of an empathic relationship with the client (Carkhuff, 1969). The overall purpose of empathy is to "understand the situation of another person from that person's perspective" (Berger, McBreen, & Rifkin, 1996, p. 210).

Client Observation

Simply observing the client provides the counselor with a rich source of "silent information." Noticing and paying attention to the *physiological cues* expressed in another person's appearance and physique provide a way to identify the internal emotional responses of the other person. These physiological cues may include changes in skin color, pupil dilation, muscle tone, and/or breathing, which can reflect the internal emotional processes and the physiologic changes occurring within the client. These physiologic messages are difficult to hide because they are generally involuntary reactions of the autonomic nervous system. Observing subtle changes in these areas can silently reveal the moments of emotional change for a client.

The points during the interview at which eye contact is broken, the voice changes, skin color changes, shifts in body posture occur, or muscle tension or facial expression changes may indicate moments when important information is being revealed.

Case Example

The counselor observes Melissa as she describes the breakup with her boyfriend. The client's voice tone drops, and she speaks more slowly. Eye contact is broken as she looks down, and her skin becomes pale. From these observations, the counselor is aware of the strong emotions connected with the breakup.

Verbal Behavior

In addition to nonverbal behavior, the client's verbal behavior can also reveal a great deal. At the most basic level, the counselor should note *topic changes* or *topic exclusions* and any *key words* that appear again and again. For example, the client's frequent use of "should" or "ought" statements may indicate a lack of control in those areas and should be explored further. Noticing topics the client avoids may also give the counselor valuable information that can be explored later with the client.

Case Example

The counselor notes that Melissa often changes the topic when the relationship with her father is mentioned. Words that continue to resurface include *alone, hurt,* and *guilty,* which may point toward themes in this client's current situation.

Sentence structure is an important clue to how the client views the world. Is the client the subject or the object of the sentence? Specifically, does the client feel he or she does the acting or is acted on? Are concerns portrayed as being in the past, the present, or the future? Are there key words and descriptions that give a clue to the client's worldview? Certain patterns of words and ideas are clues to a client's typical thought processes and self-perceptions.

Incongruities, discrepancies, and *double messages* are nearly universal in counseling interviews. They are often at the root of a client's immobility and inability to respond creatively to difficult life situations (Egan, 2007). When counselors notice such incongruities, they may choose to either hold back and say nothing or try to bring the discrepancy into the client's awareness. The emotional state of the client and the impact upon the relationship should be the main considerations in making this decision. In time-limited counseling, or within certain theoretical frameworks such as Gestalt, immediate confrontation may be the preferred intervention. Confrontation skills are discussed later in this chapter.

Case Example

The counselor notices a couple of incongruities in Melissa's communication. First, she said that she does not want to associate with her old friends because of the drug use but later revealed that she smokes marijuana from time to time. She also stated that she wishes to have a strong relationship with her father but makes excuses to avoid seeing him when possible.

Encouraging, Paraphrasing, and Summarizing

The skill of *encouraging* includes the use of both "encouragers" and "restatements," both of which punctuate the interview and provide a smooth flow. Using encouragers such as head nods, an interested facial expression, or verbal utterances such as "umm" or "uh-huh" is an active way to let clients know that they have been heard and understood. Encouragers can be used to influence the direction taken by the client and are part of selective attention as described previously.

One powerful type of encourager is the counselor's restatement of a key word or a short phrase from the client's statement, often in a questioning tone of voice.

Case Example

MELISSA: I felt alone and afraid when my boyfriend broke up with me.

COUNSELOR: Afraid?

The *paraphrase* is used to reflect the content of what the client has just said. It is not parroting the client (repeating back exactly what was said) but feeding back to the client the essence of what was said (Evans et al., 2008). It is an encapsulated rephrase of the content of the client's message in the counselor's words, sometimes containing the client's key words and constructs. The strength of the paraphrase is that the counselor is giving of self yet is paying primary attention to the client's frame of reference. The purpose of this skill is to let clients know that they have been heard accurately and to encourage them to continue discussing the issue in more detail.

Case Example

Consider the following example of a paraphrase.

MELISSA: I wish I could take back some of the mean, hurtful things I said to my friend, but now he's being deployed, and I don't have the chance. And who knows what will happen?

COUNSELOR: You wish you could talk to your friend and apologize for what you said in the past, but now you don't have that opportunity, and you think of the uncertainty of the situation with him going to fight in the war.

Summarizations are similar to paraphrasing, except that they "paraphrase" a longer period of conversation. These responses gather together a client's verbalizations—facts, feelings, meanings, and patterns—and restate them for the client as accurately as possible. Summarizations frequently give the client a feeling of movement as ideas and feelings are explored (Brammer & MacDonald, 1996).

Summarizations may be useful in the beginning of a session to warm up a client or at other times to bring closure to discussion on a theme. They can be used to add direction and coherence to a session that seems to be going nowhere (Egan, 2007). Also, summarizations are valuable to counselors as a check on the accuracy of their understanding of the information that has just been gathered.

Case Example

Here is an example of a summarization in an interview with Melissa.

> COUNSELOR: You're feeling uncertain about lots of things in your life right now—your relationships with friends, relationships with parents, and trying to figure out who you are and where you fit.

Reflection of Feelings

Besides hearing the words of the client accurately, the counselor must uncover and recognize the emotions underlying those words. The counselor listens and watches for both nonverbal messages and direct verbal communication to accurately determine the feeling(s) being expressed by the client. Reflection of feeling can help clients to feel understood, to sort out complex feelings, and to continue exploring their feelings at a deeper level (Egan, 2007; Evans et al., 2008). Seligman (2004) stated that a counselor's use of this tool is the most powerful way to communicate empathy.

The counselor also has to know how to communicate the feeling accurately by recognizing and labeling the category of emotion (i.e., anger, gladness, sadness, fear, or uncertainty), as well as the correct intensity of the emotion (Carkhuff & Anthony, 1979).

Case Example

> MELISSA: I know that Dad had an affair while he and Mom were married, and I'll never get over that. And now he wants to just trade us in for his *new* family!
>
> COUNSELOR: You're really angry with your dad and resent the fact that he's starting over with someone else.

When using reflection of feeling with clients of differing cultures, the counselor must be able to express culturally sensitive empathy by having knowledge of the client's culture and communicating respect and understanding of the culture while understanding the client's circumstances (Evans et al., 2008). Also, the counselor needs to be aware of how that specific culture views the open discussion of emotions.

Questions

The use of questions can open communication. In the helping relationship, the counselor's effective, open communication is especially necessary. It facilitates moving the client from self-exploration through increased understanding and finally to commitment to appropriate action. By using specific verbal leads, the counselor is able to bring out the major facts, feelings, and self-perceptions that a client brings to the session. Effective use of open and closed questions can encourage the client to talk more freely and openly.

Asking *open-ended questions* is considered to be the most beneficial type of questioning because the client is encouraged to talk more freely and openly. Open questions usually begin with *what, how, could,* or *would* and require the client to provide a longer, more expansive response than simply yes or no. Open questions are used to begin interviews; to encourage clients to express more information; to elicit examples of particular behaviors, thoughts, or feelings; and to increase the client's commitment to communicate. Some examples might be:

COUNSELOR: What would you like to discuss today?

COUNSELOR: How do you plan to reestablish that friendship?

Sometimes a client is very talkative and rambles or jumps from topic to topic. In such a case, *closed questions* can be used to gather information, give clarity, gain focus, and narrow the area of discussion. These closed questions usually begin with *is, are, do,* or *did.* Counselors must use caution, though, because extensive use of closed questions can hinder conversation (Egan, 2007). A questioning counselor can appear to have all the power in the relationship, and this inequality can destroy the counselor–client alliance, especially during initial encounters. With too many closed questions, clients may feel as though they are being interrogated.

Clients from some cultures are rapidly turned off by counselor questions, as are clients who have not developed trust in their counselors. The same information can frequently be obtained by asking the client what goals they have, how they feel about those goals, and how they plan to attain them. (Note that asking too many questions at once can confuse clients.) "Why" questions are especially troublesome because they may put clients on the defensive or leave them feeling they must provide a logical explanation for their behavior.

Because questions may cause resistance with some clients, the skills of encouraging, paraphrasing, summarization, and reflection of feeling may be used to obtain similar information yet seem less intrusive to the client.

Counselors must be flexible and adapt their skills to accommodate the client's culture. (See Chapter 3 for information on culture-specific issues.) To prevent counselors from making generalizations that lead to stereotyping, Hays (1996) developed a model for considering the multifaceted cultural influences that affect the helping relationship. These influences include gender, race and ethnicity, age and generation, social status, sexual orientation, religion, indigenous heritage, and national origin. Counselors must remember that the client's issues are developed in a cultural context and listen for family and cultural issues that affect the client in order to resolve the issues within that context.

Concreteness

In the process of exploring problems or issues, a client often presents an incomplete representation of what has happened. The goal of concreteness is to make the information and awareness gained through self-exploration more specific and concrete (Meier & Davis, 1993). It is the task of the counselor to help the client clarify the pieces of the puzzle and fit them together so that the whole makes sense to the client. This clarification increases the likelihood that an organized, specific, workable action plan will be accepted by the client and implemented. When encouraging concreteness, counselors attempt to focus very specifically on the situation at hand and try to make clear all facets of the issue, including the accompanying behaviors and feelings.

There are several ways to help clients become more concrete and focused. When a client makes a vague statement, the counselor can reflect in a more concrete way. At times, a rambling client may need to be focused. The effective use of concreteness in such situations may feel like interrupting but should lead to increased counselor–client interaction. When clients need to be more definite and clear, leads such as "what" and "how" rather than "why" will usually produce more relevant and specific information (Egan, 2007).

Case Example

MELISSA: I just want to feel like I belong somewhere.

COUNSELOR: Describe for me a specific time or situation in your life when you remember feeling that way.

Effective use of concreteness keeps the counseling session productively focused and aims at making vague experiences, behaviors, and feelings more specific. The more specific the information, the better the understanding and the more effective future choices and actions will be.

Self-Attending Skills

Counselors who are aware of their own values, beliefs, and assets find it easier to "be with" clients, help clients explore personal issues, and facilitate client action. Therefore, the self-attending skills are extremely important for each person who wishes to be an effective counselor. There are several components to the self-attending process. Shulman (1979) referred to these counselor components as "tuning-in." The first component in the tuning-in process is self-awareness.

Self-Awareness

The personal knowledge and understanding that the counselor has of self and the counseling setting are essential to the self-attending process. Practically speaking, the counselor should not consciously rehearse how counselors are "supposed" to be. The effective counselor acts professionally but does not put on a professional front or play-act being some imaginary expert counselor. Effective counselors know their strengths as well as their weaknesses, and by understanding themselves they are able to overcome self-consciousness and devote fuller attention to what the client is trying to disclose.

In the process of learning counseling skills, there may be times when using the skills seems awkward and uncomfortable. The learning cycle for trainees can some-times be an unsettling process. Unlearning competing behaviors and relearning new ones in their place take time, a great deal of concentration, and practice. Counselor self-awareness is crucial throughout this process.

Centering and Relaxing

Centering, or getting in touch and then in tune with oneself (Brammer & MacDonald, 1996), is an important skill for the counselor to develop. By becoming centered, the counselor is able to show more social-emotional presence (Egan, 2007) in the counseling relationship and give the client his or her undivided attention. With a keener focus than is common in most human interaction, the counselor is better able to empathi-cally understand the client's problems and concerns. Similarly, the counselor's relax-ation (both physical and psychological) helps clients relax as they face the stress and challenges of the counseling process.

Nonjudgmental Attitude Toward Self

Counselors need a broad awareness of their own value positions. They must be able to answer very clearly the questions "Who am I?" "What is important to me?" and "Am I nonjudgmental?" (Brammer & MacDonald, 1996).

This awareness aids counselors in being honest with themselves and their clients and in being free from judgments about themselves. In addition, it helps the counselor avoid unwarranted or unethical use of clients to satisfy personal needs. Although coun-selors may have opinions about the traits of people they like and want to associate with, one characteristic of effective counselors is that they try to suspend personal judg-ments about their clients' lives.

Nonjudgmental Attitude Toward Others

This attitude is respect for a client's individuality and worth as a person and very simi-lar to Rogers's (1961) concept of "unconditional positive regard." It allows clients to be open and be themselves, because they know that the counselor will not be judging them or what they say. The counselor conveys this nonjudgmental attitude by being warm, accepting, and respectful toward the client; this is especially important in the early phases of the relationship.

Case Example

MELISSA: I feel really awful. I had sex with my boyfriend, and then he broke up with me. I know my parents wouldn't approve, but I thought he really loved me. But I don't think they would understand.

COUNSELOR: You thought at the time it was the right decision because there were strong feelings involved. But you don't think that your parents could ever understand.

Respect is rarely found alone in communication. It usually occurs in combination with empathy and genuineness.

Communicating Genuineness

When counselors relate to clients naturally and openly, they are being genuine. Being a counselor is not just a role played by the individual. Instead, it is the appropriate revelation of one's own feelings, thoughts, and being in the counseling relationship. Egan (1975) cautions that "being role free is not license; freedom from role means that the counselor should not use the role or facade of counselor to protect himself, to substitute for effectiveness, or to fool the client" (p. 92).

The effective use of genuineness reduces the emotional distance between counselor and client (Cormier et al., 1997). It breaks down the role distance, links the counselor and client together, and allows the client to see the counselor as human, and a person similar to him or her. The genuine counselor is spontaneous, nondefensive, and consistent in relationships.

Case Example

MELISSA: Do you think I'm as crazy and weird as I feel?

COUNSELOR: You have been going through some difficult situations, and you're feeling confused about what to do. I don't experience you as being crazy and weird at all.

TABLE 2.3   Multicultural Considerations in Establishing a Helping Relationship

Beliefs	What are my beliefs about the client's culture, and what impact has my culture had on my beliefs?
Attitudes	Do I value cultural diversity presented by my client?
Skills	What skills and strategies do I need to work effectively with this culturally diverse client?
Knowledge	
Acculturation	What is the client's level of acculturation or assimilation into the majority culture?
Perceptions	How does my client view seeking help from a counselor?
Social philosophy	Is this client from an individualistic or collectivist society?
Approach	Will a direct or subtle approach be more effective? Will the client respond better to an equal relationship or to an expert stance?
Distance	At what physical distance is this client most comfortable?
Communication	What are the cultural norms for eye contact, vocal tone, speech rate? How does this client view silence, questioning, confrontation?
Respect	How do I express politeness and respect to this client?

Cultural Competence

It is the counselor's responsibility to learn about cultural diversity and become cultur-ally competent. This process increases the counselor's awareness and sensitivity for clients of different ethnicities. Daw (1997) emphasized several recommendations. First of all, become aware of your own cultural heritage and how it affects you as a coun-selor; also, become aware of your own biases and prejudices, including racism. Next, seek opportunities to interact with people of different cultures and learn from these experiences. Finally, examine your understanding of poverty and how it affects those of different cultures, plus take an honest look at your own positions of power and priv-ilege. (See Chapter 3 for a more thorough discussion.)

Humor

The counselor who can enjoy and use humor effectively has an invaluable asset. The healing power of humor has long been valued and can be used in counseling as an emotional release. Although counseling is serious business, there are many truly humorous dimensions to the human condition, and when humor appears as a natural outgrowth of the counselor–client relationship, it should be attended to (Prochaska & Norcross, 2003). Humor can provide a means of connecting with clients, and coun-selors need to affirm any humor clients present. Laughter and joking can release built-up tensions, and laughing at oneself can be extremely therapeutic because it requires seeing one's problems in a whole new perspective.

   When using humor with clients of a different ethnic background, the counselor needs to exercise particular caution (Maples et al., 2001). Humor can be defined, inter-preted, and valued differently by individuals from different cultures. For that reason, consider both the individual and cultural values of the client, and tailor or customize the use of humor to make it appropriate for the particular client.

Touch

Counselors should always be sensitive to the therapeutic value of touch. Using touch requires consideration of the client issues and sensitivity to the role that touch has played in creating the issue, as well as what professionals who are considered experts recommend as best practice. For example, counselors must use extreme caution when using touch with individuals traumatized by physical or sexual abuse.

   Humanistic models suggest that touch that is genuinely felt may help create within the client a willingness to be open and share. Driscoll, Newman, and Seals (1988) found that college students observing videotapes felt that counselors who touched their college-age clients were more caring than counselors who did not. It must be emphasized, though, that touch without genuine feeling behind it may be more harmful than helpful.

   The type of touch that is generally considered acceptable is one that is long enough (1–3 seconds) to make contact yet does not create uncomfortable feelings. Most professionals who do touch believe that appropriate touching is contact of the counselor's hand or forearm with the client's hand, arm, shoulder, or upper back, and recognize that gender differences may influence how such contact is interpreted. Alyn (1988) suggested that touch can reinforce the culturally prescribed unequal power relationship between genders and perpetuate the routine infringement upon women's boundaries.

There are no specific ethical standards concerning nonsexual touching; however, there are strict ethical guidelines regarding sexual contact with clients. Some counselors who oppose touch believe that nonsexual touching may lead to crossing boundaries and the gratification of the counselor's needs. The decision to touch must be based on ethical, clinical, and theoretical principles and must always be based on the client's needs (Durana, 1998).

Touch may be perceived differently from culture to culture. For example, in Hispanic and other Latin cultures, most individuals report being comfortable with touch during casual conversation. In other cultures, people are more restrained. For instance, in Asian cultures, individuals are more comfortable standing far apart and do not engage in casual touching. Cultural views of appropriate touching may transfer to the counseling relationship. However, individual personalities and levels of acculturation and assimilation always need to be taken into account and will take precedence over general norms.

Advanced Skills and Concepts

The first goal of helping is to help clients tell their story in an understandable way (Egan, 2007). This requires facilitating clients' self-understanding. Such exploration helps both counselor and client understand the client's problems and concerns. Clients begin to focus and see more clearly the puzzles of their life and are skillfully led to identify the missing pieces and blocks. This exploration involves a look at the real self and related issues. The process leads to insightful self-understanding that invites the client to change or take action.

Once the beginning counselor is adept at using the basic counseling skills, advanced skills and concepts can be added to the repertoire. These skills and concepts are more action oriented and allow the counselor to facilitate deeper client self-understanding, change, and eventual termination of the helping relationship. The advanced understanding and challenging skills include advanced empathy, self-disclosure, confrontation, and immediacy (Egan, 2007).

Advanced Understanding and Challenging Skills

Advanced Empathy. Primary empathy forms the foundation and atmospheric core of the helping relationship (Gladding, 2007). It involves listening for basic or surface messages with frequent, brief responses to those messages. The skills of paraphrasing and reflection of feeling serve counselors well when they establish an empathic base of understanding (Carkhuff, 1969). The counselor sees the world from the client's frame of reference and communicates that it has been understood. The goal is to move the client toward identifying and exploring crucial topics and feelings. During this early self-exploration phase, the counselor must be sensitive to signs of client stress or resistance and try to judge whether these arise from lack of accurate response or from being too accurate too quickly. As the counselor moves the client beyond exploration to self-understanding and action, advanced skills become more necessary.

Primary empathy gets at relevant feelings and meanings that are actually stated; the skill of *advanced empathy* gets at feelings and meanings that are hidden or beyond the immediate reach of the client (Egan, 2007). The most basic form of advanced empathy is to give expression and understanding to what the client has only implied. It challenges the client to take a deeper look at self.

Advanced empathy includes the identification of themes presented by the client. Feeling, behavioral, experiential, or combined themes may occur. Once the counselor recognizes the themes, the task is to communicate the relevant ones to the client in a way that will be heard and understood. The themes must be based solidly on an accurate understanding of the client's feelings, experiences, and behaviors and communicated as concretely as possible by using the client's experiences and communication style.

The act of bringing together and communicating relevant core material that the client has presented in only a fragmented way is part of advanced empathy. The counselor helps the client fill in the missing links in the information. When it becomes apparent that two aspects of client information are closely linked, this information should be shared, but the counselor must guard against premature speculation or unfounded linkages.

As the counselor explores the deeper, underlying meaning of an experience of the client, the skill of reflection of meaning can be used. It provides a way for the client to develop a new worldview and interpret old situations or information in new ways. Because information is always subject to individual interpretation (Gelatt, 1989), the counselor needs to reframe the situation, belief, or experience to help the client view it from a different perspective and also check that the interpretation is correct.

Advanced empathy gets at more critical, deeper, and delicate issues and, therefore, puts the client under additional stress. To avoid overwhelming the client and evoking resistance, the counselor's empathetic responses should be tentative and cautious. Leads such as "From what you have said," "Could it be that" or "It seems like" may be most helpful.

Counselors may find it helpful to reflect back to clients what they see as the meaning of an experience.

Case Example

MELISSA: I believed everything my boyfriend told me and then he dumped me. It seems as though every time I trust someone, I get hurt.

COUNSELOR: You've had several situations in your life where people that you trust have disappointed you. I'm wondering if that may be part of the reason that you're avoiding close relationships now? Maybe you've becoming more guarded because you don't want to get hurt?

Self-Disclosure. Hendrick (1988) and Peca-Baker and Friedlander (1987) have found that clients want to have information about their counselors. Sharing oneself can be a powerful intervention for making contact with clients, but it should not be an indiscriminate sharing of personal problems with clients (Egan, 2007; Sexton, Whiston, Bleuer, & Walz, 1997).

Self-disclosure is defined as any information counselors convey about themselves to clients (Cormier et al., 1997; Cozby, 1973). It can generate a more open, facilitative counseling atmosphere, encourage client talk and additional trust, and create a more equal relationship. In some instances, a self-disclosing counselor may be perceived as more caring than one who does not disclose. At times, counselor self-disclosure can present a model for clients to increase their own levels of disclosure about events and feelings (McCarthy, 1982).

The use of self-disclosure as a skill involves consideration of timing, goals, genuineness, and appropriateness. Effective self-disclosure does not add another burden to an already burdened client (Egan, 2007), and it should not distract the client from his or her own problems (Sexton et al., 1997). The counselor must consider how the client will benefit from the information shared.

Perhaps the most important type of self-disclosure focuses on the counselor–client relationship. If you are having a difficult time listening to a client, for example, it could be useful to let them know that it is difficult. However, it helps to only describe your own feelings and reactions and not judge the client. It may be fairly easy for the counselor to self-disclose, but making the disclosure relevant to the client is the important and more complex task (Ivey & Ivey, 2007). The counselor's self-disclosure should be genuine and fairly close in mood and content to the client's experience. As a counselor, you must remember that self-disclosure is appropriate only when it is genuine, benefits the client, and adds to client movement or understanding and when it does not interfere with the counseling process or contribute to raised levels of client anxiety (Cormier et al., 1997).

Case Example

MELISSA: I can't believe I was so dumb and gullible.

COUNSELOR: It seems like you're being really hard on yourself. I've found when I get in these situations that it is easy to beat myself up. I've learned instead to think of ways to be gentle on myself.

How willing are you to engage in appropriate and relevant self-disclosure? You become vulnerable when you share your own experiences, feelings, and reactions, yet can you expect your clients to become vulnerable in front of you if you rarely show them anything of yourself? Good self-disclosure is a kind of sharing that clients can use to grow, and it lets them know how you're perceiving and experiencing them (Sexton et al., 1997).

Most evidence indicates that a moderate amount of self-disclosure has more impact than too little or too much. Counselors who disclose very little risk being seen as aloof, weak, and role-conscious (Egan, 2007), whereas the counselor who discloses too much may be seen as indiscreet, untrustworthy (Levin & Gergen, 1969), preoccupied (Cozby, 1973), or needing assistance.

Concerning self-disclosure with clients of a different culture, be aware that disclosing personal information may be valued in some cultures and considered in appropriate in others. Become knowledgeable about the meaning and use of self-disclosure in that culture, and use this information to decide about the benefit of using the skill (Evans et al., 2008).

Confrontation.   Confrontation is a skill that is used when there are discrepancies, conflicts, or mixed messages being sent by the client. The mixed messages may show up in conflicts between the verbal and nonverbal messages the client sends or between two contradictory verbal messages. Egan (1975) describes confrontation as "the responsible unmasking of the discrepancies, distortions, games and smoke screens the client uses to hide both from self-understanding and from constructive behavioral change" (p. 158).

When confronting a client, the counselor must always exercise concern for the client's understanding of the challenge so that there will be client progress, not denial and flight. To do this effectively, the counselor must accurately reflect the situation. Using a tentative reflection is important, especially if it is early in the relationship. Also consider the state of the client; an already distressed, confused, or disorganized client will not benefit from a confrontation. In fact, confrontation with such clients may add to their distress or confusion.

> MELISSA: I want to have a close relationship with my dad. We have specific dates when we're supposed to meet for dinner and that's okay. But if I have anything else to do, I'll usually just make an excuse and not go.
>
> COUNSELOR: On one hand, I hear you saying that you want a close relationship with your dad, but on the other hand, you often make excuses so you don't have to meet him for dinner. Can you help me understand this?

Confrontation should be done with care and may be more effective if done gradually, which gives the client time to assimilate information. Good counselor practice demands a careful balance between confrontation and support in the form of primary empathy, positive regard, and respect (Ivey, Ivey, & Simek-Downing, 1987).

When considering cultural implications, the counselor needs to be aware that some cultures may consider confrontation to be insensitive and disrespectful. These cultures include Native North Americans, Canadian Inuit, and traditional Latino/Latina people. The counselor may need to choose alternate methods that are more culturally appropriate (Evans et al., 2008).

Immediacy.   The phenomenon of immediacy involves the counselor's sensitivity to the immediate situation and an understanding of what is occurring at the moment with clients (Pietrofesa, Hoffman, & Splete, 1984). It involves the ability to discuss directly and openly with another person what is happening in the "here and now" of an interpersonal relationship (Egan, 2007). This is sometimes referred to as "you–me" talk.

The use of immediacy combines the skills of confrontation and self-disclosure and requires the counselor to reveal feelings and/or challenge the client to deal more openly with his or her feelings. The purpose of immediacy responses is to help clients understand themselves more clearly, especially what is happening at that moment and how they are relating to the counselor in the session. The focus can be on the client, the relationship, or the counselor's own feelings and reactions (Murphy & Dillon, 2008). As interviews move more to the present tense, the counselor's presence in the interview becomes more powerful and important (Ivey & Ivey, 2007), and the counselor is modeling a kind of behavior that clients can use to become more effective in all their relationships.

Counselors usually know what is happening in a session but do not always act on it. Acting on what is happening at the moment is part of the phenomenon of immediacy. When either counselor or client has unverbalized thoughts or feelings that seem to be getting in the way of progress, the counselor should bring it up for discussion.

Case Example

MELISSA: I'm not sure I should tell you about all the other stupid things I've done.

COUNSELOR: It sounds like something is getting in the way of your trusting me to understand everything that's happened in your life.

There are many areas or issues in which the skill of immediacy might be used: Trust, differences in style, directionless sessions, dependency, counterdependency, and attraction are areas where "you–me" talk might pay off (Egan, 2007). Other areas might include concern for the client's welfare, lack of follow-through on homework, and client doubts about the value of counseling.

Carkhuff (1969) suggests that the counselor ask, during the course of the interview, "What is the client trying to tell me that he or she can't tell me directly?" The answer lies embedded in the verbal and nonverbal behavior of the client. The skilled helper can uncover it and make it an "immediacy" topic.

In considering whether to use immediacy, the counselor should decide whether it is appropriate to focus the relationship on here-and-now concerns at this specific time. If so, then counselor-initiated leads will focus on the identification and communication of feelings. The counselor must seriously consider word choice; as in many other cases, a tentative statement may be more inviting.

When considering multicultural implications in the use of immediacy, several points need to be considered (Evans et al., 2008). First of all, individuals from some cultures may need present concerns communicated in a way that permits the client to save face. Another issue of immediacy may come up if the client feels the counselor is culturally biased. The counselor should use immediacy to resolve these issues before continuing the session (Chapter 3).

Action Skills

The goal of counseling is to have a client come away from the process changed. This growth or change often entails the counselor and client working together on an action plan appropriate to the client's stated goals. These action plans should grow out of the counseling work itself and be based in part on the theoretical orientation of the counselor and what is considered the standards for practice in the profession. For instance, a behaviorally oriented counselor will be more inclined to use behavioral contracts; a cognitive therapist may emphasize thought-stopping and thought-disputing exercises.

Nevertheless, the theoretical orientation is secondary to the development of effective core helping skills. These skills seem to be shared by all effective helpers and really address the quality of the interaction between the counselor and the client. With respect to the action phase, for example, Egan (2007) has suggested that the counselor must have skills to help clients choose effective strategies for change and maintain action-based change programs.

Case Example

> **COUNSELOR:**   One of your main goals is to establish new friendships. I'm wondering how you might begin. What are some ways you've made new friends in the past?
>
> **MELISSA:**   I think I'll begin by accepting the invitation to go out Friday evening with the group from my journalism club. They seem pretty cool.
>
> **COUNSELOR:**   It sounds like you've thought this over, and you have a good idea about where to begin. I'll be interested in hearing about how the plan worked.

Termination Skills.   The ending of a helping relationship can be either gratifying or difficult and frustrating. Termination may occur either by mutual agreement or prematurely (that is, before all goals of counseling are met). When counselor and client agree that the goals of counseling have been accomplished, they may mutually agree that it is time to terminate. Sadness about parting and some client anxiety may be expected, but by exploring and sharing such feelings, each client is more likely to leave with a sense of growth and accomplishment because goals have been achieved. This process also gives clients time to prepare for the future (Murphy & Dillon, 2008). It is important to leave time to discuss feelings about ending, and for a smooth termination, both individuals must know when the last session will occur (Meier & Davis, 1993).

Either the counselor or the client may initiate premature termination. When counselor-initiated termination occurs, the client needs to be informed as early as possible or reminded that only a limited number of sessions are available. Frequently, counselors may be in the position of terminating counseling prematurely in schools and agencies with session limits. On rare occasions, it may occur because of irreconcilable differences or a perceived lack of commitment by the client. When the counselor does terminate the sessions, the reasons must be specified to the client. Most counselors agree that early termination by the counselor violates the premise that clients are in charge of solving their own problems, and early termination may make clients feel personally rejected. These feelings should be dealt with before termination is complete. Referring the individual to another agency and/or keeping the door open for future sessions is sometimes helpful.

When the client prematurely terminates the sessions, the counselor should try to explore with the client the reasons for termination. Letting clients know that they are in charge of the decision to return in the future can be beneficial, as is exploring possible referral resources.

When termination is mutual or initiated by the counselor, several steps can benefit the outcome of the relationship (Ward, 1984). There should be discussion and evaluation of the goals that have already been reached. Closure issues and feelings need to be discussed, and clients must prepared for similar happenings in the future. Clients should be prepared for self-reliance and continued self-help Finally in the last session, discussion is likely to be lighter and more social. Okun (2008), for example, often shares a poster with the client that symbolizes the significance of the client's journey. The termination process should not focus on the generation of new problems or issues but rather on an appreciation of the growth that has already occurred.

Summary

You began this chapter as a nervous client, apprehensive about your first visit to the counselor's office. Now imagine you have switched roles. You are the counselor and waiting on the other side of the door to greet that client. You have learned the importance of establishing the counselor–client relationship and the conditions essential to a therapeutic relationship, including genuineness, empathy, and nonpossessive warmth.

You know that the helping relationship has three relatively distinct phases: building the relationship, challenging the client to find ways to change, and facilitating positive action. Also important are the characteristics most effective counselors possess, including high levels of self-awareness, empathy, genuineness, and respect for others, and an ability to use themselves as vehicles of change.

You have learned that effective counselors use attending skills (eye contact, body language, and vocal tone) and basic listening skills (client observation, encouraging, paraphrasing, summarizing, reflection of feeling, and open and closed questions) throughout the helping relationship. Also vital is the use of self-attending skills, which emphasize the importance of the person of the counselor in mediating the communications skills necessary in the helping relationship.

You have been introduced to primary and advanced empathy skills, as well as the challenging skills of confrontation, self-disclosure, and immediacy. These skills deepen the helping relationship and move the client toward therapeutic change. Counselor action skills facilitate behavior change around the client's stated goals for counseling. Finally, termination skills are needed to bring closure to, and end, the helping relationship.

The following Web sites provide additional information relating to the chapter topics.

USEFUL WEB SITES

http://www.carlrogers.info/aboutCarl-Farson.html

http://www.cacd.org/ACA_2005_Ethical_Code10405.pdf

http://www.wglasser.com/reality.htm

http://counsellingresource.com/types/person-centred/index.html

http://www.carlrogers.info/

http://www.existential-therapy.com/Key-Figures.htm

REFERENCES

Alyn, J. H. (1988). The politics of touch in therapy: A response to Willison and Masson. *Journal of Counseling and Development, 66*, 432–433.

Assay, T., & Lambert, M. (1999). The empirical case for the common factors in therapy: Quantitative findings. In M. A. Hubble, B. L. Duncan, & S. D. Miller (Eds.), *The heart and soul of change: What works in therapy* (pp. 23–55). Washington, DC: American Psychological Association.

Barak, A., Shapira, G., & Fisher, W. A. (1988). Effects of verbal and vocal cues of counselor self-confidence on clients' perceptions. *Counselor Education and Supervision, 27*, 355–367.

Berger, R. L., McBreen, J. T., & Rifkin, M. J. (1996). *Human behavior: A perspective for the helping professions*. White Plains, NY: Longham.

Bohart, A. C., Elliott, R. Greenberg, L., & Watson, J. C. (2002). Empathy. In J. C. Norcross (Ed.), *Psychotherapy relationships that work* (pp. 89–108). New York: Oxford University Press.

Bozarth, J. (1997). Empathy from the framework of client-centered theory and the Rogerian hypothesis. In A. Bohart & L. Greenberg (Eds.), *Empathy reconsidered* (pp. 81–102). Washington, DC: American Psychological Association.

Brammer, L. M., & MacDonald, G. (1996). *The helping relationship: Process and skills*. Needham Heights, MA: Allyn and Bacon.

Brems, C. (2000). *Dealing with challenges in psychotherapy and counseling*. Belmont, CA: Brooks/Cole.

Carkhuff, R. (1969). *Helping and human relations* (Vols. 1–2). New York: Holt, Rinehart & Winston.

Carkhuff, R. R. (1986). *The art of helping* (5th ed.). Amherst: MA: Human Resources Development Press.

Carkhuff, R. R., & Anthony, W. A. (1979). *The skills of helping*. Amherst: MA: Human Resources Development Press.

Combs, A. W. (1986). What makes a good helper? A person-centered approach. *Person-Centered Review, 1*(1), 51–61.

Cormier, B., Cormier, L. S., & Cormier, W. H. (1997). *Interviewing strategies for helpers: Fundamental skills and cognitive behavioral interventions*. Pacific Grove, CA: Brooks/Cole.

Cormier, S., & Hackney, H. (2008). *Counseling strategies and interventions*. Boston: Pearson Education.

Cozby, P. C. (1973). Self-disclosure: A literature review. *Psychological Bulletin, 79*, 73–91.

Daw, J. (1997). Cultural competence: What does it mean? *Family Therapy News, 28*, 8–9, 27.

Driscoll, M. S., Newman, D. L., & Seals, J. M. (1988). The effects of touch on perception of counselors. *Counselor Education and Supervision, 27*, 344–354.

Durana, C. (1998). The use of touch in psychotherapy: Ethical and clinical guidelines. *Psychotherapy: Theory, Research, Practice, Training, 35*(2), 269–280.

Egan, G. (1975). *The skilled helper*. Monterey, CA: Brooks/Cole.

Egan, G. (2007). *The skilled helper: A problem-management and opportunity development approach to helping* (8th ed.). Pacific Grove, CA: Brooks/Cole.

Evans, D. R., Hearn, M. T., Uhlemann, M. R., & Ivey, A. E. (2008). *Essential interviewing: A programmed approach to effective communication* (7th ed.). Pacific Grove, CA: Brooks/Cole.

Gelatt, H. B. (1989). Positive uncertainty: A decision-making framework for counseling. *Journal of Counseling Psychology, 36*(2), 252–256.

Gladding, S. T. (2007). *Counseling: A comprehensive profession*. Englewood Cliffs, NJ: Prentice-Hall.

Hays, P. (1996). Addressing the complexities of culture and gender in counseling. *Journal of Counseling & Development, 74*, 332–333.

Hendrick, S. S. (1988). Counselor self-disclosure. *Journal of Counseling and Development, 66*(9), 419–424.

Horvarth, A. O., & Symonds, D. D. (1991). Relation between working alliance and outcome in psychotherapy: A meta-analysis. *Journal of Counseling Psychology, 38,* 139–149.

Ivey, A. E., & Ivey, M. B. (2007). *Intentional interviewing and counseling: Facilitating client development in a multicultural society* (6th ed.). Pacific Grove, CA: Brooks/Cole.

Ivey, A. E., Ivey, M. B., & Simek-Downing, L. (1987). *Counseling and psychotherapy: Integrating skills, theory and practice.* Englewood Cliffs, NJ: Prentice-Hall.

Kottler, J. A., & Shepherd, D. S. (2008). *Introduction to counseling: Voices from the field* (6th ed.). Pacific Grove, CA: Brooks/Cole.

Levin, F. M., & Gergen, K. J. (1969). Revealingness, ingratiation, and the disclosure of self. *Proceedings of the 77th Annual Convention of the American Psychological Association, 4*(1), 447–448.

Maples, M. F., Dupey, P., Torres-Rivera, E., Phan, L. T., Vereen, L., & Garrett, M. T. (2001). Ethnic diversity and the use of humor in counseling: Appropriate or inappropriate? *Journal of Counseling and Development, 79,* 1, 53–61.

McCarthy, P. (1982). Differential effects of counselor self-referent responses and counselor status. *Journal of Counseling Psychology, 29,* 125–311.

Meier, S. T., & Davis, S. R. (1993). *The elements of counseling.* Pacific Grove, CA: Brooks/Cole.

Murphy, B. C., & Dillon, C. (2008). *Interviewing in action in a multicultural world.* (3rd ed.). Pacific Grove, CA: Brooks/Cole.

Norcross, J. C. (2001). Purposes, processes, and products of the task force on empirically supported therapy relationships. *Psychotherapy, 38,* 345–356.

Okun, B. F. (2008). *Effective helping: Interviewing and counseling techniques* (7th ed.). Pacific Grove, CA: Brooks/Cole.

Peca-Baker, T. A., & Friedlander, M. L. (1987). Effects on role expectations on clients' perceptions of disclosing and nondisclosing counselors. *Journal of Counseling and Development, 66*(2), 78–81.

Pietrofesa, J. J., Hoffman, A., & Splete, H. H. (1984). *Counseling: An introduction.* Boston: Houghton-Mifflin.

Pietrofesa, J. J., Hoffman, A., Splete, H. H., & Pinto, D. V. (1978). *Counseling: Theory, research & practice.* Chicago: Rand McNally.

Prochaska, J. O., & Norcross, J. C. (2003). *Systems of psychotherapy: A transtheoretical analysis* (5th ed.) Pacific Grove, CA: Brooks/Cole.

Rogers, C. R. (1957). The necessary and sufficient conditions of therapeutic personality change. *Journal of Counseling Psychology, 21,* 95–103.

Rogers, C. R. (1961). *On becoming a person* Boston: Houghton-Mifflin.

Scherer, K. R. (1986). Vocal expression: A review and model for future research. *Psychological Bulletin, 99,* 143–165.

Seligman, L. (2004). *Technical and conceptual skills for mental health professionals.* Upper Saddle River, NJ: Pearson Education.

Sexton, T. L., & Whiston, S. C. (1994). The status of the counseling relationship: An empirical review, theoretical implications, and research directions. *Counseling Psychologist, 22*(1), 6–78.

Sexton, T. L., Whiston, S. C., Bleuer, J. C., & Walz, G. R. (1997). *Integrating outcome research into counseling practice and training.* Alexandria, VA: American Counseling Association.

Shulman, L. (1979). *The skills of helping individuals and groups.* Itasca, IL: F. E. Peacock.

Strong, S. R., & Claiborn, C. D. (1982). *Change through interaction.* New York: Wiley Interscience.

Ward, D. E. (1984). Termination of individual counseling: Concepts and strategies. *Journal of Counseling Psychology, 63*(1), 21–26.

Counseling People of Color

COURTLAND C. LEE, PhD
University of Maryland at College Park

JESSICA M. DIAZ, MA
University of Maryland at College Park

The demographic realities of the 21st century make it imperative that the profession of counseling reconsider its traditional definition of and responses to ethnic diversity. Population projections for the new century suggest that those U.S. citizens from historically minority racial/ethnic groups will supplant those citizens of European origin, identified racially as "White," as the majority of the country's population (U.S. Census Bureau, 2007). This chapter presents a 21st-century paradigm for responding to the challenges of and maximizing the opportunities inherent in counseling people of color. It begins with an overview of the demographics of people of color. Next, a historical perspective traces the evolution of the theory and practice of counseling with people of color. This is followed by a contemporary exploration of the distinction between the terms *race* and *ethnicity*. The chapter then considers a potential pitfall and the promise inherent in counseling people of color. Next are an exploration of the "cross-cultural zone" in counseling intervention and an examination of dynamics to consider when counseling with people of color. Ethical considerations for counseling people of color are then discussed. The chapter ends with important guidelines for ethnically competent counseling.

Who Are People of Color? Demographic Realities of the 21st Century

For purposes of establishing a common reference point, it is important to delineate client groups of color. In this chapter, clients of color refer to people of African American, Asian Pacific American, Hispanic/Latino, and Native American cultural backgrounds. It is impossible to detail the complexity of each ethnic group. The following descriptions of the ethnic groups are by no means exhaustive. Instead, they are a starting point for counseling-related issues with each group of people.

Latino/Hispanic Americans

According to demographers' 2006 estimates, the Latino/Hispanic community is currently the largest ethnic group of color. Currently representing 14.8% of the U.S. population, the numbers of Latino/Hispanic Americans continue to rise rapidly as a result of continuing immigration and high birthrates (U.S. Census Bureau, 2007).

The largest Latino/Hispanic ethnic groups in the United States are Mexicans, followed by Puerto Ricans and Cubans (U.S. Census Bureau, 2000). Not only do these groups differ in terms of ethnicity but also variations exist among them based on racial characteristics, as there are Latinos of African, Asian, European, and Indian heritage. Furthermore, there is significant diversity with respect to levels of acculturation, rural or urban lifestyles, educational attainment, English and Spanish proficiency, socioeconomic status, and relationship with the United States. Whereas Mexican Americans, for example, have struggled with European and U.S. colonization and forced displacement, many Cuban refugees were invited into the United States to escape Communist tyranny.

Although Mexicans, Puerto Ricans, and Cubans are the more prominent groups, Latino/Hispanic Americans also include Central Americans and those from the Caribbean (e.g., Nicaraguans and Salvadorans) and South Americans (e.g., Chileans, Argentineans). Again, each group possesses a distinct historical and contemporary relationship with the United States, which affects their worldviews.

Latino/Hispanic culture developed as a result of the fusion of Spanish culture, brought to the Americas by missionaries and soldiers, with American Indian and African (the result of the slave trade) cultures in Mexico, South America, and the Caribbean Basin. Commonality among Latino/Hispanic American ethnic groups is found in the use of the Spanish language by most, the influence of Roman Catholic religious traditions, and the strong bonds between family members (Constantine, Gloria, & Barón, 2006; Lopez-Baez, 2006; Vazquez, 2006).

African Americans

African Americans until recently were the largest ethnic group of color in the United States. Currently African Americans represent 13.4% of the U.S. population (U.S. Census Bureau, 2007). Within the social sciences literature, the African American experience has traditionally been viewed as a monolithic entity. However, there are many aspects and facets to this cultural experience. African Americans include distinct ethnic groups, such as Jamaican Americans and Nigerian Americans, as well as Black Americans who have been in the United States for almost four centuries as a result of slavery. Although these groups share discrimination and related issues, they also have their own histories and cultural realities. For example, the abominable history of slavery, the Jim Crow era, and contemporary discrimination have shaped life experiences for generations of Black Americans, and those who have immigrated in more recent decades have different backgrounds.

Despite differences among African American ethnic groups, an examination of this culture reveals that Americans of African descent have developed a worldview that is grounded in African-oriented philosophical assumptions that scholars identify as the principle of Afrocentricity (Lee, 2004). This philosophical orientation emphasizes the centrality and love of Africa and Africanness as a means to deal with one's past, present, and future. Afrocentricity includes concepts such as perceptions of time, spirituality, human relations, family membership, and holism (Lee, 2004).

Asian Pacific Americans

Asian Pacific Americans include people whose ethnic heritage originates in East Asia (e.g., Chinese, Japanese, Korean), Southeast Asia (e.g., Vietnamese, Cambodian, Burmese), South Asia (e.g., Indian, Pakistani, Nepali), West Asian (e.g., Iranian, Afghan, Turkish), and the Middle East (e.g., Iraqi, Jordanian, Palestinian). This population has doubled with each passing decade and currently is about 4% of the U.S. population (U.S. Census Bureau, 2007). The largest ethnic group within Asian Pacific American culture is Chinese followed by Filipinos, Japanese, Asian Indians, and Koreans. The first Asian Pacific Americans to arrive in the United States were the Chinese immigrants who came to work on the construction of the transcontinental railroad and the Gold Rush in the 19th century. Since then, others have followed suit and contended with discriminatory immigration laws, labor exploitation, and large-scale incarceration in the form of the Japanese internment during World War II.

Each Asian American ethnic group has its own unique cultural history and traditions. Some of their dynamics are rooted in the centuries-old Asian religious traditions of Buddhism, Confucianism, Islam, Christianity, Hinduism, ancestor worship, and animism, which play a major role in shaping the cultural values of Asian Americans regardless of ethnic background. These dynamics include moderation in behavior, self-discipline, patience, and humility. Many of these behaviors and values are dictated by family relationships that emphasize honor and respect for elders (Chang, 2006; Chung & Bemak, 2006).

Native Americans

Contemporary Native Americans are the descendants of the original inhabitants of the North American continent. Native Americans currently represent less than 1% of the U.S. population and include more than 500 different cultural communities defined as sovereign entities. The U.S. government recognizes approximately 250 nations, but another 250 Native groups go without formal acknowledgment from the government (U.S. Census Bureau, 2000). Most Native Americans identify first with a specific ancestral community and then to the larger American Indian group (Herring, 1997). Native Americans range from those who are very traditional, speak their indigenous language, live on a reservation, and practice long-standing customs to those who are very acculturated and live in metropolitan areas.

As a cultural group, Native Americans have had a long and troubled history. The basis of their trouble has been their relationship with the U.S. government—a relationship often marked by conflict and oppression. As diverse as this cultural group is, there is a shared history of displacement, matched with collective resistance.

Moreover, there are a few common values that are characteristic of Native Americans: spirituality, a strong reverence for nature, and a deep respect for one's people (Garrett, 2006).

A New Perspective on People of Color

The 21st century has brought a changing face of ethnic America. In recent years, the concepts of race and ethnicity have been continuously reinterpreted. Because of this, it has been suggested that the country has entered what can be considered a "postethnic" era (Britt-Gibson, 2007; Kotkin & Tseng, 2003). Largely spearheaded by young people, long-standing notions of ethnicity and race are being reconsidered. Old racial and ethnic distinctions are blurring and being redefined. This new period is characterized by the evolution of a new reality in which individual identity is shaped more by cultural preference than ethnic heritage.

This evolutionary process has been affected by the abolition of antimiscegenation laws and the Civil Rights Movement, which have promoted an increase in the number of interracial marriages and the resulting growing numbers of biracial and multiracial individuals (Kenney, 2006). The process has also been influenced by young people interacting in ever-growing numbers across traditional racial and ethnic lines.

The result of this process has been to push the American public to reexamine its racial and ethnic boundaries and norms. No longer can race and ethnicity be easily defined or explained: lines are blurred, and identities have begun to shift. In fact, new nomenclature indicates the blending of two cultures, for example, "Blasian," representing individuals of Asian and African heritage; "Hinjew," Indian and Jewish; and "Blaxican," African American and Mexican (Kotkin & Tseng, 2003).

Counselors today must therefore reexamine the traditional ethnic categories that have traditionally been used to identify client groups. These categories must now be expanded to include individuals whose cultural outlooks and worldviews include multiple ethnic realities.

An Historical Perspective: The Evolution of the Theory and Practice of Counseling People of Color

The concept that counseling with people of color requires awareness, knowledge, and skills that differ from the traditions of counseling practice is still evolving within the profession. Much of what is known about counseling clients from ethnic groups of color has its origins in the study of African Americans (Lee, 2004). Jackson (1977), in tracing the emergence of an African American perspective in counseling, suggests that although rudimentary notions on differential therapeutic approaches for Black people appeared in the 1940s, the bulk of the knowledge base on counseling Blacks was developed in the 1960s and 1970s. These decades, a period of social and political ferment in America, saw the rise of a generation of Black scholars who made major contributions to the profession. Many of these thinkers (Banks, 1972; Harper, 1973; Nobles, 1972; Vontress, 1969; White, 1970)—African American counterparts to Carl Rogers, Albert Ellis, and Fritz Perls—stated that Black culture with its African origins was qualitatively different from European-based White culture. Therefore, the validity of theories and techniques grounded in European/European American cultural traditions had to be questioned when applied to counseling interactions with African Americans. These pioneering scholars established new theoretical and practical directions for counseling with African Americans.

The 1970s also saw Black and White scholars initiate attempts to empirically validate new theoretical notions on and models of counseling with ethnic minority people. A body of research evidence began to emerge aimed at providing answers to questions on race as a variable in the counseling process (Harrison, 1975; Sattler, 1977). Although this research often yielded confusing and conflicting results, it stimulated thinking and continued investigation about the dynamics of counseling with Black and other client groups of color.

During the 1980s and 1990s, the knowledge base developed by African American scholars in the 1960s and 1970s contributed to an important professional trend in counseling. Because of the contributions Black scholarship has made, the total profession has come to recognize the importance of considering cultural diversity in the counseling process. A profusion of counseling professionals from diverse cultural and ethnic backgrounds are now advancing the notion of multicultural counseling. Multicultural counseling places the emphasis for counseling theory and practice equally on the cultural impressions of both the counselor and the client (Lee & Ramsey, 2006). These ideas have generated an important new knowledge base in the past two decades. This base includes the fundamental concept that cultural differences are real and must be actively considered in counseling. Counseling must be inclusive of a variety of ways of thinking, feeling, and behaving, as well as responsive to diverse worldviews (Lee, 2006c); Pope-Davis, Coleman, Liu, & Toporek, 2003; Roysircar, Arredondo, Fuertes, Ponterotto, & Toporek, 2003).

Prelude to Practice

Before we examine counseling practice with people of color, several issues must be understood if effective therapeutic intervention is to take place.

Race versus Ethnicity: A Contemporary View

The terms *race* and *ethnicity* (ethnic group) are generally used interchangeably. Often both are used to refer to groups of people who share similar physiological traits and/or personality characteristics. These traits and characteristics are either genetically transferred or have become reinforced through group association over long periods. However, these terms are not synonymous. Webster's dictionary (2004) defines *race* as "a category of humankind that shares certain distinctive physical traits." These physical traits have generally been considered hair, eyes, skin color, body shape, and the like.

Traditionally, the three primary racial categories have been labeled Caucasoid, Negroid, and Mongoloid, although many subdivisions of these are also called races. The diction-ary (2004) defines the term *ethnic* in the following manner: "Of or relating to large groups of people classed according to common racial, national, tribal, religious, linguis-tic, or cultural origin or background."

It can be argued that *race* has become an archaic anthropological/biological clas-sification of human differences that historically has been used as part of political, social, cultural, and economic brutality and exploitation in many parts of the world. A classic example is Adolf Hitler's classifying Judaism (a religion and cultural experi-ence) as a "race" and perpetrating the Holocaust in the last century. This definition of race forms the core of the heinous phenomenon known as "racism" (Lee, 2001).

What is most important from a counseling perspective, however, are not geneti-cally transferred physiological/biological traits but, rather, personality characteristics among people that become reinforced through association over time. These long-standing dynamics of thinking, feeling, and behaving form the cultural basis of "eth-nicity" or an "ethnic group" and thus a significant counseling construct. In considering a new counseling paradigm for changing population dynamics, therefore, the focus should be on the importance of ethnicity and ethnic diversity in the relationship between counselor and client (Lee, 2001). This chapter focuses on counseling issues that must be considered in counseling clients from ethnic groups of color in the con-temporary American social context.

The Pitfalls of a Monolithic Perspective

In discussing the whole concept of counseling people of color, there is a danger of assuming that all people from an ethnic group are the same and that one methodolog-ical approach is universally applicable in any counseling intervention with any of them. Indeed, someone who reviews much of the psychological or counseling literature related to issues of counseling people of color might be left with the impression that there is an all-encompassing ethnic reality and that all people from a specific group act, feel, and think in a homogeneous fashion. Such an impression invariably leads to a monolithic perspective on the African American, Asian American, Hispanic American, or Native American experience in the United States, as well as stereotypic thinking in which individuals from any of these groups are considered indistinguishable in terms of attitudes, behaviors, and values. Counseling professionals possessing such a per-spective run the risk of approaching clients of color not as distinctive human beings with individual experiences but rather merely as stereotypes.

People of color differ in terms of experiences. Each African American, Asian American, Hispanic American, and Native American is a unique individual who is the sum total of his or her common human experiences, specific cultural experiences, and personal life experiences. Indeed, attempting to identify common experiences among people of color may be a precarious enterprise because ethnic groups of color are not homogeneous (Lee, 2004). The counseling process with people of color, therefore, must incorporate the notion that there is a high degree of intragroup variability and that interventions must be client- and situation-specific. Professional counselors have to approach intervention with clients of color in an individualistic manner as opposed to monolithically.

The Promise of a Proactive Perspective

Far too often, counseling intervention with people of color is designed to counteract the negative effects of extreme environmental stress on intrapersonal and interpersonal functioning. Counseling is generally a reactionary process that focuses on remediating educational, economic, or social deficiencies that are the result of negative transactions between people of color and their environments. Counseling outcomes, therefore, are in many cases reconstructive in nature. The goal of counseling people of color traditionally has been rehabilitation and not prevention.

However, if counseling is to be a comprehensive and effective discipline for helping people of color, then the scope of services offered should be proactive. Counseling practice must move beyond merely assisting clients of color to react to negative environmental forces, to a point where the goal of intervention is helping them become empowered through the development of mastery skills. Promoting environmental mastery skills among clients of color would enable them to confront challenges in a competent and proactive manner.

Developing Cultural Competence and Ethical Considerations in the Cross-Cultural Zone

A counseling relationship with a person of color has certain unique challenges and inherent opportunities. Engaging in such a relationship entails entering an important and potentially problematic zone of helping. This helping space can be conceptualized as the cross-cultural zone. A counselor enters the cross-cultural zone whenever he or she differs from a client in terms of ethnic background and cultural realities. Traditionally conceptualized, this helping space has been entered whenever a White counselor enters a helping relationship with a client from an ethnic group of color.

Two pervasive concepts underlie the helping dynamics in the cross-cultural zone. To successfully navigate this space, a counselor must understand the impact of the concepts of *power* and *privilege* on the nature of counseling.

Power

Power is a major theme in any counseling relationship. However often counselors conceal or deny the fact, there is an inequality of power in the helping relationship. Individuals needing help with problem resolution or decision making voluntarily come, or are referred, to a counselor for that assistance. By default, therefore, that individual places the counselor in a position of power. When entering the cross-cultural zone, therefore, the counselor has to acknowledge this power and ensure that it is carefully employed to empower the client to actively take part in solving the presenting problem or making a decision. Perhaps the greatest ethical violation in the helping process is abuse of the counselor's inherent power.

Counseling in the cross-cultural zone has often been conceptualized as a sociopolitical process related to a power differential between counselor and client. Significantly, counseling practice has in many instances been perceived as a tool of power, oppression, or social control by ethnic groups of color (Holcomb-McCoy & Mitchell, 2007; Lee, 2006a; Sue & Sue, 2002). Often counseling in the cross-cultural zone is a forced experience rather than voluntary, with a counselor perceived as a culturally insensitive or unresponsive agent of the broad and repressive social welfare system. Rather than an empowering process, counseling can become disenfranchising, contributing to social marginalization for clients from ethnic groups of color.

Privilege

Upon entering the cross-cultural zone, counselors must consider the nature of the racial/ethnic privilege they may possess by virtue of the color of their skin. In this country, White Americans have generally enjoyed racial/ethnic privilege in their relationship with ethnic groups of color (McIntosh, 1989). Racial/ethnic privilege can be conceptualized along several dimensions. First, it is generally unearned. In most cases, individuals are born with it, and their racial/ethnic privilege tends to be innate. Second, individuals with racial/ethnic privilege generally tend to be unaware of the unearned benefits that accrue from their privileged status. Third, racial/ethnic privilege gives the individual who has it distinct cultural, social, and economic advantages. Individuals with racial/ethnic privilege are generally seen to be in a position of social dominance over those who lack these advantages.

Significantly, a prerequisite for entering the cross-cultural zone must be that counselors consider the nature of the possible power differential between counselor and client. Equally as important is an understanding of the extent of racial/ethnic privilege distinctions between counselor and client. The dynamics of both power and privilege may affect the counseling process. The counseling literature is replete with examples of counselors' misuse of power, their failure to acknowledge privilege, and the negative effect of counselors' disproportionate power and privilege on the counseling relationship with clients of color (Kearney, Draper, & Barón, 2005; Yeh, McCabe, Hurlburt, Hough, Hazen, Culver, Garland, & Landsverk, 2002).

What has been clearly evident in the cross-cultural zone is that the cultural and ethnic differences between counselor and client can be a significant impediment to the counseling process. Metaphorically, these counselor–client differences in the cross-cultural zone have the potential to hang between them like an impenetrable brick wall, impeding or negating counseling. This brick wall emphasizes the cultural distance between the counselor and the client. In many instances, the cultural and ethnic differences in the cross-cultural zone are ignored, thereby widening the distance between helper and helpee.

The goal, therefore, when entering the cross-cultural zone is to scale the brick wall and decrease potential cultural and ethnic distance between counselor and client. It is important that ethnic and cultural differences are acknowledged and factored into the counseling relationship. To accomplish this and increase counseling effectiveness in the cross-cultural zone, important dynamics must be considered. Competent counseling practice in the cross-cultural zone with clients of color must be predicated on an understanding of these dynamics. Implicit in these dynamics are the beliefs, social forms, and material traits that constitute distinct client worldviews. These dynamics also significantly affect the psychosocial development of clients. Dynamics that may need to be considered in culturally responsive counseling with clients of color include the relationship between ethnic identity development and degree of acculturation, language, kinship influences, gender role socialization, religious/spiritual influences, immigration experience, help-seeking attitudes and behavior, and historical hostility.

The Relationship Between Ethnic Identity Development and Degree of Acculturation

Counseling effectiveness in the cross-cultural zone may ultimately hinge upon an understanding of the concepts of ethnic identity and acculturation and the relationship between them. An appreciation of this relationship, and its influence on psychosocial development, is fundamental to culturally responsive counseling (Lee, 1997).

Ethnic identity refers to an individual's sense of belonging to an ethnic group and the part of his or her personality that is attributable to ethnic group membership (Rotheram & Phinney, 1987). Ethnic identity may be considered as the inner vision that a person possesses of himself or herself as a member of an ethnic group. It forms the core of the beliefs, social forms, and personality dimensions that characterize distinct cultural realities and worldview for an individual.

The development of ethnic identity has traditionally been conceptualized as an evolutionary linear stage process (Atkinson, Morten, & Sue, 1993; Cross, 1995) or, more recently, as a dynamic personality status process in which racial information is simultaneously interpreted and internalized at a variety of levels (Helms, 1995). It is important to point out that most models of ethnic identity development in the United States have been developed in a context where people of European origin have been in a position of social and cultural dominance with respect to other groups. This cultural privilege has profoundly influenced the attitudes of European Americans toward members of ethnic minority groups (Helms, 1995). Likewise, the perception of this cultural privilege held by people from ethnic minority groups has profoundly influenced the attitudes they hold of themselves and European Americans as racial beings (Atkinson, Morten, & Sue, 1993; Helms, 1995).

Ethnic identity development, therefore, occurs in a milieu characterized by complex social interaction among individuals from ethnic minority groups and the European American majority in the United States. The essence of this interaction for ethnic minority individuals is the concept of acculturation.

Acculturation, within the context of contemporary American society, refers to the degree to which an individual identifies with or conforms to the attitudes, lifestyles, and values of the European American–based macroculture (Lee, 1997). For individuals of color, it is generally a process of willing or unwilling attitudinal and behavioral changes brought about by overt and covert pressure from social, educational, and economic institutions within the macroculture (Lee, 1997).

Psychosocial development is greatly influenced by the sense of ethnic identity and the degree of acculturation among people of color. The relationship between these two concepts shapes attitudes, behaviors, and values. This relationship between ethnic identity development and acculturation may be conceptualized in the following four categories:

■ *Strong sense of ethnic identity and high degree of acculturation.*   This category characterizes the relationship between ethnic identity and acculturation for those individuals considered to be "bicultural." In other words, they have a strong sense of belonging to their particular ethnic group and also possess a high degree of identification with or conformity to the macroculture. Bicultural individuals can move comfortably, both physically and psychologically, between their ethnic culture and the macroculture.

   A concrete example of such movement is language competency. Bicultural individuals tend to be bilingual. They have generally mastered the "standard" English that is characteristic of the macroculture yet still maintain fluency in their ethnic language or linguistic traditions. They are usually capable of moving from the English of the macroculture to the language of their ethnic group with relative ease.

■ *Weak sense of ethnic identity and high degree of acculturation.*   Individuals in this category have a limited sense of belonging to their ethnic group, and little in the dynamics of their personality is reflective of ethnic group membership. These individuals, however, have a high degree of identification with the macroculture. People with these experiences tend to be marginal to the culture of their ethnic group. This marginalization may result from a conscious choice to adopt exclusively the attitudes, behaviors, and values of the macroculture. Often such a choice is motivated by overt or subtle macroculture messages about the unacceptability or undesirability of significant aspects of ethnic minority cultural practices. Many individuals represented in this category internalize the idea that the key to social, educational, or economic advancement in American society is predicated on a complete rejection of an ethnic minority worldview and total conformity to macroculture values.

   However, such marginalization may also be the result of a lack of contact with one's ethnic group culture. This is often the case, for example, when children are raised with little sense of their ethnic heritage because of cross-cultural adoption or other factors that remove them from contact with the experiences of their ethnic group. In such cases, the marginalization from ethnic group experiences is not by choice but rather from lack of exposure.

■ *Strong sense of ethnic identity and low degree of acculturation.*   Individuals in this category have a strong ethnic identity. On the other hand, they have little identification with or are marginal to the macroculture. An excellent example of this experience is among recent immigrants. Many new immigrants learn the language and adopt the practices of the macroculture, but many others continue to nurture the cultural customs of the "old country."

   Likewise, it may represent the reality of members of ethnic groups of color who, although born in the United States, have had limited social or economic opportunities because of systemic barriers such as racism. Effectively barred from all but superficial participation in the macroculture, many of these individuals find cultural validation exclusively within their ethnic group.

■ *Weak sense of ethnic identity and low degree of acculturation.*   People with experiences in this category are marginal to both their ethnic group and the macroculture. They have a limited sense of belonging to any group and very little of their personality is attributable to specified group membership. Such a person would be considered physically, mentally, and spiritually ill in any culture. This person would be highly dysfunctional.

Importantly, the relationship between a sense of ethnic identity and the degree of acculturation for any person may be influenced by variables such as age, gender, ethnic group, length of residence in the United States, level of education, extent of experience with racism, and socioeconomic status. The dynamic nature of human development and behavior makes it impossible to neatly place individuals into any one of these four categories and suggests that a person may experience ongoing movement across the categories. Such shifts might be due to a combination of intrapersonal and environmental factors at any given point in an individual's life.

The dynamics of ethnic identity and acculturation and the important relationship between them need to be factored into culturally responsive counseling in the cross-cultural zone. Psychosocial development is greatly influenced by an individual's sense of ethnic identity and degree of acculturation. Similarly, the relationship between these two concepts is a crucial aspect of mental health. Assessing ethnic identity and acculturation processes, therefore, can help a counselor understand the reality and issues confronting clients of color. Counselors need to be sensitive to issues of ethnic identity and carefully explore the degree of cultural similarity or dissimilarity between themselves and clients. Analysis of ethnic identity and acculturation levels should provide the focus of any counseling intervention with clients of color.

Language Preference

Counseling relies on communication between counselor and client. It is known as the "talking cure." Language, therefore, is an important variable in all counseling interactions, but it can assume complex dimensions in counseling with people of color. The practice of counseling is predicated on an understanding of standard English, but many clients from ethnic groups of color do not necessarily value this language tradition as a primary means of communication.

Language is culture. It is the cornerstone of ethnic identity. Language structures meaning, determines perception, and transmits culture. It communicates thought and subjective cultural experiences at deep and subtle levels (Sue & Sue, 2002; Westwood & Ishiyama, 1990). Acquisition and use of language is a primary aspect of psychosocial development and socialization in all cultures. Mastery of language generally implies mastery of culture.

Verbal and nonverbal communication is a cultural phenomenon involving the use of symbols of meaning that are culturally defined. The same words or gestures can have different meanings depending on the cultural context in which they are used (Gudykunst & Kim, 1984; Westwood & Borgen, 1988).

Culturally competent counseling, therefore, must be based on an appreciation of and sensitivity to possible language differences between counselor and client, including differences in language fluency, accent, dialect, and nonverbal communication (e.g., eye contact, body language, facial expressions, and emotional expressions). Failure to respect language differences in a counseling relationship invariably leads to misunderstanding and possible alienation of clients.

An appreciation for language dynamics must be a central theme in the cross-cultural zone. Clients of color must be able to tell their story in a manner that is most comfortable and appropriate for them (Roysircar et al., 2003; Westwood & Ishiyama, 1990).

Kinship Influences

Immediate and extended kinship networks must be considered as primary sources for promoting mental health and normal development among many ethnic groups of color. Such networks may include immediate and extended family, friends, or community cultural resources. Within these networks are hierarchical structures and carefully defined age and/or gender roles that promote a collective unity. This collective unity provides the basis for a worldview that emphasizes communalism rather than individualism (Lee, 1997).

Kinship support networks are crucial in providing resolution to both situational and developmental problems related to educational, career, or personal-social matters. In many instances, the supportive dynamics of these indigenous networks may keep an individual from needing to seek outside decision-making or problem-resolution assistance. Culturally responsive counselors, therefore, must understand and appreciate the role of kinship dynamics in mental health and well-being. As appropriate, counselors should find ways to use the kinship system in the counseling process (Lee, 1997, 2001).

Gender Role Socialization

Gender role socialization is sometimes an important dynamic to consider when counseling across ethnic gaps. Many ethnic groups of color have developed different perceptions of the role of men and women. These differential gender perceptions can influence the expectations considered normal for psychosocial development. Such expectations, therefore, can account for fundamental differences in personality development for men and women (Arredondo, Psalti, & Cella, 1993; Lee, 1997).

Gender role socialization and its effects on development should be considered when counseling people of color. Counselors may need to be aware of how gender-based differences in developmental expectations are manifested in decision making and problem resolution among the men and women of a particular ethnic group.

Religious and Spiritual Influences

Although religion and spirituality are universally accepted as major influences on human development, only recently have they been considered important or appropriate issues in the counseling process (Kelly, 1995; Lee & Sirch, 1994). Culturally responsive counseling may be enhanced if the influence of religion and spirituality is seen as important in the helping process. For many ethnic groups of color, there is often little distinction made between religious and secular life. The philosophical tenets inherent in religious or spiritual beliefs influence all aspects of human development and interaction.

Within the cultural traditions of many groups, religious institutions or spiritual centers are important sources of psychological support. Likewise, religious or spiritual leaders have been expected to not only provide for spiritual needs but also offer guidance for physical and emotional concerns. These institutions and their leaders have been an important indigenous source of help for decision making and problem resolution in many cultures for generations (Bond, Lee, Lowe, Malayapillay, Wheeler, Banks, Kurdt, Mercado, & Smiley, 2001). As appropriate, it might be necessary to form consultative relationships with religious or spiritual leaders or other indigenous helpers or healers for the benefit of clients.

Immigration Experience

Many individuals from ethnic groups of color are relatively recent arrivals to the United States. For these people, the immigration experience may be an important dynamic of culture that merits consideration in the counseling process.

Immigration, in some instances, has been prompted by political or social upheaval in other parts of the world. Many recent immigrants arrive here as refugees who have escaped repressive governments or political instability. In addition to cultural beliefs and practices, these people bring with them the trauma associated with forced separation from family and homeland. In other cases, individuals have been lured here by the age-old promise of economic and social opportunity. Many times, however, these immigrants enter the country without proper documentation. Two major challenges often confront so-called undocumented aliens. The first is living with the knowledge that at any time immigration officials might send them back to their country of origin. The second, which is common to all recent immigrants, is reconciling the desire to maintain cultural customs from back home with the pressure to adopt major aspects of the American macroculture.

Whatever the reason for immigration, however, the experience of suddenly finding oneself a stranger in a new land can affect human development in ways that need to be considered in culturally responsive counseling. Counseling professionals, therefore, should be aware of the possible influence immigration experiences have on the attitudinal orientations, behavioral repertoires, and value systems of clients from ethnic groups of color.

Help-Seeking Attitudes and Behavior

Counselors must recognize the great ethnic group variability with respect to help-seeking attitudes and behaviors. Not all ethnic groups traditionally value or understand the nature of formal counseling as a source of help. It might be necessary, therefore, to step outside the confines of the traditional helping setting to offer counseling services. Counselors may need to think creatively in terms of how they provide services to clients for whom the counseling process might be a totally alien experience. As previously mentioned, it might be necessary to form consultative relationships with religious or spiritual leaders or other indigenous helpers or healers for the benefit of clients (Lee, 2001).

Historical Hostility

Counseling people of color in the United States requires sensitivity to a dynamic that can be labeled historical hostility (Lee, 1997; Vontress, Johnson, & Epp, 1999). The essence of this dynamic can be observed anywhere in the world where there has been a long-term pattern of exploitation or oppression between a group of people favored on the basis of ethnicity, religion, or politics, and another devalued group in a common relationship. With respect to the United States, in their collective experience, ethnic minority people harbor conscious and unconscious negative emotions produced by traditions of brutality and frustrations that they and their forebears suffered at the hands of Europeans and their European American descendants (Vontress, Johnson, & Epp, 1999).

This concept underscores the historical reality of intergroup relations in this country. Sadly, the history of the United States is replete with examples of negative social encounters between European Americans and people from other cultural backgrounds—from the enslavement of Africans, to the systematic destruction of Native American culture, to the internment of Japanese American citizens during World War II. The motivating forces defining these encounters have generally been racism or other forms of social and economic oppression. Over time, the social and political process associated with racism and oppression in the United States has taken a collective physical and psychological toll on ethnic minority groups. This toll is reflected in intense negative feelings that members of ethnic minority groups often possess, either overtly or covertly, toward members of the majority group in the United States. Whether these feelings are justified or warranted at any given point in time is generally rendered moot by the often exploitative and destructive relationship between European Americans and people from non-European backgrounds in the United States.

With respect to counseling, historical hostility can manifest itself in resistance to the helper and the helping process. It is important to note that counseling has often been a sociopolitical process for many members of ethnic groups of color, and mental health services have been perceived as a tool of oppression and social control in many ethnic minority communities (Lee, 1997; Sue & Sue, 2002). Often counseling is a forced, involuntary experience with a culturally insensitive or unresponsive agent of some aspect of the broad social welfare system (Lee, 1997).

Historical hostility is a cultural dynamic that must be factored into counseling in the cross-cultural zone, particularly for clients whose counseling issues relate to the stress of racism, prejudice, discrimination, or socioeconomic disadvantage. Resistance to counseling might include denial of problems, viewing counseling as something that is done to them rather than with them, distrust of the counselor and the process, silence, passive-aggressive behavior, or premature termination. These phenomena may be symptomatic of generalized negative feelings about the dominant group fostered by generations of negative intergroup relations.

This list of dynamics is by no means exhaustive, but, given the demographic realities of American society, even a cursory review of ethnic groups of color suggests that these are some of the more salient influences on psychosocial development. Although the influence of these dynamics may vary across clients, a working knowledge of them and their impact on the helping process should frame the context of culturally responsive counseling intervention in the cross-cultural zone. An understanding of these dynamics can help counselors eliminate the brick wall and minimize the cultural distance often inherent in the cross-cultural zone.

Ethical Considerations in the Cross-Cultural Zone

Confronted with the challenges of the cross-cultural zone, counselors must examine their practice to ensure that it is culturally responsive. A major part of such introspective examination involves close scrutiny of the ethical standards that guide practice. Scholars have written extensively on ethical standards as they relate to counseling people of color (Delgado-Romero, 2003; LaFromboise, Foster, & James, 1996; Lee, 2006b; Pack-Brown & Williams, 2003; Ridley, Liddle, Hill, & Li, 2001). The literature suggests that counselors who are culturally responsive increase their chances of practicing in an ethical fashion with clients of color. Counselors who are not aware of cultural dynamics and their impact on client development risk engaging in unethical conduct.

Ethical standards are rules and principles of conduct designed to guide counselor practice. The codes of ethics of mental health professions, such as those of the American Counseling Association (ACA, 2005), provide such rules and principles. In a multicultural society, such standards have implications for counselor–client interactions in the cross-cultural zone. It has been asserted that counselors have an ethical responsibility to meet the needs of people of color within the context of a multicultural society (Delgado-Romero, 2003; LaFromboise et al., 1996; Lee, 2006b; Pack-Brown & Williams, 2003; Ridley et al., 2001).

In view of the dynamics that may affect counseling in the cross-cultural zone, the issue of client welfare warrants examination with respect to the potential harm that may occur when cultural dynamics are not taken into consideration. Ethically, counselors are obligated not only to protect clients from potential harm or prevent harm when possible (beneficence) but also to not inflict harm upon clients (nonmaleficence). There can be little doubt that potential harm can be inflicted when counselors do not effectively address the dynamics of culture in the cross-cultural zone.

Counselors must enter the cross-cultural zone in a manner that is both culturally competent and ethically responsible. With respect to ethical codes (ACA, 2005), therefore, whenever counselors enter the cross-cultural zone they must aspire to:

■ Recognize diversity and embrace a cross-cultural approach in support of the worth, dignity, potential, and uniqueness of people within their social and cultural contexts

- Actively attempt to understand the diverse cultural backgrounds of the clients they serve
- Explore their own cultural identities and how they affect their values and beliefs about the counseling process
- Recognize that support networks (e.g., kinship systems) hold various meanings in the lives of clients from diverse cultural backgrounds, and consider enlisting the support, understanding, and involvement of meaningful others as positive resources, when appropriate
- Take responsibility for communicating information in ways that are culturally appropriate; and consider the cultural implications of informed consent procedures and, where possible, adjust practices accordingly
- Have an awareness of one's own values, attitudes, beliefs, and behaviors and how these apply in a diverse society; avoid imposing one's own values on clients
- Understand the challenges of accepting gifts from clients, recognizing that in some cultures, small gifts are a token of respect and gratitude
- Communicate with clients about the parameters of confidentiality in a culturally competent manner, respect differing cultural views toward disclosure of information, and understand that some clients will not expect confidentiality to be upheld in traditional ways
- Practice in a manner that is nondiscriminatory
- Recognize that culture affects the manner in which clients' problems are defined and consider clients' socioeconomic and cultural experiences when diagnosing mental disorders
- Use caution when selecting assessments for culturally diverse populations to avoid inappropriate assessments that may be outside socialized behavioral or cognitive patterns
- Recognize the effects of various aspects of culture on test administration and interpretation

Questionable or unethical conduct is often due to counselors' lack of multicultural literacy. However, cultural ignorance should be no excuse for unethical counseling conduct. Providing services to clients of color by professionals not competent in understanding and providing services to such individuals should be considered unethical.

To effectively engage in ethical practice across ethnic realities, counselors must participate in an ongoing professional development process. The focus of this process should be developing and upgrading the skills to intervene effectively into the lives of clients from a variety of ethnic backgrounds. To become culturally competent in their work, counselors must become fully aware of their own heritage as well as possible biases that may interfere with helping effectiveness, gain knowledge about the history and culture of people of color, and develop new skills. Counselors who engage in ethical practice with clients of color have an awareness of their own cultural assumptions, values, and biases. They also have developed an understanding of the worldviews of clients of color, and they have acquired appropriate intervention strategies and techniques.

Ethical practice is a pervasive challenge for professional counselors. Counselors must be ever vigilant that their interventions are dedicated to promoting the worth, dignity, and potential of all clients, which is particularly crucial when clients come from ethnic groups of color. Ethical conduct in a multicultural context is predicated on awareness of and sensitivity to unique cultural realities and their relationship to optimal human development. Professional counselors who practice without such awareness and sensitivity run the danger of engaging in unethical conduct. Ignorance of cultural dynamics can be no excuse for unethical practice.

Best Practice in the Cross-Cultural Zone: Guidelines for Ethnically Competent Counseling with People of Color

If counselors are to be effective in the cross-cultural zone with clients of color, then they must approach counseling from a perspective that simultaneously acknowledges human difference and celebrates human similarity. They must adopt a philosophy that views each client as a unique individual while, at the same time, taking into consideration the client's common experiences as a human being (i.e., the universal developmental challenges that face all people regardless of ethnic background) and the specific experiences that come from his or her ethnic background. Counselors must consider each client within an ethnic group context and also within a broader global human perspective (Lee, 2001).

Counselors who are responsive to clients of color have heightened awareness, an expanded knowledge base, and culturally competent helping skills. This premise provides a framework for best practice in the cross-cultural zone (Roysircar et al., 2003).

Counselor Self-Awareness

The prerequisite for competent counseling in the cross-cultural zone is counselor self-awareness. Counselors have to fully experience themselves as racial/ethnic beings. An individual who expects to work with clients of color must first be anchored in his or her own ethnic realities. This process should start with explorations of how the counselor's own ethnic background has influenced his or her psychosocial development and the role that ethnic heritage and customs play in shaping his or her personality characteristics. Assessing one's own stage of ethnic identity development is also essential. The crucial questions to ask in this regard are "How do I experience myself as a member of Ethnic Group X?" "How do I experience others members of Ethnic Group X?" and "How do I experience people of other ethnic backgrounds?"

As part of this self-exploration process, a counselor has to evaluate the influences that have shaped the development of his or her attitudes and beliefs about people from different ethnic backgrounds. It is important to evaluate the explicit message, as well as the often subtle message, one has received throughout life about people who are ethnically "different." Counselors must reflect on how their personal attitudes and beliefs about people from different ethnic groups may facilitate or hamper counseling effectiveness.

Ethnically competent counselors explore personal issues and questions, no matter how uncomfortable, in an attempt to discern how their own ethnic heritage, values, and biases might affect the counseling process. Self-exploration leads to self-awareness, which is crucial in developing a set of personal attitudes and beliefs to guide ethnically responsive counseling practice. Ethnically responsive counselors are sensitive to ethnic group differences because they are aware of their own identity as ethnic beings.

Counselor Knowledge

Ethnically competent counselors need a knowledge base from which to plan, implement, and evaluate their services. First, they must have an understanding of how economic, social, and political systems operate with respect to their treatment of ethnic groups of color. Counselors should understand the historical impact of environmental forces such as racism on the psychosocial development of ethnic groups of color.

Second, counselors who are responsive to diverse ethnic realities acquire working knowledge and information about specific groups of people, including general knowledge about the histories, experiences, customs, and values of ethnically diverse groups. From such knowledge should come an understanding of specific ethnic contexts and how they may influence personal and social development.

Counselors should enhance their personal growth and professional development by reading the literature and exposing themselves to other forms of artistic expression (e.g., television programs, films, artwork) of ethnic groups of color. A great deal of information about lifestyles, customs, traditions, language patterns, values, and histories, as well as there impact on human development and personality, can be gained from such forms of artistic expression. In addition, the Internet can provide information about people of color.

A counselor should also go out and experience ethnic diversity firsthand. There is a limit to how much can be learned about different ethnic groups from books, classes, workshops, and films. Much more can be learned by actually being among people from diverse ethnic backgrounds and interacting with them in their cultural environments. Such in vivo experiences can raise levels of awareness, increase knowledge, and provide important dimensions to empathic style in counseling interventions.

Counselor Skills

Ethnically competent counselors have to build a repertoire of relevant skills. They should be able to use counseling strategies and techniques that are consistent with the life experiences and cultural values of clients of color.

Ethnically competent skills should be based on the following premises: First, ethnic group diversity is real and should not be ignored. Second, ethnic group differences are just that—differences. They are not necessarily deficiencies or pathological deviations. Counselors need to meet clients where they are, despite obvious cultural gaps spawned by ethnic differences between helpers and helpees. Third, when working with clients from diverse ethnic groups, counselors must avoid stereotypes and a monolithic perspective. It is crucial that counselors consider clients as individuals within an ethnic group context.

In this ethnically responsive paradigm, a counselor's repertoire includes a number of theoretical approaches. A counselor's style has to be eclectic enough to provide a variety of helping approaches. These approaches should incorporate diverse ethnic group views and practices with respect to the dynamics of ethnic identity/acculturation, language preference, kinship influences, gender role socialization, religious/spiritual influences, immigration experience, help-seeking attitudes and behavior, historical hostility, racism, and economic disadvantage, as discussed previously.

In addition to sensitivity to such dynamics, a counselor needs to understand and be willing to assume the role of systemic change agent or advocate. When working with such clients, a counselor might need to consider the negative effects of phenomena such as racism and other forms of cultural, economic, and social oppression on development. The etiology of problems is often not in clients but rather in intolerant or restrictive environments. The only way for clients to solve problems or make decisions may be to eradicate these systemic impediments. An ethnically competent counselor often must be a systemic change agent who helps clients challenge such impediments (Lee & Hipolito-Delgado, 2007).

The components of this best practice paradigm not only are the basis of ethnically responsive counseling but also can be considered the foundation of high-quality counseling in general. As counselors strive to be aware of and responsive to the needs of ethnically diverse client groups, they raise the standard of the profession for all.

Summary

This chapter has presented a 21st-century paradigm for counseling with people of color. It has explored both traditional and contemporary ethnic classifications for people of color, along with the complexity of detailing each group. It has also examined the important distinction that must be made between the terms *race* and *ethnicity* when counseling across cultures. The chapter considered the potential peril and the inherent promise in counseling people of color. The "cross-cultural zone" was introduced, along with the dynamics that must be considered for effective counseling to occur in that important helping space. Ethical considerations for counseling in the cross-cultural zone were also considered in the chapter. Finally, important guidelines for developing the awareness, knowledge, and skill for best practice in the cross-cultural zone were presented.

The cross-cultural zone can be a challenging place for counselors. It can also be a helping space of great opportunity. Demographic projections make it clear that counselors will be spending more time in this zone in the years to come, and it is incumbent on them to increase their self-awareness, obtain the knowledge, and develop the skills to be effective in counseling with people of color.

The essence of counseling is helping people solve problems and make decisions. Ethnically competent counselors should have the ability to help people do so in a manner that is both ethically responsible and consistent with a client's ethnic group realities.

The well-being of people of color and the integrity of the profession demand that counselors do no less.

The following Web sites provide additional information relating to the chapter topics.

USEFUL WEB SITES

Multicultural Counseling Competencies
www.counseling.org/Resources/

Association for Multicultural Counseling and Development
www.amcdaca.org

ACA Code of Ethics
www.counseling.org/Resources/

Dimensions of Personal Identity
www.counseling.org/Resources/

U.S. Census Bureau
www.census.gov

REFERENCES

American Counseling Association. (2005). *Code of ethics*. Alexandria, VA: Author.

Arredondo, P., Psalti, A., & Cella, K. (1993). The woman factor in multicultural counseling. *Counseling and Human Development, 25*, 1–8.

Atkinson, D. R., Morten, G., & Sue, D. W. (1993). *Counseling American minorities: A cross-cultural perspective* (4th ed.). Madison, WI: Brown and Benchmark.

Banks, W. M. (1972). The Black client and the helping professional. In R. L. Jones (Ed.), *Black psychology*. New York: Harper and Row.

Bond, T., Lee, C. C., Lowe, R., Malayapillay, A. E. M., Wheeler, S., Banks, A., Kurdt, K., Mercado, M. M., & Smiley, E. (2001). The nature of counselling: An investigation of counselling activity in selected countries. *International Journal for the Advancement of Counselling, 23*, 245–260.

Britt-Gibson, J. (2007, March 18). What's wrong with this picture? Race isn't a factor when my generation chooses friends. *Washington Post*, p. B1.

Chang, C. Y. (2006). Counseling Korean Americans. In C. C. Lee (Ed.), *Multicultural issues in counseling: New approaches to diversity* (3rd ed., pp. 171–184). Alexandria, VA: American Counseling Association.

Chung, R. C. Y., & Bemak, F. (2006). Counseling Americans of Southeast Asian descent: The impact of the refugee experience. In C. C. Lee (Ed.), *Multicultural issues in counseling: New approaches to diversity* (3rd ed., pp. 151–170). Alexandria, VA: American Counseling Association.

Constantine, M. G., Gloria, A. M., & Barón, A. (2006). Counseling Mexican American college students. In C. C. Lee (Ed.), *Multicultural issues in counseling: New approaches to diversity* (3rd ed., pp. 207–222). Alexandria, VA: American Counseling Association.

Cross, W. E. (1995). The psychology of Nigrescence: Revising the cross model. In J. G. Ponterotto, J. M. Casas, L. A. Suzuki, & C. M. Alexander (Eds.), *Handbook of multicultural counseling* (pp. 93–122). Thousand Oaks, CA: Sage.

Delgado-Romero, E. (2003). Ethics and multicultural competence. In D. B Pope-Davis, H. L. K. Coleman, W. M. Liu, & R. L. Toporek (Eds.), *Handbook of multicultural competencies in counseling and psychology* (pp. 313–329). Thousand Oaks, CA: Sage.

Garrett, M. T. (2006). When Eagle speaks: Counseling Native Americans. In C. C. Lee (Ed.), *Multicultural issues in counseling: New approaches to diversity* (3rd ed., pp. 25–53). Alexandria, VA: American Counseling Association.

Gudykunst, K. B., & Kim, K. Y. (1984). *Communicating with strangers: An approach to intercultural communication*. Reading, MA: Addison-Wesley.

Harper, F. (1973). What counselors must know about the social sciences of Black Americans. *Journal of Negro Education, 42*, 109–116.

Harrison, D. K. (1975). Race as a counselor–client variable in counseling and psychotherapy: A review of the research. *Counseling Psychologist, 5*, 124–133.

Helms, J. E. (1995). An update of Helm's White and People of Color racial identity models. In J. G. Ponterotto, J. M. Casas, L. A. Suzuki, & C. M. Alexander (Eds.), *Handbook of multicultural counseling* (pp. 181–198). Thousand Oaks, CA: Sage.

Herring, R. (1997). Counseling indigenous American youth. In C. C. Lee (Ed.), *Multicultural issues in counseling: New approaches to diversity* (pp. 53–72). Alexandria, VA: American Counseling Association.

Holcomb-McCoy, C., & Mitchell, N. A. (2007). Promoting ethnic/racial equality through empowerment-based counseling. In C. C. Lee (Ed.), *Counseling for social justice* (2nd ed., pp. 137–157). Alexandria, VA: American Counseling Association.

Jackson, G. G. (1977). The emergence of a Black perspective in counseling. *Journal of Negro Education, 46*, 230–253.

Kearney, L. K., Draper, M., & Barón, A. (2005). Counseling utilization by ethnic minority college students. *Cultural Diversity & Ethnic Minority Psychology, 11*, 272–285.

Kelly, E. W. (1995). *Spirituality and religion in counseling and psychotherapy: Diversity in theory and practice*. Alexandria, VA: American Counseling Association.

Kenney, K. (2006). Counseling multiracial individuals and families. In C. C. Lee (Ed.), *Multicultural counseling: New approaches to diversity* (3rd ed., pp. 251–266). Alexandria, VA: American Counseling Association.

Kotkin, J., & Tseng, T. (2003, June 8). Happy to mix it all up. *Washington Post*, pp. B1–B2.

LaFromboise, T. D., Foster, S., & James, A. (1996). Ethics in multicultural counseling. In P. B. Pedersen, J. G. Draguns, W. J. Lonner, & J. E. Trimble (Eds.), *Counseling across cultures* (4th ed., pp. 47–72). Thousand Oaks, CA: Sage.

Lee, C. C. (1997). Cultural dynamics: Their importance in culturally responsive counseling. In C. C. Lee (Ed.), *Multicultural issues in counseling: New approaches to diversity* (2nd ed., pp. 15–30). Alexandria, VA: American Counseling Association.

Lee, C. C. (2001). Defining and responding to racial and ethnic diversity. In D. C. Locke, J. E. Myers, & E. L. Herr (Eds.), *The handbook of counseling* (pp. 581–588). Thousand Oaks, CA: Sage.

Lee, C. C. (2004). Counseling African Americans. In R. L. Jones (Ed.), *Black psychology* (4th ed., pp. 631–650). Hampton, VA: Cobb & Henry.

Lee, C. C. (2006a). Entering the cross-cultural zone: Meeting the challenges of culturally responsive counseling. In C. C. Lee (Ed.), *Multicultural Issues in Counseling: New Approaches to Diversity* (3rd ed., pp. 13–19). Alexandria, VA: American Counseling Association.

Lee, C. C. (2006b). Ethical issues in multicultural counseling. In B. Herlihy & G. Corey (Eds.), *ACA ethical standards casebook* (6th ed., pp. 150–162). Alexandria, VA: American Counseling Association.

Lee, C. C., Ed. (2006c). *Multicultural counseling: New approaches to diversity* (3rd ed). Alexandria, VA: American Counseling Association.

Lee, C. C., & Hipolito-Delgado, C. P. (2007). Counselors as agents of social change. In C. C. Lee (Ed.), *Counseling for social justice* (2nd ed., pp. xiii–xxii). Alexandria, VA: American Counseling Association.

Lee, C. C., & Ramsey, C. J. (2006). Multicultural counseling: A new paradigm for a new century. In C. C. Lee (Ed.), *Multicultural counseling: New approaches to diversity* (3rd ed., pp. 3–11). Alexandria, VA: American Counseling Association.

Lee, C. C., & Sirch, M. L. (1994). Counseling in an enlightened society: Values for a new millennium. *Counseling and Values, 38*, 90–97.

Lopez-Baez, S. I. (2006). Counseling Latinas: Culturally responsive interventions. In C. C. Lee (Ed.), *Multicultural issues in counseling: New approaches to diversity* (3rd ed., pp. 187–194). Alexandria, VA: American Counseling Association.

McIntosh, P. (1989). White privilege: Unpacking the invisible knapsack. *Peace and Freedom, 2,* 10–12.

Nobles, W. (1972). African philosophy: Foundations for a Black psychology. In R. L. Jones (Ed.), *Black psychology.* New York: Harper & Row.

Pack-Brown, S. P., & Williams, C. B. (2003). *Ethics in a multicultural context.* Thousand Oaks, CA: Sage.

Pope-Davis, D. B., Coleman, H. L. K., Liu, W. M., & Toporek, R. L. (2003). *Handbook of multicultural competencies in counseling and psychology.* Thousand Oaks, CA: Sage.

Ridley, C. R., Liddle, M. C., Hill, C. L., & Li, L. C. (2001). Ethical decision making in multicultural counseling. In J. G. Ponterotto, J. M. Casas, L. A., Suzuki, & C. M. Alexander (Eds.), *Handbook of multicultural counseling* (2nd ed., pp. 165–188). Thousand Oaks, CA: Sage.

Rotheram, M. J., & Phinney, J. S. (1987). Introduction: Definitions and perspectives in the study of children's ethnic socialization. In J. S. Phinney & M. J. Rotheram (Eds.), *Children's ethnic socialization* (pp. 10–31). Newbury Park, CA: Sage.

Roysircar, G., Arredondo, P., Fuertes, J. N., Ponterotto, J. G., & Toporek, R. L. (2003). *Multicultural counseling competencies 2003.* Alexandria, VA: Association for Multicultural Counseling and Development.

Sattler, J. M. (1977). The effects of therapist–client racial similarity. In A. S. Gurman & A. M. Razin (Eds.), *Effective psychotherapy: A handbook of research* (pp. 252–290). New York: Pergamon Press.

Sue, D. W., & Sue, D. (2002). *Counseling the culturally different* (4th ed.). New York: John Wiley.

U.S. Census Bureau. (2000). *National Population Estimates—Characteristics.* Washington, DC: Government Printing Office.

U.S. Census Bureau. (2007). *Annual estimates of the population by sex, race, and Hispanic or Latino origin for the United States: April 1, 2000 to July 1, 2006* (NC-EST2006-03). Washington, DC: U.S. Government Printing Office.

Vazquez, J. M. (2006). Puerto Ricans in the counseling process: The dynamics of ethnicity and race in social context. In C. C. Lee (Ed.), *Multicultural issues in counseling: New approaches to diversity* (3rd ed., pp. 223–232). Alexandria, VA: American Counseling Association.

Vontress, C. E. (1969). Cultural differences: Implications for counseling. *Journal of Negro Education, 37,* 266–275.

Vontress, C. E., Johnson, J. A., & Epp, L. R. (1999). *Cross-cultural counseling: A casebook.* Alexandria, VA: American Counseling Association.

Webster's Eleventh New Collegiate Dictionary. (2004). Springfield, MA: Merriam-Webster.

Westwood, M. J., & Borgen, W. A. (1988). A culturally embedded model for effective intercultural communication. *International Journal for the Advancement of Counselling 11,* 115–125.

Westwood, M. J., & Ishiyama, F. I. (1990). The communication process as a critical intervention for client change in cross-cultural counseling. *Journal of Multicultural Counseling and Development, 18,* 163–171.

White, J. L. (1970). Toward a Black psychology. *Ebony, 25,* 44–45, 48–50, 52.

Yeh, M., McCabe, K., Hurlburt, M., Hough, R., Hazen, A., Culver, S., Garland, A., & Landsverk, J. (2002). Referral sources, diagnoses, and service types for youth in the public outpatient mental health sector: A focus on ethnic minorities. *Journal of Behavioral Health Services and Research, 29,* 45–60.

Ethics and the Beginning Counselor: Being Ethical Right from the Start

SHARON E. ROBINSON KURPIUS, PhD
Arizona State University

SARAH K. DIXON, MPH
Arizona State University

MARK D. STAUFFER, PhD
Portland State University

As you begin your coursework in counseling as a new master's-degree student, you are probably feeling overwhelmed by all you have to learn to be a competent counselor. While excited about your first counseling session and about being helpful to clients, you realize that there is much you do not know about making good professional decisions based on ethical standards and state and federal laws. The purpose of this chapter is to introduce you to the basic ethical concepts and legal guidelines that will influence your behavior as a counselor. In the end, it is up to counselors to integrate new knowledge and insight into their counseling practice. With that goal in mind, we hope to challenge preconceived notions and stimulate new understandings regarding right and wrong, moral and immoral, ethical and unethical, and legal and illegal.

Background: Basic Concepts

First, we'll clarify what the word *ethics* means. According to MacKinnon (1998), ethics is a branch of philosophy, specifically moral philosophy, that "asks basic questions about the good life, about what is better and worse, about whether there is any objective right and wrong, and how we know it if there is" (p. 5). Remley and Herlihy (2007) suggest that although ethics and morality have overlapping meanings, morality is based on one's values, and ethics is concerned with human behavior and moral decision making. The *American Heritage College Dictionary* (2002) defines *ethics* as "the rules or standards governing the conduct of a person or the members of a profession" (p. 480). Whether spoken or unspoken, codified or not, individuals and groups have beliefs about what is right and wrong, about what is ethical and unethical. These beliefs motivate day-to-day behaviors. On personal, familial, communal, and societal levels, ethics exist as part of the complex way humans create interpersonal boundaries and make choices. Ethical dilemmas arise that are not easily solved because of the multifaceted nature of life. If you consider current debate on life-and-death issues such as abortion, capital punishment, and euthanasia, it is easy to understand that ethical practice is not a formula for behavior carved in stone but rather an arena in which dilemmas arise.

As suggested by the dictionary definition of *ethics*, joining and identifying as a member of a group usually signifies that you agree to adhere to the ethical standards established by the group. In the mental health profession, that group could be the American Counseling Association (ACA), the American Psychological Association (APA), or the National Board of Certified Counselors (NBCC), to name just a few. In this chapter, the discussion of ethics is based on the guidelines provided by professional codes of ethics such as the ACA *Code of Ethics* (2005) and the APA *Ethical Principles of Psychologists and Code of Conduct* (2002) (hereafter referred to as APA *Ethical Principles*). The *useful Web sites* section at the end of this chapter includes addresses where the various ethical codes and standards of practice can be read.

Remley and Herlihy (2007) discuss the difference between mandatory ethics and aspirational ethics. Mandatory ethics are influenced and shaped in conjunction with legal standards. Aspirational ethics, as the name implies, promote ethical behavior based on broad-spectrum aspirations such as justice and respect for the rights and dignity of persons. Though not the same, principles and virtues generally fall under the rubric of aspirational ethics. Virtue ethics derive from aspirations, so importance is placed on one's internal moral process and on "who one is." Principle ethics is concerned with "what one does" and implies a certain level of obligation to act in certain ways (Sim, 1997, p. 31). Meara, Schmidt, and Day (1996) suggested that integrating both virtue and principle ethics into professional ethical standards improves counselor competence, especially in multicultural settings in which flexibility is a necessity.

Law enters into the picture when public safety, health, and welfare are jeopardized in some way. "Laws are the agreed-on rules of a society that set forth the basic principles for living together as a group" (Remley & Herlihy, 2007, p. 3). Criminal laws have to do with specific actions that are crimes (e.g., statutory rape, fraud, tax evasion), and civil laws cover disputes of personal interest to individuals, groups, or organizations, including the government. Three important types of law are legislative, constitutional, and tort or case law. Legal statutes are created by legislative bodies of government and are interpreted by court systems. Situational interpretations in court verdicts become a type of guidepost or precedent for future cases. The creation, interpretation, and enforcement of laws are not separate from cultural values and biases, and laws fluctuate with political tides. Law and judicial interpretation on the federal, state, district, and territorial level are most often in agreement, but in some situations, they do not agree.

Malpractice torts can be particularly important to professional counselors. The United States is influenced by English common law, a type of law that validates commonly held principles that are difficult to codify and allows judges to rule on actions. Through an ad hoc judicial process, tort law establishes standards for appropriate behavior and assigns responsibility for wrong done to others. Tort law usually applies to injurious actions caused by carelessness or neglect. An example is a ruling that allows an individual to receive compensation for injury inflicted by others. Based on a general principle that holds professionals responsible for practices that harm clients, a malpractice tort empowers judicial systems to establish what is unacceptable conduct for the professional (Remley & Herlihy, 2007).

Dilemmas often arise because of differences between ethical standards and law. Counselors need to understand the relationship between what is ethical and what is legal; however, should you follow or break a law that is unethical by your personal and professional standards? Counselors are sometimes forced to answer such questions with immediate action and then bear the consequences of their choices. At other times, law and ethics do not interact directly, for example, when an ethical standard is alegal—in other words, no law covers the standard. This is true because law establishes the minimum requirements for counselor behavior. Examine the following categorical graph as an exploration of the possible interplay between law and ethics. Can you add a few of your own examples?

	Legal	*Illegal*	*Alegal*
Unethical	Advertising as having unusual talents	Unwarranted disclosure of confidential information	Attempts to enhance "professional" skills at the expense of the client
Ethical	Reporting child abuse	Refusing to testify to prevent client harm	Providing some service to the profession without profit

It is best to stay current about state and federal laws, state licensing board requirements, and the ethical standards of professional counseling organizations. For new practitioners, this may seem daunting and perhaps threatening; however, remember that these standards exist to protect both the counselor and the client. They foster higher standards for the practice of counseling.

Choosing to Be a Counselor: An Ethical Beginning

What are your motivations for becoming a counselor? These motivations are often the root of a counselor's behavior, whether or not such behavior is legal or ethical. In 1972, Max Hammer discussed motivations for entering the helping profession in his classic chapter, "To Students Interested in Becoming Psychotherapists." He believed that persons often had wrong reasons, such as a need to be dominant, to be needed and loved, to be a voyeur on other's lives, to be an omnipotent healer, to escape one's own life, or to cure themselves by curing others. Corey, Corey, and Callahan (2007) also indicate that the therapeutic process can be blocked when therapists use clients to fulfill their own needs to nurture others, to feel powerful or important, or to win acceptance, admiration, respect, or awe. Acknowledging that therapists have their own needs and values, they remind us that "therapists need be aware of the possibility of working primarily to be appreciated by others instead of working toward the best interests of their clients" (p. 39).

It is unethical when counselors are primarily meeting their own needs and imposing their personal values in the counseling relationship. ACA's (2005) *Code of Ethics* specifically states under A.4.b. Personal Values that "counselors are aware of their own values, attitudes, beliefs, and behaviors and avoid imposing values that are inconsistent with counseling goals." Additionally, Standard A.4.a. states that "counselors act to avoid harming their clients." The APA *Ethical Principles* (2002) state: "Psychologists exercise reasonable judgment and take precautions to ensure that their potential biases, the boundaries of their competence, and the limitations of their expertise do not lead to or condone unjust practices" (Principle D: Justice).

Clients are harmed by counselors who meet their personal needs through "multiple relationships" with their clients. Multiple relationships occur when a counselor relates to a client in a professional role and concurrently or sequentially occupies one or more other professional or nonprofessional roles with the client (e.g., friend, intimate partner, peer, financial partner). Although not all multiple relationships are harmful or unethical, some can be devastating.

The most devastating multiple relationship occurs when a counselor engages in a sexual relationship with a client, which is unequivocally considered unethical in the counseling profession and deemed illegal in many states (Hermann & Robinson Kurpius, 2006). Having a sexual relationship with a client is the most consistently violated ethical standard among psychologists and the second most frequently claimed violation against counselors (ASPPB, 2001; Herlihy & Corey, 1992). All ethical codes ban sexual intimacies with clients. "Sexual or romantic counselor–client interactions or relationships with current clients, their romantic partners, or their family members are prohibited" (ACA, 2005, A.5.a. Current Clients). Furthermore, counselors cannot engage in "sexual or romantic counselor–client interactions or relationships with former clients, their romantic partners, or their family members . . . for a period of 5 years following the last professional contact" (ACA, 2005, A.5.b Former Clients). Counselors who engage in such a relationship after five years following the last professional contact have the responsibility to "demonstrate forethought and document (in written form) whether the interactions or relationship can be viewed as exploitive in some way and/or whether there is still potential to harm the former client" (ACA, 2005, A.5.b. Former Clients).

A client advocacy Web site posted the following comments from a client who was victimized by a therapist: "It's really hard to explain how powerful the therapist seems to the client. He is supposed to be the expert, the trusted person who knows what is best for you. I wish I hadn't ignored my uneasiness and confusion when he started touching me. I guess I wanted him to take my pain away and to take care of me. It turned out that I was taking care of his needs most of the time. I was someone for him to confide in, to hold, to be flattered by" (Public Education Work Group, 1988, p. 1).

Counselors who are emotionally healthy do not need to engage in sexual relations with a client, nor do they meet their personal needs through the counseling relationship. When sexual contact becomes part of a therapeutic relationship, the expectation of trust that is essential to the process of therapy is violated (Thoreson, Shaughnessy, Heppner, & Cook, 1993).

Research has demonstrated that a therapeutic alliance, also known as a working alliance, is one of the preeminent factors in therapeutic efficacy and outcome (Lustig, Strauser, Rice, & Rucker, 2002). An effective therapeutic alliance rests on the personal well-being and mental health of the counselor, which allows bonding, collaborative goal setting, and task accomplishment. Discussing the personhood of the counselor, Hammer (1972) stated that "the kind of person that the therapist is will be the primary determinant of whether or not there will be therapeutic results" (p. 3) and that the client "probably cannot grow beyond the level of emotional health and maturity achieved by his [her] therapist" (p. 21). Hammer further noted,

> . . . to be really effective, the therapist needs to know from *personal experience* what the "path" is that leads from internal conflict and contradiction to liberation. If you do not know how to liberate yourself from an internal conflict, fear or pain, then you are not in a position to help others do it either. . . . What right does the therapist have to ask the patient to face his [her] rejected truths and anxiety and to take risks in terms of exposing himself [herself] and making himself [herself] vulnerable, if the therapist is not willing or able to do so? (p. 12)

Therefore, your first ethical responsibility is to be as emotionally healthy as possible, to be aware of how your own "unfinished business" could potentially influence your attempts to be helpful to others, and to seek professional help as soon as you are aware that some aspect of your own life may be infringing on your work as a counselor. Your competence is limited by your own self-awareness and psychological health and maturity (Corey et al., 2007; Robinson, 1988).

Counselors integrate and use ethical principles as a way to monitor and reflect upon internal motivations and to guide their behaviors, especially when difficulties arise. The professional literature, as well as professional organizations, suggest that certain principles serve as guideposts for counselor behavior. Synthesizing the literature, Remley and Herlihy (2007) suggested six principles for counselors to consider:

1. Beneficence: do good, promote well-being and health.
2. Nonmaleficence: do no harm, prevent harmful actions and affects.
3. Autonomy: recognize and respect independence and self-determination.
4. Justice: promote fairness and equality in dealings.
5. Fidelity: be responsible to clients and honor agreements.
6. Veracity: be truthful and honest in dealings.

The APA *Code of Ethics* (2002) incorporated these principles into its ethical code: Principle A: Beneficence and Nonmaleficence; Principle B: Fidelity and Responsibility;

Principle C: Integrity; Principle D: Justice; and Principle E: Respect for People's Rights and Dignity.

Professional Responsibility

Counselors have a fiduciary responsibility to their clients and must be accountable for clients' welfare and rights. Furthermore, counselors have a responsibility to the public, to other professionals, to agencies and institutions in which they work, and to the counseling profession. In addition to respecting differences among clients, counselors must be competent, respect client rights, maintain confidentiality, and promote client welfare.

The Importance of Multiculturalism in Ethics

Although European American and "mainstream" values dominate our profession, our ethical standards are increasingly reflecting the diverse society within which we live. When asked about the 2005 ACA ethical codes, Kocet stated that multiculturalism was "the main charge of the code revision taskforce given to us by former ACA President David Kaplan" (personal communication, November 5, 2003). Continual efforts by professional organizations, educational institutions, counseling professionals, and students are necessary to represent, respect, and appropriately serve the diverse world within which we practice.

A challenge in creating ethical standards is finding standards that are specific enough to highlight proper behavior and yet broad enough that the codes are not unrepresentative or myopic. Ibrahim (1996) suggested a universalistic approach to ethical standards, that is, having ethical codes that reflect what is common across cultures while honoring the ethics of each individual culture (as cited in Atkinson, 2004). Most codes have broad aspirational goals related to multiculturalism that require counselors to act from what the code implies rather than from specific behavioral guidelines. Cottone and Tarvydas (2007) noted that "implied ethical standards are not enforceable in grievance processes, which limits the profession's ability to protect consumers from being harmed by incompetent multicultural practices" (p. 220).

Almost all beginning counselors understand that cultural insensitivity, racism, oppression, and discrimination are *wrong*. However, what often remains unclear is how such problems manifest in subtle ways in ordinary activity. For example, the guiding principles mentioned previously may indeed be useful guideposts for behavior, and yet, if counselors assert autonomy as a core value when working with a client whose worldview has collectivism as a core value, incompetent and harmful counseling may result. Beginning counselors often fail to realize how much effort is truly necessary to be a culturally competent counselor.

Several passages in both the APA (2002) *Ethical Principles* and ACA (2005) *Code of Ethics* stress that it is unethical to discriminate, harass, or demean clients on the basis of age, gender, gender identity, race, ethnicity, culture, color, marital status, national origin, spirituality/religion, sexual orientation, disability/ability, language, or socioeconomic status. Ethical codes have made it clear that discrimination is not acceptable for any reason. What is your experience with each of these identified categories? What are your preconceived notions? What are your discriminatory tendencies? When answering these questions, take into consideration individual, group, and universal levels (Sue & Sue, 2003). For example, we can recognize pain as a human phenomenon, but we also need to understand how specific groups and individuals experience pain differently. Ethics codify bases by which counselors must not discriminate, but counselors should continue to strive to understand and validate the variation, complexity, and severity of the underlying issues. There are individuals and groups who are yet to be acknowledged in their need for social justice. What other forms of discrimination are not listed? For example, one form of discrimination that is often unrecognized is discrimination based on body fat or size. The following exemplifies why respect and awareness of differences are important:

> Sandy McBrayer, the 1995 national Teacher of the Year, tells of visiting an elementary school that was proud of its ethnic diversity and the integration achieved within the school's social milieu. The principal walked her to the newly built multipurpose "cafetorium" and ceremoniously pulled open the doors to reveal children of all colors eating, talking, and laughing together. As she entered, a contrasting scene near the door caught her eye. Separated from the rest of the student body were two large children who sat at a table eating their lunches in silence, staring directly ahead. They were not laughing. They were not talking. They were just bringing their forks to their mouths and down again, trying to be inconspicuous and to finish quickly. This day, they were too slow. As other children finished their meals and exited the cafetorium, they threw their uneaten food at the two children. (Loewy, 1998)

Based on a study of 52 professionals, Loewy (1994/1995) found that mental health counselors were no less biased than the general public in that they stereotyped "fat" people negatively and "thin" people positively (as cited in Loewy, 1998). One task of the counselor is to stop malevolent action and take responsibility for harmful behavior, whatever it is.

Beginning in the late 1960s, concern was raised over counselor competence to counsel someone of a different ethnicity. According to Atkinson (2004), professional competence is still the quintessential ethical issue regarding multicultural counseling. Sue and Sue (2003) noted, "From our perspective, mental health professionals have seldom functioned in a culturally competent manner. Rather, they have functioned in a monoculturally competent manner. . . . We submit that much of the current therapeutic practice taught in graduate programs derives mainly from experience and research with middle- to upper-class White folks" (pp. 9–10). This criticism is not new to the field of counseling and comes from within the community of counselors. It is a statement that we hope challenges us to improve.

Multicultural counseling competence involves three main components: (a) an awareness of one's cultural values and biases, (b) cultural awareness of your client's worldview, and (c) culturally appropriate counseling practices (ACA, 2002). To become more skilled at meeting the needs of diverse clients, a competent counselor will proactively evolve through study, training, and supervision. Part of a counselor's job is to become secure with his or her own ethnic identity, which correlates with greater openness and acceptance of different cultural backgrounds (as noted in Semans & Stone Fish, 2000). Self-examination and accepting one's heritage are steps toward a self-awareness that requires accountability for one's intolerance, oppression, racism, and elitism. A counselor is also called on to be "aware of and respect cultural, individual, and role difference" (APA Principle E: Respect for People's Rights and Dignity). To move from being unaware to aware, didactic and experiential knowledge of individual and group differences is important.

Is it ethical to apply counseling theories, techniques, and even ethical standards without consideration of a client's cultural background? Although the easy answer is no, to practice this is another matter. For example, would your personal religious convictions or conceptualization of "appropriate" counseling prevent you from collaborating with a client's traditional healer?

The client's culture may also influence the boundaries of the counseling relationship. In some cultures, for example, sharing food or small gifts are signs of respect. The APA Code of Ethics (2002) states,

> A psychologist refrains from entering into a multiple relationship if the multiple relationship could reasonably be expected to impair the psychologist's objectivity, competence, or effectiveness in performing his or her functions as a psychologist, or otherwise risks exploitation or harm to the person with whom the professional relationship exists. Multiple relationships that would not reasonably be expected to cause impairment or risk exploitation or harm are not unethical. (3.05a Multiple Relationships)

The important point is that a skilled counselor considers client welfare and culture when using counseling interventions and applies consistent efforts to be competent while still respecting the culture of the client.

Counselor Competence

This naturally brings us to the topic of counselor competence. The notion that it is unethical to practice beyond the limits of one's competence is widely accepted. Here are some important points drawn from the 2005 ACA *Code of Ethics* (C.2. Professional Competence) regarding competence:

1. Boundaries of Competence:
   a. Provide only those services for which you are qualified.
   b. Represent accurately your professional qualifications.
2. New Specialty Areas of Practice: Practice in new specialty areas only after appropriate education, supervision and experience.
3. Qualified for Employment:
   a. Only accept employment for which you are qualified.
   b. Hire for professional counseling positions only those that are qualified.
4. Monitor Effectiveness: Make continual efforts to monitor and improve efficacy and outcomes.

5. Consultation on Ethical Obligation: Consult with colleagues and other relevant professionals regarding ethical issues.
6. Continuing Education:
   a. Grow professionally through involvement in continuing education.
   b. Take steps to insure nonmaleficence in using the new specialty area.
7. Impairment:
   a. Seek assistance in solving personal issues.
   b. Refrain from your professional services if a client may be harmed by your physical, mental, or emotional problems.
8. Counselor Incapacitation or Termination of Practice: Counselors prepare a written plan for the transfer of clients to an identified colleague in the case of incapacitation, death, or termination of practice.

To these, we would add your responsibility as counselors in training to learn basic and advanced skills, to integrate academic study with supervised practice, to develop self-understanding and awareness, to receive training in multicultural competency, and to become intimately familiar with relevant laws influencing the profession and with our ethical codes (ACA, 2005, C.1. Knowledge of Standards; APA, 2002, Introduction and Applicability).

As a student, it is your professors' responsibility to foster your learning of these aspects of competence and to provide ongoing "evaluation and appraisal" to "address the inability of some students to achieve counseling competencies that might impede performance" (ACA, 2005, F.9.b. Limitations). Counselor educators "assist students in securing remedial assistance when needed" (ACA, F.9.b. Limitations) and "recommend dismissal from training programs . . . when those supervisees are unable to provide competent services" (ACA, F.5.b. Limitations). As a student, your competence is a shared responsibility between you and your training program. However, after you graduate and enter the professional world, it is your professional and ethical responsibility to remain competent.

To work within your boundaries of competence, you must recognize your strengths and weaknesses. Defining your areas of competence occurs through both subjective and external evaluation. The subjective component involves some self-evaluation, which requires critical and honest self-examination. Calling this subjective component an internal perspective, Robinson Kurpius and Gross (1996) cautioned counselors to do everything possible to gain the skills and knowledge basic to the profession. Counselors need to stretch their skills continually by reading and attending to new and developing trends, through attaining postgraduate education, and through attending seminars and workshops aimed at sharpening and increasing both knowledge and skills.

The objective component helps solidify your identification with the profession and verifies to the profession and the public that you have achieved a minimal level of competence. The objective component typically includes completing appropriate graduate training, acquiring supervised direct-client counseling hours, and passing professional and state credentialing exams. Many choose to take the National Counselor Examination (NCE) produced by the National Board for Certified Counselors (NBCC). The NCE measures "knowledge, skills, and abilities viewed as important for providing effective counseling services. The NCE is designed to be general in nature. It is intended to assess cognitive knowledge that should be known by all counselors regardless of their individual professional specialties" (NBCC, 2001a, p. 1). The NCE assesses knowledge in eight content areas: human growth and development, social and cultural foundations, group work, helping relationships, career and lifestyle development, appraisal, research and program evaluation, and professional orientation and ethics.

Taking an exam might indicate that you have a minimum knowledge base in the profession, but it is not enough. The ACA *Code of Ethics* (2005) clearly states: "Counselors practice only within the boundaries of their competence, based on their education, training, supervised experience, state and national professional credentials, and appropriate professional experience" (C.2.a. Boundaries of Competence). The APA *Ethical Principles* (2002) makes a similar statement and adds: "Psychologists provide services, teach, and conduct research with populations and in areas only within the boundaries of their competence, based on their education, training, supervised experience, consultation, study, or professional experience" (Principle 2.01a Boundaries of Competence). Although APA requires training *or* experience, we prefer to err on the conservative side and stress that both training and experience are essential for competence.

The ethical standards are quite clear regarding what you should do if you are not competent to treat a certain client problem. You are responsible for the welfare of the client; therefore, it is your professional duty to obtain for that client the best services possible—be it from you or from a professional colleague. Clients are not subjects for your trial-and-error learning but deserve the best professional care possible. Remember, your primary ethical obligation is nonmaleficence—do no harm (Welfel & Kitchener, 1995). Here is a rough step-by-step procedure to assist you when you recognize your competency is insufficient.

1. Limit your services and refer your client to other helping professionals who can meet the needs of your client in the given area and then consider expanding your competence base. (Note: Refer to more than one professional so that the client has options and does not feel obligated to receive services from a specific professional.)
2. Suspend your services and refer to several appropriate professionals while you receive sufficient training and supervision in the specialty area.
3. Terminate professional responsibilities and make appropriate referrals.
4. If there is no one to whom you can refer (which would be an exception rather than a common occurrence), educate yourself with professional literature on the presenting problem and seek supervision of your work with the client.

Competence requires never-ending continuing education. The words of this doctoral graduate are admirable: "When I decided that I was really going to be a psychologist and do therapy, I attended every training seminar, conference, and workshop I could so that I could be really good at what I do." Like all graduates, be it from a master's or a doctoral program, he was not a finished product upon receipt of his degree. To become truly proficient at what he had chosen to do, he had to seek all the advanced didactic and experiential input he could get. Only by continually growing himself is he comfortable offering his services to others.

One area of training for which students are often not adequately prepared is diagnosis. Typically, insurance companies will not pay for service unless the client has a *DSM-IV-R* diagnosis. The ability to diagnose has been the subject of debate and court proceedings. In Arizona, a social worker diagnosed a client as paranoid, a diagnosis that was confirmed by a consulting psychiatrist (*Cooke v. Berlin*, 1987). When the client later killed a man and was diagnosed with atypical psychosis, the social worker was sued by the victim's widow. Although the case was eventually settled out of court, it left several questions unanswered. What is the appropriate scope of practice of various mental health professionals? Had there been competent diagnosis, would there have been an assessment of dangerousness resulting in a duty to warn? When can one professional, especially an unlicensed one, provide information to another without the risk of malpractice? These questions all center on knowing the limits of one's competence and behaving within the boundaries of professional training and experience.

A final area of professional competence is ethically presenting your services and credentials to the public. Most codes of ethics warn professionals against making false claims regarding expertise and qualifications and hold the professional responsible for correcting others' misrepresentation of their qualifications (ACA, 2005, C.4.a. Accurate Representation). For example, if you are called "doctor" and you do not hold a doctoral degree in counseling or a related field, you must correct this misrepresentation immediately. In advertising services, counselors "identify their credentials in an accurate manner that is not false, misleading, deceptive, or fraudulent" (ACA, 2005, C.3.a. Accurate Advertising). You cannot claim that you are a "candidate for" a degree. When trying to build a practice, client testimonials must be avoided, as well as implications of unusual or one-of-a-kind abilities (Koocher & Keith-Spiegel, 1998). The ACA *Code of Ethics* (2005, C.6.c. Media Presentations) requires that media presentation statements are appropriate and consistent with the *Code of Ethics*. Additionally, the APA *Ethical Principles* (2002) state that a paid advertisement must be acknowledged or "clearly recognizable" as such (5.02c Statements by Others).

The Federal Trade Commission has granted considerable freedom in advertising as a result of the *Goldfarb v. Virginia State Bar* (1975) ruling. How and if you advertise your services will require you to weigh carefully what is legally permitted with what is ethically acceptable. Regardless of the area of service being discussed, you are the first-line judge of your professional competence. Although credentialing bodies, professional organizations, and state legislative bodies may set standards for practice, you must be the most critical evaluator of your ability to provide service. This often becomes quite a challenge when your living depends on having clients who will pay for service. Remaining ethical is not always the easy choice.

Client Rights and Welfare

When clients enter a counseling relationship, they assume that you are competent. In addition, they have certain rights, known as client rights. These rights, which have their foundation in the Bill of Rights, particularly the First and Fourth Amendments of the Constitution of the United States, include freedom of religion, speech, and the press; the right of petition; and freedom from unreasonable searches and seizures. The concepts of confidentiality, privileged communication, and informed consent are based on the Fourth Amendment, which guarantees privacy. Privacy is defined as "the constitutional right of an individual to decide the time, place, manner, and extent of sharing oneself with others" (Corey et al., 2007, p. 212).

Privacy and Confidentiality

Confidentiality and Privileged Communications. The concept of privacy is the foundation for the client's legal right to privileged communication and the counselor's responsibility to hold counseling communications confidential. Confidentiality is a professional concept. Privileged communication is a legal term referring to a right held by clients to prevent therapeutic information from entering into a legal proceeding. Clients, not counselors, have control over who has access to what they have said in therapy, and clients are protected from having their communication disclosed in a court of law. However, a client's confidential communications may not be privileged in a court of law unless the mental health professional is legally certified or licensed in the state in which he or she practices.

Most states grant the clients of state-certified or licensed mental health professionals (e.g., psychologists, professional counselors, marriage and family therapists) the right of privileged communications. On the federal level, the U.S. Supreme Court ruled in *Jaffee v. Redmond* (1996) that communication was indeed privileged for clients of licensed social workers, which potentially has important implications for master's-level mental health professionals. Since then, privileged communication was recognized for a client of a licensed clinical social worker (see Cottone & Tarvydas, 2007). HIPAA's privacy rule, discussed later in this section, may eventually influence a definition of who is a psychotherapist. HIPPA defines the term *psychotherapy notes* as "notes recorded (in any medium) by a health care provider who is a mental health professional documenting or analyzing the contents of conversation during a private counseling session or a group, joint, or family counseling session and that are separated from the rest of the individual's medical record" (USDHHS, 2003, p. 9). Much is still uncertain regarding privileged communication for clients who seek services from certain mental health professionals in various states.

Beyond eligibility concerns, for communication to be privileged, four conditions must be met:

1. Communication must originate in confidence that it will not be disclosed.
2. Confidentiality must be essential to the full and satisfactory maintenance of the relationship.
3. In the opinion of the greater community, the relationship must be one that should be sedulously fostered or, in other words, noted by care and persistent effort.
4. Injury to the relationship by disclosure of the communication must be greater than the benefit gained by the correct disposal of litigation regarding the information (Schwitzgebel & Schwitzgebel, 1980).

If as a counselor you can claim these four conditions and your professional licensure makes your clients eligible, your clients' communications are not only confidential but also privileged and thus protected from being disclosed in a court of law. Remember, however, that there is always a balance between a client's right to privacy and society's need to know. This is often referred to as the "doctor's dilemma" (Koocher & Keith-Spiegel, 1998).

In spite of the importance given to confidentiality and privileged communication, Pope, Tabachnick, and Keith-Spiegel (1987) reported that 62% of psychologists in a national survey indicated that they had unintentionally violated a client's confidentiality, and 21% had intentionally violated a client's confidentiality. These alarming statistics suggest that mental health professionals are at risk for violating this core ethical principle. Therefore, adept mental health professionals are acutely aware of the professional standards regarding confidentiality and of their state's laws governing privileged communication. For example, in most states, if staff working in the mental health professional's office breach a client's confidentiality, the professional is guilty of breaching confidentiality. Secretaries and other staff who have access to client records are considered extensions of certified and licensed mental health professionals.

HIPAA and the "Privacy Rule."   In the late 1990s, concern over health services consumers' privacy increased because of advances in technology and the shift to managed health care. For example, service providers faxing entire health records to insurance agencies pose threats to the privacy of insured patients. In response, the U.S. Department of Health and Human Services (USDHHS) implemented the Health Insurance Portability and Accountability Act (HIPAA). The primary intent was to ensure the privacy of those who seek health services and at the same time allow client information to move freely to provide the best level of care for individuals seeking professional help. This act also sought to improve consumers' understanding and management of their personal health information (USDHHS, 2003). HIPPA affects the job requirements of both mental and physical health care providers, especially those working with health insurance companies.

The USDHHS's "Privacy Rule," formally titled Standards for Privacy of Individually Identifiable Health Information, focused on the use and disclosure of client information termed "protected healthcare information" (PHI), which is information on any past, present, or future mental or physical health of clients, including payment information. Since its final revision in 2002, movement toward compliance has posed new legal and ethical challenges for mental health professionals. Certain health service providers under the umbrella of this health regulation are called covered entities. Often, helping professionals such as counselors, psychologists, and social workers fall into this category when "they hold or transmit [PHI] . . . in any form or media, whether electronic, paper, or oral" (USDHHS, 2003, p. 3).

The Office of Civil Rights in the USDHHS has responsibility for HIPAA implementation through encouragement of voluntary compliance and enforcement through civil monetary penalties (USDHHS, 2003). Currently, agencies, including individual providers of mental health services, rely or consult with "HIPAA experts" on how to conduct business. Furthermore, the widespread adoption of these privacy standards affects all helping professionals. The nuances of operationalizing HIPPA are extensive; for this reason, a detailed and thorough explanation is beyond the scope of this chapter. Some important aspects of the privacy rule are presented, however.

The privacy rule applies to information that might identify or could be used to identify a person. A counselor may disclose information to a client or to other entities with client authorization. Difficulty arises when the disclosure of information poses potential harm to the client, for example, if a client wants to release psychotherapy notes to an unqualified and untrained person. There are also specified uses and disclosures of identifiable information without authorization (e.g., treatment, payment, health operations such as scheduling, quality assurance). However, in all cases, use and disclosure of health information should be limited to the "minimum necessary" to provide services (USDHHS, 2003, p. 10). This may mean that counselors transmit only sections of records, for example, only parts of pages or pages on which some information has been blacked out in the copying process.

The privacy rule addresses protected information related to counseling. Except in unusual circumstances, individuals have the right to review and obtain a copy of their protected health information in a counselor's "designated record set." The designated record set is that group of records "used to make decisions about individuals" (USDHHS, 2003, p. 12). The rule makes an exception for "psychotherapy notes." Descriptive of a relatively smaller portion of most mental health records, a psychotherapy note does not include "medication prescription and monitoring, counseling session start and stop times, the modalities and frequencies of treatment furnished, results of clinical tests, and any summary of the following items: diagnosis, functional status, the treatment plan, symptoms, prognosis, and progress to date" (USDHHS, p. 9). Agencies should have policies to distinguish a psychotherapy note from other records and should have separate storage for each type of record. A counselor must obtain client authorization for specific uses and disclosures of psychotherapy notes. Some important exceptions exist: for use in treatment if the originator of the note is the sole user; to conduct training programs in order to instruct and supervise students, interns, and other trainees; to defend oneself in legal proceedings activated by a client; to facilitate HHS checks for compliance; to avert a "serious and imminent threat to public health or safety"; and for lawful oversight of a counselor by a health oversight agency (USDHHS, p. 9).

The privacy rule requires professionals to inform, if not educate, clients about their privacy rights and the privacy procedures and practices used by the counseling agency. They inform clients by notice, which explains and provides examples of how protected information is used, disclosed, amended, inspected, and copied, including exceptions and prohibitions. Notices also inform clients regarding their right to restrict, revoke, and receive an accounting of disclosures. For example, a client may request that an authorization be valid for only 10 days and that he or she be informed if the transmission is completed. A general notice is also posted in reasonably clear view on counseling premises. Furthermore, notices are given to clients upon intake, promptly mailed to clients when initial communications are by phone, and sent electronically (in a proper format) when services are provided online. In the case of emergency situations, a privacy notice is given as soon as practicably possible. Written

notices have headings similar to this example: NOTICE OF PRIVACY PRAC-
TICES: THIS NOTICE DESCRIBES HOW INFORMATION ABOUT YOU
MAY BE USED AND DISCLOSED AND HOW YOU CAN GET ACCESS TO
THIS INFORMATION. PLEASE REVIEW IT CAREFULLY. Agencies should
post a notice of their privacy practices on their Web site. Furthermore, counselors
make a "good faith" effort to obtain written acknowledgment from clients that they
received a privacy notice and document efforts made when this acknowledgment is not
possible (USDHHS, 2003). Authorization forms for use and disclosure of information
should be in specific terms and allow clients to understand their privacy rights. "All
authorizations must be in plain language, and contain specific information regarding
the information to be disclosed or used, the person(s) disclosing and receiving the
information, expiration, right to revoke in writing, and other data" (USDHHS, 2003,
p. 9). In keeping with both APA and ACA ethical guidelines, when clients give authorization, they should be informed about what exact information is being released, to
whom, for what purpose, and the time period for which the signed consent for release is
valid (Robinson Kurpius, 1997). Under the privacy rule, an agency providing covered
health services must also set up procedures for the use of forms for routine disclosure
and create criteria to follow when unusual, nonroutine disclosures of information are
required. Counselors may not demand that clients give authorization for the release of
information in order to receive treatment, except in certain limited circumstances
(USDHHS, 2003).

HIPAA stipulates that training on privacy practices should be an ongoing procedure for the entire agency workforce. Training covers how and who handles protected
information. The privacy rule requires that classifications of personnel as related to
information access be clarified on the basis of workplace role and then operationalized.
For example, an agency database should not allow an office manager access to psychotherapy notes but instead limit access to the minimum information necessary to
perform his or her job (e.g., schedule clients, bill insurance). Agencies should also
appoint or identify a "privacy officer," incorporate privacy protocol and safeguards, and
instruct clients on greivance procedures (USDHHS, 2003, p. 14).

In addition to this information related to privacy, Snider (1987) makes some very
practical and useful suggestions for protecting written material such as case notes and
test data. He stresses that the absolute minimum storage is a locked file cabinet—not
just a locked office door. If a mistake is made while writing case notes, a single line
should be drawn through the written text and initialed and dated by the counselor.
Text should never be erased or whited out.

Exceptions to Confidentiality.   There are three global issues that require a breach of
confidentiality. In cases of minors, we have both a legal and ethical responsibility to
protect them from "future harm of continued abuse or neglect and to protect children
who are insufficiently autonomous to act on their own behalf" (Sattler, 1990, p. 105).
Minors are usually all individuals under the age of 18; however, some states recognize
emancipated minors who are at least 16. Counselors should know their state laws that
apply to minors and breaching confidentiality (Lawrence & Robinson Kurpius, 2000).
Every state has passed a law mandating the reporting of child abuse. Regardless of the

counselor's personal feelings about helping a client overcome his or her abusive behavior, the abuse must be reported. Society has deemed that knowing about and stopping child abuse outweigh the abuser's right to privacy. Differences exist among states, so counselors should check with their state protective service for information on what is specifically meant by abuse.

Many states also require counselors to report abuse, neglect, or exploitation of incapacitated and vulnerable adults. In Arizona, *incapacitated* is defined as "an impairment by reason of mental illness, mental deficiency, mental disorder, physical illness or disability, advanced age, chronic use of drugs, chronic intoxication, and other causes to the extent that the person lacks sufficient understanding or capacity to make or communicate responsible decisions," and a *vulnerable* adult is defined as "an individual who is eighteen years of age or older who is unable to protect himself from abuse, neglect or exploitation by others because of a physical or mental impairment" (Arizona Revised Statute 46–451).

Finally, privilege is automatically waived when a client presents with a "serious and foreseeable harm" to self or others (ACA, 2005, B.2.a. Danger and Legal Requirements). A well-known court case that established such mandatory disclosure was *Tarasoff v. Board of Regents of the University of California* (1974, 1976). A young graduate student, Poddar, from India had been working with a university psychologist regarding his depression and anger resulting from being rejected by a female peer, Tatiana Tarasoff. He told the psychologist about his intent to buy a gun. The psychologist notified the campus police both verbally and in writing about his concerns that Poddar was dangerous and should be taken to a community mental health facility. The police interviewed Poddar and released him from custody. The psychologist's supervising psychiatrist decided that the letter to the police and selected case notes should be destroyed. Shortly thereafter, Poddar shot and stabbed Tarasoff to death. The California Supreme Court held: "Once a therapist does in fact determine, or under applicable professional standards reasonably should have determined, that a patient poses a serious danger of violence to others, he bears a duty to exercise reasonable care to protect the foreseeable victims of that danger" (*Tarasoff*, 1976). This ruling has been interpreted as the duty to protect or the duty to warn. In these instances, it is the counselor's overriding responsibility to protect an intended, identifiable victim from harm that could result from a client's actions.

Other instances when the privilege is typically lost include when clients introduce their mental condition as an element in a court case, when the mental stability of either spouse is introduced in a child custody case, when the counselor is working for the court such as in conducting a court-ordered examination, when the client is suing the counselor, and when the counselor believes that the client is in need of immediate hospitalization. At the onset of therapy, counselors ought to inform clients about the limits of confidentiality and the specific instances when confidentiality must be breached. Clients can then make informed decisions about what they say in therapy.

Confidentiality and HIV. Counselors with AIDS clients face a delimma between protecting their clients' right of confidentiality and a duty to warn when clients do not inform their sexual partners of their medical condition. The APA (1991) took a leadership role in this area, and at the 1991 annual meeting, the Council of Representatives passed these resolutions:

1. A legal duty to protect third parties from HIV infection should not be imposed.
2. If, however, specific legislation is considered, then it should permit disclosure only when the provider knows of an identifiable third party who the provider has a compelling reason to believe is at significant risk for infection; the provider has a reasonable belief that the third party has no reason to suspect that he or she is at risk; and the client/patient has been urged to inform the third party and has either refused or is considered unreliable in his/her willingness to notify the third party.
3. If such legislation is adopted, it should include immunity from civil and criminal liability for providers who, in good faith, make decisions to disclose or not to disclose information about HIV infection to third parties.

This resolution provides concrete guidelines for breaching the confidentiality of clients with AIDS. The ACA *Code of Ethics* (2005 B.2.b. Contagious, Life-Threatening Diseases) addresses this same issue:

> When clients disclose that they have disease commonly known to be both communicable and life threatening, counselors may be justified in disclosing information to identifiable third parties, if they are known to be at demonstrable and high risk of contracting the disease. Prior to making a disclosure, counselors confirm that there is such a diagnosis and assess the intent of clients to inform the third parties about their disease or to engage in any behaviors that may be harmful to an identifiable third party.

Robinson Kurpius (1997) pointed out that "unless there is an identifiable victim and the client refuses to behave in a manner that protects this person, the covenant of confidentiality should not be broken" (p. 10). As Koocher and Keith-Spiegel (1998) noted, good clinical judgment is essential in making decisions regarding duty to protect. Furthermore, two thirds of the states have legislation regarding limits to confidentiality of a client's HIV status (Corey et al., 2007); therefore, counselors should be aware of the legislation in the state where they practice.

Confidentiality and Subpoenas.   It would be remiss not to discuss subpoenas and how counselors should respond to them in an attempt to protect client confidentiality. If you receive a subpoena and you are not trained as a legal professional, seek legal counsel. For example, how will you know whether a subpoena is valid? When counselors divulge information inappropriately in what seems to be a valid circumstance, they are still responsible for breaches of confidentiality. If you are unsure about a legal matter, seek help from a legal expert.

Regardless of the type of subpoena received—whether it is a typical subpoena that requires your presence at court or for a deposition or a subpoena duces tecum that requires you to bring your records with you—you should initially claim the privilege for your client (Schwitzgebel & Schwitzgebel, 1980). This forces the court or your client's attorney to require you to breach confidentiality. You then have the option of refusing to testify or producing your records, although you will most likely be ruled in contempt and have to go to jail. In these rare instances, you need to find a personally acceptable balance among what the law requires, what is ethically appropriate, and what you find to be morally correct. This is a personal decision that only you can make, because you will be the one experiencing the consequences of your decision.

Informed Consent

This brings us to a discussion of informed consent. According to Everstine et al. (1980), three elements must be present for informed consent to be legal.

1. Competence—requires that the person granting the consent is able to engage in rational thought to a sufficient degree to make competent decisions about his or her life. Minors cannot give informed consent, and consent must be sought from their parents or legal guardian. Minors give informed assent.
2. Informed—requires that the individual is given the relevant information about the procedures to be performed in a language that he or she can understand.
3. Voluntariness—requires that consent is given freely by the client.

The APA (2002) *Ethical Principles* requires a fourth element, that "Psychologists appropriately document written or oral consent, permission, and assent" (3.10d Informed Consent). The ACA (2005) *Code of Ethics* is very specific with respect to what should be disclosed to clients for them to give informed consent:

> Counselors explicitly explain to clients the nature of all services provided. They inform clients about issues such as, but not limited to, the following: the purposes, goals, techniques, procedures, limitations, potential risks, and benefits of services; the counselor's qualifications, credentials, and relevant experience; continuation of services upon the incapacitation or death of a counselor; and other pertinent information. Counselors take steps to ensure that clients understand the implications of diagnosis, the intended use of tests and reports, fees, and billing arrangements. Clients have the right to confidentiality and to be provided with an explanation of its limitations (including how supervisors and/or treatment team professionals are involved); to obtain clear information about their records; to participate in ongoing counseling plans; and to refuse any services or modality change and to be advised of the consequences of such refusal. (A.2.b. Types of Information Needed)

If you are asked by a client to disclose to a third party information revealed in therapy, have the client sign an informed consent form before making any disclosure. You may be surprised to learn that counselors are not even permitted to respond to inquiries about whether they are seeing a person in therapy—even the client's name and status in counseling are confidential, unless the client has granted permission for this information to be released.

One exception is when your services are paid through an insurance company or health maintenance organization (HMO). This automatically grants the insurance company or HMO limited access to information regarding the client. Prior to beginning therapy, the client needs to be made aware of the parameters of the information that will be shared. Again, it is evident how important it is to have potential clients sign an informed consent form before they become clients. Finally, HIPAA guidelines are to be considered in how information is handled by counselors and office staff when dealing with clients using insurance benefits to pay for services.

Right to Treatment

Having clients sign informed consent forms implies that they have a right to receive or refuse treatment. Many court cases have been based on the right-to-treatment issue. In the early 1970s, *Wyatt v. Stickney* (1971) was the first case in which the right to treatment was ruled a constitutionally protected right. The case was filed against the state of Alabama on behalf of mentally disabled institutionalized patients who were kept confined under conditions of psychological and physical deprivation. There was one physician for every 2000 patients, making adequate care impossible. The court ruled that involuntarily committed patients have a constitutional right to receive "such individual treatment as will give each of them a realistic opportunity to be cured or to improve." In addition, the court required the institution to have individualized treatment plans developed by qualified mental health professionals for each patient. Furthermore, committed patients have the right to their own clothing, to receive minimal pay for labor performed, to receive mail, to exercise several times per week, and to have an appropriate physical environment in which to live.

In *Rogers v. Orkin* (1980) and in *Rennie v. Klein* (1981), courts ruled that clients have the right to refuse treatment. In *Roger v. Orkin*, the court ruled that the "power to produce ideas was fundamental to our cherished right to communicate." The court indicated that the right to refuse medication and seclusion was a Fourth Amendment right but cited several state interests that can overrule a person's right to this privacy: police power, the right of the state to protect others from harm; *parens patriae*, the duty of the state to prevent the patient's condition from deteriorating; and consideration of the financial costs of operating facilities that may result from extended hospitalization (Levenson, 1989). *Rennie v. Klein* held that the right to refuse medication could be overruled only under due process, except in an emergency. All of these court cases have provided us with parameters for client rights with respect to treatment issues. Counselors should be constantly alert to the legal issues surrounding this very important client right.

Client Welfare

The preceding discussion rests on the premise that the counselor's primary obligation is to protect the welfare of the client. The ACA (2005) *Code of Ethics* states that "the primary responsibility of counselors is to respect the dignity and to promote the welfare of clients" (A.1.a. Primary Responsibility). A similar statement is in the Preamble to the APA (2002) *Ethical Principles*, specifically stating that it has "as its goals the welfare and protection of the individuals and groups." Inappropriate multiple relationships, counselors' personal needs, and conflicts between employing institutions and client needs all influence client welfare.

Multiple relationships and counselor needs have already been discussed. Regarding employer policy versus client needs, suppose you work in a prison setting and an inmate tells you that he or she is using drugs, which is against all prison rules. Or imagine that you are a school counselor and a 15-year-old tells you that he or she is using drugs. What is in the best interests of each of these clients? How will your behavior affect your relationship with each client, your relationship with your future clients, and your position within the institution? Similar conflicts may arise when you are employed by a business or industry and the needs of the employee and client may not be in agreement with the goals of the business (Newman & Robinson, 1991). To whom do you owe loyalty? To the employer who signs your paycheck or the employee-client? These questions are not easy to answer, nor is there always one right answer. You must decide what is ethical based on the ethical guidelines and on what is right or wrong for you personally.

Thus far, the discussion has focused on individual clients. An additional set of guidelines comes into play when you are doing group work or working with a couple or family. In a group setting, special issues include qualifications of the group leader, informed consent, limits to confidentiality and to privileged communication when third parties are present in therapy, and understanding how individuals will be protected and their growth nurtured in a group situation. Unlike individual counseling, clients who want to be involved in a group experience need to be screened before being accepted into a group. This screening not only ensures that the client is appropriate for the group but also protects other group members from a potentially dysfunctional group member.

It is evident that client welfare, whether in individual therapy or in group work, rests squarely on the shoulders of the counselor. The counselor must be cognizant of the various aspects of the counseling relationship that can jeopardize the client's welfare and take the steps necessary to alleviate the situation. Robinson Kurpius and Gross (1996) offer several suggestions for safeguarding the welfare of each client:

1. Check to be sure that you are working in harmony with any other mental health professional also seeing your client.
2. Develop clear, written descriptions of what clients may expect with respect to therapeutic regimen, testing and reports, record keeping, billing, scheduling, and emergencies.
3. Share your professional code of ethics with your clients, and prior to beginning therapy, discuss the parameters of a therapeutic relationship.
4. Know your own limitations and do not hesitate to utilize appropriate referral sources.
5. Be sure that the approaches and techniques utilized are appropriate for the client and that you have the necessary expertise for their utilization.
6. Consider all other possibilities before establishing a counseling relationship that could be considered a harmful dual relationship.
7. Evaluate the client's ability to pay and when the payment of the usual fee would create a hardship. Either accept a reduced fee or assist the client in finding needed services at an affordable cost.
8. Objectively evaluate client progress and the therapeutic relationship to determine if it is consistently in the best interests of the client.

We would be remiss if we ended the discussion of client welfare without mentioning the problems that arise from our technological society. In this age of computers and the Internet, client confidentiality is continually at risk because anyone sophisticated in computer programming can tap into insurance records, university records, and so on. Testing by computer has become popular. More and more computer-based interventions are being developed to address issues such as career indecision, lack of assertive behaviors, and irrational beliefs. The question that must be raised, however, is how secure are individual results and personal information? We must also ask whether computer testing and even computer interactive counseling are best for our clients. What about the all-important human element? Again, these questions are not easy to answer. Each of us must struggle with what we are told in the ethical guidelines, our own comfort level with the privacy afforded or not afforded by using computers, and how all of this affects client welfare.

The increasing use of the Internet to provide counseling interventions compounds these questions. Indeed, the "information highway" poses many ethical concerns that were not present just a decade ago (Cottone & Tarvydas, 2007). In 1999, the ACA Governing Council approved guidelines for computer use. Here are a few important points conveyed in their document:

1. Counselors consider the appropriateness of online counseling and explain the potential limitations of such services.
2. Counselors explain the limits of confidentiality particular to online counseling.
3. Counselors explain and notify clients about certain aspects of how confidential information is handled (e.g., who has access to the counselor's computer).
4. Counselors use only "secure" sites for confidential information and may use either secure or insecure sites for general information.
5. "Professional counselors identify foreseeable situations in which confidentiality must be breached in light of the law in *both* the state in which the client is located and the state in which the professional counselor is licensed" (A4).
6. "Professional counselors identify clients, verify identities of clients, and obtain alternative methods of contacting clients in emergency situations" (B3).
7. There are certain circumstances in which a client must waive a right to priviledged communication because of the nature of online services.

Client Rights: Summary

The rights of your clients are many and varied. Perhaps one of the best statements regarding client rights can be found at the National Board for Certified Counselors Web Site. The NBCC (2001b) listed the following client rights and responsibilities:

Your Rights as a Consumer
- Be informed of the qualifications of your counselor: education, experience, professional counseling certification(s), and license(s).
- Receive an explanation of services offered, your time commitments, fee scales, and billing policies prior to receipt of services.

- Be informed of the limitations of the counselor's practice to special areas of expertise (e.g., career development, ethnic groups) or age group (e.g., adolescents, older adults).
- Have all that you say treated confidentially and be informed of any state laws placing limitations on confidentiality in the counseling relationship.
- Ask questions about the counseling techniques and strategies and be informed of your progress.
- Participate in setting goals and evaluating progress toward meeting them.
- Be informed of how to contact the counselor in an emergency situation.
- Request referral for a second opinion at any time.
- Request copies of records and reports to be used by other counseling professionals.
- Receive a copy of the code of ethics to which your counselor adheres.
- Contact the appropriate professional organization if you have doubts or complaints relative to the counselor's conduct.
- Terminate the relationship at any time.

Your Responsibilities as a Client

- Set and keep appointments with your counselor. Let him or her know as soon as possible if you cannot keep an appointment.
- Pay your fees in accordance with the schedule you pre-established with the counselor.
- Help plan your goals.
- Follow through with agreed-upon goals.
- Keep your counselor informed of your progress toward meeting your goals.
- Terminate your counseling relationship before entering into arrangement with another counselor.

Notice that the consumer–client responsibilities require the counselor to have provided the client with informed consent at the beginning of therapy. Also note that the client cannot behave unethically—only counselors can make that mistake.

Summary

Before you know it, you will be graduating and entering the professional world of counselors, fondly known as the "real world." If you are like most mental health professionals, you will quickly find yourself involved in situations in which you will be uncertain of what is ethical and what is not. This is not unusual, and the best advice we can give you is to know the ethical guidelines, seek supervision, and consult with colleagues, professional ethics committees, and your ethics professor.

Situations that typically cause confusion, according to research by Pope et al. (1987), include performing forensic work for a contingency fee; accepting goods (rather than money) as payment; earning a salary that is a percentage of client fees; avoiding certain clients for fear of being sued; counseling a close relative or friend of a current client; sending holiday greeting cards to your clients; giving personal advice on a radio or television program; engaging in a sexual fantasy about a client; limiting treatment notes to name, date, and fee; inviting clients to an office open house; and allowing a client to run up a large, unpaid bill. From the information provided in this chapter, you should now have some idea about the ethical approach to each of these. But often the ethical answer is not crystal clear, and surrounding circumstances need to be considered.

Robinson and Gross (1989) surveyed 500 members of the American Mental Health Counselor's Association and found that those who had not had a course in ethics had a difficult time recommending ethical behaviors to a series of case vignettes. As a result, Robinson and Gross strongly recommended required graduate-level education that focuses on professional ethics. Knowing the codes is not enough. Students need experience applying the ethical guidelines to case scenarios and discussing the moral reasoning behind their decision making.

More and more clients are suing their counselors and psychologists for malpractice. Insurance rates for mental health professionals are soaring, and insurance companies and HMOs often want to settle out of court rather than endure the costs of fighting to prove your innocence. This may leave you in a vulnerable position. Your best defense is to behave as ethically as possible while doing everything in your power to promote the best interests of your client.

Most of you have entered this profession to help others while earning a living for yourself. We believe counseling is a noble profession, especially if you give your best to each of your clients by being aware of when you are burned out, stressed, or just plain tired and by limiting your contact with clients when your personal problems could interfere with the quality of your help. If you keep the ethical codes in mind at all times; strive to be as mentally, emotionally, spiritually, and physically healthy as possible; obtain a thorough graduate education that emphasizes both knowledge and practice; and seek advanced training and supervision when you are in the real world, then you should be a benefit to your clients and to your profession. With those last tidbits of advice, we welcome you to your journey and evolution as a counselor.

USEFUL WEB SITES

American Association for Marriage and Family Therapist
Ethical and legal information page
http://www.aamft.org/resources/LRMPlan/index_nm.asp

American Counseling Association
ACA Code of Ethics
http://www.counseling.org/Resources/CodeOfEthics/TP/Home/CT2.aspx

American Psychological Association
Ethics page
http://www.apa.org/ethics/

American School Counselor Association
Ethics page
http://www.schoolcounselor.org/content.asp?pl=325&sl=136&contentid=136

Association of Specialist in Group Work
Best practices page
http://www.asgw.org/PDF/Best_Practices.pdf

National Association of Social Workers
Ethics page
https://www.socialworkers.org/pubs/code/default.asp

National Board for Certified Counselors
Client rights
http://www.nbcc.org/clientrights

Ethics page
http://www.nbcc.org/ethics2

National Center on Elder Abuse
State laws page
http://www.elderabusecenter.org/default.cfm?p=statelaws.cfm

U.S. DHHS ACF Child Welfare Information Gateway
http://www.childwelfare.gov/

U.S. DHHS Office of Civil Rights
Information on HIPAA
http://www.hhs.gov/ocr/hipaa/

REFERENCES

American Counseling Association. (1999). *Approved by the ACA governing council, October 1999.* Retrieved September 1, 2003, from http://www.counseling.org/site/PageServer?pagename=resources_internet

American Counseling Association. (2002). *Cross cultural competencies and objectives.* Alexandria, VA: Author. Retrieved September 1, 2003, from http://www.counseling.org/site/PageServer?pagename=resources_competencies

American Counseling Association. (2005). *Code of ethics and standards of practice.* Alexandria, VA: Author.

American Heritage College Dictionary, 4th ed. (2002). Boston: Houghton Mifflin.

American Psychological Association. (1991). APA Council of Representatives adopts new AIDS policies. *Psychology and AIDS Exchange,* 7, 1.

American Psychological Association. (2002). *Ethical principles of psychologists and code of conduct.* Washington, DC: Author.

Arizona Revised Statute 46–451.

Association of State and Provincial Licensing Psychology Boards. (2001). *Ethics, law, and avoiding liability in the practice of psychology.* Montgomery, AL: Author.

Atkinson, D. R. (2004). *Counseling American Minorities* (6th ed.). New York: McGraw Hill.

Cooke v. Berlin, Ariz., 735 P.2d 830 (App. 1987).

Corey, G., Corey, M. S., & Callanan, P. (2007). *Issues and ethics in the helping professions* (7th ed.). Belmont, CA: Brooks/Cole.

Cottone, R. R., & Tarvydas, V. M. (2007). *Ethical and professional issues in counseling* (3rd ed.). Columbus, OH: Pearson Merrill/Prentice Hall.

Everstine, L., Everstine, D. S., Geymann, G. M., True, R. H., Frey, D. H., Johnson, H. G., et al. (1980). Privacy and confidentiality in psychotherapy. *American Psychologist,* 35, 828–840.

Goldfarb v. Virginia State Bar (1975), 421 U.S. 773.

Hammer, M. (1972). To students interested in becoming psychotherapists. In M. Hammer (Ed.), *The theory and practice of psychotherapy with specific disorders* (pp. 1–23). Springfield, IL: Charles C. Thomas.

Herlihy, B., & Corey, G. (1992). *Dual relationships in counseling.* Alexandria, VA: American Association for Counseling and Development.

Hermann, M., & Robinson Kurpius, S. E. (2006, December). New guidelines on dual relationships: A review of revisions to the ACA Code of Ethics. *Counseling Today,* 8–9.

Jaffee v. Redmond, 95–266 (U.S.C. June 13, 1996).

Koocher, G. P., & Keith-Spiegel, P. (1998). *Ethics in psychology: Professional standards and cases* (2nd ed.). New York: McGraw-Hill.

Lawrence, G., & Robinson Kurpius, S. E. (2000). Legal and ethical issues involved when counseling minors in a non-school setting. *Journal of Counseling and Development, 78,* 130–136.

Levenson, M. (1989). *Right to accept or refuse treatment: Implications for the mental health profession.* Unpublished manuscript. Arizona State University.

Loewy, M. I. (1998). Suggestions for working with fat children in the schools. *Professional School Counseling, 1,* 18–22.

Lustig, D. C., Strauser, D. R., Rice, N. D., & Rucker, T. F. (2002). The relationship between working alliance and rehabilitation outcomes. *Rehabilitation Counseling Bulletin, 46,* 25.

MacKinnon, B. (1998). *Ethics: Theory and contemporary issues* (2nd ed.). Belmont, CA: Wadsworth.

Meara, N. M., Schmidt, L. D., & Day, J. D. (1996). Principles and virtues: A foundation for ethical decision making, policies and character. *Counseling Psychologist, 24,* 4–77.

National Board for Certified Counselors (2001a). *National counselor exam.* Alexandria, VA: Author. Retrieved on September 1, 2003, from http://www.nbcc.org/exams/nce.htm

National Board for Certified Counselors. (2001b). *What can I expect from a counselor.* Alexandria, VA: Author. Retrieved September 1, 2003, from http://www.nbcc.org/clientrights

Newman, J. L., & Robinson, S. E. (1991). In the best interests of the consultee: Ethical issues in consultation. *Consulting Psychology Journal, 43,* 23–29.

Pope, K. S., Tabachnick, B. G., & Keith-Spiegel, P. (1987). Ethics of practice: The beliefs and behaviors of psychologists as therapists. *American Psychologist, 42,* 993–1006.

Public Education Work Group of the Task Force on Sexual Exploitation. (1988). *It's never ok!* Advocate Web. Retrieved September 1, 2003, from http://www.advocateweb.org/hope/itsneverok/

Remley, T. P., & Herlihy, B. (2007). *Ethical, legal, and professional issues in counseling* (2nd ed.). Saddle River, NJ: Pearson Merrill/Prentice Hall.

Rennie v. Klein, 476 F.Supp. 1294 (D. N. J., 1979, modified, Nos. 79-2576 and 70-2577 3rd Cir., July 9, 1981).

Robinson, S. E. (1988). Counselor competency and malpractice suits: Opposite sides of the same coin. *Counseling and Human Development, 20,* 1–8.

Robinson, S. E., & Gross, D. R. (1989). Applied ethics and the mental health counselor. *Journal of Mental Health Counseling, 11,* 289–299.

Robinson Kurpius, S. E. (1997). Current ethical issues in the practice of psychotherapy. In *The Hatherleigh Guide to Ethics in Therapy* (pp. 1–16). New York: Hatherleigh Press.

Robinson Kurpius, S. E., & Gross, D. R. (1996). Professional ethics and the mental health counselor. In W. J. Weikel & A. J. Palmo (Eds.), *Foundations of mental health counseling* (pp. 353–377). Springfield, IL: Charles C. Thomas.

Rogers v. Orkin, 634 F. 2nd 650 (1st Cir., 1980).

Sattler, H. A. (1990). Confidentiality. In B. Herlihy & L. Golden (Eds.), *ACA ethical standards casebook* (4th ed) Alexandria, VA: American Association for Counseling and Development.

Schwitzgebel, R. L., & Schwitzgebel, R. K. (1980). *Law and psychological practice.* New York: John Wiley & Sons.

Sim, J. (1997). *Ethical decision making in therapy practice.* Oxford: Butterworth, Heineman.

Semans, M., & Stone Fish, L. (2000). Disecting life with a Jewish scapel: A qualitative exploration or Jewish families. *Family Process, 39*(1), 121–139.

Snider, P. D. (1987). Client records: Inexpensive liability protection for mental health counselors. *Journal of Mental Health Counseling, 9,* 134–141.

Sue, D. W., & Sue, D. (2003). *Counseling the culturally diverse* (4th ed.). New York: John Wiley & Sons.

Tarasoff v. Board of Regents of the University of California, 118 Cal. Rptr. 14.551 P2d. 334 (1974).

Tarasoff v. Board of Regents of the University of California, 113 Cal. Rptr. 14.551 P.2d 334 (1976).

Thoreson, R. W., Shaughnessy, P., Heppner, P. P., & Cook, S. (1993). Sexual contact during and after the professional relationship: Attitudes and practices of male counselors. *Journal of Counseling and Development, 71,* 429–434.

U.S. Department of Health and Human Services. (2003). *OCR privacy brief: Summary of the HIPAA privacy rule.* Retrieved September 1, 2003, from http://www.hhs.gov/ocr/privacysummary.pdf

Welfel, E. R., & Kitchener, K. S. (1995). Introduction to the special section: Ethics education—An agenda for the 90's. In D. N. Bersoff (Ed.), *Ethical conflicts in psychology.* Washington, DC: American Psychological Association.

Wyatt v. Stickney, 325 F.Supp. 781 (1971).

5

Research and Writing in Counseling

TERESA M. CHRISTENSEN, PhD
Old Dominion University

What is research? How does research apply to counseling? How do I, as a beginning counseling student, incorporate research into what I am learning about counseling and my writing? What steps do I take to effectively search databases, construct literature reviews, and conduct research? At first glance, answers to these questions may seem rather simplistic and obvious; however, such issues often lead to high levels of anxiety, apprehension, and hours of wasted time for students who initially struggle with research and writing in their graduate studies (Galvan, 1999; Rechtien & Dizinno, 1997; Szuchman, 2002).

Numerous authors and presenters have addressed how to conduct research in counseling (e.g., Creswell, 1994; Herman, 1997; Merchant, 1997; Stockton & Toth, 1997). Szuchman (2002) supplied a new method for counseling students and professionals to write research papers according to the APA *Publication Manual*. Szuchman's book provides hands-on skills and instructions on constructing papers that report research, and it incorporates concepts from recent literature that pertain to selecting research topics, accessing resources, reviewing literature, critiquing research, and writing a literature review (e.g., Coelho & La Forge, 1996; Galvan, 1999; Nicol & Pexman, 1999; Nisenoff & Espina, 1999). While Szuchman (2002) was the first to devote an entire text to this topic, Heppner, Wampold, and Kivlighan (2008) were the first to publish a textbook specific to research design in counseling. They directly addressed issues specific to different methodological approaches and the process of planning and initiating a literature review and research project that pertains specifically to the field of counseling.

Other literature related to this topic suggests that many master's and some doctoral students may be hesitant and defensive and lack knowledge and confidence in their ability to understand, apply, and integrate research (Nicol & Pexman, 1999; Rechtien & Dizinno, 1997; Szuchman, 2002). The reasons for their uncertainty are multidimensional and include issues such as counseling students' confusion about professional journals and APA guidelines. Some students have difficulty distinguishing between original empirical research and anecdotal reports, theoretical articles, literature reviews, and descriptions of programs, practice strategies, or standards (Galvan, 1999). In particular, Galvan (1999) attributed students' apprehension to their lack of previous training in how to (a) search databases for reports of original research and related theoretical literature, (b) analyze these particular types of literature, and (c) synthesize them into cohesive essays. Furthermore, novice students may find it difficult to conceptualize how research relates to the theory and practice of counseling. Szuchman (2002) noted that most advanced undergraduate and beginning graduate students need training specific to writing research papers in the APA style.

This chapter attempts to incorporate various perspectives and ideas about (a) the integration of research, practice, and theory; (b) the definition of research; (c) literature reviews and conducting research; (d) legal and ethical considerations in research; and (e) program evaluations.

Integration of Research, Practice, and Theory

Many professionals in counselor education believe that research is the backbone of counseling practice and theory. Some authors go so far as to suggest that practice, research, writing, and publishing are the obligations of the professional counselor (Coelho & La Forge, 1996; Szuchman, 2002). Advocates of research contend that it defines the profession of counseling, builds on old and generates new thinking and theory, sheds light on practice strategies that are effective and ineffective, and creates a forum for communication between various professionals in the field (Coelho & La Forge, 1996; Herman, 1997; Loesch & Nicholas, 1996; Stockton & Toth, 1997). Some experts have insisted that counselors provide a service by doing research (Herman, 1997). Essentially, many believe that counseling is informed and directed by research.

Definition of Research

This chapter discusses original research in academic journals and other professional resources. Research reports are original (primary sources) when they highlight initial results and include details about methodology, findings, implications, limitations, and conclusions (Galvan, 1999), whereas secondary sources of research are generated by someone other than the researcher and typically are general descriptions of findings with few details about methodology. Some of the research on the Internet and summaries included in textbooks, magazines, and newspapers and on television and radio are secondary sources of research. To avoid misinterpretation or distortion of research methodology and findings, it is wise to rely predominately on primary research.

Quantitative Versus Qualitative

In terms of methodological procedures, research can be defined as quantitative or qualitative. Some researchers use a combination of the two, but for the purpose of this chapter, each methodology is explained separately. The usefulness of quantitative and qualitative methodology in counseling has been the topic of many controversial discussions and open debates. Recently, many experts have contended that both meth-odologies are important because the profession of counseling is in a state of transition in which the eclectic and subjective nature of humanity is appreciated (Herman, 1997). Accordingly, counseling students need to be familiar with the strengths and limitations of both types of research and must be able to accept high-quality research as informa-tive and important, regardless of its methodological underpinnings. Continuing dia-logue regarding quantitative versus qualitative research is encouraged and essential. Therefore, these two methodological approaches will be introduced and explored in terms of how they relate to each other, their unique attributes, and aspects related to the quality and credibility of each approach.

Quantitative Research

Quantitative research involves a systematic, logical, reductive, and empirically focused manner of interpreting information (Creswell, 1994). Researchers who use quantita-tive methodology utilize their worldview to develop hypotheses and test relationships of clearly defined variables that can be measured (Morse & Field, 1995). The goal is to gather information, reduce it through valid and reliable instrumentation, and produce numerical results in the form of statistics including averages, percentages, and fre-quency of occurrence. The goal of many statistical operations is to test the hypotheses and determine whether there is a relationship between variables (Morse & Field, 1995). In general, quantitative researchers seek a statistical way to determine whether a correlation exists between two or more variables (Lincoln & Guba, 1985).

To infer causal relationships, quantitative researchers believe that it is possible to extrapolate their personal values from the research process (Morse & Field, 1995). These researchers attempt to isolate specific factors, focus their investigations on pre-determined variables, and control other variables that may interfere with the research process or alter researchers' hypotheses. In working with human beings and focusing on social sciences, it can be difficult to control for all factors of the human experience and isolate variables. However, many researchers and professional journals in the field of counseling prefer research based on quantitative inquiry (Merchant, 1997; Sexton, 1996).

Coincidentally, much of the training in research for undergraduate students in psychology and sociology and many graduate students in counseling relies primarily on the positivistic, linear, and reductionistic methods of quantitative research (Hoshmund, 1989; Merchant 1997). Despite some researchers' contention that reductionistic science or quantitative research cannot capture the richness and diversity of human experience, support for quantitative research persists (Merchant, 1997). A review of articles from 1989 to 1994 in the *Journal of Marriage and Family* showed that 517 of the 527 publica-tions (98.1%) were entirely or primarily quantitative (Ambert, Adler, Adler, & Detzner, 1995). Likewise, Sexton (1996) found that of 344 current outcome studies published in 116 professional journals from 1988 to 1994, more than 95% were quantitative. Merchant (1997) suggested that professionals in psychology and counseling may be relying primarily on quantitative research methods to seek validation from those who practice research in the hard sciences.

Qualitative Research

Despite the efforts of Freud, Piaget, and other theorists in the early 1900s who used qualitative methods to construct developmental theories, research in counseling has generally neglected naturalistic methodology (Merchant, 1997). Yet the last 20 years have seen several attempts to value qualitative research and incorporate it into the field of counseling (Ambert et al., 1995; Creswell, 1994; Lincoln & Guba, 1985; Merchant, 1997; Morse & Field, 1995; Newsome, Hays, & Christensen, 2008; Polkinghorne, 1991; Sexton & Griffin, 1997; Strauss & Corbin, 1998). Flick (1998) stated, "Qualitative research is establishing itself in the social sciences and in psychology" (p. 1). Merchant (1997) devoted an entire monograph to the use of qualitative research in counseling and specifically highlighted the "relevance/fit of qualitative research" to many counselors' theoretical beliefs about human beings, ways of being with clients, and values about the process of counseling (p. 12). Shank (2002) described qualitative research as a "personal skills approach" (p. 1), and Newsome et al., 2008 (p. 87), report: "Recent changes in academic standards (i.e., Council for Accreditation of Counseling and Related Educational Programs [CACREP], 2008) set forth a movement for counseling programs to promote knowledge about various research methodologies including qualitative approaches."

Qualitative research includes various nonnumerical methods of investigating human experience and behavior (Denzin & Lincoln, 1994; Shank, 2002). Terminologies such as naturalistic inquiry, ethnography, fieldwork, observation, and systematic inquiry into meaning often accompany qualitative research (Polkinghorne, 1991; Shank, 2002). Philosophically speaking, qualitative researchers believe that knowledge is contextual and that the researcher and reader must understand the overall process and see meaning in context (Lincoln & Guba, 1985; Rubin & Rubin, 1995; Sexton, 1996; Shank, 2002). Qualitative research is process oriented; looks to explore why and how people behave, think, and make meaning as they do; and is conducted through an intense and/or prolonged contact with a life situation (Ambert et al., 1995; Merchant, 1997; Miles & Huberman, 1994; Shank, 2002). Such situations are commonly based on reflections of the everyday life of individuals, groups, societies, and organizations.

Researchers attempt to capture data based on the perceptions of those being investigated. This is accomplished through a process of deep attentiveness, empathic understanding, and suspending or "bracketing" preconceptions about the topics under exploration (Miles & Huberman, 1994, p. 6). Qualitative data analysis is done primarily with words and entails a process through which information is explicated from narratives describing a particular setting, way of life, action, process, or manner of accounting for and managing one's life (Miles & Huberman, 1994; Shank, 2002). Qualitative research is inductive in that researchers build on existing knowledge, discover and explore areas about which little is known, and construct concepts and theories as they emerge from the data (Lincoln & Guba, 1985; Maxwell, 1992; Shank, 2002; Strauss & Corbin, 1998).

In general, the objectives of qualitative research are to (a) develop theory that is based on rich description resulting from documentation, description, and identification of patterns and relationships between concepts; (b) identify the essence of experience; (c) describe the process; (d) understand meaning, context, and process;

(e) develop causal explanations; (f) explore and identify phenomena; (g) create theoretical explanations of reality; and (h) describe theory and practice (Denzin & Lincoln, 1994; Lincoln & Guba, 1985; Maxwell, 1992; Miles & Huberman, 1994; Morse & Field, 1995; Shank, 2002). The overall purpose of qualitative research is to produce vivid, dense, full, and integrated descriptions in the natural language of an experience or situation under investigation (Polkinghorne, 1994). Such objectives are accomplished through exploring the phenomena under investigation in its natural setting. This includes using words, dialogue, narratives, journals, and personal reflections as data. Accordingly, the researcher is viewed as the primary instrument for data collection (Ambert et al., 1995; Lincoln & Guba 1985; Maxwell, 1992; Shank, 2002; Strauss & Corbin, 1998). Qualitative research puts social science researchers in a position to design unique ways to explore and analyze concrete cases through the use of people's expressions and activities in their daily living (Flick, 1998; Shank, 2002).

Based on the assumption that significant contributions to the literature can be made by using any methodology that answers the research question, provided the methods are applied correctly, counseling courses must provide information about both forms of research. Furthermore, research and writing in counseling course work should be designed to enhance students' understanding of human experience, thus producing exposure to diverse methodological procedures. Counseling students involved in reviewing, reading, and designing research projects are encouraged to seek meaningful answers to their questions and to review publications that inform them about human nature through the use of both quantitative and qualitative research (Herman, 1997; Merchant, 1997; Stockton & Toth, 1997; Szuchman, 2002).

Literature Reviews and Conducting Research

Whether for a research paper, program evaluation, or thesis, students' thoughts about reviewing literature, planning and carrying out a research project, and producing a coherent essay can produce intense anxiety (Galvan, 1999; Szuchman, 2002). Anxiety can be diminished and the task of conducting research tackled through a thorough review of existing literature and a careful plan for the project. Students' perceptions may change if they shift from conceptualizing research as a complicated and overwhelming project, to a process with various phases and tasks. As students expose themselves to literature, research becomes more manageable and provokes less anxiety. Based on these assumptions, this chapter provides a five-phased process for conducting a literature review and generating a plan for doing research: (a) selecting a topic and searching for literature, (b) organizing literature, (c) analyzing literature, (d) structuring a written review of literature and developing a comprehensive essay, and (e) designing a plan for conducting research.

Many phases include steps that build from others and procedures that transfer to other parts of the writing and research processes. When doing projects, students are encouraged to carefully generate a time line with a list of important due dates, specific guidelines, and any regulations that may affect their progress. These activities are designed to assist students in preparing themselves and in gaining a clear purpose.

For example, if students are concerned with a thesis or dissertation, they must become aware of proposal and defense dates, university and departmental guidelines, and potential boundaries or resource issues that may interfere with their projects.

Specific guidelines to be aware of before beginning a project include but are not limited to the instructions of the given assignment, as provided by the professor, for example, page limitations, adherence to specific guidelines, and the use of specific journals. Other guidelines when conducting research or writing a paper may pertain to local, state, federal government, and university regulations regarding the use of human subjects in research. Other guidelines can be located through specific counseling departments, university research offices, and the appropriate publication manuals, such as the fifth edition of the *Publication Manual* of the American Psychological Association (2001), which is utilized by most counseling-related departments. Committee members, faculty advisors, and other instructors can also provide information about resources and issues related to writing and conducting research.

Phase One: Selecting a Topic and Searching for Literature

Obviously, the first step in conducting a search is to determine a specific topic. For term papers and sometimes for master's theses, a topic is predetermined or limited by an instructor. In this case, students should clarify requirements regarding data searches and use of specific journals. For example, some instructors provide a list of detailed topics to choose from and specify the use of professional journals related to the field of counseling.

If the topic is not predetermined by course instructors, selection can be difficult for counseling students. A good topic can be kept narrow, is well defined, and sparks personal interest. Ideas can be generated from classroom lectures, discussions, textbooks, professional association newsletters and Web sites, or current issues in the field. Begin a search for literature immediately in order to clarify or report potential problems. Personal interest is important for those beginning a thesis or dissertation because they will spend a great deal of time and energy on this topic and to complete the project, must be able to consistently maintain focus, desire, and interest.

Choosing a topic, narrowing and broadening that topic, and searching for literature often coincide. Constructing a literature review begins with a thorough yet manageable search of current publications in professionally prepared journals and database systems. It is wise to utilize resources related to other fields such as psychology, sociology, and education. Students are also encouraged to use information obtained from professional conferences, presentations, and organizational monographs.

Narrowing the Topic

A successful search for literature begins with a well-defined topic, yet often a topic cannot be defined until foundational information is known. Students are encouraged to start with an idea or concept that they are interested in learning more about.

As students conduct searches of various databases related to their topics, they should attempt to narrowly define and specify exactly what they are exploring. Ways to limit the topic and search include using only those articles that are presented in professional journals, within a specified time frame (the last 7 to 10 years), related to a specific course, and within a particular theory or area of practice. Another way to limit the topic is to conduct a preliminary search for literature related to a topic and then attempt to generate the first draft of a topic statement (Galvan, 1999; Szuchman, 2002). A topic statement is a well-thought-out sentence that describes what a student is going to write about and/or research.

Case Example

A student who is interested in counseling children can limit this topic by (a) specifying counseling with children who have been abused, (b) using only journal articles published in the last 5 to 7 years, (c) focusing on issues related to small-group counseling with children who have been abused, and (d) focusing on articles that address cognitive-behavioral group counseling with children who have been abused. A topic statement could be "Implications of cognitive-behavioral group counseling with children who have been abused."

As previously noted, defining a topic and conducting database searches work simultaneously. Based on information collected through searches of existing data, students may find themes that become interesting to them. They may think of questions for which they want answers. These are great reasons to narrow searches on a topic that supplies an adequate avenue for literature reviews.

Searching Counseling-Related Databases

Reviewing literature in counseling can best be accomplished by searching varying databases and utilizing multiple methods to gather relevant information. Those interested in learning about a specific topic can gain a diversified and complete cluster of information by reviewing professional journals sponsored by or affiliated with the American Counseling Association (ACA) and the American Psychological Association (APA), searching the Internet, connecting to specific Web sites, accessing computerized database programs in counseling and related fields, and attending professional conferences or seminars. Specific suggestions regarding searching databases follow.

The word *database* refers to a constellation of information and resources arranged according to specialized topics and ease of retrieval. Each library has a unique organizational system that utilizes a multitude of online electronic database search options. Students must familiarize themselves with searching features and computer resources in their libraries. Many libraries provide workshops, handouts, and attendants to inform students about effective ways to conduct electronic searches, yet many students can gain familiarity with electronic search devices and library resources on their own. With the abundance of database options, some students may be unclear about how to access those that are specific to counseling. The following is a list of databases that are appropriate for counseling-related projects (Galvan, 1999; Szuchman, 2002).

Basic Biosis—information related to life science and human behavior

CINAHL—content focused on nursing, allied health, biomedical, and consumer health

Dissertation Abstracts—primary research from doctoral dissertations on a range of academic subjects

ERIC—information related to education, counseling, and related fields

Medline—topics related to public health, medicine, and psychiatry

NCJRS—information regarding corrections, drugs, crime, juvenile justice, and victims

PAIS International—content specific to social, economic, political, and public policy issues

PsycINFO—numerous articles related to psychology, counseling, and psychiatry

PsycLit—a subset of PsycINFO including only books and journals related to mental helath

SERLINE—a subset of Medline with articles related to public health, medicine, and nutrition

Social Sciences Abstracts—articles related to sociology, psychology, and anthropology

Sociological Abstracts—information related to sociology, counseling, and psychology

Social Work Abstracts—articles focused on sociology, social work, counseling, and social sciences

Sport Discus—information on sports medicine, physical education, sports psychology, and nutrition

Online databases highlight abstracts from journal articles, doctoral dissertations, professional presentations and papers, books, newspapers, and government documents. Similar information can also be obtained through various Web sites.

The Internet

With recent advances in our technological capabilities, volumes of information can be accessed via the Internet. Specific Web sites and other online links offer a quick and cost-efficient means for gathering a multitude of information. Although access to great quantities of information is useful, such resources have shortcomings. Summaries and excerpts from journal articles or professional papers on Web pages and listservs can be incomplete and even inaccurate. It is better to rely on original work created by primary authors and researchers, rather than on secondary sources such as a Web sites, which often provide a mere synopsis of important information from a journal article. Students cannot be cautioned enough to be mindful of the validity, content, and implications suggested by sources derived from the Internet. As adapted from Nisenoff and Espina (1999), Web sites and listservs focused on issues related to counseling and mental health are listed at the end of the chapter.

Professional Journals

In hopes of exposing students to professional publications in counseling, some instructors in counselor education require students to utilize journals supported by or affiliated with the ACA. They may include a list of specific journals to be used or merely make reference to ACA-affiliated journals. These journals are numerous and cover a wide range of counseling issues. The *Journal of Counseling and Development* (*JCD*) is the official publication for the American Counseling Association. This journal is printed quarterly (winter, spring, summer, and fall) and illuminates various areas directly related to research, theory, and practice in counseling.

Advances in technology have led to the introduction of professional journals that are completely online. For example, Montana State University founded the *Journal of School Counseling* (http://www.jsc.montana.edu/) in 2005. This online journal was developed as a "forum for discussion and exchange of ideas and practices that will best serve the children in our nation's schools."

Other journals serve as official publications for one of the 19 specialized divisions within the ACA. Specialized divisions focus on a particular issue, population, or phenomenon related to counseling and therefore provide journals related to that specialized topic. Based on trends in the field of counseling and social sciences, divisions of the ACA sometimes split into independent associations, expand their focus, merge with other divisions, or cease to exist. Because some of the ACA journals are selectively available and frequently change names, a comprehensive list of all journals affiliated with the ACA can be quite difficult to provide. Consequently, the goal of this section is to introduce some of the most commonly utilized journals affiliated with the ACA and other organizations related to counseling.

1. *Adultspan*—Published twice a year (spring and fall), this official publication of the Association for Adult Development and Aging (AADA) highlights articles on current research, theory, and practice in the area of adult development, aging, and implications for counseling.
2. *Counseling and Values* (*CVJ*)—Published three times a year in January, April, and October, this official publication of the Association for Spiritual, Ethical, and Religious Values in Counseling (ASERVIC) includes articles about the relationship among psychology, philosophy, religion, social values, and counseling.
3. *Counselor Education and Supervision* (*CES*)—The official publication of the Association for Counselor Education and Supervision (ACES) is published quarterly in September, December, March, and June and includes articles on research, theory development, and program applications in the area of counselor education and supervision.
4. *Measurement and Evaluation in Counseling and Development* (*MECD*)—Published quarterly in January, April, July, and October, the official journal of the Association for Assessment in Counseling and Education (AACE) includes articles about measurement specialists, counselors, and other personnel in schools, public and private agencies, businesses, industries, and government.

5. *Journal of College Counseling* (*JCC*)—Published twice a year in spring and fall, the official journal of the American College Counseling Association (ACCA) addresses issues specific to college counselors.

6. *Journal of Counseling and Development* (*JCD*)—Published quarterly (winter, spring, summer, and fall), the official journal of the American Counseling Association (ACA) is intended to publish archival material as well as research related to counseling.

7. *Journal of Employment Counseling* (*JEC*)—This journal, published four times a year in March, June, September, and December, is the official publication of the National Employment Counseling Association (NECA). Articles highlight theory, research, and practice in employment counseling and vocational issues.

8. *Journal of Humanistic Counseling Education and Development* (*HEJ*)—The official journal of the Counseling Association for Humanistic Education and Development (C-AHEAD) is published twice a year in spring and fall and includes articles for educators and counselors interested in humanistic education and practices.

9. *Journal of Mental Health Counseling* (*JMHC*)—Published four times a year in January, April, July, and October, the official publication of the American Mental Health Counselors Association (AMHCA) includes articles on issues related to mental health counseling with various populations.

10. *Journal of Multicultural Counseling and Development* (*JMCD*)—Published quarterly in January, April, July, and October, the official publication of the Association for Multicultural Counseling and Development (AMCD) includes articles on multicultural and ethnic minority interests in counseling.

11. *Journal of Professional School Counseling* (*JPSC*)—Published five times a year in October, December, February, April, and June, the official publication of the American School Counselor Association (ASCA) addresses counseling in elementary and secondary schools.

12. *Journal for Specialists in Group Work* (*JSGW*)—Published quarterly in March, June, September, and December, the official publication of the Association for Specialists in Group Work (ASGW) includes articles on research, practice, and theory related to group work.

13. *Rehabilitative Counseling Bulletin* (*RCB*)—Published four times a year in September, December, March, and June, the official publication of the American Rehabilitation Counseling Association (ARCA) includes articles related to rehabilitative counseling.

14. *The Career Development Quarterly* (*CDQ*)—Published quarterly in March, June, September, and December, the official publication of the National Career Development Association (NCDA) covers career development and occupational resources.

15. *The Family Journal: Counseling & Therapy for Couples and Families* (*TFJ*)—Published four times a year in January, April, July, and October, the official publication of the International Association of Marriage and Family Counselors (IAMFC) has includes articles on couples and family counseling.

16. *The Journal of Addictions and Offender Counseling* (*JAOC*)—Published twice a year in October and April, the official publication of the International Association of Addictions and Offender Counselors (IAAOC) includes articles on the attitudes and behaviors of addictions and offender counselors, as well as theoretical and philosophical rationales for specific programs in these areas.

In addition to the Internet, books, journals, professional papers, and newspapers, students may also attain important information from monographs, video and audio productions, personal interviews, and professional presentations at conferences. Students should start with the most recent publication and work backwards. When they find an article that is relevant to their topic, they are encouraged to focus on the article's reference list or bibliography, where many ideas and additional literature can be discovered. Students are also encouraged to search for theoretical articles regarding their topic because these manuscripts often highlight key elements. Students should keep an eye out for existing reviews conducted on a relevant topic because previously published review articles are an excellent source for identifying additional information and expanding the scope of literature in a field of study. Finally, it is important for students to identify the most prominent studies on their topics.

After following numerous leads and spending hours at the library, quarters at the copy machine, and frustrating nights in periodicals at the library, students are now prepared to analyze and review the literature they have gathered.

Phase Two: Organizing Literature

Once students have secured literature regarding a chosen topic, they are faced with the task of organizing various pieces of information into one comprehensive essay. This can seem overwhelming and impossible to beginning counseling students. In many ways, students have already begun to unconsciously familiarize themselves with current topics during their perusal of titles, abstracts, and journals. The next step involves a more detailed review by reading the first few paragraphs of each article in order to gain an overview of the research designs and writing styles of various authors. Students should note different researchers' perspectives and approaches to inquiry, including their purposes for conducting the research and then reasons for reporting their findings.

To become even more oriented to the literature, students should explore the hypothesis section of the articles and focus on researcher hypothesis, research questions, and purpose. In the event that the article is not specifically related to research, readers are advised to scan the article for the conceptual framework or the author's rationale for writing it. Then students should continue to scan the remainder of the article and note salient information often introduced by headings, subheadings, or visual displays.

To group information into categories, cluster all articles that appear to correspond with common themes emerging from the information collected into separate stacks. A common method is to organize articles based on topics, subtopics, and then chronological order (Galvan, 1999; Szuchman, 2002). Once students have loosely organized the articles, it is time to prepare for a thorough reading and analysis of the information.

Now students should revisit their organizational schema and begin to organize in greater detail. By reading the entire article, they can summarize key points and become familiar with what the article is attempting to tell its readers. It might be helpful for students to summarize key points in a paragraph or two. Students are encouraged to develop a personalized format for recording notes and build a conceptual map that highlights common themes throughout all of the articles. By being consistent and dogmatic about a personal system of review, students can prevent disorganized or repetitive procedures. This practice will pay off later in writing the literature review (Galvan, 1999; Szuchman, 2002).

When organizing, students ought to focus on the authors' explicit definitions and terms. Questions about whether these definitions and terms match others' perceptions are important. Students are encouraged to note differences and similarities of opinion among various authors.

Next, it is time to explore methodological strengths and weaknesses in these terms: (a) Did the author provide enough information and clarify his or her purpose for conducting the study? (b) Why did the researcher utilize quantitative or qualitative methodology? (c) How does the author use his or her findings to support or reject previous findings and perspectives? (d) Does the research provide new insight regarding the topic? "Students must make sure that they understand the difference between the author's empirical evidence and his or her interpretations or assertions" (Galvan, 1999, p. 34). To avoid mistaking authors' assertions for actual findings, students should be aware of and avoid statements that are not substantiated by the research they have reviewed unless they are clearly labeled as assertions.

Students should focus on major trends, themes, or patterns in the results of the literature they review. They should identify and explore gaps and highlight such discoveries in their writeups, particularly in a literature review for a thesis or dissertation. Due to human nature and the obstacles for researchers in the field of counseling, gaps in research can be catalysts to new and innovative approaches to practice, research, and theory. If there is a lack of relationship among studies on the same topic, discuss reasons for divergent thoughts. For example, two articles may focus on the same topic but from different theoretical frameworks. Explanations and assertions as to why such differences exist are important.

Other issues to address in literature reviews include ways that specific manuscripts inform the reader about their topic. Students who experience a complete lack of research directly related to their topic may need to explore other avenues of research or literature. For example, a student who was going to conduct a literature review of group supervision with child counselors but found nothing on that topic could explore publications on group supervision, training child counselors, individual supervision of child counselors, and so on. If an article does not explicitly connect to the topic at hand, a writer must provide a clear rationale for its inclusion. Once information is read and organized, it is time to reevaluate references and ensure that a complete collection of timely, significant, and viable data exists with which to construct a well-thought-out review. As Galvan (1999) and Szuchman (2002) contend, a literature review should represent the latest work done in the subject area, present a historical overview of the topic, and communicate reasons for including articles that are not directly related to the topic. Coelho and La Forge (1996) add: "One should read extensively inside and outside the profession to ensure that the proposed contribution to the literature is a genuine one rather than merely repeating something that has already been written about" (p. 18).

At this point in the writing process, students should generate a preliminary list of references and citations. Oftentimes, throughout the writing process, students can get caught up in other organizational aspects and forget to keep track of references and appropriate citations. This lapse can lead to frustration near the end of the writing process as students find themselves in a desperate search for a specific article or citation that is missing from the volumes of information collected.

Phase Three: Analyzing Literature

During their organization of literature, students are encouraged to briefly explore the methodological section of the manuscripts collected, including an analysis of the methodology in terms of data collection and analysis procedures. Methodological approaches in counseling can be qualitative, quantitative, or a combination. The following discussion examines pertinent issues from each.

Quantitative Research

By reducing information to averages, percentages, and correlation coefficients, quantitative researchers utilize statistics and numbers to represent relationships. Readers can easily identify quantitative investigations from the title of the article or from the statistics and numbers used to present findings in the results section. Quantitative research has dominated social sciences for most of the 20th century; therefore, most counseling literature shows quantitative rather than qualitative results (Galvan, 1999; Merchant, 1997).

To analyze a quantitative study, students are encouraged to orient themselves to common themes in literature regarding effective use of quantitative methodology. Based on the following premises, students can explore the methods sections in quantitative reports and determine whether researchers adhered to basic guidelines. According to Creswell (1994) and Galvan (1999), at a minimum, effective quantitative methodology should

1. State a researcher's hypotheses at the onset of the investigation. Research hypotheses should not change throughout the study and should be evaluated only after all data are collected and analyzed.
2. Quantitative researchers serve as nonbiased individuals who can measure various aspects of human nature and counseling. Therefore, these researchers should remain objective throughout the entire investigation.
3. Use random selection in obtaining research participants from a sample of the population that is said to represent the norm. This means that participants should be randomly picked out of a larger group of representative subjects.
4. Include rather large sample sizes—between 100 to 200 and 1000, depending on the topic and resources of the researcher.

5. Indicate that specific variables of human nature, often referred to as confounding variables, were isolated, controlled for, and measured through quantifying procedures that produce numbers for data analysis.
6. Give detailed descriptions of data collection and analysis procedures. Measurements are taken with instruments that are believed to be scored objectively and deemed to be reliable and valid.
7. Present results using statistics. Use these statistical results to make inferences to correlations and relationships between variables and among groups of variables.
8. Indicate the reliability and validity of findings and address causality. Researchers must make generalizations between the study group and the general population. Researchers should never state results in terms of causes but rather correlations.

Qualitative Research

Instead of adhering to the assumptions of the physical sciences as do quantitative researchers, qualitative researchers, much like counselors, focus on assumptions that address the complex nature of human experience (Sexton & Griffin, 1997). To understand the phenomenology of such naturalistic researchers, Hill and Gronsky (1984) proposed the following assumptions: (a) There is not one truth but multiple truths or realities, depending on the perspective; (b) clinical phenomena are elusive and reactive; (c) clinical problems are deeply rooted and difficult to predict and manipulate in a controlled and rigid environment; (d) humans should be studied holistically and systematically rather than in isolated, restrictive, and incremental fashions; and (e) systematic or circular models of causality may be more appropriate and useful than linear causality for exploring humans and their unique experiences.

Much like quantitative investigations, qualitative research can be identified by the titles of the articles. Titles often contain words such as *naturalistic, exploration,* or *phenomenology,* and authors usually indicate that their study is qualitative in the abstract, introduction, or rationale for conducting the investigation. The results section of a qualitative article will be presented in terms of a narrative describing categories, themes, and trends, usually supported by quotations and comments from the actual research participants.

Similar to quantitative research, good practice in qualitative research must address questions of reliability and validity, yet these terms are replaced with parallel terms such as *dependability, trustworthiness,* and *authenticity* in qualitative research (Lincoln & Guba, 1985; Shank, 2002). Literature on how to conduct qualitative research and how to ensure appropriate qualitative procedures emphasize several aspects. Students are encouraged to familiarize themselves with the following list of qualitative concepts. They can then compare them with methodological reports in the qualitative literature they collect. Denzin and Lincoln (1994), Lincoln and Guba (1985), Maxwell (1992), Newsome et al. (in press), Shank, 2002, and Strauss and Corbin (1998) suggest that qualitative research ought to include:

1. A statement of a general purpose that does not impose rigid, specific goals and hypotheses to guide a study. Throughout data collection and analysis, this general purpose may emerge, and it is subject to change as additional data are collected.

2. Disclosure of the researcher's philosophical orientation and personal biases regarding the social and cultural context of the investigation.

3. Purposive and theoretical sampling procedures to select research participants who are accessible and appropriate for the research and topic. Purposive and theoretical sampling is a technique in which the sites, events, and participants being studied are deliberately chosen based on the purpose of the investigation and the phenomena being explored. The number of participants can fluctuate greatly, depending on the research question, population, and methodological approach. For example, the sample size can be as low as one, as in a case study of Seung-Hui Cho, the college student who massacred other students at Virginia Tech in 2007, or as many as 30, as in a phenomenological study of master's students in a multicultural counseling course or a grounded theory of the process of group supervision with internship students who are practicing group counseling skills.

4. The researcher is the primary means of data collection and uses relatively unstructured instruments such as interviews, observations, questionnaires, focus groups, and existing documents to gather information.

5. As researchers select participants, gather data, analyze data, and report their findings, they provide detailed descriptions of the internal process of the investigation.

6. The investigators have a prolonged engagement with the material and/or people they study. This includes spending extended periods with the participants to gain in-depth insights into the phenomena under investigation. How participants are experiencing themselves and the situation in which they are placed is often emphasized.

7. Interpretation and observation move in a cyclical process, thus allowing one aspect to inform the other.

8. Results are presented predominately or exclusively in words, narratives, or stories that emphasize understanding research participants' experiences and perspectives.

9. Rich descriptions enable researchers to ground their interpretations in the data by illustrating concepts through interview excerpts or describing relationships of data to theoretical concepts.

10. The focus is on "what and how" rather than "why" in analyzing and presenting data.

11. Triangulation procedures are used to confirm and verify findings. Triangulation refers to utilizing multiple sources of information, interpretation, and theory to support, challenge, clarify, and verify findings. Such sources may include, but are not limited to, existing literature, more than one researcher, experts in the field being explored, and divergent theories.

"The Seven Deadly Sins of Qualitative Research" in Shank's (2002) book offers more information on this subject.

Through exploring both quantitative and qualitative research and comparing the two methodologies, differences between the two seem blatant. Yet, both methodologies possess characteristics and procedures to ensure the credibility of findings. Differences between methodologies and unique measures to ensure trustworthiness of findings are important and must be understood to effectively evaluate the strengths and weaknesses of a study (Galvan, 1999). Other important aspects to consider in assessing the quality of either kind of study include the following:

1. Determine if the study is experimental, that is, is the purpose of the study to assess the effectiveness of something, such as an innovative counseling technique or a new drug? If so, note how the researcher selected participants, assigned treatment conditions, and measured outcomes.

2. If the study is nonexperimental (meaning that participants' traits are measured without attempting to change anything), be conscious of attempts to extrapolate correlations between outcomes and findings generated by the investigation.

3. Determine if researchers directly addressed issues related to measures of validity (Does the instrument or result seem accurate or correct?) and reliability (Would the instrument be consistent or would the same results occur over time?) for quantitative research. For qualitative research, are findings credible, trustworthy, thorough, and comprehensive? Did researchers provide a detailed explanation or a brief description of what they did to address issues of validity, reliability, credibility, and trustworthiness? Readers should attempt to make their own assessments of whether the measures were appropriate, given the purpose of the research.

4. Pay attention to the sampling procedures. In the case of a quantitative study, usually the more participants, the better, and only through random sampling can researchers generalize their findings to the overall population. In qualitative investigations, participants are purposely selected and described in detail. The number of participants is directly related to the topic at hand and may not necessarily be a factor.

5. Understand that when quantitative researchers note statistical significance, they are suggesting that there is a difference between two variables and that the difference is significantly greater than might be expected by chance alone. Because small differences can be classified as statistically significant in some studies, researchers should note the size of the differences.

6. Realize, as Peshkin (1988) contends, "Beginning with the premise that subjectivity is inevitable . . . researchers should systematically seek out their subjectivity, not retrospectively when data have been collected and analysis is complete, but while their research is actively in progress" (p. 17). Essentially, researchers should be aware of and communicate to the reader how their personal biases might have shaped their study and its outcomes.

7. Note that all empirical studies are subject to errors (Galvan, 1999). Readers should refrain from assuming that an investigation provides absolute truths or definitive answers to a given research problem. Furthermore, researchers should examine and discuss flaws of their investigations. Limitations to specific studies can often shed light on important aspects related to the topic explored, as well as supply ideas for future research.

8. Consider that implications about how the study informs the profession about the topic being explored and suggestions for future research are essential aspects in

both quantitative and qualitative research. From a qualitative perspective, researchers should discuss the transferability, and quantitative researchers should address the generalizeability of their findings.

Phase Four: Structuring a Written Review of Literature and Developing a Comprehensive Essay

It is finally time to explore how to conceptualize and synthesize review findings and writers' beliefs about literature. Students are encouraged to look at the development of a literature review as a process with a planning phase, a construction phase, and a refining phase. This section is an overview of key aspects to consider for creating a literature review.

Structuring the Literature Review

Before integrating literature into the form of a literature review, students need to clarify their purpose, their choice of voice, and the audience to whom they are writing. If the literature review is for a class assignment or term paper, instructors may set specific guidelines. For example, they may provide an outline, specify page limits, or determine the focus of the review. As far as choosing the voice in academic writing, many suggest that the first person, "I," should be avoided and that the third person or facts be allowed to speak for themselves (Galvan, 1999). Students must also take into consideration who will be reading their literature reviews. If the review is part of a thesis or dissertation, various committee members and reviewers will be reading students' work, and in most cases, literature is used to establish a framework and build a rationale for a study. Accordingly, information regarding methodology, suggestions for future research, gaps in research and literature, and other important details should be highlighted.

After clarifying the purpose and audience of the literature review, students are faced with the task of organizing their ideas into an outline or structured plan. Such a plan gives direction to the information that students have obtained throughout their review of the literature. It also allows students a forum to articulate their thoughts or judgments about the research they have reviewed (Coelho & La Forge, 1996; Galvan, 1999). This means that students should have formed judgments about the topic based on their analysis and synthesis of the research literature (Galvan, 1999). Creating an outline that exhibits the integration of information and communicates students' thoughts and judgments can be accomplished in a few basic steps.

First, students must integrate the various sources into a comprehensive summary and then clarify how all of this information is related. Next, students are encouraged to articulate their assertions, contentions, or propositions regarding the literature and research they have reviewed. Once students have established an argumentation for the reader, they should design their outlines around this set of beliefs. This includes reorganizing notes and ideas according to their assertions, contentions, or propositions.

When students have a detailed outline, they should begin connecting their beliefs to topic headings in the outline that emerged as they reviewed the literature. Students should focus on building a comprehensive and clear discussion of their line of argumentation under subheadings in the outline to define and describe each concept, clarify interrelationships among concepts, discuss connections to the topic, and discuss relationships among various studies or sources. Subheadings also address obvious gaps or areas that need further attention or research, ideas about how individual studies relate to and enhance theory, and innovative concepts that clarify misconceptions about the topic.

Writing the Literature Review

Once students have developed a detailed outline including specific headings, subheadings, and concepts, they are ready to construct the first draft. This first draft is intended to serve as a rehearsal and an opportunity to explore initial attempts at articulating the context and arrangement of information and ideas (Coelho & La Forge, 1996). If students have done their work in formulating a well-organized and specific outline, they can simply transfer concepts from that outline into a narrative with transitions, continuity, and appropriate grammar.

Students are encouraged to introduce their topic by identifying the broad area under review. They should avoid global statements and instead move from a general topic to specific concepts and ideas. This includes giving details about what the topic is and how it relates to other aspects of counseling. For example, in a discussion of group counseling with children affected by abuse, it may be logical to begin with a brief introduction to research about group work with children. Then get more specific and address issues related to counseling children who have been abused. Finally, discuss the specific topic of group work with children who have been abused.

Students should indicate the importance of the topic and comment on the timeliness in terms of a specific context. They need to identify their reasons for conducting a review of the literature and discuss why it is being done at this time. For example, when conducting a literature review for a thesis or dissertation, students may indicate that their research will address a gap in existing research. In this example, they would also need to explain why the topic is important and issues currently facing the field of counseling as a result of the topic. Students must remember to always justify their comments regarding how they determined a gap in literature and why they believe the topic is of importance now.

When students are citing a classic or landmark study, attempting to replicate it, or hoping to elaborate on it, they should indicate so. Landmark studies are those that are pivotal and influential in the historical development of the published literature and topic under investigation (Galvan, 1999; Szuchman, 2002). Such studies stimulate additional research in many instances and thus provide a solid foundation for students to build on.

Students are also encouraged to discuss other literature reviews related to the topic being explored and refer to reviews on issues related to the topic (Szuchman, 2002). In the case that earlier reviews were published about the same topic, writers are encouraged to incorporate a discussion about such reviews by focusing on how they are different, adequate, and worthy of readers' attention (Galvan, 1999). Although students should cover their topic in great detail, they may find that related concepts printed in previous reviews are important but not worthy of extended exposure. In this situation, students should simply make reference to other reviews when it may be useful to readers. On the other hand, students who locate research with an inconsistent or widely varying discussion should cite these manuscripts separately and indicate the effect on their topic and the field of counseling.

When writing a thesis, dissertation, or article for publication, students are encouraged to cite all relevant references in the literature review before they proceed to reporting original research. In this situation, students will use their review to justify and provide a rationale for conducting their studies. They should refrain from including long lists of nonspecific references within their text and instead cite only those references that provide direct quotations or essential facts needed for the text. Students should avoid the overuse of direct quotations and attempt to summarize whenever possible. Yet, it is vital that students give credit where credit is due. They should use references whenever they need to provide proper credit to an author or creator and to demonstrate the coverage given in a manuscript (Galvan, 1999). A brief discussion of legal and ethical implications follows.

Multicultural Considerations.   When writing and conducting research, students are encouraged to consider multicultural factors such as how researchers attend to gender, race, ethnicity, and sexual orientation. Likewise, students should be mindful of multicultural considerations in writing their papers. For example, appropriate terminology must be used to describe gender, racial and ethnic groups, geographic locations, and socioeconomic characteristics. Authors must avoid discriminatory language or gross generalizations about any population. Students are also responsible for remaining aware of cultural developments that emerge from professional organizations or through research in the field of counseling. For example, as of July 1, 2007, the American Counseling Association stopped referring to the Association for Gay, Lesbian, and Bisexual Issues in Counseling and began using its new name, "the Association for Lesbian, Gay, Bisexual and Transgendered Issues in Counseling (ALGBTIC)" (ACAeNews, 2007).

Noting the Legal and Ethical Implications of Writing

Copyright protection begins with the creation of a work, regardless of registration with the U.S. Copyright Office. Copyright laws acknowledge that individuals own ideas once they have created them (Remley & Herlihy, 2007). Students must give credit to sources via proper referencing and citation when they use the words and creations of others. Because of the ethical and legal implications of proper referencing, when in doubt, students should review guidelines in the most recent edition of the American Counseling Association's (ACA) *Code of Ethics and Standards of Practice* (2005) and the American Psychological Association's (APA) style manual (currently the 5th edition, 2001).

The APA manual (2001) specifies guidelines about how to properly cite the work of others, depending on the source and the way it is used. Published and unpublished sources that require citation include journal articles, books, professional presentations, personal interviews, videos, and material from the Internet. Detailed descriptions and guidelines for appropriate citation and referencing are clarified, and issues regarding manuscript organization, style, and format are included in the APA manual (2001).

Methods to Avoid Plagiarism.   There has been a steady increase in research and literature about plagiarism in academia. Studies have addressed (a) faculty members' perceptions of and response to plagiarism (Robinson-Zanartu et al., 2005), (b) Internet plagiarism (Howard, 2007), (c) how to help students avoid plagiarism (Landau, Druen, & Arcuri, 2002), and (d) the role of librarians in helping students avoid plagiarism and other forms of academic dishonesty (Mundava & Chaudhuri, 2007).

"For decades, guidelines have defined plagiarism broadly as the public misrepresentations of work as original, or any activity in which a person knowingly or unknowingly and for some form of gain, represents the work of another as his/her own" (Robinson-Zanartu et al., 2005, p. 319). The kinds of plagiarism vary, but the most common is word-for-word plagiarism, which is easily detected and most frequently punished (Martin, 1994, in Robinson-Zanartu et al., 2005). The occurrence of plagiarism has steadily increased over the last several years. Howard (2007) attributed this increase in plagiarism to the Internet and noted that the Internet has increased students' access to information and research. However, the overall lack of education about plagiarism and the inadequate preparation of many students continue to plague academia (Robinson-Zanartu et al., 2005). Despite many professors' emphasis on avoiding plagiarism and their "no tolerance" policies, cultural and language barriers have led to the increase of plagiarism in universities (Mundava & Chaudhuri, 2007).

Many experts have suggested how to address the problem of academic plagiarism. In particular, Landau, Druen, and Arcuri (2002) showed that instruction in plagiarism identification and paraphrasing skills, followed by exercises to help students practice such skills, was the most effective way to help students avoid plagiarism. Written and oral warnings against plagiarism aren't effective, they note, and they encourage faculty members to utilize exercises or feedback sessions to train students to avoid plagiarism. Professors don't have or take the time to address plagiarism directly, but students can find information and activities on Web sites and the Internet. For example, a plagiarism Web site (http://www.plagiarism.org) and the APA's publication guide offer details and examples of how to cite various resources correctly.

Overall, students are encouraged to paraphrase information appropriately and utilize direct quotes only when necessary. If specific words are necessary to preserve the meaning of a passage, students should be tenacious about citing the author, year of publication, and page number or location of such a passage as accurately as possible.

Creating a Comprehensive Essay

Because first drafts are seldom, if ever, complete, clear, and coherent, once students have completed the first draft, they must begin the process of refining their work.

Although it is often easy to get discouraged, students should be prepared to rewrite at least two or three times after the first draft is finished. Szuchman (2002) indicated that the writing process inherently includes the following process of revision: (a) first draft, (b) first rewrite, (c) second rewrite, (d) a third inspection that is not a rewrite, and (e) the final touches. Others suggest that the process of revising a research paper or manuscript usually involves at least two rewrites. As Zinsser (1990) so appropriately commented, "Writing is hard work. A clear sentence is no accident" (p. 13).

Allowing peers or others to proof first and subsequent drafts can be extremely helpful. Students are encouraged to look for people who are willing and able to read and critique their work. Feedback is the most effective way for writers to gain perspective and quality. Students who are unable to receive feedback from others are encouraged to challenge themselves and their writing as they proofread their own manuscripts. During this self-editing process, students should compare their draft with their topic statement and outline; avoid using synonyms for recurring words; spell out all acronyms when they first appear in the text; avoid contractions; set off coined terms in quotations; avoid slang expressions, colloquialisms, and idioms; and avoid plagiarism (Galvan, 1999). In addition, students must look for typical errors in typing, writing, spelling, and grammar. Students must edit and revise the first draft as many times as necessary to clarify, solidify, and edit flaws in their work.

Authors who understand that the writing process can be overwhelming have offered the suggestions to novices. Writers should develop a process of writing that is unique to them. A unique writing process takes into consideration writers' personalities and different writing styles. This process can include working at a specific time of day to enable them to write while they are fresh (Creswell, 1994). Coelho and La Forge (1996) stated that writers must avoid writing binges and instead focus on writing in small yet regular amounts. Students are also encouraged to understand that writing is a slow and tedious process requiring time, patience, and persistence. They may do well to schedule daily writing tasks, generate goals for each day, keep daily charts of writing progress, select people to proofread who will provide supportive and corrective feedback, and try to work on two or three writing projects at once (Creswell, 1994). Coelho and La Forge (1996) asserted that writing is in a constant state of evolution; therefore, writers must be flexible and open to new ideas that occur while they write. This will allow writers to fill in gaps and elaborate relationships between concepts throughout the entire process of creating an essay or manuscript for publication.

Phase Five: Designing a Plan for Conducting Research

Theses and Dissertations

At the conclusion of a literature review, those interested in conducting research need a plan for carrying out a research agenda (Cone & Foster, 1995). This can be an ideal opportunity for students to solidify their research purposes and agendas and meet with faculty advisors. Students may find that they need to reexamine parts of their research plan, including the initial research question, hypotheses, and data collection and analysis procedures. This process can often lead to a revision of the initial research plan. For example, based on suggestions regarding methodology, students may find that they need to review and incorporate additional literature regarding the use of a specific methodological approach or alter their research plan to fit a particular mode of data collection and analysis.

This is also an excellent time for master's and doctoral students to coordinate with their advisors and develop detailed and specific plans for the remainder of their investigations. Those embarking on theses or dissertations have to take ample time to decide how, when, where, and with whom they will conduct their research. Students must detail the sample population, their research purpose, specific research questions, methodological procedures, and potential barriers. A tentative time line of events and procedures must be developed before the research process can be initiated.

Legal and Ethical Considerations in Research

According to ethical guidelines and CACREP (2008), studies must be rigorously and carefully designed or they may be considered unethical on account of the waste of time and potential harm they can pose to participants and researchers (Remley & Herlihy, 2007). Therefore, students must take legal and ethical considerations into account in the initial phases of planning their investigations. Of highest priority, researchers must protect research participants from harm. This includes voluntary participation, informed consent, confidentiality, and issues of diversity.

Remley and Herlihy (2007) have discussed several of the ethical mandates pertaining to research that are supported by legal requirements. For example, any institution that receives federal funds must maintain a system to review research proposals with the intent to protect the welfare of research participants. Most universities and government-affiliated organizations require that research including human subjects must be reviewed and approved by a committee prior to the onset of data collection. Consequently, if students do not plan studies that integrate legal and ethical requirements, they will not receive approval from such review committees. This would delay students' research and could cause serious problems for students and research participants. For this and other reasons, students must familiarize themselves with ethical guidelines in conducting and reporting research prior to developing a research plan. A full discussion of such issues is provided in the ACA's *Code of Ethics and Standards of Practice* (2005).

Program Evaluations

Up to this point, this chapter has been directed toward students who are constructing literature reviews and conducting research for a thesis or dissertation. However, there are other reasons that counseling students may do research, such as program evaluation. Program evaluations look at whether the goals for implementation of a counseling program are being met and whether clients are getting what they need from the counseling experience. In many schools and agencies, counselors are asked to be accountable and produce evidence for the effectiveness of their practice. Novice and experienced counselors are faced with program evaluations and often struggle with how to accomplish this task. Counselors can satisfy such requests if they simply gather data and record information about their activities and efforts throughout their daily lives as professional counselors.

Counselors are encouraged to utilize data collection procedures outlined in both quantitative and qualitative methodologies to obtain information that testifies to their effectiveness. They should select methodological procedures that fit their individual, school, and agency needs. For example, school counselors may simply keep track of students they meet with on a weekly basis. They could set up a chart and tally the specific issues they address with students and the specific interventions or techniques they used. At the end of a semester, these school counselors could then analyze their data and produce a report highlighting the numerical results of their efforts. Such research would provide a record of what school counselors have done over a specific period of time. This information would address issues of program effectiveness for principals and school board members.

Summary

This chapter discussed writing and research in counseling. Concepts and ideas were directed toward novice and experienced counseling students who are currently encountering assignments ranging from essays, term papers, and literature reviews to theses and dissertations. Specific attention was given to the role of research in the profession of counseling. Concepts included the importance of research, the definition of research, how to use research and literature in counseling, how to construct a comprehensive essay or literature review, the legal and ethical implications for writing and research, and how to utilize research in program evaluations.

USEFUL WEB SITES

To simultaneously search more than 20 periodical databases related to humanities and educational abstracts, including Dissertation Abstracts, ERIC, Medline, PsycINFO, Social Sciences Abstracts, and Sociological Abstracts.
http://www.ishmo.org/webpsych

To obtain a preprinted professional resource bibliography on a general or specialized topic, updated annually.
http://www.counseling.org/resources/bibliographies.htm

To access the counseling and student services clearinghouse online.
http://ericcass.uncg.edu/about.htm

Counselor Net.
http://www.plattsburgh.edu/projects/cnet

Mental Health Net.
http://www.cmhc.com

American Counseling Association (ACA).
http://www.counseling.org

American Psychological Association.
http://www.apa.org

To access information specific to plagiarism and appropriate referencing techniques.
http://www.plagiarism.org/

National Association of Social Workers.
http://www.naswdc.org

National Mental Health Association.
http://www.nmha.org

Online Psychological Services.
http://www.onlinepsych.com/index.html

National Institute of Mental Health.
http://www.nimh.nih.gov

Substance Abuse and Mental Health Services Administration.
http://www.samhsa.gov

American Educational Research Association.
listserv@asuvm.inre.asu.edu—AERA—E

International Counselor Network.
listserv@utkvm1.utk.edu—ICN

Counselor Education and Supervision Network.
listserv@utkvm.utk.edu—CESNET-L

REFERENCES

ACAeNews. (2007). *9*(8).
American Counseling Association. (2005). *Code of ethics and standards of practice*. Annapolis Junction, MD: ACA Distribution Center.
Ambert, A., Adler, P. A., Adler, P., & Detzner, D. F. (1995). Understanding and evaluating qualitative research. *Journal of Marriage and Family*, *57*, 879–893.
American Psychological Association. (2001). *Publication manual* (5th ed.). Washington, DC: Author.
Coelho, R. J., & La Forge, J. (1996). Journal publication as a professional practice activity for rehabilitation counselors. *Journal of Applied Rehabilitation Counseling*, *27*(1), 17–21.
Cone, J. D., & Foster, S. L. (1995). *Dissertations and theses from start to finish*. Washington, DC: American Psychological Association.
Council for Accreditation of Counseling and Related Educational Programs (CACREP). (2008). *Revised standards*.
Creswell, J. W. (1994). *Research design: Qualitative & quantitative approaches*. Thousand Oaks, CA: Sage.

Denzin, N. K., & Lincoln, Y. S. (Eds.). (1994). *Handbook of qualitative research*. Thousand Oaks, CA: Sage.

Flick, U. (1998). *An introduction to qualitative research*. Thousand Oaks, CA: Sage.

Galvan, J. L. (1999). *Writing literature reviews: A guide for students of the social and behavioral sciences*. Los Angeles: Pyrczak.

Heppner, P. P., Wampold, B. E., & Kivlighan, D. M. (2008). *Research design in counseling* (3rd ed.). Belmont, CA: Brooks/Cole.

Herman, K. C. (1997). Embracing human science in counseling research. *Counselor Education and Supervision, 36*, 270–283.

Hill, C. E., & Gronsky, B. (1984). Research: Why and how ? In J. M. Whileley, M. Kagan, L. W. Harmon, B. R. Fretz, & F. Tanny (Eds.). *The coming decade in counseling psychology* (pp. 149–159). Schenectady, NY: Character Research.

Hoshmund, L. T. (1989). Alternative research paradigms: A review and teaching proposal. *Counseling Psychologist, 17*, 3–79.

Howard, R. M. (2007). Understanding "Internet plagiarism." *Computers and Composition, 24*, 3–15.

Landau, J. D., Druen, P. B., & Arcuri, J. A. (2002). Methods for helping students avoid plagiarism. *Teaching of Psychology, 29*(2), 112–115.

Lincoln, Y. S., & Guba, E. G. (1985). *Naturalistic inquiry*. Newbury Park, CA: Sage.

Loesch, L. C., & Nicholas, V. A. (1996). *Research in counseling and therapy* (Report No. RR93002004). Washington, DC: Office of Educational Research and Improvement. (ERIC Clearinghouse on Counseling and Student Services Co. ED404611)

Maxwell, J. A. (1992). Understanding and validity in qualitative research. *Harvard Educational Review, 62*, 279–299.

Merchant, N. (1997). Qualitative research for counselors. *Counseling and Human Development, 30*(1).

Miles, M. B., & Huberman, A. M. (1994). *Qualitative data analysis: An expanded sourcebook*. Newbury Park, CA: Sage.

Morse, J. M., & Field, P. A. (1995). *Qualitative research methods for health professionals* (2nd ed.). Thousand Oaks, CA: Sage.

Mundava, M., & Chaudhuri, J. (2007). Understanding plagiarism: The role of librarians at the University of Tennessee in assisting students to practice fair use of information. *College and Research Libraries News, 68*(3), 1–5. http://www.ala.org/ala/acrl/acrlpubs/crlnews/backissues2007/march07/plagiarism.htm

Newsome, D., Hays, D. G., & Christensen, T. M. (in press). Qualitative approaches to research. In B. T. Erford (Ed.), *Research and evaluation in counseling*. Boston: Houghton Mifflin/Lahaska Press.

Nicol, A. A. M., & Pexman, P. M. (1999). *Presenting your findings: A practical guide to creating tables*. Washington, DC: American Psychological Association.

Nisenoff, S., & Espina, M. . (1999, June). The a-b-c's of research in professional counseling. *Counseling Today*, 18.

Peshkin, A. (1988, October). In search of subjectivity—one's own. *Educational Research*, 17–21.

Polkinghorne, D. E. (1991). Qualitative procedures for counseling research. In C. E. Watkins & L. J. Schneider (Eds.), *Research in counseling* (pp. 163–204). Hillsdale, NJ: Lawrence Erlbaum.

Polkinghorne, D. E. (1994). Reaction to special section on qualitative research in counseling process and outcome. *Journal of Counseling Psychology, 41*(4), 510–512.

Rechtien, J. G., & Dizinno, G. (1997). A note on measuring apprehension about writing. *Psychological Reports, 80*, 907–913.

Reilly, R. (2000). *Trends in academic progress*. Washington, DC: U.S. Department of Education.

Remley, T. P., Jr., & Herlihy, B. (2007). *Ethical, legal, and professional issues in counseling* (2nd ed.). Upper Saddle River, NJ: Prentice Hall.

Robinson-Zanartu, C., Pena, E. D., Cook-Morales, V., Pena, A. M., Afshani, R., & Nguyen, L. (2005). Academic crime and punishment: Faculty members' perceptions of and response to plagiarism. *School Psychology Quarterly, 20*(3), 318–337.

Rubin, J. H., & Rubin, I. S. (1995), *Qualitative interviewing: The art of hearing data*. Thousand Oaks, CA: Sage.

Sexton, T. L. (1996). The relevance of counseling outcome research: Current trends and practical implications. *Journal of Counseling and Development, 74*, 590–600.

Sexton, T. L., & Griffin, B. L. (Eds.). (1997). *Constructivist thinking in counseling, practice, research, and training*. New York: Teachers College Press.

Shank, G. D. (2002). *Qualitative research: A personal skills approach*. Upper Saddle River, NJ: Pearson Education.

Stockton, R., & Toth, P. L. (1997). Applying a general research training model to group work. *Journal for Specialists in Group Work, 22*(4), 241–252.

Strauss, A., & Corbin, J. (1998). *Basics of qualitative research: Techniques and procedures for developing grounded theory* (2nd ed.). Thousand Oaks, CA: Sage.

Szuchman, L. T. (2002). *Writing with style: APA style for counseling*. Pacific Grove, CA: Brooks/Cole.

Zinsser, W. (1990). *On writing well* (4th ed.). New York: HarperCollins.

6

Technology and Counseling

MELINDA HALEY, PhD
South Texas Rural Health Services, Inc.

JASON VAZQUEZ, MA
New Mexico State University

Introduction

The use of technology in counseling has been apparent in some form or another for the last five or six decades. In the 1950s, Joyce Brothers used radio to reach millions of listeners and provide services to those in need (Brothers, 2007), and interactive video therapy, with client and therapist connected by television for the counseling session, began at the University of Nebraska (McCarty & Clancy, 2002). Telephones have been used for suicide hot lines and 24-hour counseling services, and students and counselor educators have been using audiotapes and videotapes in supervision for decades, and more recently webcams have been utilized. In the past decade, technological applications for clients and counselors have flourished.

Technology has affected the way counselors perform their job tasks (Greene, Lawson, & Getz, 2005). As of 2008, 90% of counselors are estimated to use some form of computer-related technology in 92% of their work (Cabaniss, 2001). Technology for counseling services includes (a) software to aid in report writing, (b) spreadsheets for recording client data, (c) statistical analysis packages for analyzing client data, (d) publishing software for marketing and client recruitment, and (e) software for assessment and testing (Murphy, 2003). E-mail and listservs are used for personal and professional communication, as well as for consultation, supervision, referral, and professional development. The Internet has been used for client information (professional and informational Web sites), advertising and providing counseling services, marketing, and a host of other purposes (Allen, 2004). In fact, several thousand counselors are now estimated to use Internet Web sites to advertise their counseling services (Heinlen, Welfel, Richmond, & Rak, 2003).

Realization that the technological age has profound significance for counseling has spurred debate and controversy within the profession regarding how technology will be used (Pelling, 2005). Professional associations and governing agencies have scrambled to provide counselors with guidelines, competencies, and ethics to regulate usage and provide protection to clients. For many new technological arenas such as Internet counseling, there have been no laws, regulations, or codes of conduct to initially guide counselors (Allen, 2004; Barnett & Scheetz, 2003; National Board of Certified Counselors [NBCC], 2001). This chapter will explore many of the current technological innovations counselors are using in their work today, with emphasis on discussing the benefits, consequences, considerations, and ethical implications for using these technologies in counseling.

Online Counseling and Distance Counseling

Online counseling is a growing modality for providing counseling services (Allen, 2004). It is estimated that 100 million Americans have sought help or mental health information online (Chang, 2005; Mallen & Vogel, 2005). In addition, hundreds of Web sites offer mental health information or advice, and more than a thousand counselors and mental health specialists provide some or all of their services online (Goedert, 2003; Heinlen, Welfel, Richmond, & O'Donnell, 2003; Shaw & Shaw, 2006). Online counseling is one of the fastest growing health services on the Internet and is expected to increase within the next 10 years (Allen, 2004; Mallen, Vogel, Rochlen, & Day, 2005). Although online mental health services may never replace face-to-face psychotherapy, it is clear that this modality is here to stay (Powell, 2005).

Internet behavioral health services have been called by many names: cyber counseling, e-counseling, cyber-consultations, cyber psychology, cyber therapy, online counseling, virtual couch therapy, telehealth, and telecounseling, to name just a few (Eleven & Allen, 2004). In this chapter, this form of therapy will be referred to as online counseling. A further distinction needed for this section is that online counseling is performed strictly with the use of computers via the Internet (e.g., e-mail, Web sites, or chat rooms), whereas distance counseling can use a variety of media in addition to the computer, such as the telephone, television satellite hookup, videotape, and audiotape. Distance counseling can be done with individuals, couples, or groups (Grohol, 2003; Shaw & Shaw, 2006).

When counseling is conducted online rather than in its traditional face-to-face form, it can be either synchronous or asynchronous. Synchronous counseling occurs when there is little or no gap between the responses of the counselor and the client and the interaction resembles a dialogue (Shaw & Shaw, 2006). Synchronous counseling might be delivered by telephone or a satellite hookup. In contrast, asynchronous counseling occurs when there is a gap in time between the response of the counselor and the client (Young, 2005). Asynchronous counseling uses media such as e-mail. For example, the client asks the counselor a question through e-mail, and the response might come back the next day, versus instantaneously as in face-to-face counseling or counseling done through a telephone line.

Forms of online counseling and distance counseling currently available include:

1. *Telephone Counseling:* These generally are crisis lines and 24-hour counseling lines.
2. *Radio Counseling:* This method has been made famous with such personalities as Dr. Joyce Brothers, Dr. Laura, and Dr. Sue Brown.

3. *E-mail Counseling:* The counseling experience consists of e-mail sent between counselor and client (Barack, 2005).
4. *Bulletin Board Counseling:* Users post questions to an online bulletin board, generally with an identity pseudonym for confidentially (e.g., Mickey Mouse). The mental health professional posts an answer for all users to see.
5. *Chat Room Counseling:* This allows for synchronous counseling as counselor and client(s) engage in text communication in real time. Chat room counseling is popular for group counseling because several people can communicate at the same time (Allen, 2004).
6. *Web-Telephony Counseling:* This allows for real-time speaking over the Internet via a microphone and speakers.
7. *Videoconferencing:* This is real-time (synchronous) counseling via audio and video technology that provides distance counseling but in a face-to-face manner (Allen, 2004). Generally, this is done with a camera, monitor, and computer processor. For example, technology called CU-SeeMe uses camera equipment, software, real time, and audiovisual communications. This technology allows group counseling to take place simultaneously with up to six people (Rapisarda & Jencius, 2005).
8. *Computer-Assisted or Simulated Counseling:* These are generally computer-generated answers provided to questions or concerns through software programs. The client does not receive help through a live person, although a live person may oversee the program (Wolf, 2003).
9. *E-Coaching:* This is a human-guided interactive module series for such issues as depression and anxiety. Each module might have eight or nine interactive applications that clients complete on their own. Once finished, clients send the completed application to an e-coach for process, feedback, and homework redirection (Lillis, 2004).

Discussion of each of these modes of cyber or distance counseling would be too lengthy and beyond the scope of this chapter. However, a brief discussion on videoconferencing will aid the reader in understanding the concept of this type of counseling service. Videoconferencing requires both counselor and client to have a webcam that can transmit images and sound via the Internet. In this way, counseling takes place synchronously and is similar to traditional face-to-face counseling, although participants may live in different locations and time zones (Mallen, Vogel, & Rochlen, 2005).

Counselors have used videoconferencing and other technology to treat such issues as depression, suicidal ideation, mood disorders, eating disorders, and attention-deficit disorder (Zabinski, Wilfrley, Calfas, Winzelberg, & Taylor, 2004). In addition, videoconferencing client populations have included families, older adults, teenagers with seizure disorders, and psychiatric patients (Kirk & Belovics, 2005). Evidence from numerous studies suggests that counselors are just as effective at building rapport and a working relationship via videoconferencing as in face-to-face counseling and have been similarly effective in treating disorders such as schizophrenia and obsessive-compulsive disorder (Reese & Stone, 2005).

Positives. Both online counseling and distance counseling are often more convenient for both counselor and client (Young, 2005). This is especially true for asynchronous counseling using store-and-forward technology such as e-mail. Store-and-forward systems store various types of data (e.g. text or psychological test data) on a computer, and the data can then be forwarded to another computer to be seen by another person. Because the information is actually "stored" at both the sender and receiver ends, the parties need not be present simultaneously (Mallen et al., 2005). This can be beneficial because counseling can occur without a cumbersome synchronizing of counselor and client schedules.

This form of counseling can eliminate many barriers that might keep an individual from using counseling services, such as inability to access a counselor's office because of geographical location or disability. When services are provided via e-mail, both counselor and client can respond at their convenience rather than at a prescribed time (Shaw & Shaw, 2006). In addition, although face-to-face counseling typically occurs no more than once per week, online counseling usually occurs more frequently (Casper & Berger, 2005).

One additional benefit to this type of counseling is that all communication is written and therefore automatically documented. Both client and counselor can refer back to the communication at any time for clarification (Mallen & Vogel, 2005). However, this written record also causes some ethical concerns regarding confidentiality.

Distance counseling, whether via the computer or other technological means, also appears to reduce client anxiety or embarrassment about the counseling process (Schultze, 2005; Young, 2005). This may be especially true for individuals who live in communities where there is a strong stigma against seeking mental health services (Zelvin & Speyer, 2003). Counseling performed via chat rooms also offers the client a measure of anonymity that cannot be found in face-to-face counseling (Schultze, 2005; Young, 2005). However, client anonymity can also produce profound problems for the counselor when, for example, a client discloses intentions of self-harm, harm to others, or child abuse.

Another benefit for the counselor is that distance counseling and online counseling circumvent the quagmire that has become managed care. A counselor can offer services as a provider without having to be governed by managerial systems. However, what is an advantage for the counselor is often a drawback for the client. These services are not usually covered by insurance.

Some forms of online counseling have been found to be more beneficial in some cases then typical face-to-face counseling. In couples therapy, for example, when the couple is interacting in an emotionally reactive way, slowing the communication down via e-mail and encouraging the couple to express themselves without gestures or facial expressions has been found to be effective and cathartic. In addition, having them write their story seemed to make them more reflective and obtain better understanding (Casper & Berger, 2005; Schultze, 2005).

Negatives. One major drawback to text-based communication between counselor and client is the relative lack of "presence" in the counseling situation. That is, it may be difficult to have a sense that another human being is "present" and communicating with you when using asynchronous communication (Holmes & Ainsworth, 2003). It also may be difficult for counselors to build rapport and show genuine positive regard with clients in the same manner that rapport is nurtured in face-to-face counseling (Shaw & Shaw, 2006).

In addition, the counselor cannot assess a client's nonverbal behaviors, which gives a counselor additional data upon which to confer hypotheses and diagnoses as well as identify incongruent communication and behaviors (e.g., client says she or he is angry yet is smiling) (Mallen, Vogal, Rochlen, & Day, 2005; Shaw & Shaw, 2006). Miscommunication is more likely because visual and auditory cues are missing (Zelvin & Speyer, 2003).

Furthermore, many Web sites on the Internet purport to be therapeutically inclined but are not regulated in any way. For many sites, the service provided is by someone other than a mental health specialist (Chang, 2005). It is a "buyer beware" market. According to Shaw and Shaw (2006), online counselors should identify themselves and their credentials to their clients. Shaw and Shaw list three levels of credentials: primary credentials (e.g., an earned degree from an accredited university and additional training), secondary credentials (e.g., any licensure or certification that the counselor holds), and tertiary credentials (e.g., professional associations to which the counselor belongs).

Only counselors who are certified or licensed can be held to ethical standards and guidelines. If a "counselor" is not a member of a regulating board (e.g., American Counseling Association, American Psychological Association, or National Board of Certified Counselors), complaints for violations cannot be filed. However, there are online services that can help consumers find credentialed counselors and therapists. For example, Metanoia (http://www.metanoia.org) is a site where consumers can review online practitioners' credentials, security information, and consumer ratings.

Another problem with online counseling is that many public and private health insurance carriers reimburse only for synchronous counseling services such as video-conferencing. Asynchronous counseling services (e.g., text-based consultations) are not considered a reimbursable service for many private and public health insurance carriers (Kraus, 2003). Consequently, most users of this type of service are forced to cover the costs out of their own pocket.

Furthermore, not all client populations are appropriate for online counseling (Zelvin & Speyer, 2003). For example, suicidal clients or clients who are in crisis are not appropriate for online counseling. In some cases, depending on the therapist and mode of communication, there may be a significant delay in responding to clients after initial contact, especially if the client did not provide accurate contact information. For a client seriously at risk for a suicide attempt, a delay in receiving any intervention may cost the client his or her life.

Ethical Issues.   As can be imagined, there are a superfluity of ethical concerns with both online counseling and distance counseling. Confidentiality is certainly at the forefront of these (Kraus, 2003; Shaw & Shaw, 2006). How does a counselor ensure client confidentiality? Currently, technology allows for the encryption of communication between computer systems (Zack, 2003). However, this is not a guaranteed method. In addition, how does a counselor certify confidentiality if the communications are then to be saved on the computer? Many computer systems have passwords to gain access to files or enter computers, but this is also not infallible.

Other ethical concerns pertain to client safety. How can a client ascertain that the person on the other end of the telephone or computer is actually a counselor? How does a client find out the counselor's credentials? The National Board of Certified Counselors Standards of Practice (2001) stipulates that a counselor's Web site must have all the links necessary for a client to ascertain a counselor's certification and/or licensure. However, even if a counselor's credentials are verified, how does the client know that a counselor is trained for the client's presenting issue? If the counselor states he or she is receiving supervision, how can the client verify this?

If the client resides in a different state than the counselor and a problem does arise, which state has jurisdiction? For example, if elder abuse is disclosed by the client and the client's home state does not require the counselor report it but the counselor's home state does, then what? What if the client resides in a different country? How are multicultural concerns satisfied?

Counselors are obligated to fully disclose any risks associated with a counseling modality. Online counseling is no different. Counselors must allow clients to make informed choices, and counselors providing this type of service need to be well versed in the benefits and costs of this type of counseling (Barnett & Scheetz, 2003; Goedert, 2003; Shaw & Shaw, 2006).

The National Board of Certified Counselors has provided standards for the ethical practice of Internet counseling (NBCC, 2001) that specifically address Internet counseling and do not duplicate other standards set by the NBCC for other counseling modalities. Internet counseling standards should be used in combination with the most current ethical codes (http://www.nbcc.org/extras/pdfs/ethics/nbcc-codeofethics.pdf). The American Counseling Association (ACA) and the American Psychological Association (APA) have also published standards and guidelines for services provided by telephone, teleconferencing, and the Internet. Because technology is ever expanding these standards and codes should be reviewed frequently for changes and updates.

Computer-Assisted Counseling

Computer-assisted counseling utilizes computer software to provide assessment, intervention, and specific counseling techniques to clients (Grohol, 2003; Mallen & Vogel, 2005). Today, the category of computer-assisted counseling can include any computer-based application that aids the counselor in his or her work, including software packages for assessment or treatment planning, psychoeducational software packages to provide clients information about disorders such as depression and anxiety, and computer-assisted counseling in which the computer actually provides a type of counseling service to clients.

There are many ways computers can assist in the counseling and support of a client. For example, the first computer counselor prototype was developed more than 30 years ago by Joseph Weizenbaum, who wrote a computer application named "Eliza." The program simulated natural language comprehension and approximated a nondirective counseling session by using preprogrammed responses when cued by a client (Wolf, 2003). Essentially "Eliza," in semi-Rogerian fashion, rephrased and reflected back remarks made by the client in such a way as to cause the client to think deeper about his or her issues.

In addition, computerized virtual reality systems have been used to help clients with phobias by providing a form of systematic desensitization (Zack, 2003). The client is exposed to his or her hierarchy of anxiety-provoking stimuli by computer simulation. Once the client has mastered his or her hierarchy, then in vivo exposure can begin. Another way is computer programs that use well-known cognitive behavioral techniques (e.g., thought-stopping exercises) to help clients evaluate their cognitions and reduce anxiety or depression (Anderson et al., 2004; Mallen & Vogel, 2005).

Palmtop computers have recently emerged as a promising technology for providing counseling. Palmtops are literally computers that can fit in the palm of one's hand. Compared to traditional, full-sized computers, palmtops are somewhat limited in that they have less memory and do not include disk drives. However, the user can insert disk drives, modems, memory, and other devices into many palmtops. Recently, several studies have found support for cognitive behavioral therapy (CBT) software on palmtops for clients with anxiety disorders, such as obsessive-compulsive disorder, social phobia, generalized anxiety disorder, and panic disorder (Anderson, Jacobs, & Rothbaum, 2004).

A review of studies exploring the use of computer software in cognitive behavioral applications indicates that these software systems are just as efficacious as face-to-face therapy for treating anxiety disorders such as social phobia or panic disorder (Anderson et al., 2004). Computer-assisted software is well suited for the treatment of depression and anxiety disorders because it gives the user an increased sense of mastery and control, as well as instruction in relaxation techniques, cognitive restructuring, stress management, and systematic desensitization and exposure (Anderson et al., 2004).

In addition, many counseling agencies and managed care organizations have set up online interactive consumer services, including self-help and health education programs to aid clients. For example, Cigna Behavioral Health (CBH) now provides an interactive "coaching" program for plan participants who suffer from a variety of psychological problems such as anxiety, depression, and substance abuse (Lillis, 2004). Participants are securely connected to a web-based series of exercises designed to offer confidential customized clinical feedback and access these coaching tools through their employer or the CBH' website.

Positives.   The use of computer-aided counseling can help clients when they cannot afford frequent sessions or can be used between sessions to supplement or reinforce the therapeutic gains made by face-to-face counseling. Supplementing face-to-face counseling with computer-guided self-treatment can substantially cut therapy costs for the client. In addition, because some systems can be accessed by the telephone and are often voice-activated, clients do not necessarily need a computer. These systems can also be made available 24-hours per day.

Negatives. Computers are fallible, and programs are only as good as the people who programmed them. Systems also have to be maintained and updated, which can sometimes be difficult, time consuming, and expensive. In addition, computers cannot build a relationship with a client or notice the nuances of a client's speech. Computers are literal, can process only what is typed into them, and cannot, at least at this time, respond in a spontaneous human way or show empathy, emotion, or understanding of nonverbal cues. Computers cannot assess and diagnose a client, create a treatment plan, or monitor a client's progress without human input, nor should they.

Ethical Concerns. The dangers arise when a counselor uses computer-assisted counseling as a primary means of intervention instead of as a counseling aid. Because many of the applications deal specifically with depression or severe anxiety, it would be unethical not to personally monitor a particular client and assess for suicidal ideation. With voice-activated systems, a client might be in serious trouble with no human counselor available to make an assessment. Computer-assisted counseling should be used as a supplement and not as the main provision of services.

Technology in Assessment and Diagnosis

Assessment can be defined as the accumulation of knowledge about a person from a variety of sources for purposes of providing some kind of intervention, diagnosis, or treatment for individuals seeking services. Regardless of counselor specialty, technology can be used in the assessment process. One rapidly increasing technological innovation used for assessments is the Internet, which provides professionals with continuously updated information about assessment procedures and tools that may be used free or for a fee (Barak & Buchanan, 2003).

Online Testing

Through Internet sites, counselors have access to a wide variety of assessment instruments that can be appropriate for purposes such as psychological evaluation, psychotherapeutic diagnostics, and self-exploration and can serve a diverse group of clients (Barak & Buchanan, 2003; Buchanan, Johnson, & Goldbert, 2005). These tests and assessments can measure specific factors such as level of IQ, a specific aptitude, level of emotional intelligence, or a certain attitude; others are more general and evaluate personality characteristics or help with vocational interests.

Technology has been used in the process of diagnosis with some success. McCarty and Clancy (2002) discussed a study at the Medical Center of Central Massachusetts concerning the reliability and validity of conducting diagnoses through teleconferencing methods. The study compared diagnoses for acute psychiatric patients who were involuntarily admitted. Half the group were diagnosed in a face-to-face setting, and the other half were diagnosed through teleconferencing. Results showed that the "telediagnoses" had a perfect correlation, one with another, and had a .85 correlation with the face-to-face diagnoses. Similar results were found between teleconferencing and face-to-face assessments using the Mini-Mental Status Exam, the Yale–Brown Obsessive-Compulsive Scale, the Hamilton Depression Scale, and the Hamilton Anxiety Scale (McCarty & Clancy, 2002).

A review of all the available assessments is beyond the space limitations of this chapter, but an example of an assessment used for self-exploration follows to illustrate the kinds of assessments available online. For example, an online emotional intelligence test, an online culture fair intelligence test, and online verbal or spatial intelligence tests are available (http://www.queendom.com/tests/iq). Other sites assess client interests and personalities, such as Career Keys (http://www.careerkey.org/english) and the Keirsey Temperament Sorter (http://www.keirsey.com). We as authors do not endorse any of the Web sites here, which are provided simply as examples of the types of services offered.

Test Interpretation and Scoring Software

The role of computers in psychological assessment has dramatically increased in the last 40 years (Litchenberger, 2006). Hundreds of these programs and services are available, including programs that can score and interpret the results of tests for evaluation purposes, such as personality traits and neuropsychological problems (Butcher, Perry, & Hahn, 2004). Generally, these interpretations are a result of either data ensuing from the clinical experiences of many psychodiagnosticians or from an accumulation of statistical data that define the relationships between questions answered on an inventory, and a specific typology (Litchenberger).

Some paper-and-pencil assessments that previously entailed tedious hand scoring procedures, such as the Minnesota Multiphasic Personality Inventory (MMPI), provide answer sheets that can be directly scanned into a computer and therefore allow for quicker and more accurate scoring (Barak & Buchanan, 2003). These software packages can also provide narrative assessment reports for counselors and clients (Litchenberger, 2006). In spite of the convenience of computer-based test interpretations, however, clinicians should be cautious and not use computer-generated reports as a replacement for clinical judgment (Litchenberger, 2006).

Databases

Databases can also be used in the assessment process (Farrel, 2005; "Web Tool," 2005). For example, information in the Dangerous Assessment Database helps experts decide whether to release potentially dangerous psychiatric patients (Davidson, 1991). This program's statistical information is used to predict the likelihood that a released psychiatric patient would be a danger to society. The database system works by requiring input on 1000 different questions in such areas as family background, childhood behavior, and response to therapy. The information is then weighted for reliability on a scale from unconfirmed reports (at the low end) to certified reports where there have been attempts to corroborate evidence (at the high end). Bias is accounted for by requiring input from the expert assessors to ascertain any underlying factors that might influence judgment (Davidson, 1991).

Databases can also be used for other important concerns, such as helping counselors assess for self-harm and suicidality. There are also computer programs that aid in clinical decision making by presenting a step-by-step sequence of decisions for diagnoses and symptomology (Weinhardt, Mosack, & Swain, 2007). Other uses of technology for assessment purposes include (a) databases for maintaining assessment results such as desktop spreadsheets programs (e.g., Excel or Lotus), (b) mainframe statistical packages (e.g., SAS or SPSS) for recording and analyzing information, (c) assessment programs that incorporate multiple computerized instruments, (d) electronically recorded patient-tracking software with pretreatment and posttreatment measures, (e) computerized biofeedback assessment, (f) video, audio, floppy disk, or CD-ROM to store data, and (g) e-mail and fax to transmit data.

Positives. Barak and Buchanan (2003) described several advantages of using technology for assessment purposes, especially if provided by professionals in combination with ongoing counseling. Computerized testing gives a counselor access to fast, accurate, highly accessible testing and scoring. Because the test is scored electronically the process is nearly errorless. Data are accessible as soon as the respondent finishes the test, and the data are stored in electronic form for easy transfer to a statistical package for analysis or to be incorporated into a databank. The counselor and client have immediate access to instructions, test items, and scoring techniques that can be easily updated as needed. Data from testing can be electronically submitted to a central location so norms can be updated frequently. Testing can be convenient for both counselor and client as tests can be taken at nearly any place, at any time. Assessment and testing can be conducted even when counselor and client are geographically separated by using electronic transfer of data or by using the Internet. Finally, there are no expendable materials, as everything is done electronically.

Negatives. Barak and Buchanan (2003) also noted several disadvantages to using technology in assessments. Many tests put on the Internet may not meet the American Psychological Association's psychological testing standards. Counselors using tests from the Internet often cannot verify the validity or reliability of the tests they are using. In addition, counselors may not be present when testing is conducted and therefore cannot ascertain whether the client understood the test instructions. If the client did not understand the whole test could be invalidated. Often test results and interpretations are not presented with clear explanations for the client. This could be problematic, such as when a client receives a low IQ score or has been assessed in a negative way. The counselor also has no way to verify that the client actually took the test or had an accomplice take the test for him or her.

In addition, computer software packages that help with data collection, assessment, and interpretation of tests are imperfect. Computer-generated interpretations of assessment inventories may not be correct or may not consider individual client circumstances. Software can become corrupted and information can be lost. Counselors can become lackadaisical and overly dependent upon computers to perform tasks.

Ethical Concerns.   Relatively little is known about the efficacy of online assessment (Barak & Buchanan, 2003). Therefore, the ethics of using technology for assessment represents an issue of broad concern. One of the most commonly defined problem areas is the reliability and validity of online "tests." These measures are often developed by individuals who do not have adequate training in the areas of validity, reliability, and test construction or an awareness of other psychometric issues related to the use of assessments online (Barak & Buchanan, 2003).

Paper-and-pencil tests formatted for the Internet may not retain their psychometric properties. Changing the test format to fit electronic needs may compromise an otherwise acceptable test. Just because the original test had good reliability and validity does not mean that integrity is maintained when changes are made to provide the test in electronic form. It would be prudent for a counselor to seek information regarding these concerns for any test conducted electronically. Some tests are available from large testing companies such as the Strong Interest Inventory, the Myers-Briggs Type Indicator, and the Self-Directed Search. These companies provide counselors with the online validity and reliability information (Barak & Buchanan, 2003).

In addition, clients need to understand the limits of confidentiality for online tests. They should know when they are using tests offered from unreliable sites or that the tests are exploratory in nature. Results should be presented as hypotheses because of the invalid nature of most online assessments (Barak & Buchanan, 2003; O'Halloran, Fahr, & Keller, 2002).

The security of data transmission and storage of electronic information is another commonly defined problem area. It may be difficult to verify the authenticity of electronic information (e.g., fraudulent transcripts or inaccurate Internet data) (Barak & Buchanan, 2003). Testing conducted via the Internet may have data collected by the Web site controlling the test (Barak, 1999), and these Web site owners are not held to any ethical standards.

Technological Aids for Client Interventions

Computers and the Internet have become a well-used resource for counselors in many areas of their professional duties. Many counselors have found an endless source of inspiration and resources for interventions from online sources. Zack (2003) noted that the Internet and computer software applications provide counselors with a way to use printed materials therapeutically with clients because of the ease of document sharing. Desktop publishing, paint, and animation software have been used to enable clients to draw for art therapy or find new ways to express themselves. Some software can even be used to help clients create dramas, complete with set design, wardrobe, and scripts. Online, therapists can find endless resources, possibilities, and materials.

In a review of the technological advances in online psychotherapy, Castelnuovo, Gaggioli, and Fabrizia (2003) noted the potential utility of shared hypermedia as a tool for online counseling. Shared hypermedia refers to Internet-based links that are used to present and retrieve multimedia information. Hypermedia includes numerous multimedia formats, such as visual, music, and animation. According to Castelnuovo et al. (2003), the integration of various media can enhance the client's experience because it creates a "virtual therapist's office." A device such as an electronic whiteboard allows therapist and client to exchange information in an open channel with both verbal and nonverbal language. For example, the therapist can use the electronic whiteboard to enhance explanations with diagrams and text the client can see and react to via text chat or videoconferencing technology.

Positives. The Internet makes it possible for counselors to access many free materials that might otherwise be cost prohibitive for their counseling practice. In the expressive domain, with paint and art programs, computer-animated skits that can be created, or puppets that can be downloaded and colored, a multitude of possibilities exist. All of these ideas can be used to aid a child or adult in greater expression of emotion or concerns or in the practice of new skills. Scenarios can be created, and clients can use these programs like role play to work through issues. Although computer software can be expensive, once bought, a program becomes an inexhaustible resource that the counselor can use with clients repeatedly. In addition, many programs have printable materials that can be given to a client. The counselor does not have to buy these materials redundantly but can simply print them from the software program as needed.

Negatives. These materials are all supplemental, and not many negatives are associated with them. However, some software programs are expensive, and Internet sites come and go. A counselor may find a site that fits his or her needs perfectly and then find it discontinued.

Ethical Concerns. Counselors need to be careful that the materials fit the client's needs and will be therapeutically beneficial. If the counselor becomes adamant about using materials from the Internet and selects materials that are not appropriate for the client's issue simply because the counselor is excited about using technology, or if the counselor insists upon using these materials even though the client does not want to use them, then there are ethical problems. Counselors must not to be blindsided by the excitement of using technology and use materials that does not therapeutically benefit the client.

Technologically Based Resources for Counselors and Clients

Today, research and informational resources are as close to the counselor and client as a mouse click. The Internet has created many sources for counselors to learn about counseling research and obtain information to help their clients. Counselors can access professional journals, professional organizations (e.g., the American Counseling

Association, the American Psychological Association), and electronic databases containing psychological research articles.

Online Databases

Many counseling journals are offered through online databases either free or for a cost. A counselor can type in search terms and gain access to every article listed within that database pertaining to that subject. Numerous online databases offer journals that provide hundreds of full-text articles available to print, save on disk or hard drive, or e-mail. One such database is PsycINFO, which contains more than 2.3 million records and covers 2,150 journal titles (PsycINFO Database Information, 2007).

Counselors can access the latest information on nearly any counseling topic. Most university and public libraries subscribe to databases that provide access to these professional journals, newsletters, and magazines at no cost to the user as long as that user belongs to that institution. A counselor who is not affiliated with an institution can usually subscribe to databases for a fee.

Many of the online journal databases simply offer an electronic version of the hard-copy journal article. A counselor who prefers to can still go to the library and access the same article on the shelf. One example of a hard-copy publication offered in electronic form is the American Counseling Association's *Counseling Today* (see http://www.counseling.org/publications/counseling today.aspx for more information).

More frequently, journals have no hard-copy equivalent and are available only online in electronic form. Two examples of these are the e-journals and h-journals. Members of the American Counseling Association may be familiar with one e-journal, the American Counseling Association's eNews. This is a news and practice bulletin made available to subscribers. E-journals are accessible online or are e-mailed directly to the subscriber.

The h-journals, on the other hand, are hypermedia journals that appear only online. As per their name, hypermedia journals generally have audio or video clips within the article and hyperlinks to take a reader to other sites for additional information (Castelnuovo, Gaggioli, & Riva, 2003). In addition, many of the reference articles have links so a reader can access and read them immediately. (See the *Journal of Technology in Counseling* (*JTC*) for an example of this type of h-journal.)

Information Services and Forums

The Internet houses a plethora of information to aid both counselors and clients. Sites that cater to the public usually do not expect the user to have experience or training and are more user-friendly than those catering to the professional. Some Web sites are collection points of information to help clients find counselors in their communities who specialize in that client's particular issue or concern. For example, sites such as the Psychologist USA Directory offer links to psychologists anywhere in the country (Zuckerman, 2003).

Other sites cater to the professional and expect a certain level of education and prior training when accessed. Numerous Web sites provide information on etiology, medications, the latest therapeutic treatments, and ways for the counselor to help a client cope with a variety of mental health disorders (Zuckerman, 2003). For an example of one of these types of sites, see the online dictionary of WebMD (http://www.webMD.com). In addition, counselor information forums such as PsychNet are a valuable resource for counselors that offer a great deal of information and services for subscribers (Schneider, Wantz, Rice, & Long, 2005), including:

1. Information on licensure requirements by individual state
2. Bulletin boards to provide access to consultants, equipment, private practices for sale, job openings, and the like
3. Access to computer services, computer consultants, and computer shareware
4. Opportunities for earning continuing education units through online courses, as well as information about continuing education courses, seminars, and workshops held elsewhere
5. Access to database libraries such as Knowledge Index and PsychSearch
6. Upcoming events notification and calendar
7. Access to financial services (e.g., electronic insurance billing, malpractice insurance, collection services)
8. Listings of employment opportunities and job openings by state.
9. Psychological testing with results returned by e-mail
10. Access to a psychopharmacology database and a forum where counselors can ask questions and receive answers
11. Access to a research grants database that lists grant opportunities
12. Access to special interest groups such as feminist psychology or psychology and the law

PsychNet offers more services too numerous to mention here, but this list gives a sense of what a valuable resource these information services and forums can be to a counseling practitioner or educator. However, often these types of services are membership driven, and when membership lags, information may not be updated in a timely manner.

Virtual Self-Help Groups

The Internet is an enormous resource for clients. Zuckerman (2003) reported finding 6700 mental health self-help sites online. Virtual self-help groups conducted online through chat rooms or e-mail can support individuals seeking change by providing guidance, assessment of the problem, evaluation of the severity of the problem, information on the background and development of the issue at hand, suggestions for change, and aid in goal setting (Buchanan & Coulson, 2007; Strom, Pettersson, & Andersson, 2004). A site might also suggest books, videos, or other instructional materials to help an individual work through his or her issue(s) (Bellafoire, Colon, & Rosenberg, 2003).

There are also sites online developed by individuals who have faced an experience such as abortion, have dealt with an illness such as AIDS, or have disorders such as anxiety or depression. Such sites are not professional, but conversing with others with the same issue(s) can give clients additional emotional support and information, and they can be accessed 24 hours per day (Anderson et al., 2006; Kalichman et al., 2006). Some sites offer virtual communities where people with like issues, such as addiction, can exchange ideas, information, and coping mechanisms by posting messages on electronic bulletin boards or by sending e-mail (Buchanan & Coulson, 2007).

Positives.   Many resources available online or through computer software can be downloaded and printed. Internet research is easier than ever with easy-to-use search engines and hypertextual indexed links that allow counselors and clients to access information on nearly any topic, within seconds, at any time, and in relative privacy. Professional counseling and psychology information banks are generally an accurate, easily accessed, frequently updated resource that can be used by counselors and clients alike. Counselors can research information on specific disorders, access the most current journal articles regarding treatment or theory, or converse with supervisors or colleagues, all from the convenience of home or office.

Negatives.   It is not always easy to ascertain the accuracy of information on the Web (Zuckerman, 2003). Both counselors and clients are cautioned to use information from authentic sites such as the American Counseling Association or the American Psychological Association to be certain information is correct and updated regularly. Many Web sites are individually owned and operated and are not peer reviewed or authenticated. The Internet is not a stable entity and is subject to rapid change and a lack of uniformity. Web sites may change addresses, shut down, or change contents (Zuckerman, 2003). Material may fail to download or may not be credible. However, Web sites that have the endings .gov, .edu, and .org generally are more reliable because these endings denote government, educational, or professional organization Web sites as authorized by the Internet Corporation for Assigned Names and Numbers (Gale & McKee, 2002).

Online professional journal databases are generally reliable and accurate, but unless a counselor has access to them free through an organization, the subscription cost could be prohibitive. Therefore, access to peer-reviewed sources of counseling research may be limited. Even if counselors belong to the American Counseling Association and have access to that organization's database, their access is limited to American Counseling Association journals. By comparison, many universities give students and faculty access to many different databases, each of which provide access to 10 to 50 journals.

Ethical Concerns.   Counselors must verify that information they receive or use is correct. Checking information found on the Internet with journal sources is prudent unless it is from a recognized professional source such as the American Counseling Association or PsychNet or accessed through a university or other reputable organization's database.

Client–Therapist Referrals

Technology has aided in the referral process for both counselors and clients. Today, there are many Web sites designed to provide information and guidance to individuals as to whether they should seek counseling. Sites such as the American Psychological Association's "Talk To Someone Who Can Help" (http://helping.apa.org) offer information about how counseling can help and what counseling modality works for different issues, as well as information that will aid people in counseling decisions.

Other sites such as Psyfidential (http://www.psyfidential.com) enable the consumer to enter geographical information, preferred counseling modality, and counselor practice specialties and then receive a list of counselors who meet those specifications from which the consumer can choose. These sites perform a service to both clients and counselors by providing resources and information that generate the best match.

In addition, many counselors advertise online through Web sites. A general search for "counseling" or "counselors" gives a consumer multiple listings from which to choose. Information on these sites generally includes counseling modality, counselor specialties, location of the office, contact information, operating hours, services provided, and fee schedules. Most of these sites provide the consumer with an e-mail address through which a potential client can converse and ask questions.

Positives.   These online referral sources can save a client time and provide an efficient method of finding appropriate services. In minutes, a client can enter information and obtain a list of local counselors from which to choose. Counselors can advertise services and provide a client with more information than could be included in a phone book ad. The counselor can also provide intake forms online for a client to fill out and bring to the first session, offer the client the counselor's disclosure statement, or discuss the limits of confidentiality and other pertinent information. Valuable time can be saved if the client has already read and signed these documents prior to arrival for an initial appointment. The counselor can then answer questions and ascertain client understanding once these topics have been introduced.

Negatives.   Not all counselors advertise online, nor will all counselors in a given area come up in a general Internet search. Therefore, only certain types of counselors can be found online to the exclusion of other types, which may limit a client's choices. In addition, often a client really benefits from a face-to-face visit to determine whether he or she can form a strong working relationship with a particular counselor. It is difficult to get a sense of someone from an ad or an e-mail conversation.

Ethical Concerns.   Clients might provide too much information on Web sites and compromise their confidentiality. Clients are cautioned when filling out online assessments for counselor referral to provide neutral information. In addition, counselors using these Web site referral mechanisms need to make sure the information being provided to potential clients is valid and accurate. It is unethical to represent oneself falsely. A counselor who has someone else design his or her web page needs to make sure there are no errors in representation. Counselors need to frequently update their Web sites or referral information to make sure their specialty areas, level of education, counseling modalities, and training are reflected accurately.

Technology in Counselor Supervision

Counseling students have long used some means such as audiotape and videotape to record their sessions for later perusal by their supervisor (Daire & Rasmus, 2005; Newman & Abney, 2005; Rosenberg, 2006). These forms of technology have been beneficial, but the counseling session is already over before the supervisor gets a chance to view the work that has been done—unless, of course, the student is getting live supervision. Live supervision can be provided when (Layne & Hohenshil, 2005; Rosenberg, 2006; Wood, Miller, & Hargrove, 2005):

- A supervisor views the session via one-way mirror.
- A supervisor uses the "bug in the ear" (e.g., supervisor uses a radio transmitter while the supervisee has an earphone).
- A supervisor uses the "bug in the eye" (e.g., computer screen is placed in the therapy room where the counselor can view it, but not the client).
- A supervisor uses a telephone to transmit feedback and suggestions.

Many universities use such one-on-one live supervision (Daire & Rasmus, 2005; Rosenberg, 2006). However, newer approaches eliminate the "bug in the ear," which can be highly disruptive to student trainees, and utilize instead networked computers which allows the supervisor to type in messages that can be viewed on the trainee's computer screen (Daire & Rasmus, 2005; Rosenberg, 2006). Some systems, instead of using text messages, simply present the trainee with a graph line on a computer monitor located behind and above the client's head. The graph line represents the trainee's counseling behaviors or techniques. The supervisor can indicate a trainee's performance simply by moving the graph line up or down.

Even though the VCR seems near extinction as a supervision tool because of more technological advances, the VCR has not been replaced; rather, this technology has been enhanced to include dual-track recording that allows a supervisor to record his or her own comments on the videotape track while the session's original soundtrack is preserved on the original tape (Rosenberg, 2006). This can also be done with new enhanced computerized digital recording techniques (Newman & Abney, 2005). When the counselor in training plays back the enhanced version, the supervisor's comments are superimposed on the soundtrack over and above the student's and client's voices. This technique is especially useful in distance supervision, where student and supervisor are not viewing the tapes together.

Other ways old technology has been improved for supervision include enhanced observation labs that provide a camcorder and VCR, an intercom system, and a master video monitoring system that enables a supervisor to view several counseling sessions simultaneously. This system enables simultaneous live supervision of multiple students (Braggerly, 2002). Enhanced features allow the supervising professor to increase the audio sound for one individual room, use the intercom system to intervene if a problem develops that needs immediate attention, or to alert all students to important information, such as time remaining for the session.

One exciting innovation takes this concept one step further and uses webcams on the student trainee's computer. For example, Michael Armendariz at New Mexico State University implemented a program in that university's counseling center for practicum students and interns. Counselors in training use these webcams to record counseling sessions or transmit the session live via the Internet to the supervisor's office computer. This technology allows the student immediate feedback during and after a session as well as immediate intervention from the supervisor should client or counselor safety become compromised. In addition, these digitized images can be saved for later viewing with the student.

Computers are also used in training by providing counselors with interactive, multimedia simulations of counseling sessions in which the trainee can practice when a "live" client is not available or when counselors want to practice skills for crisis situations (Schneider et al., 2005). For example, the computer simulation can be a scenario of a suicidal client. Students can then practice their skills without risking the safety of a real client. Apple's iMovie and Microsoft's Movie Maker 2 can easily be used to create these simulations (Newman & Abney, 2005).

WebCT can be used in counselor supervision for (a) posting course syllabi and calendars, (b) posting the practicum training handbook, (c) posting supervision seminar topics and relevant readings, (d) providing access to many sources of information, (e.g., home pages of ACA, NBCC, and CACREP and mental health resources), (e) easy submission and review of student journals, (f) management of supervisor–student dialogues through discussion threads and/or a chat room, (g) enhance communication among students, (h) an electronic method for student evaluations of supervisors and sites, and (i) a format for submission and review of e-portfolios (Trolley & Silliker, 2005). Digital counseling portfolios can contain a variety of multimedia artifacts such as counselor-made materials, digital photographs, student assessments, videos of classroom experiences, guidance plans, statements of philosophy, research projects, and anything else that represent a student's accomplishments (Butler & Constantine, 2006)

Technology has also made supervision easier for counselors who are not in university training programs. Often counselors who have already graduated from their counseling programs and are licensed or certified find themselves in need of supervision. Ethically, when working with a counseling issue or an ethnic population for which the counselor has not previously worked, supervision or referral is warranted. A counselor who wants to add a specialization or counseling modality or work with a diverse population will need someone trained in that area to supervise him or her until that counselor reaches a level of competence in the new area.

Technology also allows for supervision to occur even when the supervisor and supervisee are not in the same location. For example, Stamm (1998) discussed a case study of distance supervision conducted by the Veterans Affairs Cooperative Study Program. In this study, supervisors from three sites in various states supervised counselors in 10 sites from several other states in a supervisor–supervisee ratio of 20:1. All supervisees were located some distance from the supervisor location, and supervision was conducted via audiotape, videotape, weekly telephone conversations, and e-mail. A third of the way into the study, the following transmissions were counted between supervisor and counselor: 20,000 e-mails, 1800 hours of individual phone supervision, 500 hours of group phone consultations, 450 secured fax information forms, 10,000 hours of audiotaped sessions, and 3500 hours of psychotherapy videotape. Supervision conducted in this manner was deemed a success establishing that supervision, like counseling, can be done from a distance (Stamm, 1998; Wood et al., 2005).

Positives.   One benefit of using the Internet and other technology for supervision is that the counselor and supervisor do not have to reside nearby. This opens up many possibilities for counselors when choosing a supervisor. The positive attributes for audio, video, or digital taping of sessions offer a high level of accuracy of observation, provide the supervisor a high level of objective detail regarding client–counselor interaction, and give accessibility of reflection for the student (Newman & Abney, 2005). In addition, telecommunication applications make it possible to offer students a variety of instructional formats (e.g., e-mail, web resources, power point slides), that may enhance the supervisee's learning experience (Wood et al., 2005).

Negatives.   There may be instances when a counselor needs a supervisor to be accessible in person, such as during a client crisis. Distance supervision would make this difficult. Supervisors must also be cognizant of how technology-mediated communication may differ from face-to-face supervision and how that difference might affect the work they do (Wilczenski & Coomey, 2006). Depending on the type of technology used, visual and social cues may be compromised or omitted from verbal exchanges (Miller, 2006). Another negative associated with videotaping, audiotaping, and digital recording of sessions is that equipment can fail. Tapes can be accidentally erased or be "eaten" by the VCR or audiotape players, and computers can be corrupted by viruses that compromise hard drives and disks (Wood et al., 2005). Tapes can also be misplaced or lost, which compromises client confidentiality. Bug-in-the-ear and bug-in-the-eye technology can also have some disadvantages: (a) It can disrupt the flow of the session, (b) the client may feel uncomfortable, (c) the supervisee may be unduly distracted, (d) the supervisee may become dependent on the intervention of the supervisor, and (e) live supervision for providing feedback may potentially interrupt and prevent a trainee's analytical efforts, thus aborting the development of critical thinking and comprehensive problem-solving skills (Rosenberg, 2006).

Ethical Concerns.   Both counselor and supervisor need to show care in avoiding clients' identifying details when communicating via e-mail or the Internet in order to protect client confidentiality (Wood et al., 2005; Wilczenski & Coomey, 2006). E-mail is often not secure, although we might think that it is. When we have to provide a user identification and password to access it within our own office or home, we can become lulled into a false sense of security. Many counselors try to offset risk by providing a disclaimer on e-mail transmissions warning of the confidential nature of the communication such as the following:

> The information contained in this email message may be privileged, confidential, and protected from disclosure. If you are not the intended recipient, any dissemination, distribution, or copying is strictly prohibited. If you think that you have received this email message in error, please reply to the sender to that effect.

However, such a disclaimer does not erase the damage done to a client if pertinent or identifying information about a client falls into the wrong hands.

Counselor Education and Continuing Education

Online education is rapidly increasing, and current estimates are that more than 7 million people are educated online each year (Glass, Daniel, Mason, & Parks-Savage 2005). The American Council on Education (ACE) has recognized at least 300 distance learning programs offered by education institutions, including some prestigious ones such as Stanford, Purdue, and Duke (Glass et al., 2005), and more than 900 educational institutions within the United States offer full-degree programs (Carlson, Portman, & Bartlett, 2006).

More and more counselor education programs are using technology in the classroom or are considering some aspect of distance learning to educate future counselors. Technology can be used in counselor learning for a variety of applications (Glass et al., 2005). For example, Aaron Rochlen at the University of Texas at Austin designed an interactive Web site to serve as an adjunct to classroom instruction. It allows students to practice the application of theory and case conceptualization (Hall, 2005). Gale et al. (1995) developed the "group support system," an electronic dialogue that allows students to brainstorm about a client and share feedback on clinical videotape while preserving the anonymity of the responders. Some of the software and programs that can be used for distance learning and student enhancement include (a) e-learning platforms such as Web Course Tools (WebCT), Blackboard, and FaBWeb; (b) macromedia web-design programs such as Director, Authorware, Dreamweaver, Fireworks, and Coursebuilder; (c) Listserv programs, bulletin boards, shared whiteboards, and interactive television; (d) information available on the Internet; (e) departmental and program web pages, (f) Power Point lectures, (g) digitized portfolios, (h) online libraries, (i) electronic journals, (j) CD-ROM databases, and (k) e-mail discussion groups (Glass et al., 2005; Schneider et al., 2005; Wilczenski & Coomey, 2006).

A review of the research literature regarding the efficacy of distance learning indicates (Bernard et al., 2004; Jones & Karper, 2000; Woodford, Rokutani, Gressard, & Berg, 2001):

- Distance education is as effective as traditional face-to-face instruction as long as the method and technologies used are appropriate to the instructional tasks, student-to-student interaction is available, and instructor feedback to students is timely.

- Distance education is effective as long as effectiveness is measured by the achievement of learning, by the attitudes of students and teachers, and by return on the investment.
- The instructional format is not important as long as all students have equal access to resources and the delivery technology is appropriate to the content taught.

Positives.   There are many benefits for counselors who engage in distance learning, whether in fulfillment of their CEUs or to further their education. Counselors who live in rural areas can easily access educational materials through accredited programs that will fulfill their educational requirements (Kua & Srebalus, 2003; Stevens, Dobrovolny, Kent, & Shulman, 2003). Counselors can take advantage of course offerings via computer from prestigious institutions such as Stanford or Duke or from many countries around the world where it is offered: China, most of Europe, Austria, Canada, Israel, the Sudan, Ethiopia, Kenya, Zambia, India, and most of Latin America (McFadden, 2000).

When the distance educational course offers asynchronous instruction, the counselor can access materials, complete tests, and send in papers at any convenient time. This gives the counselor a lot of flexibility to work pertinent classwork into his or her schedule. Sometimes counselors are in need of CEUs and have tight schedules. They may be forced by time constraints to choose educational opportunities that fit a certain time frame or geographical location. Distance learning frees the counselor from these constraints and allows him or her to choose where and when he or she receives instruction.

Negatives.   Technology is not foolproof. Internet servers go down. Computer viruses wreak havoc. Although most students and instructors today are computer literate, some are not (Carlson et al., 2006; Wolf, 2003). Older students and instructors who did not grow up in the computer age might have a disadvantage, and some critics state that the advance of technology has forced educators to design curricula that focuses more on teaching technology and less on critical thinking or counseling skills (Glass et al., 2005).

In addition, students may theoretically have the same access to class materials, but one student might be able to utilize materials more easily or effectively than another. When this is the case, it becomes difficult to ensure the criteria of equal access. The interpersonal dynamics between teacher and student can be different in a face-to-face setting than in distance education settings, which may have an impact on instruction. For example, students may have less opportunity to ask questions in a distance format. Student-to-student interaction may also be limited, and students may censor their communication because it is recorded or because it is depersonalized. And instructors may have difficulty assuring the student is actually the person who did the work (Wilczenski & Coomey, 2006).

Ethical Concerns.   Counselors need to be aware of classes offered online and make sure the National Board of Certified Counselors (NBCC) recognizes them for CEUs. There are many unaccredited classes offered online as well as those that meet NBCC standards for continuing education (Sands, 2000). As always, it is a "buyer beware" market, and counselors considering distance learning as a method of meeting educational goals should check with the appropriate licensing or credentialing agency to make sure such classes meet requirements. Many online classes advertise if they meet CEU requirements, and if so, for which groups (e.g., social workers, psychologists, counselors). Do not make the assumption just because CEUs are offered that they meet NBCC criteria or that they are for your profession rather than another. Many professions require continuing education, and not all credentialing or licensing agencies agree on what is appropriate for continuing education.

Technology-Aided Counselor Communication

Technology has also enhanced counselor communication. Counselors have been using technology to communicate for decades via the telephone and, more recently, facsimile machines, but through computer technology and the Internet, communication between client and counselor or between counselor and supervisor or colleague has never been faster or more efficient.

Electronic Transmission and Storage

Computers can be linked into vast networks in which files and information can be shared and accessed by any individual within the network who holds the proper password. Electronic mail can be sent and received in mere seconds anywhere in the world, as opposed to the several days it takes to send a paper letter through the U.S. Postal Service (also known as snail mail). Some organizations even allow clients and counselors to make and cancel appointments via e-mail or a Web site on the Internet.

In addition, information can be put onto a 3.5-inch floppy disk to be stored or mailed. CD-ROM drives can save entire filing cabinets full of information that normally take up an inordinate amount of office space and contain it all in an area approximately 6 inches by 3 inches (CD-ROM Record Storage, 1995). When needed, this information can quickly be uploaded onto the computer screen and then e-mailed anywhere in the world.

Listservs

Counselors can also use e-mail discussion lists to communicate and receive information (Schneider et al., 2005). To subscribe, an e-mail is sent to the listserv master and then the subscriber is added to the list. Once a counselor is added to the list he or she can send and receive messages to and from the entire group. Listservs are intended to link like-minded individuals to inform, promote, and stimulate discussion and debate on a particular issue (McFadden, 2000). Normally, these discussions are specific to the users of the listservs. This is a great communication source and allows counselors to consult with colleagues all over the world who hold expertise or knowledge in different specialty areas of interest. Two examples of group specific listservs include CESNET-L for counselor educators and COUNSGRADS for graduate students in counselor education (McFadden, 2000). The American Psychological Association offers a variety of listservs for students, which can be accessed at http://www.apa.org/apags/members/listserv.html.

Synchronous Communication

Communication can also be conducted synchronously. Synchronous communication can be conducted via chat rooms or videoconferencing (Wilczenski & Coomey, 2006). There are two different types of chat environments: text-only and multimedia. Multimedia chat rooms are known as GMUKS (Graphical Multi-User Konversations) in which users choose an actual character to represent themselves onscreen (Sands, 2000), which adds a visual dimension that can mimic physicality and movement and typically is in the shape of animals, cartoon characters, or celebrities. In addition, emoticons can be used to simulate expression. The emoticon is "an ASCII glyph used to indicate an emotional state in an e-mail or transmission." Examples include (Mallen et al., 2005):

1. The smiley face :-)
2. The winking face ;-)
3. The frowning face :-(

For a dictionary of "emoticons" available for online emotional expression, see http://www.computeruser.com/resources/dictionary/emoticons.html.

Videoconferencing is more complicated and costly than mere chat room communication, but enables people to see each other visually. Videoconferencing is the "next best thing to being there" and can be used even when individuals are on opposite sides of the world (Schneider et al., 2005; Trolley & Silliker, 2005). Even though videoconferencing is more expensive than chat room communication, technological advances within the last few years have made the hardware and software to support this medium increasingly economical.

Counselors can use many types of electronic tools for supervision or collaboration purposes (Miller, DeLeon, Morgan, Penk, & Magaletta, 2006). Many of these are free, such as NetMeeting at www.webex.com or the Cu-SeeMe technology mentioned earlier. These applications allow counselors to communicate with both audio and video, exchange graphics on an electronic whiteboard, transfer files, use text-based chat rooms, and collaborate on any Windows-based program.

Computer and Internet technology has even revolutionized faxing through Web sites such as Fax4Free (www.fax4free.com). With this site, a counselor can send faxes to 2,500 cities and 27 countries from their computer free or with minimal charge. In addition, some Web sites can aid in translation when the counselor is working with a client or sending or receiving information in a foreign language. AltaVista has an online language translator (http://babelfish.altavista.com/cgi-bin/translate?) that allows a user to paste in text and choose the appropriate translation. This application will also allow a web address of a foreign site typed into the window and the application will translate the entire web page for the user.

Positives.   When using fax, computer, or Internet-based forms of communication, the sender and receiver can communicate at any time, day or night, without having to synchronize times, as is needed for communicating by telephone. Another advantage is that a person can thoroughly think through a communication before sending it.

These types of communication are also cost- and time-efficient. For example, e-mail is generally free for anyone who has Internet access. A counselor who needs to communicate with many people can send "bulk" e-mail, with no more effort or time required than sending a single e-mail, simply by adding multiple addresses for the recipient. Files can be attached to the e-mail; therefore, long prewritten information need not be typed twice or printed. Huge amounts of information can be sent in this manner, which saves money that would have been spent on postage and handling or on long-distance fees for sending faxes.

Negatives. Most communication via computers, fax, or the Internet must be type-written. This may be a hardship for counselors who do not have typing skills or who are disabled. Written communication cannot convey nonverbal subtleties, such as hand gestures, facial expression, or tone of voice. Some people do not write clearly, and a recipient who does not understand cannot gain clarity without sending another message. Counselors might receive numerous e-mail messages that must be read and perhaps responded to, which can be time consuming. Often, e-mail users get "spammed," the equivalent of receiving online junk mail. It can be difficult to ascertain which communications are "junk" and cannot be discarded until the counselor opens the e-mail. Viruses can also be sent through e-mail via Word attachments that can infect the counselor's computer, causing disruptions and headaches.

Ethical Concerns. There are certain protections in place when using the U.S. Postal Service for communication purposes that are not found when communicating electronically. For example, it is a felony to open another person's "snail mail," whereas e-mail and faxes can be intercepted and read by others with minimal or no penalties. Therefore, as discussed before, confidentiality cannot be guaranteed for electronic mediums (Barnett & Scheetz, 2003). This can cause ethical issues for counselors using this form of communication if they do not take great care to protect the identity of the client.

In addition, confidentiality concerns regarding videoconferencing and other technology have been addressed by the America Psychological Association (APA), the American Counseling Association (ACA), the National Board of Certified Counselors (NBCC), and the International Society for Mental Health Online (ISMHO), all of whom have issued statements about the use of such technology in counseling (Trolley & Silliker, 2005). Contact these organizations or access their Web sites for specific information.

Multicultural Considerations

Chapter 3 of this book provides an excellent overview of multicultural considerations in counseling. An online counselor must be just as aware of the diversity issues represented in this form of counseling as in face-to-face counseling. However, there are a few issues of diversity unique to online counseling worth mentioning, even though very little research has been devoted to these topics related to this modality of therapy

(Skinner & Latchford, 2003; Mallen, Vogel, & Rochlen, 2005; Mallen, Vogel, Rochlen, & Day, 2005).

Although a review of all the unique challenges to multiculturally competent online counseling is beyond the scope of this chapter, one issue that numerous studies have identified as a potential barrier is the lack of cultural identifiers, such as skin color, age, and language, in asynchronous forms of communication (e.g., e-mail, message board) (Skinner & Latchford, 2003; Mallen, Vogel, & Rochlen, 2005; Mallen, Vogel, Rochlen, & Day, 2005). Visual cues have been found to be important to both counselor and client in terms of building trust, rapport, and a therapeutic alliance (Sanchez-Page, 2005).

The absence of these cues may increase some counselors' reliance on stereotypical information in relating to culturally different clients online (Mallen, Vogel, & Rochlen, 2005; Sanchez-Page, 2005). As suggested in Chapter 3, there is danger in assuming that individuals from an ethnic group are all the same. In-group differences suggest a certain level of individuality within groups, and individuals may have experiences that are distinct and hold different attitudes, behaviors, and values than the group. Counselor reliance on stereotypic thinking may alienate culturally different clients and ultimately do more harm than good. In addition, it is well documented that Hispanics and African Americans use the Internet less frequently than do other populations, especially affluent Whites, and there is little research regarding the efficacy of this modality of therapy with these populations (Mallen & Vogel, 2005; Sanchez-Page, 2005).

Summary

Counselors need to build their technological knowledge and skills in order to use these tools in their work. The Association for Counselor Education and Supervision (ACES) has composed 12 counselor education technological competencies that graduates should master before leaving any program (Carrier & Haley, 2006). Technology is advancing so fast that by the time this chapter is in print, parts of it may already be obsolete. There may also be innovations that are not covered in this chapter.

Counselor education programs need to train future counselors to use the technology currently available. Otherwise, these counselors will fall behind other mental health service workers who are using this technology. There is no choice today as to whether a counselor will use technological advances in his or her practice; it is more a matter of which technology the counselor chooses. A new world has opened to counselors within the last few decades, a world that at times can be simultaneously frightening and exciting. There are so many choices to consider, as technology can be utilized in some form or another to aid nearly every aspect of a counselor's work. Counselors need to think about the benefits, the drawbacks, and the ethical considerations when implementing technology into their work.

The following Web Sites provide additional information relating to the chapter topics.

USEFUL WEB SITES

ABC's of Internet Therapy
http://www.metanoia.org/imhs/issues.htm

ACES Technology Interest Network: ACES guidelines for online instruction in counselor education
http://filebox.vt.edu/users/thohen/THOHEN/acesweb/

Counseling Center Village
http://ccvillage.buffalo.edu/ccv.html

Electronic Journals and Newsletters
http://gort.ucsd.edu/newjour/j/

John Grohol's Psych Central
http://psychcentral.com/

Index of e-mail therapy providers
http://www.metanoia.org/imhs

International Society for Mental Health Online (ISMHO)
http://www.ismho.org

Internet Mental Health
http://www.mentalhealth.com/

The *Journal of Technology in Counseling* (*JTC*)
http://jtc.colstate.edu

Mental Health InfoSource
http://www.mhsource.com/

Mental Help Net
http://www.mentalhelp.net

Mental Health Resources
http://mentalhealth.about.com/mbody.htm

Mental Health Sourcebook Online
http://mentalhelp.net/selfhelp/

Metanoia
www.metanoia.org

Michael Fenichel's Current Topics in Psychology
www.fenichel.com/Current.shtml

National Board of Certified Counselors Web Ethics
http://www.nbcc.org/webethics2

National Institute of Mental Health (NIMH)
http://www.nimh.nih.gov/

Online Dictionary of Mental Health
http://human-nature.com/odmh/

Psychologists USA Directory
www.psychologistsusa.com

Resources for Mental Health Professionals
http://www.pohly.com/admin_mh.html

SAMHSA's National Mental Health Information Center
http://www.mentalhealth.org

Specifica
http://www.realtime.net/~mmjw/

TelehealthNet
http://www.telehealth.net/index.html

Virtual Reality
http://www.virtuallybetter.com/

REFERENCES

Allen, J. (2004). Applying technology to online counseling: Suggestions for the beginning e-therapist. *Journal of Instructional Psychology, 31*(3), 223–226.

Anderson, G., Carlbring, P., Holmstrom, A., Sparthan, E., Furnmark, T., Nilsson-Ihrfelt, et al. (2006). Internet-based self-help with therapist feedback and in vivo group exposure for social phobia: A randomized controlled trial. *Journal of Counseling and Clinical Psychology, 74*(4), 675–686.

Anderson, P., Jacobs, C., & Rothbaum, B. O. (2004). Computer-supported cognitive behavioral treatment of anxiety disorders. *Journal of Clinical Psychology, 60*(3), 253–267.

Barack, L. (2005). Getting advice through bits and bytes. *School Library Journal, 51*(2), 1.

Barak, A. (1999). Psychological applications on the Internet: A discipline on the threshold of a new millennium. *Applied and Preventive Psychology, 8,* 231–246.

Barak, A., & Buchanan, T. (2003). Internet-based psychological testing and assessment. In R. Kraus, J. Zack, & G. Stricker (Eds.), *Online counseling: A handbook for mental health professionals* (pp. 219–235). San Diego, CA: Academic Press.

Barnett, J. E., & Scheetz, K. (2003). Technological advances and telehealth ethics, law, and the practice of psychotherapy. *Psychology: Theory, Research, Practice, Training, 40*(1–2), 86–93.

Bellafoire, D. R., Colon, Y., & Rosenberg, P. (2003). Online counseling groups. In R. Kraus, J. Zack, & G. Stricker (Eds.), *Online counseling: A handbook for mental health professionals* (pp. 197–215). San Diego, CA: Academic Press.

Bernard, R. M., Abrami, P. C., Lou, Y., Borokhovski, E., Wade, A., & Wozney, L. (2004). How does distance education compare with classroom instruction? A meta-analysis of the empirical literature. *Review of Educational Research, 74,* 379–439.

Braggerly, J. (2002). Practical technological applications to promote pedagogical principles and active learning in counselor education. *Journal of Technology in Counseling, 2*(2). Retrieved June 13, 2007, from http://jtc.colstate.edu/vol2_2/baggerly/baggerly.htm

Brothers, Dr. Joyce (2007). Information Please database. Retrieved June 2, 2007, from http://www.infoplease.com/ipea/A0763051.html

Buchanan, H., & Coulson, N. S. (2007). Accessing dental anxiety online support groups: An exploratory qualitative study of motives and experiences. *Patient Education and Counseling, 66*(3), 263–270.

Buchanan, T., Johnson, J. S., & Goldbert, L. R. (2005). Implementing a five-factor personality inventory for use on the Internet. *European Journal of Psychological Assessment, 21*(2), 115–127.

Butcher, J. N., Perry, J., & Hahn, J. (2004). Computers in clinical assessment: Historical developments, present status, and future challenges. *Journal of Clinical Psychology, 60*(3), 331–345.

Butler, S. K., & Constantine, M. G. (2006). Web-based peer supervision, collective self-esteem, and case conceptualization ability in school counselor trainees. *Professional School Counseling, 10*(2), 146–153.

Cabaniss, K. (2001, Feb. 21). *Counseling and computer technology in the new millennium: An Internet Delphi study.* Unpublished doctoral dissertation, Virginia Polytechnic Institute and State University, Blacksburg.

Carlson, L. A., Portman, T. A. A., & Bartlett, J. R. (2006). Professional school counselors' approaches to technology. *Professional School Counseling, 9*(3), 252–257.

Carrier, J. W., & Haley, M. (2006). Psychotherapy groups. In D. Capuzzi, D. Gross, & M. Stauffer (Eds.), *Introduction to group work* (4th ed.). Denver, CO: Love.

Casper, F., & Berger, T. (2005). The future is bright: How can we optimize online counseling, and how can we know whether we have done so? *The Counseling Psychologist, 33,* 900–909.

Castelnuovo, G., Gaggioli, A., & Fabrizia, M. (2003). From psychotherapy to e-therapy: The integration of traditional techniques and new communication tools in clinical settings. *CyberPsychology and Behavior, 6*(4), 375–382.

Castelnuovo, G., Gaggioli, A. M., & Riva, G. F. (2003). New and old tools in psychotherapy: The use of technology for the integration of traditional clinical treatments. *Psychotherapy: Theory, Research, Practice, Training, 40*(1–2), 33–44.

CD-ROM record storage has two-year payback. (1995, December). *American City & County,* p. 36.

Chang, T. (2005). Online counseling: Prioritizing psychoeducation, self-help, and mutual help for counseling psychology research and practice. *The Counseling Psychologist, 33*(6), 881–890.

Daire, A. P., & Rasmus, S. (2005). A CD-ROM supplement to practicum in counselor education. *Journal of Technology in Counseling, 4*(1). Retrieved May 3, 2007, from http://jtc.colstate. edu/Vol4_1/Daire/Daire.htm

Davidson, C. (1991, November 2). Will computers hold key to mental hospitals? *New Scientist, 22,* 16.

Eleven, R. K., & Allen, J. (2004). Applying technology to online counseling: Suggestions for beginning e-therapists. *Journal of Instructional Psychology, 31*(3), 223–226.

Farrel, E. F. (2005). Need therapy? Check your in box. *The Chronicle of Higher Education, 52*(17), 5.

Gale, A. U., & McKee, E. C. (2002). An information literate approach to the Internet for counselors. *Journal of Technology in Counseling, 2*(2). Retrieved June 13, 2007, from http://jtc.colstate.edu/ vol2_2/gale.htm

Gale, J., Dotson, D., Huber, M., Nagireddy, C., Manders, J., Young, K., et al. (1995). A new technology for teach/learning marital and family therapy. *Journal of Marital & Family Therapy, 21*(2), 183–191.

Glass, M. J., Daniel, D., Mason, R. M., & Parks-Savage, A. (2005). The integration of technology into an online doctoral program in counselor education and supervision. *Journal of Technology in Counseling, 4*(1). Retrieved May 3, 2007, from http://jtc.colstate.edu/Vol4_1/Glass/Glass.htm

Goedert, J. (2003). Is the Internet as good as the couch? *Health Data Management, 11*(2), 14.

Greene, R. T., Lawson, G., & Getz, H. (2005). The impact of the Internet: Implications for mental health counselors. *Journal of Technology in Counseling, 4*(1). Retrieved May 3, 2007, from http://jtc.colstate.edu/Vol4_1/Lawson/Lawson.htm

Grohol, J. (2003). Online counseling: A historical perspective. In R. Kraus, J. Zack, & G. Stricker (Eds.), *Online counseling: A handbook for mental health professionals* (pp. 51–68). San Diego, CA: Academic Press.

Hall, E. M. (2005). Technology in counselor training: An innovative website for building case conceptualization skills. *Journal of Technology in Counseling, 4*(1). Retrieved May 3, 2007, from http://jtc.colstate.edu/Vol4_1/Hall/Hall.htm

Heinlen, K. T., Welfel, E. R., Richmond, E. N., & O'Donnell, M. S. (2003). The nature, scope, and ethics of psychologists' e-therapy Web sites: What consumers find when surfing the web. *Psychotherapy: Theory, Research, Practice, Training, 40*(1–2), 112–124.

Heinlen, K. T., Welfel, E. R., Richmond, E. N., & Rak, C. F. (2003). The scope of WebCounseling: A survey of services and compliance with NBCC standards for the ethical practice of WebCounseling. *Journal of Counseling and Development, 81*(1), 61–70.

Holmes, L., & Ainsworth, M. (2003). The future of online counseling. In R. Kraus, J. Zack, & G. Stricker (Eds.), *Online counseling: A handbook for mental health professionals* (pp. 258–268). San Diego, CA: Academic Press.

Jones, K. D., & Karper, C. (2000). How to develop an online course in counseling techniques. *Journal of Technology in Counseling, 1*(2). Retrieved June 17, 2007, from http://jtc.colstate.edu/vol1_2/online.htm

Kalichman, S. C., Cherry, C., Cain, D., Pope, H., Kalichman, M., Eaton, L., et al. (2006). Internet-based health information consumer skills intervention for people living with HIV/AIDS. *Journal of Counseling and Clinical Psychology, 74*(3), 545–554.

Kirk, J. J., & Belovics, R. (2005). An unofficial guide to online resources for working with older workers. *Journal of Employment Counseling, 42*, 42–66.

Kraus, R. (2003). Ethical and legal considerations for providers of mental health services online. In R. Kraus, J. Zack, & G. Stricker (Eds.), *Online counseling: A handbook for mental health professionals* (pp. 123–139). San Diego, CA: Academic Press.

Kua, Y., & Srebalus, D. J. (2003). The development of a web-based career counseling course. *Journal of Technology in Counseling 3*(1). Retrieved May 3, 2007, from http://jtc.colstate.edu/vol3_1/kuo/Kuo.htm

Layne, C. M., & Hohenshil, T. H. (2005). High tech counseling revisited. *Journal of Counseling and Development, 82*(2), 222–227.

Lee, C. C., & Chuang, B. (2009). Counseling people of color. In D. Capuzzi & D. R. Gross (Eds.), *Introduction to the counseling profession* (5th ed.). New York: Allyn & Bacon.

Lillis, K. (2004). Electronically enhanced therapy. *Health Management Technology, 25*(8), 42.

Litchenberger, E. O. (2006). Computer utilization and clinical judgment in psychological assessment reports. *Journal of Clinical Psychology, 62*(1), 19–32.

Mallen, M. J., & Vogel, D. L. (2005). Introduction to the major contribution: Counseling psychology and online counseling. *The Counseling Psychologist, 33*, 761–775.

Mallen, M. J., Vogel, D. L., & Rochlen, A. B. (2005). The practical aspects of online counseling: Ethics, training, technology, and competency. *The Counseling Psychologist, 33*(6), 776–818.

Mallen, M. J., Vogel, D. L., Rochlen, A. B., & Day, S. X. (2005). Online counseling: Reviewing the literature from a counseling psychology framework. *The Counseling Psychologist, 33*(6), 819–871.

McCarty, D., & Clancy, C. (2002). Telehealth: Implications for social work practice. *Social Work, 47*(2), 153–162.

McFadden, J. (2000). Computer-mediated technology and transcultural counselor education. *Journal of Technology in Counseling, 1*(1). Retrieved June 13, 2007, from http://jtc.colstate.edu/vol1_2/transcult.html

Miller, T. W. (2006). Telehealth issues in consulting psychology practice. *Consulting Psychology Journal: Practice and Research, 58*(2), 82–90.

Miller, T. W., DeLeon, P. H., Morgan, R. D., Penk, W. E., & Magaletta, P. R. (2006). The public sector psychologist with 2020 vision. *Professional Psychology: Research and Practice, 37*(5), 531–538.

Murphy, M. J. (2003). Computer technology for office-based psychological practice applications and factors affecting adoption. *Psychotherapy: Theory, Research, Practice, Training, 40*(12), 10–19.

Myers, J., & Gibson, D. (1999). Technology competence of counselor educators (Report No. EDO-CG-99-8). Greensboro, NC: Counseling and Student Services Clearinghouse. (ERIC Document Reproduction Service No. ED 435 947)

National Board of Certified Counselors. (2001, November 3). The practice of Internet counseling. Retrieved June 12, 2007, from http://www.nbcc.org/webethics2

Newman, J. M., & Abney, P. C. (2005). The use of digital video editing software in microskills based counselor education programs: A technology perspective. *Journal of Technology in Counseling, 4*(1). Retrieved May 3, 2007, from http://jtc.colstate.edu/Vol4_1/Newman/Newman.htm

O'Halloran, T. M., Fahr, A. V., & Keller, J. R. (2002). Career counseling and the information highway: Heeding the road signs. *Career Development Quarterly, 50*(4), 371–377.

Pelling, N. J. (2005). A survey of carer's counseling wants and needs: In person, by telephone, and via the internet. *Journal of Technology in Counseling, 4*(1). Retrieved May 3, 2007, from http://jtc.colstate.edu/Vol4_1/Pelling/Pelling.htm

Powell, D. J. (2005). Trends in counseling challenge profession, but there are positives. *Addiction Profession, 3*(2), 33–37.

PsycINFO Database Information. (2007). American Psychological Association. Retrieved June 11, 2007, from http://www.apa.org/psycinfo/products/psycinfo.html

Rapisarda, C., & Jencius, M. (2005). Using high bandwidth videoconferencing to enhance technology attitudes in students. *Journal of Technology in Counseling, 4*(1). Retrieved May 3, 2007, from http://jtc.colstate.edu/Vol4_1/Rapisarda/Rapisarda.htm

Reese, C., & Stone, S. (2005). Therapeutic alliance in face-to-face versus videoconferenced psychotherapy. *Professional Psychology: Research and Practice, 36*(6), 649–653.

Rosenberg, J. I. (2006). Real-time training transfer of knowledge through computer-mediated, real-time feedback. *Professional Psychology: Research and Practice, 37*(5), 539–546.

Sanchez-Page, D. (2005). The online-counseling debate: A view toward the underserved. *The Counseling Psychologist, 33,* 891–899.

Sands, T. (2000). Student-initiated listservices. *Journal of Technology in Counseling, 1*(2). Retrieved June 13, 2007, from http://jtc.colstate.edu/vol1_2/listserv.htm

Schneider, T. M., Wantz, R. A., Rice, T., & Long, J. A. (2005). Components and implications of distance learning in counselor education: A literature review. *Journal of Technology in Counseling, 4*(1). Retrieved May 3, 2007, from http://jtc.colstate.edu/Vol4_1/Wantz/Wantz.htm

Schultze, N. G. (2005). Success factors in Internet based psychological counseling. *Cyberpsychology & Behavior, 9*(5), 623–626.

Shaw, H. E., & Shaw, S. F. (2006). Critical ethical issues in online counseling: Assessing current practices with an ethical checklist. *Journal of Counseling and Development, 84,* 41–53.

Skinner, A. E. G., & Latchford, G. (2003). International and multicultural issues in online counseling. In R. Kraus, J. Zack, & G. Stricker (Eds.), *Online counseling: A handbook for mental health professionals* (pp. 242–253). San Diego, CA: Academic Press.

Stamm, H. (1998). Clinical applications of telehealth in mental health care. *Professional Psychology: Research and Practice, 29*(6), 536–542.

Stevens, P., Dobrovolny, J., Kent, S., & Shulman, K. (2003). The development of an online graduate counseling course: Time, team, and technology. *Journal of Technology in Counseling, 3*(1). Retrieved May 3, 2007, from http://jtc.colstate.edu/vol3_1/Stevens/Stevens.htm

Strom, L., Pettersson, R., & Andersson, G. (2004). Internet-based treatment for insomnia: A controlled evaluation. *Journal of Counseling and Clinical Psychology, 72*(1), 115–120.

Trolley, B., & Silliker, A. (2005). The use of WebCT in the supervision of counseling interns. *Journal of Technology in Counseling, 4*(1). Retrieved May 3, 2007, from http://jtc.colstate.edu/Vol4_1/Trolley/Trolley.htm

Web tool can help women, counselors, assess domestic violence threat level. (2005). *Campus Crime, 15*(3), 25.

Weinhardt, L., Mosack, K., & Swain, G. (2007). Development of a computer-based risk-reduction counseling intervention: Acceptability and preferences among low-income patients at an urban sexually transmitted infection clinic. *AIDS and Behavior, 11*(4), 549–556.

Wilczenski, F. L., & Coomey, S. M. (2006). Cyber-communication: Finding its place in school counseling practice, education, and professional development. *Professional School Counseling, 9*(4), 327–331.

Wolf, A. W. (2003). Introduction to the special issues. *Psychotherapy: Theory, Research, Practice, Training, 40*(1–2), 3–7.

Wood, J. A. V., Miller, T. W., & Hargrove, D. S. (2005). Clinical supervision in rural settings: A telehealth model. *Professional Psychology: Research and Practice, 36*(2), 173–179.

Woodford, M. S., Rokutani, L., Gressard, C., & Berg, L. B. (2001). Sharing the course: An experience with collaborative distance learning in counseling education. *Journal of Technology in Counseling, 2*(1). Retrieved June 13, 2007, from http://jtc.colstate.edu/vol2_1/Sharing.htm

Young, K. S. (2005). An empirical examination of client attitudes towards online counseling. *CyberPsychology and Behavior, 8*(2), 172–177.

Zabinski, M. F., Wilfrley, D. E., Calfas, K. J., Winzelberg, A. J., & Taylor, B. (2004). An interactive psychoeducational intervention for women at risk of developing an eating disorder. *Journal of Counseling and Clinical Psychology, 72*(5), 914–919.

Zack, J. S. (2003). The technology of online counseling. In R. Kraus, J. Zack, & G. Stricker (Eds.), *Online counseling: A handbook for mental health professionals* (pp. 94–121). San Diego, CA: Academic Press.

Zelvin, E., & Speyer, C. M. (2003). Online counseling skills part 1: Treatment strategies and skills for conducting online counseling. In R. Kraus, J. Zack, & G. Stricker (Eds.), *Online counseling: A handbook for mental health professionals* (pp. 164–180). San Diego, CA: Academic Press.

Zuckerman, E. (2003). Finding, evaluating, and incorporating self help resources into psychotherapy practice. *Journal of Clinical Psychology, 59*(2), 217–225.

PART TWO

Counseling Skills

The responsibilities of counselors, regardless of the setting in which they implement their roles, require that they be competent to provide clients with a variety of services. These services cannot be implemented unless counselors have mastered a number of core knowledge and skills areas. This section provides the reader with an overview and introduction to the counseling skills and associated knowledge base that become the focus of much of the counselor education and supervision experience.

Chapter 7, "Individual Counseling: Traditional Approaches," provides information on approaches to working therapeutically with individual clients, including more in-depth descriptions of differing approaches such as Freudian, cognitive-behavioral, and Rogers's person-centered approach. Mechanisms of change within the individual are discussed, as well as rationales for understanding how individual problems develop. Chapter 8, "Individual Counseling: Brief Approaches," describes and discusses models for brief therapies. This topic is an important one to the role of the counselor, given the impact of managed care and the emphasis on cost containment, and this chapter presents an excellent overview for the beginning professional.

Chapter 9, "Group Counseling," presents the basic components of group counseling, including the history of group counseling, types of group work, qualities of the effective group leader, stages of group life, and common myths that beginning counselors and therapists often hold about the nature of group work.

Counseling as a profession had its roots in the vocational guidance movement of the early twentieth century, and working with career and vocational issues remains a significant part of many counselors' roles today. Chapter 10, "An Introduction to Career Counseling," discusses the different theories and styles of career counseling. It also outlines the stages of career exploration and the tools and interventions that the career counselor can use to assist the client in such a search. The authors describe the major vocational tests that a counselor might use to gain more information about a client's career and vocational needs.

Spirituality counseling is a topic of increasing importance to counselors all over the country, as more and more clients seek the assistance of the professional counselor with issues related to their spirituality. Chapter 11, "Counseling and Spirituality," explores the concept of spirituality in relation to religion, including similarities and

differences. It examines some of the common themes that unite counseling and spirituality and considers how some counseling theorists have challenged that a relationship should exist at all. On the basis of existing research that concludes that spirituality
and religion play an important role in culture, this chapter outlines what competencies
are important for counselors in integrating spirituality into counseling sessions. It
investigates what is important when assessing a client's spiritual domain, including the
critical need to be culturally sensitive. Throughout this chapter, the emphasis is on the
need for counselor self-awareness, including being conscious of beliefs, values, and
biases and the potential impact these issues may have on the counseling relationship.

Chapter 12, "Creative Approaches to Counseling," which describes a number of
alternative approaches to working with clients, is an important chapter. Many of these
approaches are becoming better known because their effectiveness has been demonstrated. Such alternative therapies include music and art therapy, movement therapy,
and the creative use of guided imagery. Such interventions are exciting in the possibilities they present for the counselor wishing to assist clients in self-expression and
personal growth; such approaches are becoming more widely used.

The role of testing and use of assessment instruments within the counseling profession are described in more depth in Chapter 13, "Counseling Uses of Tests." The
author presents a number of key terms and concepts and describes various categories
of tests that a counselor might have occasion to use with a client.

Chapter 14, "Diagnosis in Counseling," provides a comprehensive outline of the
major categories in the *DSM-IV-TR* currently used by the therapeutic community in
providing accurate diagnosis and assessment. The importance of diagnosis to the overall counseling process is described, as well as the benefits and risks inherent in the process of diagnosis.

7 Individual Counseling: Traditional Approaches

BENEDICT T. MCWHIRTER, PhD
University of Oregon

JENNIFER J. MIESCH, MA
University of Oregon

Although the history of counseling and psychotherapy is rich with diverse approaches to understanding and resolving human problems, the primary goal of counseling remains fostering optimal human functioning and development (Walsh, 2003). For the purposes of this chapter, we present three traditional theoretical orientations in counseling that seek to promote psychological healing and well-being (Hansen, 2002). The three approaches we focus on here are the psychodynamic approach that represents psychodynamic theory (Freud, 1915–1917, 1949; see also Kohut, 1985; Novie, 2007; Robbins, 1989; Stolorow, 1992); rational-emotive therapy, as a cognitive-behavioral approach that represents cognitive-behavioral theory (Ellis, 1962, 1995, 2004); and person-centered therapy, an approach to counseling that reflects the humanistic tradition (Rogers, 1951).

Because this chapter is designed to present a fairly simple overview of the three traditional approaches to counseling, you should be aware that our discussion is fairly restricted. Similarly, current meta-analyses of counseling outcome studies show that no particular counseling approach is most effective for all persons (Hansen, 2002). Keep in mind that the objective of counseling and psychotherapy, regardless of the therapeutic approach used, is to benefit the client (Driscoll, 1994), and at the core of any type of counseling approach is the counselor's empathy toward the client (Walsh, 2003). Empathy and involvement are critical both in developing positive therapeutic relationships and in promoting effective outcomes in counseling and psychotherapy (Walsh, 2003).

The field of counseling is constantly being redefined by new findings, changing values, and contemporary issues (Garfield & Bergin, 1994). The human experience is so complex and multifaceted that current literature reflects a strong bias toward "eclectic" or "integrative" models and approaches to counseling, or a "best fit" model, whereby counselors fit interventions to the specific needs and background of each client they work with (Petrocelli, 2002). This assumption suggests that the appropriateness of any particular theoretical orientation or intervention is dependent on the individual client, and it allows the counselor to draw upon a wider range of knowledge, rather than specifying one particular school of thought, in selecting appropriate interventions (Driscoll, 1994). As such, a review of any single theoretical approach or individual strategy, as we do in this chapter, must be read critically and with an understanding of how contemporary literature and practice comment on each of the approaches we present. At the same time, to further assist you in your in-depth study of the three approaches to counseling we discuss here, we have included a suggested reading list at the end of this chapter. In that list, we also present other counseling approaches similar to each of these major approaches. In order to describe the three counseling theories, we begin by taking a look at a client story.

The Story of Rose

Rose is a 23-year-old Mexican American woman in college who entered counseling hoping to deal with a variety of issues that she felt had been getting in the way of her academic success and her ability to have friendships. She expressed the desire to improve her academic and work performance, to choose a career path and a college major, and to improve her self-esteem. She reported being troubled by intense feelings of stress, anxiety, and depression. Rose hoped to decrease what she referred to as her "lazy" behavior, guilt, and feelings of failure; to stop interpreting messages and situations in a consistently self-critical way; to feel more successful in making her own decisions; and to be able to sustain satisfying friendships with peers.

Rose experienced what she called "a pretty good childhood," with all of her material needs met, although she did describe being verbally abused by her parents. She reported feeling guilty "for having any complaints at all when other people have it so much worse." Rose reported that she feels unable to live up to her parents' expectations. She said that her parents immigrated to the United States from Mexico before she was born and "worked very hard to make sure that [she] would have a good life." Both of her parents attended college in the United States and are now teachers, and they expect Rose to be an educator as well. Rose feels unable to live up to their expectations, and because she is not interested in being an educator, she feels paralyzed about making a career decision. Rose reported that "only certain majors and classes are acceptable" to her parents and said that they ask about her grades frequently throughout the term. She said that because they are paying her tuition and living expenses, she feels the need to comply with their wishes.

Rose expressed concern that she has become increasingly self-critical and that she now gives herself the same negative messages that she has heard all her life and still receives from her parents. She feels that no decision she makes is "good enough" for her parents' approval. She reported that she feels inadequate compared with her friends, who she perceives "have their lives together." She also said that she is unable to maintain healthy friendships because she seems to connect only with people who are critical of her lifestyle and choices. She stated that at times she really hates herself and feels like she hates her parents. She expressed strong fears of failure, feelings of guilt about spending her parents' money while not meeting their expectations, and guilt for experiencing feelings of hate toward her parents. She reported frequently skipping classes and work and rarely turning in assignments on time. She expressed frustration with her behavior and said that she feels best about herself when she does meet her responsibilities each day. Rose began counseling with an expressed desire to change or better manage these troubling thoughts and self-defeating behaviors.

Now we turn to the three counseling approaches to discover how each would identify the development of Rose's problems and intervene to modify her affect, cognition, and behavior so that she would be able to lead a more productive and satisfying life.

The Psychodynamic Approach

Most psychological theories have three basic dimensions that involve how a client thinks (cognition), feels (emotions), and acts (behavior) (Worrell & Remer, 2003). Differences among the various approaches to counseling, whether psychodynamic, cognitive-behavioral, or humanistic in orientation, depend on how much emphasis is given to one or more of these areas (Worrell & Remer, 2003). A thorough understanding of these differences is necessary to understand how we as practitioners systematically choose to perceive our clients' behaviors, interpret their experiences, and provide the appropriate intervention to fit their needs. The purpose of this section is to present an overview of psychodynamic psychology and the theoretical constructs that may be useful to beginning therapists. The psychodynamic approach discussed here is not pure Freudian psychotherapy. Although based on traditional psychoanalytic theory, this presentation is influenced by contemporary trends in psychodynamic thought; see Kohut (1985), Robbins (1989), and Stolorow (1992) for excellent discussions on more recent directions in the use of psychoanalytic theory in counseling.

In recent years, many others have expanded the scope of traditional psychoanalytic and psychodynamic theory to include a range of applications. The literature has focused on the overlap between psychodynamic and attachment theories. See Becker and Schmaling (1991) for a discussion about the interpersonal aspects of depression from the two perspectives and Dozier and Tyrrell (1998) for a discussion about the role of attachment in therapeutic relationships. Refer to Lionells (1995) for an overview of some contemporary implications and uses of interpersonal-relational psychoanalysis. See Benjamin (1998) for a discussion of psychoanalysis and feminist theory and Wheeler and Izzard (1997) for their comments on integrating difference (sexual identity, race, and culture) into psychodynamic counselor training. Lanyado and Horne (1999) provide an excellent discussion of the development and practice of psychoanalytic psychotherapy with children and young people. Finally, see Frank (1999) for a discussion on the possibility of a rapprochement between psychoanalysis and cognitive-behavior therapy, grounded in a contemporary relations perspective.

For any theory, examining how and why the theory was developed and to what extent the sociopolitical environment of the theorist's time influenced the theory conceptualization or the theorist's view of human suffering itself is critical to understanding the theory and its limits (Worrel & Remer, 2003). For example, psychoanalysis was born in Europe when Europeans needed a psychotherapy that complemented their view of their often tragic lives (Hansen, 2002). Although this chapter does not focus on multicultural or feminist perspectives, all three counseling approaches in this chapter were originally developed for and by White Europeans and European Americans. In examining research on the effectiveness of psychotherapy, Sue and Constantine (2003) caution practitioners to balance universal findings of a study (i.e., empirical studies using dominant culture populations) with culture-specific findings of a study (i.e., empirical studies using ethnic minority populations) as they relate to optimal human functioning. In other words, in an effort to facilitate human functioning and development among diverse populations, the practitioner must often critically examine and question the appropriateness of the counseling approach they choose and how this fits into the worldviews and life experiences of the diverse clients they serve. Currently, a challenge in the field of counseling and psychotherapy is to examine the effectiveness of various theoretical approaches to counseling with many different populations and cultural/ethnic groups.

Rationale: How Problems Evolve

The psychodynamic approach seeks to explain how an individual's personality expresses itself through the behavior he or she displays in various situations. An individual who is considered to be functioning in a healthy manner possesses a high degree of psychological insight into his or her functioning, and his or her behaviors reflect an increased level of awareness, or consciousness (Gelso & Woodhouse, 2003). Conversely, when an individual's behavior is driven by unrecognized defense mechanisms and levels of anxiety, the individual is often said to be driven by his or her incongruent state of unconsciousness.

The psychodynamic approach stresses the influence of genetic impulses or instincts, the concept of life energy or libido, the influence of the client's life history—psychosexual and psychosocial development—on personality formation, and the irrational, unconscious sources of human behavior (Robbins, 1989). Freud (1949) viewed people as inherently instinctual creatures, driven by their striving for infantile gratification. Throughout life, the individual is strongly motivated to seek satisfaction of one of two primitive instinctual drives: sex and aggression. Therefore, a conflict is engendered between instinctual desires and the control of these emotions that must be maintained in the social world of "reality." To cope with this conflict, defense mechanisms, some conscious and others unconscious, are used that deny, falsify, and/or distort reality. As a consequence, the ego is protected from intrusive thoughts, and instinctual energy or psychic energy is rechanneled into socially approved outlets. However, one's emotional awareness and perceptions of self and others are often inhibited by the defense mechanisms used.

Freud's (1915–1917) conceptualization of the unconscious and different levels of awareness is probably the most significant contribution of psychoanalysis. Freud held that three different levels of consciousness influence personality development and functioning: the conscious, the preconscious, and the unconscious. The conscious level consists of those thoughts the individual is aware of at the moment. The preconscious includes information that can be brought to the conscious level with relative ease. In traditional psychoanalytic theory, the third level of awareness, the unconscious, is the most important component of the mind because it largely determines human behavior but is the most difficult to access.

Some unconscious information cannot readily be brought to the conscious level because it is too anxiety-provoking to one's ego. Indeed, resistance to acknowledging its existence is blocked by employing ego defense mechanisms. For example, a person may truly hate his or her father yet be unaware that these feelings exist and/or unable to accept that they do. In psychoanalytic theory, the importance of these unconscious feelings is that they constantly strive to become conscious, and the individual then expends considerable psychic energy to keep them in the unconscious. Thus, people are in a perpetual state of internal conflict, often unaware of the cause of this struggle to prevent unacceptable, anxiety-provoking feelings and emotions from entering their consciousness.

The conflict at the unconscious level is postulated as an ongoing battle for control of psychic energy among the three structural components of the personality, the id, the ego, and the superego. The id is the original system of personality, present at birth, that is characterized as the primary source of psychic energy (libido) and the place where instincts reside; it is driven by the pleasure principle—an infantile need for immediate gratification. The second structural component of the personality is the ego, which functions to maintain an individual's contact with the external world or reality; it is governed by the reality principle—realistic and logical thinking designed to satisfy needs in a socially acceptable manner. The ego serves as a mediator between the superego and the id. In traditional Freudian theory, the ego is sometimes seen as at the mercy of the other two competing forces. In more modern theory, however, the task of the therapist is seen as helping the ego decide and balance id and superego (Kohut, 1985). The third component of the personality is the superego, the person's moral code of conduct. Analogous to the popular concept of "conscience," the superego results from the social mores and parental moral attitudes that the child internalizes during development.

Anxiety is a state of tension that serves as the motivating force within the person and frequently results from the constant conflict among the id, ego, and superego. For example, negative emotions develop from unconscious memories of past childhood experiences, from frightening impulses driven by the id (such as aggressive desires that may be forbidden), from guilt derived from an overly self-critical superego, or from the inadequacy of the ego in resolving these internal conflicts. Anxiety warns the ego that it is in danger of being overwhelmed; therefore, anxiety may be repressed by the ego defense mechanisms. However, ego defense mechanisms also tend to deny, falsify, or otherwise distort reality (Freud, 1936). Consequently, the individual's personality development is impeded, and realistic problem-solving strategies can also remain underdeveloped.

The complex task of the counselor is to help the client uncover the structure of anxiety of that personality so that reconstruction can begin. Returning to our story of Rose, the psychodynamically oriented counselor believes that the origin and solution to her problems lie deep within her unconscious. For example, her excessive anxiety and depression might well be explained by the conflict between her feelings of anger and resentment toward her parents and her superego, which continues to insist that parents are to be loved, respected, and followed. Her ego defense mechanisms of turning against self and identifying with the aggressor force her to expend considerable energy in hiding the conflicts from her and contribute to her self-defeating behavior.

A primary therapeutic task is to help Rose become more aware of her style of handling her anxiety and the underlying causes of her depression. Subsequently, more personally satisfying and socially approved ways of resolving these tensions and conflicts are discovered that help Rose develop more mature ways to use her psychic energy and to become more aware of problematic behaviors that result from unconscious impulses.

Mechanisms of Change

The goal of psychodynamic counseling with Rose is to make her conscious of unconscious material. Therefore, the counselor's goal is to help the client recognize unconscious personality characteristics that influence consistent behavior patterns across various situations. The two means by which this is done are transference and a working alliance. Gelso and Carter (1985, 1994) provide an in-depth discussion of these components of the counselor–client relationship. The scope of this chapter allows us to explore only briefly here the dynamics and importance of these change processes in psychodynamic theory.

Transference.   Transference occurs when the client reexperiences, in therapy, emotions and attitudes originally present in earlier relationships, often the parent–child relationship (but others as well) and focuses these past feelings and emotional and behavioral reactions on the counselor. In the case of Rose, transference expressed itself in Rose's resistance to counseling, missed sessions, and tendency to explain everything she had not done well during the week. She talked with and made excuses to the counselor as if the counselor would be a disapproving parent. In discussions with her about her early childhood psychosocial development (see Erikson, 1968), it became clear that this aspect of her personality was developed in her relationship with her parents. Eventually, she was able to work through her unresolved conflicts with her parents by means of understanding her transference in the relationship with the counselor.

The counselor interpreted the transference relationship to help Rose understand how she was misperceiving, misinterpreting, and misresponding to the counselor and others as a consequence of the kind of relationship she has with her parents. Talking about transference in the counseling relationship helped her achieve a corrective emotional experience by means of abreaction, or "reliving" the original tension-evoking emotional experience. This "new" emotional experience provided a catharsis—a release of tension and anxiety resulting from the process of bringing repressed ideas, feelings, wishes, and memories of the past into consciousness. Chin (1994) introduced the concept of "hierarchical transference" to describe how clients of color, particularly women of color, might offer deference to the counselor, who is seen as an authority figure. To be culturally competent, a counselor should consider how race and ethnicity could affect the transference relationship.

Working Alliance. The interpretation of the transference experience and Rose's acceptance of it were based on the therapeutic alliance developed between the counselor and Rose. Conceptually, the working alliance construct has its foundation in Freud's emphasis on the client–therapist collaboration in treatment (Connor-Greene, 1993). The primary focus of early writings emphasized the "therapeutic alliance," detailing the client's identification with the therapist and focusing on the more affective aspects of the client's collaboration in therapy. It was not until Greenson's (1967) writings that the therapeutic alliance was more comprehensively described as a working alliance, suggesting that the client's motivation and ability to work in the treatment situation were crucial for treatment success.

A more contemporary conceptualization of the working alliance identifies both the client–therapist relationship and the client's collaboration in the tasks of treatment as central to positive therapeutic outcome (Gaston, 1990; Lambert & Bergin, 1994). In fact, recent empirical work on social perception has recognized the existence and importance of countertransference processes within the therapeutic context (Andersen, Glassman, Chen, & Cole, 1995). Countertransference occurs when a counselor's reaction to her or his client is based on a past conflict with a parent or other significant person (Gelso & Hayes, 1998); that is, countertransference involves the counselor's personal characteristics and their impact on the counseling relationship. Others have suggested that the counselor represents a secure attachment figure for adult clients (Dozier & Tyrrell, 1998; Farber, Lippert, & Nevas, 1995). From the attachment perspective, the counselor provides the client with the secure base necessary for exploring repressed feelings and impulses and bringing them into consciousness. Counselors need to be aware that racial and/or ethnic differences between the client and counselor can also lead to the counselor overidentifying with the client while minimizing cultural and racial differences that are meaningful in the relationship (Chin, 1994).

Bordin (1976) took the working alliance concept out of its psychoanalytic context and reframed it from a more pantheoretical viewpoint. He built on Greenson's (1967) earlier work but separated the working alliance from its attachment to the process of transference. His focus was on the conscious partnership of the client and the therapist working together to bring about change. Although Bordin perceived the working alliance as an integrated relationship, he defined three constituent components that in combination define the quality and strength of the working alliance: tasks (in-counseling behaviors and cognitions), goals (outcomes), and bonds (the complex network of positive personal attachments between the client and the counselor).

Horvath and Greenberg (1989) stated that the significant departure for Bordin (1976) from previous theorists was to conceptualize the client–therapist interdependence along the dimension of mutuality. Bordin's concepts of task, goal, and bond involve collaboration and depend on the degree of concordance and joint purpose between the counselor and client. In other words, the client is much more a problem solver and the counselor becomes more directive in the approach to therapy (Bergin & Garfield, 1994). The counselor and the client agree on which in-therapy and outside-therapy tasks will be helpful in obtaining the goals of counseling. In the case of Rose, the working alliance was nourished by the counselor to facilitate a more positive counseling outcome.

Summary of the Psychodynamic Approach

A counselor using the psychodynamic approach tends to concentrate on the effects of past experience on shaping patterns of behavior through particular cognitions (defenses) and interpersonal styles of interaction and perception (transference) that have become repetitive and that interfere with health (Ursano, Sonnenberg, & Lazar, 1991). In the history of this approach, conceptualization of a dysfunctional personality, or psychopathology, was given the most attention, and methods of treatment were given nominal attention (Gelso & Woodhouse, 2003). In other words, the therapist often spent more time focusing on making the unconscious conscious, rather than other methods (i.e., focusing on client strengths) to effect change. Likewise, what was considered optimal human functioning and development at the time this approach was conceived was originally contrasted against White European males, and so it is essential for the counselor to understand the implicit and explicit limitations of this theoretical orientation when working with other populations (e.g., women, ethnic minorities, gay/lesbian/bisexual/transgendered clients), and how to properly work together with people with very different backgrounds and life experiences. Conversely, to be effective with their clients, counselors using a psychodynamic approach need to recognize that there are intrapsychic forces motivating people that are not entirely conscious. They must understand the significance of childhood experiences and use the concept of transference in the counseling relationship. They need to know how people defend themselves from external and internal threats with ego defense mechanisms and other methods of resistance. Finally, a counselor using this approach needs to effectively create a working alliance that facilitates the counseling process. In so doing, transference dynamics can be interpreted for clients so that they can experience an abreactive catharsis of their debilitating past history.

The Cognitive-Behavioral Approach

The history of cognitive-behavior therapy has evolved through various theoretical positions. Some of the important stages of that evolution include behavior modification (Skinner, 1938, 1953) and its expansion into applied behavioral analysis (Michael, 1991; Morris, 1992) and systematic desensitization (Wolpe, 1982). Each of these approaches represents traditional reinforcement theories whose primary, although not exclusive, focus is to modify observable behaviors without addressing other potential intervening variables.

With the advent of cognitive-behavioral therapies such as rational-emotive behavior therapy (Ellis, 1962, 1995), social learning theory (Bandura, 1977) and social cognitive theory (Bandura, 1991, 1993), cognitive therapy (Beck, 1976), and cognitive-behavior therapy (Meichenbaum, 1977), internal self-regulatory variables became pivotal determinants of behavior. Keep in mind that the list of cognitive-behavioral therapeutic approaches discussed here is only representative and not exhaustive of this broad range of approaches. The emphasis on the cognitively mediated aspects of behavior has facilitated a focus in therapy on client attributions, appraisals, expectations, and belief systems. All of these variables are integral cognitive processes that in their own way influence emotions and behaviors.

Albert Ellis is considered one of the most influential theorists in the field of cognitive-behavioral approaches to counseling. We will use his system of rational-emotive behavior therapy, or REBT (Ellis, 1995, 1999a) (formerly known as RET [Ellis, 1962, 1993a]) to illustrate one cognitive-behavioral approach and will apply REBT in conceptualizing therapeutic interventions for Rose. Ellis has applied REBT to working with elderly people (1999b), treating obsessive-compulsive disorder (OCD) (Ellis & Dryden, 1997), and counseling for stress (Ellis, Gordon, Nennan, & Palmer, 1997). Several contemporary articles and books provide comprehensive illustrations of the practice and goals of REBT (Ellis, 1997; Ellis & MacLaren, 1998).

Rationale: How Problems Evolve

Rational-emotive behavior therapy (REBT), the fundamentals of which were developed by Albert Ellis in 1955, is based on the premise that emotional disturbance has several important cognitive, emotive, and behavioral sources. Although emotional disturbance, or "neurosis," does not develop entirely from cognition or thinking, the etiology of unhealthy behaviors is heavily influenced by the process of an internal dialogue that is negatively affected by the individual's irrational beliefs. According to Ellis, human beings develop strong preferences for achievement, approval, comfort, and health, which are life goals. Because of a human innate propensity to construct absolutist demands, preferences can easily be transformed into irrational beliefs, which are dogmatic "musts," "shoulds," and thoughts that become the standard by which social situations are measured. The interaction between irrational beliefs and social stimuli creates debilitating emotional reactions for the individual. An underlying principle of REBT is that a person feels what he or she thinks (Ellis, 1993a, 1999a).

Rational-emotive behavior therapy is based on a humanist and constructivist approach to conceptualizing human agency (Ellis, 1993c). REBT is concerned with the individual's systemic, phenomenological field and suggests that people strive to achieve life goals that are usually centered on remaining alive and being reasonably happy, such as attaining success, love, and comfort. The path to achieving these goals, however, is regularly blocked by interpersonal or environmental adversities that Ellis calls activating events. Ellis proposed the ABCDE model (Ellis, 1995, 1999a) to describe this process.

During the process of maturation, the individual develops characteristic beliefs (B's) that are used to interpret and take action in response to these adversities or activating events (A's). An individual's belief system consists of rational beliefs, which are preferences that create appropriate emotional and behavioral consequences, and irrational beliefs, which are dogmatic musts and absolutist demands that create inappropriate and dysfunctional consequences. Therefore, cognitive, emotive, and behavioral consequences

(C's) are created by the imposition of the individual's belief system (B's) on the activating events (A's). Thus, when a preponderance of irrational beliefs compared to rational beliefs comprises the individual's belief system, emotional disturbance and unhealthy behaviors will result (Ellis, 1993a).

When RET (Ellis, 1962) was first practiced, an emphasis was placed on ego disturbance—that is, self-induced emotional disturbance created by self-denigrating irrational or illogical thinking. However, it was soon recognized that people also had discomfort disturbance or low frustration tolerance (LFT), again caused by irrational beliefs, that are especially characterized by the individual's belief that other people and external conditions absolutely must be a certain way (Ellis, 1993b). As a consequence, Ellis added to the idea of ego disturbance the idea of discomfort disturbance, or LFT. Throughout his writings, Ellis (1993a) has maintained that ego and discomfort disturbance often occur simultaneously and significantly interact to cause severe neurotic problems.

In short, Ellis (1993a) maintains that emotional disturbance is the result of irrational and illogical thinking that occurs in the form of internalized sentences or verbal symbols that are generated from an irrational system of beliefs. Thus, according to REBT, people are largely responsible for their emotional disturbances resulting from their irrational thinking. Ellis recognized that emotions reflect a complex mode of behavior that is intricately tied to a variety of sensing and response processes and states. Nevertheless, the process of behavior change is built on the premise that people need to change their way of thinking (cognitive restructuring) to correct their irrational belief systems. Therefore, REBT takes an active directive approach in disputing (D) a client's antiempirical and overgeneralized self-statements—the client's irrational beliefs. The objective is "to persuade and teach clients to vigorously, powerfully, and persistently think, feel, and act against their demandingness and to return to their preferences" (Ellis, 1993c, p. 199). Next we consider each of these components of REBT—A, B, and C—separately and how they might relate to Rose's concerns and behaviors. Later in this discussion of REBT, we will discuss the notion of disputing (D) the old belief system and experiencing new behavioral and emotional effects (E) as a result of increased rational thinking.

To be culturally competent, the counselor would have a discussion with Rose about her ethnic and gender identity, culture, and values. It would be important to understand how Rose's cultural values relate to her relationship with her family and her belief system. Interventions have to be culturally congruent for any client, and counselors need to have an understanding of the client's values before making assumptions about what would be considered irrational thinking within the client's cultural context. See Velásquez, Arellano, and McNeill (2004) for a discussion of Chicana/o psychology and mental health.

Activating Event. Usually a precipitating activating event or adversity is what motivates a person to enter counseling. In the case of Rose, her need to decide on a college major brought on a great deal of stress and depression. Her need to make this decision, along with the messages she received from her parents and friends, was an activating event that led Rose to start recognizing how she became paralyzed whenever she had to make an important decision or enter into new relationship. She started to recognize how she was overly self-critical and needed to change her critical self-thought and behavior patterns in her relationships.

Beliefs.   The events that brought Rose to counseling were that she started to become aware that her own emotions, thoughts, and behaviors associated with making decisions kept her feeling paralyzed and contributed to other problems in her life as well. Her system of irrational beliefs about relationships and her negative beliefs about herself led her to feel depressed. Her beliefs were characterized by self-statements such as "If I make a decision that displeases my parents or friends, they will no longer love me." Rose's failure to understand the causes of her problems are what prompted her to begin counseling, where she started working on her beliefs and self-statements and examining their consequences.

Consequences.   For many clients, the negative emotions of guilt, anger, depression, and anxiety are emotional consequences that appear to be directly caused by the activating event. REBT posits that these emotional consequences are actually caused by clients' beliefs about the activating event. In Rose's case, she strongly believed that her feelings of stress, anxiety, and depression were directly related to her need to decide on a college major and not the emotional turmoil in her relationship with her parents. Rose felt that her dreams were repeatedly rejected, and she was indirectly told that she was a terrible person. She communicated these feelings by disclosing in counseling that her parents would not allow her to "stand up for herself" when they were being critical of her. These past events, augmented by similar current events in her life, appear to be at the root of her own belief system about herself and the world around her. But in REBT, it is precisely this belief system that mediates the link between the activating event and the emotional consequence and not just the event itself, such as needing to make a decision. Therefore, REBT focuses on changing a client's system of irrational and illogical beliefs.

Mechanisms of Change

Belief System.   Identifying the client's belief system is a major focus of REBT and a key mechanism of change (Ellis, 1993a). The belief system is the mediating variable between the activating event and inappropriate consequences or emotional disturbance. Because most people draw a direct connection between activating events (A's) and consequences (C's), the main goal of the REBT counselor is to help clients identify their irrational beliefs (B's) and thinking that underlie the emotional disturbance. Ellis (1962) originally identified 10 irrational beliefs that all humans have that inevitably lead to pervasive dysfunctional behavior. Although he later added to the original list of irrational beliefs (Ellis & Whiteley, 1979), Ellis (1993a) has concluded that all these beliefs can be synthesized into three general categories of irrational beliefs, each including a rigidly prescribed must, should, or demand:

1. "I (ego) absolutely must perform well and win significant others' approval or else I am an inadequate, worthless person."
2. "You (other people) must under all conditions and at all times be nice and fair to me or else you are a rotten, horrible person!"

3. "Conditions under which I live absolutely must be comfortable, safe, and advantageous or else the world is a rotten place, I can't stand it, and life is hardly worth living!" (p. 7)

Two main tenets of REBT counseling are to (a) demonstrate to the client that self-talk is a primary source of emotional disturbance and (b) help the client restructure internal sentences to eliminate the underlying irrational beliefs. Rose felt that she had always been criticized and made statements such as "I need to prove to myself that I'm acceptable," and "I'll never be able to make a decision that will be accepted by my parents." Following the two main tenets of REBT, the counselor helped Rose clarify how she perceived events and interpreted others' and her own messages and helped her dispute her beliefs. As a consequence of this process, Rose was able to acknowledge her irrational beliefs concerning her need to be accepted and approved by others in all situations or feel that she was worthless as a person if she did not follow her parents' wishes.

Dispute. The real work of rational-emotive behavioral counseling involves disputing the client's irrational beliefs. The counselor actively challenges the client's existing belief system with the intent of eliminating the irrational beliefs and helping the client develop and internalize a set of more positive and rational beliefs. Therefore, the process of uncovering the illogical, irrational nature of Rose's internal messages was the primary focus of counseling. This is not to say that she should ignore her family and values (such as the importance of honoring her parents) but to identify when her beliefs about these values (she is worthless if she doesn't do what her parents tell her) prevented her from being well. The counselor provided new, supportive, and logical self-statements such as "I can disagree with my parents and still be a good person." As a consequence, Rose began to realize that her self-critical, irrational belief system intensified her depression and anger, which contributed to other problems in her relationships as well. By changing her belief system, she began to recognize more effective and positive ways of seeing herself and of relating with others.

Effect. Changing the client's irrational belief system is not a straightforward process. The focus on disputing irrational beliefs typically produces changes in behavior and diminishes discomfort disturbance but does so over time and as the client is able to integrate new information. Nevertheless, the client is encouraged to notice these changes and to celebrate their emergence. For example, as Rose noticed the cognitive and behavioral changes related to her irrational beliefs, she began to experience a new effect (E) or emotional consequence. Thus, in working with Rose, the REBT counselor would proceed through the process of evaluating and explaining the ABCDEs of Rose's behaviors in order to have her thoroughly incorporate a new rational belief system, while being respecting her cultural and family values.

Summary of the Cognitive-Behavioral Approach

The cognitive-behavioral approach tends to highlight the importance of irrational or dysfunctional beliefs in the creation of emotional disturbance; furthermore, this approach typically uses a range of cognitive, emotive, and behavioral strategies of challenging these beliefs and replacing them with more functional ones (Ellis, 1999b). As such, the basic assumption of the REBT approach to counseling is that most people in our society develop many irrational ways of thinking. These irrational thoughts lead to inappropriate behavior and disturbing emotional reactions that create ego and discomfort disturbance. REBT counseling is structured to facilitate clients' recognition of their irrational beliefs and alter their interpersonal patterns of behavior so that they are based on more functional, logical beliefs. Accomplishing this goal requires an active/directive counselor who is supportive yet actively engages and challenges the client (Ellis, 1993c).

The Person-Centered Approach

Person-centered therapy is one of the major theoretical approaches in the humanistic framework. This approach, developed by Carl Rogers (1951, 1957), has been known during its evolution as nondirective, client-centered, Rogerian, and person-centered therapy. The present use of the term *person-centered therapy* reflects an expanding scope of influence, including Rogers's interest in how people obtain, possess, share, or surrender power and control over others and themselves (Corey, 2005). Indeed, themes embedded in the person-centered approach have been applied to a range of settings, including care of people with Alzheimer's disease (Zeman, 1999), conflict resolution (Joyce, 1995), and therapy in Japan (Hayashi et al., 1998). Other counseling approaches, such as "relationship-centered counseling" (Kelly, 1997), have evolved out of the person-centered tradition. Some of the fundamental assumptions underlying a person-centered approach to therapy have also been examined from feminist (O'Hara, 1996) and multicultural perspectives (Brodley, 1996). Some have suggested that the approach risks "colluding with prevailing oppression and hierarchies if it fails explicitly to challenge implicit power structures within our society" (Hawtin & Moore, 1998, p. 91); others have recommended replacing client-centered counseling with "culture-centered counseling" (Laungani, 1997, p. 343). Some say a humanistic approach to counseling is compatible with multiculturalism when the counselor considers the client's cultural values and these inform different ways of expressing one's individuality (Jenkins, 2001). The person-centered approach to counseling is widely practiced.

Rationale: How Problems Evolve

A central issue in person-centered therapy is how the individual perceives the world. What the individual perceives in his or her phenomenological field is more important than the "actual" reality. In other words, what the individual perceives to be occurring is the reality. Thus, a consistent effort to understand and experience, as far as possible, the unique qualities of each client's subjective world is fundamental to person-centered therapy. The focus is not primarily with past causes of behavior; rather, person-centered therapy focuses on current experiences, feelings, and the interpersonal relationships of the individual.

Person-centered counseling is based on a belief that people act in accordance with their self-concept. One's self-concept is heavily influenced by experiences interacting with others and the environment. For a healthy self-concept to emerge, a person requires unconditional positive regard, such as love, support, respect, acceptance, and nurturing.

Often in childhood, as well as later in life, a child is given conditional positive regard by parents and significant others. In other words, parents and others communicate to the child, either directly or indirectly, exactly what the child must be or how the child must act to receive positive regard. Feelings of self-worth develop if the person behaves in accordance with these prescribed emotional and behavioral patterns because acceptance and approval are thereby achieved. Sometimes, however, children may have to deny or distort their perception of a given situation when their personal needs conflict with the expectancies of someone they depend on for approval.

The individual is thus caught in a dilemma because of the incongruence between personal growth needs and needs for positive regard. On the one hand, if a person does not do as others wish, he or she is not valued and accepted. On the other hand, if a person conforms, he or she disregards personal needs to evolve a self-concept predicated on internally derived goals. In this case, the ideal self that the person is striving to become is thwarted. The larger the discrepancy between the real self and the ideal self, the more incongruence a person experiences. In other words, conflict arises when individuals must choose between personal needs for self-actualization and the approval that significant others provide that is conditional on certain behaviors, thoughts, or feelings.

One's self-concept is a learned attribute, starting from birth and progressively developing through childhood, adolescence, and adulthood. Rose experienced a conflict between receiving positive regard and validation as a child and her evolving experience as a person with unique needs and goals. For example, she received messages from her parents that she should not have to worry about making decisions or learning skills such as time and money management. Her parents communicated, "You don't need to worry about those things; you're still a student." Yet when Rose does not meet her parents' expectations of choosing a major or budgeting money, they become very critical and threaten to stop paying her tuition and living expenses. Her parents send her conflicting messages of "you're our child, we'll take care of you no matter what" and "we'll take care of you only as long as you do what we want." Much of Rose's present negative interpersonal interactions with others reflect a self-concept that has attempted to incorporate messages that she is worthy of love and care only if she does what others expect. This message is contradictory to her need to feel safe, assertive, and protected. Therefore, Rose harbors a great deal of resentment toward her family and toward others who remind her of her family who consistently frustrated her self-actualizing potential. She frequently feels depressed and worthless, submitting to people in current relationships because they "remind" her of her parents whom she was never able to "please."

Mechanisms of Change

Self-Actualization.   Within the humanistic framework, the self-actualizing tendency is the primary motivating force of the human organism. Self-actualization is an inherent tendency in people to move in directions described by words such as *growth, adjustment, socialization, independence, self-realization,* and *fully functioning.* Thus, in the humanistic philosophy that underlies the person-centered approach, humans have an innate capacity to interact with their environment in ways designed to maintain and enhance their self-concept. Rogers (1951) emphasized that the client's natural capacity for growth and development is an important human characteristic on which counseling should focus. For example, in spite of the negative experiences that Rose has had in her life, she has an innate predisposition to be self-actualized. This predisposition can be nourished and drawn out, given a facilitative psychological climate.

Core Conditions for Constructive Personality Change.   In his classic article, Rogers (1957) identified the core conditions that must exist for constructive personality change to occur:

1. The first two persons are in psychological contact.
2. The first, whom we shall term the client, is in a state of incongruence, being vulnerable or anxious.
3. The second, whom we shall term the therapist, is congruent and integrated in the relationship.
4. The therapist experiences unconditional positive regard for the client.
5. The therapist experiences an empathic understanding of the client's internal frame of reference and endeavors to communicate this experience to the client.
6. The communication to the client of the therapist's empathic understanding and unconditional positive regard is to a minimal degree achieved. (p. 96)

Rogers identified three personal characteristics, or attitudes, of the therapist that are essential before a therapeutic relationship can be established: (a) genuineness, or congruence, (b) unconditional positive regard, and (c) empathy. These characteristics offered by the counselor to the client result in a therapeutic climate that allows the client's self-actualizing tendency to flourish. Because of the centrality of their importance to person-centered therapy, we will describe each of these characteristics.

Genuineness.   Genuineness, or congruence, is the counselor's capacity to be "real" in the relationship. Thus, genuineness is used to denote honesty, directness, sincerity, and an absence of a professional façade. Rogers (1961) defines *genuineness* as follows: "By this we mean that the feelings that the counselor is experiencing are available to his awareness, that he is able to live with these feelings, be them in the relationship, and able to communicate them if appropriate. . . . It means that he is being himself, not denying himself" (p. 417). Genuineness, then, is the counselor's ability to be psychologically open and present with the client in therapy. The counselor is "real" in the relationship, demonstrating a consistency between her or his own feeling/experiencing at the moment and her or his verbal and nonverbal communications to the client.

In Rose's case, the counselor's willingness to be genuine in the relationship with her provides Rose with a psychological climate that can be trusted, thereby facilitating her self-disclosure. The counselor's genuineness and openness to being present with

Rose are crucial elements contributing to her change process. They allow her to be real and to come into psychological contact with her counselor, expressing her feelings with the knowledge that she is and will be supported.

Unconditional Positive Regard.   This counselor characteristic has also been referred to as "nonpossessive warmth" and "regard" and is equivalent to respect, appreciation, and acceptance of another person. It can be described as the counselor's ability to experience an acceptance of every aspect of the client's personality. "Nonpossessive" or "unconditional" implies that the counselor does not qualify his or her acceptance of the client but accepts the client fully as a separate person with a right to his or her own thoughts, words, actions, and feelings.

Unconditional positive regard is a crucial component of the counseling relationship with Rose, especially because Rose's self-worth has been validated only when she has behaved in an explicitly defined manner. The counselor offers positive regard with no conditional stipulations. This caring, accepting attitude of Rose's individuality emerges from the belief that she can discover within herself the necessary resources for her own growth. Eventually, Rose will come to understand that she is capable of making decisions that feel congruent.

Empathy.   *Empathic understanding*, or *empathy*, may be defined as an active, immediate, continuous process of living another's feelings, their intensity, and their meaning instead of simply observing them. The accuracy of a counselor's empathic understanding and sensitivity to the client's feelings and experiences, as they are revealed during the moment-to-moment interaction of the counseling session, conveys the counselor's interest in appreciating the client's phenomenological world. The counselor strives to sense fully and accurately the inner world of the client's subjective experience. The concept of accurate empathy, like the other counselor attributes, has evolved over the years in the direction of freeing the counselor to be a more active participant in the therapeutic encounter. High levels of accurate empathy go beyond recognition of obvious feelings to an exploration of and communication about perceptions of underlying client messages.

In one interview, Rose said that her anxiety and feelings of resentment typically drove her to engage in self-defeating behaviors and critical, conditional relationships. Rose expressed how she behaved but failed to indicate her feelings about the consequences of her behavior. The counselor focused on these unspoken feelings, assisting Rose's process of making contact with them and, ultimately, with the more intimate aspects of her inner self. When the counselor asked Rose to describe her feelings of hopelessness, she began to cry. Because hopelessness was the result of her self-defeating behaviors but a feeling she had never previously identified, helping her recognize and deal with her hopelessness was a major factor in her continuing growth.

Summary of the Person-Centered Approach

A major assumption of the person-centered theoretical approach is the belief in the individual's innate motivation toward self-actualization and in the individual's potential to be a fully functioning person. A person will generally seek help in therapy when a significant incongruence between his or her real self and ideal self develops. The main intent in counseling is to develop a relationship between the counselor and the client that will facilitate the client's capacity for understanding his or her unhappiness and moving on to constructive personal growth. Crucial to the creation of this relationship are the counselor's characteristics of genuineness, unconditional positive regard, and accurate empathy. Therefore, creating and maintaining a nonthreatening, anxiety-free relationship in which client growth can take place is an essential component of person-centered therapy.

Summary

Three counseling theories within the psychodynamic, cognitive-behavioral, and humanistic traditions in psychology are Freudian-based psychoanalytic and general psychodynamic theory, Ellis's rational-emotive behavior therapy, and Rogers's person-centered therapy. Individual therapy from the psychodynamic perspective focuses on unconscious intrapsychic forces, childhood experiences, ego defense mechanisms, and the notion of transference and countertransference in the therapeutic relationship. Building a working alliance in therapy in order to interpret and confront transference dynamics and defense mechanisms is critical to successful counseling. Individual counseling from Ellis's approach focuses on the role of irrational thinking that people maintain about the world and self that leads to inappropriate behavior and to disturbing emotional reactions. Confronting irrational beliefs and learning more functional, logical beliefs about interpersonal patterns are central to the therapy process. Person-centered therapy is based on the belief that people have an innate motivation toward self-actualization, have the capacity for understanding their unhappiness, and can become fully functioning. Counseling focuses on developing the relationship between the client and counselor, marked by counselor genuineness, unconditional positive regard, and accurate empathy. Maintaining this nonthreatening, anxiety-free relationship is an essential component of successful person-centered therapy. Each of these traditional theoretical approaches has made enormous contributions to the process of counseling individuals toward achieving positive change, growth, and self-understanding. The case of Rose illustrates these contributions.

To aid you in putting the three approaches presented in this chapter within their theoretical and practical context, the following list contains other approaches that are similar to the three selected approaches:

Psychodynamic
Psychoanalysis (Freud)
Analytic theory (Jung)
Contemporary psychoanalytic theory (Erikson)
Individual psychology (Adler, Dreikurs)
Interpersonal theory of psychiatry (Sullivan)
Neurosis and aggression (Horney)

Social psychology (Fromm)
Personality (Murray)
Organismic theory (Goldstein)
Object-relations therapy (Otto Kernberg and James Masterson)

Behavioral (Cognitive-Behavioral)
Rational-emotive behavior therapy (Ellis)
Transactional analysis (Berne)
Reality therapy (Glasser)
Operant conditioning (Skinner)
Social modeling (Bandura)
Reciprocal inhibition (Wolpe)
Cognitive behavior modification (Meichenbaum, Beck)

Humanistic
Person-centered (Rogers)
Gestalt therapy (Perls)
Logotherapy (Frankl)
Psychology of being (Maslow)
Existential (May, Binswanger, Yalom, Jourard)

The following Web sites provide additional information about the chapter topics:

USEFUL WEB SITES

Psychodynamic psychotherapy:
http://www.guidetopsychology.com/txtypes.htm

Rational-emotive behavior therapy:
http://www.rebtnetwork.org/
http://www.albertellisinstitute.org/aei/index.html

Person-centered counseling:
http://www.person-centered-counseling.com/
http://www.personcentered.com/contents.htm

REFERENCES

Andersen, S. M., Glassman, N. S., Chen, S., & Cole, S. W. (1995). Transference in social perception: The role of chronic accessibility in significant-other representations. *Journal of Personality and Social Psychology, 69*, 41–57.

Bandura, A. (1977). *Social learning theory*. Englewood Cliffs, NJ: Prentice Hall.

Bandura, A. (1991). Social cognitive theory of self-regulation. *Organizational Behavior and Human Decision Processes, 50*, 248–287.

Bandura, A. (1993). Perceived self-efficacy in cognitive development and functioning. *Educational Psychologist, 28*(2), 117–148.

Beck, A. T. (1976). *Cognitive therapy and the emotional disorders*. New York: International Universities Press.

Becker, J., & Schmaling, K. (1991). Interpersonal aspects of depression for psychodynamic and attachment perspectives. In J. Becker & A. Kleiman (Eds.), *Psychosocial aspects of depression* (pp. 131–168). Hillsdale, NJ: Lawrence Erlbaum Associates.

Benjamin, J. (1998). *Shadow of the other: Intertsubjectivity and gender in psychoanalysis*. New York: Routledge.

Bergin, A. E., & Garfield, S. L. (1994). Overview, trends, and future issues. In A. E. Bergin & S. L. Garfield (Eds.), *Handbook of psychotherapy and behavior change* (4th ed., pp. 821–830). New York: Wiley.

Bordin, E. S. (1976). The generalizability of the psychoanalytic concept of the working alliance. *Psychotherapy: Theory, Research and Practice, 16*, 252–260.

Brodley, B. T. (1996). Uncharacteristic directiveness: Rogers and the "Anger and Hurt" client. In B. A. Farber, D. C. Brink, & P. M. Raskin (Eds.), *The Psychotherapy of Carl Rogers: Cases and Commentary* (pp. 310–321). New York: Guilford.

Chin, J. L. (1994). Psychodynamic approaches. In L. Comas-Días & B. Greene (Eds.), *Women of color: Integrating ethnic and gender identities in psychotherapy* (pp. 194–222). New York: Guilford.

Connor-Green, P. A. (1993). The therapeutic context: Preconditions for change in psychotherapy. *Psychotherapy, 30*, 375–382.

Corey, G. (2005). *Theory and practice of counseling and psychotherapy* (7th ed.). Pacific Grove, CA: Brooks/Cole.

Dozier, M., & Tyrrell, C. (1998). The role of attachment in therapeutic relationships. In J. A. Simpson & W. S. Rholes (Eds.), *Attachment theory and close relationships* (pp. 221–248). New York: Guilford.

Driscoll, R. (1994). *Pragmatic psychotherapy*. New York: Van Nostrand Reinhold.

Ellis, A. (1962). *Reason and emotion in psychotherapy*. New York: Stuart.

Ellis, A. (1993a). Fundamentals of rational-emotive therapy for the 1990s. In W. Dryden & L. K. Hill (Eds.), *Innovations in rational-emotive therapy* (pp. 1–32). Newbury Park, CA: Sage.

Ellis, A. (1993b). *The intelligent woman's guide to dating and mating*. New York: Stuart.

Ellis, A. (1993c). Reflections on rational-emotive therapy. *Journal of Consulting and Clinical Psychology, 61*(2), 199–201.

Ellis, A. (1995). Changing rational-emotive therapy (RET) to rational-emotive behavioral therapy (RETB). *Journal of Rational-Emotive and Cognitive Behavior Therapy, 13*(2), 85–89.

Ellis, A. (1997). Extending the goals of behavior therapy and of cognitive behavior therapy. *Behavior Therapy, 28*(3), 333–339.

Ellis, A. (1999a). Early theories and practices of rational emotive behavior therapy and how they have been augmented and revised during the last three decades. *Journal of Rational-Emotive & Cognitive Behavior Therapy, 17*(2), 69–93.

Ellis, A. (1999b). Rational emotive therapy and cognitive behavior therapy for elderly people. *Journal of Rational-Emotive & Cognitive Behavior Therapy, 17*(1), 5–18.

Ellis, A., & Dryden, W. (1997). *The practice of rational emotive behavior therapy* (2nd ed.). New York: Springer.

Ellis, A., Gordon, J., Nennan, M., & Palmer, S. (1997). *Stress counselling: A rationale emotive behaviour approach*. London: Cassell.

Ellis, A., & MacLaren, C. (1998). *Rational emotive behavior therapy: A therapist's guide*. The Practical Therapist Series. San Luis Obispo, CA: Impact.

Ellis, A., & Whitely, J. M. (1979). *Theoretical and empirical foundations of rational-emotive therapy*. Monterey, CA: Brooks/Cole.

Ellis, A. (2004). *Rational emotive behavior therapy: It works for me—it can work for you*. Amherst, NY: Prometheus Books.

Erikson, E. H. (1968). *Identity: Youth and crisis*. New York: Norton.

Farber, B. A., Lippert, R. A., & Nevas, D. B. (1995). The therapist as attachment figure. *Psychotherapy, 32*, 204–212.

Frank, K. A. (1999). *Psychoanalytic participation: Action, interaction, and integration*. Relational Perspectives Book Series, vol. 16. Hillsdale, NJ: Analytic Press.

Freud, A. (1936). *The writings of Anna Freud, Vol. 2: The ego and the mechanisms of defense*. New York: International Universities Press.

Freud, S. (1915–1917). *Introductory lectures on psychoanalysis*. New York: Norton.

Freud, S. (1949). *An outline of psychoanalysis*. New York: Norton

Garfield, S. L., & Bergin, A. E. (1994). Introduction and historical overview. In S. L. Garfield & A. E. Bergin (Eds.), *Handbook of psychotherapy and behavior change* (pp. 3–18). New York: John Wiley & Sons.

Gaston, L. (1990). The concept of the alliance and its role in psychotherapy: Theoretical and empirical considerations. *Psychotherapy, 27*, 143–153.

Gelso, C. J., & Carter, J. A. (1985). The relationship in counseling and psychotherapy: Components, consequences, and theoretical antecendents. *Counseling Psychologist, 13*, 155–243.

Gelso, C. J., & Carter, J. A. (1994). Components of the psychotherapy relationship: Their interaction and unfolding during treatment. *Counseling Psychologist, 41*(3), 296–306.

Gelso, C. J., & Hayes, J. A. (1998). *The psychotherapy relationship: Theory, research, and practice*. New York: Wiley.

Gelso, C. J., & Woodhouse, S. (2003). Toward a positive psychotherapy: Focus on human strength. In W. B. Walsh (Ed.), *Counseling psychology and optimal human functioning* (pp. 171–198). Mahwah, NJ: Lawrence Erlbaum Associates.

Greenson, R. R. (1967). *Technique and practice of psychoanalysis*. New York: International Universities Press.

Hansen, J. T. (2002). Postmodern implications for theoretical integration of counseling approaches. *Journal of Counseling & Development, 80*, 315–321.

Hawtin, S., & Moore, J. (1998). Empowerment of collusion? The social context of person-centred therapy. In B. Thorne & E. Lambers (Eds.), *Person-centered therapy: A European Perspective* (pp. 91–105). London: Sage.

Hayashi, S., Kuno, T., Morotomi, Y., Osawa, M., Shimizu, M., & Suetake, Y. (1998). Client-centered therapy in Japan: Fugio Tomoda and taoism. *Journal of Humanistic Psychology, 38*(2), 103–124.

Horvath, A. O., & Greenberg, L. S. (1989). Development and validation of the working alliance inventory. *Journal of Counseling Psychology, 36*(2), 223–233.

Jenkins, A. H. (2001). Humanistic psychology and multiculturalism. In K. J. Schneider, J. F. T. Bugental, & J. F. Pierson (Eds.), *The handbook of humanistic psychology: Leading edges in theory, research and practice* (pp. 37–45). Thousand Oaks, CA: Sage.

Joyce, D. P. (1995). The roles of the intervenor: A client-centered approach. *Mediation Quarterly, 12*(4), 301–312.

Kelly, E. W., Jr. (1997). Relationship-centered counseling: A humanistic model of integration. *Journal of Counseling & Development, 75*, 337–344.

Kohut, H. (1985). *Self psychology and the humanities: Reflections on a new psychoanalytic approach*. New York: Norton.

Lambert, M. J., & Bergin, A. E. (1994). The effectiveness of psychotherapy. In A. E. Bergin & S. L. Garfield (Eds.), *Handbook of psychotherapy and behavior change* (4th ed., pp. 143–189). New York: Wiley.

Lanyado, M., & Horne, A. (Eds.). (1999). *The handbook of child and psychotherapy: Psychoanalytic approaches*. New York: Routledge.

Laungani, P. (1997). Replacing client-centred counselling with culture-centred counselling. *Counselling Psychology Quarterly, 10*(4), 343–351.

Lionells, M. (1995). Interpersonal-relational psychoanalysis: An introduction and overview of contemporary implications and applications. *International Forum: Psychoanalysis, 4*, 223–230.

Meichenbaum, D. (1977). *Cognitive-behavior modification*. New York: Plenum Press.

Michael, J. (1991). Historical antecedents of behavior analysis. *Applied Behavior Analysis Newsletter, 14*(2), 7–12.

Morris, E. K. (1992). The aim, progress, and evolution of behavior analysis. *Behavior Analyst, 15*, 3–29.

Novie, G. J. (2007). Psychoanalytic theory. In D. Capuzzi & D. Gross (Eds.), *Counseling and psychotherapy: Theories and interventions* (4th ed., pp. 74–97). Upper Saddle River, NJ: Merrill Prentice Hall.

O'Hara, M. (1996). Rogers and Sylvia: A feminist analysis. In B. A. Farber & D. C. Brink (Eds.), *The psychotherapy of Carl Rogers: Cases and commentary* (pp. 284–300). New York: Guilford.

Petrocelli, J. V. (2002). Process and stages of change: Counseling with the transtheoretical model of change. *Journal of Counseling & Development, 80*, 22–28.

Robbins, S. B. (1989). Role of contemporary psychoanalysis in counseling psychology. *Journal of Counseling Psychology, 36*(3), 267–278.

Rogers, C. R. (1951). *Client-centered therapy*. Boston: Houghton Mifflin.

Rogers, C. R. (1957). The necessary and sufficient conditions of therapeutic personality change. *Journal of Consulting Psychology, 21*, 95–103.

Rogers, C. R. (1961). *On becoming a person*. Boston: Houghton Mifflin.

Skinner, B. F. (1938). *The behavior of organisms*. New York: Appleton-Century-Crofts.

Skinner, B. F. (1953). *Science and human behavior*. New York: Macmillan.

Sue, D. W., & Constantine, M. G. (2003). Optimal human functioning in people of color in the United States. In W. B. Walsh (Ed.), *Counseling psychology and optimal human functioning* (pp. 93–122). Mahwah, NJ: Lawrence Erlbaum Associates.

Stolorow, R. D. (1992). Closing the gap between theory and practice with better psychoanalytic theory. *Psychotherapy, 29*(2), 159–166.

Ursano, R. J., Sonnenberg, S. M., & Lazar, S. G. (1991). *Concise guide to psychodynamic psychotherapy*. Washington, DC: American Psychiatric Press.

Velásquez, R. J., Arellano, L. M., & McNeill, B. W. (2004). *The handbook of Chicana/o psychology and mental health*. Mahwah, NJ: Lawrence Erlbaum Associates.

Walsh, W. B. (2003). Person–environment psychology and well-being. In W. B. Walsh (Ed.), *Counseling psychology and optimal human functioning* (pp. 93–122). Mahwah, NJ: Lawrence Erlbaum Associates.

Wheeler, S., & Izzard, S. (1997). Psychodynamic counsellor training: Integrating difference. *Psychodynamic Counselling, 3*(4), 401–417.

Wolpe, J. (1982). *The practice of behavior therapy* (3rd ed.). Elmsford, NY: Pergamon Press.

Worrell, J., & Remer, P. (2003). *Feminist perspectives in therapy* (2nd ed.). Hoboken, NJ: John Wiley & Sons.

Zeman, S. (1999). Person-centered care for the patient with mid- and late-stage dementia. *American Journal of Alzheimer's Disease, 14*(5), 308–310.

SUGGESTED READING

Psychodynamic Approach

Becker, J., & Schmaling, K. (1991). Interpersonal aspects of depression from psychodynamic and attachment perspectives. In J. Becker & A. Kleinman (Eds.), *Psychosocial aspects of depression* (pp. 131–168). Hillsdale, NJ: Lawrence Erlbaum Associates.

Brenner, C. (1974). *An elementary textbook of psychoanalysis* (rev. ed.). Garden City, NY: Doubleday (Anchor).

Freud, A. (1946). *The ego and the mechanisms of defense*. New York: International Universities Press.

Freud, S. (1949). *An outline of psychoanalysis*. New York: Norton.

Gelso, C. J., & Carter, J. A. (1994). Components of the psychotherapy relationship: Their interaction and unfolding during treatment. *Counseling Psychologist, 41*(3), 296–306.

Kohut, H. (1985). *Self psychology and the humanities: Reflections of a new psychoanalytic approach*. New York: Norton.

McWilliams, N. (1994). *Psychoanalytic diagnosis: Understanding personality structure in the clinical process*. New York: Guilford.

Robbins, S. B. (1989). Role of contemporary psychoanalysis in counseling psychology. *Journal of Counseling Psychology, 36*(3), 267–268.

Storolow, R. D. (1992). Closing the gap between theory and practice with better psychoanalytic theory. *Psychotherapy, 29*(2), 159–166.

Teyber, E. (1997). *Interpersonal process in psychotherapy: A relational approach* (3rd ed.). Pacific Grove, CA: Brooks/Cole.

Ursano, R. J., Sonnenberg, S. M., & Lazar, S. G. (1991). *Concise guide to psychodynamic psychotherapy.* Washington, DC: American Psychiatric Press.

Cognitive-Behavioral Approach

Bandura, A. (1986). *Social foundations of thought and action: A social cognitive theory.* Englewood Cliffs, NJ: Prentice Hall.

Bandura, A. (1993). Perceived self-efficacy in cognitive development and functioning. *Educational Psychologist, 28*(2), 117–148.

Beck, A. T. (1976). *Cognitive therapy and the emotional disorders.* New York: International Universities Press.

Dryden, W. (1994). Reason and emotion in psychotherapy: Thirty years on. *Journal of Rational-Emotive and Cognitive-Behavior Therapy, 12*(2), 83–99.

Dryden, W., & Hill, L. K. (1993). Innovations in rational-emotive therapy. Newbury Park, CA: Sage.

Ellis, A. (1995). Changing rational-emotive therapy (RET) to rational emotive behavior therapy (REBT). *Journal of Rational-Emotive and Cognitive Behavior Therapy, 13*(2), 85–89.

Ellis, A. (1997). Extending the goals of behavior therapy and of cognitive behavior therapy. *Behavior Therapy, 28*(3), 333–339.

Heward, E. L., & Cooper, J. O. (1992). Radical behaviorism: A productive and needed philosophy for education. *Journal of Behavioral Education, 2*(4), 345–365.

Michael, J. (1991). Historical antecedents of behavior analysis. *Applied Behavior Analysis Newsletter, 14*(2), 7–12.

Morris, E. K. (1992). The aim, progress, and evolution of behavior analysis. *Behavior Analyst, 15,* 3–29.

Person-Centered Approach

Boy, A. V., & Pine, G. J. (1999). *A person-centered foundation for counseling and psychotherapy* (2nd ed.). Springfield, IL: Charles C. Thomas.

Ford, J. G. (1991). Rogers's theory of personality: Review and perspectives. *Journal of Social Behavior and Personality, 6*(5), 19–44.

Graf, C. (1994). On genuineness and the person-centered approach: A reply to Quinn. *Journal of Humanistic Psychology, 34*(2), 90–96.

Orlov, A. B. (1992). Carl Rogers and contemporary humanism. *Journal of Russian and East European Psychology, 30*(1), 36–41.

Rogers, C. R. (1951). *Client-centered therapy.* Boston: Houghton Mifflin.

Rogers, C. R. (1961). *On becoming a person.* Boston: Houghton Mifflin.

Rogers, C. R. (1980). *A way of being.* Boston: Houghton Mifflin.

Rogers, C. R., & Sanford, R. C. (1985). Client-centered psychotherapy. In H. I. Kaplan, B. J. Sadock, & A. M. Friedman (Eds.), *Comprehensive textbooks of psychiatry* (4th ed., pp. 1374–1388). Baltimore: Williams & Wilkins.

Stolorow, R. D. (1992). Closing the gap between theory and practice with better psychoanalytic theory. *Psychotherapy, 29*(2), 159–166.

Tobin, S. A. (1991). A comparison of psychoanalytic self psychology and Carl Rogers's person-centered therapy. *Journal of Humanistic Psychology, 31*(1), 9–33.

8 Individual Counseling: Brief Approaches

ROLLA E. LEWIS, EdD, NCC
California State University, East Bay

There is no singular or simple generic approach to brief counseling. Numerous brief approaches flow from diverse traditions. "Brief counseling" is an umbrella term that covers a wide array of brief approaches, each with its own history, literature, cheerleaders, and detractors. Students interested in brief counseling should recognize that the umbrella covers more than 50 brief approaches. Surveying all the literature regarding brief counseling would be too broad and have little value to students trying to develop an understanding about what brief counseling is and how it helps clients. Even with those limitations, numerous brief theories and methods compete for space in this introductory chapter, and there is neither time nor space to cover all 50-plus brief approaches.

This chapter concentrates on a few collaborative, competency-based brief approaches that recognize and begin with utilizing client strengths and cultural resources—approaches that are explicitly intentional about being effective and efficient. These brief approaches fall under a variety of names, but this chapter will refer to them as competency-based or strength-based brief counseling. Although this chapter discusses differences, it tends to lump together rather than split strength-based approaches. To give strength-based approaches a fair hearing, it might be helpful to view each approach as a dialect of the same language, the language of effective and efficient change. By concentrating on strength-based brief counseling approaches, this chapter intends to help introductory students appreciate a cluster of brief approaches and methods that can be viewed as expressing diverse dialects emerging from a common language concerned with helping clients construct more satisfying lives for themselves, enhancing their ability to choose, and utilizing their competencies and resources. The dialect analogy drawn from linguistics could help free counselors from falling into the trap of believing that there is a singular and correct dialect that all must speak. The English dialects spoken in Jamaica, England, the Midwest, the South, and in African American communities are all English, but some dialects are privileged because they are spoken and written by those in power. Linguists provide evidence to uptight language police that all dialects have consistent grammars that enable speakers to express themselves and experience the world in unique and culturally appropriate ways (Lakoff & Johnson, 1999; McWhorter, 2001). If you are a student, just use a nonstandard dialect in writing a paper and see what happens to your grade. Like dialects that are judged as less than by speakers of privileged dialects, brief counseling is viewed by some as nonstandard, less than, and not as "deep" as long-term forms of counseling. Obviously, we employ agreed-upon dialects to ensure an intellectual *lingua franca* within education, politics, and the workplace, and long-term counseling has been the *lingua franca* within the counseling community. If only to maintain contact with third-party payers, counselors oriented to long-term counseling are finding that they must be able to hang "Brief Counseling Spoken Here" next to whatever sign they are putting on their practice. In terms of the brief counseling dialects analogy, regardless of the dialect spoken, the goal in brief counseling is not about treatment duration, it is about doing what works effectively and efficiently.

What works is of great concern to therapists and counselors (Hubble, Duncan, & Miller, 1999; Wampold, 2001). Therapeutic treatment works for 80% of all clients. At least 50% of clients can benefit from 5 to 10 counseling sessions, and 20–30% require treatment lasting more than 25 sessions (Asay & Lambert, 1999). Lambert (1992) defined four broad common therapeutic factors influencing successful counseling: client and extratherapeutic factors, therapeutic relationship, expectancy and placebo effects, and therapeutic technique factors. Client and extratherapeutic events accounted for 40% of clients' counseling and therapeutic improvement. The therapeutic relationship accounted for 30%, expectancy and placebo effects accounted for 15%, and therapeutic technique accounted for 15% of clients' improvement in counseling and therapy. The strength-based approaches in this chapter draw on what works and the common factors illustrating what facilitates clients' improvement. The common factors strongly influence the brief approaches shared in this chapter because each approach presupposes clients bring strengths and competencies into the therapeutic process.

Students may want to explore the richness and variety of diverse brief counseling approaches not covered or merely touched upon in this chapter. For instance, Adlerian, rational-emotive behavior therapy, reality therapy, narrative, health realization, and psychodynamic practitioners have developed brief counseling theories and interventions that guide counselors seeking time-efficient pathways for helping others. Shulman (1989) finds similarities between Adlerian psychotherapy and some forms of brief therapy and points out that rapid assessment, flexibility, and active interpretation of emotions and goals are part of the Adlerian approach. Ellis (1989, 1990, 1996) proposes rational-emotive behavior therapy as a briefer and better form of therapy. Ellis states the ABC method is probably the most effective brief method for changing fundamental "disturbance-creating attitudes." Palmatier (1990, 1996) links reality therapy to brief approaches. Narrative therapists offer theory that guides practice intended to help clients move from problem-saturated stories to more hope-filled, culturally sensitive, alternative stories (Hoyt, 2002, 2005; Monk, Winslade, Crocket, & Epston, 1997; White & Epston, 1990; Winslade & Monk, 2007). By focusing on the nature of mind, consciousness, and thought, health realization offers a psychoeducational approach as a new paradigm for brief treatment (Pransky, 1998; Pransky, Mills, Sedgeman, & Bleven, 1997; Sedgeman, 2005). Still, those of a psychodynamic bent may want to refer to the literature that concentrates on helping clients address maladaptive inter-personal problems and related neurotic disturbances (Binder, Strupp, & Henry, 1995; Levenson, 1995; Mann, 1981, 1991; Worchel, 1990). For further exploration, inter-ested students should refer to sources cited throughout this chapter and to supplemen-tal brief counseling sources (Bertolino & O'Hanlon, 2002; DeJong & Berg, 2002; Hart, 1995; Hoyt, 2002, 2005; Lipchik, 2002; Miller, 1997; Rosenbaum, Hoyt, & Talmon, 1990; Selekman, 2005, 2006; Smith, 2006; Walter & Peller, 1992, 2000; Winslade & Monk, 2007).

A Cultural Context and Brief Background

Brief counseling approaches have been promoted for a number of reasons. For instance, time and cost are critical factors that have facilitated the proliferation of brief therapies, and when managed care approves a limited number of visits for mental health care, mental health counselors are forced to adopt short-term approaches (de Shazer, 1985; Hoyt, 2000, 2005). A simplistic dualistic argument can follow: evil and greedy corporations versus selfless professionals who care only about client well-being. But look at the issue from differing perspectives. Many practitioners complain managed care companies have rejected lengthy counseling and adopted "quick fix" approaches merely due to cost. At the same time, although it is accurate to say that many corporations focus on costs over people, studies have also found that the vast majority of clients are not long term and that the majority of clients benefit from brief treatments (Asay & Lambert, 1999; Hoyt, 2000, 2002, 2005; Koss & Shiang, 1994; Lambert, 1992; Lambert, Garfield, & Bergin, 2004a, 2004b). Only 20–30% of clients require treatment lasting more than 25 sessions (Asay & Lambert, 1999). Counselors want to advocate for necessary treatment for those clients needing more than 25 ses-sions, and they want to be aware that sometimes therapy goes beyond what is neces-sary. Efran, Lukens, and Lukens (1990) go so far as to say that some of the therapists complaining about decreasing the duration of treatment are concerned primarily with their own incomes. Exploring such issues is beyond the scope of this chapter, and such arguments should be placed in a Western cultural context.

Culturally, Westerners quantify time; we measure and count the passage of time and recognize that our lives have a limited duration, of unknown length, that makes knowing when we are going to die uncertain and makes life planning not quite as effective as the expiration date on milk containers. In the West's technological culture, clocks fetter the invisible passage of time and our lives. Clocks have influenced how we see and live in the world and created the metaphor that we live in a *machina mundi*, "world machine," that influences our very being (Crosby, 1997). Time is ticking away. To waste time is sin. Time is money. Step back briefly and consider that the philos-opher Henryk Skolimowski (1994) argues that our cultural understanding of time takes on ontological and epistemological dimensions. How we understand time influ-ences how we see reality and how we construct knowledge. For instance, stop reading briefly and think about how you are spending your time. How are you organizing your time you need to read this chapter? What do you have to give up? What do you hope to gain by "spending" your time reading this? How does your own relation with time influence how you view (and construct) reality and knowledge? Claxton (1997) points out, "Within the Western mindset, time becomes a commodity, and one inevitable consequence is the urge to 'think faster': to solve problems and make decisions quickly" (p. 5). In the West, we have a tendency to force the quick answer and instant solution, but some challenges in life cannot be met by seeking a quick or instant answer; some challenges require patience, intuition, and relaxation. Sometimes slowing down will get you where you want to go while giving you time to become more prepared for where you are. Some brief counseling approaches are efficient and effective because they draw upon this wisdom. Those that are mindful of cultural wisdom become more aligned with clients' diverse cultures. The most powerful brief counseling is culturally congruent.

Efficient and effective interventions save time because they are designed to ensure that clients attend no more sessions than necessary (Hoyt, 2000). Parsimonious interventions that are efficient and effective certainly save money and time for clients and managed care systems, but the move toward brief counseling approaches did not occur overnight or come upon the professional scene as a postmodern intellectual fashion statement. During World Wars I and II, the desire to get soldiers back to the battlefront as quickly as possible led to short-term therapeutic interventions rather than long explorations of neurotic or psychotic problems (Fisch, 1994). The therapeutic goal (if it can be called that) was to ensure the mental stamina of fighting forces. To serve the "military's institutional need for a steady supply of dependable human resources" during World War II, clinicians devised a "menu of creative psychotherapeutic alternatives and shortcuts" to ensure that the maximum number of soldiers could be returned to the active theater in the minimum of time (Herman, 1995, p. 112). More recently and on a more positive human note, the community mental health movement emphasized getting treatment to the underprivileged members of society, and brief counseling approaches naturally opened up possibilities for serving more people. Additionally, as Lambert, Garfield, and Bergin (2004a) point out, "Patients, for the most part, prefer to be helped as quickly as possible, and efficiency is also favored by funding services such as insurance companies and the government" (p. 10). The move toward brief counseling is a mixed bag. Managed care has been attracted to brief approaches because their focus on symptom relief and increased function seems pragmatic and cost effective (Hoyt, 1995, 2002). Practitioners have been attracted to brief approaches because they work and more people can be served.

The overemphasis on length of treatment may take those interested in brief counseling approaches down the wrong path. For the most part, brief therapists argue that the short duration of therapy results from using effective and efficient therapies (Bertolino & O'Hanlon, 2002; Cade & O'Hanlon, 1993; DeJong & Berg, 2002; Hoyt, 2000; Matthews & Edgette, 1997; Zeig & Gilligan, 1990). "Indeed, the actual number of hours logged in psychotherapy is much less important . . . than is the significance of the experiences that transpire during that time" (Mahoney, 1997, p. 34).

Even with an emphasis on effective and efficient therapy, there is some debate about how long brief counseling should be. For Hoyt (1995), there is "no magic number" of sessions for brief therapy, whereas Sharf (1996) offers 3 to 40 sessions as a range. Brief therapy generally ranges from 1 to 25 sessions. Some consider 25 the maximum number of sessions for brief therapy (Koss & Butcher, 1986). Using any specific, preset number of sessions is arbitrary, however, and may not be in the best interest of the client. For the purposes of this chapter, Hoyt (1995) will serve as a guide: brief therapy is not defined by "a particular number of sessions but rather the intention of helping clients make changes in thoughts, feelings, actions in order to move toward or reach a particular goal as time-efficiently as possible" (p. 1). In essence, the goal of brief therapy is not to minimize treatment but to provide effective services to those seeking help. Brief counseling does not seek to create Madison Avenue instant cures for those seeking therapeutic help but rather to facilitate meaningful change effectively and efficiently for clients.

Given the wide variety of brief approaches, it is important to consider possible common ground, where the diverse approaches can be lumped together rather than split apart. To provide some sense of common ground, Cooper (1995) offers eight technical features common to the various forms of brief counseling discussed here:

1. Maintain a clear and specific treatment focus.
2. Be conscious and conscientious about how you use time.
3. Limit goals and clearly define counseling outcomes.
4. Emphasize the present and the here-and-now.
5. Make your assessment rapidly, and integrate assessment into treatment.
6. Review progress frequently, and discard ineffective interventions.
7. Maintain a high level of therapist–client collaboration.
8. Be pragmatic and flexible when using techniques.

In a similar vein to Cooper's (1995) eight technical features, Fisch (1994) offers counselors four principles many brief approaches have in common:

1. Narrow the database regarding what counselors focus on with clients.
2. Use interactional rather than intrapsychic concepts.
3. Influence change by having a task orientation rather than an insight orientation.
4. Define goals in order to know when to stop therapy.

Cooper's (1995) common technical features and Fisch's (1994) principles illustrate a common ground and reveal how brief counselors have overlapping core values.

More importantly, research regarding the efficacy of brief approaches and the assertion that there are common factors determining therapeutic outcomes helps brief counselors to concentrate on what works in counseling (Asay & Lambert, 1999; Bertolino & O'Hanlon, 2002; Hubble et al., 1999; Koss & Butcher, 1986; Koss & Shiang, 1994). Lambert, Garfield, and Bergin (2004b) assert, "Trends in psychotherapy research indicate that almost all the psychotherapies studied in the United States are brief" (p. 814). In practice and research, brief counseling is becoming the norm. Brief counselors embrace pragmatism and parsimony in their therapeutic approach. They see human change as inevitable and build on client resources and competence. Brief counselors use homework, recognize that significant change occurs outside therapy, and believe that life outside counseling is more important than counseling itself. In addition, brief counseling practitioners recognize that there are times when therapy does not help. Brief counseling is best when it is focused in culturally appropriate ways within particular contexts and upon specific problems (Bertolino & O'Hanlon, 2002; Besley, 2003; Cade & O'Hanlon, 1993; Cooper, 1995; Durrant & Kowalski, 1993; Hoyt, 2000; Jianyi, Xuanwen, Yingping, & Weiqiang, 2006; Kurihara, 2002; Wells & Giannetti, 1990).

The rest of this chapter will introduce students to strength-based brief approaches that find roots in the work of Gregory Bateson, Milton Erickson, and others who shifted counseling from concentrating on deficits to looking for strengths, from exploring problems to creating solutions, and from fixation on the past to active construction of a preferred future (Bertolino & O'Hanlon, 2002; Hoyt, 2000, 2002, 2005).

Competency and Strength-Based Brief Approaches

This section focuses on three separate brief approaches that emerge from a common history rooted in client competencies and strengths (Amatea, Smith-Adcock, & Vallares, 2006; Berg & DeJong, 2005; Bertolino & O'Hanlon, 2002; DeJong & Berg, 2002; Fisch, 2004; Hoyt, 2000, 2002, 2005; O'Hanlon, 2003; Selekman, 2005, 2006; Smith, 2006). Returning to the dialect analogy, brief problem-solving, solution-focused, and solution-oriented approaches can claim roots within the same strength-based language of counseling, but each continues to evolve and lay claim to its own uniqueness. Even today, the strength-based approaches explored in this chapter continue to be informed by and influenced by each other and find that their therapeutic dialects are now being changed and influenced by other emerging strength-based theories, such as narrative therapy.

For all their differences, each brief approach in the remainder of this chapter draws on client strengths in solving problems, finding solutions, or discovering possibilities to altering how clients might overcome their presenting problems. The strength-based approaches do not embrace a normative model that prescribes what is normal and healthy or abnormal and deviant; the approaches move away from viewing clients as pathological and resistant and instead concentrate on working with clients to find out what works in their lives.

Focus on Problem Solving

The brief therapy model developed at the Mental Research Institute (MRI) is referred to as the MRI brief therapy approach, brief problem-solving therapy, and brief problem-focused therapy (Cooper, 1995; Fisch, 1990, 2004; O'Hanlon & Weiner-Davis, 1989). Don Jackson, in 1958, founded MRI in Palo Alto, California. A separate research group from Menlo Park, California, influenced the innovative experimental attitude at MRI. Lead by Gregory Bateson from 1952 to 1962, the group included collaboration and consultation with John Weakland, Jay Haley, Don Jackson, and William Fry Jr., and Virginia Satir.

Haley notes of Bateson's group, "Data of various types were used in the research: Hypnosis, ventriloquism, animal training, popular moving pictures, the nature of play, humor, schizophrenia, neurotic communication, psychotherapy, family systems and family therapy" (quoted in Cade & O'Hanlon, 1993, p. 2). During the 10-year project, Bateson's group investigated a variety of topics, such as cybernetics, communication, paradox, and logical types. Throughout the project's history, the Bateson group members consulted with the psychiatrist Milton Erickson, who used hypnosis, indirect suggestion, stories, metaphors, and riddles to help his clients change (Cooper, 1995; Haley, 1973; O'Hanlon, 1987, 1990; Zeig & Gilligan, 1990). The various connections involving Bateson's Palo Alto group and MRI are remarkable and would keep a counseling soap opera going for years. Bateson's Palo Alto group studied with Jackson, Haley, Weakland, and Satir. The connection with Erickson and Satir led to Bandler and Grinder's study of the practices of Fritz Perls, Erickson, and Satir and the creation of neurolinguistic programming. Haley, who was affiliated with MRI, went to Philadelphia to work with Salvador Minuchin. Haley's (1973) own work moved toward strategic or problem-solving therapy. Steve de Shazer (1985) studied at MRI and went off to develop solution-focused therapy. O'Hanlon and Weiner-Davis (1989) moved from solution-focused therapy to create solution-oriented therapy, which with O'Hanlon (1999) has evolved into possibility therapy. Even White and Epston (1990), in Australia and New Zealand, were influenced by the inquisitive openness demonstrated by Bateson's group, MRI, and the different practitioners who were connecting on the West Coast. The connection with others, sharing ideas, and the open experimental approach created a supportive context where practitioners explored innovative ways to find out what would work to help people with problems.

With as many techniques that they developed, the essence was not in the techniques. Weakland asserted that there was a fundamental principle in Erickson's work: "the Ericksonian essence . . . has nothing to do with technique. It has nothing to do with theory. It mainly had to do with Erickson being very curious" (Hoyt, 1994, p. 12). Curiosity must be emphasized because the Erickson and Bateson group's open and experimental approach clearly influenced the members at the Mental Research Institute in how they intervened with people and understood behavior change.

In 1966, Richard Fisch opened the Brief Therapy Center at MRI to see what therapeutic results could occur in a strictly limited period of a maximum of 10 1-hour sessions that focused on the main presenting complaint, used active techniques to promote change, and sought the minimum change required to resolve the presenting problem (Fisch, Weakland, & Segal, 1982). The MRI approach made no attempt to develop insight because problems were considered interactional in nature. The therapeutic goal for the brief problem-solving approach was to resolve the presenting problem as it occurs between people. The emphasis was on change and outcomes, not knowledge, insight, or other such concerns. It was assumed that change would be easier if people did something differently.

Fisch et al. (1982) cite four reasons for a client coming to therapy:

1. Clients have concerns about behavior, actions, thoughts, or feelings of themselves or someone with whom they are significantly involved.
2. The problem or concern is described as deviant in the sense of being unusual or inappropriate and "distressing or harmful, immediately or potentially, either to the behaver . . . or to others" (p. 11).
3. Clients reported their efforts or those of others about stopping or changing the behavior have been unsuccessful.
4. Clients or those concerned about them seek professional help in changing the situation because they have not been able to make the change on their own.

Clients enter therapy because they want change. In MRI's problem-focused brief therapy, problem formation and problem maintenance are seen as parts of a vicious circle process where clients' attempts to change the problem have been mishandled, leaving clients stuck (Watzlawick, Weakland, & Fisch, 1974). Because people create problems by misinterpreting ordinary life difficulties, clients' attempts to change the problems were viewed as sometimes aggravating the problem. Clients (and for that matter, therapists) can get stuck because of the way they view and behave around the problem. "We are talking only of views, not of reality or of truth, because we believe that views are all we have, or ever will have" (Fisch et al., 1982, p. 10). Thus, the therapeutic goal in problem-focused brief therapy is to interrupt the vicious circle of viewing the problem and initiate action to resolve the problem. Counselors assess where clients are stuck, what they are doing to get unstuck, and how to influence them to stop doing what they regard as logical or necessary (Fisch, 1990). The MRI approach to helping clients get unstuck has been used in a variety of contexts, including as a feminist intervention with victims of domestic violence (McCloskey & Fraser, 1997).

Helping clients get unstuck sometimes involves reframing the problem. "To reframe . . . means to change the conceptual and/or emotional setting or viewpoint in relation to which a situation is experienced and to place it in another frame which fits the 'facts' of the same concrete situation equally well or even better, and thereby changes its entire meaning" (Watzlawick et al., 1974, p. 95). The technique, drawn in large measure from the work of Milton Erickson, seeks to infuse new meaning into a situation (O'Hanlon, 1987). Watzlawick et al. (1974) cite the example of Tom Sawyer's reframing the drudgery of whitewashing the fence into something fun and attractive and then having his friends accept the "reality" that whitewashing can be pleasurable.

The Therapeutic Process

Assessment.   During the initial stages of treatment, the brief problem-solving therapist must gather adequate information seen as basic to every case. The assessment should include:

1. A clear understanding of the essential complaint. Who does the problem belong to? "Who is doing what that presents a problem, to whom, and how does such

behavior constitute a problem?" (Fisch et al., 1982, p. 70). The questioning is persistent, firm, and polite.

2. A complete and precise understanding of just what "solutions" have been attempted, especially any efforts being made currently. The basic thrust and the details regarding these "solutions" should be identified.

3. A determination of the client's minimal goals and the criteria for evaluating the achievement of those goals.

4. The use of the client's position, language, and values in the assessment. "However questionable or undesirable an aspect of the client's life may seem, we are disinclined to intervene unless the client has some complaint about it" (Fisch et al., 1982, p. 122).

5. A determination of who is most invested in change. Who is the customer? Who is the complainant? Fisch et al. (1982) state, "Get the 'window shopper' down to business" (p. 43).

Therapist Maneuverability. It is one thing to know how to best proceed, and it is quite another to have the freedom to move in the direction one thinks is best. Because clients are viewed as often hindering therapeutic efforts out of desperation or fear that things will get worse, therapists have to keep their options open. Tactics Fisch et al. (1982) suggest include:

1. Avoid taking definite positions prematurely. Taking firm positions may be aversive to the clients' sensibilities and values.

2. Take time. Defer implicit pressure to perform as therapists.

3. Help clients commit to a position. This limits clients' maneuverability. Therapists should use qualifying language to avoid making a commitment to a position. At the same time, therapists should get clients to be specific.

4. Take a one-down position and ask the client for help. The one-down position puts clients at ease and allows therapy to proceed like two people having a conversation.

5. Work with the complainant(s). Determine who is discomfited by the problem. Is it the client or another person?

Intervention. Because clients' "attempted solutions" are viewed as maintaining and perpetuating the problem, the interventions planned by the therapist are directed toward helping clients depart from their solutions. This may be accomplished by either interdicting the problem-maintaining behavior or by altering clients' view of the problem so that it is no longer viewed as a problem. Problem-solving brief therapists view problems as arising from five basic attempted solutions clients maintain. Interventions arise from therapists' responses to problems that are being maintained by these five basic solutions:

1. Attempting to force something that can only occur spontaneously. Clients' concerns with bodily functioning, personal and sexual performance, and so forth fall into this category. Clients become "enmeshed in the painful solution of trying to

coerce a performance that can only occur spontaneously" (Fisch et al., 1982, p. 130). In one example of a client complaining of obsessive ruminations, the therapist suggests that the client begin controlling the obsessive thoughts by setting a time for them to begin. Instead of resisting the ruminations, the client is given the opportunity to control them by bringing the thoughts forth at a prescribed time of day when the thoughts were normally not occurring.

2. Attempting to master a feared event by postponing it. These are usually self-referential complaints regarding shyness, creative blocks, performance blocks (stage fright), and so on. Clients basically attempt to prepare for the feared event in such a way that the event will be mastered in advance, and avoid the actual doing. The intervention involves exposing the client to the task while requiring nonmastery. One shy male client was directed to go to a public place, like a bar or skating rink, and approach the most desirable-looking woman with the introduction, "I would like to get to know you better but I am very shy talking with women" (Fisch et al., 1982, p. 139). The client was directed further to expect possible rejection and not go out with the woman, because the assignment was designed to deal with rejection, not to meet women. The essential strategy involves exposing the client to the feared task while restraining the client from successfully completing it.

3. Attempting to reach accord through opposition. These problems involve conflict in an interpersonal relationship that centers on issues requiring mutual cooperation. These problems include marital disputes, employee disputes, and other conflicts commonly referred to as power struggles. "Complainants with these problems engage in the attempted solution of haranguing the other party to comply with their demands . . . and demand that the other party treat them with respect, care, or deference" (Fisch et al., 1982, p. 140). The brief problem-solving solution in this case is to get the complainant to take a "one-down" position.

4. Attempting to attain compliance through volunteerism. These problems result from the perceived inability or abhorrence to asking something of another. "The common thread involves one person attempting to gain compliance from another while denying that compliance is being asked for" (Fisch et al., 1982, p. 154). The overall strategy here is to get the person with the problem to ask directly for what he or she wants.

5. Confirming the accuser's suspicions by defending oneself. These problems result from one person suspecting another of an act both parties view as wrong. Usually one accuses the other of infidelity, excessive drinking, dishonesty, or delinquency, and the other, by the act of denying the accusation, actually confirms the accuser's suspicions. It places both in an accuser–defender role. One technique for breaking up this interaction is to agree with the accuser. Fisch et al. (1982) share the story of an elderly couple who had been playing the game for more than 30 years. The wife accused the husband that "he was no fun," and the husband denied it. After he began agreeing with her, she stopped accusing him, and the game ended.

Additional General Interventions.   Coupled with the five approaches previously listed are four other general interventions. One, "go slow," is an intervention that is used with clients whose main attempted solution is trying too hard. The authors recommend against any overt optimism or assuming a worried expression if there is any acknowledgment of good news. Second, "dangers of improvement" might be considered an extension of "go slow" because the client is asked to recognize the possible dangers in resolving the problem. If clients lose weight, they may have to buy a new wardrobe, or if they improve their sexual performance, their partner might not be able to keep up with them. Third, making a "U-turn" is a shift to an opposite direction because the directive or strategy is not working. This tactic is especially effective when the therapist has inadvertently taken the wrong position with a client. Fourth, "how to worsen the problem" is used when advising clients to continue the ineffective approach they are using. It is generally used with clients who are having difficulty changing what they are doing (Fisch et al., 1982).

Termination is Done Without Fanfare.   Generally, goals are assessed, and the client is given a simple goodbye. In fact, according to Fisch et al. (1982), it may be important to terminate with a "doubtful and cautionary note" (p. 179).

Focus on Solutions

Solution-focused therapy is the model of brief therapy developed at the Brief Family Therapy Center (BFTC) in Milwaukee, Wisconsin, by Steve de Shazer and Insoo Kim Berg. Characterized as MRI's younger sibling, the solution-focused brief counseling approach looks closely at the pattern of interaction around the complaint, approaches for changing the pattern, and creating outcomes (Lipchik, 2002). Like MRI, the BFTC draws on Gregory Bateson's theoretical ideas and Milton Erickson's clinical work. Like MRI, solution-focused therapy has been criticized for its apparent faith in technique, and some practitioners have moved beyond atheoretical techniques toward developing a solution-focused theory that integrates language and emotion (Berg & DeJong, 2005; Lipchik, 2002; Parry & Doan, 1994).

The major difference is that solution-focused therapy offers a shift in therapeutic focus away from problems and toward solutions. Solution-focused counseling can be viewed as building upon the MRI approach, but the essential shift is on client strengths, solutions, and using whatever the client brings to the session that can promote healthy change. The counseling conversation changes from concentrating on problems to finding solutions. For solution-focused counselors, the solution-finding process holds therapeutic promise, and the therapeutic task entails helping clients to develop expectations of change and solutions. Solution-focused counselors pay relatively little attention to the details of the complaint and instead highlight how the client will know when the problem is solved. For solution-focused brief counselors, the key to brief therapy is using what clients bring to meet their needs in such a way that clients will be able to find satisfactory solutions to problems (Berg & DeJong, 2005; de Shazer, 1985,

1990, 1991; DeJong & Berg, 1998, 2002; Hoyt, 1994, 1996, 2002; Lipchik, 2002; Matthews & Edgette, 1997; Miller, Hubble, & Duncan, 1996; Walter & Peller, 1992, 2000).

More than assessing how problems are maintained or how to solve them, solution-focused counseling asserts that helping people involved in troublesome situations requires getting them to do something different, even if it seems irrational, irrelevant, bizarre, or humorous (de Shazer, 1985). No problem occurs all the time, and using clients' strengths and resources for bringing about change is crucial. One goal involves getting clients to envision their future without the presenting problem. When clients are able to do that, the problem is diminished (de Shazer, 1990).

The Therapeutic Process

Assessment. The BFTC group assumes clients want to change. "Resistance" is not an issue for solution-focused therapists because they attempt to connect the client's present with the future, compliment clients on what they are already doing that is useful, and suggest something for them to do that might be good for them. De Shazer (1985) offered 12 building blocks of complaint and 6 basic assumptions for viewing and changing clients' complaints.

The 12 complaints usually include:

1. A bit or sequence of behavior.
2. The meanings ascribed to the situation.
3. The frequency with which the complaint happens.
4. The physical location in which the complaint happens.
5. The degree to which the complaint is involuntary.
6. Significant others involved in the complaint directly or indirectly.
7. The question of who or what is to blame.
8. Environmental factors such as jobs, economic status, and living space.
9. The physiological or feeling state involved.
10. The past.
11. Dire predictions of the future.
12. Utopian expectations (de Shazer, 1985, p. 27).

The six basic assumptions that de Shazer (1985) offers to help therapists draw maps of client complaints and construct solutions are:

1. Constructing complaints to involve behavior that is brought on by the client's worldview.
2. Complaints are maintained by clients thinking the decision they made about the original problem was the only thing to do and thus getting trapped into doing more of the same.
3. Understanding that minimal changes are necessary when initiating change. There can be a "ripple effect." Once change is initiated, the client will generate additional changes to solve the complaint.

4. Using the clients' view of what reality would look like without the complaint, solution-focused therapists generate ideas for what to change.
5. Suggesting a new frame or new frames of reference and new behavior based on this new view, can promote resolution of the problem.
6. Viewing change holistically: a change in one part of the system is likely to effect changes in other parts of the system.

Intervention. Solutions, not problems, are the primary focus in solution-focused therapy. Emphasis placed on problems moves the client in the wrong direction and is based on a faulty assumption. Solution-focused brief therapy is cooperative and oriented toward change, solutions, the present, and the future.

Because solution-focused therapy assumes that therapists and clients coconstruct perspectives on the problem, establishing rapport and promoting cooperation are crucial initial moves in therapy. Change is an interactional process, and it is essential that therapists "fit" into the worldview of clients in order to jointly construct a problem that can be solved. If done effectively, therapists shape and change the process so clients can solve their own problems in therapy.

The presession change question technique involves seeking exceptions to the problem or exploring the solutions clients have been attempting. The goal is to create an expectation for change, emphasize the active role and responsibility of clients, and demonstrate that change happens outside counselors' offices. Counselors simply ask, "Since the last time we met, have you been noticing some changes in yourself or discovering a new way of looking at the problem?"

Another technique involves searching for exceptions. Finding exceptions to when clients feel stuck helps to clarify the conditions for change by reorienting clients to the hope of finding a solution, implying clients have strengths and the ability to solve problems, providing tangible evidence of resolution, and helping clients discover forgotten personal resources. Exceptions might include therapists' questions such as:

"When did you manage this problem in the past? What did you do differently?"
"Tell me when things were just a little better."

De Shazer (1985) describes working with a couple who were complaining about arguing. He asked them to describe what life would be like after they quit arguing. After the couple described what life would be like after these arguments, they no longer had an investment in arguing. Life would be better when they stopped fighting.

The miracle question is another technique that helps to clarify goals and highlight exceptions to the problem by stimulating the client to imagine a solution and remove constraints to solving the problem and by building hope for change. With this technique clients are asked, "Suppose that one night, while you were asleep, there was a miracle and this problem was solved. How would you know? What would be different?" (de Shazer, 1991, p. 113). Such questions allow clients to envision their lives without the problem.

Scaling questions is another technique designed to make the abstract concrete by quantifying intangibles, placing power with clients, and demonstrating change.

Clients are asked, "On a scale of 1 to 10, where 1 means you have no influence over your problem, and 10 means you have total influence, where would you place yourself today?" To support the initial question, therapists add further questions such as "Where would others place you on this scale?" and "What do you need to move a fraction of a point up the scale?"

These brief examples show how each technique attempts to induce doubt regarding the severity and dominance of the problem by helping clients find exceptions to the occurrence of the problem and toward helping clients understand that their lives are not constantly dominated by the problem. Finding that the problem is not always occurring or that they can imagine a future without the problem enables clients to define goals that concentrate on constructing solutions. As the name suggests, solution-focused therapy concentrates on using techniques and interventions that create the expectation that solutions exist or are imminent.

Solution-Oriented and Possibility Therapy

Solution-oriented brief therapy is the approach developed by Bill O'Hanlon and Michele Weiner-Davis that changes direction from both MRI and BFTC. Milton Erickson's influence is central. Solution-oriented brief counseling focuses on people's competence, with therapists cocreating solvable problems with clients. The approach has evolved into O'Hanlon's (1999, 2003) possibility therapy. The solution-oriented approach has a future goal orientation focused on bringing about small but positive outcomes for clients. Both solution-oriented and possibility therapy "emphasize the importance of client's internal experience" (Bertolino & O'Hanlon, 2002, p. 7). Like Rogerian counseling, clients must feel heard and understood during the counseling process if change is going to occur.

Influenced by both the MRI and BFTC approaches, solution-oriented counselors added that clients are stuck not only by how they are "doing" the problem but also by how they are "viewing" the problem. Views, actions, and context became crucial in solution-oriented counseling, and solution-oriented practitioners were encouraged to attempt three actions:

1. Changing what clients are doing in regards to their actions and interactions around the situation perceived as problematic
2. Changing the clients' frames of reference and their view of the situation they see as problematic
3. Evoking resources, solutions, and strengths to bring to the situation perceived as problematic (O'Hanlon & Weiner-Davis, 1989)

Solution-focused and solution-oriented therapies both utilize self-reinforcing patterns of thought and behavior. O'Hanlon and Weiner-Davis (1989) point out, "If the client walks into a behaviorist's office, he will leave with a behavioral problem. If clients choose psychoanalysts' offices, they will leave with unresolved issues from childhood as the focus of the problem" (p. 54). O'Hanlon and Weiner-Davis (1989) explain that clients' complaints are negotiated and "cocreated" with therapists, and the solution-oriented approach begins the therapeutic process by looking for clients' strengths, solutions, and competence. One intention in separating the two approaches is to show the continuing drift in solution-oriented and other practices away from purist thinking and toward integrating diverse ideas from the literature and using a variety of terms, such as constructivist, narrative, postmodern, collaborative, competency-based, and interactional (Bertolino, 1999; Bertolino & O'Hanlon, 2002; DeJong & Berg, 2002; Friedman, 1993; Hoyt, 2000, 2002, 2005; Matthews & Edgette, 1997; Neimeyer & Mahoney, 1995; O'Hanlon, 1999, 2003; Parry & Doan, 1994; Selekman, 2006; Walter & Peller, 1992, 2000).

Solution-focused and solution-oriented therapy are frequently confused, and the confusion resulted in O'Hanlon describing his approach as possibility therapy and inclusive therapy. Possibility therapy has three essential differences from solution-focused therapy: validating emotional experience, being flexible rather than formulaic with clients, and being mindful of cultural, political, historical, and gender influences on the problems clients bring into counseling. O'Hanlon's possibility therapy and inclusive therapy are not purist or pushing allegiance to a single model for counseling but rather open methods for using ideas and perspectives from differing approaches, such as Ericksonian, strategic, behavioral, solution-focused, and narrative (Bertolino & O'Hanlon, 2002; O'Hanlon, 1999, 2003).

O'Hanlon (1999) offers three principles that guide the work of possibility therapists:

1. Acknowledge and validate the client's perceptions and experience
2. Facilitate clients in shifting how they view things and/or do things
3. Recognize client resources, expertise, and experiences, and collaborate with them about the direction counseling is going

The Therapeutic Process

Assessment and Interventions. Assessment is viewed as directly tied to therapists' metaphors and assumptions. "We have never had a client with an unresolved Oedipal conflict or an overactive superego. Just lucky, we suppose!" (O'Hanlon & Weiner-Davis, 1989, p. 54). Furthermore, solution-oriented therapists look at problems not as pathological manifestations but as ordinary difficulties encountered in life.

Assessment and intervention are not separated into distinct steps. In fact, the initial interviewing process is viewed as an intervention. Because interviewing utilizes solution-oriented techniques, "clients can experience significant shifts in their thinking about their situations during the course of the [first] session" (O'Hanlon & Weiner-Davis, 1989, p. 77). Solution-oriented therapists use presuppositional questioning, such as "What were the good things about the dinner?" rather than "Did anything good happen at the dinner?" Such approaches begin with the way clients perceive and talk about their problems. By looking for exceptions to the problem, solution-oriented therapists attempt to normalize or depathologize problems, making problems simply a natural response to life events.

O'Hanlon and Weiner-Davis (1989) offer eight techniques for changing patterns of doing or viewing problems:

1. The frequency or rate of the performance of the complaint could be changed. Have the client who goes on candy binges slowly eat candy when not on a binge.
2. The timing of complaint performance could be changed. Have depressed clients schedule their depression for a specific time of the day.
3. The duration of the performance of the complaint could be changed. Have the compulsive handwasher wash the left hand 5 minutes and the right hand 30 seconds.
4. The location of the performance of the complaint could be changed. The authors describe a situation where a wife and husband were directed to move their arguments into the bathroom with the husband getting undressed and lying down in the bathtub and the wife sitting fully clothed on the toilet. The couple's subsequent actions and laughter broke their pattern of chronic arguments.
5. The complaint pattern could have one or more elements added to it. Clients with eating disorders are told to put on their favorite shoes or dress before bingeing.
6. The sequence of components or events in the complaint pattern could be changed. A teen was directed to tape-record her father's lectures. Then, at the appropriate time when her father was about to lecture her again, the teen was told to play the lecture back and thereby beat her father to the punch.
7. The complaint pattern could be broken into smaller pieces or elements. Spouses were told to conduct their arguments on paper, with each person taking turns to write 5 minutes, then to exchange their papers.
8. The complaint performance could be linked to the performance of some burdensome exercise. In this case, people who are chronically late may have to do something they hate to do for the same duration of time they are late. For instance, if they hate cleaning the bathroom, they must spend 1 minute cleaning the bathroom for each minute they arrive late.

In each instance, solution-oriented interventions are negotiated with the clients within a collaborative relationship where change is expected. The interventions are designed to help clients change their "doing" or "viewing" of problems, and the goal is to help clients look toward possibilities rather than problems. The approach uses what is going right rather than focusing on what is going wrong.

Solution-oriented and possibility therapy theorists augment their work with narrative interventions and have been influenced by narrative thought (Bertolino, 1999; Bertolino & O'Hanlon, 2002). Solution-focused and possibility therapists are beginning to be informed by cultural, political, historical, and gender influences on clients' problems in the same way that narrative therapists are aware that domestic abuse is something the counselor should put on the table as a problem. Both possibility and narrative approaches view humans as actively engaged in a socially constructed process of making meanings and creating stories (Monk et al., 1997; Neimeyer & Mahoney, 1995).

Brief solution-oriented and possibility therapy encourage counselors to use stories, anecdotes, parables, and humor to help clients change. This practice has been influenced by the narrative therapists White and Epston (1990), who attempt to help clients move from problem-saturated stories to more hope-filled alternative stories. Like solution-oriented therapists, Epston and White (1995) believe clients have "personal solution knowledges" that help them move beyond "expert knowledges" and toward authoring the story of their own lives.

White and Epston's (1990) theory guides their practice, helping clients achieve victory over problems that have become oppressive in their own lives; the techniques range from those designed to help clients view problems differently to giving parties, certificates, ribbons, and therapy-ending rituals. The crucial point in narrative theory is that the person is never the problem; the problem is the problem. One technique, "externalization of the problem," has been embraced by solution-oriented and possibility therapists because the problem is redefined in such a way that the problem is placed outside the clients. For example, if clients' presenting problem involves depression, therapists might ask, "How long has the depression been pushing you around?" Thus, the depression becomes a controllable object outside clients, rather than an internalized enduring condition within clients. The counselor can enlist the help of family, community, and cultural group members to unite with the identified client to fight back against the externalized problem.

An Intervention With an Adolescent

The separate brief approaches reveal the practical applications problem-focused, solution-focused, solution-oriented, and narrative approaches have for adolescent and school-age populations (Amatea et al., 2006; Bertolino, 1999; Durrant, 1995; Metcalf, 1995; Mostert, Johnson, & Mostert, 1997; Murphy, 1997; Selekman, 2005; Sklare, 2005; Winslade & Monk, 2007). Durrant (1995), Metcalf (1995), Murphy (1997), and Sklare (2005) advocate changing the way professional helpers think about difficulties by encouraging them to focus energy on solutions and competencies rather than problems. Winslade and Monk (2007) locate problems in a cultural landscape that challenges counselors to consider their own cultural positioning and the need to help youth find their own competence and life story. Amatea (1989) offers an interpretation of problem-focused therapy for school behavior problems, whereas Bertolino's (1999) possibility-oriented and Selekman's (2005) solution-oriented strategies offer an improvisational melding of all these approaches to address adolescent difficulties. Change comes from helping people (adults and adolescents) think and act differently about problematic situations. O'Hanlon (1999, 2003) offers possibility therapy and inclusive approaches that move beyond liabilities by drawing on strengths and encouraging clients to do one thing different. Such simple and pragmatic suggestions are at the heart of the strength-based approaches that work toward encouraging clients to change one small thing.

The Case of the Girl Who Knew She Was Stupid

Maria, a 16-year-old Latina, female student, met with the school counselor regarding her class selection for the upcoming school year. Maria was enrolled in a college prep program, and she had a 3.6 GPA on a 4-point scale. Neither parent had completed college, but both encouraged Maria to go to college in order to "get a good job" that would pay "good money." During an earlier session in the later part of the school year with the school counselor, Maria expressed a sense of feeling stupid and a desire to drop a class needed to meet the college entrance requirements.

MARIA: I'm stupid. I want to drop Spanish.

COUNSELOR: Drop Spanish. That's a big decision. Umm. When did stupidness start standing in your way?

MARIA: A long time ago.

COUNSELOR: By looking at your GPA, I see that stupidness certainly hasn't blocked your way to good grades.

MARIA: You just don't know.

COUNSELOR: Right, I might not know how hard you've worked. Here's what I do know. By looking at my computer screen, I see a college-prep student with a 3.6 GPA. That shows me you've outwitted stupidness and that you have a pretty full Smart Bank. It also shows me you have not let stupidness push you around or make you quit. You've pushed stupidness around.

MARIA: Maybe. I still want to drop Spanish next year. My grandma speaks Spanish but no one else in the house does. I just can't do it.

COUNSELOR: Is it stupidness or Spanish that's pushing you around?

MARIA: Spanish. My teacher doesn't help me at all. She just passes us all along, and I'm not prepared for next year. Even my grandma speaks English to me. I don't know a thing.

COUNSELOR: Not a thing? On a scale of 1 to 10, how would you rate what you know now in Spanish compared to what you knew before you took Spanish?

MARIA: About a 5.

COUNSELOR: We're halfway there. It's not a 10, but it's a solid start. Have you talked to your grandma about helping you in Spanish?

MARIA: Umm. Not really.

COUNSELOR: As I see it, you have a pretty full Smart Account. Your 3.6 GPA is just numbers on my screen, but it indicates your hard work, resources, and wealth. You are so lucky to have a grandparent who speaks Spanish, too. I think you have other accounts elsewhere, like a Knowing What to Do Account. What made you come in here to see me?

MARIA: I don't know. I just wanted to figure things out. Maybe my grandma can help, too.

COUNSELOR: Having your grandma as a learning ally would be a real help.

MARIA: Ya.

COUNSELOR: Here we are, trying to figure things out. I think you are developing a plan that begins with noticing that you have a lot going for you and you
have a grandma who can help you practice Spanish. It will take some planning
and effort but together with a learning ally or two, you have folks who will
help you make Spanish work.

MARIA: Ya, I guess I do. I'll talk to grandma tonight.

COUNSELOR: Great. Let me know how it works out and what I can do help
you work with your learning ally.

This case shows the use of externalizing the problem, scaling questions, and
metaphor. The first step in this intervention was externalizing stupidness as an object
that was standing in Maria's way. Maria then shifted the external problem to Spanish
and the Spanish teacher. Obviously, the teacher may be part of the problem, but using
scaling questions helped establish that Maria was "half-way there" in her knowledge of
Spanish. The counselor pointed out the fact that Maria made the appointment, revealing her own solution-finding skills, and that her grandmother was a learning ally. The
counselor entered into what Lee and Diaz (Chapter 3) refer to as "the cross-cultural
zone" to encourage Maria to work with her grandmother as a learning ally. Two subsequent sessions focused on strategies for dealing with her Spanish teacher, exploring
how to work with her grandmother as a learning ally, and developing a plan for continuing her success in meeting the requirements necessary to get into college.

Ethical Concerns

Brief therapy raises a number of ethical concerns, such as therapist influence,
client welfare, not addressing the underlying problem, and abandonment. Koss and
Shiang (1994) state that "no evidence exists to suggest that brief psychotherapy produces any greater negative effects than long-term psychotherapy" (p. 689). Most
people do not enter therapy to receive "overhauls." Surprisingly, given that the median
therapeutic duration is six to eight sessions, it might be said that, operationally, all
counseling is short term. Besides the pressure of third-party payments to reduce
the cost of psychotherapy, most people want to be helped as quickly as possible
without spending a great deal of time or money (Bergin & Garfield, 1994; Lambert
et al., 2004a, 2004b). At the same time, brief therapy is not a cure-all; not all clients
will benefit from brief therapy. In fact, limiting treatment duration cannot be considered a fair and equitable practice for patients who need longer therapy (Lambert
et al., 2004a).

Traditional psychodynamic therapies have been directed toward helping clients
achieve insight or awareness. Palmatier (1996) states, "Psychodynamic therapists
believe their work targets the real problem, is intensive, and results in long lasting
changes. They criticize pragmatic approaches as shallow and temporary toying with

symptoms. Therefore, symptom relief per se is not a value in therapy" (p. 91). Most brief therapies have targeted symptoms by getting clients to see and do things differently. This active relationship raises questions for some. The problem-focused approach used at MRI is frequently described as manipulative and questioned on ethical grounds. Fisch (1990) argues that manipulation is unavoidable in therapy, and the real issue is facing up to how therapists acknowledge their manipulation and assessing the therapeutic outcome. Fisch states, "Ethical and responsible therapy involves working with the client's reality (frame of reference, world view, etc.) rather than requiring clients to accept the therapist's reality" (1990, p. 430). Indeed, in a significant number of cases, brief therapy may be more ethical than long-term care if we are evaluating treatment on the basis of effective and efficient outcomes. In brief therapy, treatment is collaborative, therapists take clients' presenting complaints seriously, clients determine the success of treatment, and it is consumer oriented (Cooper, 1995). Palmatier (1996) points to core problems regarding long-term therapy: "psychodynamic therapy is nebulous, long-term, and aims to elicit insight and not behavior change" (p. 91). (Given some of the ethical concerns regarding brief therapy, brief therapists should press the ethical question around prolonged long-term care, but that is not the point.)

Professionals must advocate that clients receive adequate and effective treatment; some clients will take longer than others. Counselors are faced with the demands of third-party payers, research regarding the effectiveness of brief approaches, and clients who "do not seem to want to spend a great deal of time and money on their personal psychotherapy but prefer to be helped as quickly as possible" (Bergin & Garfield, 1994, p. 9). Models that focus on effectiveness and efficiency inform both long-term and brief approaches. Counselors may take on a role similar to a family doctor; the client might have a long-term relationship but does not see the doctor every week. Such practice is similar to using brief, intermittent psychotherapy throughout a person's life cycle. Lambert et al. (2004b) point out, "Psychotherapy is not longer viewed as a long-term process that, once completed, implies a lifetime period of mental health and adjustment" (p. 815). Counseling is moving beyond metaphors of infectious disease and ideas of permanent "cures" and toward helping people find solutions to some natural problems that are part of living. In the end, ethics are not merely lists of prescriptive rules but rather personal and professional perspectives that inform actions taken to help people seeking help (Hoyt & Combs, 1996). Counselors have a literature that points toward common factors influencing therapeutic outcomes (Asay & Lambert, 1999; Lambert, 1992). Ethical counselors look for what works to help clients.

Summary

Common assumptions in brief approaches to short-term therapy include pragmatism and parsimony, a view that human change is inevitable, that clients have resources and competence, that significant change occurs outside therapy, and that life outside therapy is more important than therapy itself.

The strength-based brief approaches point toward different forms of participation with clients, away from objectifying clients or facilitating insight, and toward collaborating with people to help them see and respond to problems differently. For strength-based brief therapists, problems are maintained by ineffective strategies for solving them. MRI facilitates clients in getting unstuck. Solution-focused counseling points clients away from problems and toward solutions. Solution-oriented therapy and possibility therapy are more concerned with cocreating with clients solvable problems or recognizing different options. Each draws on client resources and strengths.

Generally, brief therapies challenge the counseling profession to evolve. Third-party payers, research regarding the effectiveness of brief approaches, and clients who prefer to be helped as quickly as possible support continued research and experimentation with brief approaches. Although we caution against promoting any quest for instant cures, the thoughtful evolution toward therapies that are effective and efficient helps counselors look deeply at the nature of their work and the impact it has on the lives of their clients. In fact, brief therapy may press counselors to consider the deeper impact that the time variable has upon counseling designed to help clients define more meaningful and joyous lives for themselves. Indeed, some brief therapies teach clients to attend to their thinking in order to live more meaningful and joyous lives (Sedgeman, 2005). As the profession is pressed to focus on efficiencies, counselors and clients do not have time to talk about or explore meaning and joy but merely day-to-day survival. Mere survival brings us to the larger question about the roles of counselors in our culture, and the need for counselors to be mindful of the wisdom of their diverse clients' cultures. Time may be money but people matter, and wasting time may be problematic, but wasting our sense of wonder and appreciation for our incredibly rich and diverse world is even more tragic. Indeed, as moment-to-moment experience and professional counseling practice are commodified in terms of productivity, time is taken away from pointing toward simply pondering or appreciating the wonders of life. A brief intervention here might include doing one thing different—taking time to be curious about flowers, looking at and smelling flowers with someone you love, leaving work early, extending the conversation at dinner, going into a neighborhood where you are the minority, and so on. Brief or long, counselors have a role in helping individuals reach their goals and in assisting their communities to evolve in a more just, compassionate, and beautiful direction.

The following Web sites provide additional information relating to the chapter topics.

USEFUL WEB SITES

The Mental Research Institute
http://www.mri.org/

Bill O'Hanlon
http://www.brieftherapy.com/

Dulwich Centre
http://www.dulwichcentre.com.au/

European Brief Therapy Association
http://www.ebta.nu/

REFERENCES

Amatea, E. S. (1989). *Brief strategic intervention for school behavior problems.* San Francisco: Jossey-Bass.

Amatea, E. S., Smith-Adcock, S., & Villares, E. (2006). From family deficit to family strength: Viewing families' contributions to children's learning from a family resilience perspective. *Professional School Counseling, 9,* 177–189.

Asay, T. P., & Lambert, M. J. (1999). The empirical case for common factors in therapy: Quantitative findings. In M. A. Hubble, B. L. Duncan, & S. D. Miller (Eds.), *The heart and soul of change: What works in therapy* (pp. 23–55). Washington, DC: American Psychological Association.

Berg, I. K., & DeJong, P. (2005). Engagement through complimenting. *Journal of Family Psychotherapy, 16,* 51–56.

Bergin, A. E., & Garfield, S. L. (Eds.). (1994). *Handbook of psychotherapy and behavior change* (4th ed.). New York: John Wiley & Sons.

Bertolino, B. (1999). *Therapy with troubled teenagers: Rewriting young lives in progress.* New York: John Wiley & Sons.

Bertolino, B., & O'Hanlon, B. (2002). *Collaborative, competency-based counseling and therapy.* Boston: Allyn and Bacon.

Besley, T. (2003). Brief counseling in schools: Working with young people from 11 to 18. *British Journal of Guidance and Counselling, 31,* 449–452.

Binder, J. L., Strupp, H. H., & Henry, W. P. (1995). Psychodynamic therapies in practice: Time limited dynamic psychotherapy. In B. Bongar and L. E. Beutler (Eds.), *Comprehensive textbook of psychotherapy,* pp. 48–63. New York: Oxford University Press.

Cade, B., & O'Hanlon, W. H. (1993). *A brief guide to brief therapy.* New York: W. W. Norton.

Claxton, G. (1997). *Hare brain, tortoise mind: Why intelligence increases when you think less.* Hopewell, NJ: Ecco Press.

Cooper, J. F. (1995). *A primer of brief psychotherapy.* New York: W. W. Norton.

Crosby, A. W. (1997). *The measure of reality: Quantification and Western society, 1250–1600.* Cambridge, UK: Cambridge University Press.

Cummings, N., & Sayama, M. (1995). *Focused therapy: A casebook of brief intermittent psychotherapy throughout the life cycle.* New York: Brunner/Mazel.

De Shazer, S. (1985). *Keys to solution in brief therapy.* New York: W. W. Norton.

De Shazer, S. (1990). What is it about brief therapy that works? In J. K. Zeig & S. G. Gilligan (Eds.), *Brief therapy: Myths, methods, and metaphors* (pp. 90–99). New York: Brunner/Mazel.

De Shazer, S. (1991). *Putting difference to work.* New York: Norton.

DeJong, P. (2005). Teaching practice via success stories. *Journal of Family Psychotherapy, 16,* 257–262.

DeJong, P., & Berg, I. K. (1998). *Interviewing for solutions.* Pacific Grove, CA: Brooks/Cole.

DeJong, P., & Berg, I. K. (2002). *Interviewing for solutions* (2nd ed.). Pacific Grove, CA: Brooks/Cole.

Durrant, M. (1995). *Creative strategies for school problems: Solutions for psychologists and teachers.* New York: W. W. Norton.

Durrant, M., & Kowalski, K. (1993). Enhancing views of competence. In S. Friedman (Ed.), *The new language of change: Constructive collaboration in psychotherapy* (pp. 107–137). New York: Guilford Press.

Efran, J. S., Lukens, M. D., & Lukens, R. J. (1990). *Language, structure, and change: Frameworks for meaning in psychotherapy.* New York: Norton.

Ellis, A. (1989). Rational-emotive therapy. In R. J. Corsini & D. Wedding (Eds.), *Current psychotherapies* (4th ed.) (pp. 197–238). Itasca, IL: Peacock Publishers.

Ellis, A. (1990). How can psychological treatment aim to briefer and better? The rational-emotive approach to brief therapy. In J. K. Zeig & S. G. Gilligan (Eds.), *Brief therapy: Myths, methods, and metaphors* (pp. 291–302). New York: Brunner/Mazel.

Ellis, A. (1996). *Better, deeper, and more enduring brief therapy: The rational emotive behavior therapy approach.* New York: Brunner/Mazel.

Epston, D., & White, M. (1995). Termination as a rite of passage: Questioning strategies for a therapy of inclusion. In R. A. Neimeyer & M. J. Mahoney (Eds.), *Constructivism in psychotherapy* (pp. 339–354). Washington, DC: American Psychological Association.

Fisch, R. (1990). Problem-solving psychotherapy. In J. K. Zeig & W. M. Munion (Eds.), *What is psychotherapy? Contemporary perspectives* (pp. 269–273). San Francisco: Jossey-Bass.

Fisch, R. (1994). Basic elements in the brief therapies. In M. F. Hoyt (Ed.), *Constructive therapies* (pp. 126–139). New York: Guilford Press.

Fisch, R. (2004). 'So what have you done lately?' MRI brief therapy. *Journal of Systemic Therapies, 23,* 4–10.

Fisch, R., Weakland, J. H., & Segal, L. (1982). *Tactics of change: Doing therapy briefly.* San Francisco: Jossey-Bass.

Friedman, S. (Ed). (1993). The new language of change: Constructive collaboration in psychotherapy. New York: Guilford Press.

Haley, J. (1973). *Uncommon therapy: The psychiatric techniques of Milton H. Erickson.* New York: W. W. Norton.

Hart, B. (1995). Re-authoring stories we work by situating the narrative approach in the presence of the family of therapists. *Australian and New Zealand Journal of Family Therapy, 16,* 181–189.

Herman, E. (1995). *The romance of American psychology: Political culture in the age of experts.* Berkeley: University of California Press.

Hoyt, M. F. (Ed.). (1994). *Constructive therapies.* New York: Guilford Press.

Hoyt, M. F. (1995). *Brief therapy and managed care: Readings for contemporary practice.* San Francisco: Jossey-Bass.

Hoyt, M. F. (Ed.). (1996). *Constructive therapies, vol 2.* New York: Guilford Press.

Hoyt, M. F. (2000). *Some stories are better than others: Doing what works I, brief therapy and managed care.* Philadelphia: Brunner/Mazel.

Hoyt, M. F. (2002). How I embody a narrative constructive approach. *Journal of Constructivist Psychology, 15,* 279–289.

Hoyt, M. F. (2005). Why I became a (brief) psychotherapist. *Journal of Clinical Psychotherapy, 61,* 983–989.

Hoyt, M. F., & Combs, G. (1996). On ethics and the spiritualities of the surface: A conversation with Michael White. In M. F. Hoyt (Ed.), *Constructive therapies, vol 2* (pp. 33–59). New York: Guilford Press.

Hubble, M. A., Duncan, B. L., & Miller, S. D. (1999). *The heart and soul of change: What works in therapy.* Washington, DC: American Psychological Association.

Jianyi, F. Xuanwen, L., Yingping, Z., & Weiqiang, H. (2006). A new mode of counseling: Solution-focused brief counseling. *Psychological Science (China), 29,* 430–432. Retrieved Saturday, April 28, 2007 from the PsychINFO database.

Koss, M. P., & Butcher, J. N. (1986). Research on brief psychotherapy. In S. L. Garfield & A. E. Bergin (Eds.), *Handbook of psychotherapy and behavior change* (3rd ed., pp. 627–670). New York: John Wiley.

Koss, M. P., & Shiang, J. (1994). Research on brief psychotherapy. In A. E. Bergin & S. L. Garfield (Eds.), *Handbook of psychotherapy and behavior change* (4th ed., pp. 664–700). New York: John Wiley.

Kurihara, S. (2002). A study of brief counseling model by teachers in school. *Japanese Journal of Counseling Science, 35,* 30–39. Retrieved April 28, 2007, from the PsychINFO database.

Lakoff, G., & Johnson, M. (1999). *Philosophy in the flesh: The embodied mind and its challenge to Western thought.* New York: Basic Books.

Lambert, M. J. (1992). Implications of outcome research for psychotherapy integration. In J. C. Norcross & M. R. Goldstein (Eds.), *Handbook of psychotherapy integration* (pp. 94–129). New York: Basic Books.

Lambert, M. J., Garfield, S. L., & Bergin, A. E. (2004a). Introduction and historical overview. In M. J. Lambert (Ed.), *Bergin and Garfield's handbook of psychotherapy and behavior change* (5th ed., pp. 3–15). New York: Wiley.

Lambert, M. J., Garfield, S. L., & Bergin, A. E. (2004b). Overview, trends, and future issues. In M. J. Lambert (Ed.), *Bergin and Garfield's handbook of psychotherapy and behavior change* (5th ed., pp. 805–821). New York: Wiley.

Levenson, H. (1995). *Time-limited dynamic psychotherapy.* New York: Basic Books.

Lipchik, E. (2002). *Beyond technique in solution-focused therapy: Working with emotions and the therapeutic relationship*. New York: Guilford Press.

Mahoney, M. J. (1997). Brief moments and enduring effects: Reflections on time and timing in psychotherapy. In W. J. Matthews & J. H. Edgette (Eds.), *Current thinking and research in brief therapy: Solutions, strategies, narratives*. New York: Brunner/Mazel.

Mann, J. (1981). The core of time-limited psychotherapy: Time and the central issue. In S. H. Budman (Ed.), *Forms of brief therapy* (pp. 25–43). New York: Guilford Press.

Mann, J. (1991). Time limited psychotherapy. In P. Crits-Christoph & J. P. Barber (Eds.), *Handbook of short term dynamic psychotherapy* (pp. 17–44). New York: Basic Books.

Matthews, W. J., & Edgette, J. H. (Eds.). (1997). *Current thinking and research in brief therapy: Solutions, strategies, narratives*. New York: Brunner/Mazel.

McCloskey, K. A., & Fraser, J. S. (1997). Using feminist MRI brief therapy during initial contact with victims of domestic violence. *Psychotherapy, 34*, 433–446.

McKeel, A. (1996). A clinician's guide to research on solution-focused brief therapy. In S. D. Miller, M. A. Hubble, & B, L. Duncan (Eds.), *Handbook of solution-focused brief therapy* (pp. 251–271). San Francisco: Jossey-Bass.

McWhorter, J. (2001). *The power of Babel: A natural history of language*. New York: Perennial.

Metcalf, L. (1995). *Counseling toward solutions: A practical solution-focused program for working with students, teachers, and parents*. West Nyack, NY: Center for Applied Research in Education.

Miller, G. (1997). *Becoming miracle workers: Language and meaning in brief therapy*. New York: Aldine de Gruyter.

Miller, S. D., Hubble, M. A., & Duncan, B. L. (Eds.). (1996). *Handbook of solution-focused brief therapy*. San Francisco: Jossey-Bass.

Monk, G., Winslade, J., Crocket, K., & Epston, D. (Eds.). (1997). *Narrative therapy in practice: The archaeology of hope*. San Francisco: Jossey-Bass.

Mostert, D. L., Johnson, E., & Mostert, M. P. (1997). The utility of solution-focused, brief counseling in schools: Potential from an initial study. *Professional School Counseling, 1*, 21–24.

Murphy, J. J. (1997). *Solution-focused counseling in middle and high schools*. Alexandria, VA: American Counseling Association.

Neimeyer, R. A., & Mahoney, M. J. (Eds.). (1995). *Constructivism in psychotherapy*. Washington: DC: American Psychological Association.

O'Hanlon, W. H. (1987). *Taproots: Underlying principles of Milton Erickson's therapy and hypnosis*. New York: W. W. Norton.

O'Hanlon, W. H. (1990). A grand unified theory for brief therapy: Putting problems in context. In J. K. Zeig & S. G. Gilligan (Eds.), *Brief therapy: Myths, methods, and metaphors* (pp. 78–89). New York: Brunner/Mazel.

O'Hanlon, W. H. (1999). *Do one thing different: And other uncommonly sensible solutions to life's persistent problems*. New York: William Morrow.

O'Hanlon, W. H. (2003). *A guide to inclusive therapy: 26 methods of respectful, resistance-dissolving therapy*. New York: W. W. Norton.

O'Hanlon, W. H., & Weiner-Davis, M. (1989). *In search of solutions: A new direction in psychotherapy*. New York: W. W. Norton.

Palmatier, L. L. (1990). Reality therapy and brief strategic interactional therapy. *Journal of Reality Therapy, 9*, 3–17.

Palmatier, L. L. (1996). Freud defrauded while Glasser defreuded: From pathologizing to talking solutions. *Journal of Reality Therapy, 16*, 75–94.

Parry, A., & Doan, R. E. (1994). *Story re-visions: Narrative therapy in the postmodern world*. New York: Guilford Press.

Pransky, G. S. (1998). *The renaissance of psychology*. New York: Sulzburger and Graham.

Pransky, G. S., Mills, R. C., Sedgeman, J. A., & Bleven, J. K. (1997). An emerging paradigm for brief treatment. In L. Vandecreek, S. Knapp, & T. L. Jackson (Eds.), *Innovations in clinical practice: A source book* (vol. 15, pp. 401–420). Sarasota, FL: Professional Resource Press.

Rosenbaum, R., Hoyt, M. F., & Talmon, M. (1990). In R. A. Wells & V. J. Giannetti (Eds.), *Handbook of the brief psychotherapies* (pp. 165–189). New York: Plenum Press.

Sedgeman, J. (2005). Health realization/innate health: Can a quiet mind and a positive feeling state be accessible over the lifespan without stress-relief techniques? *Medical Science Monitor, 11*(12), 47–52.

Selekman, M. D. (1993a). *Pathways to change: Brief therapy solutions with difficult adolescents.* New York: Guilford Press.

Selekman, M. D. (1993b). Solution-oriented brief therapy with difficult adolescents. In S. Friedman (Ed.), *The new language of change: Constructive collaboration in psychotherapy* (pp. 138–157). New York: Guilford Press.

Selekman, M. D. (2005). *Pathways to change: Brief therapy with difficult adolescents* (2nd ed.). New York: Guilford Press.

Selekman, M. D. (2006). *Working with self-harming adolescents: A collaborative, strengths-based therapy approach.* New York: W. W. Norton.

Sharf, R. S. (1996). *Theories of psychotherapy and counseling: Concepts and cases.* Pacific Grove, CA: Brooks/Cole.

Shulman, B. H. (1989). Some remarks on brief therapy. Special issue: Varieties of brief therapy. *Individual Psychology: Journal of Adlerian Theory, Research, and Practice, 45*(1–2), 34–37.

Sklare, G. B. (2005). *Brief counseling that works: A solution-focused approach for school counselors* (2nd ed.). Thousand Oaks, CA: Corwin Press.

Skolimowski, H. (1994). *The participatory mind: A new theory of knowledge and of the universe.* London: Penguin.

Smith, E. J. (2006). The Strength-Based Counseling Model. *The Counseling Psychologist, 34*, 13–79.

Strupp, H. H. (1981). Toward the refinement of time-limited dynamic psychotherapy. In S. H. Budman (Ed.), *Forms of brief therapy* (pp. 219–242). New York: Guilford Press.

Walter, J. L., & Peller, J. E. (1992). *Becoming solution-focused in brief therapy.* New York: Brunner/Mazel.

Walter, J. L., & Peller, J. E. (2000). *Recreating brief therapy: Preferences and possibilities.* New York: W. W. Norton.

Wampold, B. E. (2001). *The great psychotherapy debate: Models, methods, and findings.* Mahwah, NJ: Lawrence Erlbaum.

Watzlawick, P., Weakland, J., & Fisch, R. (1974). *Change: Principles of problem formation and problem resolution.* New York: W. W. Norton.

Wells, R. A., & Giannetti, V. J. (Eds.). (1990). *Handbook of brief psychotherapies.* New York: Plenum Press.

White, M., & Epston, D. (1990). *Narrative means to therapeutic ends.* New York: W. W. Norton.

Winslade, J., & Monk, G. (2007). *Narrative counseling in schools: Powerful and brief* (2nd ed.). Thousand Oaks, CA: Corwin Press.

Worchel, J. (1990). Short-term dynamic psychotherapy. In R. A. Wells & V. J. Giannetti (Eds.), *Handbook of the brief psychotherapies* (pp. 193–216). New York: Plenum Press.

Zeig, J. K., & Gilligan, S. G. (Eds.). (1990). *Brief therapy: Myths, methods, and metaphors.* New York: Brunner/Mazel.

Group Counseling

DAVID CAPUZZI, PhD
Pennsylvania State University

DOUGLAS R. GROSS, PhD
Arizona State University

The 21st century poses challenges and possibilities that should be of great interest to the beginning counselor enrolled in a counselor education program and considering becoming a group work specialist. If we believe that the 1950s may have symbolized "the individual in society," the 1960s "the individual against society," the 1970s "the individual's conflict with self," and the 1980s "the individual's integration into the family," the society of the 1990s and 2000s may clearly be characterized as "the individual's integration with technology" (Greene, Lawson, & Getz, 2005). Much of the work in education, employment, and day-to-day living will be done by computers; connections between colleagues, friends, and family members will be maintained by telephones, word processors, and modems. (The reader should review Chapter 6 for more information about technology and counseling.)

As consistent social contact with friends and coworkers is replaced by e-mail, there will be a much greater need for interpersonal communication on a person-to-person basis. Groups will provide an antidote to human isolation, and more and more counselors and other human development specialists will be called upon to serve as group facilitators. The beginning counseling and human development specialist will experience an explosion of opportunities and escalating concomitant responsibilities as a group work specialist.

There are a number of reasons why the responsibilities of a group work specialist are so important to address. A facilitator must be skilled in catalyzing a therapeutic climate in a group and in monitoring therapeutic factors inherent in the group (Berg, Landreth, & Fall, 1998; Corey, 2008; Gladding, 2008; Ohlsen & Ferreira, 1994). Facilitators must also be able to assess which clients they can assist given the facilitators' level of skills, describe their services and aspects of the group experience, engender trust and confidence, and answer questions about client rights and responsibilities, confidentiality, and expectations for change.

The purpose of this chapter is to provide an introduction to group work for those interested in pursuing follow-up education and experience in the context of master's and doctoral preparation. The history of group work, types of groups, stages of group life, characteristics of group facilitators, responsibilities and interventions in groups, myths connected with group work, and the issues and ethics of group work will be reviewed.

The History of Group Work

Beginnings

As noted by Vriend (1985), the first half of the 20th century was characterized by lively interest, experimentation, and research in the promising new field of group dynamics. Behavior in small groups, leadership styles, membership roles, communication variables, and so on were all examined and studied for their application to groups in a variety of settings (Hare, Borgatta, & Bales, 1967; Johnson & Johnson, 2000). J. H. Pratt (Boston), Jesse B. Davis (Grand Rapids), J. L. Moreno, Alfred Adler, Samuel R. Slavson, Rudolf Dreikurs, Nathan Ackerman, Gregory Bateson, and Virginia Satir were all well-known practitioners who pioneered early approaches to group work (Berg et al., 1998).

In 1947, a history-making conference in Bethel, Maine, was attended by a multidisciplinary group of researchers and practitioners from university and community settings throughout North America. The National Training Laboratory (NTL) in Group Development of the National Education Association held its first "laboratory session," at which T-groups (the "T" is for training) and the laboratory method were born (Bradford, Gibb, & Benne, 1964; Roller, 1997). Using themselves as experimental subjects, participants at the conference created a laboratory situation in which the behavior of the participants was more important than any effort or technique employed. The situation created a safe place for group members to explore their own behavior and feelings and others' responses to them as people separate from social, work, and family roles. Under the direction of the NTL, such conferences continued each summer, and the T-group movement grew and achieved national visibility.

As time passed, T-groups appeared on university campuses and in other settings. The T-group provided a fresh concept with tremendous appeal, as opportunity was provided for group members to become more "sensitive," to "grow emotionally," and to "realize their human potential." The country began hearing about the "human potential movement" and of exciting developments in California, particularly at the Esalen Institute at Big Sur (Neukrug, 1999) and at the Center for the Studies of the Person, founded by Carl R. Rogers and his colleagues. Soon there were a variety of marathon and encounter groups; it was an era of openness, self-awareness, and getting in touch with feelings.

The 1960s and 1970s

The 1960s was a time of social upheaval and questioning. There were riots on campuses and in cities, and civil rights groups struggled to raise the consciousness of the nation about unfair discrimination and prejudice. Leaders such as John F. Kennedy and Martin Luther King Jr. became the idolized champions and international symbols of a people's determination to change a society and promote social responsibility. The nation united in grief-stricken disbelief as its heroes were martyred, and determination to counter the human rights violations of the decades escalated. As the 1960s ended, the encounter groups movement, emphasizing personal consciousness and connection with others, reached its zenith and then gradually waned as events such as the Charles Manson killings, the Watergate scandal, the first presidential resignation in the history of the United States, the group killings at the Munich Olympics, and the rise of fanatic cults made people question the extent to which permissiveness and "human potential" should be allowed to develop (Janis, 1972; Rowe & Winborn, 1973).

For professionals in education and mental health, however, the 1960s and 1970s were decades of maintained interest in group work, despite the highs and lows of societal fervor and dismay. Mental health centers conducted more group sessions for clients, and counselor education, counseling psychology, psychology, and social work departments on university campuses instituted more course work and supervised experiences in aspects of group work. In 1973, the Association for Specialists in Group Work (ASGW) was formed, and by 1974 (Berg et al., 1998; Neukrug, 1999) it had become a division of the American Counseling Association (at that time named the American Personnel and Guidance Association). Similar developments took place in the context of other large professional groups, such as the American Psychological Association and the National Association of Social Workers.

The 1980s

The 1980s witnessed increasing interest in group work and in working with special populations. Groups were started for alcoholics, adult children of alcoholics, incest victims, adults molested as children, persons who are overweight, underassertive persons, and those who have been victims of violent crimes. Other groups were begun for the elderly, those dealing with death and other losses, people with eating disorders, smokers, and the victims of the Holocaust (Neukrug, 1999). This increasing specialization brought an increasing need for higher standards in preparation of the group work specialist, as evidenced by the development of training standards for group work specialists (ASGW, 1983, 1992) and the inclusion in the standards of the Council for Accreditation of Counseling and Related Educational Programs (CACREP, 1988) of specific group work specialist preparation guidelines for the graduate-level university educator to follow. At the same time, this increasing specialization has brought with it a reliance on self-help groups composed of individuals who share a specific affliction. Usually, such groups are not facilitated by a professional, and this set of circumstances can conflict with the values and standards of professional group workers unless they have given some thought to how they might be involved (Corey, 2008).

The 1990s

The escalating interest in group work and in working with special populations so evident in the decade of the 1980s continued into the last decade of the century. The 1983

ASGW standards for training of group counselors was revised, and a new set of standards was adopted in 1991 (ASGW, 1991). Although the 1991 standards built on the 1983 standards in emphasizing the knowledge, skills, and supervised experience necessary for the preparation of group workers, the newer standards broadened the conception of group work, clarified the difference between core competencies and specialization requirements, defined the four prominent varieties of group work, and eliminated the previous distinctions among different kinds of supervised field experience (Conyne, Wilson, Kline, Morran, & Ward, 1993). In addition, CACREP, in its 1994 and 2001 revisions of accreditation standards, reemphasized the importance of group work by identifying principles of group dynamics, group leadership styles, theories of group counseling, group counseling methods, approaches used for other types of group work, and ethical considerations as essential curricular elements for all counselor education programs (CACREP, 1994, 2001).

Groups in the 21st Century

Technology has taken groups to computers through the use of chat rooms, computer conferencing, listservs, and news groups. Support groups on the Internet for recovering addicts, cancer survivors, individuals with eating disorders, Alzeimers caregivers, and individuals interested in a variety of other topics that can be addressed in groups are becoming more common. Online courses offered by numerous counselor education programs and departments often require course participants to engage in group work to complete course requirements. Sometimes this group work is experienced exclusively on an electronic basis; in some instances, an on-site facilitator or convener works with groups of students in a specific location to facilitate the completion of collaborative group projects and serve as consultant and supervisor.

Although the issues and ethics of group work will be reviewed at the end of this chapter, it should be noted here that the practice of the group work professional will require increasing levels of expertise and an enhanced ability to participate in and apply the results of research. The history-making national conference for group work specialists, conceptualized and sponsored by ASGW in early 1990 in Florida and repeated during subsequent years in other parts of the country, symbolizes the importance of group work to the clients served by the counseling and human development professional.

Types of Groups

Most textbooks for introductory counseling courses begin the discussion of group work by attempting to make distinctions among group therapy, group counseling, and group guidance. In general, *group therapy* is described as being longer term, more remedially and therapeutically focused, and more likely to have a facilitator with doctoral-level preparation and a more "clinical" orientation. *Group counseling* may be differentiated from group therapy by its more developmental focus on conscious problems, by the fact that it is not aimed at major personality changes, by an orientation toward short-term issues, and by the fact that it is not as concerned with the treatment of the more severe psychological and behavioral disorders (Corey, 2008; Gazda, Ginter, & Horne, 2001). The term *group guidance* usually describes a K–12 classroom setting in which the leader presents information or conducts mental health education. In contrast to a group therapy or group counseling situation involving no more than 8 to 10 group participants, a group guidance experience could involve 20 to 40 group participants, which lessens opportunities for individual participation and for facilitator observation and intervention.

For the purposes of this chapter, ASGW's definitions of the four group work specialty types are presented next as a point of departure for classifying groups (Conyne et al., 1993). Additional reading relative to group "types" is available from sources such as Corey (1985, 2008), Dinkmeyer and Muro (1979), Gazda (1984), Gladding (2008), Neukrug (1999), and Ohlsen (1977).

Task/Work Groups

The group worker who specializes in promoting the development and functioning of task and work groups seeks to support such groups in the process of improving their function and performance. Task and work group specialists employ principles of group dynamics, organizational development, and team building to enhance group members' skills in group task accomplishment and group maintenance. The scope of practice for these group work specialists includes normally functioning individuals who are members of naturally occurring task or work groups operating within a specific organizational context.

Note that graduate course work for specialists in task and work groups should include at least one specialization course in organizational management and development. Ideally, course work should be taken in the broad area of organizational psychology, management, and development to instill an awareness of organizational life and how task and work groups function within the organization. In addition, a task/work group specialist might also develop skill in organizational assessment, training, program development, consultation, and program evaluation.

Clinical instruction for training in working with task and work groups should include a minimum of 30 clock hours (45 clock hours recommended) of supervised practice in leading or coleading a task/work group appropriate to the age and clientele of the group leader's specialty area(s), such as school counseling, community counseling, or mental health counseling.

Guidance/Psychoeducational Groups

The psychoeducational group specialist educates group participants. Such participants may be informationally deficient in some area (e.g., how to cope with external threats, developmental transitions, or personal and interpersonal crises). The scope of practice of psychoeducational group leaders includes essentially normally functioning individuals who are "at risk" for, but currently unaffected by, an environmental threat (e.g., AIDS or drug use), who are approaching a developmental transition point (e.g., new parents), or who are in the midst of coping with a life crisis (such as suicide of a loved one). The primary goal in psychoeducational group work is to prevent the future development of dysfunctional behaviors.

Course work for specialization in psychoeducational groups should include at least one specialization course that provides information about community psychology, health and wellness promotion, and program development and evaluation. Ideally, psychoeducational group specialists would also take course work in curriculum design, group training methods, and instructional techniques. Psychoeducational group specialists should also acquire knowledge about the topic areas in which they intend to work (such as AIDS, substance abuse prevention, grief and loss, coping with transition and change, and parent effectiveness training).

Clinical instruction for preparing to facilitate psychoeducational groups should include a minimum of 30 clock hours (45 clock hours recommended) of supervised practice in leading or coleading a psychoeducational group appropriate to the age and clientele of the group leader's specialty area(s), such as school counseling, community counseling, or mental health counseling.

Counseling Groups

The group worker who specializes in group counseling focuses on assisting group participants to resolve the usual, yet often difficult, problems of living by stimulating interpersonal support and group problem solving. Group counselors support participants in developing their existing interpersonal problem-solving competencies so that they become better able to handle future problems of a similar nature. The scope of practice for their group work includes nonsevere career, educational, personal, interpersonal, social, and developmental concerns of essentially normally functioning individuals.

Graduate course work for specialists in group counseling should include multiple courses in human development, health promotion, and group counseling. Group counseling specialists should have in-depth knowledge in the broad areas of normal human development, problem identification, and treatment of normal personal and interpersonal problems of living.

Clinical instruction for counseling groups should include a minimum of 45 clock hours (60 clock hours recommended) of supervised practice in leading or coleading a counseling group appropriate to the age and clientele of the group leader's specialty area(s), such as community counseling, mental health counseling, or school counseling.

Psychotherapy Groups

The specialist in group psychotherapy helps individual group members remediate in-depth psychological problems or reconstruct major personality dimensions. The group psychotherapist differs from specialists in task/work groups, psychoeducational groups, or counseling groups in that the group psychotherapist's scope of practice is focused on people with acute or chronic mental or emotional disorders characterized by marked distress, impairment in functioning, or both.

Graduate course work for training in group psychotherapy should include multiple courses in the development, assessment, and treatment of serious or chronic personal and interpersonal dysfunction. The group psychotherapist must develop in-depth knowledge in the broad areas of normal and abnormal human development, diagnosis, treatment of psychopathology, and group psychotherapy. Clinical instruction for working with psychotherapy groups should include a minimum 45 clock hours (60 clock hours recommended) of supervised practice in leading or coleading a psychotherapy group appropriate to the age and clientele of the group leader's specialty area(s), such as mental health counseling, or community counseling.

Developmental Stages in Groups

Bruce Tuckman's stage model of group development (storming, norming, performing, and adjourning) was first published in 1965 and still remains one of the most commonly cited models for group program design and facilitation. In an outstanding article, David G. Zimpfer (1986) pointed out that much has been written about the developmental phases or stages through which a small group progresses over time (Bales, 1950; Braaten, 1975; Golembiewski, 1962; Hare, 1973; Hill & Gruner, 1973; Thelen & Dickerman, 1949). He noted that recent contributions to this topic range from descriptive, classificatory schemes (such as the initial, transitional, working, and final stages presented by Corey in 1985, 2004, and 2008) to detailed analyses of a single phase of group development (such as the 1965 exploration of authority relations in T-groups presented by Reid). Zimpfer's recommendation to the group work specialist is to select the theory or model of small-group development that applies to the kind of group to be conducted. This recommendation was recently endorsed by Cassidy (2007). Many additional resources that describe small-group development can be read as a follow-up to this chapter and to Zimpfer's recommendation (Donigan & Malanti, 1997; Gladding, 2008; Goldstein & Noonan, 1999; Jacobs, Masson, & Harvill, 1998; MacKenzie, 1997).

After studying a variety of models and conceptualizations of the developmental stages of groups and calling upon our own collective experience, we propose a composite conceptualization (Capuzzi, Gross, & Stauffer, 2006) of the stages of group life. In our view, the developmental process has four stages: (a) definitive stage, (b) personal involvement stage, (c) group involvement stage, and (d) enhancement and closure stage.

Definitive Stage

The length of time associated with this stage in group development varies with the group and is best explained in terms of the individual group member's definition of the purpose of the group, commitment, and involvement in it and the degree of self-disclosure he or she is willing to do. Characterizing this stage of development are questions such as Whom can I trust? Where will I find support? Will I be hurt by others knowing about me? and How much of myself am I willing to share? These questions, and the lack of immediate answers, typify members in the definitive stage as increased anxiety, excitement, nervousness, and self-protective dialogue increase. The dialogue during this stage tends to be social (small talk) as the members test the waters of group involvement. To help group members deal effectively with the definitive stage, the group leader needs skills in dealing with issues such as trust, support, safety, self-disclosure, and confidentiality.

In the definitive stage in group development, individuals define, demonstrate, and experiment with their own role definitions; they "test" the temperament, personality, and behaviors of other group members; and they arrive at conclusions about how personally involved they are willing to become. The individual's movement through this stage can be enhanced or impeded by the group's makeup (age, gender, number, values, attitudes, socioeconomic status, and so on), the leadership style (active, passive, autocratic, democratic), the group's setting (formal, informal, uncomfortable, relaxed), the personal dynamics the individual brings to the group (shy, aggressive, verbal, nonverbal), and the individual's perceptions of trust and acceptance from other group members and from the group leader.

The definitive stage is crucial in group development because this stage can determine for the individual (and, therefore, for the group) future involvement, commitment, and individual and group success or failure as the group progresses.

Personal Involvement Stage

Once individuals have drawn conclusions about their commitment and role in the group, they move into the personal involvement stage of group development. This stage is best described in terms of member-to-member interactions—the sharing of personal information, confrontation with other group members, power struggles, and the individual's growing identity as a group member. Statements such as "I am," "I fear," "I need," and "I care" are characteristic of this stage of group involvement. Through speech and behaviors, the individual member demonstrates the degree of personal sharing he or she is willing to invest and confirms the commitment made during the definitive stage.

The personal involvement stage is one of action, reaction, and interaction. Both fight and flight are represented in this stage, as individuals strive to create a role within the group. This creating process often involves intense member-to-member interactions, followed by a retreat to regroup and become involved again. The interactions that ensue not only enhance the member's place within the group but also aid in firmly establishing the group as an entity in its own right.

The personal involvement stage offers the individual the opportunity to try out various behaviors, affirm or deny perceptions of self and others, receive feedback in the form of words or behaviors, and begin the difficult process of self-evaluation. Individual involvement in this stage of group development is critical to the eventual outcome of the group.

Group Involvement Stage

As a result of the information about self gained in the personal involvement stage, group members move into the group involvement stage, characterized by self-evaluation and self-assessment of behavior, attitudes, values, and methods used in relating to others and also by members' channeling their energies to better meet group goals and purposes. During this stage the term *member* and the term *group* become more synonymous. Degrees of cooperation and cohesiveness replace conflict and confrontation as members, now more confident in their role in the group, direct more of their attention to what is best for the group and all its members. This stage reveals increasing role clarification, intimacy, problem exploration, group solidarity, compromise, conflict resolution, and risk taking. The group, with its purposes and goals, is merging with the individual purposes and goals of its members. Individual agendas are being replaced by group agendas, and members are identifying more with the group. Bonding is taking place between members as they join forces to enhance the group and, in turn, enhance self in relation to the group. References to "insider" and "outsider" differentiate the group and the member's life outside the group. Members grow protective of other group members and also of the group itself. The group and its membership take on special significance unique to those who are part of the process. This melding of member and group purposes and goals is necessary to the group's ongoing success.

Enhancement and Closure Stage

The final stage in a group's life is often described as the most exhilarating but also the saddest aspect of group work. The exhilaration stems from the evaluation and reevaluation that are so much a part of the final stage. The evaluative aspect consists of reevaluation of the group process and individual and group assessment of change, in conjunction with individual and group reinforcement of individual member change and a commitment to continue self-analysis and growth. Members have an opportunity to share significant growth experiences during the group tenure, and they receive feedback, generally positive, from other group members and the leader. Members are encouraged to review the process of the group and to measure changes that have taken place since first entering the group. Member statements at this stage of group development tend to be along the lines of "I was . . . now I am," "I felt . . . now I feel," "I didn't . . . now I do," and "I couldn't . . . now I can."

The sadness in this final stage centers on leaving an environment that provided safety, security, and support and individuals who offered encouragement, friendship, and positive feedback. A major concern seems to be whether the individual will ever be able to replace what he or she found in the group and take what was learned in the group and apply it elsewhere. The answer to both questions is generally yes, but the individual is too close to the experience to have this self-assurance. Our experience indicates that this stage often ends with members' unwritten agreement to continue group involvement and, more specifically, to continue contact with members of the present group. Most group members find, after distancing themselves from the group, that neither of these activities is essential. The gains they made from the group experience will serve them well as they move into other facets of their lives.

The movement from group initiation to group termination varies for a myriad of reasons, and no one conceptualization has all the answers or addresses all the issues inherent in the group process. This framework can provide, however, guidelines for working with groups.

Characteristics of Group Facilitators

Many writers who are expert in group counseling have described the personal traits and characteristics of effective group counselors (Corey, 1985, 2004, 2008; Dinkmeyer & Muro, 1979; Gladding, 2008; Kottler, 1983). As expressed by Gerald Corey in 2004:

> Group leaders can acquire extensive theoretical and practical knowledge of group dynamics and be skilled in diagnostic and technical procedures yet be ineffective in stimulating growth and change in the members of their groups. Leaders bring to every group their personal qualities, values, and life experiences. To promote growth in the members' lives, leaders need to live growth-oriented lives themselves. To foster honest self-investigation in others, they need to have the courage to engage in self-appraisal. If they hope to inspire others to break away from deadening ways of being, they need to be willing to seek new experiences themselves. In short, the most effective group direction is found in the kind of life the group members see the leader demonstrating and not in the words they hear the leader saying. (p. 25)

We believe that there are characteristics that the effective group leader must possess in order to do an effective job of facilitating group process. The reader is directed to sources such as Arbuckle (1975), Carkhuff and Berenson (1977), Jourard (1971), Truax and Carkhuff (1967), and Yalom (1975) for earlier readings on this topic. Corey's 2004 presentation is summarized here as a constructive point of departure for the beginning counselor.

Presence. The leader's ability to be emotionally present as group members share their experience is important. Leaders who are in touch with their own life experiences and associated emotions are usually better able to communicate empathy and understanding because they are able to relate to similar circumstances or emotions.

Personal Power. Personal power comes from a sense of self-confidence and a realization of the influence the leader has on a group. Personal power that is channeled in a way that enhances the ability of each group member to identify and build upon strengths, overcome problems, and cope more effectively with stressors is both essential and "curative."

Courage. Group facilitators must be courageous. They must take risks by expressing their reactions to aspects of group process, confronting, sharing a few life experiences, acting on a combination of intuition and observation, and directing the appropriate portion of the group movement and discussion.

Willingness to Confront Oneself.   It takes courage to deal with group members; it is not easy to role-model, confront, convey empathy, and achieve a good balance between catalyzing interaction and allowing the group to "unfold." It also takes courage on the part of the group leader to confront self. As Corey (2000) so aptly stated:

Self-confrontation can take the form of posing and answering questions such as these:

- *Why am I leading groups? What am I getting from this activity?*
- *Why do I behave as I do in a group? What impact do my attitudes, values, biases, feelings, and behaviors have on the people in the group?*
- *What needs of mine are served by being a group leader?*
- *Do I ever use the groups I lead to satisfy my personal needs at the expense of the members' needs? (p. 30)*

Self-confrontation must be an ongoing process for the leader because the leader facilitates the capacity of members in a group to ask related questions about themselves.

Sincerity and Authenticity.   Sincerity in a group counselor is usually considered to be related to the leader's genuine interest in the welfare of the group and the individual group member. Sincerity also relates to the leader's ability to be direct and to encourage each member to explore aspects of self that could easily be distorted or denied. Effective leaders are able to be real, congruent, honest, and open as they respond to the interactions in a group. Authenticity means that the leader knows who he or she really is and has a sense of comfort and acceptance about self. Authenticity results in an ability to be honest about feelings and reactions to the group in a way that is constructive to individuals as well as the group as a whole.

Sense of Identity.   Group leaders often assist members of a group in the process of clarifying values and becoming "inner" rather than "outer" directed. If the leader of a group has not clarified personal values, meanings, goals, and expectations, it may be difficult to help others with the same process.

Belief in the Group Process and Enthusiasm.   Leaders must be positive and enthusiastic about the healing capacity of groups and the benefits of a group experience. If they are unsure, tentative, or unenthusiastic, the same tenor will develop among members of the group. As will be noted in a later discussion of myths, the outcome of a group experience is not totally dependent on the leader; however, the leader does convey messages, nonverbally as well as verbally, that do have an impact on the overall benefit of the experience.

Inventiveness and Creativity.   Leaders who can be spontaneous in their approach to a group can often facilitate better communication, insight, and personal growth than those who become dependent on structured interventions and techniques. Creative facilitators are usually accepting of members who are different from themselves and flexible about approaching members and groups in ways that seem congruent with a particular group. In addition, a certain amount of creativity and spontaneity is necessary to cope with the "unexpected"; in a group situation, the leader will continuously be presented with comments, problems, and reactions that could not have been anticipated prior to a given session.

Group Facilitation: Responsibilities and Interventions

Responsibilities

One of the most important responsibilities of counselors interested in becoming group work specialists is to have a thorough understanding of what elements or factors are important in making groups effective in helping those who participate. Even though the group approach is a well-established mode of "treatment," anyone interested in facilitating a group must ask and understand the question of what about groups makes them effective. One difficulty in answering such a question is that therapeutic change from group participation is a result of a complex set of variables including leadership style, membership roles, and aspects of group process.

In a fascinating discussion of this topic, George and Dustin (1988) promote Bloch's (1986) definition of a *therapeutic factor* as "an element occurring in group therapy that contributes to improvement in a patient's condition and is a function of the actions of the group therapist, the patient, or fellow group members" (p. 679). Although this definition sounds somewhat "clinical," its application to all types of groups is apparent because it helps distinguish among therapeutic elements, conditions for change, and techniques. Conditions for change are necessary for the operation of therapeutic elements but do not, in and of themselves, have therapeutic force. An example is that a sense of belonging and acceptance—a therapeutic element that enhances personal growth in groups—cannot emerge unless the "condition" of the actual presence of several good listeners in the group exists. Likewise, a technique, such as asking members to talk about a self-esteem inventory they have filled out, does not have a direct therapeutic effect but may be used to enhance a sense of belonging and acceptance (George & Dustin, 1988).

Group work specialists have a responsibility to understand the research that has been done on therapeutic elements of groups so they can develop the skills to create a group climate that enhances personal growth. Corsini and Rosenburg (1955) published one of the earlier efforts to produce a classification of therapeutic elements in groups. They abstracted therapeutic factors published in 300 pre-1955 articles on group counseling and clustered them into nine major categories:

1. *Acceptance:* a sense of belonging
2. *Altruism:* a sense of being helpful to others
3. *Universalization:* the realization that group members are not alone in experiencing their problems
4. *Intellectualization:* the process of acquiring self-knowledge
5. *Reality testing:* recognition of the reality of issues such as defenses and family conflicts
6. *Transference:* strong attachment to either the therapist or other group members
7. *Interaction:* the process of relating to other group members that results in personal growth
8. *Spectator therapy:* growth that occurs through listening to other group members
9. *Ventilation:* the release of feelings that had previously been repressed

In 1957, in an attempt to take the classification of therapeutic elements in groups further, Hill interviewed 19 group therapists. He proposed the six elements of catharsis, feelings of belongingness, spectator therapy, insights, peer agency (universality), and socialization. Berzon, Pious, and Farson (1963) used group members rather than leaders as the source of information about therapeutic elements. Their classification included:

1. Increased awareness of emotional dynamics
2. Recognizing similarity to others
3. Feeling positive regard, acceptance, and sympathy for others
4. Seeing self as seen by others
5. Expressing self congruently, articulately, or assertively in the group
6. Witnessing honesty, courage, openness, or expressions of emotionality in others
7. Feeling warmth and closeness in the group
8. Feeling responded to by others
9. Feeling warmth and closeness generally in the group
10. Ventilating emotions

A very different set of therapeutic elements connected with group experience was proposed by Ohlsen in 1977. His list differs from earlier proposals in that it emphasizes client attitudes about the group experience. Ohlsen's paradigm included 14 elements that he labeled as "therapeutic forces":

1. Attractiveness of the group
2. Acceptance by the group
3. Expectations
4. Belonging
5. Security within the group
6. Client readiness
7. Client commitment
8. Client participation
9. Client acceptance of responsibility
10. Congruence
11. Feedback
12. Openness
13. Therapeutic tension
14. Therapeutic norms

In what is now considered a landmark classification of "curative factors," Yalom (1970, 1975) proposed a list of therapeutic elements based on research he and his colleagues conducted:

1. Instillation of hope
2. Universality
3. Imparting of information
4. Altruism

5. The corrective recapitulation of the primary family group
6. Development of socializing techniques
7. Imitative behavior
8. Interpersonal learning
9. Group cohesiveness
10. Catharsis
11. Existential factors

It is not possible to present all the possibilities for viewing the therapeutic elements of a positive group experience. It is possible, however, to encourage the beginning counselor to study the research and literature on group work (Akos, Hamm, Mack, & Dunaway, 2007) relating to these elements prior to facilitating or cofacilitating groups under close supervision.

In an interesting discussion of facilitator responsibilities, Ohlsen and Ferreira (1994) discuss the topic from a very practical perspective. Understanding which clients can be helped through participation in a group; being able to describe a potential group experience to a client; understanding how to conduct an intake or pregroup screening interview; teaching group members how to be good clients and good helpers; mastering skills for structuring, norm setting, and feedback; and recognizing when to terminate a group and assist members to continue their growth after the group terminates are among the responsibilities they address. We recommend further reading on this topic for information on the role of the group work specialist. Just as the importance of understanding the responsibilities of a group facilitator cannot be stressed enough, the topic of interventions or techniques facilitators use is important to consider.

Interventions

The literature on groups provides numerous approaches to the topic of intervention strategies. Corey (2004, 2008) discussed active listening, restating, clarifying, summarizing, questioning, interpreting, confronting, reflecting feelings, supporting, empathizing, facilitating, initiating, setting goals, evaluating, giving feedback, suggesting, protecting, disclosing oneself, modeling, linking, blocking, and terminating. Dinkmeyer and Muro (1979) focused on promoting cohesiveness, summarizing, promoting interaction, resolving conflicts, tone setting, structuring and limit setting, blocking, linking, providing support, reflecting, protecting, questioning, and regulating. Bates, Johnson, and Blaker (1982) emphasized confrontation, attending behavior, feedback, use of questions, levels of interaction, and opening and closing a session. They also presented the four major functions of group leaders as traffic director, model, interaction catalyst, and communication facilitator. Individuals new to counseling may better relate to the topic of intervention strategies by becoming familiar with circumstances during which the group leader must take responsibility for intervening in the group's "process." A helpful model (and a favorite of ours) is Dyer and Vriend's (1973) 10 occasions when intervention is required:

1. *A group member speaks for everyone.*   It is not unusual for a member of a group to say something like, "We think we should . . .," "This is how we all feel," or "We were wondering why. . . ." This happens when an individual does not feel comfortable

making a statement such as "I think we should . . ." or "I am wondering why . . ." or when an individual group member is hoping to engender support for a point of view. The problem with allowing the "we" syndrome to operate in a group is that it inhibits individual members from expressing individual feelings and thoughts. Appropriate interventions on the part of the group leader might be "You mentioned 'we' a number of times. Are you speaking for yourself or for everyone?" or "What do each of you think about the statement that was just made?"

2. *An individual speaks for another individual in the group.*   "I think I know what he means" or "She is not really saying how she feels; I can explain it for her" are statements that one group member may make for another. When one person in the group speaks for another, it often means that a judgment has been made about the capacity of the other person to communicate or that the other person is about to self-disclose "uncomfortable" information. Regardless of the motivation behind such a circumstance, the person who is allowing another group member to do the "talking" needs to evaluate why this is happening and whether the same thing occurs outside the group. In addition, the "talker" needs to evaluate the inclination to make decisions for others and/or rescue others. Appropriate interventions include saying, "Did Jim state your feelings more clearly than you can?" or "How does it feel to have someone rescue you?" Statements such as "Did you feel that June needed your assistance?" or "Do you find it difficult to hold back when you think you know what someone else is going to say?" might also be possible.

3. *A group member focuses on persons, conditions, or events outside the group.*   Often group counseling sessions can turn into "gripe sessions." Complaining about a colleague, friend, or a partner can be enjoyable for group members if they are allowed to reinforce each other. The problem with allowing such emphasis to occur is that this process erroneously substantiates that others are at fault and that group members do not have to take responsibility for aspects of their behavior. Possible interventions for the group leader include: "You keep talking about your wife as the cause of your unhappiness. Isn't it more important to ask yourself what contributions you can make to improve your relationship?" Or "Does complaining about someone else really mean you think you would be happier if he or she could change?"

4. *Someone seeks the approval of the leader or a group member before or after speaking.*   Some group members seek nonverbal acceptance from the leader or another group member (a nod, a glance, a smile). Such individuals may be intimidated by authority figures or personal strength or have low self-esteem and seek sources of support and acceptance outside themselves. One possible intervention is for the leader to look at another member, forcing the speaker to change the direction of his or her delivery. Another possibility is to say something like "You always look at me as you speak, almost as if you are asking permission."

5. *Someone says, "I don't want to hurt her feelings so I won't say what I'd like to say."*   It is not unusual for such a sentiment to be expressed in a group, particularly in the early stages. Sometimes this happens when a member thinks another member of the group is too fragile for feedback; at other times such reluctance is because the provider of the potential feedback is concerned about being "liked" by other group members. The group leader should explore reasons for apprehension about providing feedback, which can include asking the group member to check with the person to whom feedback may be directed to determine whether such fears are totally valid.

6. *A group member suggests that his or her problems are due to someone else.* Although this item overlaps with item 3, this situation represents a different problem from a "group gripe" session. A single group member may periodically attribute difficulties and unhappiness to someone else. Interventions such as "Who is really the only person who can be in charge of you?" or "How can other people determine your mood so much of the time?" are called for in such a case. We are not suggesting a stance that would be perceived as lacking empathy and acceptance. It is, however, important to facilitate responsibility for self on the part of each group member.

7. *An individual suggests that "I've always been that way."* Such a suggestion is indicative of irrational thinking and lack of motivation to change. Believing that the past determines all one's future is something that a group member can believe to such an extent that his or her future growth is inhibited. The group leader must assist such a member to identify thinking errors that lead to lack of effectiveness in specific areas. Such a member needs to learn that he or she is not doomed to repeat the mistakes of the past. Possible statements that will stimulate examination of faulty thinking and assumptions are "You're suggesting that your past has such a hold over you that you will never be any different" or "Do you feel that everyone has certain parts of their lives over which they have no control?"

8. *Someone in the group suggests, "I'll wait, and it will change."* Often, group members are willing to talk about their self-defeating behavior during a group session but aren't willing to make an effort outside the group to behave differently. At times, they take the position that they can postpone action and things will correct themselves. A competent group leader will help members develop strategies for doing something about their problems outside the group and method of "tracking" or "checking in" with members to evaluate progress.

9. *Discrepant behavior appears.* Group leader intervention is essential when discrepancies occur in a member's behavior in the group. Examples of such discrepancies include a difference in what a member is currently saying and what he or she said earlier, a lack of congruence between what a member is saying and what he or she is doing in the group, a difference between how a member sees himself or herself and how others in the group see him or her, or a difference between how a member reports feelings and how nonverbal cues communicate what is going on inside. Interventions used to identify discrepancies may be confrontational in nature because the leader usually needs to describe the discrepancies noted so the group member can begin to identify, evaluate, and change aspects of such behavior.

10. *A member bores the group by rambling.* Sometimes members use talking as a way of seeking approval. At times such talking becomes "overtalk." The leader can ask other members to react to the "intellectualizer" and let such a person know how such rambling affects others. If such behavior is not addressed, other members may develop a sense of anger and hostility toward the "offender."

Johnson and Johnson (2000) noted other situations that may require immediate intervention from the group facilitator:

11. *A member responds with a rehearsed or often used statement.*   Sometimes members don't know what to say after another member of the group has shared. This may be due to discomfort related to the speaker's topic, strong emotion precipitated by the sharing that has just taken place, "unfinished business" similar to that of speaker, or a number of other reasons. In an attempt to be responsive or fill a silence, the member may comment in a way that is similar to how he or she responds whenever discomfort or strong emotion is experienced. The comment may not fit the context and seem inappropriate, insensitive, or even unrelated. The leader may need to ask that member to clarify or respond differently so that the group can continue their work more effectively. This may even lead to some introspection and growth on the part of the member who misspoke.

12. *A member remains silent or nonparticipatory.*   When a member remains silent while other group members actively participate in the group experience, it may encourage other group members to wonder why that member has chosen to be so inactive. Sometimes other members fantasize about what the silent member is like and begin to resent the silence and resent the group leader for allowing that member to be so nonparticipatory. Members can become so agitated that they may begin to make demands on the silent member and blame or scapegoat the member for things that occur in the group. It behooves the group leader to be invitational with such a member so that the silence is not misinterpreted by members of the group.

13. *A member's expectations for the group are not met.*   Sometimes members enter groups with a preconceived idea of what the group will be like. When such expectations are not met, the member could respond in any number of ways: withdrawal, confrontation of the group leader, disagreements with other members of the group, or ventilation of anger. The group leader will need to encourage the member to share the reasons behind the discontent; sometimes doing so can lead to a resolution of the member's difficulties and enhance the quality of the group experience for all concerned.

14. *A member of the group wants all the "air time."*   There are instances in which a high-need member of the group demands to be the sole focus of the group's attention. In such a circumstance, it may be difficult for anyone else to participate unless the facilitator intervenes. Such an intervention would need to be done in a way that communicates respect for the needs of this member and, at the same time, lets other members of the group know they, too, are important. A statement such as "I know how important this is to you. Let me see if I can accurately summarize so we can come back to this after other members have a chance to participate" may be necessary from the group leader. Otherwise, members of the group will start wondering if one member will be allowed to take up all the time and question the value of the group experience.

15. *A group member blocks the expression of intense emotions by other members of the group.* Sometimes strong emotion makes a member feel uncomfortable and unsure of what to say. This could happen because of what the member has been taught about what emotions are appropriately shared or even if they should be shared. This could also occur when the emotion and experience mirrors similar unresolved issues of the member attempting to cut off such expression. The group leader would need to respond to such attempts and encourage the member to be introspective and aware of the tendencies and reasons for such "blocking."

Berg et al. (1998) and Jacobs et al. (1998) provide additional information on the leader's role in intervening in the group's "process" because of what individual members are doing or leaving unsaid.

In addition to the interventions described, the reader should be alerted to the necessity to be prepared to resolve resistance in groups. Clark (1992), Higgs (1992), Ohlsen and Ferreira (1994), and Ormont (1993) provide some excellent guidelines on this aspect of the group leader's role.

Myths Connected With Group Work

Counselors who are group work specialists are usually enthusiastic about the benefits for clients of participation in a small group. Indeed, the outcomes of a competently facilitated group experience can be such that personal growth occurs. Often the memory of such an experience has an impact on clients well into the future. On the other hand, group work, as with other forms of therapeutic assistance (such as individual or family), can be for better or for worse (Carkhuff, 1969). Many group workers follow a belief system that can be challenged by empirical facts.

Beginning counselors are well advised to be aware of a number of myths connected with group work so they don't base their "practices" on a belief system not supported by research (Anderson, 1985; Kalodner & Riva, 1997).

Myth #1: "Everyone Benefits from Group Experience"

Groups do provide benefits. The research on the psychosocial outcomes of group work demonstrates that groups are a powerful modality for learning that can be used outside the group experience (Bednar & Lawlis, 1971; Gazda & Peters, 1975; Parloff & Dies, 1978). There are times, however, when membership in a group can be harmful. Some research shows that 1 of every 10 group members can be hurt (Lieberman, Yalom, & Miles, 1973). The research findings that seem to relate most to individuals who get injured in groups suggest some important principles for the beginning counselor to understand: (a) those who join groups and who have the potential to be hurt by the experience have unrealistic expectations and (b) these expectations seem to be reinforced by the facilitator who coerces the member to meet them (De Julio, Bentley, & Cockayne, 1979; Lieberman et al., 1973; Stava & Bednar, 1979). Prevention of harm requires that the expectations members have for the group are realistic and that the facilitator maintains a reasonable perspective.

Myth #2: "Groups Can Be Composed to Ensure Effective Outcomes"

We do not know enough about how to compose groups by using the pregroup screening interview. In general, objective criteria (such as age, sex, socioeconomic status, presenting problem) can be used to keep groups homogeneous in some respects, but behavioral characteristics should be selected on a heterogeneous basis (Bertcher & Maple, 1977). The most consistent finding is that it is a good idea to compose a group in such a manner that each member is compatible with at least one other member (Stava & Bednar, 1979). This practice seems to prevent the evolution of neglected isolates or scapegoats in a group.

The essence of group process, in terms of benefit to members and effective outcomes, is perceived mutual aid such as helping others, a feeling of belonging, interpersonal learning, and instillation of hope (Butler & Fuhriman, 1980; Long & Cope, 1980; Yalom, 1975).

Myth #3: "The Group Revolves Around the Charisma of the Leader"

Although leaders influence groups tremendously, two general findings in the research on groups should be noted. First, the group, independent of the leader, has an impact on outcomes. Second, the most effective group leaders are those who help the group develop so that members are primary sources of help to one another (Ashkennas & Tandon, 1979; Lungren, 1971).

As noted by Anderson (1985), research on leadership styles has identified four particular leader functions that facilitate the group's functioning:

1. *Providing:* This is the provider role of relationships and climate setting through such skills as support, affection, praise, protection, warmth, acceptance, genuineness, and concern.
2. *Processing:* This is the processor role of illuminating the meaning of the process through such skills as explaining, clarifying, interpreting, and providing a cognitive framework for change or translating feelings and experiences into ideas.
3. *Catalyzing:* This is the catalyst role of stimulating interaction and emotional expression through such skills as reaching for feelings, challenging, confronting, and suggesting; using program activities such as structured experiences; and modeling.
4. *Directing:* This is the director role through such skills as setting limits, roles, norms, and goals; managing time; pacing; stopping; interceding; and suggesting procedures. (p. 272)

Providing and processing seem to have a linear relationship to outcomes: the higher the providing (or caring) and the higher the processing (or clarifying), the higher the positive outcomes. Catalyzing and directing have a curvilinear relationship to outcomes; too much or too little catalyzing or directing results in lower positive outcomes (Lieberman et al., 1973).

Myth #4: "Leaders Can Direct Through the Use of Structured Exercises or Experiences"

Structured exercises create early cohesion (Levin & Kurtz, 1974; Lieberman et al., 1973); they help create early expression of positive and negative feelings. However, they restrict members from dealing with such group themes as affection, closeness, distance, trust, mistrust, genuineness, and lack of genuineness. All these areas form the very basis for group process and should be dealt with in a way that is not hampered by extensive structure. The best principle around which to plan and use structured exercises to get groups started and to keep them going can best be stated as "to overplan and to underuse."

Myth #5: "Therapeutic Change in Groups Comes About Through a Focus on Here-and-Now Experiences"

Much of the research on groups indicates that corrective emotional experiences in the here and now of the group increase the intensity of the experience for members (Levine, 1971; Lieberman et al., 1973; Snortum & Myers, 1971; Zimpfer, 1967). The intensity of the emotional experiences does not, however, appear to be related to outcomes. Better outcomes in groups are achieved by members who develop "insight" or cognitive understanding of emotional experiences in the group and can transfer that understanding into their lives outside the group. The Gestaltists' influence on groups in the 1960s and 1970s (Perls, 1969) suggested that members should "lose your mind and come to your senses" and "stay with the here-and-now." Research suggests that members "use your mind and your senses" and "focus on the there and then as well as on the here and now."

Myth #6: "Major Member Learning in Groups Is Derived from Self-Disclosure and Feedback"

There is an assumption that most of the learning of members in a group comes from self-disclosure in exchange for feedback (Jacobs, 1974). To a large extent, this statement is a myth. Self-disclosure and feedback per se make little difference in terms of outcomes (Anchor, 1979; Bean & Houston, 1978). It is the use of self-disclosure and feedback that appears to make the difference (Martin & Jacobs, 1980). Self-disclosure and feedback appear useful only when deeply personal sharing is understood and appreciated and the feedback is accurate (Berzon et al., 1963; Frank & Ascher, 1951; Goldstein, Bednar, & Yanell, 1979). The actual benefit of self-disclosure and feedback is connected with how these processes facilitate empathy among members. It is empathy, or the actual experience of being understood by other members, that catalyzes personal growth and understanding in the context of a group.

Myth #7: "The Group Facilitator Can Work Effectively With a Group Without Understanding Group Process and Group Dynamics"

Groups experience a natural evolution and unfolding of processes and dynamics. Anderson (1979) labeled these stages as trust, autonomy, closeness, interdependence, and termination (TACIT). Tuckman (1965) suggested a more dramatic labeling of forming, storming, norming, performing, and adjourning. We suggested a four-stage paradigm earlier in this chapter. Two reviews, which include more than 200 studies of group dynamics and group process (Cohen & Smith, 1976; La Coursiere, 1980), revealed remarkably similar patterns (despite differences in the labels chosen as descriptors) in the evolution of group processes as a group evolves through stages. It is extremely important for group facilitators to understand group processes and dynamics to do a competent job of enhancing membership benefits from participation.

Myth #8: "Change Experienced by Group Participation Is Not Maintained Over Time"

Groups are powerful! Changes can be maintained by group members as much as 6 months to a year later, even when groups meet for only 3 or 4 months (Lieberman et al., 1973).

Myth #9: "A Group Is a Place to Get Emotionally High"

Feeling good after a group session is a positive outcome but not the main reason for being in a group in the first place. Some group members have periods of depression after group participation because they don't find elsewhere, on a daily basis, the kind of support they received from other members of the group. Group members should be prepared for this possibility and assisted in their ability to obtain support, when appropriate, from those around them.

Myth #10: "A Group's Purpose Is to Make Members Close to Every Other Member"

Although genuine feelings of intimacy and cohesiveness develop in effective groups, intimacy is the by-product and not the central purpose of the group. Intimacy develops as individual members risk self-disclosure and problem solving and other group members reach out in constructive ways.

Myth #11: "Group Participation Results in Brainwashing"

Professional groups do not indoctrinate members with a particular philosophy of life or a set of rules about how each member "should be." If this does occur in a group, it is truly a breach of professional ethics and an abuse of the group. Group participation encourages members to look within themselves for answers and to become as self-directed as possible.

Myth #12: "To Benefit From a Group, a Member Has to Be Dysfunctional"

Group counseling is as appropriate for individuals who are functioning relatively well and who want to enhance their capabilities as it is for those who are having difficulty with certain aspects of their lives. Groups are not only for dysfunctional people.

Issues and Ethics: Some Concluding Remarks

Although a thorough discussion of issues and ethics in group counseling is beyond the scope of this chapter, it is important for the beginning counselor to be introduced to this topic. *Professional Standards for Training of Group Workers* (ASGW, 1991b, 2000), *Boundary Issues in Counseling* (Herlihy & Corey, 1997), and *Ethical, Legal, and Professional Issues in Counseling* (Remley & Herlihy, 2005) are all excellent points of departure for the counselor interested in groups, as is "Principles for Diversity-Competent Group Workers," published in 1999 by the Association for Specialists in Group Work (ASGW). In addition, these resources serve as useful adjuncts to the *Code of Ethics and Standards of Practice* of the American Counseling Association (2005).

ASGW (1991, 2000) recommends that the group work specialist acquire *knowledge competencies* (for example, understanding principles of group dynamics, the roles of members in groups, the contributions of research in group work), *skill competencies* (diagnosing self-defeating behavior in groups, intervening at critical times in group process, using assessment procedures to evaluate the outcomes of a group), and *supervised clinical experience* (such as observing group counseling, coleading groups with supervision, participating as a member in a group). Interestingly, these very training standards have become an issue with some counselor preparation programs as they struggle to obtain a balance between the didactic and clinical components of the set of educational and supervisory experiences required to prepare an individual to do a competent job of group counseling. The clinical supervisory aspects of preparing the group work specialist are costly for universities, and often counselor educators are encouraged to abandon such efforts in favor of classroom didactics.

Another example of some of the issues connected with group counseling has to do with continuing education after the completion of master's and/or doctoral degree programs. Although the National Board for Certified Counselors (NBCC) requires those who achieve the National Certified Counselor (NCC) credential to obtain 100 contact hours of continuing education every 5 years, there is no specification of how much of this professional enhancement activity should be focused on aspects of group work if group work is the declared area of specialization of an NCC. In time, there may be a specific continuing education requirement for the group work specialist.

Readers should refer to ACA's *Code of Ethics and Standards of Practice* (2005) for ethical guidelines pertaining to groups. An interesting earlier document, *Ethical Guidelines for Group Leaders* (ASGW, 1991a), initially helped clarify the nature of ethical responsibilities of the counselor in a group setting. These guidelines presented standards in three areas: (a) the leader's responsibility for providing information about group work to clients, (b) the leader's responsibility for providing group counseling services to clients, and (c) the leader's responsibility for safeguarding the standards of ethical practice. One of the greatest single sources of ethical dilemmas in group counseling situations has to do with confidentiality. Except for the few exceptions delineated in ACA's *Code of Ethics and Standards of Practice* (2005), counselors have an obligation not to disclose information about the client without the client's consent. Yet, the very nature of a group counseling situation makes it difficult to ensure that each member of a group will respect the others' right to privacy.

Other issues such as recruitment and informed consent, screening and selection of group members, voluntary and involuntary participation, psychological risks, uses and abuses of group techniques, therapist competence, interpersonal relationships among the members of a group, and follow-up form the basis for considerable discussion and evaluation. In addition, these issues emphasize the necessity of adequate education, supervision, and advance time to consider the ramifications and responsibilities connected with becoming a group specialist.

Group experiences can be powerful growth-enhancing opportunities for clients, or they can be pressured, stifling encounters to be avoided. Each of us has a professional obligation to assess our readiness to facilitate or cofacilitate a group. Our clients deserve the best experience we can provide.

Summary

The use of groups of all types is increasingly important to the role of the counselor in a variety of settings. As the decades have passed, emphasis has shifted from T-groups to encounter groups to working with special populations. Self-help groups of all types are flourishing. The ASGW standards for the training of group counselors have been widely accepted.

ASGW's definitions of the four group work specialty types (task/work, guidance/psychoeducational, counseling, psychotherapy groups), information about stages of group life, and research on the characteristics of group facilitators have also enhanced the ability of the group work specialist to function in the best interests of clients in groups. In addition, the more group work specialists know about their responsibilities and the interventions they need to master, myths connected with group work, and issues and ethics associated with groups, the more competent they will be as facilitators of group experiences. The importance of broad-based education and carefully supervised group practica and other clinical experiences for group work specialists cannot be overemphasized.

The following Web sites contain additional information relating to the chapter topics.

USEFUL WEB SITES

Association for Specialists in Group Work (ASGW)
http://www.asgw.org/

American Group Psychotherapy Association (AGPA)
http://www.groupsinc.org

American Society of Group Psychotherapy and Psychodrama (ASGPP)
http://www.ASGPP.org

Group Psychology and Group Psychotherapy, Division 49 of APA
http://www.apa.org/about/division/div49.html

REFERENCES

Akos, P., Hamm, J. V., Mack, S. G., & Dunaway, M. (2007). Utilizing the developmental influence of peers in middle school groups. *The Journal for Specialists in Group Work, 32*(1), 51–60.

American Counseling Association. (2005). *Code of ethics and standards of practice*. Alexandria, VA: Author.

Anchor, K. N. (1979). High- and low-risk self-disclosure in group psychotherapy. *Small Group Behavior, 10*, 279–283.

Anderson, J. D. (1979). Social work with groups in the generic base of social work practice. *Social Work With Groups, 2*, 281–293.

Anderson, J. D. (1985). Working with groups: Little-known facts that challenge well-known myths. *Small Group Behavior, 16*(3), 267–283.

Arbuckle, D. (1975). *Counseling and psychotherapy: An existential-humanistic view*. Boston: Allyn & Bacon.

Ashkenas, R., & Tandon, R. (1979). Eclectic approach to small group facilitation. *Small Group Behavior, 10*, 224–241.

Association for Specialists in Group Work (ASGW). (1983). *Professional standards for training of group counselors*. Alexandria, VA: Author.

Association for Specialists in Group Work. (1991a). *Ethical guidelines for group leaders*. Alexandria, VA: Author.

Association for Specialists in Group Work. (1991b). Professional standards for training of group workers. *Together, 20*, 9–14.

Association for Specialists in Group Work. (1992). Professional standards for training of group workers. *The Journal for Specialists in Group Work, 17*(1), 12–19.

Association for Specialists in Group Work. (1999). Principles for diversity-competent group workers. *The Journal for Specialists in Group Work, 24*(1), 7–14.

Association for Specialists in Group Work. (2000). *Professional standards for the training of group workers*. Alexandria, VA: Author.

Bales, R. F. (1950). *Interaction process analysis: A method for study of small groups*. Reading, MA: Addison-Wesley.

Bates, M., Johnson, C. D., & Blaker, K. E. (1982). *Group leadership: A manual for group counseling leaders* (2nd ed.). Denver: Love Publishing.

Bean, B. W., & Houston, B. K. (1978). Self-concept and self-disclosure in encounter groups. *Small Group Behavior, 9*, 549–554.

Bednar, R., & Lawlis, G. (1971). Empirical research in group psychotherapy. In S. L. Garfield and A. E. Bergin (Eds.), *Handbook of psychotherapy and behavior change* (2nd ed., pp. 420–439). New York: Wiley.

Berg, R. C., Landreth, G. L., & Fall, K. A. (1998). *Group counseling: Concepts and procedures* (3rd ed.). Philadelphia: Taylor & Francis.

Bertcher, H. J., & Maple, F. F. (1977). *Creating Groups.* Newbury Park, CA: Sage.

Berzon, B., Pious, C., & Farson, R. (1963). The therapeutic event in group psychotherapy: A study of subjective reports by group members. *Journal of Individual Psychology, 19,* 204–212.

Bloch, S. (1986). Therapeutic factors in group psychotherapy. In A. J. Frances & R. E. Hales (Eds.), *Annual Review* (vol 5, pp. 678–698). Washington, DC: American Psychiatric Press.

Braaten, L. J. (1975). Developmental phases of encounter groups and related intensive groups. *Interpersonal Development, 5,* 112–129.

Bradford, L. P., Gibb, J. R., & Benne, K. D. (Eds.). (1964). *T-group theory and laboratory method: Innovation in re-education.* New York: John Wiley.

Butler, T., & Fuhriman, A. (1980). Patient perspective on the curative process: A comparison of day treatment and outpatient psychotherapy groups. *Small Group Behavior, 11,* 371–388.

Capuzzi, D., Gross, D. R., & Stauffer, M. D. (2006). *Introduction to group work* (4th ed.). Denver: Love Publishing.

Carkhuff, R. R. (1969). *Helping and human relations: A primer for lay and professional helpers.* Vol. 2: *Practice and research.* New York: Holt, Rinehart & Winston.

Carkhuff, R. R., & Berenson, B. G. (1977). *Beyond counseling and therapy* (2nd ed.). New York: Holt, Rinehart & Winston.

Cassidy, K. (2007) Tuckman revisited: Proposing a new model of group development for practitioners. *Journal of Experiential Education, 20*(3), 413–417.

Clark, A. J. (1992). Defense mechanisms in group counseling. *The Journal for Specialists in Group Work, 17*(3), 151–160.

Cohen, A. M., & Smith, D. R. (1976). *The critical incident in growth groups: Theory and techniques.* La Jolla, CA: University Associates.

Conyne, R. K., Wilson, F. R., Kline, W. B., Morran, D. K., & Ward, D. E. (1993). Training group workers: Implications of the new ASGW training standards for training and practice. *The Journal for Specialists in Group Work, 18*(1), 11–23.

Corey, G. (1985). *Theory and practice of group counseling* (2nd ed.). Pacific Grove, CA: Brooks/Cole.

Corey, G. (2000). *Theory and practice of group counseling* (5th ed.). Belmont, CA: Brooks/Cole.

Corey, G. (2004). *Theory and practice of group counseling* (6th ed.). Belmont, CA: Brooks/Cole.

Corey, G. (2008) *Theory and practice of group counseling* (7th ed.). Belmont, CA: Brooks/Cole.

Corsini, R., & Rosenberg, B. (1955). Mechanisms of group psychotherapy: Processes and dynamics. *Journal of Abnormal and Social Psychology, 51,* 406–411.

Council for Accreditation of Counseling and Related Educational Programs (CACREP). (1988). *Accreditation procedures manual and application.* Alexandria, VA: Author.

Council for Accreditation of Counseling and Related Educational Programs (CACREP). (1994, 2001). *CACREP accreditation standards and procedures manual.* Alexandria, VA: Author.

De Julio, S. J., Bentley, J., & Cockayne, T. (1979). Pregroup norm setting: Effects on encounter group interaction. *Small Group Behavior, 10,* 368–388.

Dinkmeyer, D. C., & Muro, J. J. (1979). *Group counseling: Theory and practice* (2nd ed.). Itasca, IL: Peacock.

Donigan, J., & Malanti, R. (1997). *Systemic group therapy: A triadic model.* Pacific Grove, Ca: Brooks/Cole.

Dyer, W. W., & Vriend, J. (1973). Effective group counseling process interventions. *Educational Technology, 13*(1), 61–67.

Frank, J., & Ascher, E. (1951). The corrective emotional experience in group therapy. *American Journal of Psychiatry, 108,* 126–131.

Gazda, G. (1984). *Group counseling* (3rd ed.). Dubuque, IA: Brown.

Gazda, G. M., Ginter, E. J., & Horne, A. M. (2001). *Group counseling and psychotherapy: Theory and application.* Needham Heights, MA: Allyn & Bacon.

Gazda, G. M., & Peters, R. W. (1975). An analysis of human research in group psychotherapy, group counseling and human relations training. In G. M. Gazda (Ed.), *Basic approaches to group psychotherapy and group counseling* (pp. 38–54). Springfield, IL: Thomas.

George, R. L., & Dustin, D. (1988). *Group counseling: Theory and practice.* Englewood Cliffs, NJ: Prentice-Hall.

Gladding, S. T. (2008). *Groups: A counseling specialty* (5th ed.). Upper Saddle River, NJ: Merrill/ Prentice Hall.

Goldstein, E. G., & Noonan, M. (1999). *Short-term treatment and social work practice: An integrative perspective.* New York: The Free Press.

Goldstein, M. J., Bednar, R. L., & Yanell, B. (1979). Personal risk associated with self-disclosure, interpersonal feedback, and group confrontation in group psychotherapy. *Small Group Behavior, 9,* 579–587.

Golembiewski, R. T. (1962). *The small group: An analysis of research concepts and operations.* Chicago: University of Chicago Press.

Greene, R. T., Lawson, G., & Getz, H. (2005). The impact of the Internet: Implications for mental health counselors. *Journal of Technology in Counseling, 4*(1). Retrieved May 3, 2007, from http:// jtc.colstate.edu/Vol4_1/Lawson/Lawson.htm

Hare, A. P. (1973). Theories of group development and categories for interaction analysis. *Small Group Behavior, 4,* 259–304.

Hare, A. P., Borgatta, E. F., & Bales, R. F. (Eds.). (1967). *Small groups: Studies in social interaction* (rev. ed.). New York: Knopf.

Herlihy, B., & Corey, G. C. (1997). *Boundary issues in counseling: Multiple roles and responsibilities.* Alexandria, VA: American Counseling Association.

Higgs, J. S. (1992). Dealing with resistance: Strategies for effective group. *The Journal for Specialists in Group Work, 17*(2), 67–73.

Hill, W. F. (1957). Analysis of interviews of group therapists' papers. Provo *Papers, 1,* 1.

Hill, W. F., & Gruner, L. (1973). A study of development in open and closed groups. *Small Group Behavior, 4,* 355–381.

Jacobs, A. (1974). The use of feedback in groups. In A. Jacobs & W. W. Spradline (Eds.), *The group as an agent of change* (pp. 31–49). New York: Behavioral Publications.

Jacobs, E. E., Masson, R. L., & Harvill, R. L. (1998). *Group counseling: Strategies and skills.* Pacific Grove, CA: Brooks/Cole.

Janis, I. L. (1972). *Victims of groupthink: A psychological study of foreign-policy decisions and fiascos.* Boston: Houghton Mifflin.

Johnson, D. W., & Johnson, F. P. (2000). *Joining together: Group theory and group skills.* Boston: Allyn & Bacon.

Jourard, S. (1971). *The transparent self* (rev ed.). New York: Van Nostrand Reinhold.

Kalodner, C. R., & Riva, M. T. (1997). Group research: Encouraging a collaboration between practitioners and researchers: a conclusion. *Journal for Specialists in Group Work, 22*(4), 297.

Kottler, J. A. (1983). *Pragmatic group leadership.* Pacific Grove, CA: Brooks/Cole.

La Coursiere, R. (1980). *The life-cycle of groups: Group development stage theory.* New York: Human Sciences.

Leiberman, M. A., Yalom, I. D., & Miles, M. B. (1973). *Encounter groups: First facts.* New York: Basic Books.

Levin, E. M., & Kurtz, R. P. (1974). Participant perceptions following structured and nonstructured human relations training. *Journal of Counseling Psychology, 21,* 514–532.

Levine, N. (1971). Emotional factors in group development. *Human Relations, 24,* 65–89.

Long, L. D., & Cope, C. S. (1980). Curative factors in a male felony offender group. *Small Group Behavior, 11,* 389–398.

Lungren, D. C. (1971). Trainer style and patterns of group development. *Journal of Applied Behavioral Science,* 689–709.

MacKenzie, K. R. (1997). *Time-managed group psychotherapy: Effective clinical applications.* Washington, DC: American Psychiatric Press.

Martin, L., & Jacobs, M. (1980). Structured feedback delivered in small groups. *Small Group Behavior, 1,* 88–107.

Neukrug, E. (1999). *The world of the counselor: An introduction to the counseling profession.* Pacific Grove, CA: Brooks/Cole.

Ohlsen, M. M. (1977). *Group counseling* (2nd ed.). New York: Holt, Rinehart & Winston.

Ohlsen, M. M., & Ferreira, L. O. (1994). The basics of group counseling. *Counseling and Human Development, 26*(5), 1–20.

Ormont, L. R. (1993). Resolving resistances to immediacy in the group setting. *International Journal of Group Psychotherapy, 43*(4), 399–418.

Parloff, M. B., & Dies, R. R. (1978). Group therapy outcome instrument: Guidelines for conducting research. *Small Group Behavior, 9,* 243–286.

Perls, F. (1969). *Gestalt therapy verbatim.* New York: Bantam.

Reid, C. H. (1965). The authority cycle in small group development. *Adult Leadership, 1,* 308–310.

Remley, T. P., Jr. & Herlihy, B. (2005). *Ethical, legal, and professional issues in counseling* (2nd ed.). Upper Saddle River, NJ: Pearson, Merrill/Prentice Hall.

Roller, B. (1997). *The promise of group therapy: How to build a vigorous training and organizational base for group therapy in managed behavioral healthcare.* San Francisco, CA: Jossey-Bass.

Rowe, W., & Winborn, B. B. (1973). What people fear about group work: An analysis of 36 selected critical articles. *Educational Technology, 13*(1), 53–57.

Snortum, J. R., & Myers, H. F. (1971). Intensity of T-group relations as function of interaction. *International Journal of Group Psychotherapy, 21,* 190–201.

Stava, L. J., & Bednar, R. L. (1979). Process and outcome in encounter groups: The effect of group composition. *Small Group Behavior, 10,* 200–213.

Thelen, H., & Dickerman, W. (1949). Stereotypes and the growth of groups. *Educational Leadership, 6,* 309–316.

Truax, C. B., & Carkhuff, R. R. (1967). *Toward effective counseling and psychotherapy: Training and practice.* Chicago: Aldine.

Tuckman, B. W. (1965). Developmental sequences in small groups. *Psychological Bulletin, 63,* 384–389.

Vriend, J. (1985). We've come a long way, group. *Journal for Specialists in Group Work, 10*(2), 63–67.

Yalom, I. D. (1970). *The theory and practice of group psychotherapy.* New York: Basic Books.

Yalom, I. D. (1975). *The theory and practice of group psychotherapy* (2nd ed.). New York: Basic Books.

Zimpfer, D. G. (1967). Expression of feelings in group counseling. *Personnel and Guidance Journal, 45,* 703–708.

Zimpfer, D. G. (1986). Planning for groups based on their developmental phases. *Journal for Specialists in Group Work, 11*(3), 180–187.

10 An Introduction to Career Counseling

ELLEN HAWLEY MCWHIRTER, PhD
University of Oregon

CHRISTINA L. ARANDA, BA
University of Oregon

JENEKA JOYCE, BA
University of Oregon

*Trying to eliminate her nervous fidgeting by clasping her hands under the table,
the novice counselor watches as the cards are handed out.
Who will this first client be? Am I going to know what to say?
The anticipation builds as each member of the group is provided with
demographics and a single phrase describing the client's main concern. She
releases a hand to reach for the blue index card and quickly skims its contents.
Female, OK, age 23, great, concern. . . .
The counselor stifles a sigh of disappointment. No thrill, no challenge here.
"Seeking career counseling."*

Introduction

Graduate students in counseling and counseling psychology and beginning counselors
have been shown to have negative attitudes about career counseling and to be uninter-
ested in spending counseling time engaged in career counseling activities (Heppner,
O'Brien, Hinkelman, & Flores, 1996; Pinkney & Jacobs, 1985). Some of these negative attitudes may be based on an impression that career counseling is no more than a
process of going through endless inventories and reference material to locate the right
job for a rather dull, helpless person. Contrary to these impressions, however, career
counseling is an intriguing and complex area of counseling that requires an in-depth
knowledge of human nature and involves an active, collaborative relationship between
the counselor and the client. Although there may be some distinctions between

personal and career counseling, most authors agree that there is considerable overlap (e.g., Betz & Corning, 1993; Croteau & Thiel, 1993; Pace & Quinn, 2000; Sharf, 2006). We hope that the information in this chapter will diminish any unfounded negative impressions the reader may have and illustrate the variety and challenge inherent in the tasks of career counselors.

Condensing the theory and practice of contemporary career counseling into a single chapter is a formidable task that requires little or no coverage of many important aspects of career counseling. The purpose of this chapter is to introduce the beginning counselor to a developmental perspective of career counseling and to introduce the basic components and activities in the territory of the career counselor. To accommodate this purpose within space limitations, we minimize evaluation and critique of current theories and interventions and emphasize description, with references provided for more detailed analysis of the history, theory, and research related to career counseling. The beginning counselor is urged to consult contemporary career textbooks such as those by Brown and Associates (2002), Reardon, Lenz, Sampson, and Peterson (2005), Sharf (2006), Walsh and Heppner (2006), and Walsh and Savickas (2005), as well as journals such as the *Journal of Vocational Behavior, Career Development Quarterly*, the *Journal of Career Assessment*, the *Journal of Counseling and Development*, the *Journal of Career Development*, and the *Journal of Counseling Psychology*.

Before proceeding with a discussion of career development theories, *work, career,* and *career development* must be defined. Recognition of the pervasive nature of work in human lives has led to broader and more developmental definitions of *career.* Stemming from the work of Blustein, McWhirter, and Perry (2005) and Miller and McWhirter (2006), *work* is defined as the primary human activity that may be either paid or unpaid and serves to ensure survival and the completion of daily living tasks. Drawing from the National Vocational Guidance Association (1973), we define *career* in this chapter as "a time-extended working out of a purposeful life pattern through work undertaken by the individual." Miller and McWhirter (2006) expand the definition and state that *career* is "a subset of work characterized by volition, pay, hierarchal and thematic relationships among various jobs that constitute a career" (p. 3). Career development refers to "the total constellation of psychological, sociological, educational, physical, economic, and chance factors that combine to shape the career of any given individual" (NVGA, 1973). Finally, career counseling may be described as:

> . . . a series of general and specific interventions throughout the life span, dealing with such concerns as self-understanding; broadening one's horizons; work selection, challenge, satisfaction, and other intrapersonal matters; work site behavior, communication, and other interpersonal phenomena; and lifestyle issues, such as balancing work, family, and leisure. Thus, career counseling primarily involves career planning and decision making while encompassing many other matters, such as integrating life, work, family and social roles, discrimination, stress, sexual harassment, bias, stereotyping, pay inequities, and "tokenism" (Engels, Minor, Sampson, & Splete, 1995, p. 134).

Thus, presenting problems in career counseling might include difficulty responding to homophobic and/or discriminatory workplace policies and colleagues, marital dissatisfaction related to a dual-career situation, poor decision-making skills, lack of knowledge about wheelchair-accessible leisure options, role conflicts and poor stress management skills, or any of the more traditional issues brought to career counseling, such as fear of interviews, lack of occupational information, need to develop a resume, or desire to choose or change a career.

The knowledge and skills required for competent career counseling have been specified in the context of preparation standards (Council for Accreditation of Counseling and Related Educational Programs [CACREP], 2001; National Career Development Association [NCDA], 1997). Along with the career counseling competencies of CACREP and NCDA, the beginning career counselor should be knowledgeable of multicultural counseling competencies (Sue et al., 1998), applicable multicultural guidelines (American Psychological Association [APA], 2003), and the ethical codes for the American Counseling Association (ACA, 2005).

Theories of Career Counseling

John Krumboltz (1989) stated that the purpose, emphasis, and vocabulary of the major theories of career counseling may differ, but there are no fundamental disagreements between them. Comparing theories to maps, Krumboltz (1994b) points out how they are similar: both represent an oversimplification of reality, both distort certain features, both employ symbols to depict reality and are intended to provide a big picture, and the usefulness of both maps and theories depends on the purpose for which they are used. The various career counseling theories represent different aspects of the same territory; no one theory covers the entire area, and the theories overlap. Although further development is needed in career theory, the ultimate goal is not to develop a "perfect" theory but theories that are "perfect" for given purposes.

Among the implications that might be drawn from Krumboltz's analogy is one very pertinent to the beginning career counselor. Theoretical viewpoints cannot be adopted or rejected on the basis of their "goodness" or "badness" without specifically considering their intended scope, emphasis, and purpose. A theory useful for understanding one aspect of the career development process may shed little light on another. Rigid adherence to one particular theory may, therefore, be detrimental to understanding the career process in its entirety. This is not to say that one should carry about a hodgepodge of unrelated concepts and explanations but that theories should be used according to their intended purposes.

Some of the major theories of career development are briefly described here. Although only the most central concepts of each have been presented, more detailed reviews of each theory and critiques of the related research are available in the texts mentioned previously.

Trait-and-Factor Theory

Frank Parsons. The trait-and-factor approach to career counseling was established in the work of Parsons (1909), and most authors credit the origin of vocational counseling to Frank Parsons. Although his era was witness to a variety of innovative guidance programs, Parsons conceptualized a model for career guidance that is still viable in contemporary formulations of career counseling. Parsons was concerned about the difficult social problems experienced by immigrants new to the United States and viewed assistance with vocational selection as one means of alleviating their impoverished status. Hawks and Muha (1991) argued that recommitment to the social change orientation characterized by Parsons is critical to optimizing the educational and occupational attainment of young people, especially ethnic minority youth, in our still-stratified society. A special section of *Career Development Quarterly* (vol. 50, number 1, 2001) was devoted to discussing Parsons's contribution to the field of career development, including his commitment to social change (O'Brien, 2001).

Parsons proposed a three-step model for helping individuals choose a vocation: (a) develop knowledge about self, including aptitudes, interests, and resources; (b) develop knowledge about the world of work, including the advantages, disadvantages, opportunities, and requirements associated with different occupations; and (c) find a suitable match between the individual and the world of work (Parsons, 1909). His work stimulated increased interest in vocational guidance nationwide (Miller & McWhirter, 2006), and elements of trait-and-factor theory can be found in most contemporary theories of career development.

A career counselor following the trait-and-factor approach would structure the counseling experience according to the three steps outlined by Parsons (1909). First, the counselor would generate information about the client's aptitudes, interests, goals, resources, and so on. Next, the counselor would use his or her knowledge of occupations to assist the client's exploration of possible career alternatives. After the client has enough self-knowledge and occupational knowledge, the counselor would facilitate the client's choice of an occupation that is consistent with the identified personal qualities and interests.

John Holland.   The work of John Holland has been classified under both trait approaches to career development (Swanson, 1996) and personality-based theories of career (Sharf, 2006). Holland (1996a, 1996b, 1997) assumes that people develop relatively permanent sets of behaviors or personalities that they seek to express through occupational choices. In addition, he asserts that people project their views of themselves and of the work world onto occupational titles. Assessment of these projections identifies information about the occupational areas that might be most satisfying for an individual and illuminates relevant aspects of the individual's personality.

According to Holland's theory (1996a, 1996b, 1997), there are six basic types of work environments in U. S. society and six corresponding modal personal orientations. Modal personal orientations are the way the person typically responds to environmental demands. People achieve the most work satisfaction when their work environment matches their modal personal orientation. For example, positions in education or social welfare are considered "social" occupational environments most suited to "social" personal orientations, that is, people who perceive themselves to be sociable, skilled at dealing with others, and concerned with helping others and solving human problems. Some people are dominant in one particular orientation; others exhibit a combination of orientations in their interactions with the environment. The six orientations are often referred to as "Holland's hexagon" because they are depicted with the most similar orientations adjacent and the most distinct opposite each other on the hexagon. Research on the Strong Interest Inventory provides some evidence for the validity of Holland's hexagon with college women and men of diverse racial/ethnic minority backgrounds (Fouad, 2002, 2007; Hansen & Lee, 2007; Lattimore & Borgen, 1999) and with high school students (Flores, Spanierman, et al., 2006). Additionally, recent research examined the validity of the 2005 Strong Interest Inventory in relation to gender and college major (Gasser, Larson, & Borgen, 2007). There have also been a number of studies investigating the use of Holland's theory cross-culturally (Fouad, 2007; Fouad & Mohler, 2004; Leung & Hou, 2001; Soh & Leong, 2001).

In addition to the social orientation, there are five other orientations: realistic, investigative, conventional, enterprising, and artistic. "Realistic" persons are described as practical, concrete, and rugged; interested in activities requiring physical strength; and less likely to be sensitive and socially skilled. Corresponding work environments are found in the skilled trades, such as plumbing or machine operation, and in the technical trades, such as mechanics and photography.

"Investigative" persons are described as preferring to think rather than act and as intellectual, abstract, and analytical. Work environments most suited to the investigative orientation are scientific, such as those of the chemist or mathematician, and the technical environments of the computer programmer and the electronics worker.

"Conventional" persons are practical, well-controlled, and conservative and prefer structure and conformity to the abstract and the unique. Conventional environments are typified in those of the office worker, the bookkeeper, and the credit manager.

An "enterprising" individual is likely to prefer leadership roles and to be aggressive, extroverted, persuasive, and dominant. Managerial positions in personnel and production and work in real estate, life insurance, and other sales areas correspond most closely to the enterprising work environment.

Holland's final personality orientation, "artistic," corresponds to persons who are imaginative, independent, expressive, and introspective; their preferred work environments include those of the artist, the musician, and the writer. Holland (1996b) and Blake and Sackett (1999) provide detailed descriptions of the modal orientations, which may be helpful for the counselor interested in further exploration of these concepts.

Counselors grounded in Holland's approach generally attempt to determine the client's modal personal orientation and then explore corresponding work orientations. In this sense, the trait-and-factor approach is represented. Instruments that assess modal orientations include the *Strong Interest Inventory* and Holland's *Self-Directed Search*. Lofquist and Dawis's (1969, 1984) Work Adjustment Theory is another extension of trait-and-factor approaches to career counseling.

Social Learning Theory

Perhaps the foremost proponent of the social learning approach to career counseling is John Krumboltz (Krumboltz, 1994; Krumboltz & Henderson, 2002). Krumboltz identifies four factors that influence career decision making: (a) genetic endowment and special abilities, (b) environmental conditions and events, (c) learning experiences, and (d) task-approach skills. He defines task-approach skills as the skills an individual applies to new tasks and problems, including cognitive processes, work habits, and values. Every individual is born into specific environmental conditions with certain genetic characteristics; these interact to influence the life experiences, opportunities, and learning of the individual. Learning experiences are followed by rewards or punishments that also influence the individual's development. According to Krumboltz, career choice is influenced by individuals' unique learning experiences in the course of their lifetimes.

Task-approach skills, self-observation generalizations, and actions are the result of an individual's learning experiences. Self-observation generalizations are the self-statements individuals make after assessing their performance or potential performance against learned standards. They are expressed in the form of interests. Actions are decision-related behaviors that emerge from the individual's task-approach skills and self-observation generalizations.

A counselor approaching career clients from a social learning perspective would be interested in the learning experiences that have influenced the client's career development. Often a client's inaccurate self-observations, maladaptive beliefs (Krumboltz & Vosvick, 1996), or deficient task-approach skills are a barrier to exploring potential career choices and to making career decisions. The counselor's role may include a strong psychoeducational component in helping the client revise faulty beliefs or observations and learn new skills that will facilitate the career exploration and choice process, including decision-making skills.

Social Cognitive Career Theory

Lent, Brown, and Hackett (1994, 2002) proposed a theoretical model of career choice and implementation grounded in Bandura's (1986, 1997) general social cognitive theory. Their model emphasizes the importance of personal agency in the career decision-making process and attempts to explain how both internal and external factors enhance or constrain this agency. Lent et al. (1994, 2002) suggest that career interests directly influence career choice goals (e.g., career aspirations), which increases the likelihood of certain career choice actions (e.g., declaring an academic major). Contextual and social cognitive factors are hypothesized to directly influence the development of career interests, goals, and actions. Contextual factors include discrimination, socioeconomic status, job availability, educational access, perceived and real barriers, and other influential environmental factors. Lent et al. argue that the particular effect that contextual factors have on an individual's career choice often depends on her or his personal appraisal of and response to those factors. The social cognitive factors (Bandura, 1997) include self-appraisals such as self-efficacy expectations, or beliefs about one's performance abilities in relation to specific tasks, as well as outcome expectations, or beliefs about the likely consequences of given behaviors.

Lent et al. (1994, 2002) propose that contextual and social cognitive factors are responsible for shaping the experiences that lead to the development of interests and choices as well as the relationship between interests and choices and between career choices and attainments. Even if an individual possesses high levels of career self-efficacy, high outcome expectations, and interests that are congruent with those expectations, she or he may still avoid selection of a particular career if she or he perceives insurmountable barriers to career entry or career goal attainment. This model represents an important contribution to understanding career interests, choices, and implementation because it integrates the social forces of racism, sexism, classism, and homophobia that shape the career development process of all individuals, as well as related contextual/environmental factors such as role models, socialization, and perceived opportunities and barriers (Fouad, 2007). The growing body of literature on the career development of people of color (e.g., Bowman, 1998; Brown & Lavish, 2006; Byars, 2001; Flores, Lin, & Huang, 2005; Leong & Gupta, 2007; McWhirter, Hackett, & Bandalos, 1998; Walsh, Bingham, Brown, & Ward, 2001; Walsh & Heppner, 2006), as well as the broader literature on counseling people of color (see Atkinson, Morten, & Sue, 1998; Comas-Diaz & Greene, 1994; Lee, 1997; Pedersen, 2000; Sue & Sue, 2003), consistently stresses the influence of contextual factors. Implications for career counseling include acknowledging and clarifying the role of environmental factors and cognitions in the career development process and providing opportunities to test and enhance self-efficacy and outcome expectations.

Developmental Theories

Developmental career theories view the selection and implementation of careers as part of a long-term developmental process that begins early in life and ends with death. Developmental theorists recognize the contributions of early experiences, life events and opportunities, and the maturation process on the development of interests, the exploration process, and career outcomes. Most contemporary theories of career choice incorporate elements of the developmental perspective. In this chapter, *career* has been defined from a developmental perspective in recognition of the widespread acceptance of career as an ongoing, lifelong process.

Ginzberg, Ginsburg, Axelrad, and Herma (1951) were among the first theorists to link the developmental theory with occupational choice. Their work, along with the work of Teideman and O'Hara (1963) and others, has been valuable in shaping developmental theories. Two developmental approaches are briefly discussed in this section. First, major components of the work of Donald Super are presented. Readers may wish to consult a special issue of the *Career Development Quarterly* (1994, volume 43, issue 1) devoted to Super's tremendous contributions to career development theory. Next, Linda Gottfredson's (1981) theory of circumscription and compromise is presented.

Donald Super. Super (1957, 1963, 1990) contended that individuals select occupations consistent with their self-concept. Self-concept is fluid and influenced by the dynamic interplay of biological, psychological, and social factors. Super (1990) highlighted how societal variables such as family, school, social policy, and peer groupings interact with psychological variables such as values, interests, personalities, and skills to affect career development. He argued that the manner in which people implement their self-concepts into occupational choices is a function of their developmental life stage. It therefore follows that vocational behaviors should be examined in the context of the particular demands of a person's developmental life stage. The vocational developmental stages formulated by Super are as follows: (a) growth (ages 0–14) is characterized by the development of interests, aptitudes, and needs in conjunction with the self-concept, (b) exploration (ages 15–24) is a tentative phase of narrowing down options, (c) establishment (ages 25–44) is characterized by choosing and implementing a career and stabilization within that career, (d) maintenance (ages 45–64) involves continued efforts to improve work position, and (e) disengagement (ages 65 and above) is characterized by preparation for retirement and retirement itself. Despite the age ranges, Super recognized individual variation in passage through the stages; he also noted that recycling of the stages often occurs during reconsideration of career plans or career changes. Each stage has a corresponding set of developmental vocational tasks.

Throughout the lifespan, individuals are called upon to fulfill the demands of a variety of roles, such as child, student, leisurite, citizen, worker, and homemaker. The life–career rainbow (Super & Neville, 1986) provides a physical representation of how these roles may overlap with and influence vocational development and behaviors. Career maturity, another important concept proposed by Super (1974), refers to the readiness of individuals to make good vocational choices. Assessment of the client's career maturity often helps to set the stage for appropriate interventions (Sharf, 2006). Fouad and Arbona (1994) review research on the applicability of Super's model to people of color. Osborne, Brown, Niles, and Miner (1998) comprehensively analyze Super's theory and its application to career counseling.

Linda Gottfredson.   Gottfredson's (1981, 1996, 2002) theory of circumscription and compromise incorporates elements of a social systems approach into a developmental perspective and focuses on the influence of gender, social class, and intelligence on career aspirations and choices. Her theory concerns the manner by which children "seem to re-create the social inequalities of their elders long before they themselves experience any barriers to pursuing their dreams" (p. 85). According to her theory, all people have a unique "zone of acceptable alternatives"—a range of occupations acceptable for consideration and reflecting their view of where they fit in society. This zone is bounded by the greatest and least amount of effort individuals are willing to expend to attain that career, as well as by their willingness to pursue careers nontraditional for their gender. For example, an individual might consider a range of occupations perceived to be more prestigious than secretarial work, such as nursing or management, but not as demanding as becoming a physician or a lawyer. A man might automatically rule out nursing because it is a traditionally female profession and inconsistent with his perceived gender role. Gottfredson and Lapan (1997) found that occupational roles based on gender typing have the potential to be broadened within specific vocational exploration activities.

Gottfredson postulates that as the self-concept develops, people become oriented to the implications of size and power (ages 3–5), gender roles (ages 6–8), social valuation (ages 9–13), and finally, as their interests emerge, their internal unique self (ages 14 and older). The zone of acceptable alternatives is narrowed (circumscribed) as age increases. That is, occupations that are perceived as incongruent with the child's view of appropriate gender roles are the first occupations to be eliminated, followed by occupations perceived as too low in prestige for young person's social class, and then occupations requiring too much or too little effort are eliminated. When compromise in occupational choices is required, Gottfredson argues that people first sacrifice their interests related to work—for example, their internal unique self—followed by prestige. Gottfredson (2002) provides a detailed summary as well as recent extensions of her theory, including further attention to the impact of individual and group differences and a discussion of how biosocial theory best addresses these concepts. Under the umbrella of the nature–nurture partnership theory, Gottfredson (2002) highlights individual and group difference considerations for career counselors to utilize when working with clients.

Assumptions and Diversity

The majority of career counseling theories were based on the behaviors of able-bodied, heterosexual, middle- to upper-class white men, and numerous implicit assumptions are embedded in many contemporary approaches to career counseling. Our ability to work effectively as career counselors is contingent on our awareness of these assumptions and our willingness to critically reflect on the appropriateness of any theory, technique, or strategy when working with a given individual. Additionally, any given individual has multiple identities, and career interventions should be tailored for the salient identities of an individual. Career interventions suited for white middle-class men will not necessarily be appropriate for or meet the needs of others. Phillips, Ingram, Smith, and Mindes (2003) cite the lack of empirical data on multiple intersecting identities, such as gender, race/ethnicity, and sexual orientation; however, theoretical developments such as the social cognitive career theory (Lent, Brown, & Hackett, 1994) are critically important because they integrate critical factors shaping the reality of women, ethnic minorities, gay and lesbian individuals, and people with disabilities, such as the influence of discrimination, perceived barriers, self-efficacy and outcome expectations, and environmental support. The small number of resources that are offered here is by no means an exhaustive list, and the reader is encouraged to explore far beyond these resources in developing competencies consistent with the needs of our diverse society.

Contemporary researchers have increased emphasis on women's career development in the last several decades. Society has come a long way since advice such as the following, on supervising women workers, was considered professionally acceptable: "General experience indicates that 'husky' girls—those who are just a little on the heavy side—are more even-tempered and efficient than their underweight sisters" (from *Transportation Magazine*, July 1943). Nonetheless, considerable gender role stereotyping of occupations and gender stratification continue to influence career patterns and expectations for both women and men. Considerations and recommendations for career counseling with women are provided in special issues of the *Journal of Career Assessment* (1997, Vol. 5, No. 4; 1998, Vol. 6, No. 4) and *Career Development Quarterly* (2002, Vol. 50, No. 4). Chronister, McWhirter, and Forrest (2006) and Cook, Heppner, and O'Brien (2002) address the intersections between women's career development, ethnic identity, and contextual constraints. Finally, classic texts such as

Betz and Fitzgerald's (1987) *The Career Psychology of Women*, Worell and Remer's (2003) *Feminist Perspectives in Therapy: Empowering Diverse Women*, and more recently, Walsh and Heppner's (2006) *Career Counseling for Women* are excellent resources.

Resources for career counseling with ethnic minority clients have accumulated much more slowly despite repeated calls within the literature to address the career development needs of ethnic minority populations (Arbona, 1990; Carter & Cook, 1992). Flores, Berkel et al. (2006) conducted a content and trend analysis of racial/ethnic minority vocational research. They found an upward trend in the percentage of research scholarship pertaining to racial/ethnic minorities and also located the most frequently researched content areas: contextual factors (e.g., background influences), racial issues (e.g., racial discrimination) gender issues, and assessment. Texts by Gysbers, Heppner, and Johnson (2003); Osipow, Leong, and Barak (2001), Sharf (2006); and Walsh, Bingham, Brown, and Ward (2001) and a chapter by Dillard and Harley (2002) address this topic with varying amounts of detail. Leong's (1995) *Career Development and Vocational Behavior of Racial and Ethnic Minorities* is a comprehensive text that covers a range of cultural implications within career development and counseling for ethnic minorities. More recently, a special issue of the *Journal of Multicultural Counseling and Development* (2005, volume 33, issue 3) addressed multiculturalism within career issues. Articles addressing cultural issues in the context of career counseling include Brown (2002); Byars-Winston and Fouad (2006); Flores, Spanierman, and Obasi (2003); Hackett and Byars (1996); McWhirter, Torres, and Rasheed (1998); Pearson and Bieschke (2001); Rivera, Anderson, and Middleton (1999); and Worthington, Flores, and Navarro (2005).

The Americans with Disabilities Act (ADA) of 1990 has raised consciousness among employers, counselors, and to some extent, the general public about the rights of people with disabilities. The implications of this act for career counselors are numerous, and career counselors must be familiar with the ADA to properly serve their clients. Nagler's (1993) *Perspectives on Disability* is a helpful and comprehensive resource that includes a focus on the multidimensional impact of the ADA. Additionally, Szymanski and Parker's (2003) *Work and Disability: Issues and Strategies in Career Development and Job Placement* offers insight on disability legislation that affects the career development of individuals with disabilities. Other resources addressing the career counseling needs of individuals with disabilities include Alston, Bell, and Hampton (2002); Dipeoulu, Reardon, Sampson, and Burkhead (2002); Favian and Liesener (2005); Hershenson and Liesener (2003); Moxley, Finch, Tripp, and Forman (2003); National Center on Secondary Education and Transition (2002); Szymanski and Hershenson (2005); and Wehman (2001).

Only quite recently has the literature addressed career counseling with gay, lesbian, and bisexual adolescents and adults. Issues related to bullying and harassment in schools, coming out, identity management, workplace outing, fear of AIDS, job discrimination based on sexual orientation, workplace homophobia, and dual career and parenting versus career issues illustrate the intersection between sexual orientation and career counseling. Hunt, Jaques, Niles, and Wierzalis (2003) describe a variety of career issues and concerns relevant to individuals with HIV/AIDS. Gelberg and Chojnacki's (1995) article on the process of becoming gay, lesbian, and bisexual affirmative career counselors offers a realistic perspective of the challenges this endeavor represents. Other helpful references include Bieschke and Toepfer-Hendey (2006); Chung (2003); Croteau, Anderson, Distefano, and Kampa-Kokesch (2000); Morrow, Gore, and Campbell (1996); Prince (1997); Pope et al. (2004); and Ritter and Terndrup (2002). Gay/lesbian career development was the focus of a special issue of the *Career Development Quarterly* (volume 44, number 2, 1995) and the *Journal of Vocational Behavior* (volume 48, number 2, 1996). Additionally, Fassinger (2000); Morrow (1997); Nauta, Saucier, and Woodard (2001); and Schmidt and Nilsson (2006) address the unique career development needs of gay, lesbian, and bisexual adolescents. In addition to issues related to sexual orientation, gender identity, and expression within vocational development are emerging issues within the literature. For a summary of transgender concerns within vocational counseling see O'Neil, McWhirter, and Cerezo (2007).

Is it possible to be knowledgeable about all cultures and all types of disability or to fully understand the complexities of gender and sexual orientation as they interact with career development? Of course, the answer to this question is no. It certainly is possible, and in fact is a professional obligation, to develop an approach to all clients that explores and honors their multiple identities and orientations. Such an approach requires continuous education through reading, contact with diverse clientele, consultation with colleagues, seminars and workshops, and ongoing critical self-reflection. Career counselors risk perpetuating limiting stereotypes and discrimination when they fail to understand the dynamics of privilege and oppression and the role of such environmental factors as poverty, access to education and health care, homophobia, and racism in the career development process (Blustein, 2006; McWhirter, 1994, 2001; O'Ryan, 2003).

Intervention

Once the nature of career counseling has been clarified and specific goals have been established, the intervention phase of career counseling may begin. Interventions vary, depending on the specific needs and characteristics of the client, the theoretical framework of the counselor, and the counselor's knowledge of available resources. The number of assessment instruments, references, and resources related to career development has expanded so rapidly in the past three decades that the beginning counselor may find the prospect of intervention a bit overwhelming. In this section, some of the most common intervention approaches and instruments will be presented.

Because most career interventions are useful across several theoretical frameworks, they will not be discussed in reference to specific theoretical orientations. Instead, this section is divided according to the five stages presented by Salomone (1988). Although this arrangement is more applicable to clients interested in career exploration and selection than those with concerns related to dual careers and other issues, it remains an efficient way to present information central to career counseling in a limited space. Readers should note that interventions discussed with respect to one stage will not always be associated with that stage of counseling in actual practice; individual client needs, rather than adherence to a formula, should influence the type and order of the interventions employed.

Stage 1: Knowledge About Self

Interests.   Because of the important relationship between interests and occupations, many career interventions incorporate a process of identifying and exploring the client's interests. Approaches to interest measurement can be either qualitative or objective (Gysbers, Heppner, & Johnston, 2003). Several qualitative approaches are presented first, followed by descriptions of several popular objective interest inventories. More detailed information about inventories and the other tests discussed in this chapter is available in the Buros *Mental Measurements Yearbook* series, Kapes and Whitfield's (2002) *A Counselor's Guide to Career Assessment Instruments*, Osborn and Zunker's (2005) *Using Assessment Results for Career Development*, and the *Journal of Career Assessment*. Finally, several computer programs with an interest assessment component are described.

Qualitative approaches to interest assessment include structured interviews, such as the Life Career Assessment (LCA), which is discussed in detail by Gysbers et al. (2003). Career genograms, the detailed analysis of a family's work-related history, may help clients identify concrete areas of interest, as well as the complex work, gender, and cultural socialization that helped shape their interests (Gibson, 2005; Gysbers et al., 2003; Heppner, O'Brien, Hinkleman, & Humphrey, 1994; Moon, Coleman, McCollum, Nelson, & Jensen-Scott, 1993; Okocha, 1998). As there may be differences between the interests assessed by objective inventories and those verbally expressed by the client, measures such as the self-administered Vocational Card Sort (Slaney, 1978) have been recommended to identify career interests (McWhirter, Torres, & Rasheed, 1998; Osborn & Zunker, 2005; Peterson, 1998). Review of the client's previous jobs, activities, and accomplishments may provide another starting point for discussion of interests. The counselor must be sure to break down each experience into its component parts to avoid erroneous conclusions. For example, the client who enjoys volunteering at a nursing home may like interacting with the elderly; on the other hand, attractive features of the job could be related to autonomy, being in charge of other volunteers, or working in the kitchen. The counselor and client should attempt to draw up a highly specific list of interests to facilitate the task of identifying potential options. Martin and Farris (1994) offer an excellent framework for qualitative, culturally appropriate career assessment with Native Americans. According to Goldman (1990), the advantages of qualitative assessment include a greater degree of adaptability with respect to individual characteristics such as gender and ethnicity. McMahon, Patton, and Watson (2003) note that although assessment is a fundamental part of career counseling, qualitative assessments have received little attention within the career counseling literature. They provide several suggestions as a guide for the career counselor developing qualitative assessments for use with clients.

Qualitative approaches may be used alone or in conjunction with formal or published inventories. The counselor should provide the client with information concerning the use of assessment instruments so that they can determine together if this is a desirable option. The decision to use objective assessment instruments should be carefully considered. Although they often save time, objective instruments typically require less activity on the part of the client and may indirectly communicate to clients that they are not capable of identifying their own interests. In addition, indiscriminate reliance on instruments can lead to a "gas station" style of counseling: drive in, take test, explain, drive out, "thank you for shopping at the counseling center." Finally, objective assessment instruments have been plagued by gender and racial bias, and evidence of reliability and validity should be a prerequisite for using such instruments with women and people of color. Leong's (1995) *Career Development and Vocational Behavior of Racial and Ethnic Minorities* offers an overview of the issues concerning the validity of career assessments as applied to ethnic minority groups. Walsh and Heppner's (2006) *Career Counseling for Women* includes attention to gender bias in career assessment. Career assessment with people of diverse cultural backgrounds is frequently featured in the *Journal of Career Assessment,* including lesbian, gay, and bisexual persons, people of diverse racial and ethnic groups, and women (Chung, 2003; Flores, Spanierman, & Obasi, 2003; Whiston & Bouwkamp, 2003). Other valuable references include the career assessment chapters of the *Handbook of Multicultural Assessment* (Gainor, 2001), *Career Counseling for African Americans* (Ward & Bingham, 2001), and a chapter on career assessment and diversity in the *Handbook of Vocational Psychology* (Subich, 2005). The counselor should employ a system of self-checks to continuously assess whether the client is receiving optimal service with the use of an objective instrument.

The Strong Interest Inventory.   The Strong Interest Inventory (SII) is among the most widely used interest inventories. It was created by Strong in 1927 and most recently revised by Donnay, Morris, Schaubhut, and Thompson in 2005. The results of the 291-item SII permit clients to contrast their interest patterns with those of people in more than 100 different occupations. Separate scales for males and females reduce bias related to gender differences. Contrary to many a client's hopes, the SII does not predict how successful a person might be in a chosen field, nor does it indicate a career area that a client should or should not pursue. What it does provide is a launching point for exploration of career options that have never been considered and a point of departure for discussing why certain career interests are congruent or incongruent with those of persons employed in that field. The SII is organized according to Holland's (1973) typology of modal orientations, so the client can easily determine the orientations with which his or her interests most closely coincide. This may help the client to focus on a particular group of careers to explore more thoroughly. Research investigating the validity of the SII with Latinos, African Americans, Native Americans, and Asian Americans has produced mixed findings (Chartrand, Borgen, Betz, & Donnay, 2002; Flores et al., 2006; Fouad, 2007; Fouad & Walker, 2005; Hansen & Lee, 2007).

Self-Directed Search.   The Self-Directed Search (SDS) was developed by John Holland (1991a, 1991b) and published by Psychological Assessment Resources. The SDS is a self-administered inventory that assesses an individual's activities, competencies, and career interests and translates this information into matching career options. The results of the inventory correspond with Holland's occupational typology and are also cross-referenced with the *Dictionary of Occupational Titles* (DOT). The SDS is thorough and relatively easy to administer.

Kuder Occupational Interest Survey.   The Kuder Occupational Interest Survey (KOIS) was developed by G. Frederick Kuder in 1966 and revised by Donald Zytowski in 1985. The current version of the Kuder interest assessment instrument is available online and is published by National Career Assessment Services, Inc. (http://www. kuder.com/). Assessments include skills and work values, as well as career and educational planning tools.

Computer Programs.   There are several interactive computer programs designed to facilitate a client's self-exploration of interests. Each program also contains other components, such as values assessment, occupational information, and skills assessment. A brief review of three such programs follows.

SIGI+ is an extension of SIGI, the System of Interactive Guidance and Information, which is described later in this chapter. SIGI+ contains nine components, beginning with a system overview followed by a self-assessment section where users are guided through an inventory of their interests, values, and skills. Other sections of SIGI+ allow users to learn about careers that correspond to the results of their inventory and provide advice on financial assistance, suggestions for decision making, training requirements for specific occupations, and a large amount of additional occupational information.

The Discover program, like SIGI+, contains interest, ability, and values inventories to facilitate the user's self-assessment. Strategies for identifying occupations, occupational information, and information about educational institutions are available with the Discover program. In addition, Discover contains a section that incorporates Holland's Self-Directed Search. A newer version of Discover, called Discover for Adult Learners, was developed for unemployed adults and those in the process of school or job market reentry or career changes. Among other developments, Discover for Adult Learners contains a skills inventory that incorporates the user's previous work experiences.

Eureka's Micro SKILLS is a computer program that begins with a skills inventory similar to the process described in Bolles's *What Color Is Your Parachute? A Practical Manual for Job-Hunters and Career-Changers* (2006). This inventory is useful for adults reentering the workforce or changing careers, owing to its focus on experiences as well as interests.

Aptitudes.   Gathering knowledge should also include assessment of the client's aptitudes and skills. Knowing what the client does well facilitates the identification of career-related skills or careers at which the client may succeed. One common informal way to assess aptitudes is by reviewing grades in various subject areas. However, this presents only a limited amount of information. Clients should be encouraged to identify the specific types of class activities in which they were successful: oral presentations, group projects, detailed note taking, debates, and so on. Work-related successes should also be noted: Was the client ever complimented for achievements in productivity, facility cleanliness, or record keeping? Clients might be encouraged to interview others for additional information about their special talents or skills. Be wary of the client who claims a general lack of proficiency because such a claim may be more reflective of a low self-concept or low self-efficacy expectations than of actual performance.

The counselor should be prepared to dig deeply and specifically to obtain information about aptitudes because obvious signs of success such as grades and awards are often the only signs to which people attend. In addition to informal information gathering, some circumstances may warrant the use of an aptitude test.

Differential Aptitude Test. The Differential Aptitude Test (DAT) was developed by Bennet, Seashore, and Westman. The DAT was most recently updated in 1990 and is published by the Psychological Corporation. Several forms have been developed and revised. The DAT is widely used across the country by schools and counseling services and has proven extremely useful to high school students trying to determine how they might fare in future educational endeavors. Counselors should be aware that although this instrument is useful in predicting general academic success, it is not useful for predicting success in specific academic areas, nor does prediction extend to the area of occupational success.

General Aptitude Test Battery. The General Aptitude Test Battery (GATB) was developed and published by the U.S. Employment Service in 1947, with periodic revisions since then. A unique advantage of the GATB is that this test allows clients to compare themselves with actual workers in specific occupations with respect to nine aptitudes (e.g., motor coordination and clerical perception). The GATB has often been used to assist in job placement, and can be used in conjunction with the new Employment Service Interest Inventory to facilitate the exploration of job possibilities in the DOT and the *Occupational Outlook Handbook* (OOH) (U.S. Department of Labor, 2006). Osborn and Zunker (2005) note that concerns have been raised about test bias against racial and ethnic minority groups, as well as concerns about the need to update the test to reflect changes in technology. Additional aptitude tests are reviewed in the Buros Mental Measurement Yearbook series.

Values. Values clarification is an important component of career counseling (Zytowski, 1994). To make realistic decisions about future occupational pursuits, an individual should have a good idea about the relative importance of values such as family time, income, prestige, and autonomy that are affected by the nature of an occupation. For example, an individual who highly values family time is not likely to be satisfied with a traveling sales position, nor would someone valuing autonomy fare well in a job that involves constant scrutiny by a supervisor. Mael (1991) offers an excellent discussion of the factors influencing career-related behaviors of observant Jews, illustrating the interaction of specific values and religious practices with the world of work.

Often clients begin career counseling without ever having considered the relationship between occupational choices and value satisfaction. The counselor must be prepared to initiate and accompany the client's exploration of values, as well as anticipate the potential value conflicts and means of satisfaction in the occupations under consideration. By bringing value exploration into the counselor–client interaction, the cultural factors underlying the career development process can be used as a tool for culturally appropriate intervention. Dominant culture values are embedded in many of the theories and practices of career counseling, limiting their appropriateness for use with those whose values are different than those of the dominant culture, such as members of ethnic minority groups (Byars-Winston & Fouad, 2006). Hartung (2002) posits that the career counselor should examine cultural factors influencing values by (a) identifying sets of values that delineate the influence of broader cultural values on the individual and (b) examining the individualistic and/or collectivistic cultural value orientations of the client. McCloskey and Mintz (2006) explore the values that may affect career counseling with Native American women. Shin (1999) provides a discussion of career-relevant personality characteristics and values among Asian Americans that may affect career counseling; exploration of such resources is especially important when working with an individual of a sociocultural background distinct from that of the counselor.

Changing values are not infrequently the impetus of a decision to seek career counseling. Loss due to death, divorce, or changes in health status may necessitate a reprioritization of values. In such a case, income may replace helping others, or job security may supersede autonomy in an individual's values hierarchy. Counselors should be sensitive to the changing nature of values over an individual's lifespan and the implications of value changes for career choices.

The basic processes involved in many values clarification exercises include one or a combination of the following: identification and analysis of the values issue; examination of past experiences, preferences, behaviors, and decisions that are related to the present issues; investigation of how others view the issue (by direct questioning or imagining what respected others would do in a similar situation); testing or self-confrontation about tentative choices, positions, or resolutions; finding personal environments that are conducive to clear thought about, or temporary escape from, the issue ("sleeping on it" or quiet meditation); and making the "best" tentative resolution, living in accordance with it, and revising if needed (Brown, 1995; Kinnier & Krumboltz, 1984). Counselors can use widely available strategies devised and published by others or create their own variations of values clarification techniques (Kinnier, 1995).

Some clarification exercises involve consideration of values in light of one's mortality. The "lifeline" exercise requires the client to imagine having a terminal illness and to review priorities from this mindset. "Epitaph" and "obituary" exercises require clients to write down their own version of how they want to be remembered after they have died (Kinnier & Krumboltz, 1984).

The Work Values Inventory developed by Super (1970) is one example of an objective instrument for assessing work-related values. Other available instruments include the Work Environment Preference Schedule, the Salience Inventory, the Study of Values, and the Survey of Interpersonal Values. The latter two instruments are designed to explore both work-related and personal values.

The System of Interactive Guidance and Information (SIGI) is a computer program primarily geared toward helping users clarify their most important values and providing information about careers consistent with the values identified. There are 10 values that the user must evaluate in terms of importance: income, prestige, independence, helping others, security, variety, leadership, interest field, leisure, and early entry. Peterson, Ryan-Jones, Sampson, and Reardon (1994) found that SIGI users report a positive impact on their career exploration.

Stage 2: Knowledge About the World of Work

Career counselors are responsible for introducing clients to resources for occupational information. More specifically, part of the counselor's job is to ensure that clients are able to obtain career-related information independently in the future. Occupational information is vast and constantly changing, and keeping up to date can be a staggering task. Fortunately, many resources significantly reduce the amount of time and research required of both the counselor and the client. In this section, informal, formal, and computer sources of career information will be presented.

Informal processes of obtaining career information can be interesting and rewarding for the client. The most direct way to find out about a career of interest is to talk to someone already doing it! The client can locate potential interviewees from a variety of sources including friends, relatives, and classmates; local alumni associations; service and professional organizations; and even the local phone directory. The counselor may help the client formulate a set of questions that will maximize the amount and value of the information the client gains from the interview. "Shadowing," or following a worker on the job, is an option that provides an even more concrete idea of what a particular career involves.

College and university campuses are another rich source of occupational information. Clients may wish to ask instructors in their field of interest for insights into the nature of specific occupations. Libraries offer journals and magazines that serve professional audiences and provide information on current developments and the cutting edge of research in the field. Additionally, libraries contain reference materials such as labor market statistics, occupational forecasts, and descriptive information.

A number of excellent reference materials are typically found in counseling centers, career development centers, and libraries. The most recent version of the *Occupational Outlook Handbook* (OOH), as of this writing, is the 2006–2007 edition, and an online edition is available at http://www.bls.gov/oco/. *The Guide for Occupational Exploration: Linking Interests, Learning, and Careers* (GOE, 2005), like the OOH, is updated regularly. In addition, the U. S. Department of Labor published the *Dictionary of Occupational Titles* from 1939 until 1991 and since replaced this resource with a database called O*NET that can be accessed online at http://online.onetcenter.org/. O*NET provides information about careers and requirements and a host of other services, such as online skills assessments. The first state-based computerized career information system was Oregon Career Information Systems (Oregon CIS). Developed to provide Oregonians with integrated, timely, and comprehensive information useful in career development, planning, and decision making, there are now similar information systems in most states, as well as a national CIS office located at the University of Oregon (http://oregoncis.uoregon.edu/home/). Resources such as those described here provide databases that are highly useful for individuals and organizations seeking information, such as the nature of specific jobs, the skills and abilities required, how to prepare for entry into the field, forecasts for employment, and how to determine whether such work might be of interest to an individual. Counselors should be familiar with the particular classification system used in each source before introducing these references to clients.

The Internet has become an important and rich source of information on the world of work. For example, the University of California at Berkeley Career and Education Guidance Library maintains a Web site of career exploration links (http://www.uhs.berkeley.edu/Students/CareerLibrary/Links/Occup.cfm). Other Web sites of interest include the U.S. Department of Labor (http://www.dol.gov) and state departments of education. For a review of the impact of the Internet and technological advances on career counseling and assessment, the beginning counselor is encouraged to read Gore and Leuwerke (2000), and Harris-Bowlsbey (2002).

Computerized guidance programs are widely used sources of occupational information in middle, secondary, and higher education settings (Fowkes & McWhirter, in press) and include CIS, SIGI, Guidance Information System (GIS), and Discover. The relative ease with which computer files can be updated and accessed makes computers an invaluable source of current occupational information.

Stage 3: Creating a Match

For the client interested in choosing an occupation, this stage of career counseling refers to the process of deciding which occupations are consistent with the client's skills, interests, and values. Eventually, the client has to narrow down the list of occupations, and career counselors often assist in the decision-making process.

Decision making is a part of life, but unfortunately many people lack the skills for making effective decisions. Decision making within career counseling has been conceptualized in terms of four components: (a) conceptualization of the problem as one of choice, (b) enlargement of the response repertoire, (c) identification of discriminative stimuli, and (d) response selection (Olson, McWhirter, & Horan, 1989). Enlargement of the response repertoire refers to the process of generating many alternative actions. Identification of discriminative stimuli involves weighing the advantages and disadvantages of each potential course of action, as well as assessing the probable results of each. For example, although the advantages of writing a Pulitzer Prize–winning book are many, the probability of doing so is quite slim. Teaching clients this or other decision-making models provides them with a skill generalizable to a multitude of situations and helps ensure subsequent satisfaction with the decisions they make. It is important to integrate cultural values into the decision-making process. For example, the involvement of parents and other family members in career decision making varies quite a bit across cultures, and counselors should not assume that mainstream middle-class Western values such as "independent decisions" and "whatever makes me happy" are salient for a given client (e.g., see Arthur & McMahon, 2005; Sue et al., 1998; Sue & Constantine, 2005).

Career decision making has been the focus of an enormous amount of empirical and conceptual literature. Some recent examples, including those that focus on career decision-making measures or instruments, are Albion and Fogarty (2002), Chope (2006), Chung (2002), Cohen (2003), and Thompson and Subich (2006).

Stage 4: Implementation of a Decision

Salomone (1988) notes that even when a decision has been made, the task of the career counselor is not over. The client may lack the specific skills, support, or information necessary for successful implementation of the decision. The counselor should be prepared to assist the client in developing these skills, locating sources of support, and obtaining information in areas such as resume writing, interviewing, assertiveness, and communication. If part of the client's decision involves actions such as changing a behavior, developing a hobby, or participating in a new organization, the counselor can be a valuable source of support and encouragement. Often simply scheduling tasks is enough motivation for the hesitant client to follow through on decisions.

The stages of change model, along with other transtheoretical models of counseling, can be used to assess a client's readiness for decisions involving action and assist in the development of interventions tailored to the client's stage of change (Prochaska & DiClemente, 1984, 1992; Prochaska, DiClemente, & Norcross, 1992). The stages of change model outlines the different stages that an individual must undergo to follow through with a particular change process. Individuals in the *precontemplation* stage have little or no awareness of the need or intention to change (an adult, Chris, is living in his parents' home, without a job or source of income, and with no intention to seek education or employment). In the *contemplation* stage, awareness of the need/desire for change surfaces; however, a commitment to change has not yet evolved (Chris's parents ask Chris to either contribute to the household income or move out, but Chris does not think that this "threat" is serious and has no plans for action). Once the individual reaches the *preparation* stage, the decision to make a change has been made (Chris accepts that getting a job is probably necessary and decides to begin seeking a job . . . within the next couple of weeks). In the *action* phase, the behaviors necessary for change are enacted (Chris engages in job seeking). The final step is the *maintenance* phase, in which the change is maintained over time. If Chris discontinues job seeking without finding a job or finds a job but is then fired or laid off, the cycle begins again. Prochaska, DiClemente, and Norcross (1992) explain that individuals may cycle through these stages a number of times before entering and sustaining maintenance of the change; the duration of any particular stage can vary widely.

As discussed by Dolan, Seay, and Vellela (2006), the stages of change model was modified by Freeman and Dolan in 2001 to increase its specificity so that targeted, effective interventions can be implemented and evaluated. When clients enter career counseling, they may not be ready to change behaviors that become the focus of intervention. Understanding the nature of change processes can help the career counselor meet clients where they are and assist them in taking the next step toward change. When clients are not achieving their own goals, examining their process by using the stages of change model can be very useful to both counselor and client.

Anxiety may interfere with the client's motivation to carry out a plan of action. Anxiety is often based on irrational beliefs or expectations. According to Krumboltz, maladaptive or irrational beliefs are a common obstacle to career development, and he recommends cognitive restructuring as one means to address this problem (Krumboltz & Worthington, 1999). Cognitive restructuring involves identifying irrational beliefs such as "There's only one perfect job for me" and replacing them with rational and realistic thoughts. The Career Beliefs Inventory is a counseling tool that may help identify clients' beliefs and assumptions about careers that may be preventing action (Krumboltz, 1994; Krumboltz & Vosvick, 1996). The counselor's familiarity with the world of work and with the client's skills and personality can be used to reduce anxiety and encourage action.

Stage 5: Adjustment to New Settings

Sometimes the goals established in career counseling result in the client moving into a new environment. This may be the result of a job promotion, the start of a new job, enrollment in an academic program, a change of residence, or a combination of these and other changes. The client may be challenged to cope with a new set of demands and expectations, as well as to interact with unfamiliar groups and individuals. The new environment may be characterized by racism and sexual harassment, support and professional challenge, or widespread demoralization, or it may simply differ radically from the prior environment and require a major adjustment. Issues often perceived as the sole territory of personal counseling are commonly encountered in career counseling. Often clients are dealing with career concerns as a result of or in conjunction with developmental issues such as divorce, changes in ethnic identity status, children leaving home, coming out as gay or lesbian, changing financial circumstances, or changes in health.

Training in skills such as communication, human relations with diverse groups, and giving or receiving supervision may help the client interact in a healthy and productive way with new coworkers, supervisors, and acquaintances. Assertiveness training may help clients secure what they need from the environment and safeguard their rights without infringing upon the rights of others. Stress inoculation and relaxation training may help clients deal with the anxiety associated with these new situations. Strategies for dealing with loneliness, frustration, and feelings of inadequacy may also be important at this time of transition.

Keep in mind that the arrangement of specific interventions with specific stages in career counseling is by no means set in stone. For example, cognitive restructuring may be called for as the client begins the self-assessment process and at a variety of other points in the career counseling process. In addition, career counseling interventions need not follow each and every one of the five steps identified by Salomone (1988). Rather, the process should be dictated by the nature of the client's concern and the plan that the counselor and client establish together.

Evaluation

Evaluation is a sorely neglected aspect of career counseling. Although many career counselors are aware of the immediate outcomes of counseling, such as the choice of a college major or a reduction in job stress, in general practice there is very little formal follow-up. In addition, it is good practice for counselors to end every counseling relationship with an evaluation of the process. Such an evaluation may be incorporated into one of the final sessions and yield important information for both the counselor and the client. Potential closing topics to cover are similar to those of personal counseling: the relative helpfulness of the interventions, the degree of support the client experienced throughout the process, the extent to which the client felt respected and understood, the extent to which the client felt like an active participant and collaborator, topics on which the client might have wanted to spend more or less time, and what the client might like to have done differently. Feedback for clients might include the counselor's perceptions of their relevant strengths and weaknesses, changes and progress noted, and suggestions for future directions.

There is also a need in career counseling for more formal evaluations of the relative effectiveness of various interventions (Fowkes & McWhirter, 2007). Surprisingly little is known about how various career interventions affect the vocational development process. Brown and McPartland (2005) describe the results of several meta-analyses of the effects of career interventions and noted five specific intervention components that appear to be associated with positive career counseling outcomes: written exercises, individualized interpretation and feedback, world of work information, modeling opportunities, and attention to building support within a social network. Their review is a promising step forward in understanding the complexity of career counseling and vocational choices.

Summary

Career counseling is a vital and dynamic area of counseling. Although a variety of theoretical perspectives currently inform the career counselor, a developmental perspective has been emphasized in the definition and description of career counseling. The framework in this chapter may serve as an initial organizer for viewing the roles and activities of the career counselor, and the references listed may guide future, more in-depth exploration of career development theories and career interventions. We hope that beginning counselors will continue to pursue the vast resources of available information in the area of career counseling. Further exploration and utilization of these resources can make the process of career counseling a productive, challenging, and enjoyable experience for both the counselor and the client. The following Web sites provide additional information relating to the chapter topics.

USEFUL WEB SITES

Society for Vocational Psychology
http://www.div17.org/vocpsych/

National Career Development Association
http://www.ncda.org/

U.S. Department of Labor
http://www.dol.gov/

Kuder Career Planning System
http://www.kuder.com/

Bureau of Labor Statistics *Occupational Outlook Handbook*
http://www.bls.gov/oco/

Buros Institute of Mental Measurements
http://www.unl.edu/buros/

O*NET Online
http://online.onetcenter.org

Career Information System (CIS)
http://cis.uoregon.edu/

Career Exploration Links
http://www.uhs.berkeley.edu/Students/CareerLibrary/Links/Occup.cfm

REFERENCES

Albion, M. J., & Fogarty, G. J. (2002). Factors influencing career decision making in adolescents and adults. *Journal of Career Assessment, 10*, 91–126.

Alston, R. J., Bell, T. J., & Hampton, J. L. (2002). Learning disability and career entry into the sciences: A critical analysis of attitudinal factors. *Journal of Career Development, 28*, 263–275.

American Counseling Association. (2005). *Code of ethics and standards of practice.* Alexandria, VA: Author.

American Psychological Association. (2003). Guidelines on multicultural education, training, research, practice, and organizational change for psychologists. *American Psychologist, 58*, 377–402.

Arbona, C. (1990). Career counseling research and Hispanics: A review of the literature. *The Counseling Psychologist, 18*, 300–323.

Arthur, N., & McMahon, M. (2005). Multicultural career counseling: Theoretical applications of the systems theory framework. *The Career Development Quarterly, 53*, 208–222.

Atkinson, D. R., Morten, G., & Sue, D. W. (1998). *Counseling American minorities: A cross-cultural perspective* (5th ed.). Boston: McGraw-Hill.

Bandura, A. (1986). *Social foundations of thought and action: A social cognitive theory.* Englewood Cliffs, NJ: Prentice-Hall.

Bandura, A. (1997). *Self-efficacy: The exercise of control.* New York: Freeman.

Betz, N. E., & Corning, A. F. (1993). The inseparability of "career" and "personal" counseling. *The Career Development Quarterly, 42*(2), 137–142.

Betz, N. E., & Fitzgerald, L. (1987). *The Career Psychology of Women.* Orlando, FL: Academic Press.

Bieschke, K. J., & Toepfer-Hendey, E. (2006). Career counseling with lesbian clients. In W. B. Walsh & M. J. Heppner (Eds.), *Handbook of career counseling for women* (2nd ed., pp. 351–385). Mahwah, NJ: Lawrence Erlbaum Associates.

Blake, R. J., & Sackett, S. A. (1999). Holland's typology and the five-factor model: A rational-empirical analysis. *Journal of Career Assessment, 7*, 249–279.

Blustein, D. (2006). *The psychology of working: A new perspective for career development, counseling, and public policy.* Mahwah, NJ: Lawrence Erlbaum Associates.

Bolles, R. N. (2006). *What color is your parachute? 2007: A practical manual for job-hunters and career-changers.* Berkeley, CA: Ten Speed Press.

Bowman, S. L. (1998). Minority women and career adjustment. *Journal of Career Assessment, 6*, 417–431.

Brown, C., & Lavish, L. A. (2006). Career assessment with Native Americans: Role salience and career decision-making self-efficacy. *Journal of Career Assessment, 14*, 116–129.

Brown, D. (1995). A values-based approach to facilitating career transitions. *The Career Development Quarterly, 44*, 4–11.

Brown, D. (2002). The role of work and cultural values in occupational choice, satisfaction, and success: A theoretical statement. *Journal of Counseling & Development, 80*, 48–56.

Brown, D., & Associates (Eds.). (2003). *Career information, career counseling, and career development* (8th ed.). Boston: Allyn & Bacon.

Brown, S. D., & McPartland, E. (2005). Career interventions: Current status and future directions. In W. B. Walsh & M. L. Savickas (Eds.), *Handbook of vocational psychology: Theory, research, and practice* (3rd ed., pp. 195–226). Mahwah, NJ: Lawrence Erlbaum Associates.

Byars, A. M. (2001). Rights-of-way: Affirmative career counseling with African American women. In W. B. Walsh, R. P. Bingham, M. T. Brown, & C. M. Ward (Eds.), *Career counseling for African Americans* (pp. 27–48). Mahwah, NJ: Lawrence Erlbaum Associates.

Byars-Winston, A., & Fouad, N. (2006). Metacognition and multicultural competence: Expanding the culturally appropriate career counseling model. *The Career Development Quarterly, 54,* 187–201.

Career assessment for a new millennium. (2000). Special section of the *Journal of Career Assessment, 8*(4), 56–88.

Career development of women of color and white women. (2002). Special issue of the *Career Development Quarterly, 50*(4).

Carter, R. T., & Cook, D. A. (1992). A culturally relevant perspective for understanding the career paths of visible racial/ethnic group people. In H. D. Lea & Z. B. Leibowitz (Eds.), *Adult Career Development* (2nd ed., pp. 192–217). Alexandria, VA: National Career Development Association.

Chartrand, J. M., Borgen, F. H., Betz, N. E., & Donnay, D. (2002). Using the Strong Interest Inventory and the Skills Confidence Inventory to explain career goals. *Journal of Career Assessment,10,* 169–189.

Chope, R. (2006). Assessing family influence in career decision making. In G. Walz, J. Bleuer, & R. Yep (Eds.), *Vistas: Compelling perspectives on counseling* (pp. 183–186). Alexandria, VA: American Counseling Association.

Chronister, K. M., McWhirter, E. H., & Forrest, L. (2006). A critical feminist approach to career counseling with women. In W. B. Walsh & M. J. Heppner (Eds.), *Handbook of career counseling with women* (2nd ed., pp. 167–192). Mahwah, NJ: Lawrence Erlbaum Associates.

Chung, B. Y. (2002). Career decision-making self-efficacy and career commitment: Gender and ethnic differences among college students. *Journal of Career Development, 28,* 277–284.

Chung, B. Y. (2003). Career counseling with lesbian, gay, bisexual, and transgendered persons: The next decade. *The Career Development Quarterly, 52,* 78–85.

Cohen, B. N. (2003). Applying existential theory and intervention to career decision-making. *Journal of Career Development, 29,* 195–210.

Comas-Diaz, L., & Greene, B. (1994). *Women of color: Integrating ethnic and gender identities in psychotherapy.* New York: Guilford Press.

Cook, E. P., Heppner, M. J., & O'Brien, K. M. (2002). Career development of women of color and White women: Assumptions, conceptualization, and interventions from an ecological perspective. *Career Development Quarterly, 50,* 291–305.

Council for Accreditation of Counseling and Related Educational Programs. (2001). *The 2001 standards.* Alexandria, VA: Author. Retrieved October 1, 2003, from http://www.counseling.org/cacrep/2001standards700.htm

Croteau, J. M., Anderson, M. Z., Distefano, T. M., & Kampa-Kokesch, S. (2000). Lesbian, gay, and bisexual vocational psychology: Reviewing foundations and planning construction. In R. M. Perez, K. A. DeBord, K. J. Bieschke, & L. S. Brown (Eds.), *Handbook of counseling and psychotherapy with lesbian, gay, and bisexual clients* (pp. 383–408). Washington, DC: American Psychological Association.

Croteau, J. M., & Thiel, M. J. (1993). Integrating sexual orientation in career counseling: Acting to end a form of the personal-career dichotomy. *The Career Development Quarterly, 42,* 174–179.

Dillard, J. M., & Harley, D. A. (2002). Working with ethnic minority employees in the workplace. In D. S. Sandhu (Ed.), *Counseling employees: A multifaceted approach* (pp. 131–149). Alexandria, VA: American Counseling Association.

Dipeolu, A., Reardon, R., Sampson, J., & Burkhead, J. (2002). The relationship between dysfunctional career thoughts and adjustment to disability in college students with learning disabilities. *Journal of Career Assessment, 10,* 413–427.

Dolan, M., Seay, T., & Vellela, T. (2006). The revised stage of change model and the treatment planning process. In G. Walz, J. Bleuer, & R. Yep (Eds.), *Vistas: Compelling perspectives on counseling* (pp. 129–132). Alexandria, VA: American Counseling Association.

Donney, D., Morris, M., Schaubhut, N., & Thompson, R. (2005). *Strong Interest Inventory Manual revised edition*. Mountain View, CA: CPP.

Engels, D. W., Minor, C. W., Sampson Jr., J. P., & Splete, H. H. (1995). Career counseling specialty: History, development and prospect. *Journal of Counseling and Development, 74*, 134–138.

Fabian, E. S., & Liesener, J. J. (2005). Promoting the career potential of youth with disabilities. In S. D. Brown & R. W. Lent (Eds.), *Career development and counseling: Putting theory and research to work* (pp. 551–572). Hoboken, NJ: John Wiley & Sons.

Fassinger, R. E. (2000). Applying counseling theories to lesbian, gay, and bisexual clients: Pitfalls and possibilities. In R. M. Perez, K. A. DeBord, & K. J. Bieschke (Eds.), *Handbook of counseling and psychotherapy with lesbian, gay, and bisexual clients* (pp. 107–131). Washington, DC: American Psychological Association.

Flores, L. Y., Berkel, L. A., Nilsson, J. E., Ojeda, L., Jordan, S. E., Lynn, G. L., et al. (2006). Racial/ethnic minority vocational research: A content and trend analysis across 36 years. *The Career Development Quarterly, 55*, 2–21.

Flores, L. Y., Lin, Y., & Huang, Y. (2005). Applying the multicultural guidelines to career counseling with people of color. In M. G. Constantine & D. W. Sue (Eds.), *Strategies for building multicultural competence in mental health and educational settings* (pp. 73–90). Hoboken, NJ: John Wiley & Sons.

Flores, L. Y., & O'Brien, K. M. (2002). The career development of Mexican American adolescent women: A test of social cognitive career theory. *Journal of Counseling Psychology, 49*, 14–27.

Flores, L., Spanierman, L., Armstrong, P., & Velez, A. (2006). Validity of the Strong Interest Inventory and Skills Confidence Inventory with Mexican American high school students. *Journal of Career Assessment, 14*, 183–202.

Flores, L., Spanierman, L., & Obasi, E. (2003). Ethical and professional issues in career assessment with diverse racial and ethnic groups. *Journal of Career Assessment, 11*, 76–95.

Fouad, N. A. (2002). Cross-cultural differences in vocational interests: Between-group differences on the Strong Interest Inventory. *Journal of Counseling Psychology, 49*, 283–289.

Fouad, N. A. (2007). Work and vocational psychology: Theory, research, and applications. *Annual Review of Psychology, 58*(5), 1–22.

Fouad, N. A., & Arbona, C. (1994). Careers in a cultural context. *The Career Development Quarterly, 43*, 96–104.

Fouad, N. A., & Mohler, C. J. (2004). Cultural validity of Holland's theory and the Strong Interest Inventory for five racial/ethnic groups. *Journal of Career Assessment, 12*, 423–439.

Fouad, N. A., & Walker, C. M. (2005). Cultural influences on responses to items on the Strong Interest Inventory. *Journal of Vocational Behavior, 66*(1), 104–123.

Fowkes, K. M., & McWhirter, E. H. (2007). Evaluation of computer-assisted career guidance in middle and secondary education settings: Status, obstacles, and suggestions. *Journal of Career Assessment, 15*(3), 388–400.

Frank Parsons's continuing legacy to career development interventions. Special section of *The Career Development Quarterly, 50*.

Gainor, K. A. (2001). Vocational assessment with culturally diverse populations. In L. A. Suzuki, J. G. Ponterotto, & P. J. Meller (Eds.), *Handbook of multicultural assessment: Clinical, psychological, and educational applications* (2nd ed., pp. 169–189). San Francisco: Jossey-Bass.

Gasser, C. E., Larson, L. M., & Borgen, F. H. (2007). Concurrent validity of the 2005 Strong Interest Inventory: An examination of gender and major field of study. *Journal of Career Assessment, 15*, 23–43.

Gelberg, S., & Chojnacki, J. T. (1995). Developmental transitions of gay/lesbian/bisexual-affirmative, heterosexual career counselors. *The Career Development Quarterly, 43*, 267–273.

Gibson, D. (2005). The use of genograms in career counseling with elementary, middle, and high school students. *The Career Development Quarterly, 53*, 353–362.

Ginzberg, E., Ginsburg, S. W., Axelrad, S., & Herma, J. L. (1951). *Occupational choice: An approach to a general theory.* New York: Columbia University Press.

Goldman, L. (1990). Qualitative assessment. *The Counseling Psychologist, 18*, 205–213.

Gore, P. A., & Leuwerke, W. C. (2000). Information technology for career assessment on the Internet. *Journal of Career Assessment, 8*, 3–19.

Gottfredson, L. S. (1981). Circumscription and compromise: A developmental theory of occupational aspirations. *Journal of Counseling Psychology, 28*, 545–579.

Gottfredson, L. S. (1996). Gottfredson's theory of circumscription and compromise. In D. Brown, L. Brooks, & Associates (Eds.), *Career choice and development* (3rd ed., pp. 179–232). San Francisco: Jossey-Bass.

Gottfredson, L. S. (2002). Gottfredson's theory of circumscription, compromise, and self-creation. In D. Brown & Associates (Eds.), *Career choice and development* (4th ed., pp. 85–148). San Francisco: Jossey-Bass.

Gottfredson, L. S., & Lapan, R. T. (1997). Assessing gender-based circumscription of occupational aspirations. *Journal of Career Assessment, 5*, 419–441.

Gysbers, N. C., Heppner, M. J., & Johnston, J. A. (2003). *Career counseling: Process, issues, and techniques* (2nd ed.). Boston: Allyn & Bacon.

Hackett, G., & Byars, A. M. (1996). Social cognitive theory and the career development of African American women. *The Career Development Quarterly, 44*, 322–340.

Hansen, J., & Lee, W. (2007). Evidence of concurrent validity of SII scores for Asian American college students. *Journal of Career Assessment, 15*, 44–54.

Harris-Bowlsbey, J. (2002). Career planning and technology in the 21st century. In S. Niles (Ed.), *Adult career development: Concepts, issues and practices* (3rd ed., pp. 157–165). Columbus, OH: National Career Development Association.

Hartung, P. J. (2002). Cultural context in career theory and practice: Role salience and values. *Career Development Quarterly, 51*, 12–25.

Hawks, B. K., & Muha, D. (1991). Facilitating the career development of minorities: Doing it differently this time. *The Career Development Quarterly, 39*, 251–260.

Heppner, M. J., O'Brien, K. M., Hinkelman, J. M., & Flores, L. Y. (1996). Training counseling psychologists in career development: Are we our own worst enemies? *The Counseling Psychologist, 24*, 105–125.

Heppner, M. J., O'Brien, K. M., Hinkelman, J. M., & Humphrey, C. F. (1994). Shifting the paradigm: The use of creativity in career counseling. *Journal of Career Development, 21*(2), 77–86.

Hershenson, D. B., & Liesener, J. J. (2003). Career counseling with diverse populations: Models, interventions, and applications. In E. M. Szymanski & R. M. Parker (Eds.), *Work and disability: Issues and strategies in career development and job placement* (2nd ed., pp. 281–316). Austin, TX: PRO-ED.

Holland, J. L. (1973). *Making vocational choices: A theory of careers*. Englewood Cliffs, NJ: Prentice Hall.

Holland, J. L. (1991a). *Self-Directed Search (SDS) Form CP: Computer Version*. Tampa, FL: Psychological Assessment Resources.

Holland, J. L. (1991b). *Self-Directed Search (SDS) Form CP: Interpretive Report*. Tampa, FL: Psychological Assessment Resources.

Holland, J. L. (1996a). Exploring career with typology: What we have learned and some new directions. *American Psychologist, 51*, 397–406.

Holland, J. L. (1996b). Integrating career theory and practice: The current situation and some potential remedies. In M. L. Savickas and W. B. Walsh (Eds.), *Handbook of career counseling theory and practice* (pp. 1–11). Palo Alto, CA: Davies-Black.

Holland, J. L. (1997). *Making vocational choices*. Tampa, FL: Psychological Assessment Resources.

Holland's theory. (1999). Special issue of the *Journal of Vocational Behavior, 55*(1).

Hunt, B., Jaques, J., Niles, S. G., & Wierzalis, E. (2003). Career concerns for people living with HIV/AIDS. *Journal of Counseling & Development, 81*, 55–60.

Kapes, J. T., & Whitfield, E. A. (Eds.). (2002). *A counselor's guide to career assessment instruments* (4th ed.). Tulsa, OK: National Career Development Association.

Kinnier, R.T. (1995). A reconceptualization of values clarification: Values conflict resolution. *Journal of Counseling and Development, 74*, 18–24.

Kinnier, R. T., & Krumboltz, J. D. (1984). Procedures for successful career counseling. In N. Gysbers (Ed.), *Designing careers: Counseling to enhance education, work and leisure* (pp. 307–335). San Francisco: Jossey-Bass.

Krumboltz, J. D. (1989, August). *The social learning theory of career decision making*. Paper presented at the annual convention of the American Psychological Association, New Orleans, LA.

Krumboltz, J. D. (1994a). The Career Beliefs Inventory. *Journal of Counseling and Development, 72*, 424–428.

Krumboltz, J. D. (1994b). Improving career development theory from a social learning perspective. In M. L. Savickas & R. W. Lent (Eds.), *Convergence in career development theories* (pp. 9–31). Palo Alto, CA: Consulting Psychologists Press.

Krumboltz, J. D., & Henderson, S. J. (2002). A learning theory for career counselors. In S. G. Niles (Ed.), *Adult career development: Concepts, issues and practices* (3rd ed., pp. 39–56). Columbus, OH: National Career Development Association.

Krumboltz, J. D., & Vosvick, M. A. (1996). Career assessment and the career beliefs inventory. *Journal of Career Assessment, 4,* 345–361.

Krumboltz, J., & Worthington, R. (1999). The school-to-work transition from a learning theory perspective. *The Career Development Quarterly, 47,* 312–325.

Lattimore, R. R., & Borgen, F. H. (1999). Validity of the 1994 Strong Interest Inventory with racial and ethnic groups in the United States. *Journal of Counseling Psychology, 46,* 185–195.

Lee, C. C. (Ed.). (1997). *Multicultural issues in counseling: New approaches to diversity* (2nd ed.). Alexandria, VA: American Counseling Association.

Lent, R. W., Brown, S. D., & Hackett, G. (1994). Toward a unifying social cognitive theory of career and academic interest, choice, and performance. *Journal of Vocational Behavior, 45,* 79–122.

Lent, R. W., Brown, S. D., & Hackett, G. (2002). Social cognitive career theory. In D. Brown & Associates (Eds.), *Career choice and development* (4th ed., pp. 255–311). San Francisco: Jossey-Bass.

Leong, F. T. (Ed.). (1995). *Career development and vocational behavior of racial and ethnic minorities.* Hillsdale, NJ: Lawrence Erlbaum.

Leong, F. T., & Gupta, A. (2007). Career development and vocational behaviors of Asian Americans. In F. T. Leong, A. Ebreo, L. Kinoshita, A. G. Inman, & L. H. Yang (Eds.), *Handbook of Asian American psychology* (2nd ed., pp. 159–178). Thousand Oaks, CA: Sage.

Leung, S. A., & Hou, Z. (2001). Concurrent validity of the 1994 Self-Directed Search for Chinese high school students in Hong Kong. *Journal of Career Assessment, 9,* 283–296.

Levinson, E. M., Ohler, D. L., Caswell, S., & Kiewra, K. (1998). Six approaches to the assessment of career maturity. *Journal of Counseling & Development, 76,* 475–482.

Lofquist, L. H., & Dawis, R. V. (1969). *Adjustment to work.* Englewood Cliffs, NJ: Prentice-Hall.

Lofquist, L. H., & Dawis, R. V. (1984). Research on work adjustment and satisfaction: Implications for career counseling. In S. Brown & R. Lent (Eds.), *Handbook of counseling psychology.* New York: John Wiley.

Mael, F. A. (1991). Career constraints of observant Jews. *The Career Development Quarterly, 39,* 341–349.

Martin, W. E. Jr., & Farris, K. K. (1994). A cultural and contextual decision path approach to career assessment with Native Americans: A psychological perspective. *Journal of Career Assessment, 2,* 258–275.

McCloskey, C., & Mintz, L. (2006). A culturally oriented approach for career counseling with Native American women. In W. B. Walsh & M. J. Heppner (Eds.), *Handbook of career counseling for women* (pp. 319–349) New Jersey: Lawrence Erlbaum Associates.

McMahon, M., Patton, W., & Watson, M. (2003). Developing qualitative career assessment processes. *Career Development Quarterly, 51,* 194–202.

McWhirter, E. H. (1994). *Counseling for empowerment.* Alexandria, VA: American Counseling Association Press.

McWhirter, E. H. (2001, March). *Social action at the individual level: In pursuit of critical consciousness.* Invited keynote address, 5th biennial conference of the Society for Vocational Psychology, Houston, TX.

McWhirter, E. H., Blustein, D., & Perry, J. C. (2005). Annunciation: Implementing an emancipatory communitarian approach to vocational psychology: Response. *The Counseling Psychologist, 33,* 215–224.

McWhirter, E. H., Hackett, G., & Bandalos, D. L. (1998). A causal model of educational plans and career expectations of Mexican-American high school girls. *Journal of Counseling Psychology, 45,* 166–181.

McWhirter, E. H., Torres, D., & Rasheed, S. (1998). Assessing barriers to women's career adjustment. *Journal of Career Assessment, 6,* 317–332.

Miller, D. S., & McWhirter, E. H. (2006). The history of career counseling: From Frank Parsons to twenty-first-century challenges. In D. Capuzzi & M. D. Stauffer (Eds.), *Career counseling: Foundations, perspectives, and applications* (pp. 3–39). Boston: Pearson/Allyn and Bacon.

Moon, S., Coleman, V., McCollum, E., Nelson, T., & Jensen-Scott, R. (1993). Using the genogram to facilitate career decisions: A case study. *Journal of Family Psychotherapy, 4,* 45–56.

Morrow, S. L. (1997). Career development of lesbian and gay youth: Effects of sexual orientation, coming out, and homophobia. In M. B. Harris (Ed.), *School experiences of gay and lesbian youth: The invisible minority* (pp. 1–15). Binghamton, NY: Harrington Park Press/Haworth Press.

Morrow, S. L., Gore Jr., P. A., & Campbell, B. W. (1996). The application of sociocognitive framework to the career development of lesbian women and gay men. *Journal of Vocational Behavior, 48,* 126–148.

Moxley, D. P., Finch, J. R., Tripp, J., & Forman, S. (2003). Strategic career development for people with disabilities. In D. P. Moxley & J. R. Finch (Eds.), *Sourcebook of rehabilitation and mental health practice* (pp. 77–91). New York: Kluwer Academic/Plenum.

Nagler, M. (1993). *Perspectives on disability* (2nd ed.). Palo Alto, CA: Health Markets Research.

National Career Development Association. (1997). *Career counseling competencies.* Retrieved September 28, 2003, from http://ncda.org/about/polccc.html

National Center on Secondary Education and Transition. (2002). *Policy update: Youth with disabilities and the Workforce Investment Act of 1998.* Minneapolis, MN: Author.

National Vocational Guidance Association, American Vocational Association. (1973). *Position paper on career development.* Washington, DC: Author.

Nauta, M. M., Saucier, A. M., & Woodard, L. E. (2001). Interpersonal influences on students' academic and career decisions: The impact of sexual orientation. *Career Development Quarterly, 49,* 352–362.

O'Brien, K. M. (2001). The legacy of Parsons: Career counselors and vocational psychologists as agents of social change. *Career Development Quarterly, 50,* 66–76.

Okocha, A. A. (1998). Using qualitative appraisal strategies in career counseling. *Journal of Employment Counseling, 35*(3), 151–159.

Olson, C., McWhirter, E. H., & Horan, J. J. (1989). A decision making model applied to career counseling. *Journal of Career Development, 16*(2), 19–23.

O'Neil, M., McWhirter, E. H., & Cerezo, A. (in press). *Transgender identities and gender variance in vocational psychology: Recommendations for practice and social advocacy. Journal of Career Development.*

O'Ryan, L. (2003). Career counseling and social justice. *Counselors for Social Justice Newsletter, 4,* 1–3.

Osborn, D. S., & Zunker, V. G. (2005). *Using assessment results for career development* (7th ed.). Boston: Thompson-Wadsworth.

Osborne, W. L., Brown, S., Niles, S., & Miner, C. U. (1998). *Career development, assessment, & counseling: Applications of the Donald E. Super C-DAC approach.* Alexandria, VA: American Counseling Association.

Osipow, S. H., Leong, F. T., & Barak, A. (Eds.). (2001). *Contemporary models in vocational psychology: A volume in honor of Samuel H. Osipow.* Mahwah, NJ: Lawrence Erlbaum.

Pace, D., & Quinn, L. (2000). Empirical support of the overlap between career and mental health counseling of university students. *Journal of College Student Development, 14*(3), 41–50.

Parsons, F. (1909). *Choosing a vocation.* Boston: Houghton Mifflin.

Pearson, S. M., & Bieschke, K. J. (2001). Succeeding against the odds: An examination of familial influences on the career development of professional African American women. *Journal of Counseling Psychology, 48,* 301–309.

Pedersen, P. (2000). *Handbook for developing multicultural awareness.* Alexandria: ACA Press.

Peterson, G. W. (1998). Using a vocational card sort as an assessment of occupational knowledge. *Journal of Career Assessment, 6,* 49–67.

Peterson, G. W., Ryan-Jones, R. E., Sampson, J. P., & Reardon, R. C. (1994). A comparison of the effectiveness of three computer-assisted career guidance systems: Discover, SIGI, and SIGI PLUS. *Computers in Human Behavior, 10,* 189–198.

Phillips, J. C., Ingram, K. M., Smith, N. G., & Mindes, E. J. (2003). Methodological and content review of lesbian-, gay-, bisexual-related articles in counseling journals: 1990–1999. *The Counseling Psychologist, 31*(1), 25–62.

Pinkney, J. W., & Jacobs, D. (1985). New counselors and personal interest in the task of career counseling. *Journal of Counseling Psychology, 32,* 454–457.

Pope, M., Barret, B., Szymanski, D. M., Chung, B. Y., Singaravelu, H., McLean, R., et al. (2004). Culturally appropriate career counseling with gay and lesbian clients. *The Career Development Quarterly, 53,* 158–177.

Prince, J. P. (1997). Career assessment with lesbian, gay, and bisexual individuals. *Journal of Career Assessment, 5,* 225–238.

Prochaska, J. O., & DiClemente, C. C. (1984). *The transtheoretical approach: Crossing the traditional boundaries of therapy.* Homewood, IL: Dow-Jones-Irvin.

Prochaska, J. O., & DiClemente, C. C. (1992). The transtheoretical approach. In J. C. Norcross (Ed.), *Handbook of psychotherapy integration* (pp. 300–334). New York: Basic Books.

Prochaska, J. O., DiClemente, C. C., & Norcross, J. C. (1992). In search of how people change: Applications to addictive behaviors. *American Psychologist, 47,* 1102–1114.

Reardon, R. C., Lenz, J. G., Sampson, J. P., & Peterson, G. W. (2005). *Career development and planning: A comprehensive approach* (2nd ed.). Belmont, CA: Thompson Wadsworth.

Ritter, K. Y., & Terndrup, A. I. (2002). *Handbook of affirmative psychotherapy with lesbians and gay men.* New York: Guilford Press.

Rivera, A. A., Anderson, S. K., & Middleton, V. A. (1999). A career development model for Mexican-American women. *Journal of Career Development, 26,* 91–106.

Salomone, P. R. (1988). Career counseling: Steps and stages beyond Parsons. *The Career Development Quarterly, 36,* 218–221.

Schmidt, C. K., & Nilsson, J. E. (2006). The effects of simultaneous developmental processes: Factors relating to the career development of lesbian, gay, and bisexual youth. *The Career Development Quarterly, 55,* 22–37.

Seligman, L. (1994). *Developmental career counseling and assessment* (2nd ed.). Thousand Oaks, CA: Sage.

Sharf, R. S. (2006). *Applying career development theory to career counseling* (4th ed.). Pacific Grove, CA: Wadsworth.

Shin, S. L. A. (1999). Contextualizing career concerns of Asian American students. In Y. M. Jenkins (Ed.), *Diversity in college settings: Directives for helping professionals* (pp. 201–209). New York: Routledge.

Slaney, R. B. (1978). Expressed and inventoried vocational interests: A comparison of instruments. *Journal of Counseling Psychology, 25,* 520–529.

Soh, S., & Leong, F. T. (2001). Cross-cultural validation of Holland's theory in Singapore: Beyond structural validity of the RIASEC. *Journal of Career Assessment, 9,* 115–133.

Special issue on career assessment with women of color. (1998). *Journal of Career Assessment, 6*(4).

Special issue on gay and lesbian career development. (1995). Special issue of *The Career Development Quarterly, 44*(2).

Special issue on multiculturalism within career issues. (2005) *Journal of Multicultural Counseling and Development, 33*(3).

Special issue on Super's contribution to career development theory. (1994). Special issue of *The Career Development Quarterly, 43*(1).

Special issue on the vocational issues of lesbian women and gay men. (1996). Special issue of *The Journal of Vocational Behavior, 48*(2).

Special issue on theory into practice in career assessment for women. (1997) *Journal of Career Assessment, 5*(4).

Subich, L. M. (2005). Career assessment with culturally diverse individuals. In W. B. Walsh & M. L. Savickas (Eds.), *Handbook of vocational psychology: Theory, research, and practice* (pp. 397–421). New Jersey: Lawrence Erlbaum Associates.

Sue, D. W., Carter, R. T., Casas, J. M., Fouad, N. A., Ivey, A. E., Jensen, M., et al. (1998). *Multicultural counseling competencies: Individual and organizational development.* Thousand Oaks, CA: Sage.

Sue, D. W., & Constantine, M. G. (2005). Effective multicultural consultation and organizational development. In M. G. Constantine & D. W. Sue (Eds.), *Strategies for building multicultural competence in mental health and educational settings* (pp. 212–226). New Jersey: John Wiley & Sons.

Sue, D. W., & Sue, D. (2003). *Counseling the culturally diverse: Theory and process* (4th ed.). New York: John Wiley & Sons.

Super, D. E. (1957). *The psychology of careers.* New York: Harper & Brothers.

Super, D. E. (1963). Self-concepts in vocational development. In D. E. Super R. Starisheusky, N. Maitlin, & E. J. Jordan (Eds.), *Career development: Self-concept theory.* New York: CEEB Research Monograph No. 4.

Super, D. E. (1970). *Manual for the Work Value Inventory.* Boston: Houghton Mifflin, Boston.

Super, D. E. (1974). *Measuring vocational maturity for counseling and evaluation.* Washington, DC: National Vocational Guidance Association.

Super, D. E. (1990). A life span, life-space approach to career development. In D. Brown, L. Brooks, & Associates (Eds.), *Career choice and development: Applying contemporary theories to practice* (2nd ed., pp. 197–261). San Francisco: Jossey-Bass.

Super, D. E., & Neville, D. D. (1986). *The Salience Inventory.* Palo Alto, CA: Consulting Psychologists Press.

Swanson, J. L. (1996). The process and outcome of career counseling. In W. B. Walsh & S. H. Osipow (Eds.), *Handbook of vocational psychology* (2nd ed., pp. 217–259). Mahwah, NJ: Erlbaum.

Szymanski, E. M., & Hershenson, D. B. (2005). An ecological approach to vocational behavior and career development of people with disabilities. In R. M. Parker, E. M. Szymanski, & J. B. Patterson (Eds.), *Rehabilitation counseling: Basics and beyond* (4th ed., pp. 225–280). Austin, TX: PRO-ED.

Szymanski, E. M., & Parker, R. M. (Eds.). (2003). *Work and disability: Issues and strategies in career development and job placement* (2nd ed.). Austin, TX: Pro-Ed.

Teideman, D. V., & O'Hara, R. P. (1963). *Career development: Choice and adjustment.* Princeton, NJ: College Entrance Examination Board.

Thompson, M. N., & Subich, L. M. (2006). The relation of social status to the career decision-making process. *Journal of Vocational Behavior, 69,* 289–301.

U.S. Department of Labor (2006). *Occupational outlook handbook 2006–2007.* Washington, DC: Jist Works Publishing.

Walsh, W. B., Bingham, R. P., Brown, M. T., & Ward, C. M. (Eds.). (2001). *Career counseling for African Americans* (pp. 27–48). Mahwah, NJ: Erlbaum.

Walsh, W. B., & Heppner, M. J. (2006). Career counseling for women (2nd ed.). Mahwah, NJ: Lawrence Erlbaum Associates.

Walsh, W. B., & Savickas, M. L. (2005). *Handbook of vocational psychology: Theory, research, and practice* (3rd ed.). Mahwah, NJ: Lawrence Erlbaum Associates.

Ward, C. M., & Bingham, R. P. (2001). Career assessment for African Americans. In W. B. Walsh, R. P. Bingham, M. T. Brown, & C. M. Ward (Eds.), *Career counseling for African Americans* (pp. 27–48). Mahwah, NJ: Lawrence Erlbaum.

Wehman, P. (2001). *Pursuing postsecondary education opportunities for individuals with disabilities.* Baltimore, MD: Paul Brookes Publishing.

Whiston, S. C., & Bouwkamp, J. C. (2003). Ethical implications of career assessment with women. *Journal of Career Assessment, 11,* 59–75.

Worell, J., & Remer, P. (2003). Feminist perspectives in therapy: Empowering diverse women (2nd ed.). New York: John Wiley & Sons.

Worthington, R. L., Flores, L. Y., & Navarro, R. L. (2005). Career development in context: Research with people of color. In S. D. Brown & R. W. Lent (Eds.), *Career development and counseling: Putting theory and research to work* (pp. 225–252). Hoboken, NJ: John Wiley & Sons.

Zytowski, D. G. (1985). *Kuder DD Occupational Interest Survey manual supplement.* Chicago: Science Research Associates.

Zytowski, D. G. (1994). A super contribution to vocational theory: Work values. *Career Development Quarterly, 43,* 25–31.

11 Counseling and Spirituality

LAURA R. SIMPSON
Delta State University

A seeker after truth must shun no science, scorn no book, nor cling frantically to a single creed.

— Muslim Proverb

Helping professionals have come to value, even demand, sensitivity to cultural diversity. That is, we emphasize taking into consideration and respecting the specific customs of our clients in the design, planning, and implementation of counseling interventions. Yet practice remains harder than preaching. Beliefs, values, and ideals are all part of an individual's culture. For some, these principles are manifested through spiritual or religious practice. Yet, there is vast discord about the meaning of spirituality and ongoing arguments about whether it should be included in the process of counseling. This chapter focuses on the issue of counseling and spirituality. It explores the concept of spirituality in relation to religion, including similarities and differences. It examines some of the common themes that unite counseling and spirituality and considers how some counseling theorists have challenged that a relationship should exist at all. This includes support for the practice of incorporating the spiritual dimension into the counseling process. On the basis of existing research that concludes that spirituality and religion play an important role in culture, this chapter outlines what competencies are important for counselors when integrating spirituality into counseling sessions. It investigates what is important when assessing a client's spiritual domain, including the critical need to be culturally sensitive. Throughout this chapter, emphasis is placed on the need for counselor self-awareness, including being conscious of your own beliefs, values, and biases and the potential impact these issues may have on the counseling relationship.

Spirituality in the Context of Counseling

During the past decade, ongoing research suggests that the majority of Americans value spirituality and religion (Cashwell & Young, 2005; Ivey, Ivey, Myers, & Sweeney,

2005; Miller, 2003; Myers & Williard, 2003). Despite a plethora of evidence to suggest this is true all around the world, for the purposes of this chapter, we will focus on the United States. Surveys suggest that 84–96% of Americans believe in God, with 85–90% reporting the use of prayer as a coping response to life stressors (Cashwell & Young, 2005; Miller, 2003). Spirituality or religion as part of a way of life, together or separately, may provide individuals and families with an effective framework for coping with life's challenges. Counselors will often find that individuals consider these values to be an important part of counseling when the need for help arises.

Spiritual and religious issues are potentially significant topics in counseling, thus counselors must be equipped to determine which issues are therapeutically relevant and ethically appropriate. Additionally, counselors may need to be prepared to aid clients in applying spiritual or religious perspectives as a coping resource in their lives. This may include using every technique available that will support a client's progress, including interventions intended to promote healthy spiritual development. This does not suggest that all counselors should be "spiritual counselors" (i.e., pastoral counselors) but, instead, that counselors need the ability to accurately assess a client's existing spiritual and religious values and the potential impact on the client's success of including these issues within the counseling process (Cashwell & Young, 2005). Counselors are best served by being prepared to work with clients with particular religious or spiritual values, including the ability to affirm the significance of spirituality in the client's life and utilize verbal communication and descriptions in problem solving and treatment that are congruent with the client's worldview. This may include the need to consult with resources for education about a particular view but definitively includes the need for cultural sensitivity and ethical practices of the highest standards.

Religion and spirituality have been increasingly supported as relevant to both physical and mental wellness (Simpson, 2005). When spiritual and religious practices have been measured, they have consistently been positively associated with health and inversely related to physical disorders, mental disorders, and substance use disorders (Cooper, 2003).

Professional counseling organizations such as the American Counseling Association (ACA) have become progressively more focused on the significance of the spiritual domain in counseling. Specialized divisions related to spirituality such as ACA's Association for Spiritual, Ethical, and Religious Values in Counseling (ASERVIC) speak to the importance of the spiritual dimension in counseling and the commitment professional counseling organizations are making to promote competence in this arena. Additionally, the Council for Accreditation of Counseling and Related Educational Programs (CACREP) has included this subject as a requirement for inclusion within the curriculum of accredited programs. Counselors need to become proficient at working effectively with this realm of clients' lives, and professional organizations are promoting the aptitude to do so.

Spiritual and religious needs of clients are addressed within the code of ethics and standards of practice (2005) of the American Counseling Association. In an effort to regulate the profession of counseling and promote the growth and development of clients, Section A: The Counseling Relationship, addresses the need to respect diversity including the following subsection (ACA, 2005):

> a. *Nondiscrimination*. Counselors do not condone or engage in discrimination based on age, color, culture, disability, ethnic group, gender, race, *religion*, sexual orientation, marital status, or socioeconomic status.

The section goes on to include an additional subsection that supports the concept of counselor self-awareness in relation to spiritual and religious identity as follows (ACA, 2005):

> b. *Respecting differences*: Counselors will actively attempt to understand the diverse cultural backgrounds of the clients with whom they work. This includes, but is not limited to, learning *how the counselor's own cultural/ethnic/racial identify impacts her or his values* and beliefs about the counseling process.

The problem is, stating the need for spiritually competent counselors is one thing, and translating that into skills is another. There have been a number of efforts to identify the competencies counselors need to properly address the spiritual or religious concerns of the clients they serve. One of the initial efforts to promote the appropriate integration of spirituality into counseling was ASERVIC's 1995 Summit on Spirituality. A group of counseling professionals examined the role of spirituality in counseling, and a compilation of skills was developed as a foundation of desirable expertise that counselors ought to possess to successfully assist clients in the exploration of their spiritual lives as they relate to their mental health concerns. Miller (1999) also addressed the development of spiritual focus in counseling and counselor education and provided an expanded list of competencies.

The following list represents the merging of the proposed competencies by the Summit on Spirituality (1995) and Miller (1999). Counselors should possess the following skills to assist clients with spiritual or religious concerns:

1. The counselor can explain the relationship between spirituality and religion, including the similarities and differences.
2. The counselor can describe religious and spiritual beliefs and practices in a cultural context.
3. The counselor engages in self-exploration of religious and spiritual beliefs in order to increase sensitivity, understanding, and acceptance of various belief systems.
4. The counselor can articulate his or her personal spiritual and religious belief system and explain various models of religious or spiritual development across the lifespan.
5. The counselor demonstrates sensitivity and acceptance of a variety of religious and spiritual expressions in client communication.
6. The counselor can identify limits of his or her understanding of a client's religious and/or spiritual expressions and demonstrate the ability to make appropriate referrals, including generating referral resources if needed.

7. The counselor is receptive to spiritual or religious topics and can assess the relevance of the religious or spiritual themes in the counseling process as befits each client's expressed preference.

8. The counselor uses the client's religious or spiritual beliefs as part of the pursuit of the client's therapeutic goals as befits each client's expressed preference.

Spirituality and Religiosity

Many researchers consider the concepts of religiosity and spirituality to be closely associated. Distinguishing spirituality from religion is a slippery task. Counselors who have difficulty conceptualizing spirituality or religion may have trouble addressing related issues in a suitable and insightful way. Thus, beginning with a clear conceptualization is important. However, the nature of human spirituality is ineffable, which makes it difficult to study. Theologians and researchers alike agree on one thing: spirituality is not the same thing as religion. Religion and spirituality do share some qualities; however, the two are distinctly separate concepts.

Spirituality

Spirituality is a complex, multidimensional concept that is a challenge to define. To operationalize a topic that is both developmental and highly personal is difficult. It is further complicated by often being equated with religion. For some, spirituality includes religion, and for others it is highly unstructured. Spirituality is typically represented by a broad perspective that reflects the need for transcendence and connectedness; religion is a view that incorporates the tenets of specific faith traditions. It has been suggested that spirituality is "what individuals find sacred in their lives, what is most important to them at the essence of their being. It is a context for understanding things" (Ganje-Fling & McCarthy, 1996 p. 254). This suggests that spirituality is individualized by each person's meaning system and values, and a definition is "simply a starting point that cannot fully represent the entire concept" (Ceasar & Miranti, 2005, p. 242). Simultaneously, a definition must be useful to counselors if they are to understand how the issue relates to working with their clients.

As a concept, spirituality includes an ongoing search for meaning and purpose in life, an individualized belief system (Chandler, Holden, & Kolander, 1992), a profound sense of oneness, wholeness, connectedness, or belonging in the universe, and believing in a power outside one's self (Pargament, 1997; Ryan, 1998). Wiggins-Frame (2005) concludes that "spirituality includes one's beliefs, awareness, values, subjective experience, sense of purpose and mission, and an attempt to reach toward something greater than oneself. It may or may not include a deity" (p. 13). An individual's spirituality is considered personal and private and may not involve religious practice in any way. As for how that translates into working with a client, it means examining "willingness to seek meaning and purpose in human existence, to question everything, and to appreciate the intangibles which cannot be explained or understood readily" (Chandler et al., 1992, p. 168). Spirituality allows individuals to define and understand occurrences in their lives and provides them with a sense of meaning and purpose in their existence. "As a concept, spirituality usually refers to a unique, personally meaningful experience of a transcendent dimension that is associated with wholeness and wellness" (Gladding, 2005, p. 109).

So, I offer you this: Meditation is a form of spirituality, lighting candles for the Sabbath is spirituality, giving to the homeless could be a form of spirituality, and going to church or the mosque is spiritual. Private or public prayer is spirituality. The creation of Kwanzaa was a spiritual act. Spirituality means beyond the self: it is mindfulness, connectedness, and community.

Religiosity

Religion is easier to define. It is often represented by one's chosen denomination and is public in nature. It is typically characterized by "an organized system of worship, cumulative traditions and prescribed rituals" (Ceasar & Miranti, 2005, p. 242). Frequently, religion is considered a segment of spirituality and often includes a faith system and commitment to one of the major religions of the world, including the rituals, creeds, and traditions connected to that religion. Religious groups all have systems of meaning that give individuals a sense of coherence and connection with others. The doctrine often makes meaning of difficult situations and provides support.

Although not synonymous, both religion and spirituality include a sense of transcendence. This belief in something greater than us may be part of religion's social process or spirituality's more personal, internal process. Thus, religion may be a part of spirituality, and for many it is an expression of their spirituality. For some, participation in organized religion provides a community context for their spiritual lives. For others, participation in organized religion seems to surface from a sense of duty or habit. These individuals may indeed be religious, but not spiritual at all. On the contrary, many individuals consider themselves spiritual as opposed to religious and find that the organizations of religion infringe into their ideas of spirituality. Thus, spirituality and religion may be similar in many ways yet demonstrated very individualistically. For example, a person may actively examine the meaning of life, have willful direction and purpose in his or her choices, and may even engage in spiritual practices such as meditation, yet choose not to be connected to any religious organization at all. Conversely, another person may be an active member of a church, attend services regularly, and sing in the choir but never really associate personal meaning to these practices. This individual may be participating in the activity of being religious without being spiritual. A third option could be participating as an active member of a congregation, attending worship routinely, reading religious doctrine, praying regularly, and finding great meaning and purpose in these activities, including a sense of support during times of stress. This individual could be described as simultaneously spiritual and religious.

Regardless of an individual's position with regard to spiritual or religious practice, our quality of life is deeply affected by the degree of purpose and engagement we feel at any given time (Cherniss, 1995). Research suggests that individuals who have a sense of meaning and well-being in their lives cope with stress in healthier ways (Pargament, 1997). "Thus, there is value in conscious, periodic consideration of what we find significant, what has priority, and what most deserves care and protection in our lives" (Baker, 2003, p. 64). Ryan (1998) theorized that individuals who lack spiritual beliefs are at risk of experiencing unbearable pain and feelings of rejection as they search for meaning in the world. Thus, spirituality is potentially a source of hope, meaning, and purpose, particularly during difficult times. As suggested by Bullock (2002), "a person's spiritual needs are inextricably related to their growth, development, and healing" (p. 4).

Case Illustration: Marsha

Marsha, a 76-year-old woman, is referred to counseling after receiving a diagnosis of terminal cancer. Marsha has been through an exhaustive round of chemotherapy and radiation, only to find out that her cancer continues to grow. Marsha knows she is dying and finds herself struggling with facing her own mortality. In particular, Marsha's grief includes anger with God over being terminally ill, which leads to a sense of overwhelming guilt. Marsha is consumed by intrusive thoughts about issues she feels are unresolved in her life, as well as fear about the actual experience of death and her views of the afterlife. For many years, Marsha has been an active member of a conservative Christian church whose doctrine includes the belief that only individuals who have been "saved" will go to heaven.

Marsha's distress includes both grief issues and theological issues. Her grief is acute and complicated by the guilt she feels over being angry with God about her illness. This leads to Marsha questioning whether she is assured a place in heaven following her death. Although spirituality is an issue here, it is also expressed as a religious issue, as her beliefs have become intertwined with her emotions. Additionally, Marsha has angst related to issues she defines as unresolved and because of her illness feels a sense of urgency to address these issues.

Marsha's counselor is in a position to support her through active listening and empathy. Her counselor can acknowledge Marsha's sadness and fear about her impending death. The counselor could engage Marsha in a dialogue about her views on God, faith, and the afterlife. By doing so, Marsha has an opportunity to explore her beliefs. Allowing her the opportunity to examine her viewpoint and express her frustration and conflicting emotions in a safe environment could result in a sense of acceptance that reduces Marsha's pain.

It is important for the counselor to be clear about the difference between spirituality and religion. Marsha has clearly stated a religious belief about the afterlife and attached a spiritual meaning to it. The counselor must be careful not to impose alternative values on the client through introducing ideas about alternative views of afterlife or trying to get Marsha to change her views. Of greater importance is helping Marsha explore more fully the meaning and implications of her religious beliefs. It is essential for the counselor to recognize that Marsha is engrossed in a religious system that is shaping her worldview and causing her anguish. It is critical for the counselor to create a safe, nonjudgmental environment in which Marsha can explore beliefs that are troubling her as she faces her own mortality.

Questions for Counselor Self-Exploration

1. What emotional reactions do you have to the client's story?
2. What reactions do you have to her church doctrine as she describes it?
3. What would be your therapeutic approach with her issues in counseling?
4. Would you require supervision or consultation with a colleague to proceed in counseling? If so, what specific areas would you need to address?

The Relationship Between Counseling Theory and Religion/Spirituality

Historically, science and religion have often been deemed incompatible because science is based on fact and religion on faith. As a consequence, clinicians and counselor education programs have been reluctant to include attention to religious and spiritual domains in counseling practice. One of the largest obstacles has been pervasive confusion between the concepts of spirituality and religion, which is further complicated by existing religiosity associated with mental illness. However, psychology and religion have been traditionally associated because psychology has emerged as the study of the human mind, soul, or spirit (Wiggins-Frame, 2005). Thus, counselors are left to navigate the murky overlap between science and theology.

Some of the earliest counseling theory equated religiosity and mental illness, resulting in a negative outlook on clients' inclusion of religious concerns in counseling. Many psychologists and mental health practitioners have been critical of religion or dismissed it as an example of pathology. For example, Sigmund Freud was a well-known opponent of religion. Psychoanalytic theory declared that religion is an illusion that is the result of yearning and desire and necessary to the functioning of an immature person (Miller, 2003). Another critic of religion was Albert Ellis, the founder of rational-emotive behavior therapy (REBT). Ellis posited that atheism was the only avenue to optimal human functioning and that religiosity represents irrational thinking and emotional disturbance (Ellis, 1980). This position led to the trend of cognitive-behavioral counselors treating all spiritual and religious beliefs as illogical distortions that clients should dispose of. Behavioral counselors, led by B. F. Skinner, claimed that religious behavior is the result of stimulus-response reactions of the client as participation in certain behavior or adherence to particular beliefs is rewarded (Skinner, 1953).

The link between religiosity and mental illness has also promoted the separation of spiritual and religious values from counseling. This idea is partially based on the idea that many mental health disorders were once believed to be a result of extreme religiosity (Bergin, 1991). Individuals experiencing depression and anxiety were accused of experiencing shame and guilt as a result of behaving sinfully.

The movement to incorporate the spiritual dimension into counseling was introduced into Western psychology by Carl Jung and existential theory (Chandler,

Holden, & Kolander, 2001). Jung viewed the traditions of religions as facilitating the development of the self and suggested that counselors incorporate spiritual issues and experiences into counseling sessions in a form and rate proportionate to the client's level of personal development. Thus, counselors enter the subjective reality of their clients and work within their perspectives.

Additional support for the inclusion of spiritual and religious topics into counseling was provided by the humanistic school of psychology, which viewed individuals as having positive potential and behavior made more complex with the incorporation of spiritual needs and values. Fromm (1950) in particular supported the notion that religion can be helpful to people as a coping mechanism in response to life stressors. Frank Parsons (1909) and vocational counseling looked at the individual within the entirety of his or her life development and viewed religion and spirituality as assisting in positive development. Cognitive psychology promoted the concept of self-control, creating yet another link for the inner world of clients and the potential inclusion of spirituality as part of that world.

Consider that we turn to spirituality and religion when we are in pain. Counseling seeks what spirituality seeks: a restoration to our brokenness, some comforting reprieve for our fear or indecision. To investigate the spiritual or religious principles that our clients utilize in efforts to be healthy seems both logical and practical.

Further reinforcing the inclusion of spiritual and religious issues into the practice of counseling is research suggesting that the counseling profession views spirituality as an important factor in wellness. Graham, Furr, Flowers, and Burke (2001) reported on a survey conducted by the American Counseling Association that indicates counseling professionals view spirituality as an important component of mental health. These authors conducted additional research that examined the relationship between religion and spirituality in coping with stress and found a positive correlation between spiritual health and immunity to stressful situations (Graham et al., 2001). Spirituality is often cited in the literature as a resource of strength, comfort, and coping in clients' lives (Bullock, 2002).

A growing body of research has established a relationship between diverse spiritual principles and multiple aspects of health. Collective interpretations of studies have concluded that there is a protective feature of spirituality to health (Meisenhelder & Chandler, 2002). Spiritual commitment appears to play a role in preventing physical and mental illness, in facilitating coping with illness, and in facilitating recovery (Matthews, McCullough, Larson, Koenig, & Swyers, 1998). Spirituality exerts a primary prevention effect against morbidity in multiple populations, and there is a positive association with psychological well-being (Ellison & Levin, 1998; Koenig, 1999; Levin, Larson, & Puchalski, 1997; Levin & Vanderpool, 1987). Multiple studies have shown the positive effect of spirituality on various aspects of health such as cardiac surgery (Ai, Dunkle, Peterson, & Bolling, 1998; Harris et al., 1995), mortality (Clark, Friedman, & Martin, 1999; Oman & Reed, 1998), and immune function (Woods, Antoni, Ironson, & Kling, 1999).

Studies have shown similar results in relation to mental health. Higher self-esteem (Krause, 1995), less depression (Fehring, Miller, & Shaw, 1997; Koenig, 1998), and lower alcohol use (Musick, Lazer, & Hays, 2000) have been associated with spirituality.

The addictions counseling field has frequently used a 12-step program that incorporates spirituality since the 1935 inception of Alcoholics Anonymous (AA), a self-help recovery group. A mounting number of studies have reported that those who are more spiritual experience greater well-being and life satisfaction (Ellison, 1991), cope better with stress (Pargament, 1997), and are less likely to commit suicide (Cooperman & Simoni, 2005).

Case Illustration: Paul

Paul is a 55-year-old man who seeks counseling at the suggestion of his brother. For approximately 1 year, Paul has become increasingly withdrawn. He has eliminated most contact with family members and has ceased all social interactions. After losing his job because of downsizing, Paul virtually eliminated all daily activities. For example, Paul stopped coaching his son's baseball team and stopped volunteering for the animal shelter. In spite of being an active member of the choir, Paul is no longer attending the church where he has been a member for many years. Paul reports feeling worthless and like a failure. He feels he has let his family down.

Paul's presenting problems include symptoms of depression such as loss of appetite, sleep disturbance, and loss of interest in activities. When Paul discloses his discontinuation of church activity, his counselor inquires about his spiritual beliefs, and Paul expresses a belief in God. He shares that he feels abandoned by God in his time of need. Paul believes that he has always tried to do the right thing, and now he is being unjustly punished. Paul describes having lost the sense of meaning and purpose in his life.

Paul's counselor is in a position to encourage him through active listening and empathy. His counselor can acknowledge Paul's anger and frustration over the loss of his job. The counselor could engage Paul in a discussion about his altered relationship with God following his loss of employment. By doing so, Paul has an opportunity to explore his beliefs, including his stand that God has abandoned him.

It is important for the counselor to examine the timing between the onset of Paul's depressive symptoms and the emergence of spiritual and religious conflict related to the loss of his job. Paul has clearly identified the existence of a relationship with God and indicated that it has changed radically during the past year. The counselor must be mindful of Paul's problems in the spiritual domain. This does not suggest that the counselor must not thoroughly address the symptoms of depression, including referring Paul for a medication evaluation if necessary. From a holistic perspective, however, it is of great importance to assist Paul in exploring more fully the meaning and implications of his religious beliefs. The counselor must recognize that Paul's depression is linked to the lack of meaning in his life. The counselor has to create a safe, nonjudgmental environment in which Paul can explore his views and not feel like a failure.

Questions for Counselor Self-Exploration

1. What is your first comment in response to his story?
2. What concerns would you have in approaching this topic with this client?

3. What would be your goal with regard to exploring the client's spiritual and religious domains?
4. Would you require supervision or consultation with a colleague to proceed in counseling? If so, what specific areas would you need to address?

Assessment of Spiritual Dimensions

Spirituality is a way of life. It is not something we simply think about or feel. We live it through our beliefs and behaviors. It affects the way we perceive our world, the way we think about humanity, and the choices we make based on our perceptions and sensations. Counselors need to be prepared to assess the client's religious and spiritual views because of the potential impact on the presenting problem or because the presenting problem is spiritual or religious in nature.

The counselor's efforts to define the problem typically include consideration of all components of the problem, including contributing factors, length and duration of symptoms, and the client's coping resources. In relating counseling issues to spiritual dimensions, the counselor will identify how elements of the spiritual domain, such as the client's conscience, beliefs, values, spiritual principles, meaning, responsibility, and practices, contribute to the way the client is experiencing the problem and to ways the client could cope with the issue (Harper & Gill, 2005). Once the counselor establishes a link between the presenting problem and the client's spiritual dimension, the elements associated with the spiritual domain become counseling issues.

Assessing a client's religious or spiritual views necessitates addressing a number of issues. Family history of spiritual or religious values is critical in this assessment process. Specifically, emphasis on certain spiritual or religious views during the client's childhood may have a current impact on the problems being addressed in counseling. For example, if there was an expectation to choose a partner of the same religion, a client may have difficulties with having chosen a partner from a different religion. Additionally, issues related to sexual orientation or behavior may have roots in spiritual or religious perspectives from a client's upbringing. Clients may have received deep-seated messages about the inherent acceptability or morality associated with particular behaviors or choices. Religious or spiritual conflicts may also arise associated with issues such as death, divorce, life-threatening illness, or suicide. Making spiritual and religious views a typical part of the intake process is one way to assist clients in identifying issues that need to be addressed.

Models

Models can be valuable because they offer structure for conceptualizing how clients may be experiencing their spiritual or religious concerns. They can also aid in determining where clients are in their spiritual growth (Frame, 2003). The following descriptions, adapted from the work of Ceasar and Miranti (2005), examine three models and suggest how counselors might approach spirituality within a counseling setting.

The Developmental Model.   The developmental model approaches spirituality as an internal outlook that underscores vigor, creative choice, and a potent energy for living. This model endorses a partnership with a higher power (Ingersoll, 1994). It suggests that individuals grow and change over the course of life and equates spiritual growth with psychological growth (Genia, 1995; Hinterkopf, 1994). Throughout stages of immense change or transition, individuals may experience uncertainty, insecurity, or suffering. During these times of struggle, the incorporation of spiritual concepts may emerge as individuals search to clarify their position and next move in life. As the client experiences changes, the spiritual challenge may be present to move to a higher level of faith. Thus, spirituality is a dimension in an individual's life that develops, matures, and evolves through life's triumphs and hurts, challenges and growth.

The Systemic Model.   The systemic model suggests that spiritual awareness emerges through the experience of connectedness to others (Steere, 1997). Individuals develop spiritual presence as a product of ongoing relationships with others that help to construct new ways of thinking and interacting. As a result, individuals are capable of healing, overcoming impasses, and enhancing their meaning and purpose in relation to the larger environment of other systems. This level of understanding is part of a greater and higher order of intelligence. The translation of this model into counseling is to assist clients in achieving a deeper awareness and understanding of their place in the world and the role they play within their universe.

The Wellness Model.   Built on developmental constructs, the wellness model merges theological and psychological concepts into a holistic perspective (Witmer, Sweeney, & Myers, 1993). This perspective has a collective and synergistic belief that maintains the sum of the parts is greater than the whole. This model includes a broader perspective because it integrates research in sociology, psychology, anthropology, religion, education, and behavioral medicine. It defines the mind-body-spirit connection as a window through which to view a complete picture of an individual, including what has meaning and impact in each individual's life. The wellness model views individuals as evolving and growing throughout the lifespan. Spirituality is conceptualized as one of the core characteristics of healthy persons. Counseling from this perspective assists individuals in examining how spiritual and religious domains in their lives help them cope with issues from the past, present, and future. It emphasizes what works for an individual that can be encouraged or further developed in counseling. Counselors strive to understand the connectedness and interrelationship of all internal and external elements.

Instruments

A variety of assessment instruments related to spiritual and religious domains are available. The tests vary by content and may be designed to measure beliefs, values, or behaviors. It is important to examine each instrument with regard to validity and reliability, as well as factors such as cost, level of client functioning, and intended purpose within the counseling process. The following list represents a sample of instruments available for use or purchase.

- The Human Spirituality Scale (Wheat, 1991)
- The Spirituality Assessment Scale (Howden, 1992)
- Spirituality Scale (Jagers & Smith, 1996)
- The Spiritual Health Inventory (Veach & Chappell, 1992)
- The Spiritual Involvement and Beliefs Scale (Hatch, Burg, Naberhaus, & Hellmich, 1998)
- The Spiritual Well-Being Scale (Ellison, 1983)
- The Wellness Evaluation of Lifestyle (Witmer et al., 1993)

Questions for Counselor Consideration

Now that I have explored why it is important to assess a client's spiritual domain and some ways to go about doing that, I challenge you to pause for a moment and think about how this information can serve you as the counselor. Here are some questions for consideration:

1. If clients define themselves as spiritual, religious, or both, how is this information helpful to you?
2. In what ways do spiritual or religious issues relate to diagnosis or intervention selection?
3. What role do spiritual and religious beliefs or practice have in validating a client's culture?
4. Does inclusion of a spiritual or religious assessment in the counseling process have the potential to harm the client?
5. Will exploration of spiritual/religious values assist in understanding what messages your client has internalized and what drives his or her belief system?
6. How do past or present spiritual values and practices contribute to presenting problems or block healing and growth?
7. How has adversity or trauma wounded your client's spirit?
8. How might spiritual emptiness or disconnectedness from religious roots intensify distress or isolation?

Cultural Considerations

Spirituality and religion are at the center of culture. Although your clients may not express interest in addressing these topics, their worldview probably reflects spiritual roots in some way. One ultimate goal of the counselor is to affirm and appreciate the differences among people. Spirituality and religious beliefs provide personal avenues for people to construct meaning and purpose in life. These personal avenues are greatly influenced by social and cultural traditions, family values and customs, and individual experiences. Understanding the strengths of a client's spiritual or religious culture can be instrumental in promoting healthy development. Understanding any history of oppression within your client's spiritual or religious culture may help you in defining issues that challenge your client. Addressing such dimensions requires an examination of spiritual or religious values as part of a client's culture. Thus, counselors need to learn to communicate effectively with clients about their full range of values in order to promote insight into the connection among these values, how they view their problems, and determining possible counseling interventions.

"Often counselors will omit certain information or avoid asking particular questions out of fear of being perceived as ignorant, racist, insensitive, or discriminatory" (Robinson, 2005, p. 18). This apprehension can hinder the counseling session and interfere with the client's growth and support in dealing with problems. It is unrealistic to believe it is possible to help clients explore complex issues regarding race, sexual orientation, gender, religion, and culture if counselors are reluctant to talk about such topics. Individuals have multiple identities, including spiritual and religious perceptions of self and others. "Counseling a broad clientele demands an understanding of how these identities, for both the client and counselor, interact and influence self-concept development and life choices" (Schmidt, 2006, p. 160).

Case Illustration: Daniel

Daniel is a 32-year-old Asian man. He resides with his wife of 6 years and their two small children. Daniel has lived in the United States since he was in elementary school. He identifies himself as Christian and is actively involved in the church he attends with his family within their community.

Daniel is taking a class at a local university. His time away from home has increased, and he says he is studying with a classmate. Daniel's relationship with his wife has become strained, and his wife suggests they meet together with their minister to address the issue. Daniel refuses and ultimately admits he has been engaging in a sexual relationship with a male classmate. He reports that he has prayed these feelings will go away, but they have not. Daniel would prefer to talk to a man, and although he is close to his family, he does not feel the freedom to discuss this topic. Daniel decides to seek counseling with a clinician at the university counseling center.

Daniel's dilemma is complex, and he is in need of a safe place to sort out his feelings. As a father, husband, Christian, and Asian man, some of his identities conflict. For example, his church doctrine rejects homosexuality. He believes good fathers are not homosexual. Daniel also feels there are clear expectations of him as an Asian man. Kinship ties are very strong, and Asian families are traditionally hardworking and loyal and demonstrate respect for parents and other elders (Robinson, 2005). Daniel and his family maintain traditional attitudes toward a number of issues, including that disclosure of private, personal information is reflective of lack of discipline. Daniel also feels ashamed for placing emphasis on his own individual interests as opposed to making decisions based on the good of his entire family.

Daniel's counselor must find balance between assisting with the struggle with sexuality issues and respecting his spiritual and religious views as a crucial part of his life. His religion also contributes to his guilt. The counselor would be wise to assist Daniel with sorting through the collision of his sexuality, his Asian identity, and his religion.

Questions for Counselor Self-Exploration:

1. What do you view as the dominant conflicts between Daniel's ethnicity, marital status, gender, and religion?
2. How could a counselor's personal bias affect the counseling relationship?
3. Where would you begin your work with Daniel if you were his counselor?
4. What changes would need to take place for you to view counseling as a success?

Counselor Self-Awareness

Before counselors inquire about their clients' spiritual lives, it is good practice to be aware of their own spiritual and religious beliefs, values, and spiritual journey. Counselors are not exempt from having their own biases and views when it comes to religion or spirituality. As addressed earlier, many counseling theorists take a negative view of spirituality and religion. As a result of education, training, or supervision, counselors may view religious behavior with a theoretical bias. Personal life experience may also play a role in a counselor's ability to receive and process a client's issues with neutrality. These personal or professional experiences can have an impact on the counselor and result in biases toward religion or spirituality, either positively or negatively. Counselors may not pick up on their clients' concerns because of their own bias or may pick up on these themes too readily to the exclusion of other issues. Counselors and clients benefit from the helpers' self-awareness of their perspective on spirituality and the inherent biases of that perspective. Without sensitivity toward personal bias, counselors may inadvertently neglect the welfare of the client and potentially cause harm. Having an awareness of bias may assist a counselor in addressing issues within spiritual domains while maintaining an emphasis on respect and care for the client's well-being. Ultimately, counselors can facilitate a helping relationship that includes spiritual issues simply by being aware of their own perspective. Therefore, counselors must be aware of their own personal perspectives within spiritual and religious domains.

I challenge you to pause and consider what spiritual self-awareness actually includes. I offer that it begins with an examination of your personal value system. "Understanding one's own value system also increases sensitivity to the value system of others. Without self-awareness, ignoring others' value systems is unfortunately a potential consequence" (Hagedorn, 2005, p. 70). This is of utmost importance because the counselor's personal values become a part of the counseling process and there is a risk that a helper will impose her or his values onto clients. Being aware of one's own values helps counselors avoid making value judgments or invalidating client's feelings. Values also assist counselors in conceptualizing client issues and in choosing theoretical orientations. Without self-awareness, counselors may inadvertently affect the conditions necessary for the counseling alliance or invalidate the client's experiences, resulting in harm to the client or the counseling relationship.

Potential Barriers to the Incorporation of Spirituality Into Counseling

Lack of Training

Unfortunately, there are many potential barriers for counselors in training and for practicing helping professionals who are considering incorporating religious or spiritual issues into the counseling experience. Lack of training may cause counselors to avoid addressing particular concerns or even result in the counselor becoming fixated with this area. Sometimes having a client simply mention religious or spiritual practice may result in strong reactions from the counselor. Although counselor education programs may emphasize the importance of self-awareness as a component of professional development, there may be little or no emphasis placed on religious or spiritual awareness. Counseling professionals may find themselves practicing in an environment that offers limited opportunities to consult with colleagues or receive supervision on religious or spiritual issues. Therefore, without taking a very proactive position of seeking opportunity for religious or spiritual exploration, counselors may find themselves unprepared to integrate religious or spiritual domains into the counseling process.

Countertransference

Another potential barrier to effective practice is countertransference. Two types related to spirituality and religion are interreligious and intrareligious countertransference (Abernathy & Lancia, 1998). When counselors deduce that they have different religious backgrounds from their clients, it can result in *interreligious countertransference*. This may result in counselors distancing themselves from these clients because of their self-doubt about being capable of understanding the client's perspective. This problem can be intensified if the client questions the counselor's spiritual orientation. Conversely, *intrareligious countertransference* may occur when counselors observe that their religious or spiritual histories are similar to those of their clients. This can result in a counselor placing too much emphasis on religious or spiritual views.

Other countertransference issues include the potential for making personal projections on client issues, particularly those relating to themes of mortality, afterlife, or meaningfulness. Counselors must attempt to maintain balance and neither avoid discussion about particular topics nor turn too readily to the spiritual realm for an answer. For example, assisting a client with a concern relating to grief may cause a counselor to reflect on issues in his or her own life. If a counselor has an unresolved grief issue or has experienced a meaningful life circumstance related to the topic, it may cause the counselor to react within a particular context.

The value of understanding one's ideals, biases, and competencies cannot be overstated. With this knowledge, counselors increase their effectiveness in assessing and treating particular issues and recognize the need to refer when necessary. Hagedorn (2005) summed it up nicely, stating:

> When working with spiritual values, counselors need more than an education in skills and techniques, more than devouring religious/spiritual literature, and more than supervision/consultation with religious and spiritual leaders to assist in the exploration of that which is crucial and yet intangible. Those counselors who have made significant movement towards awareness of their own values, who are in touch with deeper spheres of being, and who are familiar with the spiritual world are those who can successfully facilitate this discovery process with clients. (p. 71)

Questions for Counselor Reflection

Authors have suggested a number of questions for self-reflection when making a personal exploration of spirituality and religion (Fukuyama & Sevig, 1997; Hagedorn, 2005; Miller, 2003). These questions could be used in a classroom setting, as part of supervision, or through a process of personal journaling. There is no need to answer them all at once. Take as much time as needed to thoroughly examine each one.

1. What is my personal definition of spirituality? Of religion?
2. Do I identify myself as spiritual, religious, or both? Do I see a distinction between religion and spirituality? Why or why not?
3. What are some of my earliest childhood memories of religion, of God, of the sacred or holy?
4. What are the spiritual/religious values of my parents? Did this influence my current beliefs and values?
5. What were the major spiritual/religious influences outside my immediate family, including the beliefs common to my peers?
6. What are my earliest recollections of spiritual/religious practice?
7. How have my religious/spiritual beliefs changed through my personal growth process? How has the practice of these beliefs changed?
8. What influenced me to accept or reject the religious/spiritual values of my family or peer group?
9. Have any significant turning points, crises, or transitions affected the development of my religious/spiritual beliefs and values?
10. What are my current challenges/concerns in relation to my spiritual/religious beliefs and values?
11. Has spirituality or religion ever frightened or confused me? Has spirituality or religion ever made me feel joyful or energized?
12. Recall a situation, event, or moment that felt spiritual and describe it.

Use of Spiritual or Religious Interventions in Counseling

Assuming a counselor chooses to address spiritual or religious issues within the counseling process, it then becomes necessary to consider the development of skills and resources for working within this domain. Prior to utilizing specific techniques, a counselor must consider whether the client is ready for the technique and verify that the client is comfortable with the approach. Once a counselor determines that the technique is appropriate, it is then ethically pertinent that the counselor has the ability to use the technique accurately and appropriately.

Using ethical guidelines of practice and focusing on the client's goals may provide a rough map toward choosing the technique, yet it falls on the counselor to develop the competence to utilize a technique. In terms of developing skills and training, this presents a bit of a conundrum. How do you learn to use the techniques, and when is training adequate? Is it enough for student counselors to take a course as part of a program of study or to attend a seminar? Should practicing counselors consult with colleagues or seek supervision with clinicians who are experienced in this arena? Each counseling professional must individualize his or her approach to learning techniques for working with spiritual or religious issues, but a combination of education, consultation, and supervision is a reasonable consideration.

The following examples are techniques regularly utilized in countless forms of counseling. A description of how these commonly used interventions could be implemented to address spirituality and/or religion in the counseling process is provided. As part of your own efforts to develop self-awareness, you might consider completing each of the exercises prior to using them with a client. Also keep in mind that each intervention could require adaptation to meet the specific cultural position of the client. Choosing an intervention that does not fit the client could result in an upset client, unrealistic goals, or a breakdown of the counseling alliance. Thus, competent counselors will work in collaboration with their client to find an intervention that is the best fit.

Techniques

Bibliotherapy. The use of books or other reading material as part of the counseling process is certainly not a new concept. Typically, counselors "assign" reading to a client and facilitate discussion regarding how the content applies to the individual. This dialogue may include how the client reacts to the material, insight the client gained through the exposure to the reading, or the reading as a foundation for goal setting. When a client identifies with the material, it can promote a sense of feeling validated or hopeful about a situation or even inspire a client to address a situation. Used as a means for self-exploration, bibliotherapy is a technique counselors can use to help clients explore their spiritual or religious life. Simply remember that readings of a spiritual or religious nature must be carefully chosen to complement the client's values and beliefs.

Exploration/Focusing. Exploration of an issue as part of the counseling experience is also useful. Encouraging exchange related to a client's spiritual and religious beliefs will assist the counselor in understanding what the client values, how important those values are, and to what degree they are associated with the client's presenting problem. This exploration may merge spiritual or religious beliefs into the counseling process as it helps the counselor understand the nature and depth of the client's values, provides the client with an occasion to discover and divulge those values, and enables the counselor to make accurate choices about which additional techniques to employ.

Focusing allows clients to learn to listen to themselves without judgment and facilitates openness and curiosity toward the unknown. This approach promotes new growth and assists clients in identifying and labeling their thoughts and feelings.

Journaling. Sometimes an individual needs a platform for expressing thoughts freely without fear of the judgment of self or others. Journaling offers just such an opportunity. There is no "right" way to journal, and the greater emphasis is on expression without regard for grammar or logic. A counselor might choose to request journaling on a particular topic or encourage the client to be spontaneous and record whatever comes to mind. The self-exploration aspect of journal writing can assist the client in exploring his or her spiritual world.

Meditation/Relaxation. There are a variety of meditation practices, and many are a common component of religions all around the world (Kelly, 1995). Some meditation practices promote freedom of ideas or cessation of concentrated thought, resulting in a state of mind that is free from awareness or conscious thought. Other practices are more cognitive, focusing on a particular issue and resulting in clarity or insight about the matter. Counselors can make choices based on what fits best with the client and employ techniques with the potential to change "perspective, reduce stress or anxiety, or provide new avenues for exploration of issues" (Basham & O'Connor, 2005, p. 154).

Relaxation techniques are also commonly the foundation to working with many mental health complaints, such as anxiety or panic attacks. Existential psychologists such as Rollo May have used the term *existential anxiety* to refer to angst that occurs when individuals have been unable to reach their full potential in life (Bourne, 1995). Living with a sense of incompleteness, lack of purpose, or meaningless can provide fertile ground for the development of panic attacks. Learning to achieve a deep state of relaxation may help clients learn to be introspective and develop insight into their full potential and life purpose.

Summary

Counseling that incorporates the spiritual dimension can help clients have a sense of hope, view their issues from a different perspective, become more focused on what is important to them, discover who they are, and have an opportunity to feel less alone in the world. Throughout this chapter, the concepts of spirituality and religion were examined, including similarities and differences. Reasons to incorporate spiritual and religious domains into the counseling process were explored through investigation of the theological and psychological foundations that support the inclusion of these dimensions into counseling. A list of suggested competencies for counselors working with spiritual and religious domains was provided. Case examples illustrated common patterns and themes that demonstrate the overlap between spiritual pain and emotional pain. Further, the need to assess not only the spiritual thoughts, feelings, and beliefs of our clients but also our own was emphasized. Personal reflection was encouraged through questions for consideration. A variety of models and assessment instruments were offered to assist in conceptualizing client issues that include a spiritual or religious dimension. Finally, a number of techniques for use with clients were presented in an effort to introduce you to how to actually work on spiritual or religious concepts with clients. How clients process these factors and incorporate these beliefs into their daily lives may play a significant role in the counseling relationship. Of equal importance is the extent to which counselors understand their own spiritual existence and religious principles and the influence these values have on relationships with other people. I invite you to consider the meaning of spirituality for yourself and its value for the people you serve, teach, and learn from.

USEFUL WEB SITES

The official Web site of the American Counseling Association. This site includes the complete counseling code of ethics and a link to the religion interest division. There is also a link to ASERVIC competencies related to counseling and spirituality.
http://www.counseling.org

The Web site for the Association for Spiritual, Ethical, and Religious Values in Counseling, a division of the American Counseling Association.
http://www.aservic.org

This Web site promotes religious freedom and diversity as positive personal values.
http://www.religioustolerance.org

This Web site is a nonprofit organization that describes itself as deeply committed to ongoing spiritual formation for people of all ages and all backgrounds, living in countries around the world.
http://www.explorefaith.org

Spirituality and Health reports on the people, practices, and ideas of the current spiritual resurgence and offers self-tests; guidance on spiritual practices; reviews of the latest resources for people on spiritual journeys; inspiration and insights from leading teachers, researchers, and practitioners; and a forum for the active exchange of ideas among various disciplines and communities. This Web site reports being open to all points of view on spiritual questions, drawing on the world's wisdom traditions as well as science, psychology, sociology, and medicine.
http://www.spiritualityhealth.com

REFERENCES

Abernathy, A. D., & Lancia, J. J. (1998). Religion and the psychotherapeutic relationship. *Journal of Psychotherapy Practice and Research, 7,* 281–289.

Ai, A. L., Dunkle, R. E. Peterson, C., & Bolling, S. F. (1998). The role of private prayer in psychological recovery among midlife and aged patients following cardiac surgery. *Gerontologist, 23*(5), 591–601.

American Counseling Association. (2005). *ACA code of ethics.* Alexandria, VA: Author.

Baker, E. K. (2003). *Caring for ourselves: A therapist's guide to personal and professional well-being.* Washington, DC: American Psychological Association.

Basham, A., & O'Connor, M. (2005). Use of spiritual and religious beliefs in pursuit of clients' goals. In C. Cashwell and S. Young (Eds.), *Integrating spirituality and religion into counseling: A guide for competent practice.* Alexandria, VA: American Counseling Association.

Bergin, A. E. (1991). Values and religious issues in psychotherapy and mental heath. *American Psychologist, 46*, 394–403.

Bourne, E. J. (1995). *The anxiety and phobia workbook* (2nd ed.). Oakland, CA: New Harbinger Publications.

Bullock, L. E. (2002). The role of spirituality in the personal and professional lives of clinical social workers: An examination of coping and well-being. *Dissertation Abstracts International* Publication AAT 1410136 (UMI No. 1410136) http://O-wwwlib.umi.com.umiss.lib.olemise.edu/dissertations/preview_all/1410136

Cashwell, C. S., & Young, J. S. (2005). Integrating spirituality and religion into counseling: An introduction. In C. Cashwell & S. Young (Eds.), *Integrating spirituality and religion into counseling: A guide to competent practice*. Alexandria, VA: American Counseling Association.

Ceasar, P. T., & Miranti, J. G. (2005). Counseling and spirituality. In Capuzzi, D. & Gross D. (Eds.), *Introduction to the counseling profession* (4th ed.). Boston: Allyn & Bacon.

Chandler, C., Holden, J., & Kolander, C. (1992). Counseling and spiritual wellness. *Journal of Counseling and Development, 71*, 168–176.

Chandler, C., Holden, J., & Kolander, C. (2001). Counseling for spiritual wellness: Theory and practice. *Journal of Counseling & Development, 92*(71), 168–175.

Cherniss, C. (1995). *Beyond burnout.* New York: Routledge.

Clark, K. M., Friedman, H. S., & Martin, L. R. (1999). A longitudinal study of religiosity and mortality risk. *Journal of Health Psychology, 44*(2), 113–117.

Cooper, A. E. (2003). An investigation of the relationships among spirituality, prayer, and meditation, and aspects of stress and coping. *Dissertation Abstracts International* Publication AAT 3084474 (UMI No. 3084474) http://0-wwwlib.uml.com.umiss.edu/dissertations/preview_all 3084474

Cooperman, N., & Simoni, J. (2005). Suicidal ideation and attempted suicide among women living with HIV/AIDS. *Journal of Behavioral Medicine, 28*(2), 149–156.

Ellis, A. (1980). Psychotherapy and atheistic values: A response to A. E. Bergin's "Psychotherapy and Religious values." *Journal of Consulting and Clinical Psychology, 48*, 635–639.

Ellison, C. G. (1991). Religious involvement and subjective well-being. *Journal of Health, 32*, 80–99.

Ellison, C. G., & Levin, J. S. (1998). The religion-health connection: Evidence, theory, and future directions. *Health Education and Behavior, 25*(6), 700–720.

Ellison, C. W. (1983). Spiritual well-being: Conceptualization and measurement. *Journal Psychology and Theology, 11*, 330–340.

Fehring, R. J., Miller, J. F., & Shaw, C. (1997). Spiritual well-being, religiosity, hope, depression, and other mood states in elderly people coping with cancer. *Oncology Nursing, 24*, 663–671.

Frame, M. W. (2003). *Integrating religion and spirituality into counseling.* Pacific Grove, CA: Brooks/Cole–Thompson Learning.

Fromm, E. (1950). *Psychoanalysis and religion.* New Haven, CT: Yale University Press.

Fukuyama, M. A., & Sevig, T. D. (1997). Spiritual issues in counseling: A new course. *Counselor Education and Supervision, 36*, 233–245.

Gange-Fling, M. A., & McCarthy, P. (1996). Impact of childhood sexual abuse on client spiritual development: Counseling implications. *Journal of Counseling & Development, 74*(3), 253–258.

Genia, V. (1995). *Counseling and psychotherapy of religious clients: A developmental approach.* Westport, CT: Praeger.

Gladding, S. (2005). *Counseling: A comprehensive profession* (5th ed.). Upper Saddle River, NJ: Prentice-Hall

Graham, S., Furr, S., Flowers, C., & Burke, M. T. (2001). Religion and spirituality in coping with stress [Electronic version]. *Counseling and Values, 46*(1), 2–14.

Hagedorn, W. B. (2005). Counselor self awareness and self exploration of religious and spiritual beliefs: Know thyself. In C. Cashwell and S. Young (Eds.), *Integrating spirituality and religion into counseling: A guide for competent practice*. Alexandria, VA: American Counseling Association.

Harper, M. C., & Gill, C. S. (1995). Assessing the client's spiritual domain. In C. Cashwell and S. Young (Eds.), *Integrating spirituality and religion into counseling: A guide for competent practice*. Alexandria, VA: American Counseling Association.

Harris, R. C., Dew, M. A., Lee, A., Amaya, M., Buches, L., Reet, D., et al. (1995). The role of religion in heart transplant recipients' long-term health and well-being. *Journal of Religion and Health, 34*(1), 17–32.

Hatch, R. L., Burg, M. A., Naberhaus, D. S., & Hellmich, L. K. (1998). The spiritual involvement and beliefs scale: Development and testing of a new instrument. *The Journal of Family Practice, 46*(6), 476–486.

Hinterkopf, E. (1994). Integrating spiritual experiences in counseling. *Counseling and Values, 38,* 165–175.

Howden, J. W. (1992). Development and psychometric characteristics of the spirituality assessment scale. *Dissertation Abstracts International, 54*(01), 166B. (UMI No. AAG9312917)

Ingersoll, R. E. (1994). Spirituality, religion, and counseling: Dimensions and relationships. *Counseling and Values, 38,* 98–111.

Ivey, A., Ivey M. B., Myers, J., & Sweeney, T. (2005). *Developmental counseling and theory.* Boston: Houghton Mifflin.

Jagers, R. J., & Smith, P. (1996). Further examination of the spirituality scale. *Journal of Black Psychology, 23,* 429–442.

Kelly, E. W. (1995). *Spirituality and religion in counseling and psychotherapy: Diversity in theory and practice.* Alexandria, VA: American Counseling Association.

Koenig, H. G. (1998). Religious attitudes and practices of hospitalized medically ill older adults. *International Journal of Geriatric Psychiatry, 13*(4), 213–224.

Koenig, H. G. (1999). *The healing power of faith.* New York: Simon & Schuster.

Krause, N. (1995). Religiosity and self-esteem among older adults. *Journal of Gerontology, 50*(5), 236–246.

Levin, J. S., Larson, D. B., & Puchalski, C. M. (1997). Religion and spirituality in medicine: Research and education. *Journal of the American Medical Association, 278*(9), 792–793.

Levin, J. S., & Vanderpool, S. Y. (1987). Is frequent religious attendance really conducive to better health? Toward an epidemiology of religion. *Social Science Medicine, 24*(7), 589–600.

Matthews, D. A., McCollough, M. E., Larson, D. B., Koenig, H. G., & Swyers, J. P. (1998). Religious commitment and health status: A review of the research and implications for family medicine. *Archives in Family Medicine, 7*(2), 118–124.

Meisenhelder, J. B., & Chandler, E. N. (2002). Spirituality and health outcomes in the elderly. *Journal of Religion and Health, 42*(3), 243–252.

Miller, G. (1999). The development of the spiritual focus in counseling and counselor education. *Journal of Counseling & Development, 77,* 498–501.

Miller, G. (2003). *Incorporating spirituality in counseling and psychotherapy.* Hoboken, NJ: John Wiley & Sons.

Musick, M. A., Blazer, D. G., & Hays, J. C. (2000). Religious activity, alcohol use, and depression in a sample of elderly Baptists. *Research on Aging, 22*(2), 91–116.

Myers, J. E., & Williard, K. (2003). Integrating spirituality into counselor preparation: A developmental wellness approach. *Counseling and Values, 47,* 142–155.

Oman, D., & Reed, D. (1998). Religion and mortality among the community dwelling elderly. *American Journal of Public Health, 88,* 1469–1475.

Pargament, K. I. (1997). *The psychology of religion and coping.* New York: Guilford Press.

Parsons, F. (1909). *Choosing a vocation.* Boston: Houghton Mifflin.

Robinson, T. L. (2005). *The convergence of race, ethnicity, and gender: Multiple identities in counseling.* Upper Saddle River, NJ: Pearson Education.

Ryan, P. (1998). Spirituality among adult survivors of childhood violence: A literature review. *The Journal of Transpersonal Psychology, 30*(1), 39–51.

Schmidt, J. J. (2006). *Social and cultural foundations of counseling and human services.* Boston, MA: Allyn & Bacon.

Simpson, L. R. (2005). Level of spirituality as a predictor of the occurrence of compassion fatigue among counseling professionals in Mississippi. *Dissertation Abstracts Online Database, 66*(09A), 3223–3332.

Skinner, B. F. (1953). *Science and human behavior*. New York: Macmillan.

Steere, D. A. (1997). *Spiritual presence in psychotherapy*. New York: Brunner/Mazel.

Summit on Spirituality. (July 1995). Spiritual competencies for counselors. *Counseling Today*, p. 30.

Veach, T. L., & Chappell, J. N. (1992). Measuring spiritual health: A preliminary study. *Substance Abuse, 13*, 139–147.

Wheat, L. W. (1991). Development of a scale for the measurement of human spirituality. *Dissertation Abstracts International, 52*(09), 3230A.

Wiggins-Frame, M. (2005). Spirituality and religion: Similarities and differences. In C. Cashwell and S. Young (Eds.), *Integrating spirituality and religion into counseling: A guide for competent practice*. Alexandria, VA: American Counseling Association.

Witmer, J. M., Sweeney, T. J., & Myers, J. E. (1993). *Wellness evaluation of lifestyle: The WEL inventory*. Palo Alto, CA: Mind Garden.

Woods, T. E., Antoni, M. H., Ironson, G. H., & Kling, D. W. (1999). Religiosity is associated with affective status in symptomatic HIV-infected African-American women. *Journal of Health Psychology, 4*(3), 317–326.

12 Creative Approaches to Counseling

ANN VERNON, PhD
University of Northern Iowa

Introduction

Effective counseling establishes a therapeutic relationship to help clients think, feel, and behave in more self-enhancing ways. This relationship enables clients to work through difficulties (Nugent, 2000) and empowers them to cope more effectively with life circumstances to "enhance their present and future opportunities" (Welfel & Patterson, 2005, p. 1). Wagner (2003) stressed that counselors should not only focus on eliminating problems but also look for opportunities to facilitate optimal development. In effect, this occurs when the counselor helps clients develop more options for their lives and encourages them to accept more responsibility for their choices and actions (Kottler, 2004). Through counseling, clients become more aware, conceptualize their experiences differently, and see themselves and their ways of being more constructively. According to Thompson, Rudolph, and Henderson (2004), counseling is "a process in which people learn how to help themselves and, in effect, become their own counselors" (p. 22). This implies that the counselor won't "fix it" so that the client will feel and act better, but rather, through a collaborative process, the client can be empowered to work through the dysfunctional aspects that interfere with her or his life in order to engage in more growth-producing activities.

Counseling has basically been a mental arena, characterized by a predominantly verbal orientation, which, according to Dunn and Griggs (1995), can be very limiting. Gladding (2005) concurred, noting that verbal techniques alone are not sufficient for reluctant or nonverbal clients. He emphasized that effective counselors "are aware of the multidimensional nature of the profession and are able to work with a variety of populations by using appropriate interventions" (preface). In his opinion, the creative arts, often referred to as the expressive arts, have been overlooked as one of the most effective approaches for helping clients. In effect, using dance and movement, the visual arts, music, imagery, literature and writing, drama, and psychodrama, as well as play and humor, enables clients to invest more in the counseling process, resulting in growth and development that helps them experience their world in different ways.

Many practitioners are now recognizing that for many clients who seem relatively unaffected by the counseling process, standard techniques alone are inadequate. Consequently, there is more emphasis on expressive therapies (Malchiodi, 2005). While the goal is to facilitate change and problem solving, these approaches combine theory and practice in more flexible, creative ways, while focusing on the unique as well as universal qualities of clients (Gladding, 2005). Malchiodi noted that expressive therapies such as the use of the arts and play involve the "purposeful, active participation of the individual and are often complemented by verbal interventions" (p. xiv). According to Malchiodi, expressive therapies have been applied to many different client populations for a variety of issues, such as trauma and loss, addictions, developmental and psychiatric disorders, and relationship problems. Gladding stressed that this approach is emotionally sensitive and process oriented, making it applicable in numerous ways for clients throughout the life span. These nontraditional methods are especially relevant for children and adolescents, whose developmental needs are different and who may not be verbally proficient, according to Vernon and Clemente (2005). These authors also emphasized that because reading, writing, and speaking can be difficult for some clients because of language differences, the expressive arts are more universally and culturally appropriate.

"Effective therapists understand both their clients' styles of communication as well as how to bring out the best in their clients within the helping relationship" (Malchiodi, 2005, p. xiv). The importance of understanding individual communication and learning styles—the way a person perceives and responds to the learning environment—began appearing in the literature in the 1980s and supported Nickerson and O'Laughlin's (1982) contention that verbal approaches to counseling are often ineffective (Griggs, 1983, 1985; Griggs, Price, Kopel, & Swaine, 1984). In the 1990s, Myrick stressed the importance of taking learning styles into account, noting that failure to do so may result in less success with some clients. According to Myrick (1997), counselors must be "flexible, adaptive, and learn how to use different counseling approaches" (p. 111).

The learning style approach assumes that individuals have unique learning patterns that should be accommodated in the counseling process. Because counseling is primarily a talking process, if this is not done, some clients may feel inundated with words and feel overwhelmed, insecure, or lost (Myrick, 1997). Furthermore, the client may resist. Dunn and Griggs (1995) emphasized that this resistance is due in part to the "mismatch between the counseling interventions, strategies, and techniques used by the counselor and the learning-style preferences of the counselee" (p. 29). This mismatch may be more pronounced for clients from diverse cultures, particularly if they are not proficient in the language the counselor is using. Integrating the creative expressive arts into counseling has limitless possibilities for overcoming this mismatch because of the multidimensional aspects to this approach. As Malchiodi (2005) noted, the expressive arts engage clients in self-expression in their own creative and unique way that cannot always be accomplished verbally.

This chapter describes a variety of creative, expressive counseling approaches that may be used either as a complement to a predominantly verbal orientation with a client or as the primary therapeutic method. These approaches may be used with clients of all ages and in a variety of settings, such as schools, hospitals, and mental health centers. As previously noted, these approaches are often more appropriate for clients from diverse cultures (Vernon & Clemente, 2005), as well as for nonverbal clients or anyone else who "needs to explore and to integrate their behavior in a comprehensive and effective fashion" (Nickerson & O'Laughlin, 1982, p. 7). Gladding (2005) concurred with Nickerson and O'Laughlin and noted that creative approaches help clients as well as counselors see things from a different, more positive, perspective. According to Gladding (1995), "Clients from all backgrounds can benefit from using a creativity approach regardless of whether the form is fixed, such as with some creative exercises, or spontaneous" (p. 4). Gladding (2005) cited several compelling reasons for using the creative arts in counseling: they help clients become connected and integrated, they are participatory and involve energy and process, they help clients clearly see their goals, they enhance creativity for both the client and the counselor, they give clients a new way to experience themselves, they are very concrete and help clients conceptualize more effectively, they promote insight, they focus on cooperation and socialization, and they are culturally sensitive.

Art

Art therapy, derived from art and psychology (Vick, 2003), literally means using art in a therapeutic way (Jennings & Minde, 1993). Although art has been used since the beginning of history as a means of communication and healing, it has been used in evaluation and treatment as a definable method of practice since the mid-20th century (Malchiodi, 2005). The American Art Therapy Association (as cited in Malchiodi, 2005) stated that art therapy is based on the belief that the "creative process of art making is healing and life enhancing" (p. 18), and Vondracek and Corneal (1995) defined *art therapy* as "the use of art in a therapeutic setting to foster an individual's psychological growth and well-being" (p. 294). These authors referred to art within the therapeutic context as a means of bringing subconscious material into awareness, which in turn leads to perception and interpretation.

Lev-Wiesel and Daphna-Tekoha (2000) noted that art therapy techniques allow the counselor to examine the client's inner language, which leads to increased insight, and Kwiatowska (2001) stressed that art helps clients perceive themselves more clearly. Malchiodi (2005) cited several other advantages of using art therapy, including the fact that it is experiential because it utilizes the senses; it is a "hands-on" activity (p. 19). In addition, it promotes catharsis, can alleviate stress by inducing relaxation, and provides a tangible product that can be referred to at other times. Silver (2001) noted that an advantage of using art in therapy is that it is a way for clients to articulate thoughts and express experiences that they cannot put into words. Gladding (2005) emphasized that art is an effective approach because it is perceived as nonthreatening and can readily be used in conjunction with other creative arts, which makes it very flexible and widely applicable.

A distinction is made between using art techniques in counseling as opposed to pure art therapy, which focuses more on artistic eloquence as opposed to creating art and looking at the symbolism (Kramer, 1998). Typically, counselors focus on the latter.

As Malchiodi (2005) discussed, art therapy is a profession with specialized education and credentials, whereas counselors use art to help clients express themselves. Although the majority of research on art therapy has focused on making the unconscious material explicit, art therapy can also be used to increase understanding of conscious material. For example, a client can be encouraged to express his or her anger resulting from a loss in a drawing, and the client and therapist can discuss what the drawing symbolizes and the feelings it evoked.

Malchiodi (2005) noted, "While art expression may be used as another form of language in therapy, the actual act of making art taps the universal human potential to be creative, a capacity that has been related to health and wellness" (p. 18). Cited as being particularly effective with reluctant, nonverbal clients, Bush (1997) stated that painting and drawing can facilitate growth and change as the counselor helps the client focus on symbolic areas of pain and growth in an accepting, understanding manner. Gladding (1998) indicated that art provides an emotional outlet for people who have difficulty expressing their needs, feelings, and desires and is an effective way to help them begin to understand their confusion. Catharsis and growth, as well as assessment, are the three major purposes of art, according to Brems (2002).

According to Gladding (2005), counselors use art in therapy with children, adolescents, college students, adults, and the elderly. It has also been used with groups, couples and families, and with people from all ethnic backgrounds. Gladding noted that because art transcends cultural boundaries, it is especially effective with diverse populations. Silver (2001) described using art with various client populations such as abused, emotionally disturbed, hearing-impaired, or brain-injured individuals. Malchiodi (2005) indicated that it is used to treat ADHD, autism, substance abuse, eating disorders, trauma and loss, domestic violence, physical and sexual abuse, and most forms of mental illness. Art therapy is used in a variety of settings, such as schools, prisons, rehabilitation centers, day-treatment centers, hospitals, and clinics. It is now not only being used to work with people who have problems (Landgarten & Lubbers, 1991) but also is more prevalent in helping "normal" clients, where the emphasis is on growth and self-development (Vondracek & Corneal, 1995).

The Process

Many art forms can be used to help clients gain self-awareness and work through emotional conflicts: painting, sculpting, modeling with clay, photography, drawing, printing/designing, collages, or graphic art. Gladding (2005) identified using already existing artwork as a means of introducing images that facilitate communication and understanding. In addition, Gladding discussed the use of body outlines and serial drawing as visual art forms that can be used with clients to help uncover troublesome issues.

According to Kenny (1987), the goal is communication between the helper and the client rather than mastery of art form or content. In the process, the client is encouraged to express feelings symbolically through an art form. As Allan (1982) noted, the counselor's role is basically that of a listener who responds to the client and allows him or her time and space to initiate interaction. After a given interval, the counselor might invite the client to share by issuing a simple invitation such as "Would you like to tell me what's happening in your picture?" If working with a more seriously disturbed client with whom art media is used in each session, Allan indicated that the counselor's role may change. After several sessions, the counselor might become more active by relating the art to what is occurring in real life, as well as emphasizing positive aspects that indicate growth.

Art is an effective means of initiating contact with a client, as illustrated in the following example. Amanda, a third-grader, was referred by her teacher because she seemed preoccupied and unhappy. In the initial meeting, the counselor noted that Amanda seemed quite anxious and hesitant. To establish rapport and facilitate expression, the counselor put some modeling clay on the table and invited Amanda to play with it. At first Amanda just rolled the clay around without molding it. The counselor made no comment but simply communicated an attitude of acceptance. Presently Amanda began to shape the clay into a bridge. Next she made a car and attached small clay dots to the car. As she placed the car on the bridge, the bridge collapsed. At this point the counselor asked Amanda if she would like to tell her about what was happening. Amanda explained that the dots were people—her family. The counselor reflected that something must have happened to the family in the car, and Amanda began to talk about how her family had had an accident because her Dad and Mom were drunk. She shared her feelings of fright and how she took care of her brothers and sister after the accident. As she talked, she began to roll the clay and pound it, tears streaming down her cheeks. As the counselor supported her, it became apparent that the feelings Amanda needed to express would be more readily verbalized in future sessions as the counselor began to help Amanda deal with her painful situation.

Art media can be used in the manner previously illustrated or in a more directed manner to facilitate a process. For example, clients could be instructed to draw their family, paint their life story or their dreams, or illustrate a book that describes a situation with which they are dealing. They could be asked to sketch and color themselves in moods that they experienced recently or be invited to draw a picture representing something that they need in their life. Designing a T-shirt, a banner, or a bumper sticker with a motto they feel describes them is a good way to encourage personal growth and sharing, particularly with resistant adolescent clients.

Photography can also be used effectively to elicit feelings and create awareness. Amerikaner, Schauble, and Ziller (1982) outlined a method of using 12 client-created photographs describing how the client sees self to stimulate self-awareness. Gladding (2005) described using old photographs to help the elderly participate in a life review process, and Vernon and Clemente (2005) explained how photographs were used with an adolescent to help her more realistically assess experiences with her peers. Photographs can also help clients assess their goals, as in the case of Mandy.

Mandy, 17-year-old female, was referred for counseling by her parents, who were concerned about her behavior, specifically her alcohol abuse, low grades, and her association with peers they felt were a bad influence. Although Mandy's parents felt that her behavior was very much out of control, Mandy did not share this same opinion. To the contrary, she did not want to be in counseling and saw nothing wrong with the way she was living her life. Because of her reluctance, the counselor felt that it would be more effective to use a variety of approaches to help her evaluate her goals and her current behaviors.

After establishing rapport by having her client share artifacts from her backpack that told something about her, as well as acknowledging her resistance, the counselor asked Mandy if she had any goals for these counseling sessions. Mandy's reply was that she wanted her parents to leave her alone and let her make her own decisions. The counselor replied that she thought one way of doing this would be for Mandy to "prove" to her parents that her present behaviors would help her achieve future goals. She suggested that Mandy take photographs of what her life would be like if she continued her present course of action (substance abuse, low grades, associating with peers who were encouraging her to drop out of high school, move away from home, etc.) and to take photos that represented a life she might like to have, in case it would be different from the one she would have if she continued along the same path.

This visual intervention proved to be very enlightening for Mandy, who took the task seriously. Her photographs depicting how her life would be if she continued her present lifestyle reflected working at fast-food chains, living in substandard housing, and having her driver's license taken away for driving while intoxicated. Her pictures of how she wanted her life to be were considerably different: graduating from high school, getting a new car, and going to college. After discussing the differences between the two sets of pictures, Mandy and her counselor were able to set realistic goals for behavioral and attitudinal changes.

Implementation Considerations

In employing art, Rubin (1988) cautioned that experience and skill are necessary if working at a sophisticated level but that specific training in art is not essential with simple expressive work and minimal interpretation. Brems (2002) emphasized that there are various approaches to the use of art and that it can be used exclusively or in combination with other strategies.

Rubin (1988) also noted that therapeutic work through art may be one way for clients to feel in charge when other parts of their life are overwhelming. As a trusting relationship is established, the counselor invites the client to share the meaning from his or her perspective. In essence, the counselor observes the client's work as it develops, attends to the nonverbal and verbal communication offered, and responds to clarify.

Kenny (1987) identified the following factors that may help the counselor understand clients' artwork by considering the larger context of their world:

1. In Western culture, dark colors or heavy shading generally indicate sadness, depression, or anger; excessive use of white may indicate emotional rigidity.
2. Small figures, particularly of self, may indicate insecurity, anxiety, or low self-esteem.
3. Sadness, violence, aggression, or other emotional disturbance are often represented with dark images, storms, accidents, fighting, or murder.

4. Texture of materials can provide insight: aggressive, angry clients might select bold or tough materials, whereas a nonassertive client might choose watercolors or something softer.
5. Clients with emotional disturbances tend to depict figures more grotesquely, stiff and rigid, or unintegrated, with some body parts being exaggerated. Excessive shading may indicate high anxiety.

The basic function of art therapy is to facilitate emotional expression from clients who do not communicate well verbally and to execute the counseling process more effectively through visual representation. Art therapy can be used to reduce resistance and put the client at ease during an initial session, can be used strategically in later sessions to help the client clarify and gain awareness, or can be used over a period of several sessions as the main vehicle to work through painful issues. Brems (2002) added that it is an effective means of introducing and discussing difficult topics or affects. Gladding (2005) emphasized that art helps awaken clients to "a new sense of self and deeper understanding of their intra- and interpersonal relationships" (p. 105). Bush (1997) noted that as clients liken themselves to artists who can repaint canvasses they do not like after the paint is dry, they can, in effect, learn to paint over their problems to attain new solutions" (p. 4).

Art Therapy: An Introduction (Rubin, 1998), and *Handbook of Art Therapy* (Malchiodi, 2003) are excellent resources for the professional interested in learning more about using art in a counseling relationship.

Imagery

Imagery, described as "seeing with the mind's eye or as having an inner vision" (Gladding, 2005, p. 66), has been defined as "perception that comes through any of the senses—sight, smell, touch, taste, hearing, and feeling" (Kanchier, 1997, p. 14, as cited in Gladding, 2005). The use of imagery is especially effective in helping people deal with life changes and has increasingly been used in career counseling and life planning (Skovholt, Morgan, & Negron-Cunningham, 1989), as well as with children and adolescents (Gladding, 2005; Plummer, 1999). It also has been used to help clients deal with posttraumatic stress (Smucker & Dancu, 1999), bulimia (Ohanian, 2002), physical pain (Cupal & Brewer, 2001), and marital issues (Morrison & Rasp, 2001). Witmer and Young (1987) noted that imagery facilitates awareness of personal values, emotions, goals, conflicts, and spiritual desires. Gladding (2005) emphasized that imagery is a "universal and natural modality for helping people engender change" (p. 66).

There are good rationales for using imagery in counseling. First of all, many clients already use imagery to help them learn new material or remember things (Gladding, 2005). Second, imagery can help people change behavior. Plummer (1999) noted that because the body cannot distinguish between a vivid mental experience and an actual physical experience, clients who use imagery may actually perform better. The use of imagery also teaches clients how to stimulate creativity and develop cognitive flexibility. In addition, because many client problems are connected to images of self and others, using imagery to change perspectives is helpful. Finally, imagery promotes a holistic approach (Gladding, 2005) and is especially effective with Native Americans, according to Dunn and Griggs (1995).

Although free daydreams are often cited as one form of imagery, this section describes the use of guided imagery and concrete images to help a client reconceptualize events and change behavior.

Guided Imagery

Guided imagery is a structured, directed activity designed to increase artistic expression, personal awareness, and concentration (Myrick & Myrick, 1993). In guided imagery, the counselor orchestrates a scenario for the client with stimulus words or sounds to serve as a catalyst for creating a mental picture (Myrick & Myrick, 1993). Sometimes called guided fantasy, the process involves inducing relaxation, the actual fantasy, and processing the fantasy (Skovholt et al., 1989). The inclusion of relaxation is important because it helps bridge the gap between prior activities and the imagery experience to move the client's focus from external to internal.

Myrick and Myrick (1993) identified the following guidelines for using guided imagery:

1. Create a scripted story. This is particularly helpful because it allows the counselor to select words that connote vivid textures and other senses.
2. Introduce the concept of guided imagery, and instruct the client to sit or lie in a relaxed position, focusing on breathing.
3. Read the script slowly, using a quiet and soothing voice to help create vivid images.
4. Bring closure to the experience by stopping at a pleasant place accompanied by positive feelings. Inform the client that you are getting ready to stop, and as you count to 3 slowly, have the client open her or his eyes and stretch.
5. Invite the client to discuss the experience, focusing on positive aspects of the activity, as well as his or her experiences with obstacles and how he or she overcame them.

The following script was used with a middle-aged woman who suffered from anxiety and procrastinated about completing housework and other chores. After being instructed to relax by imagining a peaceful scene and engaging in deep breathing to release tension, Jana was invited to involve herself in this imagery experience.

SETTING: Imagine that it is next Monday. (pause) You are waking up in the morning. What time is it? (pause) You get up and eat breakfast. Who is there? (pause) You finish breakfast. You don't have to leave for work until noon. What needs to be done? What do you do first? (pause) How do you see yourself doing this task, and how long does it take? Is anyone helping you? If not, how are you feeling about that? (pause) You finish this activity. What do you do now? (pause) It is now time to get ready to leave for work. (pause)

> WORK: You are now at work. Are you working alone, or are you interacting with others? What tasks are you doing? Are you enjoying them? (pause)
>
> HOME: You have left work and are home again. Are you alone? (pause) If not, who is there? Do you interact with them? (pause) It is time to get dinner. Do you do this alone, or does anyone help you? (pause) Now it is after dinner. What do you do? Who is with you? (pause) Now it is time for bed. Tomorrow you will not work and will be at home all day. What will you do? How will you do it? (pause)
>
> END: You may open your eyes, and we will discuss your experience.

In processing the imagery exercise, Jana said that it was not difficult to see what needed to be done, but it was hard to visualize what she would do first. Once she did select a task, it wasn't too difficult to see herself taking the necessary steps to complete it. She saw herself alone in doing the housework and resented that. She described the work portion of her day, where she had no trouble completing necessary tasks, as basically enjoyable.

In reflecting on the exercise, it seemed helpful for Jana to list the chores that needed to be done each day so she wouldn't become anxious about deciding what to do. It was also appropriate to begin teaching her some assertiveness skills so that she could negotiate for equity with the housework. The guided imagery effectively helped the counselor and client clarify issues and pinpoint target areas for goal setting and skill development.

Guided imagery has also been used successfully in career counseling where clients are asked to imagine "A Day in the Future"; "The Opposite Sex," growing up as the opposite sex and holding a job usually held by the opposite sex; or "Mid-Career Change or Retirement," focusing on shifting from the present career focus (Skovholt et al., 1989). Omizo, Omizo, and Kitaoka (1998) suggested using guided imagery with children to help clarify problems, reduce anxiety, enhance self-concept, and make behavioral changes. Bourne (1995) described its usefulness with athletes to achieve peak performance and as a part of a treatment program for various diseases, and Pearson (2003) suggested using guided imagery to help counseling graduate students transition from student to professional.

Use of Concrete Images

Images can also be used therapeutically in isolation to help stimulate thinking that can lead to more productive behavior. When using images this way, the counselor tries to relate the image to something familiar to the client or something that conveys a type of metaphor, as in the following example.

Eighteen-year-old Nat was in counseling for depression. Irrational beliefs in the form of exaggerations, overgeneralizations, and awfulizations contributed to his depression. In the session when the image was introduced, Nat was discussing an incident with his girlfriend. He assumed that because she didn't call him every day, she didn't care about him. He said he couldn't stand it if she found someone else.

In previous sessions, the counselor had helped Nat dispute these irrational beliefs, but they continued to be quite prevalent. As Nat and the counselor were working on these irrational beliefs in the present session, the counselor glanced out the window and noticed a bug zapper. She called it to Nat's attention and asked him to watch the zapper and describe how it operated. The counselor explained to Nat that he could image that his head was a zapper, when he started to think irrationally, he should visualize these irrational thoughts being deflected, just like the bugs were when they hit the zapper. Although this may seem simplistic, it helped Nat stop the irrational thinking more effectively because he could quickly recall the bug zapper image and use this to trigger his disputations before he felt the negative effects of the irrational beliefs.

In listening carefully to the client's problem, counselors do not find it difficult to think of helpful images. Children who have difficulty controlling impulsive behavior might be asked, when they start to feel out of control, to visualize a stop sign. Pairing the visualization with self-statements such as "I don't have to hit; I can walk away" increases the effectiveness of the image. A child who is reluctant to go to bed because she or he is afraid of monsters can visualize herself or himself in a scary Halloween costume, frightening away any monsters that might come into the room.

Gladding (1998, 2005) pointed out these benefits of imagery: it can be performed anywhere, it is an available resource that most clients already employ, it teaches clients how to use their imaginations to stimulate creative problem solving, it is a powerful type of mental practice, and it is holistic. In addition, many client problems, such as eating disorders, are connected to clients' images of self and others. Imagery helps clients learn about themselves, and although it might not work for everyone, it can be an extremely effective method to access information and resolve problems.

Hypnotherapy

In hypnotherapy, hypnosis is used in conjunction with various forms of psychotherapy (Vondracek & Corneal, 1995). Havens and Walters (2002) stressed that in everyday life, everyone has experiences that resemble hypnosis. Consequently, professionals should utilize it in a therapeutic manner. Plummer (1999) asserted that hypnosis is an effective way to help clients become more aware of their inner experiences, reexperience past events, and envision new possibilities. Hypnotherapy also helps clients assume responsibility for healing themselves, noted Havens and Walters (2002). Olness and Kohen (1996) suggested that clients often feel passive and helpless about their problems and that hypnotherapy can "teach an attitude of hope in the context of mastery" (p. 89).

Winsor (1993) cited three styles of hypnosis: directive, which is based on simple commands; Ericksonian, which relies on indirect methods such as stories, confusion techniques, and metaphors; and permissive, in which the client and hypnotherapist contract to help the client gain access to an altered state of consciousness.

Hypnosis is generally induced as part of counseling or in conjunction with pain reduction. Havens and Walters (2002) contended that the common denominator of all problems presented in counseling is emotional pain. The presenting concern may be relationship issues, feelings of inadequacy, depression, or anxiety. In any case, the counselor's job is to help clients describe their specific pain, and counseling involves "replacing that suffering with comfort" (p. 6). Olness and Kohen (1996) cautioned against using hypnosis for "fun" (p. 95), using hypnosis if it could exaggerate existing emotional problems, or using this form of treatment if the real problem should be treated in another way.

Because hypnosis is used in conjunction with counseling, the specific procedures used in hypnotherapy depend on the theoretical framework of the counselor. Hypnotherapy is often used in conjunction with behavior therapy, eclectic therapy, and supportive therapies (Weitzenhoffer, 1989), as well as in psychoanalysis (Vondracek & Corneal, 1995).

According to Olness and Kohen (1996), there are three broad categories of hypnotherapy: supportive, ego-enhancing methods; symptom-oriented methods; and dynamic, insight-oriented methods. The main goal of supportive, ego-enhancing methods is to help the client feel more capable of dealing with problems and challenges, more worthy, and better able to be in control of internal and external circumstances. This method might be particularly helpful for clients who have pervasive anxiety or who are afraid of surgery. Supportive phrases such as "I think you can get through this" are used to help the client gain control.

In the symptom-oriented method, the effort is directed at removing, changing, or alleviating physical or emotional symptoms. This method is especially useful for treating phobias, pain control, and habit control. Dynamic, insight-oriented methods are used for symptom relief and ego strengthening, but special methods are also used to help the client understand the issues that create and maintain the problem. In this method, they gain insight into and work through underlying conflicts.

The Process

There are four phases of hypnotherapy, according to Olness and Kohen (1996): the preinduction interview, induction, hypnotherapeutic intervention, and arousal after the hypnotic state has been terminated. Wagner (2003) stressed the importance of developing a good relationship and exploring reservations about the procedure during the preinduction interview before moving to the induction phase. During the induction phase, a variety of strategies can be used, according to Wagner: visual imagery (imagining a favorite place or activity), auditory imagery (imagining a favorite musical selection), ideomotor techniques (hand levitation), progressive relaxation, and eye fixation techniques. After the induction, the counselor proceeds to the intervention stage, using developmentally appropriate suggestions to facilitate symptom reduction. Kohen (1997) recommended having clients describe their experience when they are no longer in the trancelike state.

Cautions and Applications

Critics have raised questions about the use of posthypnotic suggestions and other hypnotic practices because they represent undue influence over the client's behavior or encourage antisocial behavior. Weitzenhoffer (1989) noted that under hypnosis, a client's defenses may be reduced before he or she is ready to deal with the repressed material. This author stressed the importance of proper training for practitioners who use hypnotherapy. When used appropriately, hypnotherapy has been used successfully with weight control, anxiety disorders, sexual dysfunction, eating disorders, obsessive-compulsive disorders, substance abuse disorders, and smoking cessation (Sapp, 2000). It has also been used to treat common childhood problems such as nail biting, enuresis, encopresis, phobias, sleep disorders, and thumb sucking (LaBaw & LaBaw, 1990). Winsor (1993) stated that hypnosis has regained scientific credibility in the past 50 years and is used to treat a growing number of medical as well as psychological problems.

Music

Music, which has played an important role in healing and nurturing for centuries, is another effective counseling approach to use with a variety of populations (Horden, 2000; Wigram, Pedersen, & Bonde, 2002). Music is a "therapeutic ally to verbal approaches to counseling" (Gladding, 2005, p. 23); it is a creative experience that can be used to initiate other counseling processes. Music has also been described as a "universal multicultural experience" (Brown, 2001, as cited in Gladding, 2005, p. 22). According to Gladding (2005), the effectiveness of this intervention depends on the client's involvement with music, but because most clients enjoy singing, dancing, or listening to music, this can be an ideal approach for clients who have difficulty expressing themselves verbally (Newcomb, 1994). It is important to distinguish between music therapy, which Peters (2000) described as "a planned, goal-directed process of interaction and intervention, based on assessment and evaluation of individual clients' specific needs, strengths, and weaknesses, in which music or music-based experiences are specifically prescribed to be used by specially trained personnel to influence positive changes in an individual's condition, skills, thoughts, feelings, or behaviors" (p. 2), and using music techniques in counseling. Gladding (1998, 2005) stated that music therapy is more direct and implemented by therapists who are specialists in music and human behavior, whereas counseling that includes music involves listening, improvising, performing, and composing that are therapeutic but not as encompassing as music therapy.

Music has been used in individual as well as group settings to help geriatric clients with advanced Alzheimer's (Forinash, 2005), encourage healing (Clarkson, 1994) and wellness (Peters, 2000), reduce depression and increase self-esteem (Hendricks, 2000), facilitate social interaction and self-expression in older adults (Rio, 2002), and help children deal with the trauma of abuse (Ostertag, 2002). Music has also been used successfully with the mentally challenged, institutionalized elderly; emotionally disturbed, sensory impaired clients; and with depressed clients in a hospital setting (Davis, Gfeller, & Thaut, 1999), as well as with physically and/or developmentally delayed clients (Wigram et al., 2002) and with behaviorally disturbed or socially maladjusted children and adolescents (Peters, 2000). Maranto (1993) recommended using music with the elderly and to treat stress disorders. Davis et al. (1999) stressed the importance of music therapy in treating individuals with psychological disorders, delinquent behavior, or drug addiction. Gladding (2005) discussed the effectiveness of music with children, adolescents, families and couples, the elderly, and clients with chronic illnesses. Music is a catalyst for self-expression and can result in a number of therapeutic changes, including heightened attention and concentration, stimulation and expression of feelings, and insight into one's thinking, feeling, and behavior (Thaut, 1990). It can be used to alleviate burnout (Peters, 2000) and plays an important role in preventive care and health maintenance (Guzzetta, 1991). Gladding (2005) noted that music is a versatile tool that can reduce anxiety, elicit memories, communicate feelings, develop rapport, and intensify or create moods. Music is energizing and also has a calming effect.

Although music can be used as the primary method of treatment, it can also be incorporated into the counseling experience to facilitate the process more effectively. Gladding (2005) noted that music can be used in conjunction with other creative arts such as music and play, music and storytelling, and music and poetry. Music can also be used to introduce or convey messages in classroom guidance sessions and to clarify issues as a "homework" assignment. Song lyrics or CDs are perhaps the most accessible form of music, but for improvisation purposes, a guitar, drum, shakers, xylophone, or keyboard are useful.

Applications

Music can effectively establish rapport, particularly with teenagers, who are often not self-referred. Having the radio softly tuned into a popular rock station when the client walks into the office can facilitate communication and relaxation. Generally, it is best left to the client to initiate conversation about the music, but if she or he doesn't, the counselor might comment on the song, inquire whether the client likes to listen to music, and then ease into the traditional get acquainted phase of the session. After a first session, one teenager commented to me that he was surprised to hear the music and that it didn't make it seem like he was "going to a shrink." This helped establish trust by communicating to the client that the counselor had some understanding of where he was coming from.

To help clients get more in touch with what they are thinking and feeling, music can be a useful homework assignment. The client is invited to bring in CDs or record songs that illustrate how she or he is thinking or feeling that week. Clients can also find songs that express who they are, their conflicts, or their hopes. This is effective especially for teenagers, in that music is such an important part of their life experience.

This approach was used with 14-year-old Annette, a depressed, nonverbal client who asked to see a counselor because of home conflicts. Despite the fact that she had initiated the counseling, it was difficult for Annette to express what was happening at home and why she was so upset. Annette was very willing to do the music assignment and came back the following week with several tapes. The counselor invited her to play the tapes, briefly reflected on what she thought was expressed through the music, and then encouraged Annette to share how the songs related to her experiences. She opened up some, which facilitated verbal exchange about the problems.

After several sessions of discussing and working through some of her difficulties, Annette was again asked to bring in songs that told more about her current feelings. This time the songs were less conflictual and more hopeful. The use of music homework had helped the counselor understand Annette's pain and confusion so they could begin dealing with it. The music also provided a useful way to determine therapy progress.

Vernon (2002) suggested using music in the counseling session and described having depressed adolescents "take a sad song and make it better," by selecting a song that conveyed elements of their own depression and rewriting the lyrics to convey a more hopeful outlook. She also developed the concept of "silly songs," where children take a familiar song and write silly lyrics to help them gain new perspective. For example, this song, sung to the tune of "This Old Man, He Played One" helps sad children develop different coping strategies:

This sad kid, he sat and cried,	This sad kid, he no longer cried,
All he wanted was to hide;	He went to play and did not hide,
With a knickknack patty-whack,	With a knickknack-patty-whack,
Give this boy some hope;	Sensible thinking was the key
Now this kid knows how to cope	Now the boy can sing with glee (Vernon, 2002, p. 130)

Newcomb (1994) described using songwriting to promote increased self-awareness and facilitate emotional release. She noted that song lyrics can be used to teach children about positive interpersonal relationships and suggested pairing children up and having them draw to music as a way to increase communication and cooperation. Peters (2000) indicated that music can be used to encourage team work.

Music can also be used with children in classroom guidance lessons (DeLucia-Waack, 2001). DeLucia Waack (2001) created songs to help children learn how to cope with divorce, and Peter Yarrow (2000) wrote songs to promote acceptance of others. Dan Conley (1994) developed a series of children's songs to help children deal with typical problems such as anxiety, perfectionism, and guilt. Using the song "I Worry" from the Dan Conley album can introduce a lesson in classroom guidance about how everyone worries from time to time. After playing the recording, children can be invited to sing the song, and a discussion can follow about the main points in the song. Follow-up activities include making a "worry box" to contain the worries, writing advice columns about how to handle typical worries, or incorporating bibliotherapy.

Advantages

Because music is a popular medium and readily available, counselors are limited by only their creativity to specific applications. Music can easily be integrated into counseling sessions to help clients clarify issues, communicate problems, or monitor progress. It can also be used improvisationally to encourage risk taking, self-expression, spontaneity, playfulness, and creative expression (Forinash, 2005). Clients might be invited to experiment with various musical instruments to create a piece of music that is meaningful to them. Putting words to the music adds yet another dimension. Improvisations in a group setting encourage cooperation and cohesiveness.

If clients respond to the use of music, it provides a pleasurable way to connect with them to stimulate personal awareness and growth. Whether they listen, compose, or move to music, the benefits of this approach are multifaceted.

Writing or Scriptotherapy

According to Gladding (2005), scriptotherapy means writing in a therapeutic way. Writing, an effective self-help approach, offers a powerful way for clients to clarify feelings and events and gain a perspective on their problems. Bradley, Gould, and Hendricks (2004) noted that writing contributes to personal integration and provides a cathartic experience. For many clients, seeing something in writing has more impact than hearing it.

Writing as a therapeutic experience can take numerous forms, and the reader is encouraged to experiment with the variations later described to meet a client's needs most effectively. Obviously, for very young children, writing must be more simplistic, or the counselor may choose to serve as the recorder. Also, writing may not be appropriate with some clients from diverse cultures who may struggle to write in a language that is not their primary language (Vernon & Clemente, 2005). In addition, some clients don't find certain forms of writing helpful, and the assignment ought to be geared to what the counselor deems will be most useful for achieving the therapeutic goals. Therapeutic writing approaches range from structured to open-ended. Examples of each are described in the following sections.

Autobiographies

Autobiographies are generally written in one of two ways: describing a particular segment or aspect of one's life or writing a chronicle that covers all of one's life history (Bradley et al., 2004). How the autobiography is used depends on which approach better helps the client clarify concerns, express feelings, and work toward resolution. In either case, once the client provides the written material, the counselor helps the client clarify the issues by asking questions, probing for feelings, confronting discrepancies in the writing, identifying specific concerns, and setting goals for change.

In one case in which this approach was used, the counselor determined that because the client was struggling with a relationship with her spouse, it would help her to chronicle all past significant relationships, including how these relationships were established, what was meaningful about them, how they were terminated, and how the client felt. The client and counselor then identified patterns in the way the client reacted to significant others. In other instances, it might benefit the client to write a more detailed account of her or his life to see how perceptions and values change over time and to develop some perspective about the future.

Correspondence

We typically think of correspondence as appropriate when face-to-face contact isn't possible. However, correspondence can also help clarify concerns in other ways. White and Murray (2002) noted that letter writing can allow for self-exploration and change. For example, clients can be encouraged to write letters to themselves to give positive feedback about an accomplishment or some advice about how to handle a particular problem. Or correspondence between client and counselor can elaborate important points that occurred during the session (White & Murray, 2002).

Clients may also find it useful to write a letter (probably unsent) to a person with whom they are in conflict to help them express thoughts and clarify issues. This approach was used with an elderly client who was angry with his sister. To help him diffuse the anger and develop some perspective about the problem, he first put his thoughts on paper and then discussed his feelings with the counselor. The counselor helped him identify the behaviors that upset him and speculate on alternative viewpoints. As a homework assignment, the client rewrote the letter. When he brought it in the following week, the concerns were more succinctly expressed and the anger was more focused. The counselor showed the client ways to express the anger more assertively and how to dispute overgeneralizations and exaggerated thinking.

In this example, the client sent his letter, and it did not affect the relationship negatively, as the first letter might have. Instead, the first letter served as a valuable catharsis and a tool for the counselor to help the client clarify the problem and develop skills to address it more effectively.

In other cases, clients may not use the counselor as an editor but simply write a letter as a way of dealing with feelings. After they have written the letter, they may keep it, give it to the person with whom they are in conflict, or tear it up. It is important for clients to realize that an unedited angry letter may create more problems when it is received. On the other hand, such a letter can serve as a springboard for getting problems out in the open.

Writing a letter to one's disease, such as cancer or Crohn's disease, is an exceptionally helpful form of catharsis for clients who suffer from illnesses but often keep their feelings to themselves. Likewise, writing a letter to a deceased loved one, a hope or dream, or a major transition such as retirement or moving can be very therapeutic.

Riordan and Ketchum (1996) discussed another form of writing they call therapeutic correspondence, when the client and/or counselor writes notes in the form of letters after the session. These letters can motivate the client to work on particular issues and also are a good refresher of topics addressed during counseling.

Journaling

Journaling, either structured or unstructured, is a form of expressive writing that helps clients reflect on their personal experiences and identify where growth has occurred (Gladding, 2005). Journaling is particularly helpful with clients who are not very verbal because it can illuminate issues to encourage discussion. It is also an appropriate multicultural approach because in some cultures people are not encouraged to share their feelings. Journaling allows self-expression and the acceptance of feelings, relieves emotional pain, and allows clients to start dealing with emotions cognitively and objectively (Mercer, 1993). Recording thoughts and feelings enables both client and counselor to understand the dimensions of the problem and monitor behavior.

When unstructured journaling is used, the client is invited to write down thoughts and feelings about events each day. The journal can then be used as catharsis. During each session, the counselor can invite clients to share anything from the journal that they felt was significant, anything they would like help with, or items they want to talk more about.

Journaling can also be more structured; for example, the counselor can present the client with a list of suggestions—identifying events that were pleasurable or upsetting, goals that were accomplished, people they did or did not enjoy being with, and feelings about each of these topics to guide the writing. Often clients initially need these guidelines but don't generally rely on the structure for long. Regardless of the form, Gladding (2005) recommended reviewing the journal material on a regular basis to increase reflection and insight. He also stressed that an audiotaped journal may be an alternative for clients who process information auditorily or are not very adept at writing.

Structured Writing

Structured writing can be open-ended sentences, questionnaires, or writing in session. Hutchins and Cole (1992) cautioned that writing does not replace counselor–client interaction but rather is a starting point for discussion as well as a way to help the client generate and synthesize data.

Open-Ended Sentences.   Open-ended sentences may be used to establish rapport or to determine areas of concern to address during the counseling sessions. Children or adolescents, who are often more nonverbal, may readily respond to open-ended sentences, but these techniques can also be very effective with adults, such as in couple counseling. Open-ended sentences can provide a valuable source of information and set the client at ease by supplying a structure to which she or he can respond. With very young children, the counselor can serve as the recorder so the child doesn't have to labor over writing.

Open-ended sentences can be general starters such as the following, which are good to use in initial sessions to learn more about the client:

"I get upset when . . ."
"If I could change something in my life, it would be . . ."
"I am happiest when . . ."
"In my free time I like to . . ."

Or the starters may be geared more specifically to an area of concern the client previously expressed such as:

"I wish my spouse would . . ."
"Three things I consider important in our relationship are . . ."

"The biggest change in our relationship over the years has been . . ."
"The thing I most appreciate about my spouse is . . ."

Both strategies effectively collect information about thoughts and feelings that can be used as the counselor helps the client sort through concerns. In employing open-ended sentences, it is important to make sure the starters are appropriate for the client's developmental level. It is not necessary to have a long list of starters; the real purpose is to elicit information that can be used in the counseling session, not simply to collect data.

Stories. Writing personal stories with different endings is an effective way for clients of all ages to make a difficult decision among alternatives. With this strategy, the client is first invited to write the personal dilemma and then encouraged to write several different endings to the same story. Dialogue between counselor and client should focus on the advantages and disadvantages of each ending, as well as consequences. This technique facilitates problem resolution, as in the case of Enrique, age 18, who was struggling with the decision of what to do after high school. After writing about several alternatives, including attending college, joining the armed forces, and working in town and attending the local community college, Enrique had a much clearer idea about his immediate and long-term future relative to each option.

Writing in Session. For many clients, seeing things in print has more impact than hearing them. For this reason, clients might be encouraged to take notes during the counseling session and refer to these notes between sessions to work on aspects of the problem. In working with young children or clients who labor over writing, the counselor may opt to record key ideas that might be useful to the client

Poetry

Poetry therapy is the use of poetry in counseling, and a distinction is made between trained poetry therapists and counselors who use poetry as a therapeutic tool (Gladding, 2005). Gorelick (2005) described poetry as speaking the "language of the heart" (p. 118), and Sloan (2003) noted that poetry helps clients "sift through the layers of their lives in search of their own truths" (p. 35). According to Gorelick (2005), poetry is a form of healing that began with shaman incantations long ago. And although poetry conjures up a negative reaction for some, it is more widely embraced now because it has returned to its lyrical roots.

With clients who are unsure about writing poetry, Woytowich (1994) suggested asking specific questions about the event. As clients tell their story, the counselor writes down what is shared and gives it back to them in the form of verses. Gladding (1995) discussed the idea of prescribing a specific poem related to a client's problem. Reading the poem helps the client understand that she or he is not alone in experiencing this emotion. After reading the poem, the client is encouraged to do her or his own writing for further self-expression. It is critical that the poem be pertinent or relevant to the client's situation, age, and culture.

Poetry can be a form of catharsis and can also provide a liberating, therapeutic effect that increases understanding and contributes to more accurate self-perceptions (Bates, 1993). In addition, poetry enables clients to use words to reconstruct reality; it is "a way of seeing and ultimately, a way of knowing" (Bates, 1993, p. 155).

Poetry can be used to help clients understand themselves and others, improve interpersonal and communication skills, and promote change and coping skills (National Coalition of Creative Arts Therapies Associations, as cited in Gorelick, 2005). Counselors can use it themselves to prevent their own burnout and promote self-renewal (Gladding, 1987). It can also be used as a catalyst for growth and healing in hospitals, nursing homes, prisons, adult education centers, and chemical dependency units (Hynes, 1990). Gladding (1998) described having elderly residents in long-term care facilities read poems aloud as a group and react to the content with their own opinions and emotions, which enhances self-concept and group cohesiveness.

Poetry can be used to facilitate healing for clients dealing with change and loss, substance abuse, and depression. The following poem was written by a 16-year-old girl who struggled with depression. It was often difficult for her to describe how she was feeling, so she accepted the invitation to write about her feelings through poetry, and this poem became the vehicle for discussing her pain.

What Is Happiness?
So many things, so many worries,
In a life where pain isn't a wonder,
Where happiness is unknown.
But I wonder most of all,
Is there such a thing as happiness,
Or is it just a word?
I see it in their eyes, as well as mine,
That anger, that darkness, that emptiness,
That eats you up inside.
But yet no one cares,
Because it is just a part of life,
Or is it?
Is there a better way; another world,
Where everything, everybody is happy,
And pain is unknown?
But what is happiness?
Is it worry, or wonder?
Does anybody know?
Is dying happiness?
I often think so,
No other way; no other world,
Out of this hell where happiness is unknown,
And you cry yourself to sleep every night,
But no one knows; no one is there.
And as I lie here, I wonder,
Am I the only one, or are there more?
And I dream, I dream of a place where I do not exist,
And that to me is happiness.

After a year of counseling, in which she typically described her feelings through her poetry, she began to feel better, as reflected in the following poem:

> *A finalizing day has yet to arrive.*
> *Everyday the same obstacles,*
> *But now we can overcome.*
> *The shadow upon me is slowly drifting away,*
> *To where I can actually see myself, and all that lies around me.*
> *So this will all end*
> *And I will finally get my wish of happiness,*
> *Now and forever.*

Limericks

Limericks, a form of poetry written with precise rhythm (Sloan, 2003), can be a good way to help clients think outside the box and discover their own problem-solving and coping strategies. In writing limericks, the first and second lines rhyme, the third and fourth lines rhyme, and the last line rhymes with the first. An example of a limerick to help young clients handle teasing is as follows:

> *You can throw your sticks and stones*
> *But they will not break my bones.*
> *What you say is not okay*
> *And you are wrong in every way.*
> *So stay away and don't invade my zones. (Vernon & Clemente, 2005, p. 86)*

Bibliotherapy

The term *bibliotherapy* refers to the use of literature as a therapeutic process (Vernon & Clemente, 2005). It is an interactive process designed to help individuals gain control over their lives as they solve problems, learn new skills, practice new behaviors (Jackson, 2001), and better understand themselves through their response to literature or media (Doll & Doll, 1997). Jackson (2000) noted that literature has been used to establish relationships with clients as well as promote insight. According to Pardeck (1998), the goals of bibliotherapy include (a) providing information and insight about problems, (b) communicating new values and attitudes, (c) creating an awareness of how others have dealt with similar problems, (d) stimulating discussion about problems, and (e) providing solutions.

Bibliotherapy has been used to increase academic and emotional development for children with serious emotional disturbances (Bauer & Balius, 1995; Pardeck & Pardeck, 1993), to enhance self-esteem in learning disabled children (Gladding, 1998), to help clients cope with stress and change (Pardeck, 1994), and to assist adolescents in dealing with the transition from childhood to adulthood (Gladding, 2005). Nugent (2000) discussed bibliotherapy as a way of helping clients deal with unfinished business and alleviate depression. Bradley and Gould (1999) described it as a helpful process for clients needing to work through grief, and Pardeck (1998) identified ways in which bibliotherapy increased socialization and self-actualization.

According to Gladding (1998), bibliotherapy can be practiced with disturbed clients, with clients who have moderate emotional and behavioral problems, and with a normal population to enhance development. Borders and Paisley (1992) discussed the developmental approach and stressed the importance of using bibliotherapy in classroom guidance sessions with children.

Bibliotherapy is especially effective for clients who process things visually as opposed to auditorily. I recall working with a couple experiencing relationship difficulties. I was attempting to stop the cycle of blame and increase this couple's understanding of their communication differences and ways of perceiving the world. Because verbal efforts had not been successful, I suggested they read a book as a homework assignment. When the couple arrived for the next session, they were eager to share their insights. The information they had learned provided them with new perspectives and information they needed to move to the next level of problem solving regarding their relationship issues.

In addition to literature in print, such as fiction, nonfiction, poetry, self-help books, and fairy tales, Caron (2005) described benefits of using movies as a bibliotherapy tool. This approach is particularly effective with adolescents who spend a great deal of time watching movies but who may not pick up a book. Movies that depict events or emotions like the client's can facilitate insight and emotional catharsis in addition to identifying coping strategies. Higgens and Dermer (2001) discussed having clients watch a movie as a homework assignment to gain insights they might not glean in face-to-face counseling sessions. Alternately, the counselor and client can view a movie together, stopping in key places to discuss insights and feelings (Patrick, 2007).

The Process

Gladding (2005) noted that the bibliotherapy process is a triadic connection among the piece of literature, the client, and the facilitator who helps the client process an insight and apply it to his or her own life. There are four stages to the bibliotherapy process, according to Kelsch and Emry (2003, as cited in Gladding, 2005): identification with the characters, situation, and setting; catharsis, which involves becoming emotionally connected with the characters; insight, which evolves from the emotional identification and catharsis and enables the client to apply concepts from the literature to his or her own life; and universality, in which clients are more empathic and sensitive, moving beyond their immediate situations.

Before bibliotherapy is used, a relationship built on trust and rapport is necessary. Also, the client and the counselor should agree on the presenting problem and complete some preliminary problem exploration (Pardeck & Pardeck, 1993). It is also important to consider the presenting problem in selecting books for treatment and to select books that contain believable characters, situations that are relevant to the client's situation, and an outlook that offers realistic hope. The selections should be developmentally appropriate (Wagner, 2003) and reflect the client's culture, gender, and age. Pardeck (1994) noted that it is often more effective to suggest rather than prescribe books. This author also emphasized that discussion, counseling, and follow-up activities are an essential part of the bibliotherapy process.

Play

"Play therapy is an approach to counseling young children in which the counselor uses toys and play as the primary vehicle for communication" (Kottman, 2004, p. 111). Homeyer and DeFrance (2005) noted that through play, children learn about their experiences and communicate them. Consequently, play is an ideal modality to help children know and accept themselves, as well as work out problems and communicate with others. Generally used with children age 3–10, play provides a way for children to express their experiences and feelings through a natural, self-healing process (Landreth, 1993). Through play, children are able to act out confusing or conflicting situations, make choices (Thompson, Rudolph, & Henderson, 2004), learn and practice problem-solving and relationship-building skills (Kottman, 2004), master their fears (Kottman, 2001), explore alternative perceptions of problems and difficult relationships (Kottman, 2004), and learn to communicate more effectively (Brems, 2002). According to Brems, "play is perhaps one of the most common techniques utilized by child therapists" (p. 248).

Play Therapy Approaches

Kottman (2004) described four approaches to play therapy: child-centered, Adlerian, cognitive-behavioral, and Theraplay. Child-centered play therapy, which Homeyer and DeFrance (2005) noted is very nondirective, is based on the philosophy that children have an innate capacity for growth and maturity and that they are capable of being constructively self-directing. In this form of play therapy, the therapist builds a warm, genuine relationship with the child to facilitate a strong therapeutic bond. The therapist is totally accepting of the child and respects the child's ability to solve problems. Although the therapist maintains an active role, he or she does not manage or direct the experience. Rather, the child-centered play therapist believes that by communicating acceptance and belief in the child, the child will tap into his or her innate capacity for solving problems.

In Adlerian play therapy, the play therapist utilizes the principles and strategies of individual psychology along with the skills and concepts of play therapy. The Adlerian play therapist develops an egalitarian relationship with the client and then uses play to gain an understanding of the child's lifestyle and how the child conceptualizes his or her world. Next, the therapist helps the child gain insight into his or her lifestyle by using stories, artwork, metaphors, and metacommunication. Finally, the therapist provides reorientation and reeducation for the client, which can involve learning and practicing new skills.

Cognitive-behavioral play therapy combines play therapy approaches with cognitive and behavioral strategies. The cognitive-behavioral play therapist involves the child in the therapeutic process through play and examines the thoughts, feelings, and environment of the child. Next, the therapist helps the child develop more adaptive thoughts and behaviors, along with more effective problem-solving strategies. This form of play therapy is problem-focused, structured, and directive. Specific behavioral and cognitive interventions that have been proven to be successful for particular problems are employed.

Theraplay is directive, intensive, and brief. This type of play therapy is a treatment method that is modeled on the healthy interaction between parents and their children. It actively involves parents as observers and later as cotherapists. Play therapists use activities and materials that facilitate structure, challenge, intrude and engage, and nurture to remedy children's problems. The therapist is in charge of the session, and the sessions are predictable and structured.

Uses of Play

Play can be used in several ways to meet the developmental needs of all children. Orton (1997) identified the following uses of play:

1. To aid in the assessment process. The counselor notes the child's interactions, inhibitions, preoccupations, perceptions, and expressions of feelings and ideas.
2. To establish a working relationship. For children who may be fearful, nonverbal, or resistant, play can establish an accepting relationship, as in the case of Ryan.

Ryan, age 6, was referred for inability to relate effectively to others. In the initial interview, he sat as far away from the counselor as possible and only shook his head in response to questions. Instead of continuing to talk, the counselor got out a can of shaving cream and squirted some onto a large tray. Then she started playing with it, shaping it into different forms. Ryan watched for a few minutes and then hesitantly approached the table and began to play. The counselor added more shaving cream and some food coloring. Ryan's eyes widened, and he began making pictures out of the cream and chatting about what he was creating. By initiating the play that stimulated Ryan to interact, the counselor was able to establish a working relationship.

3. To help children express their concerns. Frequently, children will not or are not able to verbalize feelings about events. Play can facilitate verbalization, as well as provide a means of dealing with the issue. In the following situation, the counselor used a dart game to elicit angry feelings.

Dan was a behaviorally disordered third-grader who was hostile and aggressive with other children and adults. After Dan's angry confrontation with the principal, she and the teacher requested the counselor to work with Dan. Knowing that he would be defensive, the counselor set up a dartboard equipped with rubber-tipped darts. When Dan entered the office, the counselor simply invited him to play darts. After several minutes of play, the counselor commented to Dan that he was really throwing the darts as if he were angry. Dan didn't comment and simply continued to play. After a while he stopped and sat down. The counselor asked if there was anything he'd like to talk about, and Dan began to share situations in which other kids picked on him, he'd call them names, and then he got in trouble for name-calling. After discussing this for a while, the counselor asked Dan if he'd like to come back again to talk more about his anger and what he could do about it. He agreed to come but expressed a desire to play darts again. Using the dartboard initiated verbalization and let Dan express his hostile, angry feelings.

4. To promote healing and growth.

For example, 6-year-old Amelia was the youngest in her family. The teacher reported that several children had complained that every time Amelia played a game, she had to win. If she wasn't winning, she changed the rules. The counselor invited Amelia to play a board game, and when she tried to change the rules, the counselor commented on this. They discussed Amelia's need to win and what it said about her if she didn't win. After several sessions of this nature, the counselor invited several of Amelia's friends in to play. Amelia played the game without changing the rules. This experience seemed to successfully teach her alternative behaviors to help her interact more appropriately.

Regardless of how play is used, the therapeutic relationship is extremely important. Showing interest in what the child chooses to do and being patient and understanding are crucial.

Selection of Materials

Landreth (1993) discussed the importance of selecting play materials that facilitate (a) exploration of real-life experiences, (b) expression of a wide range of feelings, (c) testing of limits, (d) expressive and exploratory play, (e) exploration and expression without verbalization, and (f) success without prescribed structure. Landreth warned against mechanical or complex toys or materials that required the counselor's assistance to manipulate. Kottman (2003) suggested that toys should represent five different categories: family/nurturing toys, scary toys, aggressive toys, expressive toys, and pretend/fantasy toys. Kottman (2003, 2004) listed specific examples of toys to facilitate exploration of family/nurturing, including dolls of different ethnicities, dollhouses and furniture, play dishes, and soft blankets. Scary toys, which help children express their fears and how to cope with them, include rubber snakes, monsters, insects, and fierce animal puppets. Dart guns, play swords and knives, toy soldiers, and a pounding board or bop bag were identified as toys that allow children to express anger and aggression. Crayons, clay, paints, pipe cleaners, chalk, and newsprint were cited as examples of materials to facilitate creative expression. Pretend/fantasy toys that help children express their feelings and explore roles and behaviors include masks, costumes, hats, jewelry, telephones, magic wands, and people figures.

Toys selected should be in good condition. It is also important not to have so many toys that the room is cluttered and junky. The specific use of the toys depends on whether the approach is structured, in which the counselor selects the toys to fit the child's problem, or nondirective, in which the child has more freedom to choose materials.

Games

Board games provide another way to establish rapport, facilitate verbalization, release feelings, and teach new behaviors (Vernon, 2002). Bradley et al. (2004) noted that games are familiar and nonthreatening and have diagnostic value. Schaefer and Reid (2000) cited their usefulness in addressing specific topics in counseling. Games allow clients to gain a sense of mastery and receive positive feedback. For preadolescents and adolescents in particular, board games can make counseling more enjoyable and thus more productive.

Games such as checkers or chess generally work well in establishing rapport, as do other commercial board games. Once rapport has been established, the counselor may want to develop or select games that specifically address the concerns with which the child is working. The case of Stephanie illustrates this point.

Stephanie, a fourth-grader, was frequently upset because she made assumptions about what her peers were thinking and, therefore, assumed that they didn't like her, were upset with her, or didn't ever want to be her friend. To help her recognize how she upset herself by mistaking what she thought for factual information, the counselor engaged Stephanie in a game called "Fights with Friends" (Vernon, 2002, pp. 225–227). They took turns drawing assumption cards and coping strategies cards, identifying whether the child in the situation was thinking rationally (not making assumptions) and was demonstrating effective behavioral coping strategies. If not, Stephanie or the counselor had to identify what the assumptions or ineffective coping strategies were and discuss how to change them before putting an X (client) or O (counselor) on the game board (like tic-tac-toe).

After the game, the counselor asked Stephanie to identify the difference between a fact and an assumption and how making assumptions negatively affected her relationships with her friends. She then invited her client to make a set of new assumptions and coping strategies cards that pertained specifically to her situation. They were able to discuss Stephanie's tendency to mistake a fact ("My friend didn't sit by me in the lunchroom") from an assumption ("Because she didn't sit by me, there must be something wrong with me and she must not like me anymore"). The game was a concrete way of helping this fourth-grader work through her problem.

The value of play therapy is undisputed; research supports its use with a wide range of presenting problems (LeBlanc & Richie, 1999). Because the actual process of play therapy is complex and needs more explanation than this brief overview, the reader is encouraged to read *Play Therapy: Basics and Beyond* (Kottman, 2001) or *The Play Therapy Primer* (O'Connor, 2000).

More Creative Approaches

The number of creative approaches that can be used in a counseling session is endless. The only limiting factors are the counselor's own creative abilities to develop effective methods of helping the client resolve issues. I have found the following approaches helpful in the process of working with clients.

Props

Using props during a session can stimulate thinking or elicit emotion about a problem. Props are a way, other than words, to reach the client. For example, a woman who was constantly pessimistic was given a set of old eyeglasses and four round circles of paper: two gray and two pink. She was instructed to tape the gray paper on the glasses and talk about her day from a "doom and gloom" perspective. Next she was asked to substitute the pink paper and describe her day as if she were looking through "rose-colored glasses." She and the counselor then discussed the difference in the two perspectives and set some goals for developing a more optimistic perception of events.

In working with a young adult on her tendency to procrastinate, the counselor brought a pile of newspapers to the session. She invited her client to make a list of all the things she procrastinated about. Next, she asked her to lie on the floor, and one by one, she read off the list of things about which the client procrastinated. As she read each one, she piled a bunch of newspapers on the client until the pile was quite high after all of the items on the list had been read. Next, they talked about how she felt with everything "all piled up," applying it to her personal experiences with procrastination. She then identified what she could do or say relative to each item on the list to resolve the procrastination problems, and as she did so, the counselor lifted newspapers from the pile. This was a very graphic way to help this client remember that it is better not to let things pile up by procrastinating one (Vernon, 2002).

With another young client, a tape recorder helped him become less dependent on the counselor and more skilled at solving his own problems. Adam had lots of worries, such as what he should do if someone teased him, what he should do if his mother wasn't home after school, and what he should do if he didn't understand how to do his schoolwork.

Because Adam's father was concerned that Adam might be "inventing" some problems because he really liked coming to counseling, the counselor decided to teach Adam how to be his own counselor. When he arrived for his session, she asked Adam what was bothering him that week. He shared a situation about his friend teasing him, and the counselor helped Adam develop some tease tolerance techniques. Adam was to ask himself if he was what his friend said he was, if names could hurt him, and how he could handle the situation if he couldn't control what came out of the other person's mouth. Next the counselor said that she would pretend to be Adam and that Adam could be the counselor. As the counselor, Adam was asked to solve a problem similar to his real one. After role-playing this, Adam was given a tape recorder and a blank tape. During the week, whenever he had a problem, he could use the tape recorder and first be the person who has the problem and then switch roles and pretend to be the counselor who helps him solve the problem. When Adam returned for his next session, he played the tape for the counselor. He had recorded several problems and had done a good job of helping himself deal with his problems.

Props were useful in a marriage counseling session when a rope helped a couple see the "tug of war" state of their marriage and understand how they each felt controlled. Each person held one end of the rope, pulled on it, and verbalized one of the ways she or he felt controlled by the partner. The counselor wrote down each of the statements so the couple could see what both said. This simple activity was a good stimulus for mobilizing some energy and illuminating some of the issues that needed to be solved.

Homework Suggestions

To facilitate self-reliance, homework assignments can effectively extend the concepts dealt with during the counseling session. The following ideas can be adapted and expanded on, depending on the client's age:

1. Have clients make a "mad pillow" that they decorate with pictures of things or people with whom they feel angry. When they experience anger, they can pound the pillow rather than act aggressively toward another person.
2. Suggest that when clients worry excessively about minor, as opposed to major, problems, they can buy a bubble pipe. As they use it, they can visualize the minor problems "blowing away."
3. Invite clients who are dealing with a lot of anger to write down on separate pieces of paper situations in which they have been angry. They should then collect as many rocks as they have slips of paper and take them to a river or open field. As they throw a rock away with force, they can yell out the name of the anger-provoking situation.
4. If clients have difficulty accomplishing tasks because they're overwhelmed with the amount of work to be done, invite them to buy a timer and set it for a given amount of time to work and a given amount of time to relax. They can also incorporate their own punishment and reward system, rewarding themselves with something they like to do after tasks have been accomplished and doing something they hate to do when they fail to complete a task.
5. Recommend that clients make books of written text and/or illustrations to express their perceptions about a problem and their methods of solving it.
6. For clients who think the "grass is greener on the other side of the fence" (e.g., spouses who think they would be better off single, adolescents who think they would be better off living with their friends' parents), have them interview people to find out more what it is "really like" on the other side.

Group Applications

The creative individual counseling approaches previously described can usually be applied in a group context. Each of the approaches is discussed with a brief explanation of group applicability.

Art

Malchiodi (2005) described how group art therapy is used to enhance communication and interaction in hospitals, community agencies, and outpatient clinics. She noted that this approach has "curative potential" for group members (p. 39).

In a group setting, art can facilitate group cohesiveness. Participants can make a collage to represent their group by using finger paint and scraps of fabric and paper. In a self-awareness group, members can tear a shape out of construction paper that tells something about themselves as a way to introduce themselves to the group. To teach cooperation, group participants can be given paper, tape, magazines, and instructions to design an object of beauty. Roles that members play in developing this project could then be discussed. In a group setting, members might take turns drawing symbols they feel represent other group members as a way to provide feedback on how they come across to others.

Imagery

Guided imagery can be readily applied to a group setting. In a classroom or small group, students could be led in guided imagery relative to test taking, task completion, stress management, or cooperative behavior with classmates. Guided imagery has also been used extensively in career development (Gladding, 1998). Heppner, O'Brien, Hindelman, and Humphrey (1994) described using guided imagery in life planning to spur their clients' imagination. Jacobs (1992) used projective fantasies in a group setting where participants were encouraged to imagine themselves as a common object and to describe what their lives would be like if they were this object. As a result of this activity, they were able to see their lives differently.

Music

Musical activities facilitate self-awareness and interpersonal relationships. In a classroom setting, students can compose and perform their own compositions related to guidance topics: feelings, self-concept, decision making, friendship, or values. Newcomb (1994) noted that music can be used in classroom guidance as an energizer, to set the mood, to develop group cohesiveness, or as a way of emphasizing the theme of a lesson.

Bowman (1987) described the "feelings ensemble." A group is divided into smaller groups of five or six, and each group is given a feeling word that becomes the title of their composition. They are instructed to make up and perform a song in front of the large group that describes their feeling word. They may use sound makers such as pencils or rulers, or the counselor can provide them with whistles, horns, harmonicas, or kazoos. After several minutes of planning, each group performs while other members attempt to guess what feeling they are expressing.

Music is also a good way to build group identity and cohesiveness. Group members can compose a song or select a recording that expresses who they are. An alternative activity is the musical collage. Each individual group member selects short segments of songs that have meaning and tapes each of these segments to create a collage. After listening to each person's collage, group members discuss how the music represents that individual (Bowman, 1987).

Writing

Various forms of writing can be adapted for group use. Open-ended sentences can become a get-acquainted activity or prompt discussion and sharing. Questionnaires are also used this way, or they can be adapted to the specific focus of the group. For example, members of a stress management group might be given a questionnaire about ways they deal with stress. As responses are shared, members benefit from hearing others' ideas.

In a classroom setting, students can be given journal topics related to self-awareness, clarification of values, or feelings about various issues. Examples of topics include:

> "Something I like best about myself is . . ."
> "Something I feel strongly about is . . ."
> "Something I'm good at doing is . . ."
> "Something I value highly is . . ."

Topics of this nature encourage self-exploration. Journal writing can be further shared in student dyads or triads to clarify responses. In such a situation, participants must feel comfortable with the sharing and have the option to pass if they wish.

Bibliotherapy

Borders and Paisley (1992) suggested that bibliotherapy be used not only in problem-centered interventions in individual or small-group counseling but also with children in classroom guidance to promote developmental growth. Their research indicated that the use of stories is an effective approach to help children solve problems and enhance personal growth.

Gladding (2005) noted that poetry and other literary works are frequently used in group settings as a therapeutic tool, especially in psychiatric and self-help groups. Poetry and other forms of literature may also be used to open and close groups, according to Gladding.

Play

For younger children, particularly in a school setting, play can be highly effective in a small group of four or five children to improve socialization skills. One or two children in the group are selected as good models; the targeted individuals may need to develop cooperative versus competitive behavior, learn to control aggression, become more comfortable with group interaction, or learn to share.

In the group setting, the play is generally more structured, and the toys used are selected to help children work on the desirable behaviors. For instance, if two of the children in the group have difficulty sharing, the counselor may have only one can of blocks for all group members to use. As the children play with the blocks, the counselor reflects on the interaction and involves the children in discussing how it feels when friends share or don't share, thus seeking to develop behaviors that will transfer to other situations.

Board games can also be developed for group use. A game called "Road to Achievement" (Vernon, 2002, p. 202) helps children identify effective study skills. "Feelings-Go-Round" (Vernon, 2006, p. 127) is a game like musical chairs; children identify ways to handle negative feelings.

Bradley et al. (2004) described the multicultural circle, which is an effective game for a group setting. Students stand in a circle, and as the facilitator calls out various topics, such as "is a Native American," "was born in another country," "speaks Spanish," or "attends the synagogue," students enter the center of the circle if that topic applies to them. This activity builds multicultural awareness and fosters communication about culture and religion.

Conclusion

Using the expressive arts in counseling offers a creative alternative to the traditional verbal approaches. These approaches are particularly beneficial for younger clients and those whose learning style may be more auditory or kinesthetic. Most important, culturally competent counselors will find these approaches to be more effective with clients whose diverse background necessitates something other than the traditional verbal counseling styles. Furthermore, the culturally sensitive counselor recognizes that for many clients, not just those from diverse cultures, using music, art, literature, or play, either as an adjunct or an alternative to traditional approaches, may be the most meaningful and effective way to engage clients of all ages.

The expressive arts approaches are not limited to the descriptions in this chapter. Movement, dance, drama, humor, and puppetry are other approaches that can meet client needs. No "universal" format exists for application; the creativity of the counselor and an assessment of what would most effectively engage the client guide the implementation. The training needed to use these specialized approaches depends on whether they are used to supplement a verbal approach or constitute the major aspect of the counseling. As Nickerson and O'Laughlin (1982) noted, the issue is perhaps one of degree. In other words, a counselor does not have to be an artist to use some art with clients who are not able to express themselves verbally, but if art were the primary modality, further training would be needed.

Creative approaches have been used successfully with children and adolescents (Bradley et al., 2004; Bush, 1997; Gladding, 1998, 2005; Vernon & Clemente, 2005), the borderline client (Silverman, 1991), the elderly (Gladding, 2005), Alzheimer's patients (Forinash, 2005), clients with eating disorders (Brown, 1991; Sapp, 2000), and children from violent homes (Malchiodi, 1997). They can be used to treat specific problems or can be applied preventively, particularly in school settings.

The diversity of creative counseling approaches can effectively address a wide range of client needs. These methods move counseling beyond the mental arena, which relies on verbal techniques, to a more comprehensive orientation using a multitude of approaches.

Summary

Although counseling has traditionally been characterized by a verbal orientation, practitioners are now encouraged to explore other methods to help people cope with psychological problems. In this chapter, a variety of creative approaches to counseling were described. These approaches have been found to be effective for problems presented by both children and adults.

As discussed in this chapter, creative approaches to counseling can be adapted to fit the client's learning style. Art, imagery, and writing were identified as appropriate strategies for clients of all ages. Specific ways to use music, bibliotherapy, and play were also described. Implementing approaches of this nature can enhance the counseling process because they combine theory and practice in flexible ways to focus on the unique aspects of the client and the problem.

The following Web sites provide additional information relating to chapter topics.

USEFUL WEB SITES

An online community for creative arts therapists
http://www.artsintherapy.com

Phototherapy techniques in counseling
http://www.phototherapy-centre.com

American Music Therapy Association
http://www.musictherapy.org

National Association for Drama Therapy
http://www.nadt.org

Changing Images Art Foundation
http://www.changingimages.org

REFERENCES

Allan, J. (1982). Social drawing: A therapeutic approach with young children. In E. T. Nickerson & K. O'Laughlin (Eds.), *Helping through action: Action-oriented therapies* (pp. 25–32). Amherst, MA: Human Resource Development Press.

Amerikaner, M., Schauble, P., & Ziller, R. (1982). Images: The use of photographs in personal counseling. In E. T. Nickerson & K. O'Laughlin (Eds.), *Helping through action: Action-oriented therapies* (pp. 33–41). Amherst, MA: Human Resource Development Press.

Bates, M. (1993). Poetic responses to art: Summoning the adolescent voice. *Journal of Poetry Therapy, 3,* 149–156.

Bauer, M. S., & Balius, F. A. (1995). Storytelling: Integrating therapy and curriculum for students with serious emotional disturbances. *Teaching Exceptional Children, 27,* 24–29.

Borders, S., & Paisley, P. O. (1992). Children's literature as a source for classroom guidance. *Elementary School Guidance and Counseling, 27,* 131–139.

Bourne, E. J. (1995). *The anxiety and phobia workbook.* Oakland, CA: New Harbinger Publications.

Bowman, R. P. (1987). Approaches for counseling children through music. *Elementary School Guidance and Counseling, 21,* 284–291.

Bradley, L. J., & Gould, L. J. (1999). Individual counseling: Creative interventions. In A. Vernon (Ed.), *Counseling children and adolescents* (2nd ed., pp. 66–95). Denver: Love Publishing.

Bradley, L. J., Gould, L. J., & Hendricks, P. B. (2004). Using innovative techniques for counseling children and adolescents. In A. Vernon (Ed.), *Counseling children and adolescents* (3rd ed., pp. 75–110). Denver, CO: Love Publishing.

Brems, C. (2002). *A comprehensive guide to child psychotherapy* (2nd ed.). Boston: Allyn & Bacon.

Brown, M. H. (1991). Innovations in the treatment of bulimia: Transpersonal psychology, relaxation, imagination, hypnosis, myth, and ritual. *Journal of Humanistic Education and Development, 30,* 50–60.

Bush, J. (1997). *The handbook of school art therapy.* Springfield, IL: Charles C. Thomas.

Caron, J. C. (2005). DSM at the movies: Use of media in clinical or educational settings. In G. R. Walz & R. K. Yep (Eds.), *VISTAS: Compelling perspectives on counseling 2005* (pp. 179–182). Alexandria, VA: American Counseling Association.

Clarkson, G. (1994). Creative music therapy and facilitated communication: New ways of reaching students with autism. *Preventing School Failure, 38,* 31–33.

Conley, D. (1994). *If you believe in you.* Treehouse Publishing.

Cupal, D. D., & Brewer, B. W. (2001). Effects of relaxation and guided imagery on knee strength, reinjury anxiety, and pain following anterior cruciate ligament reconstruction. *Rehabilitation Psychology, 46,* 28–43.

Davis, W. B., Gfeller, K. E., & Thaut, M. H. (1999). *An introduction to music therapy: Theory and practice* (2nd ed.). Boston: McGraw-Hill.

DeLucia-Waack, J. L. (2001). *Using music in children of divorce groups: A session-by-session manual for counselors.* Alexandria, VA: American Counseling Association.

Doll, B., & Doll, C. (1997). *Bibliotherapy with young people.* Englewood, CA: Libraries Unlimited.

Dunn, R., & Griggs, S. A. (1995). *Multiculturalism and learning style.* Westport, CT: Praeger.

Forinash, M. (2005). Music therapy. In C. A. Malchiodi (Ed.), *Expressive therapies* (pp. 46–67). New York: Guilford Press.

Gladding, S. T. (1987). The poetics of a "check out" place: Preventing burnout and promoting self-renewal. *Journal of Poetry Therapy, 1,* 95–102.

Gladding, S. T. (1995). Creativity in counseling. *Counseling and Human Development, 28*(1), 1–12.

Gladding, S. T. (1998). *Counseling as an art: The creative arts in counseling* (2nd ed.). Alexandria, VA: American Counseling Association.

Gladding, S. T. (2005). *Counseling as an art: The creative arts in counseling* (3rd ed.). Alexandria, VA: American Counseling Association.

Gorelick, K. (2005). Poetry therapy. In C. A. Malchiodi (Ed.), *Expressive therapies* (pp. 117–140). New York: Guilford Press.

Griggs, S. A. (1983). Counseling high school students for their individual learning styles. *Clearing House, 56,* 293–296.

Griggs, S. A. (1985). Counseling for individual learning styles. *Journal of Counseling and Development, 64,* 202–205.

Griggs, S. A., Price, G. E., Kopel, S., & Swaine, W. (1984). The effects of group counseling on sixth-grade students with different learning styles. *California Journal of Counseling and Development, 5,* 28–35.

Guzzetta, C. E. (1991). A method for conducting improvised musical play with children both with and without developmental delays in preschool classrooms. *Music Therapy Perspectives, 9,* 46–51.

Havens, R. A., & Walters, C. (2002). *Hypnotherapy scripts* (2nd ed.). New York: Brunner-Routledge.

Hendricks, P. B. (2000). A study of the use of music therapy techniques in a group for the treatment of adolescent depression. *Dissertation Abstracts International, 62,* 107.

Heppner, M. J., O'Brien, K. M., Hindelman, J. M., & Humphrey, C. A. (1994). Shifting the paradigm: The use of creativity in career counseling. *Journal of Career Development, 21,* 77–86.

Higgens, J. A., & Dermer, S. (2001). The use of film in marriage and family counselor education. *Counselor Education and Supervision, 40,* 182–192.

Homeyer, L. E., & DeFrance, E. (2005). Play therapy. In C. A. Malchiodi (Ed.), *Expressive therapies* (pp. 141–161). New York: Guilford Press.

Horden, P. (2000). *Music as medicine: The history of music therapy since antiquity.* Aldershot, UK: Ashgate.

Hutchins, D. E., & Cole, C. G. (1992). *Helping relationships and strategies.* Pacific Grove, CA: Brooks/Cole.

Hynes, A. (1990). Poetry: An avenue into the spirit. *Journal of Poetry Therapy, 4,* 71–81.

Jackson, T. (2000). *Still more activities that teach.* Salt Lake City, UT: Red Rock Publishing.

Jackson, T. (2001). Using bibliotherapy with clients. *Journal of Individual Psychology, 57*, 289–297.

Jacobs, E. (1992). *Creative counseling techniques: An illustrated guide*. Odess, FL: Psychological Assessment Resources.

Jennings, S., & Minde, A. (1993). *Art therapy and dramatherapy: Masks of the soul*. Philadelphia: Jessica Kingsley Publishers.

Kenny, A. (1987). An art activities approach: Counseling the gifted, creative and talented. *Gifted Child Today, 10*, 33–37.

Kohen, D. P. (1997). Teaching children with asthma to help themselves with relaxation/mental imagery. In W. J. Mathews & J. H. Edgette (Eds.), *Current thinking and research in brief therapy: Solutions, strategies, narratives* (Vol. 1, pp. 169–191). New York: Brunner/Mazel.

Kottler, J. A. (2004). *Introduction to therapeutic counseling: Voices from the field*. Pacific Grove, CA: Brooks/Cole.

Kottman, T. (2001). *Play therapy: Basics and beyond*. Alexandria, VA: American Counseling Association.

Kottman, T. (2003). *Partners in play: An Adlerian approach to play therapy*. Alexandria, VA: American Counseling Association.

Kottman, T. (2004). Play therapy. In A. Vernon (Ed.), *Counseling children and adolescents* (3rd ed., pp. 111–136). Denver, CO: Love Publishing.

Kramer, E. (1998). *Childhood and art therapy* (2nd ed.). Chicago: Magnolia Street.

Kwiatowska, H. (2001). Family art therapy: Experiments with new techniques. *American Journal of Art Therapy, 40*, 27–39.

LaBaw, J. L., & LaBaw, W. L. (1990). Self-hypnosis and hypnotherapy with children. In R. P. Zahourek (Ed.), *Clinical hypnosis and therapeutic suggestion in patient care* (pp. 127–153). New York: Brunnel/Mazel.

Landgarten, H. B., & Lubbers, D. (1991). *Adult art psychotherapy: Issues and applications*. New York: Brunner/Mazel.

Landreth, G. L. (1993). Child-centered play therapy. *Elementary School Guidance and Counseling Journal, 28*, 17–29.

LeBlanc, M., & Richie, M. (1999). Predictors of play therapy outcomes. *International Journal of Play Therapy, 8*(2), 19–34.

Lev-Wiesel, R., & Daphna-Tekoha, S. (2000). The self-revelation through color technique: Understanding clients' relationships with significant others through the use of color. *American Journal of Art Therapy, 39*, 35–41.

Malchiodi, C. A. (1997). *Breaking the silence: Art therapy with children from violent homes* (2nd ed.). Bristol, PA: Brunner/Mazel.

Malchiodi, C. A. (2003). *Handbook of art therapy*. New York: Guilford Press.

Malchiodi, C. A. (Ed.). (2005). *Expressive therapies*. New York: Guilford Press.

Maranto, C. D. (1993). Music therapy and stress management. In P. M. Lehrer & R. L. Woolfolk (Eds.), *Principles and practice of stress management* (2nd ed., pp. 407–422). New York: Guilford Press.

Mercer, L. E. (1993). Self-healing through poetry writing. *Journal of Poetry Therapy, 6*, 161–168.

Morrison, N. C., & Rasp, R. R. (2001). The application of facilitated imagery to marital counseling. In B. J. Brothers (Ed.), *Couples, intimacy issues, and addiction* (pp. 131–151). New York: Haworth Press.

Myrick, R. D. (1997). *Developmental guidance and counseling: A practical approach*. Minneapolis, MN: Educational Media.

Myrick, R. D., & Myrick, L. S. (1993). Guided imagery: From mystical to practical. *Elementary School Guidance and Counseling, 28*, 62–70.

Newcomb, N. S. (1994). Music: A powerful resource for the elementary school counselor. *Elementary School Guidance and Counseling, 29*, 150–155.

Nickerson, E. T., & O'Laughlin, K. (Eds.). (1982). *Helping through action: Action-oriented therapies*. Amherst, MA: Human Resource Development Press.

Nugent, S. A. (2000). Perfectionism: Its manifestations and classroom based interventions. *Journal of Secondary Gifted Education, 11*, 215–221.

O'Connor, K. (2000). *The play therapy primer* (2nd ed.). New York: Wiley.

Ohanian, V. (2002). Imagery rescripting within cognitive behavior therapy for bulimia nervosa: An illustrative case report. *International Journal of Eating Disorders, 31,* 352–357.

Olness, K., & Kohen, D. (1996). *Hypnosis and hypnotherapy with children.* New York: Guilford Press.

Omizo, M. M., Omizo, S. A., & Kitaoka, S. K. (1998). Guided affective and cognitive imagery to enhance self-esteem among Hawaiian children. *Journal of Multicultural Counseling and Development, 26,* 52–62.

Orton, G. L. (1997). *Strategies for counseling with children and their parents.* Pacific Grove, CA: Brooks/Cole.

Ostertag, J. (2002). Unspoken stories: Music therapy with abused children. *Canadian Journal of Music Therapy, 9,* 10–29.

Pardeck, J. T. (1994). Using literature to help adolescents cope with problems. *Adolescence, 29,* 421–427.

Pardeck, J. T. (1998). *Using books in clinical social work practice: A guide to bibliotherapy.* New York: Haworth Press.

Pardeck, J. T., & Pardeck, J. A. (1993). *Bibliotherapy: A clinical approach for helping children.* New York: Gordon and Breach.

Patrick, P. K. S. (2007). *Contemporary issues in counseling.* Boston: Pearson.

Pearson, Q. M. (2003). Polished rocks: A culminating guided imagery for counselor interns. *Journal of Humanistic Counseling, Education, and Development, 42,* 116–120.

Peters, J. S. (2000). *Music therapy: An introduction* (2nd ed.). Springfield, IL: Charles C. Thomas.

Plummer, D. (1999). *Using interactive imagework with children: Walking on the magic mountain.* Philadelphia: J. Kingsley.

Rio, R. (2002). Improvisation with the elderly: Moving from creative activities to process-oriented therapy. *Arts in Psychotherapy, 29,* 191–201.

Riordan, R. J., & Ketchum, S. B. (1996). Therapeutic correspondence: The usefulness of notes and letters in counseling. *Georgia Journal of Professional Counseling,* 31–40.

Rubin, J. A. (1988). Art counseling: An alternative. *Elementary School Guidance and Counseling, 22,* 180–185.

Rubin, J. A. (1998). *Art therapy: An introduction.* Philadelphia: Taylor & Francis.

Sapp, M. (2000). *Hypnosis, dissociation, and absorption: Theories, assessment, and treatment.* Springfield, IL: Charles C. Thomas.

Schaefer, C. E., & Reid, S. E. (2000). *Game play: Therapeutic use of childhood games.* New York: Wiley.

Silver, R. (2001). *Art as language.* Lillington, NC: Edwards Brothers.

Silverman, D. (1991). Art psychotherapy: An approach to borderline adults. In H. B. Langarten & D. Lubbers (Eds.), *Adult art psychotherapy.* New York: Brunner/Mazel.

Skovholt, T. M., Morgan, J. I., & Negron-Cunningham, H. (1989). Mental imagery in career counseling and life planning: A review of research and intervention methods. *Journal of Counseling and Development, 67,* 287–292.

Sloan, G. (2003). *Give them poetry!* New York: Teachers College Press.

Smucker, M. R., & Dancu, C. V. (1999). *Cognitive-behavioral treatment for adult survivors of childhood trauma: Imagery rescripting and reprocessing.* Northvale, NJ: Jason Aronson.

Thaut, M. H. (1990). Neuropsychological processes in music relevance in music therapy. In R. F. Unkefer (Ed.), *Music therapy in treatment of adults with mental disorders: Theoretical bases and clinical interventions* (pp. 3–32). New York: Macmillan.

Thompson, C., Rudolph, L., & Henderson, D. (2004). *Counseling children.* Belmont, CA: Brooks/Cole.

Vernon, A. (2002). *What works when with children and adolescents: A handbook of individual counseling techniques.* Champaign, IL: Research Press.

Vernon, A. (2006). *Thinking, feeling, behaving: An emotional education curriculum for children (Grades 1–6).* Champaign, IL: Research Press.

Vernon, A., & Clemente, R. (2005). *Assessment and intervention with children and adolescents: Developmental and multicultural approaches.* Alexandria, VA: American Counseling Association.

Vick, R. M. (2003). A brief history of art therapy. In C. A. Malchiodi (Ed.), *Handbook of art therapy* (pp. 5–15). New York: Guilford Press.

Vondracek, F. W., & Corneal, S. (1995). *Strategies for resolving individual and family problems.* Pacific Grove, CA: Brooks/Cole.

Wagner, W. G. (2003). *Counseling, psychology, and children.* Upper Saddle River, NJ: Merrill-Prentice Hall.

Weitzenhoffer, A. M. (1989). *The practice of hypnotism, Vol. 2: Applications of traditional and semitraditional hypnotism-nontraditional hypnotism.* New York: Wiley.

Welfel, E. R., & Patterson, L. E. (2005). *The counseling process: A multitheoretical integrative approach.* Belmont, CA: Thompson Brooks/Cole.

White, V. E., & Murray, M. A. (2002). Passing notes: The use of therapeutic letter writing in counseling adolescents. *Journal of Mental Health Counseling, 24*(2), 166.

Wigram, T., Pedersen, I. N., & Bonde, L. O. (2002). *A comprehensive guide to music therapy: Theory, clinical practice, research and training.* London: Jessica Kingsley.

Winsor, R. M. (1993). Hypnosis: A neglected tool for client empowerment. *Social Work, 38,* 603–608.

Witmer, J. M., & Young, M. E. (1987). Imagery in counseling. *Elementary School Guidance and Counseling, 22,* 5–15.

Woytowich, J. M. (1994). The power of the poem in the counseling office. *School Counselor, 42,* 78–80.

Yarrow, P. (2000). *Don't laugh at me.* Los Angeles, CA: Warner Brothers Records.

13

Counseling Uses of Tests

LINDA H. FOSTER, PhD, NCC
University of Alabama at Birmingham

Goldman (1971) proposed, in the introduction of his historically significant text, *Using Tests in Counseling*, that testing and counseling are inextricably linked. He wrote, "The types of tests used, and the ways in which testing is conducted, differ to some extent, but all have in common a relationship between counselor and counselee in which the latter's well-being, adjustment, and choices are paramount" (p. 1). Goldman's prophetic words are pertinent today. Today's counselors have ever increasing needs and requirements for valid and reliable information about their counselees. Thus, the importance of the relationship between counseling and testing continues to increase, perhaps reaching its pinnacle at the point of test interpretation. Lichtenberg and Goodyear (1999) wrote, "Test interpretation can have real consequences. That is, interpretations of test data are used to make decisions related to such matters as psychological diagnosis, treatment planning, hiring, career choice, occupational classification . . . and so on. In each of these instances, a person's life can be affected, sometimes profoundly" (p. 2). Testing is indeed an important part of the work of professional counselors and a part that requires substantive knowledge and well-honed skills.

Unfortunately, some counselors have been reluctant to accept the suggestion that testing is an integral part of counseling, instead viewing it as an unnecessary component of their counseling practice. This perspective ignores the reality that counselors quite routinely, but usually subjectively, gather and interpret information from and about their counselees. Effective counselors not only acknowledge that gathering and interpreting subjective information are important parts of counseling processes but also recognize that effective assessment and evaluation (i.e., testing) procedures can facilitate and enhance achievement of counseling goals and the efficiency of their counseling.

Some counselors' attitudes toward testing, in part, reflect confusion about semantics. *Measurement* may be considered the assignment of numeric or categorical values to

---

This chapter is respectfully dedicated to the memory of Dr. Nicholas A. Vacc and in honor of Dr. Larry C. Loesch for coauthoring the first four versions.

human attributes according to rules (Aiken & Groth-Marnat, 2006). *Assessment* includes measurement and also can be considered the data-gathering process or method (Drummond & Jones, 2006). *Evaluation* subsumes assessment and can be considered the interpretation and application of measurement data according to rules (Vacc & Loesch, 2000). *Appraisal* is sometimes considered synonymous with assessment (Vacc & Loesch, 2000), but more frequently with evaluation. Unfortunately, *testing* has been and today is still used as a synonym for each and all of these terms!

Testing (particularly when used as a synonym to appraisal/evaluation) can involve value judgments being made about measurement results and therefore about people. For this reason, testing has become equated with "labeling" people. Most counselors do not want to be viewed as labeling people because it connotes being "nonhumanistic" or "uncaring." Therefore, counselors often complain about testing based on incorrect understandings of what it really is. However, it is not the act of making value judgments that must be avoided, because the counseling process certainly incorporates such subjective judgments. Rather, it is making unfounded and/or invalid value judgments that must be avoided. Counselors are well advised to seek the best assessment procedures available because there is substantial evidence that clinicians' subjective judgments correlate poorly with more objective indices of human attributes (Groth-Marnat, 2003). Thus testing, when properly understood and used, is a significant aid, not a hindrance, to the counseling process.

Uses of Tests in Counseling

Kaplan and Saccuzzo (2005) and Gregory (2007) have listed general uses for testing, and others (e.g., Drummond & Jones, 2006; Hood & Johnson, 2004; Lichtenberg & Goodyear, 1999; Vacc & Loesch, 2000) have identified more specific counseling applications. The following summarizes primary counseling-related uses of testing.

Preliminary (Problem) Exploration and/or Diagnosis

For counseling processes to be efficient, counselors must gain accurate information about counselees as rapidly as possible. In fact, counselors typically must make a "diagnosis" soon after initial contact with their respective counselees. Unfortunately, the term *diagnosis* is not interpreted consistently in the counseling profession. In some contexts, it simply means "trying to find out what's going on with the counselee" (i.e., to determine rather general information about a counselee or the counselee's problem). In other contexts, it means to determine a very specific mental health syndrome for the counselee. For example, Gregory (2007) wrote, "Diagnosis consists of two intertwined tasks: determining the nature and source of a person's . . . behavior, and classifying the behavior pattern within an accepted diagnostic system" (p. 38). However, in either case, one efficient means of gaining accurate information from which to understand a person's behavior is testing.

Testing in this context has several distinct advantages over other types of counselor interactions and data gathering with counselees. First, it enhances comprehensive and systematic inquiry. Second, testing (in most cases) enables normative comparison of a counselee's personal data with that of similar persons. Third, it typically results in a relatively concise summary of counselee characteristics. Finally, testing *may* "uncover" counselee characteristics about which the counselee is unaware. Thus, substantive information about counselees' characteristics, behaviors, or problems can be gained expeditiously when testing is an integral part of initial counseling activities (Drummond & Jones, 2006).

Selection or Screening

Using test results in a selection or screening process helps to identify persons who might benefit from counseling or who are eligible for counseling services. For example, in large-scale testing programs (such as those conducted in schools), identification of outliers in score distributions *may* suggest persons in need of counseling or other services. In individualized situations, test results *may* be used to determine if a person meets particular criteria for the receipt of counseling services.

Using test information for selection or screening usually involves measurement and evaluation of applicant attributes for use in educational, business/industry employment, or counseling agency decision making. Thus, test results often are used to supplement more subjectively obtained information (i.e., personal judgments) so that decision making is improved and more efficient, thereby benefiting all involved.

Testing for selection or screening purposes has advantages similar to those for preliminary exploration or diagnosis. Comprehensive information can be obtained systematically and rapidly. For example, it is common in employment screening for applicants to complete a test battery as part of the application process. The ability to make normative comparisons of test results is particularly important in selection or screening processes. In this context, counseling professionals often establish statistical decision-making rules, based on numeric test result criteria, to supplement personal judgment criteria in decision-making processes.

Placement and/or Planning

Counselors often use test results to help them determine the most appropriate situations (e.g., educational programs or occupational categories) in which to place people. This use of testing is closely related to the selection or screening use, except that the focus of placement is typically narrower than that for a selection process. For example, determining assignment to a particular program of studies within an institution of higher education is usually a narrower focus than determining eligibility for admission to the institution. Similarly, determining an applicant's appropriate job classification is narrower in scope than determining the applicant's suitability for employment.

Testing for placement usually involves obtaining data about level of aptitude or competency. Tests used for such purposes may assess general attributes (e.g., when intelligence test scores are used as one of the criteria for placement in an academically gifted student program) or relatively specific abilities (e.g., when work sample tests are used to determine the speed with which a person can perform a job-specific task).

Testing for planning also usually involves the assessment of level of an ability or competency, and often the process is indistinguishable from that for placement. However, in this case, tests are used specifically to determine areas of functioning where increased competency is needed. Testing for planning thus involves identifying the best ways to facilitate the necessary improvement.

Facilitation of Self-Understanding

A primary reason counselees seek counseling services is for the facilitation of self-understanding. One of the roles of the counselor in this regard is as an information gatherer, transmitter, and interpreter. This role necessitates the integration of both communication and assessment skills in order to provide clients with multiple sources of information. Whiston (2005) wrote that "assessment is an integral part of counseling, it is crucial that practitioners become competent in this area" (p. 10). Counselors' effectiveness in this role is largely contingent upon counselees' trust in the counselor. Counselees must strongly trust their counselors before they will agree to exploration leading to self-understanding. This trust is difficult to achieve in early stages of the counseling process. However, testing is one means by which counselors can obtain information that enhances feedback to counselees. Using "objective" test information may then increase counselors' credibility with their counselees.

Test results also may be used to normalize aspects in turn leading to counselees' self-understanding. For example, counselees often wish to know how their characteristics, attributes, abilities, or behaviors compare with those of other people. Test results provided in normative contexts can be a basis for comparison. Another possible use for counselees in this regard is to use test results to identify specific aspects of themselves they may wish to change. Therefore, testing to facilitate self-understanding may help counselees identify counseling goals.

The testing process, when focusing upon characteristic behaviors, also facilitates counselees' self-understanding. Many tests incorporate logical, systematic, and relatively transparent approaches to analysis of human behavior. Thus, actually engaging in the testing process may enable counselees to learn new ways of evaluating themselves.

Assessment of Individual Progress

With increasing frequency and urgency, counselors are being required to demonstrate the effectiveness of their counseling activities to others, particularly others outside the counseling profession. Although counselors can generate evidence of their counseling effectiveness in a wide variety of ways, use of tests is clearly one of the more accepted and expeditious methods. Effective counseling is synonymous with counselee change, which presumably is perceived by counselees as positive. However, demonstration of counselee change is difficult if left to subjective interpretations by counselees or counselors. The use of test data provides an objective way to document counselee change. For example, precounseling and postcounseling assessments of counselee characteristics, attributes, and/or behaviors can provide data for evaluating the degree of change.

Counselors also have a professional responsibility to demonstrate their effectiveness to their counselees. Use of tests in this context may have a very subtle added benefit. One of the more difficult aspects of counseling is maintaining a high level of counselee motivation throughout the counseling process, a difficulty that increases as the length of the counseling process increases. The counselor's provision of encouraging feedback, as well as counselee's self-monitoring, helps to maintain counselee motivation. However, again, these are subjective processes. Periodic use of tests that yield "objective" indications of counselee change can be a powerful reinforcer of counselee motivation.

Licensure or Certification

Testing has become a significant factor in many professional counselors' personal careers. A greatly increased emphasis on counselor credentialing in the past three decades has resulted in the development of several major national counselor certifications. In addition, counselor licensure laws now exist in 49 states, the District of Columbia, and Puerto Rico. All these procedures require some type of performance evaluation, and most require successful performance on a credentialing examination. The examinations used encompass a variety of measurement formats, including multiple-choice, essay, and simulation tests. Typically, counselors have to exceed a minimum criterion score on an examination to become certified and/or licensed and/or otherwise credentialed. Thus, the counseling profession has embraced testing as an effective and efficient method for obtaining useful information for professional purposes.

Basic Concepts in Testing

Tests used for counseling and related purposes are usually evaluated by three major attributes: validity, reliability, and appropriateness.

Validity

Validity is commonly defined as the extent to which a test measures what it purports to measure (Aiken & Groth-Marnat, 2006; Drummond & Jones, 2006; Hood & Johnson, 2004; Kaplan & Saccuzzo, 2005). Messick (1998) clarified that common definition when he wrote, "Validity is an integrated evaluative judgment of the degree to which empirical evidence and theoretical rationales support the *adequacy* and *appropriateness* of *inferences* and *actions* based on test scores or other modes of assessment" (p. 13). Messick's definition emphasizes that ultimately, validity is based on judgment and is the most important consideration of how test results are used. It also is the most important criterion upon which any test should be evaluated (Kaplan & Saccuzzo, 2005; Gregory, 2007).

Historically, validity was usually considered as a generalized characteristic of a test. However, the most recent edition of the *Standards for Educational and Psychological*

Testing (AERA/APA/NCME, 2000) includes a significant change in how validity is viewed, which in turn has significant implications for how it is established. Validity is now viewed as "contextual," which means that the validity of a test must be specified *for a particular purpose and for use with a particular group of people.* If a test is to be used for a purpose or with a group of people other than those for which current validity information exists, then additional evidence of validity must be generated before the test can be considered valid for use in the new situation.

Three major types of validity typically have been discussed in most of the professional literature on testing. *Content validity* refers to the extent to which a test is an adequate representation of a conceptual domain that it is designed to query (Kaplan & Saccuzzo, 2005). Domains of interest to counselors include human attributes, characteristics, behaviors, attitudes, and abilities. Content validity evaluation is usually associated with measures of cognitive abilities. *Construct validity* is the accuracy with which test scores reflect levels or degrees of psychological constructs (Aiken & Groth-Marnat, 2006). Construct validity is particularly important for evaluating measures of personality dynamics, attitudes, or interests. *Criterion-related validity* refers to the extent to which test scores are predictably associated with other, often behavioral, criteria (Aiken & Groth-Marnat, 2006). Performance and competency measures in particular need to have criterion-related validity.

The newer interpretation of validity emphasizes the importance of substantive documentation and research to establish test validity for a particular use with a particular group of people. Within this perspective, a test's validity must be based on *evidence* of (a) representativeness of a content domain, (b) appropriate response processes, (c) appropriate internal structure, or (d) appropriate relationships to other variables, or some combination of these types of evidence.

Reliability

The consistency of measurement in terms of accuracy, dependability, consistency, or repeatability of test results is known as reliability (Kaplan & Saccuzzo, 2005). Similar to validity, three types of reliability are usually described in the literature. *Stability*, sometimes called test–retest reliability, indicates the likelihood of a group of people achieving the same or similar test scores if the test is administered on two or more occasions. *Equivalence*, sometimes called parallel forms reliability, indicates the extent to which two versions of a measure yield the same or essentially similar results. *Internal consistency* reliability indicates the extent to which items within a test (or subscale) correlate with one another (i.e., are internally consistent). The type of reliability deemed most important depends on the nature of the testing situation (Gregory, 2007).

Appropriateness

A test is appropriate if factors extraneous to the purpose and nature of the test itself (e.g., size of print type used, testing conditions, test delivery format, or reading level of test content) do not influence performance on or responding to the test. Validity, reliability, and appropriateness are interrelated but not necessarily interdependent.

A valid test is necessarily reliable and appropriate. However, a test can produce reliable (i.e., consistent) but invalid results. Similarly, an inappropriate test (e.g., one for which the response format is inappropriate for the respondents) can produce reliable but not valid results.

General Testing Vocabulary

Tests have been characterized and/or differentiated through the use of a wide variety of terms. The following are brief clarifications of terms commonly used in the testing literature.

Interpretation Basis

Norm-referenced and *criterion-referenced* are two terms commonly used to describe tests. The distinction between the two types of tests is usually made in regard to the interpretation of the results from each type (Gregory, 2007). In norm-referenced testing, a respondent's test score is reported in comparison with performance on the same test by other persons. Percentiles, or other standardized scores such as T scores or deviation IQs (which are different from the original intelligence quotient, which was defined as the person's mental age divided by the person's chronological age times 100), are commonly used to indicate *relative* performance. For example, a person whose score is at the 85th percentile is interpreted to have performed on the test at a level equal to or surpassing 85% of the persons in the norm group for the test. These persons presumably are similar to the respondent in important ways. Norm-referenced testing necessitates establishment of normative data but not of specific behavioral criteria.

In criterion-referenced testing, a respondent's test score is interpreted in comparison with some specified behavioral domain or criterion of proficiency. A respondent's score indicates how many criterion-specific tasks (i.e., items) the respondent completed successfully and, therefore, how many of the specific criteria (e.g., identified skills) the respondent has achieved. Criterion-referenced testing involves the development of specific behavioral criteria and careful specification of the relationships of test items to those criteria.

Standardized Tests

According to Aiken and Groth-Marnat (2006), *standardized tests* usually are commercially prepared by measurement experts and incorporate uniform sets of items and administration and scoring procedures. In general, a test is standardized if it is used in the same way for all respondents. Gregory (2007) also emphasized that "standardized" does not mean that the test *necessarily* accurately measures what it is intended to measure. So-called nonstandardized tests frequently are user-prepared, and administration procedures may vary depending on the situation. The validity of standardized and nonstandardized tests must be evaluated on an individual basis; a test is not necessarily valid by designation as standardized or invalid by designation as nonstandardized.

Individual and Group Tests

Individual tests are designed and intended to be administered to one person at a time by a single administrator. These tests usually involve the administrator tailoring the testing procedure (e.g., determining the time allowed for responding) to a specific respondent and/or testing situation. A group test is designed and intended to be administered to more than one person at a time.

Power and Speed(ed) Tests

In most types of testing, maximum respondent performance is preferred. Therefore, testing time allotments exceed time needed by most respondents to complete the test. Such tests are called power tests. Intellectual ability, aptitude, and achievement tests are common examples of power tests. In contrast, speed(ed) tests involve speed of performance as a dynamic in the assessment process. Task completion tests (e.g., typing or other manual dexterity skills tests) are common examples of speed tests.

Vertical and Horizontal Tests

Tests that have different but conceptually and structurally related forms based on some hierarchy (e.g., age category, developmental level, or grade) are known as vertical tests. Horizontal tests are conceptually and structurally related and assess within a number of different domains simultaneously within a defined category (e.g., age group or grade level). Some tests, such as aptitude or achievement test batteries commonly used in schools, are both vertical and horizontal tests.

Structured and Unstructured Tests

Tests also differ by response task. In a structured test, the respondent is presented with a clear stimulus (e.g., an item stem) and instructed to select the appropriate response from those presented (e.g., response choices, sometimes known as distractors in a multiple-choice test). In an unstructured test, the respondent is presented with either a clear or an ambiguous stimulus and instructed to construct a response. This differentiation is evident in different types of personality inventories.

Computer-Based Tests

Rapid technologic advancements are being made in the uses of computers for testing. In computer-based testing, the respondent interacts with a computer by providing responses (through keyboard, joystick, or touch screen input) to stimuli (e.g., questions or graphics) presented on a computer monitor. Both the number and type of tests being transformed to computer application are increasing at an exponential rate.

The major advantages of computer-based testing are that responses are made easily, sophisticated visual and/or graphical effects can be incorporated into testing paradigms, respondents have considerable control over the rate of interaction (i.e., responding), test scoring and data analyses are completed rapidly, and local data sets (e.g., local normative data) are easily established. Historically, the major limitations of computer-based testing concerned the security of the tests and testing procedures. However, significant recent improvements in computer-based testing have helped to minimize these concerns.

Computer-based testing clearly is the method of choice for the future. In particular, the increasing use of the Internet as a communications modality is likely to increase dramatically both the nature and types of computer-based testing. In addition, increasingly sophisticated technologies will allow a diverse array of testing approaches to be used.

Paper-and-Pencil Tests

Currently, a majority of tests are paper-and-pencil tests, for example, wherein respondents provide responses directly on tests, test booklets, or accompanying answer or response sheets. However, the connotation of the term *paper-and-pencil tests* has been broadened beyond the restrictive (literal) definition to encompass almost all structured tests, including computer-based versions of those tests.

Performance Tests

Tests that require respondents to complete physical tasks to allow evaluation of skill or competence levels are known as performance tests. They also are sometimes referred to as work sample tests. Performance or work sample tests are used most frequently in the context of vocational or vocational rehabilitation counseling. However, they are increasingly becoming part of other assessment procedures. For example, the in-basket technique used in employee screening procedures calls for prospective employees to actually respond to a sample of what might be found in the person's in basket if hired (e.g., the potential employee could be asked to write a letter of response to a customer complaint or to write an informative memo to other employees). The responses of the potential employee are then evaluated by the employer.

High-Stakes Testing

Tests are increasingly used as the basis for decisions about individuals' education and whether individuals may progress in an environment that utilizes "high standards." The testing enterprise in this context is referred to as *high-stakes* testing. The most common example of high-stakes testing is statewide achievement testing. For example, based on some of these testing processes, students who do not perform well may be denied a diploma, their teachers' employment may not be continued or may be altered significantly, or their schools may receive differentiated funding. Credentialing examinations, such as those for counselors, also fall in the realm of high-stakes testing because failure to surpass a score criterion may mean that an applicant may not be able to practice as a counselor. Increasingly sophisticated assessment techniques in combination with increasing societal demand for performance-based evidence of competence are the driving forces behind the rapidly increasing emphasis on high-stakes testing.

Additional Assessment Methods

The following are methods that may be thought of as tests because they yield data for evaluation purposes. However, they differ in that the data are not necessarily provided by the person to whom the data applies.

Structured and Open-Response Interviews

In a structured interview, the interviewer asks the interviewee a predetermined set of questions. Responses from the interviewee are classified (or coded) into predetermined potential response categories. Questions posed in an open-response interview are also predetermined, but categories of potential responses are not. Rather, post hoc analyses are made in the attempt to sort out respondent information.

Rating Scales

The use of rating scales involves a rater providing an indication of another person's *level* or *degree* of an attribute, attitude, or characteristic in terms of predetermined stimuli (e.g., items or criteria). Rating scales may be used to assess "live" behavior or through media (e.g., audiotape, videotape, or photographs) that record the behavior.

Behavior Observations

In making behavior observations, an observer views (sometimes on videotape) a person in a situation and records *frequencies* with which predetermined behaviors occur. Behavior observation and rating techniques are often used in the same contexts. For example, counselor trainees' verbal responses in counseling sessions are typically counted by type and rated for level of effectiveness by supervisors. Behavior observations also are used commonly in determination of a diagnostic classification.

Checklists

When used as assessment techniques, checklists contain either sets of behaviors or attributes. For behaviors, responses usually reflect *perceived* frequencies of occurrence. For attributes, responses usually reflect *perceived* presence or absence. Checklist responses can be self-reported, provided by another person (e.g., a counselor, teacher, or parent), or both.

Writing or Essay Examinations

In a composition (usually essay format) examination, respondents are required to create responses to questions or other stimuli and to communicate their responses using written communication skills, including proper use of grammar, spelling, and information organization. These types of examinations have the advantage of allowing each respondent to develop a highly personalized response. However, they have the disadvantage of allowing significant variation in the responses presented, which in turn hinders determination of an effective or successful response to the stimulus presented, which then makes scoring difficult. Standardization in presentation of writing examinations and in scoring responses to them is increasingly being achieved through the use of computer-based test formats.

Major Types of Tests

Specific tests are usually described according to their respective individual characteristics. More commonly, however, tests are grouped according to the general human dynamic being assessed. Therefore, counselors typically use five major types of standardized tests: achievement, aptitude, intelligence, interest, and personality.

Achievement Tests

Achievement tests are developed to measure the effects of relatively specific programs of instruction or training (Aiken & Groth-Marnat, 2006; Gregory, 2007; Kaplan & Saccuzzo, 2005). Accordingly, achievement tests are used widely in educational systems and institutions. However, achievement tests are also used in business and industry settings to determine the need for or effects of on-the-job or other specialized training. In either case, achievement tests are designed to provide information about how much has been learned up to the date of assessment as a result of educational or training experiences.

Structured or guided learning activities, such as school curricula, are intended to enable participants to learn the content of specific knowledge and skill domains. Achievement tests are developed to be related to those domains. Thus, content validity considerations are particularly important in evaluating achievement tests. Because achievement tests are generally administered one time, usually at the end of an instructional period, internal consistency reliability is a primary consideration in their evaluation.

Achievement tests typically are subdivided into three types: single subject matter, survey batteries, and diagnostic. The purpose of *single-subject-matter* achievement tests is to assess level of knowledge retention for a specifically defined content domain. This type of test is most commonly used in schools. However, they are sometimes used in other specialized training programs such as construction or trade apprenticeship programs. *Survey battery* achievement tests are collections of single-subject-matter tests. Achievement test batteries contain subtests, each of which is designed to measure achievement in a specific area. Achievement test batteries have several advantages over a collection of single-subject-matter tests. Administration procedures are simplified by the format similarity in each subsection. Testing costs often are less for achievement test batteries because printing, test booklet binding, answer sheet printing, and overall processing costs are usually minimized. The greatest advantage of achievement test batteries, however, is that all subtests in the battery have the same norm group. This commonality facilitates comparisons among a respondent's relative levels of achievement across areas tested.

Diagnostic achievement tests are primarily concerned with measuring skills or abilities. For example, diagnostic tests can be used to determine which reading, writing, or mathematical skills students are able to perform. Diagnostic achievement tests are sometimes referred to as deficit measurement tests because they reveal skills that have not yet been mastered. Subsequent instruction can be focused specifically upon the development of these skills. It should be noted that although diagnostic tests identify skills that have not yet been achieved, they do not reveal *why* the skills have not been achieved. Achievement tests yield descriptive but not causal relationship results.

Clearly there is a trend toward the development of criterion-referenced achievement tests paralleling the trend toward development of curricular competency objectives in schools. This latter trend should help clarify the objectives schools are trying to accomplish. However, it may result in greater tendencies to "teach to the test," particularly when curricular and test objectives and competencies are highly similar. Therefore, counselors using achievement tests should consider the instruction underlying results.

Aptitude Tests

Traditionally, *aptitude tests* have been defined as tests intended for the prediction of an individual's future behavior. For example, aptitude tests have been used to predict future performance in an academic curriculum area or in a specialized vocational activity. The traditionally used definition has the advantage of implying how the tests are to be used (i.e., for prediction). However, the definition does not clarify why aptitude tests have greater predictive power than other types of tests, or how they differ from other types of tests.

The nature and purposes of aptitude testing are best conceived within the global context of evaluation of human abilities. Within that context, intelligence testing is considered to be the measurement and evaluation of potentially generalized human functioning. Aptitude testing within that context is conceived as measurement and evaluation of potential functioning within more specific domains of human behavior. In general, the narrower the domain of human functioning for which prediction is to be made, the easier it is to develop effective predictive tests. Thus, aptitude tests have greater predictive power because they usually focus on specific areas of human functioning.

The physical formats of most aptitude tests are similar to other measures of cognitive functioning (e.g., intelligence or achievement tests). They frequently contain multiple-choice items, with a few tests containing manual or other dexterity tasks. The difference between aptitude and achievement tests lies in the criteria to which the items are theoretically related. Items in achievement tests are presumed to be related to academic and other learning experiences to which respondents have been *previously* exposed. Items in aptitude tests are presumed to be related to learning or occupational tasks that respondents will be *expected* to master or accomplish in the future.

Although theoretical distinctions can be made between aptitude and achievement tests, practical distinctions are difficult to operationalize. All human performance on tests is contingent upon respondents' previous learning and life experiences. For example, there is considerable debate as to whether the Scholastic Assessment Test (SAT; formerly the Scholastic Aptitude Test) is an achievement or an aptitude test. Ostensibly, it is an aptitude test because it is used primarily to predict secondary school students' performance in college curricula. Presumably, individual items are closely related to the types of mental functioning tasks that college students are required to master. However, SAT scores have high positive correlations with students' high school grade-point averages (GPAs), which have high positive correlations with secondary school level achievement tests. Further, most students who complete the SAT have been enrolled in college prep curricula that focused on mastery of academic skills (i.e., skills necessary for successful performance in college). School systems publicize increases in the average SAT scores for graduates (as if the SAT were an achievement test), whereas colleges extol the positive correlations between SAT scores and GPAs (as if the SAT were an aptitude test). The debate probably will not be ended soon.

Aptitude tests are usually categorized into either single-domain or multifactor batteries. The differentiation is the same as that for achievement tests. Single-domain aptitude tests focus on a specific aspect of human performance, such as a particular type of academic performance or job behavior. Aptitude (multifactor) test batteries are assemblies of single-domain tests having a common format, administration procedure, and norm group. Regardless of type, criterion-related validity (specifically *predictive* validity) is most important for aptitude tests. Like achievement tests, internal consistency reliability is the most important type for aptitude tests. For large-scale testing programs, equivalent forms reliability also is important.

Counselors use aptitude test results primarily in academic and/or vocational counseling contexts. Because of the faith many people place in aptitude test results, it is imperative that counselors establish that aptitude tests have validity for the respective contexts in which predictions are made. Erroneous predictions of performance can have significant, long-term detrimental effects for counselees.

Intelligence Tests

No area in testing has resulted in more heated debate than the meaning and effective measurement of intelligence (Kaplan & Saccuzzo, 2005). Professionals are interested in being able to evaluate an individual's level of mental ability because of the many significant implications that could be derived from such knowledge. However, although many of these implications serve the benefit of humankind, some can be construed as highly unethical. Therefore, it may be best that neither a definitive explanation nor a fully valid measurement of intelligence has yet been, or will be, conceived.

The voluminous literature on intelligence testing prohibits more than cursory coverage of the topic. Therefore, only a few of the major concepts are addressed here. At the core of intelligence testing is how intelligence is defined. Some, following the lead of Binet, conceive of intelligence as a *unitary* (also called unifactor) construct. In brief, they believe that intelligence is a single, generalized (probably inherited) human ability that underlies all human functioning. The best-known example of a test based on this conceptualization is the Stanford-Binet Intelligence Test (S-B). In contrast, others, following the lead of Wechsler, believe that intelligence is the sum total of a large and diverse set of more specific (probably inherited) mental abilities. That is, they believe that intelligence is a *multifactor* construct. A variety of intelligence tests have been developed based on this conceptualization, such as the Wechsler Intelligence Scale for Children (WISC) or Wechsler Adult Intelligence Scale (WAIS). Still others, such as the Kaufmans, believe that intelligence is multifactored but inseparable from prior experiences and/or learning and have developed tests such as the Kaufman Assessment Battery for Children (K-ABC) or Kaufman Adolescent and Adult Intelligence Test (KAIT) to reflect this integrated perspective. The pragmatic result is that different intelligence tests yield from 1 to 20 or more (subscale) scores, depending on the definition used as the basis for the respective tests.

Intelligence tests also are classified as *group* or *individual* tests. Group intelligence tests are usually of the paper-and-pencil variety. They are heavily dependent on facility in use of language and are designed to be administered to large groups of persons during a single administration. As the name implies, individual intelligence tests are *designed* to be administered to one person at a time. Individual intelligence tests also typically include performance tasks to be completed by respondents. The significant advantage of individual intelligence tests over group intelligence tests is that competent administrators can learn much about *how* a person responds to a testing task (i.e., method of problem solving and/or affective reactions) by careful observation during the testing session. The significant disadvantage of individual intelligence testing is the cost of administering tests on an individual basis.

Intelligence tests (or subsections of them) also are described as verbal or nonverbal. A "verbal" intelligence test employs the use of language, such as providing definitions of words in a vocabulary subtest. In a nonverbal intelligence test, persons can respond without having to interpret written or spoken language. Traditionally, such tests have been composed of a variety of tasks involving figures, diagrams, symbols, or drawings (e.g., the Raven's Progressive Matrices). However, the term also has come to include performance tests (or subtests) in which respondents physically manipulate objects (e.g., the Leiter International Performance Scale). Most well-accepted individual intelligence tests include both verbal and nonverbal subtests. Most group intelligence tests are verbal, although a few nonverbal ("culture-fair") group intelligence tests have been developed.

The immense general interest in intelligence assessment has subjected intelligence testing to intense scrutiny, which has resulted in substantial criticism being aimed at intelligence tests. A common criticism is that intelligence tests are really academic aptitude tests; items in them seem closely related to the types of abilities needed to be successful in academic systems. Another criticism is that intelligence tests are biased; they favor persons from upper socioeconomic classifications because of the types of values reflected in the tests. However, the most significant criticism for counselors is that intelligence tests are culturally and/or racially biased. Arguments and counterarguments have emerged as to whether, how, and why intelligence tests are racially or culturally biased. At the very least, there is a basis for questioning possible bias in intelligence tests. Therefore, counselors who intend to use intelligence tests should study available expository and empirical information about intelligence testing.

Interest Inventories

Interest inventories were developed as a means to assess a person's relative preferences for (i.e., feelings about) engaging in a variety of conceptually related activities (Drummond & Jones, 2006; Hood & Johnson, 2004; Kaplan & Saccuzzo, 2005). Among the best-known interest inventories are the Strong Interest Inventory, Kuder Occupational Interest Survey, and Jackson Vocational Interest Survey. Although the vast majority of interest inventories focus on assessment of vocational interests, leisure (or avocational) interest inventories are sometimes useful to counselors. However, the following discussion relates only to vocational interest inventories because of their predominance.

Vocational interest inventories are intended to provide information on a person's interests in various vocations or occupations. To achieve this goal, respondents indicate their degree of preference on a scale with incremental values for each of a large set of activities. The activities that respondents prefer are obtained and related to types of work activities that are characteristic of various occupations. Noteworthy is that activities for which preference information is obtained may not be obviously related to particular occupations. That is, respondents typically do not know which activities are conceptually and/or empirically related to particular occupations.

Associations between activities and occupations are established by having persons who report being satisfied in an occupation indicate their preferences for a variety of activities. Activities that are most frequently preferred by satisfied workers become associated with the respective occupations. Thus, vocational interest assessment typically is a comparison of a respondent's pattern of activity preferences with those of persons reporting satisfaction in various occupations. Vocational interest assessment has reached a degree of sophistication such that interest levels in a wide variety of occupations are achieved through responses to a relatively small number of items (i.e., activities).

For counseling purposes, the basic assumption underlying interest assessment is that people are prone to engage in activities they prefer. Thus, a *very* simplistic view of vocational counseling is that of pairing people's interests with activities inherent in occupations, with interest assessment as a major component of the process. However, such a simplistic view belies the limitations of vocational interest assessment.

Chief among the limitations of interest assessment is that "high interest in" an occupation is not necessarily synonymous with "aptitude for" an occupation. Unfortunately, counselees who are poorly counseled often erroneously assume that interest and aptitude are equivalent and may subsequently make misinformed decisions. Another limitation of interest assessment is susceptibility to response sets. For example, some people report high levels of interest in particular activities because they believe it is socially acceptable to do so. Perhaps this explains why many young people overselect the "higher" professions as occupational goals, although they do not have the requisite aptitudes for those professions. A third limitation is reliability. Interests often fluctuate because of the influences of life experience, maturation, social context, and/or economic need. Thus, even the best of vocational interest inventories have low stability reliability coefficients. Finally, there is the potential for gender bias in interest assessment. Clearly, gender roles and situations in the workplace are changing. These changes result in gender-specific or non-gender-specific normative data for interest inventories. Development costs restrict frequencies of instrument and/or normative refinements. Therefore, the continuing possibility exists that vocational interest inventory results can be misinterpreted because of gender bias.

These limitations notwithstanding, counselors frequently assess vocational interests. Several reasons underlie this trend. One is that counselees seek the most expedient means of finding satisfying and rewarding work. A second reason is that interest assessment is nonthreatening to counselees; it is acceptable to lack interest in an area. A third is that counselees view interest assessment as a way to understand themselves without fear of disclosing their "deficiencies." In summary, counselors and counselees favor interest assessment because it provides information that is easily obtained and accepted in counseling processes.

Personality Inventories

Defining *personality assessment* is difficult because of its multifaceted nature. In general, however, personality inventories are designed to yield information about a person's characteristics, traits, behaviors, attitudes, opinions, and/or emotions (Gregory, 2007; Hood & Johnson, 2004; Kaplan & Saccuzzo, 2005). Personality assessment is particularly germane to the work of counselors, but it is the most complex type of assessment; counselors must be knowledgeable in both psychometric principles and personality theory. Additionally, they should have substantive supervised practice before using personality assessment instruments.

Personality inventories are classified as *structured* or *unstructured*. Structured personality inventories contain a set of items that are interpreted in the same way by all respondents. These inventories also contain a set of potential item responses from among which a respondent selects one as most appropriate (i.e., pertinent to or characteristic of self). Structured personality inventories are sometimes referred to as self-report inventories (Kaplan & Saccuzzo, 2005). Responses are selected by respondents, not made from the interpretations of administrators. Structured personality inventories yield quantitative scores based on predetermined scoring criteria. They are intended to be interpreted in comparison to normative data. The Myers–Briggs Type Inventory, Minnesota Multiphasic Personality Inventory–2, Sixteen Personality Factor Questionnaire, and California Psychological Inventory are among the better-known self-report personality inventories.

Unstructured personality inventories contain stimuli that can be interpreted in different ways by different respondents. Unstructured personality inventories are sometimes referred to as projective tests because in many of them respondents are required to "project" thoughts or feelings onto the stimuli presented. The Rorschach Inkblot Test, Thematic Apperception Test, House-Tree-Person, and Kinetic Family

Drawing Test are well-known examples of projective personality inventories. Although scoring procedures have been developed for some unstructured personality inventories, results are more commonly "clinical interpretations" of responses made.

Personality inventories have a number of limitations, many of which are similar to those for interest inventories. For example, personality inventories are susceptible to faking. In these instances, counselees subvert the validity of the assessment by providing responses they believe will make them "look good" or "look bad." Personality inventories also are susceptible to invalidity through contextual bias. What is a "perfectly normal" response in one context may be evaluated as an exceptionally deviant response in another (Dana, 1993; Whiston, 2005). Counselees also may perceive personality inventories as threatening. Although counselees may be intrigued about the nature of their personalities, fear of negative attributes often outweighs curiosity-based motivation to respond openly and honestly.

Personality inventories can help counselees gain insights into their functioning. However, most counselors do not receive extensive training in personality assessment. Therefore, they should restrict their use of personality inventories to persons who are functioning normally but who have areas of concern they want to address. In general, most counselors will derive the most benefit from use of structured or self-report inventories.

Test Bias

No discussion of basic concepts in testing would be complete without some reference to test bias. Anastasi and Urbina (1997) wrote, "The principal questions that have been raised regarding test bias pertain to validity coefficients . . . and to the relationship between the group means on the test and on the criterion" (p. 165). Test bias *appears* evident when at least two distinctly identifiable groups achieve different results on a test. These differences may be attributed to factors (e.g., gender, race, or physical condition) that, theoretically, *should not* be bases for the differences. Although test bias is usually thought of as a characteristic of test items, its most significant (and usually detrimental) impact concerns interpretations of test data and the actions taken on the basis of those interpretations.

A variety of methods have been developed to alleviate test bias, including empirical means. Test developers are conscientiously striving to produce nonbiased tests. Nonetheless, there remain some tests that are biased. Therefore, counselors must be sensitive to test results that may be biased and strive to ensure that their interpretations of test results are not flawed by being based on biased data.

Documents Pertinent to Testing

There are at least five types of informational documents pertinent to testing with which counselors should be familiar. The first type is sections of relevant ethical standards pertaining to testing (see Chapter 4). In particular, counselors should be thoroughly familiar with the measurement and evaluation sections of the ACA *Code of Ethics* and *Standards of Practice* and the NBCC *Code of Ethics*. These standards are available in written form from the parent organizations and in electronic form at their respective

Web sites (http://www.counseling.org and http://www.nbcc.org). The second type, documents related to *appropriate practices for test users*, is covered later in this chapter.

The third type is *test manuals*. A good test manual contains the theoretical bases of the test; evidence of validity, reliability, and appropriateness; normative or criterion data; and other information necessary for proper use of the test. Good tests have good test manuals, and good counselors make good use of those manuals. Indeed, maximum benefit cannot be derived from a test unless the test user is familiar with the material presented in the test manual.

Specific information about tests, such as that usually found in test manuals, increasingly is being conveyed from test publishers' Web sites. Typically, this information can be found by first visiting the appropriate publisher's home page and then linking to the needed information for a particular test. Determination of the appropriate test publisher, as well as other substantive information about tests, can be found by visiting Web sites such as the ERIC Clearinghouse on Assessment and Evaluation (http://ericae.net).

The fourth type is a single document, *Standards for Educational and Psychological Testing* (AERA/APA/NCME, 2000). It was developed initially, and subsequently revised, through the collaborative effort of the American Psychological Association (APA), American Educational Research Association (AERA), and National Council on Measurement in Education (NCME) and are now published by AERA. These standards are the recognized criteria against which tests, testing procedures, test manuals, and other test information should be evaluated. Counselors should become thoroughly familiar with these standards in order to critique, select, and use tests effectively for counseling purposes.

The fifth type is the set of documents that have to do with broad-scale professional practices pertinent to testing. For example, both the Fair Access Coalition for Testing (http://www.fairaccess.org/) in the United States and the International Test Commission (http://www.intestcom.org/) headquartered in Paris have developed documents clarifying appropriate professional practices for test use, including qualifications of various types of test users. The documents and other information provided by organizations such as these frequently are focused upon specific problematic situations, such as ideological conflicts about tests and/or their use among professional groups interested in testing or perspectives on cross-cultural testing practices. These types of documents most commonly are presented as a link off the home page of a sponsoring organization. Counselors should be familiar with the contents of these types of documents because they suggest boundaries and guidelines for the appropriate uses of tests.

Recent Trends in Testing

A recent and highly significant trend in testing is application of item response theory (IRT) in test development practices. McKinley (1989) wrote:

> The attractiveness of IRT as both a research and measurement tool is derived primarily from its *parameter invariance* properties. The property of invariance means that the

item statistics that are obtained from the application of the IRT model are independent of the sample of examinees to which a test (or other instrument) is administered. Likewise, the personal statistics obtained for examinees are independent of the items included in the test. This is in marked contrast to more traditional statistics, such as item and examinee proportion-correct or number-correct scores. (p. 37)

In classical (i.e., traditional) test theory and practices based on it, resultant test statistics are, technically, applicable only to the norm group from which the response data were derived; other groups would have other item and/or test statistics. Thus, item and test statistical data in traditional analyses are unique to the set of items included and to the particular norm group. In comparison, use of IRT models yields data that are, theoretically, invariant with regard to both the sample of examinees and the sample of items.

Thorough discussion of IRT models is beyond the scope of this chapter. However, interested readers are referred to McKinley (1989) for a good overview of IRT or to Hambleton (1998) for a complete discussion. The important point is that the use of IRT models has resulted in significant improvement in the development of tests, particularly in testing for achievement, aptitude, and credentialing (Anastasi & Urbina, 1997; Gregory, 2007).

A related recent trend is use of so-called *adaptive testing* models. Adaptive testing is quite literally what the term implies: each test is "adapted" for each respondent. Currently, adaptive testing is used almost exclusively for ability testing (although other applications are possible). In a typical adaptive testing situation (e.g., the SAT or GRE), the first item to which the examinee responds is a relatively arbitrarily selected starting point, usually based on a generalized presumption about the examinee (e.g., based on the examinee's age or grade level). However, selection of the next and all subsequent items is based on performance on the preceding item. For example, the examinee who provides an incorrect response to the first item is next presented with an item of lesser difficulty. Conversely, if the examinee provides the correct response to an item, the examinee is next presented with an item having a higher difficulty level.

Adaptive testing is theoretically sound because of advances in the use of IRT models and computers. That is, IRT models allow development of item difficulty indices that are *theoretically* sample and item set free. The use of computer-based formats for adaptive testing allows rapid determination of the next item to which the examinee should respond.

An examinee's experience with adaptive testing is significantly different than that for traditional testing. For example, in adaptive testing, not all examinees respond to the same items or even the same number of items for a given test; each response pattern is individualized. Examinees responding to adaptive tests also are not permitted to go backwards in the item sequence, which means that test respondents are not permitted to skip an item and then go back to it later.

It is clear that adaptive testing yields a highly personalized test for each examinee, reduces testing time (and therefore costs), and facilitates more rapid provision of feedback (which in some cases is immediate upon completion of the test). Adaptive testing is becoming much more common, even though many persons find the unidirectional task sequencing to be disconcerting. Nonetheless, it is likely that adaptive testing will be used more frequently as computer-based testing becomes more common.

Another recent trend in testing that the testing community appears to be being rapidly embracing is generalizability theory. In generalizability theory, a test score is considered a single sample from a universe of possible scores for the respondent. "The degree of accuracy with which the test score estimates the universe score depends on the nature of the universe, that is, the particular facets that define it" (Aiken & Groth-Marnat, 2006, p. 96). Both a *generalizability coefficient* (which is similar to a traditional reliability coefficient) and a *universe value of the score* can be calculated. The primary application of generalizability theory is exploration of how factors such as the nature of the items; administration, motivational, and environmental conditions; and other facets of performance influence the generalizability coefficient (and therefore reliability of measurement).

So-called *authentic assessment* is actually a subtype within the more general category of performance assessment. Authentic assessment also is sometimes referred to as alternative assessment to emphasize that it is different from traditional paper-and-pencil testing (Aiken & Groth-Marnat, 2006). In brief, performance assessment involves evaluation of the products of some behavior or action (such as the use of an identified skill). The most common representation of authentic assessment is the use of *portfolios* in educational systems. As an alternative to traditional written tests, students are asked to create a portfolio and to fill it with "products" or "physical evidence" that represent their best work in different areas (e.g., math, science, art, or language arts). The contents of the portfolio are then examined and evaluated by the instructor.

The use of portfolios and other authentic assessment techniques was heralded as a more caring, individualized, and outcome-based alternative to traditional assessment practices during the late 1980s and throughout much of the 1990s. Whether this popularity will continue is unknown. However, it appears to be waning in at least the scientific community because authentic assessment procedures simply have not fared well when reasonable psychometric scrutiny has been applied. For example, both intrarater and interrater (e.g., teacher) reliability coefficients for portfolio evaluations are astonishingly low. Further, there remains considerable debate as to how much structure should be imposed on the composition of the portfolio materials. That is, to what extent should students be told what has to be included in their respective portfolios? Authentic assessment is an alternative to traditional assessment, but it is far from an equivalent alternative.

As the demographics of the United States change, it is incumbent on the counseling profession to acknowledge the challenges and impact of a changing population. Clearly, multicultural sensitivity must be incorporated into the assessment process as well. Historically, assessment has been mired in an *etic* perspective, for example, a "perspective that emphasizes universals among human beings by using examination and comparison of many cultures from a position outside those cultures" (Dana, 1993, p. 21). The alternative is to adopt an *emic* perspective, which is one that is "culture specific and examines behavior from within a culture, using criteria relative to the internal characteristics of that culture" (Dana, 1993, p. 21). The emic perspective suggests that test results must be considered in the context of the cultural characteristics of the person(s) from whom the results were obtained. A particularly striking example of the need for multicultural sensitivity in testing is when tests are used to support or confirm a diagnosis of mental illness. Obviously, the appropriateness of behavioral reactions to life stressors is determined in part by the cultural context in which the reactions are evident. Being a culturally responsive counselor entails self-awareness, knowledge, and multiculturally sensitive skills in order to work effectively with people of color (Lee & Chuang, 2005). If testing is done without due consideration to potentially influential and/or important cultural factors, how can the test results possibly be valid (Dana, 1993; Lee, 2001; Whiston, 2005)? A more comprehensive discussion of culturally responsive counselors can be found in Chapter 3.

Appropriate Practices for Test Users

Counselors' effective use of tests is directly related to the degree of responsibility they assume for using the tests. Historically, guidelines for responsible uses of tests had to be extrapolated from statements of ethical standards. A vast majority of counselors have attempted to use tests ethically and, therefore, responsibly. However, their effort was limited by lack of specificity in ethical standards statements. In response to this situation, in 1989 the American Counseling Association (ACA; formerly the American Association for Counseling and Development, AACD), through its Association for Assessment in Counseling and Education (AACE; formerly the Association for Measurement and Evaluation in Counseling and Development, AMECD) division, developed the guidelines titled *Responsibilities of Users of Standardized Tests* (RUST). The following are comments on major sections of those guidelines.

With regard to test decisions, counselors (as test users) are responsible for determination of information assessment needs and clarification of the objectives for and limitations of testing for each circumstance. Thus, counselors (not counselees or others) have the final authority for decisions about test use in their profession. Qualifications of test users are also an important factor in the testing process. They should be considered with regard to the purposes of testing, characteristics of the tests, conditions of test use, and the roles of other professionals.

Emphasized in the test selection guidelines is that careful consideration should be given to each test's validity, reliability, appropriateness, and other technical characteristics and psychometric properties. Also, respondent participation in the test selection process is desirable, if appropriate and/or possible. Test administration procedures should be conducted by qualified administrators who give proper test orientation and directions in appropriate testing conditions. Test scoring should be conducted only by fully qualified persons to ensure accurate results.

Provided within the guidelines are test interpretations in the contexts of uses for placement, prediction, description, assessment of growth, and program evaluation. The importance of appropriate norms, technical factors, and the effects of variations in administration and scoring are emphasized. Guidelines for communicating test results in individual or group contexts also are presented.

Unfortunately, only these brief comments on the RUST statement can be provided here. Counselors who use tests should carefully read the entire document, which is available through the Resources link at http://aac.ncat.edu.

Another document of significance to counselors in using tests is the *Code of Fair Testing Practices in Education*. This noncopyrighted document was developed by the Joint Committee on Testing Practices (JCTP). The JCTP includes member representatives from a variety of professional organizations, notably including the ACA and AACE. The code is distinct in that it delineates responsibilities of both test users and test developers. Major sections of the code present guidelines for topics such as test development or selection, test score interpretation, fairness in testing, and informing test takers of results. The code is available as a link from either http://aac.ncat.edu or http://ericae.net.

Although the code was developed specifically to address testing practices in educational settings, the important points in it extend beyond that limitation. That is, the code contains useful information and sound suggestions for use of tests in any circumstance. Counselors should use the code both for guidance about good testing practices and for clarification of responsibilities among test users and developers.

Testing in Program Evaluation

Counselors should be familiar with the counseling program evaluation literature. However, many counselors mistakenly believe that generating and reporting test results is synonymous with program evaluation. Testing is an aspect of program evaluation, but a "testing program" does not replace program evaluation. Effective program evaluation involves gathering a wide variety of both objective (empirical) and subjective information about program impacts (Loesch, 2001). Test results are just one part of this process.

Formative and *summative* are the two major types of program evaluation processes. In formative program evaluation, data are gathered while the program is in progress so that process adjustments and modifications can be made to maximize the program's (eventual) effectiveness. Summative program evaluation involves gathering data at the conclusion of a program to determine the extent of the program's overall impact. Carefully and effectively designed program evaluation processes usually encompass both types.

Testing and test results can be used in either type of program evaluation process. For example, test data derived while counseling and/or other programmatic activities are being conducted can be used to identify needed changes in those activities. Test data obtained after a program has been concluded can be used for analysis and evaluation of which activities were effective. In either case, if tests are used within appropriate guidelines they can be invaluable resources in program evaluation processes.

Just as program evaluation is not synonymous with testing, neither is it synonymous with research. However, research designs and principles often are incorporated into program evaluation processes. Specifically, summative program evaluation processes typically involve "pre-post" testing, which includes administering tests before a program begins and administering the same (or equivalent) tests at the program's end. In addition to any concern about test validity, this type of procedure requires concern for the appropriateness and reliability of tests used. Thus, the major concerns regarding test use for counseling purposes are at least equally important for research and program evaluation purposes.

The need for counselors to be accountable for their activities has been widely publicized. Program evaluation processes should be a part of counselors' accountability efforts because these processes reflect the full scope of services rendered by counselors. However, counselors need to be involved in program evaluation activities because competent counselors know about tests and testing and therefore should serve as resources for development of program evaluation procedures.

Summary

Testing is an integral and legitimate part of a counselor's professional functioning. However, counselors have a choice about the attitudes they adopt toward testing. They can view it as a necessary evil and employ minimal effort toward testing functions, or they learn psychometric principles, tests, and testing processes and therefore reap the benefits of effective testing practices. Counselors who adopt this latter perspective will find that testing is a valuable resource, and one that enhances many of their professional activities. The following Web sites provide additional information relating to the chapter topics.

USEFUL WEB SITES

American Counseling Association
www.counseling.org

American Educational Research Association
www.aera.net

American Psychological Association
www.apa.org

Association for Assessment in Counseling and Education
http://aac.ncat.edu

Association of Test Publishers
www.testpublishers.org

ERIC Clearinghouse on Assessment
www.ericae.net

Fair Access Coalition on Testing
www.fairaccess.org/

International Test Commission
www.intestcom.org/

National Board for Certified Counselors
www.nbcc.org

National Council on Measurement in Education
www.ncme.org

Test Reviews Online
http://buros.unl.edu/buros/jsp/search.jsp

Note that almost all testing companies have their own Web sites; search by company name, test name, or type of test.

REFERENCES

Aiken, L. R., & Groth-Marnat, G. (2006). *Psychological testing and assessment* (12th ed.). Boston: Allyn and Bacon.

American Educational Research Association, American Psychological Association, & National Council on Measurement in Education. (2000). *Standards for educational and psychological testing.* Washington, DC: American Educational Research Association.

Anastasi, A., & Urbina, S. (1997). *Psychological testing* (7th ed.). New York: Macmillan.

Association for Assessment in Counseling and Education. (1989). *Responsibilities of users of standardized tests* (3rd ed.). Retrieved June 6, 2007, from http://aac.ncat.edu/resources.html.

Dana, R. H. (1993). *Multicultural assessment perspectives for professional psychology.* Boston: Allyn and Bacon.

Drummond, R. J., & Jones, K. D. (2006). *Appraisal procedures for counselors and helping professionals* (6th ed.). Saddle River, NJ: Pearson Prentice Hall.

Goldman, L. (1971). *Using tests in counseling* (2nd ed.). New York: Appleton-Century-Crofts.

Gregory, R. J. (2007). *Psychological testing: History, principles, and applications* (5th ed.). Boston: Allyn and Bacon.

Groth-Marnat, G. (2003). *Handbook of psychological assessment* (4th ed.). New York: Wiley.

Hambleton, R. K. (1998). Principles and selected applications of item response theory. In R. L. Linn (Ed.), *Educational measurement* (3rd ed. reprint; pp. 147–200). New York: American Council on Education & Oryx Press.

Hood, A. B., & Johnson, R. W. (2004). *Assessment in counseling: A guide to the use of psychological assessment procedures* (4th ed.). Alexandria, VA: American Counseling Association.

Kaplan, R. M., & Saccuzzo, D. P. (2005). *Psychological testing: Principles, applications, and issues.* Belmont, CA: Thomson Wadsworth.

Lee, C. C. (2001). Assessing diverse populations. In G. R. Walz & J. C. Bleuer (Eds.), *Assessment issues and challenges for the new millennium* (pp.115–124). Greensboro, NC: ERIC/CAPS.

Lee, C. C., & Chaung, B. (2005). Counseling people of color. In D. Capuzzi & D. R. Gross (Eds.), *Introduction to the counseling profession.* New York: Pearson Education.

Lichtenburg, J. W., & Goodyear, R. K. (1999). *Scientist-practitioner perspectives on test interpretation.* Boston: Allyn and Bacon.

Loesch, L. C. (2001). Counseling program evaluation: Inside and outside the box. In D. C. Locke, J. E. Myers, & E. L. Herr (Eds.), *The handbook of counseling* (pp. 513–525). Thousand Oaks, CA: Sage.

McKinley, R. L. (1989). An introduction to item response theory. *Measurement and Evaluation in Counseling and Development, 22,* 37–57.

Messick, S. (1998). Validity. In R. L. Linn (Ed.), *Educational measurement* (3rd ed. reprint) (pp. 13–104). New York: American Council on Education & Oryx Press.

Vacc, N. A., & Loesch, L. C. (2000). *The profession of counseling* (3rd ed.). Philadelphia: Taylor & Francis.

Whiston, S. C. (2005). *Principles and applications of assessment in counseling* 2nd ed.). Belmont, CA: Wadsworth.

14 Diagnosis in Counseling

LINDA SELIGMAN, PhD, LPC

Walden University

Professor Emeritus, George Mason University

Introduction

Alice, age 20, consulted a counselor at her college because of feelings of depression. She told the counselor that she has barely been able to get out of bed for the past month. She has been eating little, has strong feelings of unexplained guilt, has not attended most of her classes, and has thought about committing suicide. She could offer no explanation for her mood change and said she had never felt like this before.

Michael, age 28, sought help for depression from a community mental health center. Although he has been going to work and fulfilling his family obligations, he has felt hopeless for more than a month. Michael reported a 10-year history of unstable moods, with long periods of depression as well as episodes of elation, high energy, and distractibility.

Susan, age 11, was brought to her pediatrician by her mother, who stated that Susan has been sad and tearful for the past month, since her parents separated. Although Susan does become much more cheerful when her father visits and has been going to school regularly, she was moody and irritable much of the time.

Robert, age 45, sought help from a psychiatrist for long-standing depression, coinciding with a history of alcohol and drug abuse. He has multiple physical complaints and had several alcohol-related automobile accidents. He has begun several treatment programs but has not been able to remain drug- or alcohol-free for more than a few weeks.

Cheryl, too, sought counseling for depression. At 35, she had achieved a great deal. Married with two children, she was a successful writer and photographer. However, she has been troubled by feelings of sadness of at least 2 years' duration that she has been unable to dispel on her own. Although she has been able to function relatively well and conceal those feelings from others, she finally decided to seek help.

All five of these people sought help for depression. However, their depressions differ in several respects: presence of an apparent precipitant, duration, frequency, severity, and accompanying symptoms. Similarly, the diagnoses, the treatments, and the prognoses for each person's disorder differ.

Alice probably is experiencing a Major Depressive Disorder, Single Episode. This form of depression tends to respond fairly quickly to several types of counseling (e.g., cognitive, brief psychodynamic), often in combination with antidepressant medication. Michael is suffering from a Bipolar I Disorder, Most Recent Episode Depressed. This disorder is frequently chronic without treatment but can be alleviated through a combination of counseling and medication. Susan has experienced a recent loss and is reacting to that loss with an Adjustment Disorder with Depressed Mood. Family counseling seems most likely to alleviate Susan's sadness. Robert, on the other hand, may be suffering from a Substance-Induced Mental Disorder, linked to his long-standing substance use. Prognosis here is far less favorable, and treatment may entail hospitalization. Dysthymic Disorder probably is the diagnosis for Cheryl's symptoms. Hospitalization is usually not needed for treatment of this disorder, but its response to counseling, perhaps accompanied by medication, varies and is difficult to predict.

The importance of diagnosis can be seen from these examples. Without an accurate diagnosis, counselors will probably have difficulty determining the proper treatment for a disorder and assessing whether a person is likely to benefit from counseling. In these examples, Susan and probably Cheryl are good candidates for counseling. Alice and Michael are also likely to benefit from counseling, but as part of a team effort, with counselors and psychiatrists working together to ameliorate the depression. Robert's case is too complicated by physiological concerns for counseling to be a primary focus of treatment at present. Perhaps once he has been medically evaluated and detoxified, counseling can facilitate his adjustment to a healthier lifestyle and complement other forms of treatment.

Benefits of Diagnosis

Estimates indicate that 40–50 million Americans have mental or addictive disorders (Maxmen & Ward, 1995). An accurate diagnosis is essential in determining the appropriate treatment for a mental disorder and in indicating when counseling is likely to be effective and when a referral for medication and other sources of help is necessary. These are not the only reasons why diagnosis is a fundamental skill in the counselor's repertoire (Seligman, 2004).

- A diagnostic system provides a consistent framework as well as a set of criteria for naming and describing mental disorders.
- Knowing the diagnosis for a client's concerns can help counselors anticipate the course of the disorder and develop a clearer understanding of the client's symptoms.
- Knowledge of diagnosis enables counselors to make use of the literature on treatment effectiveness (Seligman & Reichenberg, 2007) (e.g., what types of interventions are most likely to ameliorate a given disorder) and to formulate a treatment plan that is likely to be effective.

- The process of counseling employs a common language, used by all mental health disciplines, thereby facilitating parity, credibility, communication, and collaboration.
- Diagnoses are linked to several standardized inventories (e.g., the Minnesota Multiphasic Personality Inventory, the Millon Clinical Multiaxial Inventory), enabling counselors to use inventories as a source of information on their clients.
- Counselors can more easily demonstrate accountability and effectiveness and are less vulnerable to malpractice suits if they make diagnoses and treatment plans according to an accepted system.
- Using a standardized system of diagnosis helps counselors obtain third-party payments for their services, thereby making counseling affordable to many people who would not otherwise be able to receive help.
- The use of standard diagnostic terminology helps counselors research the nature and effectiveness of their practice and improve their treatment skills.
- Sharing diagnoses with clients, when appropriate, can help them to understand their symptoms and experience less guilt and take more appropriate responsibility for themselves. Knowing that others have experienced similar symptoms and that information is available about their difficulties can also be reassuring.
- Explaining to clients that they have a diagnosable mental disorder can unbalance previously established views of their difficulties and help them take a fresh look at their issues and perhaps increase their openness to treatment.
- The use of diagnoses helps counselors determine those clients they have the skills and training to help, as well as those who would benefit from a referral.

Risks of Diagnosis

Although many benefits come from the use of a standard diagnostic system, some risks also are inherent in the use of such a system.

- Attaching a diagnostic label to someone can be stigmatizing, if misused, and can lead to negative perceptions of that person at school, at work, or in the family.
- In some cases, knowing the diagnostic term for a person's symptoms can be more discouraging and threatening than viewing the problem in lay terms. For example, parents may be more comfortable dealing with a child they view as behaving badly than with one who has a Conduct Disorder.
- Diagnosis can lead to overgeneralizing, to viewing clients as their mental disorders (e.g., a Borderline, a Depressive) rather than as a person with a particular set of concerns, and promote a focus on pathology rather than on health.
- Although the process of diagnosis can facilitate information gathering and treatment planning, it also can make it more difficult to think about people in developmental and systemic terms and to take a holistic view of clients and their environments.
- Similarly, attaching a diagnostic label to one person puts the focus of treatment on the individual rather than on a family or social system. This can reinforce the

family's perception of that person as its only problem and make it more difficult for a family to work together on shared issues and concerns.

■ The diagnosis of some mental disorders can have a negative impact on people's ability to obtain health or disability insurance and can affect their employment if they are in high-risk or security-related positions.

■ In addition, the widely accepted systems of diagnosis have all grown out of a Western concept of mental illness and may not be as relevant to people from other cultures.

Although clearly some risks are inherent in the process of diagnosis, most of the risks can be avoided by skillful counseling, judicious presentation of diagnostic information to avoid misunderstanding by clients and their families, and maintenance of the clients' confidentiality whenever possible. Particularly important in reducing risks is counselors' knowledge of diagnosis, as well as their multicultural competence and sensitivity. "Barriers to effective counseling in the postmodern era lie more within the counselor than between the pages of a book. The *DSM*, when used properly, can enhance rather than detract from skills and culturally sensitive counseling" (Seligman, 1999a, p. 6). Resources such as *Diagnosis in a Multicultural Context* (Paniagua, 2001) and *Diagnosis and Treatment Planning in Counseling* (Seligman, 2004) can help counselors maximize the benefits and minimize the risks of diagnosis. Chapter 3 of the present book, Counseling People of Color written by Cortland Lee, also provides guidelines that help counselors make accurate diagnoses of multicultural clients.

Growing Importance of Diagnosis

Some counselors and students in counseling, particularly those who are primarily interested in school or business settings, may feel uncomfortable with the idea of making diagnoses. They may view their role as emphasizing support, crisis intervention, and information giving and may refer people who have mental disorders to other mental health practitioners. Consequently, they may feel little need to learn about diagnosis. Other counselors may have a strongly humanistic, multicultural, or family systems emphasis in their counseling and may believe that the process of labeling clients is antithetical to their conception of the counselor's role.

However, developments in the field of counseling make it important for all counselors to be familiar with the process and tools of diagnosis, and most counselors seem to recognize that. A study by Mead, Hohenshil, and Singh (1997), in which 334 Certified Clinical Mental Health Counselors were surveyed on their use of the *Diagnostic and Statistical Manual of Mental Disorders (DSM)*, reflected the importance of this resource to counselors. Mead et al. found that 91% of respondents "indicated that the *DSM* is their most frequently used professional reference" (p. 394). Most believed they were skilled in the use of the *DSM*, and 93% reported that they believed they were usually able to provide accurate diagnoses using the *DSM*. Although respondents did note shortcomings in the *DSM*, including bias, labeling, and difficulty of use, they found the *DSM* particularly helpful with case conceptualization, treatment planning, billing, communication with other professionals, education, and meeting employers' requirements. Mastery of diagnosis not only can improve the effectiveness of mental health counselors but also is required by many places of employment where diagnoses are needed for accountability, determination of treatment effectiveness, record keeping, and third-party payments.

Although knowledge of diagnosis is essential to mental health counselors, counselors in schools and businesses should also be familiar with the process of diagnosis for somewhat different reasons. Knowledge of diagnosis enables counselors to determine whether they can provide services that will help a client or whether a referral is needed, it can help them select the most appropriate referral, and it can help them anticipate the client's probable response to treatment. Making a diagnosis also can help counselors in schools and businesses to assess whether clients should remain in that setting, possibly with some extra help, or whether the client needs an environment providing more support and assistance. Diagnosis, therefore, is an important skill for all counselors.

The *DSM-IV-TR* and Other Diagnostic Systems

The most widely used diagnostic system in the United States is the *Diagnostic and Statistical Manual of Mental Disorders (DSM)*. The most recent edition of this volume, the *DSM-IV-TR*, was issued in 2000 by the American Psychiatric Association. The first edition of the *DSM*, containing 108 categories of mental disorder, was published in 1952 (Hohenshil, 1993). Developed primarily by and for psychiatrists, it presented a psychobiological view of the nature of emotional disorders. It was replaced in 1968 by the *DSM-II*, a landmark publication in the field of mental health that looked at mental disorders primarily in terms of psychoses, neuroses, and personality disorders.

The *DSM-III* was introduced in 1980. Field tests involving more than 500 clinicians were used to maximize the validity of that volume. In addition, psychologists, as well as a small number of social workers and counselors, worked along with psychiatrists to develop this revision of the *DSM*. The *DSM-III* was more comprehensive and detailed than its predecessor and was designed to be more precise and less stigmatizing in its language. The *DSM-III* made some major changes in definitions and terminology used for mental disorders. For example, the term *neurosis*, which had become a pejorative and common term in the language, was no longer used. Schizophrenia was defined more narrowly and was used to describe only severe disorders involving evident loss of contact with reality.

A revised version of the *DSM-III*, the *DSM-III-R*, was published in 1987. The *DSM-III-R* reflected changes arising from increased knowledge of mental disorders as well as from changes in attitudes and perceptions. For example, the diagnosis of homosexuality was excluded from this edition, reflecting greater understanding as well as increased acceptance of homosexuality.

The primary justification for a change in content from the *DSM-III-R* to the *DSM-IV*, published in 1994, was compelling empirical support. Three criteria were used to determine revisions: extensive literature reviews, clinical trials, and feedback on two drafts of the *DSM-IV* to determine whether support was available for a suggested change. The *DSM-IV*, like the *DSM-III* and *DSM-III-R*, was deliberately atheoretical. The *DSM-IV* included more than 300 categories of mental disorders, as well as extensive descriptive information, much of which focused on gender, ethnicity, and cultural patterns in mental disorders. This reflects great progress in making the *DSM-IV* sensitive to differences related to group membership and diversity. The current edition, the *DSM-IV-TR*, is called a text revision of the *DSM;* further text was added describing diagnoses and their manifestations. No substantive changes in diagnostic criteria were made in the *DSM-IV-TR*. A more detailed discussion of the development of the *DSM* can be found in "Twenty Years of Diagnosis and the *DSM*" (Seligman, 1999b). Work is already underway on the *DSM-V*, with publication currently anticipated in 2011.

Revisions of the *DSM* demonstrate that knowledge of mental disorders is a vital and changing body of information. New material is constantly discovered about biochemistry, the emotions, and their interaction and impact. In many ways, we are still novices in our understanding of the psychology of people. As a result, our current information is often inadequate and imprecise. Although the *DSM* makes an important contribution to clarifying and organizing mental disorders, it is a complex publication whose skillful use requires sound clinical judgment as well as experience. A subsequent section of this chapter introduces the major types of mental disorders and gives readers some familiarity with the *DSM-IV-TR*. Browsing through the volume, reading about diagnoses of interest, and making diagnoses of case studies will increase all counselors' comfort and familiarity with this sometimes intimidating volume. However, true ease of use of the *DSM* rarely comes without considerable clinical experience.

Although the *DSM-IV-TR* is the standard for diagnostic nomenclature in the United States, another system of diagnosis is also used, particularly in medically oriented settings. The *ICD-10 Classification of Mental and Behavioural Disorders* (World Health Organization, 2004), known in the United States as the *ICD-10*, is an international publication of the World Health Organization. The code numbers of the *ICD-10* are coordinated with the *DSM-IV-TR*, and clinicians can refer to Appendix H of the *DSM-IV-TR* to determine the appropriate *ICD-10* diagnosis, if required by a managed care organization.

Definition of a Mental Disorder

The *DSM-IV-TR* defines a *mental disorder* as "a clinically significant behavioral or psychological syndrome or pattern that occurs in an individual" (p. xxxi) (American Psychiatric Association, 2000). Responses that are expectable or culturally sanctioned are not considered mental disorders. According to the *DSM-IV-TR*, at least one of three features—distress, impairment, and/or significant risk—must be present for a person to be diagnosed with a mental disorder. Although these features are often present in combination, illustrations of the features in isolation are provided to clarify their nature.

Beth sought counseling after her fiancé broke their engagement for the third time. She was a successful lawyer who continued to perform well at her job despite her turmoil. A very private person, Beth continued to see friends and family and go to work every day and showed little or no evidence of her distress. However, every night she cried herself to sleep and even had fleeting suicidal thoughts. Although Beth manifested no impairment nor was she really at risk, she was certainly experiencing considerable distress and met the criteria for a mental disorder, Adjustment Disorder with Depressed Mood.

On the other hand, Frank, a 14-year-old who was brought to counseling by his parents, reported that life was great; he saw his only problem as his parents' nagging. For the past year, Frank had cut classes frequently and spent several days each week hanging out at the neighborhood shopping center with his friends. He disobeyed his parents' rules, had frequent arguments with family and teachers, and usually seemed angry and annoyed. Frank had little distress about his situation and was not currently at risk. Frank's diagnosis, Oppositional Defiant Disorder, was characterized primarily by impairment.

Hilda reported neither distress nor impairment when she consulted a counselor at the suggestion of her family physician. At 5 feet, 6 inches tall, Hilda weighed 100 pounds and was quite pleased with her figure, estimating that she had only another 5 to 10 pounds to lose. Hilda had the diagnosis of Anorexia Nervosa, Restricting Type, and had dieted herself into a physical condition that posed considerable risk to her health and life.

Some symptoms that do not cause significant distress, impairment, or risk and are expectable responses are not viewed as mental disorders. For example, Jessica consulted a counselor after the birth of her third child within the past 5 years. Although she was a caring and knowledgeable parent, she had difficulty asking for help and managing her time. Counseling could certainly help Jessica handle the many demands on her and her husband, but Jessica did not have a mental disorder. Her reactions caused no risk to herself or the children, did not reflect impairment, and were characterized by appropriate, understandable, and manageable concern. Jessica would be described as experiencing a Phase of Life Problem rather than a mental disorder.

Multiaxial Assessment

Whether or not people who present for counseling have mental disorders, a multiaxial assessment offers counselors a way to organize information on clients' symptoms, their physical conditions, their levels of coping, and the stressors they are experiencing. A full multiaxial assessment involves viewing a person according to five axes.

Axis I includes what the *DSM* calls Clinical Disorders and Other Conditions That May Be a Focus of Clinical Attention. All disorders and conditions in the *DSM-IV-TR* are included in Axis I with the exception of the Personality Disorders and both Mental Retardation and Borderline Intellectual Functioning, which are listed on Axis II. These Axis II listings may actually involve less severe symptoms than some of the diagnoses on Axis I, but they have a pervasive and enduring impact on a person's life.

People may have one or more diagnoses or conditions on Axis I or Axis II, or one or both of these axes may have no diagnosis or condition listed. Each diagnosis has a code number provided in the *DSM*. When a diagnosis is listed, both the name and the code number are specified (e.g., 307.51 Bulimia Nervosa). In addition, clinicians generally describe the severity of a mental disorder, using the terms *Mild, Moderate,* and *Severe*. Three additional specifiers describe disorders a person had previously that no longer meet the full criteria for the disorder. *In Partial Remission* describes symptoms that once met the criteria for a mental disorder but now are manifested in more limited ways. *In Full Remission* describes disorders whose symptoms no longer are evident but remain clinically relevant, perhaps because the person still receives medication for the disorder. *Prior History* characterizes past disorders, no longer treated or in evidence, that remain noteworthy, perhaps because they have a tendency to recur under stress. Disorders characterized as Prior History are one step removed from those described as In Full Remission, but both would be viewed as important to keep in mind. The *DSM* also provides terminology to be used when no diagnoses are listed on Axis I or on Axis II (e.g., V71.09 No Mental Disorder on Axis II). When more than one diagnosis is listed on an axis, they are listed in order of treatment priority. The *Principal Diagnosis* is assumed to be the first diagnosis on Axis I unless otherwise specified. The *DSM-IV-TR* also offers the option of the descriptor *Reason for Visit*, used if the presenting concern is not the principal diagnosis.

Axis III includes *General Medical Conditions*. On this axis, clinicians list physical disorders that may be relevant to a person's emotional condition. This would include such conditions as migraine headaches that might be related to stress, as well as conditions such as cancer or diabetes that might have an impact on a person's emotional adjustment. Although clinicians may informally list signs and symptoms on Axis III in their own notes, an official multiaxial assessment should include only medically verified physical conditions on Axis III. Until that verification is obtained, clinicians should state on Axis III that the medical symptoms and conditions are provided *by client report*.

On Axis IV, clinicians list *Psychosocial and Environmental Problems* that may be affecting a person. Clinicians may use their own labels for these stressors and also can organize them according to the *DSM* categories of stressors. These include problems with one's primary support group; problems related to the social environment; problems related to educational, occupational, or housing concerns; economic problems; and problems related to access to health care services or to interaction with the legal system. Counselors generally list on Axis IV only stressors that have occurred within the past year, unless an earlier stressor is especially relevant to the current diagnosis, such as combat experiences related to a diagnosis of Posttraumatic Stress Disorder.

Axis V includes a *Global Assessment of Functioning* rating on a scale ranging from 1 to 100. Here, counselors rate clients' current functioning, paying particular attention to symptoms associated with mental disorders and conditions listed on Axes I and II. (Highest level of functioning also can be rated if the clinician chooses.) Ratings below 50 indicate people with severe symptoms who need close monitoring and probably medication and even hospitalization. Ratings above 50 indicate higher levels of functioning. Most people who are seen for counseling in outpatient settings seem to have ratings between 50 and 70.

Axes IV and V are particularly useful in treatment planning. People with many stressors listed on Axis IV and low ratings on Axis V are experiencing considerable stress and have poor levels of functioning. They typically require a multifaceted treatment plan, including counseling, medication, and possibly hospitalization. On the other hand, people with an opposite profile, few stressors on Axis IV and high ratings on Axis V, are experiencing more manageable stress and probably have good coping mechanisms. Such clients are likely to make good use of brief counseling.

The following example of a multiaxial assessment illustrates how such a diagnosis can quickly provide a broad and rich picture of a client:

Axis I: V71.01 Adult Antisocial Behavior
315.2 Disorder of Written Expression, Mild
Axis II: 301.20 Schizoid Personality Disorder
Axis III: 346.20 Headaches, cluster
Axis IV: Psychosocial stressors: Problems related to interaction with the legal system/crime (Arrest)
Axis V: Current global assessment of functioning (GAF): 45
Highest GAF in the past year: 60

This multiaxial assessment was made on a 37-year-old man, Dennis Roth, who had been arrested and charged with assault and battery. Mr. Roth lived alone and earned a living by raising dogs. One of his dogs had escaped to a neighbor's yard, where he damaged some plants and frightened the neighbor's son. The neighbor dealt with this by shooting and killing the dog. When Mr. Roth discovered this, he smashed the window of his neighbor's car and physically attacked the neighbor.

Prior to this, Mr. Roth had no legal problems and was viewed by his neighbors as a loner but someone who was always available to help when cars or other machinery broke down. Mr. Roth had left high school when he was 16, reporting poor grades and discouragement. He had lived on a small farm, raising dogs, since that time. He had little contact with others, except that necessitated by his business and other daily activities, but reported being content with his life.

The multiaxial assessment provides insight into the dynamics of this client's attack on his neighbor. Mr. Roth's primary source of success and gratification and the focus of his life were his dogs. Consequently, Mr. Roth's strong response to the shooting of his dog reflected the impact this event had on his life. He had no history of criminal or violent behavior and was unlikely to present a danger to others in the future.

Axis I reflects the current incident (Adult Antisocial Behavior) and this client's long-standing learning disorder that limited his success in school as well as his career opportunities. Axis II lists his Schizoid Personality Disorder, reflected in his lack of interest in interpersonal relationships, his preference for solitary activities, and his usual detached state. Mr. Roth's medically diagnosed headaches are listed on Axis III, contributing to his constricted lifestyle. The primary stressor, listed on Axis IV, was his arrest and the threat of incarceration that would prevent him from caring for his dogs. Axis V indicates that this man's highest, and usual, level of functioning is moderately impaired, particularly in terms of relationships. Current GAF of 45 reflected his aggressive behavior toward his neighbor and Mr. Roth's continued rage. This multiaxial assessment was instrumental in obtaining probation for Mr. Roth, with the condition that he seek counseling to help him with impulse control and communication skills.

Review of the *DSM-IV-TR*

The mental disorders and conditions described in the *DSM-IV-TR* are divided into 17 broad categories. Although this chapter is not designed to teach or interpret the *DSM*, a brief review of the 17 sections is provided here to give readers a familiarity with the major types of mental disorders. Many specific mental disorders and conditions included in each broad category are not cited here. Readers planning to use the *DSM* with their clients should study that book and probably complete course work or training in its use. Professional organizations offer training related to the *DSM*, and the American Counseling Association offers a home study program to teach diagnosis and treatment planning (Seligman, 1995). In addition, study guides and other texts are available: *Study Guide to DSM-IV-TR* (Fauman, 2002), *DSM-IV Made Easier* (Morrison, 2006), the *DSM-IV-TR Casebook* (Spitzer, Gibbon, First, Skodol, & Williams, 2002), *Diagnosis and Treatment Planning in Counseling* (Seligman, 2004), and *Selecting Effective Treatments* (Seligman & Reichenberg, 2007).

Disorders Usually First Diagnosed in Infancy, Childhood, or Adolescence

This is the largest and most comprehensive category in the *DSM* and includes disorders that typically begin during the early years, although many of these may persist into adulthood. Many of the other diagnoses described in the *DSM* can be applied to children and adolescents, but most of the disorders young people experience are included in this first category. Categories of disorders in this section include Mental Retardation, Learning Disorders, Motor Skills Disorder, Pervasive Developmental Disorders such as Autism and Asperger's Disorder, Attention-Deficit/Hyperactivity Disorder, Disruptive Behavior Disorders (e.g., Conduct Disorder and Oppositional Defiant Disorder), and Communication Disorders (e.g., Stuttering, Phonological Disorder). Also included in this section of the *DSM-IV-TR* are Feeding and Eating Disorders of Infancy or Early Childhood such as Pica, Tic Disorders including Tourette's Disorder, and the Elimination Disorders (Encopresis and Enuresis). Other disorders in this section include Separation Anxiety Disorder, Selective Mutism, Reactive Attachment Disorder, and Stereotypic Movement Disorder.

Of the disorders in this section, Learning Disorders, Attention-Deficit/Hyperactivity Disorder, Conduct Disorder, Oppositional Defiant Disorder, and Separation Anxiety Disorder are particularly important to school counselors and others working with children of elementary school age. Children with Learning Disorders typically have both social and academic impairment. Although they are usually of normal intelligence, they have inordinate difficulty mastering a particular area of learning, such as reading or mathematics, and consequently may experience teasing, criticism, and frustration. They usually need both counseling and academic help. Children diagnosed with Attention-Deficit/Hyperactivity Disorder also tend to have academic, social, and often family problems as a result of their symptoms, such as a high level of motor activity, distractibility, and impulsivity, which impair their efforts to concentrate and engage in rewarding activities with family and friends. Conduct Disorder, involving repeated violations of laws and rules (e.g., stealing, vandalism, truancy), is sometimes the precursor of adult antisocial or criminal behavior. Consequently, rapid treatment of this disorder is important, although client resistance and mistrust may be high. Oppositional Defiant Disorder involves angry, defiant, and argumentative behavior and sometimes accompanies Attention-Deficit/Hyperactivity Disorder and Conduct Disorder. Family counseling is especially important in treating Oppositional Defiant Disorder. Separation Anxiety Disorder has been known as school phobia and typically involves difficulty separating from parents or caregivers, accompanied by an avoidance of school. Early intervention is critical here, too, because the longer this disorder persists, the more difficult it is for the child to return to school. Additional information on disorders in this section of the *DSM* can be found in books such as *Counseling Treatment for Children and Adolescents with DSM-IV-TR Disorders* (Erk, 2008).

Delirium, Dementia, and Amnestic and Other Cognitive Disorders

These cognitive disorders all involve some type of transient or permanent damage to the brain. Causes can include an injury, drug or alcohol use, exposure to a toxic chemical or other substance, disease such as AIDS or Parkinson's, or an abnormal aging process as in Alzheimer's disease.

Counselors rarely are qualified to diagnose or treat either the cognitive disorders discussed here or the disorders due to general medical conditions discussed in the next section. However, they should be familiar with the nature and typical symptoms of these disorders in order to refer clients they suspect of having such disorders to a psychiatrist or neurologist for a conclusive diagnosis. Counselors may work with people with these disorders as part of a treatment team; the counselor may provide therapy to the family of the affected person or may counsel the client to facilitate social and occupational adjustment in light of any limitations that may be imposed by the disorder. Primary treatment, however, usually will come from a physician.

Mental Disorders Due to a General Medical Condition

This section in the *DSM* includes disorders that directly and physiologically result from medical conditions listed on Axis III. Examples of these disorders include Personality Change Due to a General Medical Condition, such as that caused by temporal lobe epilepsy, and Catatonic Disorder Due to a General Medical Condition, which might result from encephalitis.

Substance-Related Disorders

This section includes psychological and behavioral disorders associated with substance use (Substance Abuse and Substance Dependence), as well as the induced or physiological disorders resulting from drug or alcohol use, such as Intoxication, Substance-Induced Sexual Dysfunction, and Substance-Induced Mood Disorder. Counselors should specify whether a person with Substance Abuse or Dependence is experiencing Physiological Dependence, is in remission, is on agonist therapy such as Antabuse, or is in a controlled environment such as a halfway house.

The Substance Use Disorders are divided into Substance Abuse and Substance Dependence (usually the more severe and pervasive of the two). These diagnoses describe people who use alcohol or other substances (e.g., amphetamines, cannabis, cocaine, hallucinogens, inhalants, nicotine, opioids, and sedatives) in a self-damaging way, usually with the knowledge that they are being harmed by their substance use. Although these people may continue to maintain employment and present a positive façade to friends and family, their performance and relationships usually are adversely affected by their substance use, and they may be endangering their lives through their use of these substances. Counselors in nearly all settings should be familiar with the diagnosis and treatment of these prevalent disorders, particularly counselors working in employee assistance programs. Treatment for substance use disorders typically involves a multifaceted approach including group, individual, and family counseling; education; participation in a self-help group such as Alcoholics Anonymous; and relapse prevention.

Schizophrenia and Other Psychotic Disorders

The disorders included in this section are all characterized by symptoms of loss of contact with reality, including hallucinations and delusions. Schizophrenia involves a severe, pervasive loss of contact with reality, often including auditory hallucinations, and lasting at least 6 months. Types of Schizophrenia include Paranoid, Disorganized, Catatonic, Undifferentiated, and Residual. Schizophreniform Disorder has the same criteria as Schizophrenia, but the symptoms are less than 6 months in duration. Delusional Disorders are characterized by nonbizarre (possible) delusions lasting at least 1 month. An example is a man who became convinced, without reason, that his wife was having a series of affairs. Delusional Disorders typically are circumscribed and are more likely than Schizophrenia to have an apparent precipitant and to begin abruptly. Brief Psychotic Disorder is characterized by symptoms of Schizophrenia or Delusional Disorder that are less than 1 month in duration. When psychotic symptoms have a precipitant—for example, the loss of one's family in an accident—and when the symptoms begin suddenly rather than gradually, the prognosis for recovery is generally good. This usually is the case with Brief Psychotic Disorder. Schizoaffective Disorder includes criteria for the diagnosis of both Schizophrenia and a Mood Disorder (Major Depressive Disorder or Bipolar Disorder). Shared Psychotic Disorder involves two people, usually in a close relationship, who have a shared delusional belief. Psychotic Disorders Due to a General Medical Condition are included in this section, such as psychosis resulting from lupus.

Mood Disorders

This section of the *DSM* includes disorders characterized primarily by manic or depressive features. Manic features are less commonly presented by clients than are depressive ones. Mania is typified by an elevated, expansive, or irritable mood; grandiosity; distractibility and agitation; and excessive pleasure seeking. One client, a man in his mid-20s, employed as a teacher and planning to get married, reported during a manic episode that he realized he was destined to be a Hollywood film star. He resigned from his job, bought an expensive sports car, enrolled in three acting classes, and prepared to move to California. Clearly, manic features can be very disruptive and self-destructive. Their treatment usually involves both medication and counseling.

Clients experiencing depression present quite different symptoms. They may feel helpless, discouraged, and even suicidal; experience excessive guilt and self-blame; and usually take little interest or pleasure in anything. Sleeping and eating problems, as well as fatigue, are also common. Irritability may reflect depression, especially in children and adolescents. Cognitive-behavioral and brief psychodynamic approaches to treatment are often used to treat depression, frequently in combination with medication.

Diagnoses in the Mood Disorders category include Major Depressive Disorder (severe depression of at least 2 weeks' duration), Dysthymic Disorder (long-standing moderate depression), and Bipolar I and II Disorders and Cyclothymic Disorder, which combine depressive and manic or hypomanic (similar to but milder than manic) symptoms. Specifiers such as Seasonal Pattern, Postpartum Onset, or Melancholic Features, indicating the patterns and features of the disturbance, further describe each diagnosis. This section is an important one for counselors because of the prevalence of Mood Disorders, especially Major Depressive Disorders, in both inpatient and outpatient settings.

Anxiety Disorders

Anxiety is another symptom that is frequently presented in counseling. Several of the anxiety disorders in the *DSM* involve a phobia, characterized by a persistent and exaggerated fear of an object or situation, leading to impairment through avoidance of the feared stimulus. Examples of these disorders include Social Phobia (fear of social embarrassment), Agoraphobia (fear of places from which escape is difficult, such as crowds or public transportation), and Specific Phobia (fear of a specific object or situation, such as heights or snakes). Also included in this section are Panic Disorder, characterized by brief (usually less than 20 minutes), unexpected feelings of physical and emotional panic; Obsessive-Compulsive Disorder, characterized by recurrent unwanted thoughts or impulses; Posttraumatic Stress Disorder and Acute Stress Disorder, triggered by exposure to traumatic experiences such as rape and natural disasters; and Generalized Anxiety Disorder (pervasive and excessive anxiety and worry lasting at least 6 months). Acute Stress Disorder and Posttraumatic Stress Disorder are frequently encountered by counselors on hotlines or in crisis centers; these disorders involve a cluster of symptoms (e.g., withdrawal, reexperiencing the trauma, anxiety) following a traumatic experience. Anxiety symptoms sometimes mimic those of physical conditions, and a thorough diagnostic evaluation of people experiencing anxiety is important. Properly diagnosed, most anxiety symptoms respond well to a multifaceted treatment plan including improving coping mechanisms, desensitization, cognitive strategies, relaxation, and, in some cases, medication (Seligman, 2004).

Somatoform Disorders

People with Somatoform Disorders are commonly referred for counseling by their physicians. These clients strongly believe they are experiencing a physical ailment; however, medical examinations fail to find any medical cause for their complaints. People with these disorders typically have difficulty managing stress and expressing themselves verbally; their physical complaints often reflect their negative feelings. Types of Somatoform Disorders include Somatization Disorder, characterized by many unverified physical complaints; Conversion Disorder, involving impairment in motor or sensory function, such as paralysis or blindness without medical cause; Pain Disorder; Hypochondriasis, typified by preoccupation with the idea of having a serious illness; and Body Dysmorphic Disorder, characterized by an imagined or exaggerated flaw in one's appearance.

Factitious Disorders

People with Factitious Disorders rarely present for counseling in a straightforward fashion (Seligman & Reichenberg, 2007). These people enjoy the role of patient and deliberately feign physical or psychological symptoms so that they can assume a sick role. Often, the histories of people with Factitious Disorders involve experiencing illness as rewarding, and they learn this dysfunctional way of getting attention. A subtype of Factitious Disorder is Factitious Disorder by Proxy, in which the client causes another person (e.g., a child, an elderly person, or one with disabilities) to feign or experience medical complaints. Little is known about treatment for this disorder because people with this disorder tend to resist treatment and typically leave treatment prematurely. Building a therapeutic alliance and promoting motivation to change is essential to successful treatment of people with Factitious Disorders.

Dissociative Disorders

The best known of these disorders is Dissociative Identity Disorder (DID), previously called Multiple Personality Disorder. This disorder was illustrated on television and film through the cases of Eve and Sybil. Dissociative Amnesia, Dissociative Fugue, and Depersonalization Disorder are also types of Dissociative Disorders. All of these disorders involve an alteration in consciousness (e.g., memory loss, alternate personality states) that is neither organic nor psychotic. Until recently, these disorders were believed to be rare. However, new information on their prevalence is providing a different picture, although DID remains a controversial diagnosis.

Sexual and Gender Identity Disorders

The *DSM-IV-TR* divides these disorders into three groups: Sexual Dysfunctions, Paraphilias, and Gender Identity Disorders. The three are very different in terms of their nature and treatment. People with Sexual Dysfunctions, such as Sexual Desire Disorder, Arousal Disorder, Orgasmic Disorder, or Sexual Pain Disorder, usually are eager for help, although they may be encouraged to seek treatment by an unhappy partner. Paraphilias, on the other hand, involve sexual urges or behaviors that interfere with social adjustment and relationships. Examples are Exhibitionism, Fetishism, Sexual Sadism, Voyeurism, and Pedophilia (sexual activity with children). People with these disorders are often reluctant to change but may seek treatment because of a court mandate or the insistence of an unhappy partner. Gender Identity Disorders (GID) are characterized by strong and persistent cross-gender identification, accompanied by discomfort with one's assigned sex. GID is a controversial diagnosis and many people believe that it should not be retained in the next edition of the *DSM*.

Eating Disorders

Eating Disorders are especially prevalent among adolescent and young adult females, although these disorders are increasing in both younger and older females and in males. If left untreated, eating disorders can be physically harmful and even fatal. A body weight that is 85% or less than expected, as well as an intense fear of weight gain, characterize Anorexia Nervosa (Restricting, Binge Eating, or Purging Type). Bulimia Nervosa (Purging or Nonpurging Types) entails frequent consumption of large quantities of food, often accompanied by self-induced vomiting or excessive use of laxatives or diuretics to avoid weight gain. Treatment of Eating Disorders often is conducted in a group setting and typically involves both cognitive-behavioral and psychodynamic interventions.

Sleep Disorders

Sleep Disorders may be described as Primary (not related to other medical or mental disorders) or as related to other specific diagnoses. Emotions, environment, lifestyle, and physiology can all be causative factors in these disorders. Sleep Disorders include Insomnia; Hypersomnia, characterized by excessive sleeping or fatigue; Narcolepsy, in which a person suffers from sudden and irresistible sleep; Breathing-Related Sleep Disorder, in which a person stops breathing many times during sleep; Circadian Rhythm Sleep Disorder, usually caused by an irregular or unusual sleep schedule; and Nightmare, Sleep Terror, and Sleepwalking Disorders. Sleep disorder clinics are available to facilitate diagnosis of these disorders by tracing the client's brain wave activity while monitoring sleep patterns.

Impulse-Control Disorders Not Elsewhere Classified

Disorders in this section typically involve a repetitive cycle in which people have a buildup of tension and anxiety linked to a craving to engage in some harmful behavior. They release the tension via the behavior and then may be apologetic and promise change, only to repeat the cycle. Disorders described in this section of the *DSM* include Intermittent Explosive Disorder (describing symptoms of people who repeatedly engage in impulsive, aggressive or destructive behaviors, such as partner abuse), Kleptomania (stealing objects that are not needed), Pathological Gambling, Pyromania (fire setting), and Trichotillomania, a disorder that involves pulling out the hairs on one's own head or body. Treatment for these disorders typically involves behavioral counseling as well as help with stress management and interpersonal relationships.

Adjustment Disorders

People who respond to a stressor with mild to moderate, but clinically significant, impairment within 3 months of the stressor are described as having an Adjustment Disorder. The type of Adjustment Disorder (e.g., With Depressed Mood, With Anxiety, With Disturbance of Conduct) is specified when the diagnosis is made. This diagnosis can be maintained for a maximum of 6 months following the termination of the stressor. If symptoms persist beyond that time, the diagnosis must be changed. These disorders, among the mildest mental disorders found in the *DSM-IV-TR*, are common in people going through negative life experiences (e.g., a divorce, illness, being fired from a job) but can also be found in people experiencing positive life changes (e.g., marriage, the birth of a child, graduation). Adjustment disorders generally respond well to crisis intervention and solution-focused brief counseling.

Personality Disorders

Personality Disorders, listed on Axis II of a multiaxial assessment, are long-standing, deeply ingrained disorders, typically evident at least by adolescence or early adulthood. Although most of these disorders are not as severe as such disorders as Schizophrenia and Bipolar I Disorder in terms of the impairment they cause, they are among the most treatment-resistant disorders. Personality Disorders typically are manifested by pervasive patterns of dysfunction that show up in all areas of a person's life. People with Personality Disorders usually do not have a clear and positive self-image, a set of effective coping mechanisms, or an array of healthy peer relationships. Consequently, counseling for people experiencing Personality Disorders is often either a lengthy and challenging process or is terminated prematurely by the client.

   Personality Disorders take many forms. For example, they can be characterized by patterns of suspiciousness, isolation, antisocial behavior, mood instability, grandiosity, dependence, or perfectionism. Many people with histories of criminal and irresponsible behavior, dating back to childhood, are diagnosed as having Antisocial Personality Disorder, often seen by counselors working in corrections or substance abuse settings. Other Personality Disorders frequently treated in counseling include Dependent, Borderline, Histrionic, and Narcissistic Personality Disorders. Less often seen in counseling are people with Paranoid, Schizoid, Schizotypal, Avoidant, and Obsessive-Compulsive Personality Disorders. For more information on personality disorders, see Millon, Millon, Meagher, and Ramnath (2004).

Other Conditions That May Be a Focus of Clinical Attention

These conditions are not viewed as mental disorders but may be a focus of attention in counseling. Conditions listed in the *DSM* may be used alone to describe a person who does not have a mental disorder, or they may be used along with one or more mental disorders on a multiaxial assessment to indicate important areas to be addressed in treatment. Included among the conditions are Psychological Factors Affecting Medical Condition, in which emotional or behavioral patterns adversely affect a medical disorder; Medication-Induced Movement Disorders, such as Neuroleptic-Induced Tardive Dyskinesia; Relational Problems including Partner, Parent–Child, Sibling, and other interpersonal difficulties; and Problems Related to Abuse or Neglect. Additional conditions include Acculturation Problem, Age-Related Cognitive Decline, Identity Problem, Religious or Spiritual Problem, Occupational Problem, Phase of Life Problem, and Borderline Intellectual Functioning (listed on Axis II), among others. Although people who present with conditions and who do not have accompanying mental disorders may seek counseling and may derive considerable benefit from that process, they typically are emotionally healthy people with good resources who have encountered a difficult period in their lives. Often people such as these, like people with Adjustment Disorders, learn and grow considerably from the counseling process.

Diagnosis in Context

This chapter has focused primarily on diagnosis. However, diagnosis is only one of three steps counselors should take before counseling a person. The other two steps, intake interviews and treatment planning, are discussed briefly here.

Intake Interviews

Intake interviews precede diagnosis and provide much of the information needed to make an accurate diagnosis. Some agencies have a formal intake process in which a prospective client goes through a structured interview, completes some forms and inventories, and possibly even meets with more than one clinician (e.g., a counselor and a psychiatrist). In other settings, such as private practices and college counseling settings, the first counseling session usually serves as an intake interview. In a less structured way, the counselor orients the client to the counseling process and gathers information in order to assess the urgency of the client's situation, determine the client's suitability for counseling in that setting, formulate a diagnosis, and develop a treatment plan.

Intake interviews vary widely in terms of their duration and thoroughness. They may be as brief as 15 minutes, focusing on presenting concerns and their development, or they may extend over several sessions of an hour or more to provide a comprehensive and in-depth picture of the client. Topics typically covered in an intake interview include identifying information (e.g., client's age, occupation, marital status), presenting concerns, previous emotional difficulties, treatment history, present life situation, information on family of origin and present family, developmental history, cultural and spiritual background, leisure activities, relationships, education, career, and medical history (Seligman, 2004). While conducting intake interviews, counselors should gather information not only from clients' words but also from their appearance, their behavior during the interview, their interactions with the counselor, their mood and display of emotion, their contact with reality, and their thinking processes. That information can be summarized in a mental status evaluation and is important in helping counselors develop a full picture of their clients and make an accurate diagnosis.

Treatment Planning

Treatment planning is the third step in the process that begins with the intake interview and continues with a multiaxial assessment according to the *DSM-IV-TR*. This three-step process has been compared with the shape of an hourglass (Hershenson, Power, & Seligman, 1989). The information collected during the intake interview provides a broad picture of the client. This information is processed and condensed into a diagnosis, analogous to the narrow part of the hourglass. The focus is then expanded once again with treatment planning. Beginning with the establishment of mutually agreed-upon objectives, the treatment plan provides counselors with a map to guide their work with their clients.

Many models have been developed for treatment plans. One I developed, the DO A CLIENT MAP, is presented here (Seligman, 2004; Seligman & Reichenberg, 2007). The title of the model is a mnemonic device with each letter in the name reflecting 1 of the 12 important areas to be addressed in treatment planning:

1. Diagnosis according to the *DSM-IV-TR*
2. Objectives of treatment
3. Assessment procedures
4. Clinician characteristics
5. Location of treatment
6. Interventions (both theoretical framework and specific interventions)
7. Emphasis of treatment (e.g., supportive, probing)
8. Numbers (individual, group, or family counseling)
9. Timing (duration and scheduling of sessions)
10. Medication
11. Adjunct Services
12. Prognosis

By responding to each item in the outline of a treatment plan, counselors can develop a comprehensive and useful guide for working with a client. Of course, effective treatment planning requires that counselors become knowledgeable not only about diagnosis but also about other elements. For example, counselors should be well informed on empirically supported treatments when determining interventions (Messer, 2001).

Illustration of the Three-Step Process

The following case provides an abbreviated version of the three-step process of intake interview, multiaxial assessment, and treatment plan. The case begins with a short summary of information obtained from the intake interview with the client, continues with a multiaxial assessment, and finishes with a brief treatment plan.

Intake Information.   Amber, a 15-year-old African American female, requested help from her school counselor, who referred her and her family to a community mental health center. Amber lived with her mother, her 12-year-old brother, and her step-father of 2 months. Amber's father died 3 years ago in an automobile accident. Amber stated that she was very angry with her mother for remarrying and could not understand what attracted her to her new husband, Jeff. Amber reported that her mother expected Amber to call Jeff "Dad" and to participate in family outings. Amber spent as much time away from home as she could and reported sadness and loss of interest in academic and social activities since her mother's marriage.

Before that event, Amber had been a quiet and capable student, earning satisfactory grades and participating in several school clubs. She had a small circle of girlfriends and had recently begun to date. Other than some expectable grief and withdrawal around the time of her father's death, Amber had been well adjusted, and no history of problem behavior was reported. She was in good health and rarely missed school. She was above average in intelligence and was well-oriented to reality.

1. **D**iagnosis according to the *DSM-IV-TR*
   Axis I: 309.0 Adjustment Disorder with Depressed Mood, Acute
   Axis II: V71.09 No diagnosis on Axis II
   Axis III: No physical disorders or conditions reported
   Axis IV: Psychosocial stressors: Problems with primary support group (death of father, mother's remarriage)
   Axis V: Current GAF: 65
2. **O**bjectives of treatment
   a. Reduce Amber's level of sadness as measured by the Beck Depression Inventory
   b. Improve her relationships with her mother and stepfather as reflected in increased amounts of rewarding time spent together and on the Family Functioning Scale
   c. Increase Amber's interest and involvement in academic and social activities, as reflected by a daily journal of activities, improved grades, and ratings of mastery and pleasure
3. **A**ssessment procedures: Beck Depression Inventory, Family Functioning Scale
4. **C**linician: No specific counselor variables are indicated here; arguments could be made for assigning Amber to either a male or a female counselor. Her preference for counselor's gender and ethnicity will be considered when selecting her clinician
5. **L**ocation: Outpatient private practice or community mental health center
6. **I**nterventions: A cognitive-behavioral orientation will be emphasized; Amber is telling herself that she must not allow anyone to usurp her father's position in the family, and this is causing dysfunction. Affect (sadness, anger) and behavior (avoidance of family, destructive patterns of communication) also need to be addressed. Such techniques as cognitive restructuring, practicing improved communication skills, monitoring mood levels, and planning activities would be used

in individual counseling. Family counseling will follow a communications approach such as that of Virginia Satir, helping Amber's parents to allow a more gradual development of the stepfather–stepdaughter relationship, helping Amber to reestablish her close tie to her mother and understand her mother's decision to remarry

7. **Emphasis of treatment:** Counseling will initially be supportive and accepting but will encourage Amber to address her grief and develop her coping skills
8. **Numbers:** Individual counseling will be combined with family counseling with the whole family, as well as with Amber and her mother, Amber and her stepfather, and Amber and both parents
9. **Timing:** Weekly 45- or 50-minute counseling sessions will be scheduled for approximately 3–4 months
10. **Medication:** A referral for medication is not indicated
11. **Adjunct services:** Involvement in a rewarding and ongoing peer activity will be encouraged. Tutoring might be needed in any school subjects in which Amber has fallen behind
12. **Prognosis:** Excellent, in light of her relatively mild diagnosis and Amber's previously high level of functioning, as well as her family support

The Future of Counseling and Diagnosis

Diagnosis has become an essential skill of the counselor (Seligman, 1999b). According to the American Counseling Association *Code of Ethics and Standards of Practice* (2005), counselors are careful to provide proper diagnosis of mental disorders.

The 1990s witnessed the growth of private practice and managed care, an increasing emphasis on accountability for counselors, the expansion of the counselor's role to include helping both relatively well-functioning people and those with severe mental disorders, and the growth of most master's degree programs in counseling to 48 or more credits. During the first decade of the 21st century, these trends have continued, along with increased collaboration between school and mental health counselors and an emphasis on empirically supported treatment and brief solution-focused treatment. These trends suggest that diagnosis and treatment planning will continue to grow in importance and will remain important skills for counselors in all settings.

Summary

This chapter has reviewed the important benefits that knowledge of diagnosis and the *DSM* can bring to counselors and their clients. It also cites some possible pitfalls of the diagnostic process that counselors should try to avoid. An overview was presented of the process of multiaxial assessment according to the *Diagnostic and Statistical Manual of Mental Disorders–Text Revision* (American Psychiatric Association. 2000). The 17 categories of mental disorders and conditions also were described.

Diagnosis is one piece of a three-step process that facilitates effective counseling. An intake interview and review of any records is the first step, yielding information that is needed for a diagnosis, which is the second step. A treatment plan then can be developed, based on the diagnosis or multiaxial assessment, and reflecting knowledge of the appropriate use of counseling.

The following Web sites provide additional information relating to the chapter topics. For additional sites, see *Quick Guide to the Internet for Counseling* (Pachis, Rettman, & Gotthoffer, 2001) and *DSM-IV Internet Companion* (Morrison & Stamps, 1998).

USEFUL WEB SITES

Resource for information on mental health
http://www.mentalhealth.com

Source of free newsletters containing useful information on mental disorders and their treatment
http://www.athealth.com

Provides information on *DSM* codes, diagnostic criteria, decision trees to facilitate diagnosis
www.PsychiatryOnline.com

Includes information on mental disorders included in the *DSM*
http://psychcentral.com/disorders/

Discusses the diagnosis of symptom clusters and mental health problems
http://www.mentalhealth.about.com/od/problems/

REFERENCES

American Counseling Association. (2005). *Code of ethics and standards of practice.* Retrieved June 25, 2007, from http://www.counseling.org/resources/code of ethics

American Psychiatric Association. (1980). *Diagnostic and statistical manual of mental disorders* (3rd ed.). Washington, DC: Author.

American Psychiatric Association. (1987). *Diagnostic and statistical manual of mental disorders–text revision* (3rd ed.). Washington, DC: Author.

American Psychiatric Association. (1994). *Diagnostic and statistical manual of mental disorders* (4th ed.). Washington, DC: Author.

American Psychiatric Association. (2000). *Diagnostic and statistical manual of mental disorders–text revision.* Washington, DC: Author.

Erk, R. R. (2008). *Counseling treatment for children and adolescents with DSM-IV-TR disorders* (2nd ed.). Upper Saddle River, NJ: Pearson Education.

Fauman, M. A. (2002). *Study guide to DSM-IV-TR.* Washington DC: American Psychiatric Press.

Hershenson, D. B., Power, P. W., & Seligman, L. (1989). Mental health counseling theory: Present status and future prospects. *Journal of Mental Health Counseling, 11*(1), 44–69.

Hohenshil, T. H. (1993). Teaching the DSM-III-R in counselor education. *Counselor Education and Supervision, 32*(4), 267–275.

Maxmen, J. S., & Ward, N. G. (1995). *Essential psychopathology and its treatment.* New York: W. W. Norton.

Mead, M. A., Hohenshil, T. H., & Singh, K. (1997). How the *DSM* system is used by clinical counselors: A national study. *Journal of Mental Health Counseling, 19,* 383–401.

Messer, S. B. (2001). Empirically supported treatments. In B. D. Slife, R. N. Williams, & S. H. Barlow (Eds.), *Critical issues in psychotherapy* (pp. 3–19). Thousand Oaks, CA: Sage.

Millon, T., Millon, C. M., Meagher, S., & Ramnath, R. (2004). *Personality disorders in modern life.* New York: John Wiley and Sons.

Morrison, J. (2006). *Diagnosis made easier.* New York: Guilford Press.

Morrison, M. R., & Stamps, R. F. (1998). *DSM-IV Internet companion.* New York: W. W. Norton.

Pachis, B., Rettman, S., & Gotthoffer, D. (2001). *Quick guide to the Internet for counseling.* Boston: Allyn and Bacon.

Paniagua, F. A. (2001). *Diagnosis in a multicultural context.* Thousand Oaks, CA: Sage.

Seligman, L. (1995). *DSM-IV:* Diagnosis and treatment planning home study. Alexandria, VA: American Counseling Association.

Seligman, L. (1999a, November). The *DSM-IV:* An essential tool in the hands of skilled clinicians. *Counseling Today,* pp. 6, 37.

Seligman, L. (1999b). Twenty years of diagnosis and the *DSM. Journal of Mental Health Counseling, 21,* 229–239.

Seligman, L. (2004). *Diagnosis and treatment planning in counseling* (3rd ed.). New York: Kluwer.

Seligman, L., & Reichenberg, L. (2007). *Selecting effective treatments* (3rd ed.). San Francisco: Jossey-Bass.

Spitzer, R. L., Gibbon, M., First, M. B., Skodol, A. E., & Williams, J. B. W. (2002). *DSM-IV-TR casebook.* Washington, DC: American Psychiatric Association.

World Health Organization. (2004). *International statistical classification of diseases and health related problems (ICD-10).* Geneva, Switzerland: Author.

PART THREE

Counseling in Specific Settings

This section describes the basic environments in which counselors today are most likely to work. Chapter 15, "Professional School Counseling," describes the unique setting of professional school counseling and provides insight into the role and function of today's school counselor. School counseling, as a specialty area of counseling, differs from other areas in a variety of ways, and these differences are discussed. A brief history of school counseling is given, followed by a comprehensive examination of the current status of school counseling. Information from the American School Counselor Association (ASCA), the premier association for school counseling, is shared throughout the chapter, along with details regarding the ASCA National Model for School Counseling programs and other influential movements and documents in professional school counseling literature.

Chapter 16, "Counseling in Mental Health and Private Practice Settings," describes the other major settings in which the counselor may practice. The history of mental health counseling is outlined, and the process of how counseling expanded from its early educational/vocational focus to encompass therapeutic mental health activities is described. Major events that have influenced this process, such as the Community Mental Health Act of 1963, which provided federal funding for community mental health agencies and programs, are presented, and the possibilities for the future of mental health counseling in the 21st century are considered. Mental health counselors have engaged in a continuing process to earn recognition as mental health professionals similar to social workers, psychologists, and psychiatrists, and this process has supported the movement toward counselor licensure. As more states have passed legislation enabling counselors, both in mental health and in other specializations, to be recognized as practicing professionals, more counselors have chosen to go into private practice, either as a full-time career option or as an adjunct to their other work. This chapter also depicts the expanding roles and work settings of community/ mental health counselors in the 21st century.

As these chapters indicate, the role of counselors has continuously expanded and will inevitably continue to do so. As the opportunities for therapeutic mental health professions increase in our society, so will the settings and environments in which counselors may choose to practice.

15 Professional School Counseling

TAMARA DAVIS, EdD
Marymount University

Everyone had noticed that Paul's behavior and academic performance at school had been deteriorating since the holiday break. The rumor was that Paul's parents had announced their intent to separate and divorce after the family had "gotten through Christmas." Paul's geometry teacher was especially concerned that he had not turned in any homework since returning from break. His swimming coach noted that Paul had been consistently late for practice and had even missed a swim meet with no excuse. Some students said that Paul had been hanging with a new group of friends (referred to as the "potheads") and that his moods were either depressed or almost manic. Although the parental separation might explain some of this, there was great concern that Paul's downward spiral could cost him academically and ultimately affect his postsecondary plans.

Paul's case demonstrates when a professional school counselor is needed. Often referred to as a guidance counselor, the professional school counselor has a unique and pivotal role in today's education system. A professional school counselor serves as a member of the educational team of qualified professionals whose specialty is the enhancement of students' academic, personal/social, and career development as they experience their school life. We know that students do not leave their personal lives at the schoolhouse door; school counselors have a distinct opportunity to help students deal with issues that could hamper their academic progress. A counseling plan for Paul is offered at the end of this chapter.

This chapter reveals the unique field of professional school counseling and provides insight into the role and function of today's school's counselor. School counseling, as a specialty area of counseling, differs from other areas in a variety of ways, and these differences are detailed. A brief history of school counseling is followed by a comprehensive examination of the current status of school counseling. Information from the American School Counselor Association (ASCA), the premier association for school counseling, is shared throughout the chapter, and details regarding the ASCA National Model for School Counseling Programs (ASCA, 2005a) and other influential movements and documents in professional school counseling are given.

The role of the school counselor within the framework of the ASCA National Model (ASCA, 2005a) is discussed, as is collaboration with faculty, administrators, parents, and community members as a critical role for school counselors. Throughout the chapter, examples and graphics illustrate key concepts and ideas in school counseling. Finally, credentials for becoming a school counselor and considerations for a career in school counseling are discussed.

In this chapter, "professional school counselor" is used to describe school personnel who are typically referred to as guidance counselors. *Guidance* is a function of what school counselors do but does not define who they are. Further, in most counseling fields, the persons receiving services are called clients. Because school counselors work in the school setting, the clients are students and here are referred to as "students." Finally, any discussion of school counseling refers to school counselors who work in K–12 settings and not higher education types of counseling.

School Counseling as a Specialty Area in Counseling

The role of school counselors has changed significantly over the years. School counseling as a specialty differs from other types of counseling in specific ways. One of those ways has already been mentioned: the setting in which counseling occurs (schools) and the clients being served (students). Another difference is the logistics of how, when, and where counseling is conducted. In agency or mental health counseling, most clients are seen by appointment, for a designated period of time, and then leave to go about their daily lives. For school counselors, most counseling occurs when students drop by to check in or when a student is in crisis. There are rarely scheduled appointments because of the structure of the student's academic schedule. An advantage that school counselors have is the opportunity to see students on a daily basis, which gives them ample time to follow up and check on students' progress. On the other hand, school counselors sometimes have difficulty meeting with students because pulling them from class interferes with their academic learning, which brings up another difference between school counseling and other types of counseling: the goal of counseling.

The major goal of school counseling is to help students be in the best frame of mind possible to be effective lifelong learners. Other counseling professionals typically do not have a major goal in mind other than to help clients work through their presenting issues or concerns. Because the focus of schools is on academic success, school counselors must also focus on student academic success. However, it is difficult for Johnny to do well on his algebra test if he cannot focus because he is so distraught about the police coming to his house the night before to break up a parental dispute. The overarching goal of academic achievement is not typically found in other counseling specialty areas.

A final difference between school counseling and other specialty areas of counseling is that school counselors are bound by the external policies and protocol of the school and school district. Although this may also be true in some other settings, it is more binding in the school setting. For example, if a student comes to the school counselor to talk about becoming sexually active but the school board's policy is that school personnel advocate for abstinence as the only sexual practice, school counselors are put in the position of deciding how to respond: Should they defy the policies of the school district (employer) and risk dismissal, or should they try to address the students' needs without breaking school district policies? Although there are ways to make decisions in compliance with policies or respond in ways that do not defy rules and regulations, being policed by a third party is another obstacle that school counselors face that may not be present in other counseling specialty areas.

More positively, school counselors also have some distinct advantages over other types of counselors: (a) A large group of students can be served through counseling (a captive audience), (b) there tends to be support for counseling in schools because the ultimate goal is student success, and (c) the stigma that surrounds other areas of counseling may not be present for school counselors because school counseling programs are offered in most schools. An important resource for school counselors is the Ethical Standard for School Counselors, an ethical code written specifically for school counselors (ASCA, 2004a). The ethical standards are applicable to situations and circumstances that are relevant in the school setting and serve as a guide for school counselors as they work with students, parents, peers, administrators, and community members. Anyone considering becoming a school counselor should review the ethical standards to understand the unique features of ethical practices for school counselors.

History of School Counseling

Chapter 1 provides a comprehensive history of the counseling field in general. More specifically, school counseling grew out of the field of vocational counseling, which began in the early 1900s. Frank Parsons, often considered the "father of counseling," began the movement toward counseling by creating a bureau to help students get jobs. The purpose of counseling in this context was to meet societal needs for trained, productive workers.

Over the years, the role of guidance personnel in schools began to include testing young men for the purposes of classification to serve in the armed forces. The emphasis on vocations was still the predominant role, but the war required placement of many young men in service to their country. One specific event that gave credence to school guidance personnel (as they were called at the time) was the advent of state certification for guidance counselors in 1924 (Baker & Gerler, 2004). The need for trained personnel to assist in placement for jobs or for service continued in the 1920s and 1930s.

Beginning with the 1940s, school counseling services were influenced by several events. Changes in support for school counseling and the role of school counselors has been shifting with each decade until the present. Table 15.1 provides a snapshot of key events, legislation, and movements that influenced school counseling from the 1940s until the end of the 20th century.

TABLE 15.1   Key Events in School Counseling, 1940–2000

Year/Decade	Event	Impact on School Counseling Profession
Early 1940s	Carl Rogers are published.	Seminal works altered the public's perception of the counselor's role and promoted more personal counseling rather than vocational counseling.
1946	George Barden Act was passed.	This legislation supported the development and implementation of guidance and counseling activities in schools.
1953	The American School Counselor Association (ASCA) is chartered.	ASCA began as a small organization for school counselors; it has grown to more than 20,000 members.
1955	The Guidance and Personnel Services section of the U.S. Office of Education was reestablished (Schmidt, 2008).	The government began to recognize the importance of professional school counselors in schools and created a section specifically to support guidance personnel.
1958	National Defense Education Act (NDEA) was passed.	The United States was threatened by the launching of Sputnik. NDEA mandated greater funding for academic programs and support services (like school counseling) to improve students' academic and vocational preparation.
1962	Gilbert Wrenn's *The Counselor in a Changing World* was published.	This book provided support for role refinement for school counselors and encouraged school counselors to respond to the needs of students in an ever-changing society.
1964	NDEA was amended to include elementary school counselors.	Up until now, school counselors were present only at secondary levels. The amendment allowed for the hiring of elementary school counselors for the first time.
1975	Education Act for All Handicapped Children was passed.	There were no specific implications for school counseling, but the legislation focused on the need for individualized support services for all students, particularly those with challenging conditions.
1983	"A Nation at Risk" report was published.	The report indicated the declining performance of American's students; as a result, school counselors were asked to be more accountable for their services and to provide more effective support services.
1997	*National Standards for School Counseling Programs* (Campbell & Dahir, 1997) was published.	This was the first document to unify the profession by providing objectives for the *academic, personal/social, and career development* of all students.

Since the millennium, school counseling movements and trends have hit an all-time high. Never has there been a more active period in the history of the school counseling profession. The most current events in school counseling have forever altered the way school counselors function in education settings. In particular, three major events have influenced the school counseling profession: the Transforming School Counseling Initiative (Education Trust, 1996), the No Child Left Behind Act of 2001 (U.S. Department of Education, 2002), and the *ASCA National Model for School Counseling Programs* (2005a).

Tranforming School Counseling Initiative

The Transforming School Counseling Initiative (TSCI), sponsored by the Education Trust, began in 1996 as a grant initiative of the DeWitt Wallace–Reader's Digest fund (Education Trust, 1996). The goal of the initiative was to refine school counselor training programs and current school counseling practices to expand beyond the traditional roles of school counseling (classroom guidance, counseling, consultation, coordination) and include competencies in advocacy, leadership, systemic change, teaming and collaboration, and use of data. The TSCI initiative partnered higher education institutions who were training school counselors with local school districts to improve the academic progress of all students. The initiative focused on greater involvement and the use of data to allow school counselors to become more actively involved in closing the achievement gap through providing increased equity and access for students. The TSCI put its stamp on the world of school counseling and contributed to the future development of the *ASCA National Model for School Counseling Programs* (ASCA, 2005a).

No Child Left Behind Act of 2001

The No Child Left Behind Act of 2001 (U.S. Department of Education, 2002), endorsed by President George Bush in 2002, indicated the nation's focus on education reform, particularly greater accountability for student performance and closing the gap between majority and minority students in terms of achievement. Although school counselor responsibilities are not prescribed in the act, it is critical that school counselors understand their role in helping students during this era of change and engage in practices that support the educational program and student success (Davis, 2005). Dahir and House (2002) suggested that school counseling programs must respond to No Child Left Behind in the following ways: (a) closing the achievement gap between groups, (b) identifying best practices in school counseling that facilitate student success, (c) recognizing the school counselor's role as leader and advocate, and (d) increasing student options by providing services and programs to address academic, personal/social, and career needs.

The ASCA National Model for School Counseling Programs

Perhaps no document has affected school counseling more than the *ASCA National Model for School Counseling Programs* (2005a). The diamond's four quadrants are the basis for developing comprehensive school counseling programs (see Figure 15.1).

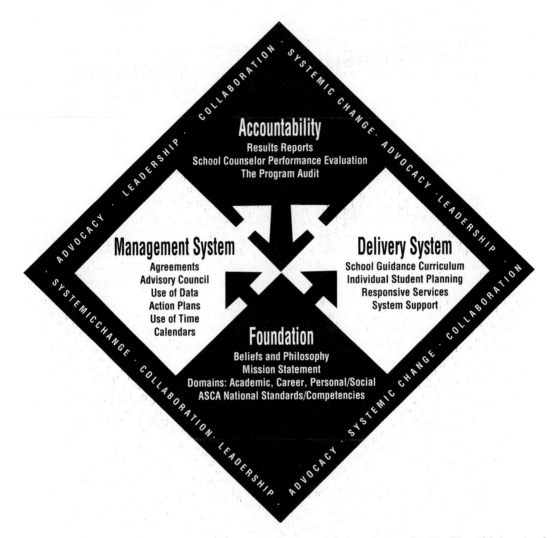

FIGURE 15.1 The ASCA model. American School Counselor Association. (2005). *The ASCA national model: A framework for school counseling programs* (2nd ed.). Alexandria, VA: Author.

The ASCA Model approaches counseling in schools from a systemic perspective rather than from the individualistic model of traditional counseling. Walsh, Barrett, and DePaul (2007) described the shift and related it to other education reform movements:

> The shift in focus from providing services predominantly for individual students to working systematically to serve all students centralizes the role of school counselors in supporting the teaching and learning mission of schools and situates them as essential figures in the nation's goal to reform education and leave no child behind. (p. 377)

Overview of the ASCA National Model. The ASCA Model (ASCA, 2005a) contains four elements that are necessary for the creation of effective and comprehensive school counseling programs. The diagram indicates that the Foundation of the model contributes to the Delivery and Management Systems, which are connected to Accountability. Accountability then flows back to Foundation because the results of data collected about the school counseling program ultimately influence the foundation of the program.

The ASCA Model (ASCA, 2005a) is the professional framework that provides structure for what school counselors do in schools. Many of the tasks, particularly those in the delivery system, involve direct work with students. Other components assist in the planning, organization, and evaluation of the school counseling program. The connection between the model and the role of school counselors is evident in ASCA's (2004c) *The Role of the Professional School Counselor*, and it is important to understand the role of professional school counselors in the context of the ASCA Model.

The Role of the Professional School Counselor: Alignment with the ASCA National Model

The ASCA Model (ASCA, 2005a) offers a framework in which the school counseling program should be developed, implemented, sustained, and improved. The traditional roles of classroom guidance, counseling coordination, and consultation are infused into the transformed roles of advocacy, leadership, systemic change, assessment, use of data, and teaming and collaboration (Education Trust, 1996). An exploration of these roles within each component is critical to understanding the important work of professional school counselors.

Foundation

At the crux of school counseling are the beliefs and philosophies about how students benefit from school counseling. According to ASCA (2004c), these beliefs and philosophies "guide the development, implementation and evaluation of a comprehensive school counseling program" (p. 1). The professional school counselor asks: What do I believe about student success? What is my philosophy of education on student learning? What do I believe about students today? These personal beliefs and philosophies are at the core of why people choose school counseling as a career and also affect the development of a mission statement for the school counseling program. The mission statement of the school counseling program should align with the school's mission statement and should encompass the ultimate goals of promoting student academic, personal/social, and career development. One way this is achieved is through the alignment of the school counseling program with state and national standards (Campbell & Dahir, 1997). Once these tasks are completed, the foundation for a comprehensive school counseling program is laid.

Delivery System

The delivery system indicates how the school counseling program will be delivered or carried out and includes many roles of the school counselor. The delivery of counseling services is probably the area in which most school counselors spend the majority of their time.

School Counseling Curriculum.   The first component of the delivery system is the *school counseling curriculum*, which concurs with a traditional role in school counseling: classroom guidance. According to the ASCA (2004c): "The school guidance curriculum is delivered throughout the school's overall curriculum and is systematically presented by professional school counselors in collaboration with other professional educators in K–12 classroom and group activities" (p. 1). Classroom guidance, which is teaching lessons in the classroom or large group setting, is a unique feature of school counseling. The teaching component of school counseling may be intimidating for school counselors who do not have teaching experience. The debate over school counseling with or without teaching experience is ongoing, and the literature in school counseling has provided mixed results (Olson & Allen, 1993; Quarto, 1999; Smith, Crutchfield, & Culbreth, 2001). Davis (2005) compared the benefits and challenges of having or not having prior teaching experience before becoming a school counselor. However, teaching or speaking in front of large groups is a reality in school counseling, so many counseling preparation programs provide training specific to classroom instruction, such as classroom management strategies.

Classroom guidance topics for school counselors at each level may vary by the development needs in students. For example, elementary school classroom guidance lessons tend to be more preventive in nature, whereas middle and high school topics may be more instructional. Table 15.2 lists topics that may be addressed at each school level.

Individual Student Planning.   One of the reasons most people have for selecting a career in school counseling is the opportunity to influence students on an individual

TABLE 15.2   Developmental Classroom Guidance Topics for Each Level

Elementary	Middle	High
Developing Friendships	Friendship Issues	SAT/ACT Prep Strategies
Bully Prevention	Peer Pressure	Postsecondary Options
Conflict Resolution Skills	Academic Planning	Applying for Scholarships
Test-Taking Strategies	Relationship Issues	Relationship Issues (family, dating)
Character Education	Bullying/Harassment	
Uniqueness/Differences	Fitting in	Academic Planning (yearly)
Responses to Peer Pressure	Test Preparation Skills	Career Decision Making
Career Awareness	Career Exploration	

basis. Individual student planning is often conducted through individual counseling sessions and, while planning may be academic in nature, includes addressing students' personal and social needs. As students begin to plan for their futures, there are often issues or concerns that arise. Family issues, personal issues, or other external concerns may become barriers to the student's academic progress. Individual planning includes important actions, such as establishing goals and planning for the future, while addressing personal/social issues. The developmental nature of education–career planning across levels is indicated by Trusty, Niles, and Carney (2005): "Ideally, students get a solid introduction to education–career planning at the elementary school; planning becomes increasingly specific and involved through middle school, resulting in appropriate plans for high school" (p. 142).

Responsive Services. The majority of the school counselor's day is spent responding to the needs of students, faculty, parents, and community. According to ASCA (2004c), the roles of the school counselor in responsive services include "individual or group counseling, consultation with parents, teachers, and other educators, referrals to other school support services or community resources, peer helping, [providing] information" (p. 1).

Individual and small group counseling are often the roles that attract people to the school counseling profession. Individual counseling may be ongoing or may be a drop-in or "fly-by" encounter with a student. A distinction between individual counseling in schools and in community or agency counseling is that school counselors rarely keep students in a session for a long time. Because most individual counseling occurs during the school day, it is critical to keep students in class whenever possible. The time issues involved in school counseling have facilitated more frequent use of solution-focused brief counseling interventions because counseling must be efficient as well as effective, and solution-focused strategies have proven to be effective in school counseling (Birdsall & Miller, 2002; Gingerich & Wabeke, 2001; Mostert, Johnson, & Mostert, 1997; Schmidt, 2008; Thompson, 2002).

Small group counseling is another role of school counselors. It involves gathering smaller groups (usually 6–8 students) to work on specific skills. Two specific types of groups in schools are *remedial* and *support* groups (Davis, 2005). Remedial groups include topics such as study skills, social skills, anger management, and behavior management and activities that provide skill development to address issues. Support groups focus more on personal issues such as changing families, grief, or life transitions. School counselors solicit referrals for group counseling from teachers, parents, or the students themselves. Parent consent for participation is secured, and small groups typically last from 6 to 8 weeks, although some school counselors have support groups (such as "Girls Group" or "Relationship Issues") on an ongoing basis, with changing student membership each session. Research supports the efficacy of small group counseling in schools (Glaser & Shoffner, 2001; McEachern & Bornot, 2001; Rowell & Hong, 2002; Schectman, 2002; Zinck & Littrell, 2000). There is also evidence that small group counseling interventions, combined with classroom guidance interventions, are associated with positive improvements on student achievement and behavior (Brigman & Campbell, 2003).

Consultation.   A traditional role for school counselors is consultation with parents, teachers, other educators and school personnel, and community members. The school counselor is often a consultant for teachers who are seeking help with students. "Counselors often handle situations by meeting with the student, calling a parent, or establishing a working alliance with the teacher to help meet the needs of the student" (Davis, 2005, p. 82). Consultation with parents is another common role for school counselors, who are often the first to be contacted when parents have a concern about their child. The school counselor becomes the facilitator for action that is taken to address parent concerns or student needs. Finally, the school counselor serves as a consultant and liaison to the community. "Given the movement toward integration of school and community services and school–community partnerships, collaborative consultation adds a critical dimension to the school counselor's consultative function" (Keys, Bemak, & Lockart, 1998, p. 385). The school counselor must be accessible, available, and willing to serve as a consultant to others and has a crucial role to play in the development of strategies and solutions for concerns that are expressed.

When school counselors are not sure how to respond to a situation or do not have the expertise needed to address a problem, they have an ethical obligation to refer the student or person to other school personnel services or community resources. This role may involve coordinating or facilitating the connection between the school and the community. Coordination of services is another role of school counselors and requires organization, knowledge, and the ability to connect constituents with the services they need.

System Support.   "System support consists of management activities establishing, maintaining and enhancing the total school counseling program" (ASCA, 2004c, p. 1). As the profession of school counseling has evolved, greater emphasis has been placed on professional development and alliance with professional organizations. Many school counselor preparation programs require students to obtain professional liability insurance prior to their on-site school experiences. In response to the need for greater professionalism, ASCA includes professional liability insurance in their membership fee. Further, ongoing education to increase knowledge and awareness of relevant issues and practices in school counseling is paramount. State and national counseling organizations offer training through workshops on a variety of topics relevant to school counselors. Through participation in professional development activities, school counselors support their program through increased knowledge of current trends in the field and improved delivery of counseling services.

Management

An important role for school counselors is the overall management and organization of the school counseling program. The management system (ASCA, 2005a) is (a) agreement with administrators in terms of school counseling services and service delivery, (b) the development of an advisory council to provide input and feedback to the school counseling program, (c) use of student data to make decisions regarding the counseling services that are needed to effectively meet student needs, (d) development of action plans to address student needs, and (e) use of master and weekly calendars to keep others informed of the activities and events in the school counseling program. The management of the school counseling program requires organizational skills as well as effective communication to implement the school counseling program.

Because management responsibilities can be time-consuming, school counselors must be careful that the management duties do not undermine the delivery of counseling services. ASCA (2004c) has recommended that 80% of the school counselor's time be devoted to direct service (i.e., counseling, consultation) with students. The tasks and responsibilities of management should enhance the delivery of counseling services, not replace them.

Accountability

As education has become increasingly standards-based, the emphasis on high-stakes testing has also affected school counseling. School counseling services are often considered ancillary to the education program, and school personnel are reluctant to allow school counselors to pull students from class. School counselors may find themselves in the position to have to rationalize or *prove* that school counseling programs make a difference in student success, According to Whiston (2002), "School counselors may believe they make a difference, but without 'hard data' to support these claims, school counselors run the risks of losing their positions" (p. 153).

The emphasis on accountability practices in school counseling is a relatively new phenomenon in school counseling.

> Professional school counselors use data to show the impact of the school counseling program on school improvement and student achievement. Professional school counselors conduct school counseling program audits for all students. The performance of the professional school counselor is evaluated based on standards of practice expected of professional school counselors implementing a school counseling program. (ASCA, 2004c, p. 1)

Current research practices in school counseling include action research (Rowell, 2006) and the development of assessment instruments that can reflect the results of school counseling programs and interventions (Studer, Oberman, & Womack, 2006). The development of the National School Counseling Research Center (Sabella, 2006) and the Center for School Counseling Outcome Research (Carey & Dimmitt, 2006) is evidence of the need for greater results data and accountability in school counseling programs. The following is an example of how a school counselor might use data to support the efficacy of the school counseling program.

Mr. Ledford, a middle school counselor, was concerned about having so many students on the D/F list for English during the first 9-week grading period. In his caseload alone, there were 20 students already at risk of failing for the semester if things did not improve. Mr. Ledford decided he would implement a variety of counseling services to support these students. His plan included: (a) small group counseling sessions with the students to work on study skills such as time management, organization, and study skills; (b) individual counseling or "check ins" with students weekly; (c) consultation with teachers of the students at risk of failure; and (d) contact with parents to enlist their help in making sure homework was completed and returned. He implemented this plan for the second 9-week grading period. Mr. Ledford also conducted a pretest survey to see if students could name three effective strategies for help with studying (12 students could identify three strategies).

At the end of the second 9 weeks, Mr. Ledford checked the students' grades and found that 15 of 20 had successfully raised their grades to at least a "C" in English. Mr. Ledford could conclude that 75% of the students had improved their grades after counseling interventions were implemented to specifically address areas of weakness. Mr. Ledford also completed a posttest survey and found a 50% increase in the number of students who could identify three successful study strategies (18 students could identify three study strategies).

Mr. Ledford can feel good about his success! However, his role as a professional school counselor does not end with his findings. He should let others know of his success with these students. All educational stakeholders need to know that allowing students to participate in counseling services can positively affect success. The sharing of information with key stakeholders demonstrates other important roles for the professional school counselor—advocacy and leadership.

Role of the School Counselor: Leadership and Advocacy

The roles of advocacy and leadership in school counseling go hand in hand. Most people who think about school counseling do not consider leadership an obvious role. However, school counselors have opportunities to be included in important decisions that benefit students.

Brown and Trusty (2005) discuss leadership in school counseling in terms of power. In particular, they refer to *expert power* (the school counselor possesses the knowledge and skills to achieve goals), *referent power* (the school counselor possesses professional characteristics that others would like to emulate), and *informational power* (the school counselor can identify and deliver critical information to teachers and others) (pp. 211–213). School counselors who possess these qualities are inclined to leadership and can gain respect for their roles.

School counselors lead by involvement and example. For example, involvement on curriculum and/or discipline committees gives school counselors the opportunity to have a voice in school programs and activities. Often, people equate leadership with being in charge. Effective leadership includes being visible, being an advocate, and being around the table in important conversations that involve decision making about educational programs and school climate. Leadership in school counseling means taking big steps: School counselors must: (a) step up and participate in important conversations about student development, (b) step out and be visible so that people know who the school counselor is and what school counseling is all about, and (c) step in and get involved in all areas of student development.

Advocacy in school counseling is necessary at many levels. Davis (2005) identified areas of student advocacy, program advocacy, and educational advocacy as required

TABLE 15.3 Advocacy Roles of School Counselors

Advocacy Area	Examples
Student advocacy: supporting the academic, personal/social, and career development of students	Educating students about their personal and educational rights, representing students in administrative hearings, testifying in court on behalf of a student, representing students in decisions that affect their student life
Program advocacy: providing evidence that the school counseling program is effective and essential to student success	Distributing newsletters or brochures that highlight current and future school counseling programs and services; developing accountability reports that demonstrate the efficacy of school counseling programs and sharing the reports with key stakeholders
Educational advocacy: supporting the goals of education and ascertaining that the educational program benefits students.	Learning how the school and school system work; becoming aware of protocol for reporting concerns about the educational program; supporting curricular or program decisions that benefit students

Source: Adapted from Davis, 2005.

roles of school counselors. Table 15.3 summarizes the types of advocacy that are necessary roles of school counselors.

Research supports the need for school counselor advocacy to maximize the student learning experience (Davis, 2005; Erford, 2007; House & Martin, 1998), but perhaps the best definition is offered by Kuranz (2002):

> A good advocate listens, communicates, embraces different points of view, sets goals, develops strategies, provides feedback, works with people no matter who is in charge, thinks on his or her feet, coordinates, mediates, juggles more than one job at a time, identifies resources, and sticks with a task until a solution is found. (p. 178)

Leadership and advocacy are school counseling roles that are necessary to promote student, program, and professional goals. Being an effective leader requires advocacy efforts, and being an effective advocate requires leadership efforts.

Role of the School Counselor: Working with Students

The role of the school counselor that most attracts people to the field is the opportunity to affect and enhance the lives of young people. As has been mentioned, the school counselor assists in the academic, personal/social, and career development of students. An exploration of these domains will provide insight into the comprehensive role of K–12 school counselors. A discussion of students with special needs and minority youth will follow.

Academic Development.   First and foremost, school counselors are committed to helping students become effective, lifelong learners (Davis, 2005). Because school counseling occurs within the school environment, it makes sense that academic success, the goal of education, is also the goal of school counseling. At the elementary school level, the school counselor contributes to the development of effective study skills and student appreciation for learning. Early intervention is necessary so that students make the connection between academic success and the future. Classroom guidance that focuses on study skills or test-taking strategies can help students perform better on academic tasks. At both elementary and secondary levels, individual and small group counseling often addresses specific learning problems, provides strategies to facilitate learning, and encourages goal setting for academic progress. Brown (1999) identified several direct interventions to use in academic counseling with students: contracting, study skills groups, time management training, classroom guidance units, achievement/motivation groups, standardized testing preparation courses, peer/volunteer tutoring programs, and homework support networks (p. 4).

School counselors may also provide schoolwide programs that create a positive climate for learning. Brown (1999) suggested that conducting awards programs and recognizing student achievement may reinforce student academic success. Other schoolwide programs that facilitate a positive climate for learning are those that ensure student safety, such as bullying or violence prevention programs.

Personal/Social Development.   One of the biggest barriers to students' academic achievement is personal/social events that often overwhelm them to the point of distraction and apathy regarding their academic progress. Student issues run the gamut from family issues (divorce, poverty, moving, abuse, etc.) to social issues (friendships, dating, peer pressure, etc.) and may even result in destructive behaviors such as eating disorders and self-mutilation (e.g., cutting).

Although most people believe that young children do not have problems in their lives, elementary school counselors often help students who are going through problems either at home or at school. These issues may range from a disagreement with friends to the incarceration of a parent. Regardless of the severity, the impact of life events is a reality for students, regardless of age. School counselors are uniquely trained to help students process their feelings about their personal and social circumstances, with the ultimate goal of putting the student in the best frame of mind to be successful in class. The appropriate delivery service, may be individual counseling, small group counseling, or in some situations, classroom guidance. Counseling may also include consultation and collaboration with parents and teachers to provide a network of support for students. Davis (2005) provides some general guidelines for counseling students around personal/social issues:

- Listen to the story: Students need to be heard.
- Help students identify their concerns: What are the major issues or concerns?
- Meet the student where the student is: Empathize with their issue.
- Help the student set goals: What would the student like to have happen?

- Consider challenges to achieving goals: What are the consequences of acting toward the goals?
- Be available and check in with the student: Provide support and follow-up.
- Consider referral: Recognize the extent of professional knowledge and expertise and refer to outside counseling if necessary. (pp. 119–120)

One caution about referrals to outside counseling is that school counselors may only *suggest* outside counseling services rather than *recommend*. Recommendations from school personnel have fiscal implications; therefore, a suggestion to seek outside therapy does not financially obligate the school district to pay the costs of therapy.

Career Development. Because school counseling got its start in the career and vocational arena, it seems appropriate that career development is still a primary focus of school counseling. Career counseling is helping students with postsecondary planning, whether students are headed for college or planning to enter the world of work. ASCA (2006) posited: "Professional school counselors collaborate with administrators, teachers, staff, parents and the community to ensure that all students have the opportunity to design a rigorous and relevant academic and career program" (p. 1).

At the elementary level, school counselors perform career counseling by promoting *awareness* of the world of work. Students learn the connection between getting an education and getting a job. School counselors may coordinate a career day, when professionals from a variety of jobs come to share their careers with students. Also, classroom guidance lessons may focus on interests and skills as they are related to specific careers.

Middle school counselors focus more on career *exploration* and typically spend time learning about a variety of careers. Middle school counselors may use technology and career exploration programs that are available via the Internet. Career lessons might include interest inventories or skill assessment so that students may begin to consider careers of interest. Also, middle school may be the first time that a student's course selections might influence postsecondary plans, and decisions about the type of diploma or course of study might be affected by the middle school student's decisions. School counselors may facilitate important sessions with students as they consider their academic plans.

As one might expect, career *decision making* is necessary for high school students. Many high schools have a career center dedicated to helping students explore and decide on postsecondary options. Even though the career center may have personnel available for students, this does not take away the important role of career counseling from school counselors. As Davis (2005) stated, "the school counselor's role is to assist in any way possible to alleviate the anxiety and worry that often comes with making major life decisions" (p. 126).

Special Needs

For the purposes of this discussion, *special needs* will refer to students who qualify for special education services under the Individuals with Disabilities Education Act (2004).

According to the National Center for Education Statistics (U.S. Department of Education, 2006a), students with special needs were 13.7% of the entire enrollment of students (pre-K through grade 12) in 2005. Quigney and Studer (1998) noted that school counselors work with students with special needs in two ways: (a) working with the nonchallenged students to help them understand the unique qualities and needs of challenged students and (b) working with students with special needs to help them deal with the academic/personal/social and career challenges that may result from their condition (p. 79). School counselors may have a variety of roles in working with students with special needs: individual counseling, group counseling, collaboration and consultation with parents of students with special needs, and serving on the multidisciplinary team that makes decisions about special education services. Because special education has legal implications, it is important for the school counselor to become familiar with the state and federal laws that pertain to serving students with special needs. According to ASCA (2004b):

> Professional school counselors work with students with special needs both in special class settings and in the regular classroom and are a key component in assisting with transitions to post-secondary options. It is particularly important that the professional school counselor's role in these procedures is clearly defined and is in compliance with laws and local policies. (p. 1)

Student advocacy is a primary role for school counselors who work with students with special needs. Persons who are pursuing school counseling jobs would benefit from coursework specific to students with special needs to become familiar with special needs categories, as well as the laws around services for students with special needs.

Multicultural/Minority Students

According to Shore (2001), there are more than 180 different language groups among the students in American schools, with the number of non-English-speaking students growing 2.5 times faster than that of native English-speaking students. According to the U.S. Department of Education (2006b), in the 2003–2004 school year, English language learner (ELL) services were provided to 3.8 million students (11% of all students). Projections are that by the year 2020, 20% of children will be of Hispanic descent (Federal Interagency Forum on Child and Family Statistics, 2001). Capuzzi and Gross (2007) identified language, identity, generational difference, cultural customs, geography, family history, and traditions as issues that school counselors (and all school personnel) face in schools. School counselors must be prepared to deal with the myriad of issues that often surface around multiculturalism.

Lee (2001) recommended that culturally responsive schools take a "salad bowl" approach when considering multiculturalism in schools; that is, school counselors should consider each diverse student group as a separate but necessary part of the student body (p. 258). It is imperative that school counselors develop multicultural competence to work with students from various cultural backgrounds. Providing counseling services for students, such as support groups, transition groups, and individual counseling, supports minority students. Clemente and Collison (2000) asserted that school counselors help ESL/ESOL students develop the following skills: "(a) problem-solving skills to develop self-confidence and cultural pride, (b) planning skills consistent with the student's family system to establish goal setting, (c) leadership skills that go across ethnic groups, and (d) integration skills to develop self-acceptance" (p. 346). In addition, school counselors reach out to non-English-speaking parents and offer to act as a consultant or liaison with other school personal (e.g., ESL/ESOL teachers) to provide comprehensive support for diverse students and their families. "Advocacy activities also can take the form of educating other school personnel about the importance in fostering culturally supportive environments so that youth of color can attain personal and academic success" (Shin, Daly, & Vera, 2007, p. 386).

Other diversity issues, such as working with sexual minority youth, are also part of the educational setting. School counselors, especially those in middle and high school, will be working with students as they develop their sexual identity and begin to explore dating relationships. For sexual minority youth, the consequences of coming out may include harassment, parental rejection, and dealing with homophobia. Research supports the school counselor's role in working with sexual minority youth (Davis, 2005). The school counselor is also an integral person in helping to create a climate of tolerance for all students, regardless of sexual orientation. ASCA (2005b) asserted that:

> Professional school counselors promote affirmation, respect and equal opportunity for all individuals regardless of sexual orientation or gender identity. Professional school counselors also promote awareness of issues related to sexual orientation/gender identity among students, teachers, administrators, parents and the community . . . work to eliminate barriers that impede student development and achievement and are committed to the academic, career and personal/social development of all students. (p. 1)

There are many student populations in schools that need the assistance of school counselors to address issues and situations that occur naturally in schools; only two were discussed here. Professional school counselors strive to meet the needs of *all* student populations in order to provide equitable access to educational and counseling services.

Role of the School Counselor: Collaboration with Others

Collaborating with School Personnel. The nature of counseling in schools is that there are many other people with whom the counselor may interface on a daily basis. Collaboration with others in the school and also outside the school (parents, community members) is an important role for school counselors. Building relationships with school personnel and working as a team in the best interest of students are primary goals for school counselors. Although school counselors primarily support students, they are also in a unique position to provide support for colleagues (teachers and administrators). Davis (2005) emphasized the need for effective communication skills with school personnel so that connections are made that will ultimately benefit students as everyone works together to ensure student success.

School counselors may work with a variety of school personnel, depending on the need to be involved with student situations. It is not unusual for the school counselor to work closely with the school psychologist (Simcox, Nuijens, & Lee, 2006), the school social worker, the school nurse, or the student resource office (a police officer in the school). Because school counselors become acquainted with a large number of students, it makes sense that they are involved with personnel who interact with these students. The forging of these relationships will ultimately benefit students. As Davis (2005) concluded:

> In order to provide effective and comprehensive services to students, which may require the input and expertise of many school professionals, school counselors should initiate dialogue and interactions that will benefit students. It is only through . . . effective working relationships and team efforts toward student development and success that everyone wins. (p. 193)

Collaborating with parents/families/guardians.   Parents are an integral part of student academic success and, therefore, should be involved in their child's education. School counselors build positive relationships with parents by being available, accessible, and flexible (Davis, 2005). Often, parents do not participate in a student's education program because of a variety of reasons, such as work schedule or avoidance due to a negative educational experience in their own past. School counselors should try to connect with parents and emphasize that everyone wants the same goal—the academic success of their student.

Davis (2005) suggested that school counselors can provide support for parents in a variety of ways, such as parent education programs, parenting skills workshops, and developing a parenting resource library. In addition, participating in parent–teacher conferences on behalf of the student can also alleviate some of the anxiety that parents may experience in consultation with teachers. Supporting parents is necessary as they focus on supporting their child in school. School counselors develop important relationships with parents in order to effectively bridge the gap between home and school.

Obviously, school counselors have many roles to play as they facilitate the academic, personal/social, and career development of students. Because students bring their unique stories to the school setting, school counselors have to be prepared to work with students through their school careers and facilitate healthy and positive growth toward life goals.

Credentialing in School Counseling

A professional school counselor typically has a graduate degree in school counseling, although some states allow counselors with degrees in related counseling fields to be given a license in school counseling. Each state has different criteria for licensure as a school counselor; information by state may be found on the ASCA Web site (listed at the end of this chapter), and information is also provided on each state's department of education Web site.

Many school counseling graduate programs are accredited by the Council for the Accreditation of Counseling and Related Education Programs (CACREP, 2001). The standards that are required for the accreditation of a school counseling graduate program (in addition to the eight core areas of CACREP for all counseling programs) are:

- Foundations of school counseling
- Contextual dimensions of school counseling
- Knowledge and skill requirements in program development, implementation, and evaluation and counseling and guidance
- Consultation
- Clinical Instruction (a 600-hour internship in a school counseling setting under the supervision of a qualified site supervisor). (CACREP, 2001)

Coursework in CACREP-accredited school counseling graduate programs must meet objectives in the core areas, in addition to school counseling–specific standards. School counselor preparation programs that are CACREP-accredited are typically 48 credits, although some may be more, depending on other licensure requirements in each state. It is best to consult with university preparation programs to see what requirements are needed to complete a graduate degree in school counseling, and also consult state department of education Web sites to see what other experience or criteria are required.

Considerations for a Career as a Professional School Counselor

Given the recent events across our country and in the world, the need for school counselors is evident. Schools are a constant in our society. Youth, by virtue of being students in schools, will bring many issues, concerns, and joys into the education setting. School counselors are specifically trained in counseling skills to provide mental health services for students in schools. Although professional school counselors are not *therapists* in schools, they are trained to begin to address the mental, physical, social, and emotional health of students as they pursue their academic goals.

When considering an employment setting as a school counselor, one must consider the personal and professional challenges that might arise. Consider the following case example.

Samantha was completing her undergraduate degree in psychology. The looming question that haunted her as graduation approached was "What next?" Samantha had been examining graduate programs in several counseling specialties. One of the areas she was strongly considering was becoming a professional school counselor. When weighing the feasibility of this career, Samantha wrote a list of pros and cons about being a school counselor.

Pros	*Cons*
I enjoy working with kids.	*Not sure if I want to only work with kids.*
I had a positive school experience.	*Will I be stifled by the structure of schools?*
I would like to help students achieve academic and career goals.	*How much personal counseling will I get to do?*
I enjoy working in a collaborative environment.	*I don't like confrontation; how will I handle an irate parent?*

Samantha's lists contain valid comments and questions as she explores the option of becoming a professional school counselor. The effective school counselor is able to balance the personal qualities and goals of helping students and the political and structural nature of schools. School counseling is a profession in which each day is different; planned events may go by the wayside because of a crisis or emergency that must be addressed immediately. Professional school counselors must be flexible and able to respond to crises in appropriate ways. Being able to multitask and keeping informed about many student situations simultaneously are other qualities of effective school counselors.

Perhaps one of the biggest stressors for school counselors is being unable to leave student problems and issues at school when it is time to go home. Often, school counselors burn out emotionally because they spend both working and nonworking hours concerned about students. Siebert (2002) offered the following advice about developing *caregiver resiliency.*

> As a school counselor, a big part of your job is that of caregiver. You provide people in need with a shoulder to cry on, someone to listen to their concerns and advise on how to deal with adversity. However, it can be a fine line to walk between helping others with their problems and letting others' problems have a negative impact on your own mental health. You not only owe it to yourself but to your students to be a role model for resiliency. (p. 11)

Although the rewards of being a professional school counselor are many, the challenge is meeting the daily demands of students, parents, peers, and administrators who often believe that the school counselor is the remedy for many issues. This challenge, while often exhausting, is exhilarating, as the school counselor has the capacity to forever influence the healthy development of students.

Summary

The world of professional school counseling is one of great opportunity and challenge. Unlike other specialty areas in counseling, professional school counselors have, as an ultimate goal, the academic success of students. The role of professional school counselors is multifaceted and includes many activities related to providing services for students, parents, and other school personnel. The school counseling profession continues to respond to the needs of a diverse and ever-changing society. Issues related to diverse student populations, equitable access to education, technology, and the role definition of the school counselor will continue to permeate the profession (Jones & Granello, 2002). Outcome-based program evaluation (Green & Keys, 2001) and finding time for counseling in an age of testing and accountability (Baker & Gerler, 2004) also challenge school counselors. However, the professional school counselor will confront these challenges head-on and continue the positive course of recent events in school counseling, resulting in more positive futures for today's youth.

So, how would a professional school counselor work with Paul, the struggling student in the beginning of the chapter? First, the school counselor might consult with Paul's teachers to try to understand what specific behaviors Paul has been demonstrating in class and what changes they have observed in his school performance. Second, the school counselor would conduct individual counseling with Paul to assess his perspective on what is going on in his life. Using effective counseling skills, the school counselor would try to get Paul to be open about his life situation and the effect his home life might be having on his school performance. The school counselor would encourage Paul to express his feelings about things and then ask what Paul would like to have happen. In this session, the school counselor is also going to address Paul's decline in academic performance and generate strategies to provide support for him at school. If necessary, the school counselor will help Paul identify resources he can use to improve his academic performance. Finally, the school counselor would seek Paul's consent to speak with his parents so that everyone can be informed about the impact of the family situation on his academic progress. If Paul gives consent, the school counselor would arrange a meeting with the parents (with Paul present if he wishes) and perhaps include teachers as well so that everyone is collaborating to help Paul experience success at school. A comprehensive school counseling plan, involving the roles of counseling, consultation, and coordination of services, as well as monitoring and assessing the effectiveness of the interventions will highly increase Paul's chances of school and personal success.

The following Web sites provide additional information relating to the chapter topics.

USEFUL WEB SITES

American School Counselor Association (some information is limited to members)
http://www.schoolcounselor.org

Education Trust
http://www.edtrust.org

Center for School Counseling Outcome Research
http://www.umass.edu/schoolcounseling

National Center for Education Statistics
http://www.nces.ed.gov

REFERENCES

American School Counselor Association. (2004a). *Ethical standards for school counselors.* Retrieved June 12, 2007, from http://www.schoolcounselor.org/content.asp?contentid=173

American School Counselor Association. (2004b). *Position statement: Special-needs students.* Retrieved June 12, 2007, from http://www.schoolcounselor.org/content.asp?contentid=218

American School Counselor Association. (2004c). *The role of the professional school counselor.* Retrieved June 7, 2007, from http://www.schoolcounselor.org/content.asp?contentid=240

American School Counselor Association. (2005a). *The ASCA national model for school counseling programs* (2nd ed.). Alexandria, VA: Author.

American School Counselor Association. (2005b). *Position statement: Gay, lesbian, bisexual, transgendered, and questioning youth.* Retrieved June 14, 2007, from http://www.schoolcounselor.org/content.asp?contentid=217

American School Counselor Association. (2006). *Position statement: Academic and career planning.* Retrieved June 12, 2007, from http://www.schoolcounselor.org/content.asp?contentid=205

Baker, S. B., & Gerler, E. R. (2004). *School counseling for the twenty-first century* (4th ed.). Upper Saddle River, NJ: Merrill/Prentice Hall.

Birdsall, B. A., & Miller, L. D. (2002). Brief counseling in the schools: A solution-focused approach for school counselors. *Counseling and Human Development, 35,* 1–10.

Brigman, G., & Campbell, C. (2003). Helping students improve academic achievement and school success behavior. *Professional School Counseling, 7,* 91–97.

Brown, D. (1999). *Improving academic achievement: What school counselors can do.* Greensboro, NC: ERIC Clearinghouse on Counseling and Student Services. (ERIC Document Reproduction Service No. ED435895)

Brown, D., & Trusty, J. (2005). *Designing and leading comprehensive school counseling programs: Promoting student competence and meeting student needs.* Belmont, CA: Brooks/Cole.

Campbell, C. A., & Dahir, C. A. (1997). *National standards for school counseling programs.* Alexandria, VA: American School Counselor Association.

Capuzzi, D., & Gross, D. R. (2007). *Counseling and psychotherapy: Theories and interventions* (4th ed.). Upper Saddle River, NJ: Merrill Prentice Hall.

Carey, J. C., & Dimmitt, C. (2006). Resources for school counselors and counselor educators: The Center for School Counseling Outcome Research. *Professional School Counseling, 9,* 416–420.

Clemente, R., & Collison, B. B. (2000). The relationships among counselors, ESL teachers, and students. *Professional School Counseling, 3,* 339–348.

Council for the Accreditation of Counseling and Related Educational Programs. (2001). *2001 standards.* Retrieved June 13, 2007, from http://www.cacrep.org/2001Standards.html

Dahir, C. A., & House, R. (2002, October). *Connecting pre-service with practice: CACREP-TSCI-National standards.* Presentation at the biannual conference of the Association for Counselor Education and Supervision, Park City, UT.

Davis, T. E. (2005). *Exploring school counseling: Professional practices and perspectives.* Boston: Lahaska Press/Houghton Mifflin.

Education Trust. (1996). *Transforming school counseling initiative.* Retrieved June 13, 2007, from http://www2.edtrust.org/EdTrust/Transforming+School+Counseling/main

Erford, B. T. (Ed.). (2007). *Transforming the school counseling profession* (2nd ed.). Upper Saddle River, NJ: Merrill Prentice Hall.

Federal Interagency Forum on Child and Family Statistics. (2001). *America's children: Key indicators of well-being.* Washington, DC: U.S. Government Printing Office.

Gingerich, W. J., & Wabeke, T. (2001). A solution-focused approach to mental health intervention in school settings. *Children & Schools, 23,* 33–47.

Glaser, J. S., & Shoffner, M. F. (2001). Adventure-based counseling in schools. *Professional School Counseling, 5,* 42–48.

Green, A., & Keys, S. (2001). Expanding the developmental school counseling paradigm: Meeting the needs of the 21st century student. *Professional School Counseling, 5,* 84–95.

House, R. M., & Martin, P. J. (1998). Advocating for better futures for all students: A new vision for school counselors. *Education, 119*, 284–291.

Individuals with Disabilities Education Act. (2004). *Building the legacy: IDEA 2004.* Retrieved June 18, 2007, from http://idea.ed.gov/

Jones, S., & Granello, D. H. (2002). School counseling now and in the future: A reaction. *Professional School Counseling, 5*, 164–171.

Keys, S. G., Bemak, F., & Lockart, E. J. (1998). Transforming school counseling to serve the mental health needs of at-risk youth. *Journal of Counseling & Development, 76*, 381–388.

Kuranz, M. (2002). Cultivating student potential. *Professional School Counseling, 5*, 172–179.

Lee, C. C. (2001). Culturally responsive school counselors and programs: Addressing the needs of all students. *Professional School Counseling, 4*, 257–261.

McEachern, A. G., & Bornot, J. (2001). Gifted student with learning disabilities. *Professional School Counseling, 5*, 34–41.

Mostert, D. L., Johnson, E., & Mostert, M. P. (1997). The utility of solution-focused brief counseling in schools: Potential from an initial study. *Professional School Counseling, 1*, 21–24.

Olson, M. J., & Allen, D. N. (1993). Principals' perception of the effectiveness of school counselors with and without teaching experience. *Counselor Education & Supervision, 33*, 10–21.

Quarto, C. J. (1999). Teachers' perceptions of school counselors with and without teaching experience. *Professional School Counseling, 2*, 378–383.

Quigney, T. A., & Studer, J. R. (1998). Touching strands of the educational web: The professional school counselor's role in inclusion. *Professional School Counseling, 2*, 77–81.

Rowell, L. L. (2006). Action research and school counseling: Closing the gap between research and practice. *Professional School Counseling, 9*, 376–384.

Rowell, L. L., & Hong, E. (2002). The role of school counselors in homework intervention. *Professional School Counseling, 5*, 285–291.

Sabella, R. A. (2006). The ASCA national school counseling research center: A brief history and agenda. *Professional School Counseling, 9*, 412–415.

Schmidt, J. J. (2008). *Counseling in schools: Comprehensive programs of responsive services for all students* (5th ed.). Boston: Allyn & Bacon.

Shechtman, Z. (2002). Child group psychotherapy in the school at the threshold of a new millennium. *Journal of Counseling & Development, 80*, 293–299.

Shin, R., Daly, B., & Vera, E. (2007). The relationships of peer norms, ethnic identity, and peer support to school engagement in urban youth. *Professional School Counseling, 10*, 379–388.

Shore, K. (2001). Success for ESL students. *Instructor, 110*, 30, 32, 106.

Siebert, A. (2002). Caregiver resiliency. *ASCA School Counselor, 39*, 10–13.

Simcox, A. G., Nuijens, K. L., & Lee, C. C. (2006). School counselors and school psychologists: Collaborative partners in promoting culturally competent schools. *Professional School Counseling, 9*, 272–277.

Smith, S. L., Crutchfield, L. B., & Culbreth, J. R. (2001). Teaching experience for school counselors: Counselor educators' perceptions. *Professional School Counseling, 4*, 216–224.

Studer, J. R., Oberman, A. H., & Womack, R. H. (2006). Producing evidence to show counseling effectiveness in the schools. *Professional School Counseling, 9*, 385–391.

Thompson, R. A. (2002). *School counseling: Best practices for working in schools* (2nd ed.). New York: Brunner-Routledge.

Trusty, J., Niles, S. G., & Carney, J. V. (2005). Education-career planning and middle school counselors. *Professional School Counseling, 9*, 136–142.

U.S. Department of Education. (2002). *No child left behind: A desk reference.* Washington, DC: Office of Elementary and Secondary Education.

U.S. Department of Education, National Center for Education Statistics. (2006a). *Digest of education statistics, 2005.* Retrieved June 12, 2007, from http://nces.ed.gov/fastfacts/display.asp?id=64

U.S. Department of Education, National Center for Education Statistics. (2006b). *Public elementary and secondary students, staff, schools, and school districts: School year 2003–04.* Retrieved June 12, 2007, from http://nces.ed.gov/fastfacts/display.asp?id=96

Walsh, M. E., Barrett, J. G., & DePaul, J. (2007). Day-to-day activities of school counselors: Alignment with new directions in the field and the ASCA national model. *Professional School Counseling, 10,* 370–378.

Whiston, S. C. (2002). Response to the past, present, and future of school counseling: Raising some issues. *Professional School Counseling, 5,* 148–155.

Wrenn, C. G. (1962). *The counselor in a changing world.* Washington, DC: American Personnel and Guidance Association.

Zinck, K., & Littrell, J. M. (2000). Action research shows group counseling effective with at-risk adolescent girls. *Professional School Counseling, 4,* 50–59.

16 Counseling in Mental Health and Private Practice Settings

JANE E. RHEINECK
Northern Illinois University

Introduction

Historically, counselors have been teachers, social reformers, and advocates. Just as counseling is a process, the profession itself is also a developmental work in progress (Gladding, 2007). From Frank Parsons and vocational guidance, to its growth through the educational systems and the recognition by the National Institute of Mental Health (NIMH) in 1992 as a primary mental health profession (Manderscheid & Sonnenshein as cited in Gladding, 2007), counseling has a rich past. Regardless of the counseling trajectory, counselors have always focused on the social factors and constellations significant in an individual's development (2007).

During the 1960s, as counselors began to look for professional opportunities in addition to the traditional positions in educational settings, they moved into the community. Initially, community counseling focused on the needs of individuals (and occasionally couples and families) who were essentially healthy but struggling with normal conflicts, uncertainties, or developmental transitions. Following the Community Mental Health Centers Act of 1963, counselors were employed to provide service to clients who had previously been hospitalized for various mental disorders. The last three decades of the 20th century brought rapid and remarkable change to the practice of community mental health counseling (Browers, 2005).

Today, professional mental health counselors respond to clients facing a more complex world, a pluralistic society, changing views on families, and a shifting economic structure. Today, counselors work with a variety of people from diverse backgrounds.

I would like to express my appreciation to the author who wrote the previous version of this chapter: Rebecca T. Browers, EdD, NCC, LPC. Her knowledge and scholarly contributions are reflected in the present version.

Clients range from small children to older adults with complex issues from a diversity of backgrounds. These clients may be burdened by troubling circumstances within their homes, on the job, or in their communities. Some face situations such as parenting grandchildren, caring for incapacitated older parents, or living with domestic violence and seek assistance from counselors for needs of varying severity.

Community mental health counselors provide counseling in a wide variety of settings. Government-funded agencies, clinics, and programs can be found in most communities, where various services are usually supported by state or county funds or a combination of the two. In recent years, it has become typical for community mental health care to focus on the more severe needs of adults and children in a community or a region, frequently as the primary resource for the chronically mentally ill, those diagnosed with a substance abuse, or more severely troubled adults and youth (Browers, 2005). Some communities are also fortunate enough to have public or private nonprofit agencies, primarily dependent on funding from grants, contributions, or public campaigns like United Way (Nugent, 2000). Examples of these services include shelters and rape crisis centers.

The American Counseling Association (ACA) defines *counseling* as "the application of mental health, psychological, or human development principles, through cognitive, affective, behavioral or systematic intervention strategies, that address wellness, personal growth, or career development, as well as pathology" (ACA, 2005). Clients seek counseling services for many different reasons and may turn for assistance to practitioners in independent private practice, group practices, or for-profit clinical settings. Counseling is provided to individuals, couples, families, or groups and addresses common concerns associated with stresses in daily living such as decision making, transitions, developmental concerns, and building communication skills. Some clients may be dealing with issues of a more severe nature requiring longer term counseling as well. Likewise, counselors in private practice may specialize in specific problems, such as depression, anxiety, phobias, substance abuse, posttraumatic stress disorder (PTSD), or eating disorders, or a particular population, such as children with attention deficit disorder or gay, lesbian, bisexual, or transgendered individuals.

Professional mental health counselors hold master's degrees and may pursue a variety of professional credentials. In 49 states, counselors must have a license regulated by the state to be in private practice and to qualify for third-party payments. Licensed professional counselors are sometimes called upon to testify in court, may receive contracts to conduct assessments and evaluations, provide consulting services in the schools, and consult with other mental health care professionals. Depending on areas of specialty, they may also be referral sources for physicians, other health care professionals, and managed health care systems. A counselor in private practice, in addition to being a competent practitioner who is able to assess and effectively treat a broad range of client needs, must also possess, or be able to hire someone who possesses skills in managing a business. The demands of a practice include promoting the practice, scheduling appointments, maintaining accurate client records, handling the financial details of billing, bookkeeping, filing tax reports, and communicating with insurance providers (Browers, 2005).

History of Professional Counselors

Mental health counselors have diversified from their roots in educational and vocational guidance, have adapted to the demands of the clinical environment, and have responded to the needs of the community. Prior to the 1960s, those pursuing graduate education to become counselors generally went on to provide counseling services in traditional educational settings, such as public and private schools, colleges, and universities. School counselors were almost guaranteed a secure position in the nation's elementary, junior high, and high schools as a result of federal funding that accompanied the passage of the National Defense Education Act of 1958 and the subsequent Secondary Education Act of 1964.

During the 1960s and 1970s, counselors were also employed in colleges, universities, and junior colleges (which evolved into community colleges). Traditionally (as well as today), the role of the counselor was associated with student affairs and was quite diverse, including career development, academic planning, academic assessment, advising, and residence life support, while also responding to the general mental health needs of all students. Occasionally, counselors in higher education filled a more narrowly defined function, with student counseling services distributed among several offices (Levine, 1980).

However, as the 1960s neared an end, the escalating war in Vietnam reduced the amount of federal dollars available for many human services programs, including school counseling programs (Brooks, 1997). Positions available decreased for school counselors, as well as counselors in postsecondary settings, leading to a bleak job market for several graduating classes and limiting the necessity for new hires in counselor education.

A resurgence of sorts has taken hold. Because of government programs such as No Child Left Behind that mandated a high-quality education for all children (U.S. Department of Education, n.d.) and the increase of college students with documented diagnoses (Beamish, 2005; Collins & Mowbray, 2005, 2006; Nolan, Ford, Kress, Anderson, & Novak, 2005), the demand for professional counselors is on the rise. Educational institutions at all levels are recognizing their need for trained professionals to work with students to promote optimal learning and, in the case of higher education, student retention.

The Emergence of Mental Health Counselors

The difficulties faced by counselors in traditional educational settings and the struggles faced by new graduates with ambitions to enter the ranks of school counselors led to a growing interest in mental health counseling opportunities outside school settings. Fortunately, community awareness, employment opportunities, and emerging sources of funding began to evolve around the same time. The Community Mental Health Centers Act of 1963 signaled a significant shift in attitudes about counseling and the delivery of mental health care services. The intent of the act was to establish community-based treatment centers as alternatives to the overstressed, marginally effective state hospital system that had prevailed since the 19th century. The transition to community mental health care was believed to be more humane and effective than the mental health "warehouses" that many state hospitals had become (Brooks, 1997; Brooks & Weikel, 1986).

In the beginning, community mental health care centers were staffed by multidisciplinary treatment teams that included the four "core provider" professions of psychiatry, psychology, social work, and nursing, as well as a variety of paraprofessionals whose training was varied. As the centers began hiring staff, master's-level counselor education graduates filled many of the undesignated "paraprofessional" positions. Counselors trained at the doctoral level, but increasingly denied licensure as psychologists by state boards, also found receptivity from the community mental health centers, which were frequently exempt from licensure requirements (Brooks, 1997).

The cultural shift in mental health care that increased the demand for trained mental health care providers from multiple disciplines and compatible perspectives presented both a challenge and an opportunity for the counseling profession. It was clear that to compete in a shifting job market, counselor education programs needed to expand their training, and counselors would need to reassess their professional goals to include community-based mental health counseling, an opportunity welcomed by many.

Emerging Opportunities in Community Counseling

The social concerns and political movements of the decades of the 1960s, 1970s, and even the 1980s contributed to a need for more community-based counseling services. The civil rights movement, the women's movement, returning Vietnam veterans, antiwar activism, the sexual revolution, changing demographics in the home and the workplace, and the counseling profession's increased emphasis on human growth and development all raised public awareness of the value of counseling for individuals, couples, and families. The emerging needs reflected a continuum of care to include supportive services, crisis intervention and response, assessment and referral, and short- or long-term counseling. In response to the growing trend for community mental health care services, counselor education programs revised their curricula, and graduate students broadened their training in some cases, became more specialized in other cases, and increased their credentials to better prepare them to work in community mental health care, both public and private.

Professional Growing Pains

As the counseling profession was undergoing a period of rapid change and productive growth, it understandably experienced some professional growing pains. In 1978, the American Mental Health Counselors Association (AMHCA) became the 13th division of the American Counseling Association (ACA), which was then known as the American Personnel and Guidance Association (APGA). From the beginning and well into the 1980s, AMHCA's rapidly growing membership paralleled the tremendous increase in numbers of counselors working in public and private community mental health care. From the very beginning, AMHCA consistently assumed an active role in the professionalization of the mental health counseling field by proposing and supporting standardization of counselor education programs, state licensure, and certification requirements. A primary goal of AMHCA has always been to professionally and politically advocate for the recognition of counselors as equal to other nonmedical mental health disciplines: clinical psychology, social work, and psychiatric nursing (Brooks, 1997).

Although membership has declined, AMHCA continues to be a powerful voice at the local, state, and national levels, actively involved in efforts to promote and secure gains in public policy and legislation that ensure professional status for mental health counselors. ACA and its divisions work together to educate the public regarding the role of counselors in community mental health care and advocate for the needs of the consuming public. The basis for some of the earlier organizational conflicts, ironically, reflects one of the major strengths of the counseling profession; namely, included among the professional ranks are counselors who fill many distinctly different roles in community settings but respectfully collaborate to serve the needs of those in the community. ACA, with its 19 divisions, is a reflection of that diversity.

The Need for Community-Based Mental Health Counseling

Professional mental health counselors face greater demands and have been challenged with more opportunities for practice in today's market. As more acute inpatient adult psychiatric facilities are closing, community-based mental health care providers are striving to serve the priorities of a broader client population who present with more severe clinical issues than a generation ago. Although some agencies are responding to increasing budget demands and a reduction in crucial programs and services, community needs are not diminishing, and it is clear that the necessity for competent and accessible mental health counseling services will continue to grow (Browers, 2005).

In 2002, the president's New Freedom Commission on Mental Health confirmed that many who suffer from mental health problems have unmet needs. It went on to say that no community is untouched by mental illness, and those in need are young or old, and of any socioeconomic status, race, disability, or sexual orientation. The challenges are found in schools, homes, and the workplace. In a given year, according to the National Institute of Mental Health (NIMH) (2007), 26.2% of the adult population suffers from a diagnosable mental disorder. Of those individuals, about 6%, or 17 million people, suffer from what is considered a serious mental illness. Statistics for children and adolescents (4–17 years) vary depending on age and gender. As reported by parent(s), from 2001 to 2004 the overall rate of emotional and behavioral difficulties rose from 5.1% to 5.4%. Interestingly, the percentage for males decreased from

6.2% to 5.8%, while females increased from 4.1% to 4.8%. Some differences were also evident when race was considered. Parents who identified as Hispanic reported the lowest incidences at 3.3%; both Black and White parents reported 6%. Family structure also appears to have an impact on emotional and behavioral disturbances among children and adolescents. Statistics from 2004 indicate minors with two parents had an incidence rate of 4.4%, while children and adolescents with no parents had a rate of 9.4% (NIMH, 2007).

In fact, mental illness ranks first among illnesses that cause disability in the United States, Canada, and Western Europe, taking a serious toll on the health and well-being of families and communities while creating a major economic dilemma in the direct and indirect costs in the workplace—reportedly as much as $79 billion in the United States alone. Included in that figure is almost $12 billion in mortality costs and $4 billion in productivity costs due to incarcerated individuals and for the time of those who provide family care. It is a public health challenge to be taken seriously (U.S. Department of Health and Human Services, n.d.b).

According to NIMH (2007), the most frequent occurrences are anxiety disorders at 18.1%, followed by mood disorders at 9.5%. Although fewer individuals are affected by more serious conditions such as schizophrenia at 1.1% (ACA, 1999; NIMH, 2007) and antisocial personality disorder at 1.5% (ACA, 1999), the disruption to the individual is more severe, and counseling interventions are likely to be longer in duration. Although individuals may have more than one disorder in a year, less than 7% of the population experiences symptoms for a full year or longer (ACA, 1999).

Depression affects sufferers by impairing their ability to function effectively in their environment. It can also complicate other medical conditions and be serious enough to lead to suicide. The National Institute of Mental Health reported 32,439 adult suicides in 2004; 90% of those had a diagnosed disorder, usually a depressive disorder or substance abuse. It is also true that the illness affects families, productivity, and communities. In a study conducted by the World Health Organization, the World Bank, and Harvard University (as reported by NIMH, 2007), mental illness (including suicide) accounts for 15% of the burden of disease in established economies such as the United States. In fact, according to the National Mental Health Association (2007), major depression is considered the leading cause of disability in the world (2007).

The Substance Abuse and Mental Heath Services Administration (SAMSHA), a division of the Department of Health and Human Services, combined data from SAMHSA's 2004 and 2005 National Surveys on Drug Use and Health and used the data to examine co-occurring alcohol use and depression, as well as treatment for these disorders in adults aged 18 or older. The following prevalences were found: An estimated 7.6% of adults 18 or older (approximately 16.4 million adults) had experienced at least one major depressive episode during the past year. An estimated 8% (17.3 million adults) met criteria for alcohol use disorder in the past year. An estimated 1.2% (2.7 million adults) had co-occurring major depressive episode and alcohol use disorder in the past year (SAMHSA, 2007). Those who interact with or are affected by someone with a substance abuse problem may also experience stress, anxiety, depression, or related concerns that are alleviated by counseling.

Mental Health Needs of Children and Adolescents

Over the last 20 years, the emphasis of service delivery has shifted to systems of care that are designed to provide culturally competent, coordinated services; community-based services; new financing arrangements in the private and public sectors; family participation in decision making about care for their children; and individualized care drawing on treatment and social supports called wraparound services.

The MECA study (Methodology for Epidemiology of Mental Disorders in Children and Adolescents) estimated that almost 21% of U.S. children age 9 to 17 had a diagnosable mental or addictive disorder associated with at least minimum impairment (U.S. Department of Health and Human Services, n.d.a). The surgeon general's report also stated that most children in need of mental health services do not receive them. This, of course, carries implications for costly and potentially tragic consequences for those not treated. To improve retention of children receiving services, the office recommends better education of frontline providers, such as teachers, health care workers, and school counselors.

But the fact is, school counselors will continue to have caseloads and responsibilities that make it unlikely that they can sufficiently respond to the number of needs and the severity of problems experienced by children and adolescents, without the support and collaboration of mental health counselors in the community. Effective comprehensive treatment mandates the integration of services between schools and community mental health care services. An increasing trend is for individual schools or school districts to contract with community services for student needs that are specialized in nature or exceed the resources of the school. School counselors and community mental health counselors work together in an atmosphere of mutual respect to meet the needs of children and adolescents, link with families, and consult regarding environmental and situational concerns of the school.

Current statistics suggest that children and adolescents are currently underserved, indicating a critical need for even further support for community-based programming to supplement the strained school-based resources and to better address severe and long-term needs. The National Institute on Mental Health (2007) reported that in 2004 approximately 5.4% or 2.7 million children between 4 and 17 years of age suffer from some type of emotional or behavioral difficulties (as reported by caregivers), and according to Hoagwood (1999), only 20% of youth with mental disorders, or their families, receive help. A major concern is the potential for tragic consequences when the urgent needs of youth are neglected—the increased risk for suicide, homicide, or other forms of violence. In 2004, the NIMH (2007) estimated that 1.3 per 100,000 children age 10–14 died of suicide, and 8.2 per 100,000 of children 15–19 years of age took their own lives. Males are four times more likely than females to commit suicide, with non-Hispanic Whites the highest risk group (12.9 per 100,000). The second highest risk group is Native Americans/Native Alaskans (12.4 per 100,000). The lowest risk groups are (a) non-Hispanic Blacks at 5.3 per 100,000, (b) Asian/Pacific Islanders at 5.8 per 100,000, and (c) Hispanics at 5.9 per 100,000.

Approximately 90% of teenagers who commit suicide have a psychiatric diagnosis, most often a form of a mood disorder (depression), and have problems with alcohol or other substances (ACA, 1999; NIMH, 2007). These statistics do not reflect the young people who attempt suicide, or seriously contemplate it and are in need of mental health counseling to move them out of such a high-risk state.

The consequences of failing to provide adequate mental health counseling and related services to children and adolescents with severe emotional needs are significant and affect not only the individual but also his or her family, their school, and all of our communities. Communities must continue to support and increase the mental health resources available to young people. In addition to school counselors, professional counselors outside the educational system must be prepared to respond to the psychological and emotional needs of the young people they serve.

Mental Health Needs of Older Adults

Because of the rapidly changing demographics in the United States, addressing the mental health needs of older adults is imperative. In recognition of this growing area of need, standards have been developed that include the unique considerations of counseling the older population (Myers, 1995). According to the U.S. Census Bureau (2004), approximately 12% of the U.S. population is over the age of 64, and 22% of the population is at least 55 years old. Residents of the United States are anticipating longer life spans, and the population is predicted to include 20% over the age of 65 before 2050. The 85 and over group is the fastest growing segment of our society (Newman & Newman, 1999). Unfortunately, less than a third of older adults who have a mental illness receive treatment (Karlin & Fuller, 2007).

As the life span increases, there are implications for community counseling practice. Counselors who focus on families, careers and lifestyles, and addictions will experience changes in their client base to include more older adults. Older persons (people age 65 and older) are already affected by major depression, estimated between 1% and 5%, with that number increasing to 13.5% of those who require home health care and 11.5% for those in nursing homes (NIMH, 2007). Older Americans also die of suicide at disproportionate rates. Although they are 12% of the overall U.S. population, they accounted for 16% of the suicides in 2004. In fact, the highest rates of suicide are among White men over the age of 85 (NIMH, 2007).

It is logical and necessary that the counseling profession and community mental health counselors continue their efforts to ensure access for older adults to comprehensive mental health care and increase their emphasis on individuals in later life, in addition to the traditional focus on adults, children, and adolescents.

Mental Health Counseling in Community Settings

Initially, when counselors began to seek counseling positions outside traditional educational institutions, most positions they found were in publicly funded community mental health centers. Many professional counselors still find challenging and rewarding opportunities in such agencies today. The agencies fulfill a necessary and important function in communities. Counselors who work in community agencies gain experience working with very diverse client populations who present with moderate to severe problems and often enjoy the variety afforded them in such a setting. Because of the significant number of clients with acute needs, counselors working in community agencies must be competent in diagnosis and treatment planning and must be knowledgeable about psychotropic medications (Nugent, 2000). The work is demanding, fast paced, and challenging.

Most communities have a municipally funded mental health care facility. These agencies (whether broadly or narrowly focused) may collaborate with a community system of care, serve as referral sources, or function completely independent of other programs within the community. The agency, by virtue of its location, its affiliation, or its source of funding, may serve particular population or community needs (e.g., county-funded court diversion programs, county youth services, or a community halfway house). Counselors who have a specialty or want to increase their experience in a specific area of practice may work in one of these programs or agencies.

Public Nonprofit Agencies

In many cases, state, local, or county funds, government grants, or some combination of those sources support agencies or programs. Government-funded or -sponsored services tend to be multipurpose and available to the general public. Even with the prevalence of a major publicly supported community mental health care center in most communities, mental health care services are found in many different programs scattered throughout the community and are not necessarily coordinated in the most efficient manner. Those seeking services are likely to find different requirements for eligibility depending on their particular need, diagnosis, ability to pay, or limitations associated with insurance or managed care companies. Accessing counseling services can be a complicated and frustrating process at a time when the individual may have a diminished capacity to navigate the maze.

In spite of the obvious challenges to be overcome, there are some clear advantages to utilizing a community-based "system" of mental health care. Individuals seeking counseling will find many different areas of specialization available among practitioners in the community. Not only are different clinical needs addressed but also an array of treatment options are offered, different theoretical perspectives respected, flexible delivery systems utilized, and diverse counseling environments represented. Services may be interdisciplinary or emphasize certain specialty areas that are not available elsewhere in community settings. Community mental health care agencies and counselors usually are strong advocates for their clients. Examples of community mental health services other than centralized community mental health centers include the following:

1. Drop-in crisis centers
2. Outpatient substance abuse treatment and support programs
3. Day treatment programs for severely and persistently mentally ill individuals
4. Support services for Alzheimer's patients and their caregivers

5. Counseling services aimed toward ethnic and culturally diverse communities
6. Child and family agencies
7. Homeless shelters
8. Anger management groups

Private Nonprofit Agencies

Nonprofit agencies include those supported by the United Way, religiously affiliated nondenominational organizations (e.g., Catholic Family Services, Jewish Family Services, Samaritan Counseling Centers, Lutheran Social Services), charities, private endowments, or grants. There is occasionally overlap or even a duplication of service provided by public and private nonprofit mental health counseling services, but private nonprofit agencies tend to include programs that would otherwise be absent from the community.

Because of the diverse sources of funding, private nonprofit agencies reflect the greatest range of services, employment opportunities, and wages in the professional counseling community. Mental health counseling professionals with less traditional interests or those dedicated to working with a specific population or clinical interest may be drawn to opportunities with private counseling services.

Whether public or private, nonprofit programs often function more independently and more autonomously and, therefore, are sometimes not bound by institutional policies and restrictions. Finally, because increased credentialing requirements (namely, licensing and certification), consumers of nonprofit services can feel confident that mental health counselors have been professionally trained and are receiving professional supervision and consultation.

For-Profit Mental Health Care

The concept of community mental health care encapsulates a myriad of community-based services in both centralized and specialized programs that offer an alternative to hospitalization; in truth, the majority of mental health care services are provided in the community. Very few clients receive hospitalization, inpatient treatment, or residential treatment today, and in most cases, the present practice is considered preferable (Brooks & Weikel, 1986). Whereas many services are provided through nonprofit agencies, others are accessed by clients from mental health counselors in private, for-profit settings. Clients receiving mental health counseling services pay a fee for service, either out of pocket or by their insurance provider. The private agency or counselor in private practice intends to make a profit, and the fee structure is usually quite different from that of nonprofit services. An advantage of private practice includes the freedom to be broad or narrow in the services offered or the clients served.

Private Agencies.   Services provided by professional counselors in private agencies range from individual, group, marital, or family counseling to programs offered through contractual arrangements for other private companies or occasionally public institutions (Male, 1990). An example of contractual arrangements is an employee assistance program (EAP) provided to a corporation or an industry by a private counseling agency. Specific time-limited service might be enlisted from a private agency to provide counseling and support to employees during a time of major or unanticipated layoffs.

Some private mental health care agencies specialize in specific areas of clinical need (e.g., eating disorders, substance abuse, sex abuse) and may "market" their services to public or private concerns that offer general counseling services but are unprepared to respond to certain client needs requiring special knowledge, training, or resources. In the case of private agencies that operate for profit, the mental health counselor is generally employed by the agency and receives a salary. In some arrangements, the counselor receives a percentage of the fees collected from their clients.

Private Practice. Prior to the advent of insurance, third-party payment, and managed care, counselors' professional lives in private practice were relatively simple (Gladding, 2007). Professional counselors in private practice may work independently, affiliate with other private practitioners to share administration and supervision services and costs, or have part-time or full-time practices. It should be stressed that it is neither typical nor advisable for mental health counselors to go into independent practice without significant postgraduate experience in working with a range of clients and counseling concerns. To do so without sufficient preparation is a violation of quite a few professional ethical standards but most clearly would not meet the ACA standard (C.2.a.) that states, "Counselors practice only within the boundaries of their competence, based on their education, training, supervised experience, state and national professional credentials, and appropriate professional experience. Counselors gain knowledge, personal awareness, sensitivity, and skills pertinent to working with a diverse client population" (ACA, 2005, p. 9).

Most counselors in private practice have spent time in community or agency practice and have acquired an appropriate license prior to pursuing an independent practice. Whether working in an independent private practice or affiliating with other private mental health care providers, it is essential to have a well-developed resource and referral network and a system in place for assessing and responding to clients in crisis. That system should include a process for admitting a client to a hospital or treatment facility, should it become necessary.

Depending on your point of view, mental health counselors in private practice have either maximum freedom and flexibility or maximum limitations in their professional work. Gladding (2007) provided a brief overview of some advantages and difficulties in establishing a successful private practice. In addition to clinical proficiency, Gladding identified (a) strong business skills, (b) strong networking skills, and (c) the desire to donate services for the "public good" (p. 485). The benefits of private practice can be rewarding as well. According to Gladding, private practice provides a chance for counselors to be specialists, provide flexibility, and gain individual recognition for their quality of services. In the extreme, private practice affords the freedom of choosing to whom service will be provided and the ability to work with those clients using whatever theoretically sound methods and interventions are considered most effective, without external influences on the format or duration of treatment. Some counselors feel when they are not dependent on third-party payment, they can be more responsive to the needs of the client, determining (with the client) how frequently to schedule appointments and the duration of the counseling process. It should be noted that mental health counselors who exercise this "maximum freedom" generally are in the White upper-middle class (Nugent, 2000, 2005), although in theory, the independent counselor in private practice could offer services to the most diverse client population, depending on counselors' range of competency and their flexibility in setting fees. Service fees should be determined judiciously and within the scope of the *ACA Code of Ethics* A.10 (2005).

Successful mental health counselors in private practice are more likely to be financially successful if they are eligible for third-party reimbursement (i.e., insurance payments) and are recognized as core providers by managed health care systems. Their client roster includes some clients who pay out-of-pocket, and the counselor is effective in counseling different clients with a variety of concerns. Professional mental health counselors who are trained in group counseling techniques may provide effective services and increase their income by offering counseling groups. Most counselors in private practice are generalists, but some counselors with advanced training and experience in specific areas may develop lucrative practices because of those specialties. In addition to a general practice, counseling specialties may include the following:

1. Marital and family counseling
2. Child and adolescent counseling
3. Treatment of eating disorders
4. Lesbian, gay, bisexual, and transgendered clients
5. Gerontological counseling
6. Addictions and substance abuse counseling
7. Divorce mediation

Other Roles in Private Practice: Supervision, Consulting, and Teaching.   Most mental health counselors engage in professional responsibilities in addition to direct service to their clients. Although the primary emphasis is often on counseling, counselors in private practice may also provide clinical supervision, professional consultation, and teaching and training to other professional counselors or counselors in training.

The ACA *Code of Ethics* and the states that issue licenses to professional mental health counselors require them to receive appropriate supervision and consultation (2005). Counselors must also participate in ongoing continuing educational experiences to maintain their professional credentials, as well as strengthen their skills. Although all counselors, regardless of their years of experience or their level of competence, must continue to meet these professional obligations, those who are more experienced or who have knowledge in an area of specialization sometimes use that knowledge and experience to offer service to other mental health professionals. This is a service to the profession and could be a means of increasing income.

Counselors must meet stringent qualifications to become licensed and sometimes certified in areas of specialization such as supervision. Part of the process requires counselors to accrue a specific number of hours of clinically supervised postgraduate counseling practice. Qualifications to serve as a supervisor vary from state to state. Some states require a particular certification; other states require only a specified number of hours of professional experience. The credentials of supervisors can also differ. A number of states specify that a qualified supervisor must be a professional counselor, and other states require only that the supervisor be a licensed mental health professional (e.g., social worker or psychologist). This supervision is conducted both in one-on-one arrangements and with small groups of counselors, and the counselor receives a fee for this contracted service, usually the same as the hourly rate charged for counseling services in the counselor's private practice.

Like counseling, effective supervision requires specific knowledge, training, and skills. Counselors who provide supervision may hold the credential Approved Clinical Supervisor, established by the National Board for Certified Counselors (NBCC). Counselors who engage in supervision must be clear about any acquired risk of liability that accompanies their supervisory role and should verify that they have sufficient coverage in professional liability insurance policies.

Consultation is a form of supervision that occurs in several different contexts. Peer consultation takes place on a regular basis and can be either formal or informal. Informal consultation describes the activity whereby counselors communicate, respecting the ethical principles of confidentiality (ACA, 2005) regarding the well-being of their clients. The communication may be oriented toward case management or to address a specific client issue or need. The consultation is sometimes intended to bounce ideas off each other and other times to seek professional advice from someone with an area of expertise. Although it is a professional responsibility to engage in consultation, in most cases, there is usually not an associated fee for the service, and none of the participants in the consultation have any increased responsibility based on the communication.

A different method of consultation is when a professional counselor provides a contracted service to another mental health professional, mental health agency, or those in a different field seeking counseling or other human services. This is described as *expert* or *process* consultation. Some examples of consultation services that might be requested from a mental health counselor are coming to a job site to facilitate a conflict resolution process or being available for counseling and support to employees for a time following a violent incident resulting in loss of life and injuries to workers on the job.

Teaching or training provides those in private practice with another, often rewarding professional activity and an additional means of enhancing income. Of course, through the formal and informal consultation process, counselors always, in a sense, engage in teaching and learning. However, professional mental health counselors may be asked or seek opportunities to teach, particularly if they are recognized as having a relevant or unusual area of special knowledge or practice. Professional counselors may teach counselors in training by accepting appointments as adjunct faculty members in counselor education programs. The perspective of field-based or community mental health counselings is valuable in the classroom environment because the hands-on experience of the practitioner enhances the academic component of the counselor education program.

Counselors teach courses for other counseling professionals and those working in related fields, usually offered in association with an educational institution or professional association, available for credit as continuing professional education. Additionally, mental health counselors are sometimes called upon to teach courses, provide skills training, offer workshops and seminars, prepare materials, or make professional speeches for businesses, agencies, and community organizations. Popular topics include stress management, effective parenting skills, and communication training. In addition to supplementing their income, counselors who consult, train, and teach experience the added benefit of becoming more recognized in the community. To a large degree, the success of a private practice depends on effective marketing strategies. Word of mouth is typically the most valuable marketing tool, and a respected reputation in the community can be the best advertising (Gladding, 2007).

Some Final Thoughts on Private Practice. The entrepreneurial opportunities afforded counselors who have a private practice are considerable. Counselors who work independently can create a practice that utilizes their own professional and personal strengths, allows them to respond to individuals and counseling and clinical issues that most interest them, and removes many of the restrictions associated with being part of a system of care.

Counselors working in private practice must be creative, energetic, and comfortable with risk taking. Maintaining clinical competence is a professional, ethical, and in the case of the private practice, essential responsibility in order to be successful. Conditions may sometimes conspire to make those previously listed responsibilities difficult to meet. For example, because private practitioners' income is tied directly to how much work they do, they cannot depend on a regular or predictable salary and often work long hours, sometimes 50–60 hours per week, while establishing a practice (Male, 1990). Challenges such as these run counter to what is considered best practice, can become a stressor, and constitute a block to therapeutic effectiveness (Brooks, 1997). Professional mental health counselors must take responsibility for self-care and take measures to remedy such a situation in order to provide competent counseling for their clients.

Because a private practice is a business, mental health counselors in independent practice must be able to attend to the development and operating needs of the practice. In most cases, this means handling those responsibilities themselves. Like any other business, managing a private counseling practice means arranging for and maintaining office space, paying bills, and hiring and supervising any employees. Counselors promote their services, communicate with referral sources, consult with other professionals, and navigate the maze of insurance and managed health care systems. Some responsibilities idiosyncratic to the counseling profession are maintaining client records, remaining current in therapeutic practice developments, and keeping abreast of frequently changing licensing, insurance, and tax regulations that affect the counselor and the client. Professional mental health counselors who succeed in private practice enjoy the opportunity to be independent, find the tasks exciting, and especially enjoy the incredible variety that comes with the territory (Browers, 2005; Gladding, 2007).

Hospitals and Health Care Facilities. Although not strictly defined as community-based mental health care, community hospitals and other comprehensive health care facilities may operate for-profit or nonprofit and may be private or public. They certainly interface with mental health services in the community and should be considered as a viable service under the community umbrella.

Although the majority of hospitals' services are provided inpatient, some are provided on site or in communities. In either case, hospitals and health care facilities are a major component of most community health care systems—medical and psychological. Opportunities for counselors may be found in general hospitals, psychiatric facilities, Veteran's Administration facilities, rehabilitation centers, and substance abuse treatment programs.

Residential treatment facilities/hospitals serve a variety of conditions and populations. Adult inpatient treatment can be acute (1–5 days) or specialized programs such as drug and alcohol rehabilitation. Specialized programs consist of more long-term treatments, often several weeks. Child and adolescent residential treatment programs may have a variety of different services that include, but are not limited to, psychiatric residential treatment and group homes.

Although some hospitals may not include any counseling programs (usually called behavioral medicine in hospital settings), many provide preventative and maintenance programs. Traditionally, medical care facilities relied on clinical psychologists, social workers, psychiatric nurses, and occupational therapists to address the counseling and psychological needs of the patients in hospitals (Browers, 2005). In the past 20 or 30 years, hospitals and related health care facilities have expanded to include services to clients whose medical conditions may be complicated by psychological conditions or, conversely, whose medical diagnosis may cause or contribute to emotional problems. As a result, many mental health counselors are now finding employment in hospitals and medical settings where they collaborate with health care professionals to provide comprehensive treatment that includes counseling.

Counselors in hospital and health care settings focus on crisis work, preventative counseling, remediation, or supportive counseling with patients or clients (outside medical settings, it is not considered appropriate to refer to clients as patients). Many health care facilities provide services to patients oriented toward wellness, especially for patients with cardiac disease, diabetes, injuries, and strokes. Counselors can effectively assist clients in identifying and changing behaviors or patterns of thinking, which may have complicated their medical concerns, and can contribute to their recovery. Additionally, counselors may help clients address the emotional issues of fear, anxiety, anger, or depression that often accompany or result from a medical diagnosis. The comorbidity of a physical ailment and psychological distress is especially relevant with older adults.

Other wellness and prevention programs in hospitals that employ mental health care counselors are often available to patients in the hospital and open to the community as well. Such programs and education focus on smoking cessation, nutrition, exercise, stress reduction, pain management, and sleep disorders.

Counselors have long been part of the medical team that provides counseling for clients or patients in treatment for alcohol and substance abuse and for eating disorders. More recently, health care facilities have begun to offer counseling and support services to patients (and their loved ones) who are critically or chronically ill, are facing or recovering from major surgery, or have a terminal illness.

Managed Health Care

Managed health care systems (HMOs) are more difficult to define but clearly are influential in access to services and the quality of care available to communities. A health management organization is a large, privately run comprehensive system of health care that usually includes mental health care services. Several states have also developed systems that resemble HMOs as a means of providing comprehensive health care services. The emergence of these systems of care is an effort to curb escalating health care costs, primarily by restricting access to care or the amount of care that can be utilized. Professional mental health counselors may be employed directly by a managed care system or may be an approved contractor. Relatively speaking, managed health care systems are new on the scene, but most health care providers believe that they are here to stay (Corey, Corey, & Callanan, 2003).

There are obvious disadvantages to such systems. Often seen as gatekeepers, HMOs determine how health care providers, including counselors, deliver services and what rights and resources consumers have in treatment (Gladding, 2007). The most frequently cited concern is that determinations regarding clients' care will be made by nonclinical personnel, although treatment decisions are best made by mental health professionals in consultation with their clients (Nugent, 2000; Nugent & Jones, 2005). There is anxiety that quality of care may be negatively affected by cost-cutting measures now in place or established in the future. Understandably, many health care providers, including mental health counselors, have reacted to the real and perceived threat of limitations to service with resentment, frustration, and legitimate concerns about potential neglect of clients' needs based on limited access to appropriate services (Browers, 2005).

Although it is true that when a managed health care system determines access to and the nature and duration of mental health care service, a client faces potential risks, it has also served to motivate mental health counselors to become more accountable. Counselors are responsible for assessing client needs and developing effective (and consistent with managed health care directives—efficient) treatment plans. Accountability is good for the client; however, having access to care and control over the nature of treatment and the duration of service determined by individuals who are not trained as mental health care providers or knowledgeable about diagnosis, treatment, and effective counseling practices is very disturbing (Browers, 2005).

Since managed health care is a reality of life for community mental health counselors, practitioners must be competent in rapid assessment, identifying client needs and establishing goals, and pairing the client with the counselor and intervention most likely to provide assistance. Counselors working as part of a managed health care system should be highly skilled in the use of brief therapy models and also must be well informed about additional community resources, should their client require service beyond or different from what is approved by their HMO (Browers, 2005).

Mental Health Counseling and Mental Health Counselors: A New Identity

A considerable amount of space in this chapter has been devoted to reviewing the likely settings where professional mental health counselors are providing services. Even a cursory reading of the material should make it very clear that the counseling profession has been in an evolutionary process and that professional mental health counselors have an important role in a cluster of disciplines that make up the professional community of mental health care providers. While the profession has been evolving, there have been profound changes in government policies and a restructuring of comprehensive health care delivery systems (including mental health care). Those changes make it clear that mental health counseling, while necessary and important, must be provided in ways that are compatible with current systems and structures. Current revisions in public policy influence the nature of the work of counselors, the client populations served, the counseling needs that can be addressed, and the settings where they work (Browers, 2005).

It may seem misplaced to address the issue of professional identity *after* focusing on the settings and opportunities for counseling practice. The reality is the counseling profession has a history of examining and refining the definition of its professional role, a history that could not be more evident than it is today. With today's climate of change, the ability to adapt is a valuable and necessary skill. To prepare to be a counselor in community and private practice settings, it is crucial to have a clear understanding of what services are consistent with mental health counseling and how mental health counselors view their role in that process. In the last 35 years, the counseling profession, counselor educators, and counselors in particular have entered a new world. Today, counselors can be found in public or private agencies, clinics, and residential and outpatient treatment facilities. They provide a broad range of general counseling services, work in settings that focus on specific clinical issues, or specialize to better meet a particular need. The rapid changes in the mental health counseling profession necessitate a reexamination of the identity of the mental health counselor and the definition of mental health counseling.

Mental Health Counselors and Mental Health Counseling

Because the profession is relatively young and dynamic, the definition of mental health counseling and counselors continues to evolve and be refined to accurately reflect the needs of the mental health community and the clients being served, while also describing the roles and functions of the mental health practitioner. In 1997, the Governing Council of the American Counseling Association adopted the following definition of professional counseling:

The Practice of Mental Health Counseling: The application of mental health, psychological, or human development principles, through cognitive, affective, behavioral, or systemic intervention strategies that address wellness, personal growth, or career development, as well as pathology (ACA, 1997, p. 8). The governing counsel further defined a professional counseling specialty as:

> A professional counseling specialty is narrowly focused, requiring advanced knowledge in the field founded on the premise that all Professional Counselors must first meet the requirements for the general practice of professional counseling. (ACA, 1997, p. 8)

It is important, as mental health counselors, to operate out of a common understanding of how professionals define the task of counseling and the roles and responsibilities of counselors in that task. It is equally important that professionals are in agreement when presenting that definition to other related disciplines in the mental health practice community and especially to the public. However, the definition is likely to be revised periodically as the profession changes along with the rapidly changing systems that deliver mental health care systems to our communities.

Professional Identity.   Unlike other professions in the mental health care arena, the mental health counseling profession may actually resemble a group of professions. Contributing to that perception is the tradition of counselor education programs admitting applicants from many different academic disciplines. Another factor in that perception is that the counseling profession embraces practitioners representing a broad array of counseling specialties; counselors may focus on group counseling, families, be certified as school counselors or mental health counselors, work in substance abuse treatment, and so on, and still be a professional counselor. Arguably, the interdisciplinary history counselors share and the integrated methods used in practice create a broader perspective through which counselors can consider the individuals they serve.

A similarity that professional mental health counselors share with other mental health care providers is that all offer counseling that is intentionally therapeutic in nature. The distinctions are more apparent in the methods and approaches employed. Professional counselors retain the historical roots of responding to client needs by using a wellness model, that is, accessing existing and underlying strengths to help clients make positive changes in functioning. But like other mental health care professions, the profession of mental health counseling has clearly become more clinically oriented during the last 20 or 30 years. This is both necessary and consistent with increased community-based treatment for individuals who traditionally were treated in inpatient facilities. Whereas in the early days of the profession, counselors worked primarily with individuals considered more mentally healthy, today's professional counselor is prepared to respond to mental health needs ranging from severe and persistent mental illness to clients who are considered to be mentally healthy. Fortunately, counselor education programs, accreditation and licensing boards, the American Counseling Association and its divisions, and professional mental health counselors themselves reflect this transition.

Professional Preparation and Credentials for Mental Health Counselors.   Professional counselors have a master's or doctorate degree in counseling from a counselor education or closely related program. The academic and supervised clinical experiences that comprise counselor education programs create the foundation from which mental health counselors draw throughout their professional life. The professional credentials that they hold help to clarify the parameters of the education and skills counselors bring to the many and varied roles they fill in the mental health care arena. Furthermore, clients seeking service from a counselor who has earned professional credentials as a mental health counselor can feel confident that the practitioner has received advanced training and abides by the ethics and standards consistent with the credential held.

Council for the Accreditation of Counseling and Related Educational Programs (CACREP). The Council for the Accreditation of Counseling and Related Educational Programs (CACREP) was established in 1981 and is the primary accreditation body for counseling programs (Schmidt, 1999). Its purpose is to establish educational standards and evaluate master's- and doctoral-level degree programs for accreditation. It evaluates counselor education programs at the master's level in the areas of school counseling, community counseling, career counseling, student affairs practice in higher education, marriage and family counseling, and mental health counseling. It also accredits doctoral-level programs in counselor education and supervision.

Although a voluntary process, the number of accredited counselor preparation programs is increasing, and the trend is continuing. As of January 2007 there were 543 individual programs accredited by CACREP (all categories) at the master's level, housed in 210 institutions, and 52 at the doctoral level (CACREP, 2007a). Faculty and administrators recognize that CACREP accreditation is respected as a standard of excellence. In a study conducted by Adams (2005), students who graduate from CACREP programs scored higher on the National Counselors Exam (NCE) than those students who did not graduate from a CACREP-accredited program.

Graduates of CACREP-accredited counselor education programs gain advantages in addition to assurance of a quality education. Most states specify CACREP-accredited or CACREP-like counseling programs when specifying the educational requirements for obtaining a state license. By completing the rigorous and standardized CACREP curriculum, counselors have more ease in securing a professional counseling license when they must move across state lines (Nugent, 2000). Entrance into accredited counselor education doctoral programs may be enhanced by graduation from CACREP master's programs. Despite a grassroots movement currently taking place, licensure does not carry portability from state to state.

Licensing and Certification for Mental Health Counselors. Licensure is a state-regulated process, created by statute, and it regulates the activities of the professional and occupational activities of the holder of the license. At the time of this writing, 49 states and the District of Columbia have licensing laws for professional counselors. Unfortunately, there is currently very little consistency in the licensing laws across the nation that regulate counseling. At least 39 states and the District of Columbia have practice acts or practice and title acts, an act that does not permit one to practice as a counselor without holding a license. Several states have a title act, protecting only the title, and allow anyone to practice counseling, as long as he or she does not represent themselves as licensed. One state, California, does not have a specific credential for professional mental health counselors. For obvious reasons, a practice act is preferable; it assures a more professional community of mental health counselors and is a clearer designation for the community to understand. Although not a guarantee of third-party reimbursement, it is highly unlikely that an unlicensed counselor would qualify for payment.

Certification is a rather generic term or designation, potentially referring to a status granted by a state, an agency, a professional organization, or a professional board. Counselors can earn a variety of certifications, including designations that attest to their knowledge in areas of specialized practice. The most common and easily recognized certification in the counseling profession is available from the National Board for Certified Counselors (NBCC). Nationally certified counselors (NCCs) have earned master's or doctorate degrees that meet the academic requirements and have satisfied the experiential and supervision requirements designated by NBCC. Those seeking certification in a specialty area from NBCC may pursue a credential in the areas of mental health counseling, school counseling, career counseling, substance abuse counseling, and supervision.

One might ask, "Why seek a license and certification?" There are several good reasons. Like those who graduate from CACREP programs, nationally certified counselors experience some advantages, should they seek a counselor's license in more than one state during the course of a new career. Many states having licensing laws require the National Counselor Exam (NCE) or accept the NCE as partial fulfillment of the standards for obtaining a license. Professional certification is another means of demonstrating to the public that qualified counselors practice according to the high standards established by the counseling profession.

Those in the counseling profession have experienced increasing opportunities, and not so subtle pressure, to continually upgrade their professional status by seeking standard and specialized credentials. In the field of mental health care, professional credentials help to clearly identify the niche occupied by professional mental health counselors. The maintenance of credentials ensures the public that mental health counselors are continuing to upgrade their knowledge, collaborate with other professionals, and strictly adhere to the accepted standards of the profession.

New Dimensions in Counseling

Much change still lies ahead for the counseling profession. Individuals, partners, families, and communities will continue to struggle with experiences that are part of the human condition—loss, grief, transition, conflict, and self-doubt—and counselors will continue to respond to the emotional, psychological, and psychosocial needs that arise as a result. In some cases, the changes are a reflection of shifts in society and, in other cases, may be a result of those changes. Mental health counselors can expect transitions in the profession that are philosophical in nature, some that are technical, a continuing evolution of mental health care delivery systems, and optimistically, growth in the understanding of how to best use counseling skills to assist others in improving their quality of life.

Trauma and Crisis Counseling

Events such as the Virginia Tech shootings (2007), Hurricane Katrina (2005), and the terrorist attacks on September 11, 2001, have become defining moments in how professional counselors are preparing and responding to trauma and crisis. These types of tragedies entail specialized training for both direct victims and indirect victims (i.e., family, friends, emergency responders). Diagnoses such as Acute Stress Disorder (ASD) and Posttraumatic Stress Disorder (PTSD) may result from such experiences, and counselors need to be prepared and trained to assess the unique symptomology and the critical needs of those affected.

Recognizing the vital role counselors play in national emergencies, CACREP was awarded an "historic first of its kind federal contract to consider establishing guidelines and standards that will prepare counselors to work with health care providers" (CACREP, 2007b). This initiative will implement a network of counseling professionals to create those standards and guidelines within educational programs training counselors.

Technology and Counseling

As in other professions, computers and technology figure prominently in the work of mental health counselors. In recent years, many mental health counselors have become proficient in the use of computer-assisted diagnostic programs. Community agencies and managed health care systems maintain some or all of clients' records in computer files. Counselors regularly go online to connect with other professionals, access their professional organizations, and search the Internet for the most current information and resources to better serve their clients.

Web-based online counseling is a reality and could become an important means of providing access to mental health services. It provides greater access to rural clients, those who are housebound or disabled, and those with particular needs not available in their own community, such as non-English speakers. Recognizing the potential risks, the ACA established guidelines within its code of ethics governing the uses and restrictions of online counseling. The National Board of Certified Counselors (NBCC) also developed *The Practice of Internet Counseling* that encompasses electronic mail-based, chat room-based, and video-based services (NBCC, n.d.). The standards for both address the issues of secured sites, confidentiality and its limits, record keeping, and the counseling relationship. Counselors providing information or engaging in counseling and counseling-related activities via the Internet should seek appropriate legal, professional, and technical consultation to be certain that they are not in violation of any state, federal, or professional regulations or statutes, and to ensure that the activities are included in their liability coverage.

Another significant event in the increased use of technology is the implementation of HIPAA (Health Insurance Portability and Accountability Act of 1996). It is designed to protect the privacy of all client health data, including mental health records. It had resulted in mental health practitioners becoming knowledgeable in all the new regulations and revisions in record maintenance and transfer procedures.

Health Management Organizations and Advocating

Although no longer a new concept, managed health care systems will exert considerable influence on the practice of mental health counseling for the foreseeable future, regardless of whether a professional counselor elects to work within or outside health maintenance organizations. To work as part of the system, counselors are going to professionally and politically advocate for full recognition as core providers of mental health care. To work outside of managed care, counselors again must advocate and collaborate to develop creative ways to provide counseling services to the community that serve the needs of all clients, while meeting the income requirements of the practitioner (Browers, 2005).

Ethics for the Future

The counseling profession is at a crossroads. Graduate training assures a solid preparation for entry into the field, increased credentialing options define for the public what they can expect from mental health counseling, and professional counselors have gained recognition and status as professionals in mental health care. With a bright future, it is important to not lose touch with the rich history of the profession. First and foremost, counselors care about those they serve and respect the dignity of each human being.

In a new age, those roots will serve the profession well. The nature of advocacy is descriptive of the challenges faced by counselors in a new century. The pluralistic nature of America makes it imperative that the profession be mindful of its own biases, increase the knowledge and understanding of differing systems (especially families), and broaden counseling approaches to be more useful to more of the community. Along the same lines, the counseling profession itself would be well served to increase the diversity within its own ranks.

The concept of advocacy expands to include the responsibility of speaking on behalf of the clients we serve and those we don't, seeking services and resources for those who may otherwise fall through the cracks. As economic diversity continues to create greater disparity between the haves and the have-nots, professionals must lend their clout to improving the conditions of their communities.

Summary

Mental health counselors have a specific role in the larger profession of counseling. The role has evolved out of a rich history and is supported by specific academic and clinical training. Mental health counselors collaborate with other mental health care professionals and have opportunities to practice counseling in many diverse settings. Some of these settings include community agencies (public and private), hospitals and health care facilities, government-sponsored programs and services, and private practice. Professional counselors have available to them many different professional credentials, which helps to define for the public what counselors do and increases their professional recognition in the mental health care community. Forty-nine states offer some form of professional counseling license, and all counselors who qualify can seek certification as a national certified counselor (NCC). Some professional counselors hold credentials in counseling specialties.

Mental health counselors have made many advances during the relatively brief history of the counseling profession. That history reflects ongoing efforts to make sure the definition of counseling accurately reflects the competencies of counseling practitioners, as well as the roles fulfilled in the mental health profession. The future of mental health counseling promises exciting challenges as mental health counselors use new resources in their work, gain greater access to managed health care systems, and engage with a more diverse society. The following Web sites provide additional information relating to the chapter topics:

USEFUL WEB SITES

American Counseling Association (ACA)
www.counseling.org

American School Counselor Association (ASCA)
www.schoolcounselor.org

American Mental Health Counselors Association (AMHCA)
www.amhca.org

National Board of Certified Counselors (NBCC)
www.nbcc.org

Council for Accreditation of Counseling and Related Educational Programs (CACREP)
www.cacrep.org

National Institute of Mental Health (NIMH)
www.nimh.nih.gov

Substance Abuse and Mental Health Services Administration (SAMHSA)
www.samhsa.gov

REFERENCES

Adams, S. A. (2005). Does CACREP accreditation make a difference? A look at NCE results and answers. *Journal of Professional Counseling: Practice, Theory, & Research, 33*(2), 60–76.

American Counseling Association. (1997, October). *Governing council minutes.* Alexandria, VA: Author.

American Counseling Association. (1999, March). The effectiveness of professional counseling services (Office of Public Policy and Information). Alexandria, VA: Author.

American Counseling Association. (2005). *ACA code of ethics.* Alexandria, VA: Author.

Beamish, P. M. (2005). Introduction to the special section—severe and persistent mental illness on college campuses: Considerations for service provision. *Journal of College Counseling, 8*(2), 138–139.

Brooks, D. K., Jr. (1997). Counseling in mental health and private practice settings. In D. Capuzzi & D. R. Gross (Eds.), *Introduction to counseling* (2nd ed., pp. 309–327). Boston: Allyn and Bacon.

Brooks, D. K., Jr., & Weikel, W. J. (1986). History and development of the mental health counseling movement. In A. J. Palmo & W. J. Weikel (Eds.), *Foundations of mental health counseling* (pp. 5–28). Springfield, IL: C. J. Thomas.

Browers, R. T. (2005). Counseling in mental health and private practice setting. In D. Capuzzi & D. R. Gross (Eds.), *Introduction to the counseling profession* (4th ed., pp. 309–330). Boston: Allyn and Bacon.

Collins, M., & Mowbray, C. (2005). Higher education and psychiatric disabilities: National survey of campus disability services. *American Journal of Orthopsychiatry, 75*(2), 304–315.

Collins, M., & Mowbray, C. (2006). Campus mental health services: Recommendations for change. *American Journal of Orthopsychiatry, 76*(2), 226–237.

Corey, G., Corey, M. S., & Callanan, P. (2003). *Issues and ethics in the helping professions* (6th ed.). Pacific Grove, CA: Brooks/Cole.

Council for Accreditation of Counseling and Related Programs. (2007a). Retrieved May 20, 2007, from http://www.cacrep.org/directory-current.html

Council for Accreditation of Counseling and Related Programs. (2007b). Retrieved May 20, 2007, from http://www.cacrep.org/epp.html

Gladding, S. T. (2007). *Counseling: A comprehensive profession* (5th ed.). Upper Saddle River, NJ: Prentice Hall.

Hoagwood, K. (1999, March 15). *Major research findings on child and adolescent mental health* (Summary sheet). Alexandria, VA.: National Institute on Mental Health.

Karlin, B. E., & Fuller, J. D. (2007). Meeting the mental health needs of older adults: Implications for primary care practice. *Geriatrics, 62,* 26–35.

Levine, A. (1980). *When dreams and heroes died: A portrait of today's college student.* San Francisco: Jossey-Bass.

Male, R. A. (1990). Careers in public and private agencies. In B. B. Collison & N. J. Garfield (Eds.), *Careers in counseling and human development* (pp. 81–89). Alexandria, VA: American Counseling Association.

Myers, J. E. (1995). From "forgotten and ignored" to standards and certification: Gerontological counseling comes of age. *Journal of Counseling and Development, 74,* 143.

National Board of Certified Counselors. (n.d.). Retrieved June 17, 2007, from http://www.nbcc.org/webethics2

National Institute of Mental Health. (2007). *National institutes of health.* Retrieved May 20, 2007, from http://www.nimh.nih.gov

Newman, B. M., & Newman, P. R. (1999). Development through life: A psychosocial approach (7th ed.). Belmont, CA: Brooks/Cole.

Nolan, J. M., Ford, S. J. W., Kress, V. E., Anderson, R. L., & Novak, T. C. (2005). A comprehensive model for addressing severe and persistent mental health illness on campuses: The new diversity initiative. *Journal of College Counseling, 8*(2), 172–179.

Nugent, F. A. (2000). *Introduction to the profession of counseling* (3rd ed.). Upper Saddle River, NJ: Prentice Hall.

Nugent, F. A., & Jones, K. D. (2005). *Introduction to the counseling profession* (4th ed.). Upper Saddle River, NJ: Prentice Hall.

President's New Freedom Commission on Mental Health. (2002, December 2). *Final report to the president.* Retrieved June 17, 2007, from http://www.mentalhealthcommission.gov/

Schmidt, J. J. (1999). Two decades of CACREP and what do we know? *Counselor Education and Supervision, 39,* 34–46.

Substance Abuse and Mental Health Services Administration. (2007). Retrieved May 20, 2007, from http://www.samhsa.gov

U.S. Census Bureau. (2004). Table 1.1 population by age, sex, race and Hispanic origin: 2004. Retrieved May 20, 2007, from http://www.census.gov/population/socdemo/age

U.S. Department of Education. (n.d.). *No child left behind.* Retrieved May 20, 2007, from http://www.ed.gov/nclb/landing.jhtml

United States Department of Health and Human Services. (n.d.a). *Reports of the surgeon general, U.S. public health service; Chapter 3: Children and mental health.* Retrieved May 20, 2007, from http://www.surgeongeneral.gov/library/mentalhealth/chapter3/sec1.html

United States Department of Health and Human Services. (n.d.b). *Reports of the surgeon general, U.S. public health service; Chapter 6: Organizing and financing mental health services.* Retrieved May 20, 2007, from http://www.surgeongeneral.gov/library/mentalhealth/chapter6/sec1.html

PART FOUR

Counseling Special Populations

In the previous sections, the basic skills and theoretical bases for counseling were described. In Part Four, "Counseling Special Populations," these skills are applied to specific groups with whom a counselor may work. Each of these special populations demands different combinations of skills, knowledge, and experience from the counselor.

Demographic statistics predict that the percentage of individuals over the age of 55 will be increasing in the coming decades. A knowledge of the specific counseling needs of older individuals will become increasingly more important as our society moves into the 21st century and beyond. Chapter 17, "Counseling the Older Adult," presents a detailed description of the field of gerontological counseling. The specialized needs and social realities of older individuals are presented. The importance of viewing older clients as individuals—and not from the basis of cultural stereotypes about aging and the elderly—is stressed. Specific developmental challenges with which older individuals must cope are also outlined. The current therapeutic approaches most widely used with older clients, such as reality orientation, reminiscence groups, and remotivation therapy, are described.

Family therapy assumes a systems approach to counseling and stresses the overall interpersonal context in which the client's problems are occurring. Chapter 18, "Counseling Couples and Families," provides a historical framework for viewing the development of couples and family counseling and outlines the central concepts of family systems theory. The author presents an overview of the different schools of family therapy and stresses the importance of maintaining an integrative and eclectic approach to understanding and learning from these approaches. Core issues that often emerge in family counseling, such as boundary problems, low self-esteem, and inappropriate family hierarchies, are described. Stages in couples and family counseling are outlined, with descriptions of appropriate interventions for each particular level. This chapter concludes with discussions of professional issues connected with couples and family counseling and research in family therapy.

Chapter 19, "Counseling Lesbian, Gay, Bisexual, Transgendered, and Questioning Clients," surveys a field of growing importance to counselors. Issues involving gay individuals are becoming more visible in our society. Although clients who happen to be gay should be viewed as individuals first and as gay persons second, the importance for the counselor to maintain a sensitivity to the special concerns of gay clients is stressed. Self-identity, self-esteem, and relationship concerns may take on an enhanced intensity with gay clients, owing to the significant social, psychological, and interpersonal stresses they may experience.

This section concludes with Chapter 20, "Counseling Clients with Disabilities," in which an overview of both the goals and the major interventions for working with clients with disabilities are discussed. Physical, cognitive, and emotional factors in understanding disability are reviewed, with emphasis on helping clients improve their overall quality of life and come to terms with the conditions of their particular disability. Counseling clients with psychiatric disorders and the professional qualifications and necessary training for counselors wishing to pursue rehabilitation as a career choice are described to complete a realistic depiction of the scope and practice of the rehabilitation counselor.

Although Part Four of the text introduces the reader to only four selected special populations, the possibilities for roles and responsibilities of the professional counselor are well presented and illustrative of the growth and maturation of the counseling profession. Individuals preparing to enter the profession can expect to be part of a demanding and exciting career field requiring continuing education and supervision beyond the confines of the university and completion of graduate requirements.

CHAPTER

17 Counseling the Older Adult

DOUGLAS R. GROSS, PhD
Arizona State University

DAVID CAPUZZI, PhD
Pennsylvania State University

Paul was in the final semester of his master of counseling program and was just beginning his internship. With the advice of his program chairperson, Paul had purposely selected a clinic setting that served people 65 years of age and older. He was interested in working with older adults and had taken several courses designed to provide him with information and experience in working with this population. His orientation to the setting had been completed 2 days ago; today, he was to see his first client.

As he prepared for the session, Paul reviewed many of the things he had learned in his university coursework. His office had been arranged so that the client, a 79-year-old widower, would have both easy access and a comfortable chair. The time scheduled for the appointment had been arranged to accommodate both the client's concerns regarding transportation and an appointment with a physician in the same complex. He knew that the client was somewhat resistant to seeking help and that he would need to reassure him of the benefits of counseling. He was also aware that their age difference—he was 29 and the client was 79—might be a barrier to communication, and he would need to take this into consideration.

An intake interview and an orientation meeting had been conducted by the intake person in the clinic, and the schedule of fees had been explained to the client. Paul had reviewed the material collected during the intake interview, which included a medical history documenting the client's physical limitations due to issues of neuropathy, arthritis, diabetes, mobility, and medications. There was also information related to the client's past history of alcohol addiction, lack of social involvement, periods of depression, and lapses in memory. The client's presenting problem centered around his fear and anger at being forced to move from his home to a care facility Paul's role was to explore with the client his feelings regarding the move and possible alternatives.

The client arrived at the clinic a few minutes prior to the scheduled time. He was accompanied by his son and asked that the son be allowed to join him in the counseling session. Paul had not anticipated this but, wishing to make the client feel more comfortable, agreed. Paul's office was quickly rearranged to accommodate the son, and the session began.

During the session, the son told Paul that his father's health no longer allowed him to live alone. Based upon the physician's recommendation and with his father's agreement, arrangements had been made to move him to a full-care facility. In the past 2 weeks, however, his father had become very disturbed about this move. He now felt that with more assistance from his son and family, he could remain in his home. Based upon his physical condition, however, this would not be possible. His son stated that his father was aware of this and was denying the reality of the situation. Depression, fear, and anger were obvious as the client discussed how much he loved his home and its memories and how he needed to remain independent as long as possible. The session had reached a stalemate, with both parties holding to their positions. Paul decided to talk with each person separately, and the son said that he would wait outside.

In the session with the client, Paul explored the depression, fear, and anger that the client was feeling. He was afraid of losing independence and angry that his son was not willing to take care of him as he had always taken care of him. He felt that he was being placed in the facility to die. He knew that he needed a lot of special care but felt that with the son's help he could remain at home. Paul understood his strong need for independence rather than dependence, and he wanted to do what he could to make this a possibility.

During his session, the son explained his father's physical limitations, the dangers of living alone, and the fact that his father could no longer care for himself or his large home. The move had been discussed at length, and he felt that his father was accepting the fact that he could no longer remain alone. He was surprised by his current reaction and was at a loss as to what could be done to make the transition as positive as possible. He stated that he loved his father and would do nothing to hurt him. The move was both supported and encouraged by his physician.

Paul brought the client and his son together and shared with them his perceptions of the situation. He encouraged them to talk with each other, as each had talked with him, and asked if they would be willing to return to the clinic to continue to discuss the situation. The client seemed somewhat hesitant, but did agree to return the following Tuesday.

Paul sat for a short time after the client and son left reviewing what had taken place. He decided that he needed to talk with his supervisor regarding the session and what he had done. Questions such as Should he have done more to resolve the situation? Are there comorbidity factors related to the client's physical condition, past addiction, and his depression? Based upon the depression, is there danger of suicide?—needed answers. He could see both sides of the issue, but his feelings were more strongly on the side of the client. He wanted him to be able to remain independent as long as possible and felt that he needed to develop more of an advocacy role in assisting the client and his son to bring a more positive solution to the situation.

This scenario is occurring more and more in various mental health settings. Counselors and mental health workers are being asked to work with a clientele for whom many are ill prepared. The clientele are older adults who, owing to the lengthening of the life span, are increasing in numbers and will continue to have a profound impact on all areas of counseling and therapy. Today, there are more than 35 million people age 65 or older. Based on the projections of the Administration on Aging (AOA), in its 2001 report, "A Profile of Older Americans, 2001," this figure will climb to more than 70 million by the year 2030. The impact of this growing population has been addressed by numerous authors (Gross and Capuzzi, 2005; Maples & Abney 2006; Thomas & Martin, 2006). According to Gross and Capuzzi (2005), "The growing body of literature in the area of counseling and intervention strategies for the elderly address the emerging recognition that this population will continue to represent itself in growing numbers to the counseling professional" (p. 385).

The purpose of this chapter is to present information relative to counseling the older adult. This information will enable the reader to develop an understanding of the demographics, the general and unique nature of the problems presented, research into individual and group counseling approaches that have proven to be effective, and recommendations that should aid the counseling/mental health professional to serve this population more effectively. In this chapter, the term *older adult* refers to people 65 years and older.

Demography of Aging

To understand the demographics of the aging population in the United States, the reader has to understand the numerical increase and its growing diversity in relation to age, sex and marital status, geographic distribution, race and ethnicity, retirement, employment, income, and physical and mental health status. It is not the purpose of this chapter to present an in-depth analysis of these diverse issues. Each is presented to provide the reader with an overview that should aid counselors and other mental health professionals to better understand this growing population that is and will continue to become an ongoing part of their caseloads.

The growing number of older adults within the United States constitutes an escalating portion of our total population. According to Myers and Harper (2004), "The total population of older persons in the United States numbered 34.5 million in 1999, representing 1 in every 8 persons—an 11-fold increase during the twentieth century" (p. 207). Projecting these figures into the 21st century, the AOA 2001 report indicates that this population will reach 70 million by the year 2030, more than twice their number in 1999. This number would represent approximately 20% of the total population and reflect a 7 percentage point increase over the 13% this population currently constitutes.

A Composite Picture

Older adults are too often viewed as a fairly homogeneous group of individuals (Thornton, 2002). A closer look at variations in this grouping will prove this view to be far from the truth. This population is quite diverse and parallels the diversity found in other segments of our population. The following discussion of these demographic variations highlights this diversity. The data reported are taken from *A Profile of Older Americans* (AOA, 2001).

Age, Sex, and Marital Status

The older adult population itself is aging. One of the most rapidly growing age categories is that of people 85 years and older (the old-old). This population (4.2 million) will increase to 8.9 million by the year 2030. This population is 32 times larger in 2001 than in 1900. Within this same time frame, the 75–84 age group (middle-old) was 16 times larger, and the 65–74 age group (young-old) was 8 times larger than their counterpart in 1900.

Variation is also noted in the percentage of males to females. In 2001, there were 20.6 million older women and 14.4 million older men, for a sex ratio of approximately 143 women for every 100 men. The sex ratio increased with age ranging from 117 women for every 100 men for the 65–69 group to a high of 245 women for every 100 men for persons 85 and over.

These figures are probably not too surprising, given the data related to the greater life expectancy of women. What is surprising, however, is the fact that older men tend to remarry if they lose a spouse and women do not. In 2001, older men were much more likely to be married than older women: 74% of men, 41% of women. Almost half of all older women in 2001 were widows (46%). There were four times as many widows (8.49 million) as widowers (2.0 million). Although divorced and/or separated older persons represented only 10% of all older persons in 2001, this represents a 4% increase since 1990.

Geographic Distribution

There is a degree of similarity between the distribution of older adults and the distribution of the general population. States with the largest populations tend to have the largest number of older adults. In 2001, about half (52%) of persons age 65 and older lived in nine states. California had more than 3.4 million, Florida 2.8 million, New York 2.4 million, Texas and Pennsylvania each had almost 2 million, and Ohio, Illinois, Michigan, and New Jersey each had more than 1 million.

Persons 65 and older were slightly less likely to live in metropolitan areas in 2001 than younger persons (75% of the elderly, 80% of persons under 65). About 27% of older persons lived in central cities, and 48% lived in the suburbs. The belief that a majority of older adults uproot themselves and move is not supported by the data. The majority of older adults continue to live in the same location. In 1999, only 4.2% of persons 65 and older had moved since 1998, compared with 16.5% of persons under 65.

Race and Ethnicity

Racial and ethnic differences provide yet another variation within this population (Harris, 1998). In 2001, about 16.4% of persons 65 and older were minorities: 8% were Black, 2.4% were Asian or Pacific Islander, 5.6% were of Hispanic origin, and less than 1% were American Indian or Native Alaskan. Only 6.16% of racial and ethnic minority populations were 65 and older in 2001. In the general population, 85% are White and 15% are non-White. Minority populations are projected to represent 25.4% of the elderly population in 2030, up from 16.4% in 2001.

Retirement, Employment, and Income

Retirement, which at one point in our history was considered a luxury, is today the norm. According to the Special Committee on Aging (SCOA, 1983), 66% of older men were employed in the labor force in 1900. Today, less than 16–18% of this population is employed, and the projections are that this percentage will continue to decline. The percentages for females for this same period show a much more stable pattern: 10% in the labor force in 1900 and 10.8% in 2001. The percentage for females has been around 8–10% since 1988. The people who tend to remain in the labor force after they are 70 are those classified as professionals and those who are craftspeople. Both these categories are descriptive of the self-employed.

Retirement brings with it a set of unique circumstances surrounding the older adult related to employment and income. According to Butler, Lewis, and Sunderland (1991), a majority of those who retire do so with incomes stemming from pensions (16%), Social Security (38%), savings (26%), employment (17%), and assistance from relatives (3%). For the most part, this income is "fixed" and generally represents approximately 40% of the income the individual was receiving prior to retirement. With inflation generally on the rise in this country, the reductions, coupled with the "fixed" nature of the income, place the individual in a position of having to manage income more carefully to meet not only the basic costs of living but also the added costs, specifically those that deal with increasing taxes and the expenses associated with health care that come with retirement (Taylor-Carter, Cook, & Weinberg, 1997).

In 2001, the median income of older persons was $19,688 for males and $11,313 for females. Households containing families headed by persons over age 65 reported a median income of $33,936 ($34,661 for Whites, $26,610 for Blacks, and $24,287 for Hispanics). Approximately one of nine (10.7%) family households with an elderly head had incomes below $15,000, and 40.1% had incomes of $35,000 or more. According to Myers and Harper (2004), 10% of older people are poor, with poverty rates higher for older women than for older men. These authors also indicate that older members of ethnic minorities are more likely to live at or near the federal poverty level.

Maples and Abney (2006) paint an interesting picture of the "baby boomer" generation. The approximately 76 million adults who compose this population bring with them differing perspectives on health, life expectations, worldviews, retirement, and income. According to the authors, "As baby boomers move into their 60s in 2006, the face of counseling will become more complex. Increasing numbers of highly skilled professionals will be needed to meet the mental, physical, social, emotional, career and leisure needs of this population" (p. 8).

Physical and Mental Health

One of the stereotypical pictures of older adults is people who are frail, weak, and suffering from a myriad of chronic disorders. Like all stereotypes, nothing could be further from the truth (Myers, 2003; Thornton, 2002). According to Lemme (1995), "Most adults are in good health and experience few limitations or disabilities. Nearly 71 percent of adults over age 65 living in the community (that is not in institutions) report their health as excellent, very good, or good" (p. 374). Based on findings such as these, a high percentage of older adults are able to maintain the activities of daily living without the necessity of medical assistance.

In 2001, older people had about four times the number of days of hospitalizations (1.8 days) as did the under-65 population (0.4 days) The average length of a hospital stay was 6.4 days for older people, compared with only 4.6 days for all people. In 2001, older consumers averaged $3,493 in out-of-pocket health care expenditures, an increase of more than half since 1990. In contrast, the total population spent considerably less, averaging $2,182 in out-of-pocket costs. Older Americans spent 12.6% of their total expenditures on health, more than twice the proportion spent by all consumers (5.5%).

The mental health picture for older adults indicates that even though 27% of all admissions to public mental hospitals are over 65, only 2 to 4% are represented in outpatient mental health treatment facilities (Schwiebert, Myers, & Dice, 2000; Tice & Perkins, 1996). These percentages may reflect a variety of factors. It could be that, based on values and attitudes, older adults do not see the benefit in seeking such treatment. They may not understand the concepts that underlie counseling and therapy. It could be that the mental health facility, based on personnel and facilities, is not prepared to work with this population or that older adults place more emphasis on physical versus mental health. Regardless of the reasons, older adults, like their younger counterparts, can benefit from such assistance and need to receive information and encouragement from the mental health professional.

Mental Health Problems and Developmental Issues of Older Adults

From a psychological viewpoint, the emotional and psychological problems of older adults differ slightly from the emotional and psychological problems of their younger counterparts (Burlingame, 1995; Myers, 2003; Tueth, 1995). For example, feelings of anxiety, depression, loneliness, despair, worthlessness, fear, and suicide are prevalent across all age levels. Substance abuse, violence, and domestic abuse are not limited to the young but find equal applicability across the older adult population (Kleinke, 1998; Myers & Harper, 2004; Zalaquett & Stens, 2006). The young as well as the old must learn to cope daily with a multitude of life situations that test their emotional stability. For the older adult, however, many of these emotional and psychological problems may have a comorbid relationship to physical illness, disability, and chronic pain common in later life. For example, emotions such as anxiety, depression, fear, despair, and suicide ideation may stem from a physical rather than situational base. Counselors need to be able to distinguish whether symptoms are caused by a medical condition or a psychiatric disorder. This being the case, it may be necessary to make adaptations (request for medical evaluations, working more closely with the client's physician, etc.) when working with this population (Knight, 1999).

From a situational perspective, the process of aging also brings with it a set of developmental factors not only unique but also telescoped into a brief period of years. These factors—physiological, situational, and psychological—force older adults into changing patterns of behavior and lifestyles that have been developed and ingrained over long periods. Any one of these may serve as a basis for emotional distress. In combination, they will certainly challenge the emotional stability of the older adult and account for the high incidence of depression and suicide in this population. The following are examples of these developmental factors.

Loss of Work Role Identity, Increased Leisure Time, and Decreased Financial Support

For older adults, the onset of retirement, either by choice or law, removes them from activities that for many years have been the focus of their self-identity (Moen, 1998). This work/career identity shaped not only their family life and their interactions with family members but also their social life outside the family. What they did for a living was so much a part of who they were and how they were valued both by self and by others that this loss often creates an identity crisis. The degree of severity that surrounds this issue is related to the older adult's ability to create a new identity.

With retirement comes increased amounts of leisure time—time for which many older adults are ill prepared. Leisure time, the dream of the full-time employee, often becomes the nightmare of retirees. What will they do with this time? What will be done to replace the daily routines so much a part of their working years? How will they relate to significant others now that they are together for extended periods of time? These and other questions need to be addressed, and education and planning are necessary if older adults are to make a positive transition from work to leisure (Gee & Baillie, 1999; Wong, 2002)

Retirement also brings a significant reduction in income. The majority of older adults enter this period of life on fixed incomes representing approximately 40% of their incomes prior to retirement. With increasing inflation, added expenses for health care, and rising taxes, they often move from a financially independent state to a financially dependent state, needing more support from family, friends, and state and federal agencies. They may also find their lifestyles restricted so that they may better conserve their fixed resources today to meet the continually escalating financial world of tomorrow (Hershey, Mowen, & Jacobs-Lawson, 2003)

Loss of Significant Person(s) and Increased Loneliness and Separation

The aging process brings with it a series of negative life events and the reality of the terminal nature of relationships (Kraaij & de Wilde, 2001). Loss of significant people, due to geographical relocation or death, occurs often during this period of life. Marital and social relationships on which much of the significance of life centered end, and older adults are called on to cope and to find meaning in other aspects of life. Sometimes this can be done with the support of family and friends. Sometimes it requires the intervention of helping professionals trained to work with this aspect of the aging process. In either case, the loss and its accompanying separation from the secure and familiar are issues that aging people must confront.

Geographic Relocation and Peer and Family Group Restructuring

Although the majority of older adults do not relocate during this period of life, those who do by choice or by extenuating circumstances find themselves adjusting both to new environments and to the building of new family and social relationships. The reasons for such relocations vary with the individual. Often they represent movements to areas that are more climatically conducive to leisure lifestyles, areas that are less demanding based on physical and physiologic disabilities, or areas that are closer to significant family members. Even when the relocation is by choice, the reconstruction process that follows is never easy and often brings with it stress, frustration, loneliness, separation, and regret.

Increased Physiologic Disorders and Increasing Amounts of Dependence

Health often becomes a major issue for older adults. Even though, as reported earlier, the majority report their health as good to excellent, it is a period marked by physiological decline. The body, like any complex machine, is beginning to wear down. The stress, anxiety, and frustration of this process takes a heavy toll. Older people are often called on to cope with health-related situations, both their own and those of loved ones, that demand both personal stamina and financial resources. Either or both of these may not be in great abundance during this period of life.

Dementia, common in older persons, is yet another physiological disorder that places stress not only on the individual but also on his or her family system. Alzheimer's disease, the most common cause of dementia, lacks both a known cause and effective treatment and according to Myers and Harper (2004), "affects 4 million persons at present and increases in incidence each decade after 60" (p. 212).

To compensate for any physiological disorders, older adults are often forced to depend on others both for support and for financial resources. Such dependence, following a life characterized by productivity and independence, is often difficult to accept. The resulting anger, depression, and loss of self-esteem need to be addressed if the individual is to cope effectively with the situation (Pinquart & Sorensen, 2001; Santrock, 2002).

When these major life changes are viewed in terms of the rapidity of their onset, the lack of preparation for their encounter, and society's negative attitudes regarding older adults, the prevalence of emotional and psychological problems is brought into clear focus. Any one of these changing life situations can produce emotional and psychological difficulties for the individual. In combination, they place the individual in an "at risk" situation in which he or she must develop coping strategies to survive (Whitty, 2003).

The Impact of Ageism and the Increasing Abuse and Maltreatment of Older Persons

Ageism, society's negative attitudes regarding older persons, affects many aspects of the daily life of the elderly. Ageism, which is often presented in terms of age-based expectations, stereotypes, myths, and prejudices, sets forth an image of older persons as being in poor health, disabled, lacking mental sharpness, depressed, lonely, sexless, lacking vitality, and unable to learn or change. Such beliefs, which are biased, unfounded, and untrue, serve to discriminate against older adults and often displace and prevent their active involvement within society (Gladding, 2003. Thornton, 2002).

Elder abuse is a growing problem in the United States. The National Center on Elder Abuse (NCEA, 1998) notes that nearly 600,000 cases of abuse and maltreatment were reported in 1996. Projecting this figure to the year 2030, when the older population will reach nearly 70 million, the incidence of abuse and maltreatment would reach into the millions. According to Reynolds-Welfel, Danzinger, and Santoro (2000), the abuse and maltreatment of older adults takes at least five major forms: neglect, physical violence, psychological abuse, financial exploitation, and violation of inalienable or legal rights. Any one of these may result in physiological, situational, and/or psychological problems for the older person; in combination, they may prove to be life-threatening.

To cope with the myriad of physiological, situational, and psychological changes that are part of the aging process, older adults turn for assistance to family, friends, the church, physicians, counselors, and government agencies. In doing so, they encounter both personal and societal barriers that include, but are not limited to, the following:

- Lack of recognition of the need for help
- Personal values and fears regarding seeking assistance
- Ageism on the part of helping professionals
- Lack of personnel trained to work with older adults
- Society's negative attitudes regarding older adults
- Practical problems such as transportation and financial limitations
- Lack of awareness of existing support services
- Family pressure to keep problems within the family
- Separation from family members who could provide assistance
- Personal mistrust and fear based on abuse and maltreatment

Basic Counseling Goals and Approaches

A basic premise of this chapter is that there is a common core of counseling approaches that are applicable across the life span. Skills in rapport building, active listening, and ability to demonstrate caring, support, respect, and acceptance are as applicable to the 80-year-old client as to the 8-year-old client (Warnick, 1995). According to Waters (1984),

Regardless of the age of your client, you as a counselor need to communicate clearly, respond both to thoughts and feelings, ask effective questions, and confront when appropriate. It also is important to help people clarify their values and their goals in order to make decisions and develop action plans to implement these decisions. (p. 63)

The basic goals and approaches of counseling are not age related. These goals and approaches assist the individual in problem resolution and behavior change, regardless of age. When working with older adults, counselors need not put aside their basic skills and techniques and adopt a new set. What they need to do is develop an awareness of the aging process and the factors within it that may necessitate adapting existing skills and techniques to more effectively meet the needs of this population (Myers & Harper, 2004; Zucchero, 1998).

Such adaptations are best understood in terms of a set of general counseling recommendations that are more applicable to the older adult than, perhaps, to the younger client (Altekruse & Ray, 1998). Such recommendations are directed at compensating for some of the "developmental factors" and "barriers" discussed earlier. The following recommendations, applied to basic goals and approaches, have general applicability to both individual and group counseling.

- *Counselors should expend more effort in enhancing the dignity and worth of the older adult.* Given ageist attitudes within society and often within the helping professions, these clients are often led to believe that they are less valuable than younger people. Counselors need to devote time and energy to restoring self-esteem and encouraging clients to review their successes and accomplishments and the positive aspects of their changing lifestyles (Gross & Capuzzi, 2005; Myers, 2003; Strawbridge, Wallhagen, & Cohen, 2002).

- *Counselors need to expend more effort in "selling" the client on the positive benefits to be derived from counseling.* Given long-established values and attitudes, the client may well view counseling and seeking such assistance as a sign of weakness and place little value on the positive results of such a process. The counselor needs to reinforce the client's willingness to seek assistance and to demonstrate, through actions, the positive results that are possible through counseling (Gladding, 2003; Maples & Abney, 2006; Thomas & Martin, 2006).

- *Counselors must attend more to the "physical environment" of counseling than might be necessary with a younger client.* Because of these clients' decreasing physical competencies, attention needs to center on factors such as noise distractions and counselor voice levels to compensate for hearing loss, adequate lighting for those with visual impairments, furniture that will enhance clients' physical comfort, thermostatic control to protect against extremes in temperatures, office accessibility, and removal of items that impair ease of movement. Shorter sessions may also be appropriate, because older adults may experience difficulty sitting in one position for a long time (Gross, 1991; Gross & Capuzzi, 2005; Zucchero, 1998).

- *Counselors should address counselor–client involvement and the role of the counselor as advocate.* The counselor in this situation needs to take a much more active/doing role to better serve the client. This active/doing role may involve contacting agencies, family, attorneys, and other support personnel for the client. It may also entail serving as advocate to represent the older adult's needs and grievances. It might also mean transporting the client or taking the counseling services to the client, as would be the case with shut-ins or those who are incapacitated (Gladding, 2003; Myers, Sweeney, & White, 2002).

■ *Counselors need to think in terms of short-term goals that are clear-cut and emphasize the present life situation for the client.* Many of the problems the client presents deal with day-to-day living situations. The counselor, in helping the client find solutions to these problems, not only reinforces the positive aspects of the counseling process but also encourages the client to continue seeking assistance (Burlingame, 1995; Kennedy & Tanenbaum, 2000).

■ *Counselors should pay attention to the dependence–independence issue characteristic of work with older adults.* Changing life situations often force the older adult into a more dependent lifestyle. The reasons vary from client to client but may be centered around health, finances, and family. The counselor needs to realize that a certain degree of dependence may benefit the client and needs to be encouraged until the client is ready once again to assume an independent role. The majority have functioned somewhat independently most of their adult lives. They often need assistance in seeing that it is still possible (Baltes, 1996; Myers, 2003).

■ *Counselors must be sensitive to the possible age differential between themselves and the clients and to the differing cultural, environmental, and value orientations that this difference in age may denote.* With the exception of peer counseling, the counselor generally is younger than the client. This age difference can generate client resistance, anger, or resentment. The counselor has to be aware of this and learn to deal with it in an appropriate manner. The counselor, depending on his or her attitudes regarding aging, may also experience feelings of resistance, anger, or resentment toward the client. Dealing with this at the beginning should enhance the probability of success (Gladding, 2003; Gross & Capuzzi, 2005).

■ *Counselors need to have some perspective on the client's place in history and the significance this place holds in determining values and attitudes.* People whose significant developmental period took place during the Depression years of the 1930s or the war years of the 1940s may well be espousing values characteristic of that era. The counselor needs to accept this and not expect this person to easily incorporate values and attitudes descriptive of the year 2008 (Gross & Capuzzi, 2005; Shmotkin & Eyal, 2003).

■ *Counselors should be cautious in the selection of diagnostic tools (tests) to be used with this population.* The diagnostic instruments selected have to be appropriate for older adults in terms of norm groups, reliability, and validity. Instruments such as the Geriatric Depression Scale (GDS), the Zung Self-Rating Depression Scale, the Mental Status Questionnaire (MSQ), the Folstein Mini-Mental Status Examination (MMSE), and the Confusion Assessment Method (CAM) were designed for working with older adults. These instruments, often referred to as screening tools, focus on two problematic areas for older adults, namely, depression and dementia. Assessment formats also exist in areas such as elder abuse and neglect, sexuality, sleep quality, and chronic pain. The counselor should select only those tools he or she has been trained to use and, before using them, determine whether they are the best means of gaining the types of data needed (Birren & Schaie, 1996; Gintner, 1995).

■ *Counselors need to be aware of the multicultural factors that affect the lives of older adults.* Counselors need not only background information regarding the racial, cultural, and ethnic backgrounds of older adults but also competencies that allow them to implement this knowledge. Diversity plays the same significant part in the values, beliefs, attitudes, and behaviors of older adults as it does for younger clients (Delgado-Romero, 2003; Lee & Chuang, 2005; Roysircar, Arredondo, Fuertes, Ponterotto, & Toporek, 2003).

Theoretical Counseling Interventions With Older Adults

Because the basic goals and approaches of counseling are not age related, all theoretical systems, techniques, and intervention styles should be applicable to this older adult population. Selecting which is most applicable remains a somewhat subjective issue. One of the earlier reviews of outcome research in counseling interventions with older people was conducted by Wellman and McCormack (1984), who reported the results of more than 90 studies. In this report, a myriad of approaches, including psychoanalytic (Brink, 1979), developmental (Kastenbaum, 1968), brief task-centered therapy (Saferstein, 1972), behavior management (Nigl & Jackson, 1981), and cognitive behavioral (Meichenbaum, 1974) were cited. The results varied, but all approaches appear to support the use of psychological intervention with this population. According to the authors, much of the research reviewed suffered from methodological weaknesses centering on controls, sampling, and sound theoretical rationales. They indicate, however, that procedures such as (a) regular continued contact, (b) brief psychotherapy approaches, (c) task-oriented and structured activities, (d) high levels of client involvement, (e) multidisciplinary team and peer counseling, and (f) group work all seem to hold promise in working with older adults. The following goals for counseling older adults appear often in their review:

- To decrease anxiety and depression
- To reduce confusion and loss of contact with reality
- To increase socialization and improve interpersonal relationships
- To improve behavior within institutions
- To cope with crisis and transitional stress
- To become more accepting of self and the aging process (p. 82)

Birren and Schaie (1996), Butler et al. (1991), Burlingame (1995), and Warnick (1995) also address differing theoretical approaches in working with older adults. According to Butler et al. (1991):

All forms of psychotherapy—from "uncovering" to "supportive" to "reeducative" and from Freudian to Jungian to Rogerian—can contribute to both a better understanding of the psychology and psychotherapy of old age. Further integration and eclectic utilization of all contemporary personality theories and practices, including the life-cycle perspective of human life along with the use of medication, when appropriate, are needed. (p. 407)

More recent reviews, Myers and Harper (2004) and Zalaquett and Stens (2006), also address the issue of effective counseling interventions and differing theoretical approaches for older adults. In an attempt to determine evidenced-based effective practices, Myers and Harper (2004) reviewed outcome research for both diagnosable conditions and late-life transitions. Utilizing information from PsycINFO, the ERIC database, and counseling journals, they reviewed the work of Black, Rabins, German, McGuire, and Roca (1997); Blow (1998); Kennedy and Tanenbaum (2000); Lubin, Wilson, Petren, and Polk (1996); Roth and Fonagy (1996); Smyer and Qualls (1999); and Stanley and Novy (2000). Some of their findings regarding effective counseling practice and theoretical utilization are:

- There is sufficient evidence to support specialized approaches to clinical work with older adults.
- Longevity, life circumstance, social supports and resources, and health need to be considered when developing appropriate interventions.
- Older adults are not only more receptive to receiving assistance but also respond better than younger persons.
- Both longer sessions and longer periods of intervention may be required.
- Prevention and early intervention are necessary with an older adult population.
- Dual diagnosis and team approaches are applicable with this population.
- Group counseling is effective for both developmental and remedial issues associated with aging and late-life development.
- Normalizing disorders such as anxiety, depression, and sleep disturbances is necessary because of their high incidence in older adults.
- Advocacy by the helping professional is mandatory.
- Cognitive behavioral and brief psychodynamic therapies are applicable when treating depression.
- Life review therapy is effective for older adults with depression and those living in institutional settings.
- Cognitive behavioral interventions are applicable for sleep disorders.
- Cognitive retraining is effective for older persons with dementia.
- Problem solving, bibliotherapy, and psychoeducational and social support groups have proven effective with several diagnoses and situations.
- Relaxation training has been associated with positive outcomes for older adults.

Zalaquett and Stens (2006) examined the outcome literature to identify research addressing psychosocial treatments of depression and dysthymia in older adults. Two electronic databases, PsycINFO and MEDLINE were used to gather data. The review produced 26 articles that met the authors' criteria of age, design, and treatment. Their findings, although cautionary, included the following:

- Older adults who have major depression and dysthymia can benefit from psychosocial treatments.

- Cognitive behavioral therapy (CBT) is probably effective as a treatment for depression in older adults who are cognitively intact and not suicidal.
- Reminiscence therapy (RT) seems to be potentially useful for treating older adults with major depression.
- Brief diagnostic therapy (BDT) is probably effective for treating major depression in older adults.
- For dysthymia, only CBT and interpersonal therapy (IPT) have been shown to be potentially helpful treatments with older adults.
- IPT combined with medication appears to aid older adults in maintaining their mood improvements after initial treatment.
- Necessary adjustments must be made for older adult clients regardless of psychosocial treatment used.

Other interesting data reported in their study included:

- Researching nearly 21,000 Medicare claims between 1992 and 1998, they found that persons 75 years and older, those of Hispanic ethnicity, and those without supplemental coverage received significantly less treatment and, if treated, were less likely to receive psychotherapy (Stephen, Sambamoorhi, Walkup, & Akincigil, 2003).
- Men, African Americans, Latinos, and those who preferred counseling to antidepressant medications reported significantly lower rates of depression care (Unutzer et al., 2003).
- When working with older adults, counselors should be flexible, take into account sensory and cognitive impairment and family/caregiver participation, and accept improved function and symptom reduction as valuable therapeutic goals (Kennedy & Tanenbaum, 2000).

Based on the previously cited work, both individual and group approaches to working with older adults are supported in the literature. Which is the most appropriate depends on the client, the nature of the presenting problem, the resources available to both the client and the counselor, and the setting in which the counseling takes place. Along with the developmental factors and barriers identified earlier, keep in mind that treatment for older adults presents the same variety of problems presented by younger clients. Issues dealing with alcohol and drug usage, abuse, loss, family, marriage, divorce, suicide, crime victimization, and career and avocational areas are often continuing concerns.

Individual Approaches

In providing individual counseling or therapy to older adults, counselors have a variety of techniques, intervention strategies, and theoretical systems available to them. The only limitations seem to be those related to the skills and expertise of the counselor. Keeping in mind the nine counseling recommendations mentioned previously, the following counseling skills are highly applicable to this population (Burlingame, 1995; Gladding, 2003).

Active Listening Skills.   Older adults, like their younger counterparts, need to be heard. Techniques such as visual contact, encouragers, reflection of both content and feeling, paraphrasing, clarifying, questioning, and summarizing are all appropriate. Such techniques, when used appropriately, serve as encouragers; demonstrate caring, concern, and interest; and provide the client with an opportunity to share, vent feelings, be understood, and gain self-respect.

Nonverbal Skills.   Work with older adults is enhanced if the counselor is aware of and able to make use of nonverbal communication patterns. Attention paid to body posture, eye contact, tone level, and rate of speech, although not the royal road to a person's inner self, is one road that helps the counselor understand the client's communication more completely.

Relationship Variables.   Relationship building with older adults may demand more effort from the counselor. The active listening and nonverbal skills mentioned in this section should facilitate this process, but establishing trust with a much older person may require the counselor to consider his or her language, appearance, solicitous attitude, and values and attitudes related to aging.

A second factor related to relationship building centers on the client's need for both support and challenge. Counselors working with this population need to understand that their view of older adults as fragile may temper their ability to provide the challenge. If challenge is not part of the counseling process, the client may be denied the opportunity for change and growth.

Counseling Strategies

The following strategies are not presented in any priority order. Each needs to be given careful consideration in working individually with this population.

- Take into consideration the longevity of the client's life. In doing so, stress the positive accomplishments, and encourage the client to use the many coping skills that he or she has demonstrated in reaching this stage of life.
- Stress the benefits that counseling can provide. Often older adults view such assistance as weakness on their part and believe counseling carries with it a stigma. Perhaps the words used to describe the service will need to be changed to attract this population. It might be more acceptable for the person to attend a discussion group rather than a therapy group.
- Give attention to the physiologic needs of the client as these relate to mobility, hearing loss, visual acuity, and physical condition. For example, sessions may need to be of shorter duration owing to the client's inability to sit for extended periods of time.
- Work to establish a more collaborative relationship with the various other professionals who may be working with the client, for example, physician, social worker, and agency personnel.
- Consider problem areas that you believe are applicable only to a younger population. Drugs, alcohol, and relationships are all viable issues in dealing with older

adults. Also keep in mind that loss and its impact are more often experienced by this population.

■ Use what is most workable in the selection of intervention techniques, based on the client's special needs and attitudinal set. Certain techniques, owing to their physical nature or affective emphasis, may not be appropriate for this population

■ Keep in mind the "historical period" that has shaped the thinking, behavior, and moral development of the client. Understand that current reactions, behaviors, and general outlook have historical antecedents. Shmotkin and Eyal (2003) present an intriguing approach to this in their article dealing with "psychological time."

■ Revisit the ethical standards related to working with older adults. A recent publication (Schwiebert et al., 2000) identified three unique areas for which few or inadequate ethical guidelines exist: (a) older adults with cognitive impairments, (b) victims of abuse, and (c) those with a terminal illness. The authors propose a model for ethical decision making that has application to these unique areas and suggest that this model has applicability to other unique situations faced by counselors working with older adults.

Group Approaches

Counselors who decide to use a group approach with the older adult can gain a great deal of information and direction from reviewing the work of such authors as Lubin et al. (1996), Thomas and Martin (2006), and Toseland (1990). These authors not only offer special considerations for working with older adults in groups, such as time parameters, member selection, and group size, but also specify the types of groups that have proven to be particularly helpful with this population. Some of the advantages of the group approach mentioned by these authors include (a) discovering common bonds, (b) learning social skills, (c) decreasing feelings of loneliness, (d) giving mutual assistance, (e) sharing feelings, and (f) providing shared purposes.

Whether selecting an individual or group modality for working with older adults, keep in mind that certain approaches to both individual and group work have been designed specifically to deal with this population from a rehabilitative perspective. The needs of the individual in a life care facility may be quite different from the individual who maintains an independent lifestyle. In working with the individual in the life care facility, the following selected approaches have proven to be helpful (Thomas & Martin, 2006; Vernon, 2006).

Reality Orientation Therapy Groups. Reality orientation therapy groups, which combine both individual and group work, are directed at the individual who has experienced memory loss, confusion, and time-place-person disorientation. The thrust of reality orientation therapy is the repetition and learning of basic personal information, such as the individual's name, the place, the time of day, the day of the week and date, the next meal, and time of bath. If the therapy is done on an informal basis within the care facility, it should be done on a 24-hour basis, and it should be used by all people who have contact with the person. On a formal basis, this is done in a class setting.

Milieu Therapy Groups.   Milieu therapy groups, which may make use of both individual and group work, are based on the concept that the social milieu of the care facility itself can be an instrument for treatment. The environment is organized to provide a more homelike atmosphere, with the individual taking more responsibility, trying new skills, and being involved in decision making in a somewhat safe environment. Levels of activity, self-care, and sense of self-worth have increased with this approach.

Reminiscence Therapy Groups.   Reminiscence therapy groups are designed to encourage groups of six to eight members to share memories and are conducted in both institutional and noninstitutional settings. This approach is similar to the "life review" process and in a group setting enhances a cohort effect; it helps members identify and share accomplishments, tribulations, and viewpoints as it increases opportunities for socialization. Music, visual aids, and memorabilia are often used to stimulate group discussion.

Remotivation Therapy Groups.   Remotivation therapy, which can be done either in a group or in an individual setting, seeks to encourage the moderately confused person to take a renewed interest in his or her surroundings by focusing attention on the simple, objective features of everyday life. Common topics are selected, such as pets, gardening, and cooking, and people are encouraged to relate to these topics by drawing on their own life experiences.

Topic and Theme-Focused Groups.   In working with the majority of older adults who continue to live independent lives, self-help groups, assertiveness training groups, growth groups, support groups, and special topic groups are as applicable as they are with a younger client population. Although these types of groups may be provided in institutionalized settings, they are often directed at older people who are living independently. According to Thomas and Martin (2006), these groups that have a specific focus have proliferated with the increase in these types of groups for other populations. These groups target such areas as loss, grief, health, retirement, career skills, sexuality, and caregiving and focus on developing coping strategies and skill building related to these specialized areas. Most topic and theme-focused groups can be offered in a variety of settings. The size, composition, duration, and meeting frequency depend upon the needs of the group and the member competencies. Is group counseling with older adults different from work with younger clients? The answer seems to be one of selective emphasis. In both individual and group work, all counseling interventions have applicability. The counselor needs to adapt his or her approach to accommodate the unique factors that parallel the aging process.

Summary

As older adults increase in number, more will be seen in counseling. Counselors whose preparation has primarily focused on working with a younger population need to seek the type of preparation that will allow them to work more effectively with older adults. Counselor educators need to revise existing preparation programs to provide a curriculum that incorporates both didactic and experiential programming related to this population (Durodoye & Ennis-Cole, 1998; Myers, 2003; Thomas & Martin, 2006).

The counseling needs of older adults are very similar to those of younger clients. When differences exist, they are best described in terms of a set of developmental factors that are characteristic of the aging process. The following recommendations can help the beginning counselor better understand what he or she needs to do to prepare for this clientele:

- Counselors need to secure special training and information regarding the aging process and physiological, sociological, and psychological factors that have an impact on this process.
- Counselors need to be aware of the comorbid relationship between physical illness and psychological disorders.
- Counselors must be alert to the fact that suicide and suicide ideation are prevalent in older adults. For more information in this area, see Capuzzi (2004).
- Counselors need to address the issues of loss and grief with older adults and educate not only themselves but also clients regarding normalizing the various stages of this process. Further information can be found in Vernon (2006).
- Counselors need to understand the negative effects of "ageism" and clarify their values regarding aging from both self and other person perspectives. These values and attitudes will either enhance or impede their success with the older adult.
- Counselors need to be aware of the client's "place in history" and the significance this place holds in formulating values and attitudes that affect the client's view of the counseling process.
- Counselors need to emphasize short-term goals with older adult clients. These goals need to be clearly understood and accepted by the client and should emphasize the client's present life situation.
- Counselors need to be aware of the various diagnostic tools that have special application to the older adult. Counselors may need to seek out more creative ways of data gathering.
- Counselors need to pay more attention to the physical setting in which counseling takes place. This environment needs to encourage, not discourage, the older adult's participation.
- Counselors need to view their role with the client more from an advocacy perspective. They need to be more actively involved with the day-to-day life of the client. Based upon the increasing incidence of abuse and maltreatment, older persons represent a population "at risk." As with any "at risk" population, efforts to reduce this risk call for more active participation.
- Counselors need to be willing to go to the client and not always expect the client to come to them. It may be necessary to take counseling to the client's home or to other settings because of the physical limitations of the older adult.

- Counselors need not fear or be apprehensive about involvement with older adults. They differ from their younger counterparts generally in increased life experiences and the rapidity of change descriptive of the aging process.
- Counselors need to use the longevity and the developed coping strategies that accompany the aging process to enhance clients' present life situation. These clients have an advantage inasmuch as they have proven qualities of survival that the counselor can use to improve self-esteem, interpersonal relations, family problems, loneliness, and questions of dependence versus independence.

The common theme of these recommendations is that counselors must pay more attention to and show more concern for the older adult. They must recognize their unique needs and, more important, treat them as fully deserving of the care counselors provide younger people. If counselors are to effectively deal with older adults, then specialized training is necessary. Perhaps it is the lack of such specialized training that places older adults in an "underserved" category for counseling. According to the Council for Accreditation of Counseling and Related Educational Programs (CACREP, 2003), there are only two counselor training programs accredited to provide gerontological counseling.

In the case that introduced this chapter, Paul did his best to apply what he had learned regarding working with the older adult client. He had paid attention to the physical environment and time considerations. He had studied the intake interview information and felt prepared to work with the client's concerns about his relocation. Paul had not anticipated the two clients who arrived but was flexible in attempting to deal with the situation. Both the individual sessions with the client and his son and the joint meetings left Paul questioning what he had done, and he felt perhaps he should have done more. A meeting with his supervisor was scheduled to address some of these questions.

It is our hope that the information in this chapter will provide answers to some of these questions and that counselors such as Paul will enter the counseling relationship with more assurance that they have both the information and the skills to work with the older adult client.

USEFUL WEB SITES

AARP
http://www.aarp.org/research/ageline

Grief healing
http://www.griefhealing.com/index.htm

Group work
http://www.asgw.org

Senior citizens
http://www.seniorjournal.com/seniorlinks.htm

REFERENCES

Administration on Aging (AoA). (2001). *A profile of older Americans 2001.* Washington, DC: U.S. Department of Health and Human Services.

Altekruse, M. K., & Ray, D. (1998). Counseling older adults: A special issue. *Educational Gerontology, 24,* 303–307.

Baltes, M. M. (1996). *The many faces of dependency in old age.* New York: Cambridge University Press.

Birren, J. E., & Schaie, K. W. (1996). *Handbook of the psychology of aging* (4th ed.) San Diego: Academic Press.

Black, B. S., Rabins, P. V., German, P., McGuire, M., & Roca, R. (1997). Need and unmet need for mental health care among elderly public housing residents. *The Gerontologist, 37,* 717–728.

Blow, F. C. (1998). *Substance abuse among older adults. Treatment improvement protocol (TIP), Series 26* (DHHS Publication No. SMS 98–3179). Rockwell, MD: Substance Abuse and Mental Health Services Administration.

Brink, T. L. (1979). *Geriatric psychotherapy.* New York: Human Sciences.

Burlingame, V. S. (1995). *Gerocounseling: Counseling elders and their families.* New York: Springer.

Butler, R. N., Lewis, M., & Sunderland, T. (1991). *Aging and mental health: Positive psychosocial and biomedical approaches* (4th ed.). New York, Macmillan.

Capuzzi, D. (Ed.). (2004). *Suicide across the life span: Implications for counselors.* Alexandria, VA: ACA Press.

Council for Accreditation of Counseling and Related Educational Programs. (2003). *Directory of CACREP accredited programs.* Alexandria, VA: Author.

Delgado-Romero, E. (2003). Ethics and multicultural competence. In D. B. Pope-Davis, H. L. K. Coleman, W. M. Liu, & R. L. Toporek (Eds.), *Handbook of multicultural competencies in counseling and psychology* (pp. 313–329). Thousand Oaks, CA: Sage Publications.

Durodoye, B. A., & Ennis-Cole, D. (1998). Empowering counselors to work with senior adult clients in the computer age. *Educational Gerontology, 24,* 359–371.

Gee, S., & Baillie, J. (1999). Happily ever after? An exploration of retirement expectations. *Educational Gerontology, 25,* 109–128.

Gintner, G. G. (1995). Differential diagnosis in older adults: Dementia, depression, and delirium. *Journal of Counseling and Development, 73*(3), 346–351.

Gladding, S. T. (2003). *Counseling: A comprehensive profession* (4th ed.). Englewood Cliffs, NJ: Merrill/ Prentice Hall.

Gross, D. R. (1991). Counseling the elderly. In J. Carlson and J. Lewis (Eds.), *Family counseling: Strategies and issues* (pp. 209–223). Denver: Love Publishing.

Gross, D. R., & Capuzzi, D. (2005). Counseling the older adult. In D. Capuzzi & D. R. Gross (Eds.), *Introduction to the counseling profession* (4th ed.) (pp. 383–400). Boston: Allyn and Bacon.

Harris, H. L. (1998). Ethnic minority elders: Issues and interventions. *Educational Gerontology, 1*(24), 309–324.

Hershey, D., Mowen, C., & Jacobs-Lawson, A. (2003). An experimental comparison of retirement planning intervention seminars. *Educational Gerontology, 29,* 339–359.

Kastenbaum, R. (1968). Perspectives on the development and modification of behavior in the aged: A developmental field perspective. *Gerontologist, 8,* 280–283.

Kennedy, G. J., & Tanenbaum, S. (2000). Psychotherapy with older adults. *American Journal of Psychotherapy, 54,* 386–407.

Kleinke, C. (1998). *Coping with life's challenges* (2nd ed.). Pacific Grove, CA: Brooks/Cole.

Knight, B. G. (1999). The scientific basis for psychotherapeutic intervention with older adults: An overview. *Journal of Clinical Psychology, 55,* 927–934.

Kraaij, E., & de Wilde, J. (2001). Negative life events and depressive symptoms in the elderly: A life span perspective. *Aging and Mental Health, 5*(1), 84–91.

Lee, C. C., & Chuang, B. (2005). Counseling people of color. In D. Capuzzi & D. R. Gross (Eds.), *Introduction to the counseling profession* (pp. 465–483). Boston: Allyn and Bacon.

Lemme, B. H. (1995). *Development in adulthood.* Boston: Allyn and Bacon.

Lubin, B., Wilson, C. D., Petren, S., & Polk, A. (1996). *Research on group treatment methods: Selectively annotated bibliography.* Westport, CT: Greenwood.

Maples, M. F., & Abney, P. C. (2006). Baby boomers mature and gerontological counseling comes of age. *Journal of Counseling and Development, 84*, 3–9.

Meichenbaum, D. (1974). Self-instructional strategy training: A cognitive prosthesis for the aged. *Human Development, 17*, 273–280.

Moen, P. (1998). Recasting careers: Changing reference groups, risks and realities. *Generations, 22*(1), 40–45.

Myers, J. E. (2003). Coping with caregiving stres: A wellness-oriented strengths-based approach for family counselors. *The Family Journal, 11*, 1–9.

Myers, J. E., & Harper, M. C. (2004). Evidence-based effective practices with older adults. *Journal of Counseling and Development, 82*, 207–218.

Myers, J. E., Sweeney, T. J., & White, V. A. (2002). Advocacy for counselors and counseling: A professional imperative. *Journal of Counseling and Development, 80*, 394–402.

National Center on Elder Abuse. (1998). *National Elder Abuse Incidence Study: Final Report.* Washington, DC: Author.

Nigl, A. J., & Jackson, B. (1981). A behavior management program to increase social responses in psychogeriatric patients. *Journal of the Geriatrics Society, 29*, 92–95.

Pinquart, M., & Sorensen, S. (2001). How effective are psychotherapeutic and other psychosocial interventions with older adults? A meta-analysis. *Journal of Mental Health and Aging, 7*, 207–243.

Reynolds-Welfel, E., Danzinger, P., & Santoro, S. (2000). Mandated reporting of abuse/maltreatment of older adults: A primer for counselors. *Journal of Counseling and Development, 78*(3), 284–292.

Roth, A., & Fonagy, P. (1996). *What works for whom? A critical review of psychotherapy research.* New York: Guilford Press.

Roysircar, G., Arredondo, P., Fuertes, J. N., Ponterotto, J. G., & Toporek, R. L. (2003). *Multicultural counseling competencies 2003: Association for Multicultural Counseling and Development.* Alexandria, VA: Association for Multicultural Counseling and Development.

Saferstein, S. (1972). Psychotherapy for geriatric patients. *New York State Journal of Medicine, 72*, 2743–2748.

Santrock, J. (2002). *Life span development.* New York: McGraw Hill.

Schwiebert, V., Myers, J., & Dice, C. (2000). Ethical guidelines for counselors working with older adults. *Journal of Counseling and Developmen, 78*(2), 123–136.

Shmotkin, D., & Eyal, N. (2003). Psychological time in later life: Implications for counseling. *Journal of Counseling and Development, 81*(3), 259–267.

Smyer, M. A., & Qualls, S. H. (1999). *Aging and mental health.* Malden, MA: Blackwell.

Special Committee on Aging (SCOA). (1983). *Developments in aging: 1983* (Vol. 1). Washington, DC: U.S. Government Printing Office.

Stanley, M. A., & Novy, D. M. (2000). Cognitive-behavior therapy for generalized anxiety in late life: An evaluative overview. *Journal of Anxiety Disorders, 14*, 191–207.

Stephen, C., Sambamoorthi, U., Walkup, J. T., & Akincigil, A. (2003). Diagnosis and treatment of depression in the elderly Medicare population: Predictors, disparities and trends. *Journal of the American Geriatrics Society, 51*, 1718–1728.

Strawbridge, W., Wallhagan, M., & Cohen, R. (2002) Successful aging and well-being: Self-rated compared with Rowe and Kahn. *The Gerontologist, 42*, 727–733.

Taylor-Carter, M. A., Cook, K., & Weinberg, C. (1997). Planning and expectations of the retirement experience. *Educational Gerontology, 23*, 273–288.

Thomas, M. C., & Martin, V. (2006). Group counseling with the elderly and their caregivers. In D. Capuzzi, D. R. Gross, & M. Stauffer (Eds.), *Introduction to group counseling* (4th. ed., pp. 483–513). Denver, CO: Love Publishing.

Thornton, J. (2002). Myths of aging or ageist stereotypes. *Educational Gerontology, 28*, 301–312.

Tice, C. J., & Perkins, K. (1996). *Mental health issues and aging: Building on the strengths of older persons.* Pacific Grove, CA: Brooks/Cole.

Toseland, R. W. (1990). *Group work with older adults*. New York: New York University Press.

Tueth, M. J. (1995). *DSM-IV* disorders most commonly seen in the elderly. *Clinical Gerontologist, 16*, 74–76.

Unutzer, J., Katon, W., Callahan, C. M., Williams, J. W. Jr., Hunkeler, E., Harpole, L., et al. (2003). Depression treatment in a sample of 1,801 depressed older adults in primary care. *Journal of the American Geriatrics Society, 51*, 505–514.

Vernon, A. (2006). Group work: Loss. In D. Capuzzi, D. R. Gross, & M. Stauffer (Eds.), *Introduction to group counseling* (4th ed., pp. 417–451) Denver, CO: Love Publishing.

Warnick, J. (1995). *Listening with different ears: Counseling people over 60*. Fort Bragg, CA: QED Press.

Waters, E. (1984). Building on what you know: Techniques for individual and group counseling with older people. *Counseling Psychologist, 12*(2), 63–74.

Wellman, R., & McCormack, J. (1984). Counseling with older persons: A review of outcome research. *Counseling Psychologist, 12*(2), 81–96.

Whitty, M. (2003). Coping and defending: Age differences in maturity of defence mechanisms and coping strategies. *Aging and Mental Health, 7*(21), 123–132.

Wong, F. (2002) Preparing to meet the needs of an aging American public. *Nation's Health, 32*(8), 3.

Zalaquett, C. P., & Stens, A. N. (2006). Psychosocial treatments for major depression and systhymia in older adults: A review of the research literature. *Journal of Counseling and Development, 84*, 192–201.

Zucchero, R. A. (1998). A unique model for training mental health professionals to work with older adults. *Educational Gerontology, 24*, 265–278.

18 Counseling Couples and Families

CASS DYKEMAN
Oregon State University

Introduction

The placement of this chapter in a section called "Counseling Special Populations" confirms Duncan Stanton's (1988) contention: "Non-family therapists often view family therapy as (a) a modality, that (b) usually involves the nuclear family" (p. 8). He goes on to point out the inaccuracy of this conception, explaining that family therapy is based on a point of view that emphasizes the contextual nature of psychological problems.

> More fundamentally, it [family therapy] is a way of construing human problems that dictates certain actions for their alleviation. Its conceptual and data bases differ from most other (especially individually oriented) therapies in that the interpersonal context of a problem and the interplay between this context and the symptoms are of primary interest. An index patient is seen as responding to his or her social situation; those around the patient are noted to react to this response; the patient then reacts "back," and so on, in an on-going, give and take process. Interventions designed to alter this process derive from such interactional formulations. (p. 8)

It is, of course, possible for a counselor who is oriented to the treatment of individuals to interview the members of a client's family in the course of treatment. However, this rarely occurs, because the individual orientation places the source of dysfunction within the client rather than focusing on the context in which the symptoms occur. Table 18.1 illustrates some of the other differences in perspective between psychodynamic and family therapy points of view. The psychodynamic approach is based in Freudian theory and emphasizes internal constructs such as the id, ego, and superego; in contrast, family therapy is primarily based in systems theory and emphasizes interpersonal behavior. To further illuminate this paradigm shift, several concepts from systems theory will be illustrated within a human behavioral context.

> *Fundamental unity.* The universe is one system with infinite levels of subsystems; analysis at any level needs to consider the levels above and below. To understand the individual, it is essential to analyze both the interindividual context and the

TABLE 18.1 Two Contrasting Views of Therapy: Psychodynamic and Family Systems

	Psychodynamic	**Family Systems**
Causality	Linear	Recursive
Time Focus	Past	Present
Pathology	Intrapsychic	Interpersonal
Assessment	Individual	Systemic
Therapy	Long-term	Brief
	catharsis	reframing
	transference	restructuring
	abreaction	problem solving
	insight	behavior change
Therapist	Passive	Active

intraindividual subsystems. A person's strange behavior may be due to dysfunctional family interactions or may be due to a chemical imbalance in the individual's blood.

System change. Change in any part of a system will impact the whole system. If therapy with an individual is successful, the system of which the client is a part will be affected. Unfortunately, we will know of those changes only through the selective filter of our client, and that our chances of success are diminished by the homeostatic drag of the system.

Recursive causality. Inherent in the first two concepts is a nonlinear epistemology. Thus, our observation that A causes B is due only to our punctuation of a behavioral sequence that fails to see what follows from B or what preceded A. Every act (or nonaction) provokes feedback, which alters the nature of the next act. In a family, "does he drink because she nags?" (his punctuation); or "does she nag because he drinks?" (her punctuation).

Homeostasis. Systems use negative feedback to maintain a steady state; positive feedback creates change in the system. If one member of a family begins to change, perhaps as the result of individual therapy, the usual routine interactions of the family will be disrupted, and the family will send messages designed to bring the person in therapy back into line.

Viability. The viability of a system is based on order and structure; entropy is disorder. In addition to structure, which is a static quality, the system must also be open to new input if it is to be capable of accommodating to its changing environment. A family with young children needs a generational hierarchy, but the hierarchy must also be open to modification as the children mature. (Adapted from Sieburg, 1985)

With this brief description of systems concepts, perhaps the following definition of family therapy, as stated by Wynne (1988), can be presented:

Family therapy is a psychotherapeutic approach that focuses on altering interactions between a couple, within a nuclear family or extended family, or between a family and other interpersonal systems, with the goal of alleviating problems initially presented by individual family members, family subsystems, the family as a whole, or other referral sources. (pp. 250–251)

The History Of Family Therapy

The history of family therapy is relatively brief. It begins in the 1950s, with the seminal contributions of Nathan Ackerman, Theodore Lidz, Lyman Wynne, Murray Bowen, and Carl Whitaker. All of these psychiatrists, originally trained in the prevailing psychodynamic model, broke away from its restrictive influence and began to see that dysfunctional behavior was rooted in the individual's past and present family life. Each of these pioneers arrived at this insight relatively independently: Ackerman through his research on the mental health problems of the unemployed in Pennsylvania; Lidz studying the families of schizophrenics at Yale; Wynne treating patients with psychosis and ulcerative colitis in Massachusetts, and later doing research on the families of schizophrenics at the National Institute of Mental Health (NIMH); Bowen through his work with families at the Menninger Foundation and later with Wynne at NIMH; and Whitaker through seeing families at Oak Ridge and his later work with families with a schizophrenic member at Emory. In his preface to *The Psychodynamics of Family Life* (1958), the first book-length treatment of this point of view, Ackerman said:

> This approach attempts to correlate the dynamic psychological processes of individual behavior with family behavior in order to be able to place individual clinical diagnosis and therapy within the broader frame of family diagnosis and therapy. It has been necessary, therefore, to explore a series of interrelated themes: the interdependence of individual and family stability at every stage of growth from infancy to old age; the role of family in the emotional development of the child; the family as stabilizer of the mental health of the adult; the family as conveyor belt for anxiety and conflict and as a carrier of the contagion of mental illness; the interplay of conflict between family and community, conflict in family relationships, and conflict within individual family members; and breakdown in adaptation and illness as symptoms of the group pathology of the family. (p. viii)

With this statement he did much to set the agenda for the next three decades.

During this same period, an unusual group of people assembled in Palo Alto to study the communication processes of schizophrenics. The project was headed by Gregory Bateson, an anthropologist, who hired Jay Haley, a recent graduate in communications theory; Don Jackson, a psychiatrist; and John Weakland, whose initial training was in chemical engineering. Early in the project, Haley began consulting with Milton Erickson, who was known at that time primarily as a hypnotherapist. From this rich mélange emerged the beginnings of strategic family therapy. In 1959, Jackson founded the Mental Research Institute (MRI) in Palo Alto and invited Virginia Satir to join him. When the Bateson project ended in 1961, Haley and Weakland also joined the staff at MRI.

Satir diverged from the pragmatic approach of strategic therapy when she left MRI to join the human potential movement at the Esalen Institute. With the publication of her book *Conjoint Family Therapy* in 1964, she established her own approach to family treatment, which incorporated elements of the thinking of the group at MRI within a framework of Gestalt and experiential therapy.

Structural family therapy emerged on the East Coast in the work of Salvador Minuchin and his colleagues at Wyltwick School and later the Philadelphia Child Guidance Clinic (PCGC). At Wyltwick, Minuchin worked with the families of delinquent boys, and at PCGC he did research on families with a member who was psychosomatic. Each of these projects resulted in a book that enriched our understanding of family functioning (Minuchin, Montalvo, Gurney, Rosman, & Schumer, 1967; Minuchin, Rosman, & Baker, 1978). He was joined by Haley in 1967, and they worked together for 10 years. As might be expected, the concepts of strategic and structural therapy have much in common. Haley, who met his second wife, Cloe Madanes, at the PCGC, left with her in 1977 to found the Family Therapy Institute of Washington, D.C.

Murray Bowen began his career at the Menninger Foundation and focused his research on families with a schizophrenic member. He continued this at the NIMH, where, in 1954, he had the families of schizophrenic youngsters actually live in the hospital so that he could observe their interactions. In 1959, he moved to Georgetown University Medical Center, where he worked for the rest of his career.

Carl Whitaker is often referred to as the "clown prince of family therapy." Whitaker began his career as a gynecologist but soon switched to psychiatry. He was chief psychiatrist at Oak Ridge, Tennessee, where he first began bringing the family into treatment with his patients. He moved from Oak Ridge to the chair of the Department of Psychiatry at Emory University in 1946. The publication of his first book, *The Roots of Psychotherapy* (Whitaker & Malone, 1953), led to his dismissal, and he went into private practice for 10 years. The book, which he coauthored with his colleague, Thomas Malone, challenged much of traditional psychodynamic thinking and was resoundingly condemned by the psychiatric establishment. In 1965, Whitaker began teaching at the University of Wisconsin. He would remain at this institution through the rest of his professional life. He referred to his work as Symbolic-Experiential Family Therapy.

For a more complete treatment of the history of family therapy, see Becvar and Becvar's *Family Therapy: A Systematic Integration* (2005) or Gladding's *Family Therapy: History, Theory, and Practice* (2006).

Chapter Overview

Although it would be possible to follow this brief historical introduction with a detailed description of each of the major therapeutic approaches, I have elected to take a different approach. It is my contention that family therapy has moved beyond the "schools of therapy" orientation and that a systematic eclecticism is now possible. For the reader who is interested in a comparison of the various approaches, Table 18.2 presents a comparative assessment of some of the relevant aspects of family therapy.

TABLE 18.2   A Comparison of Family Therapy Approaches

	Strategic (*Haley*)	Structural (*Minuchin*)	Transgenerational (*Bowen*)	Experiential (*Whitaker*)	Conjoint (*Satir*)
Who is included in therapy?	Everyone involved in the problem	Whoever is involved and accessible	The most motivated family member(s)	Who he decides should come	The pattern is flexible
What is the theory of dysfunction?	Confused hierarchy; communication; rigid behavioral sequences	Boundaries (enmeshed or disengaged); stable coalitions; power	Fusion (emotions control; symbiosis with family of origin); anxiety; triangulation	Rigidity of thought and behavior	Low self-esteem; poor communication; triangulation
What are the goals of therapy?	Solve the problem; restore hierarchy; introduce flexibility	Solve the problem; change the structure; increase flexibility	Greater differentiation of self; reduced anxiety	Increase family creativity; greater sense of belonging and individuation	Improved communication; personal growth
What is the method of assessment?	Structured initial interview; intervene and observe the reaction; focus on the present	Joining the family to experience its process; chart the family structure; focus on the present	Detailed family history over several generations using the genogram; focus on the past	Informal; not separated from treatment; focus on both past and present	Family life chronology is used to take history and assess present functioning
What are the intervention procedures?	Directives are used to change behavior; they may be straightforward, paradoxical, or ordeals	Reframing is used to change the perception of the problem; structure is changed by unbalancing and increasing stress	Reducing anxiety by providing rational, untriangulated third party; coaching to aid in differentiation from family of origin	Increasing stress to force change; reframing symptoms as efforts at growth; affective confrontation	Modeling and coaching clear communication; family sculpting; guided interaction
What is the stance of the therapist?	Active, directive, but not self-revealing; planful, not spontaneous	Active, directive, personally involved; spontaneous; humorous	Interested but detached; reinforces calmness and rationality	Active, personally involved; encourages and models "craziness," cotherapy	Active, directive, matter-of-fact, nonjudgmental; models open communication

The present attempt to reduce the emphasis on the differences between various approaches to family therapy has the support of at least one of the major figures in the field. Salvador Minuchin, writing in 1982, also decried the tendency to fragment the field into schools of therapy:

> In early explorations of family therapy, the field increased its sophistication and expanded its territory. Naturally, the early explorers staked the unmarked corners with their trade names: strategic, systemic, structural Bowenian, experiential, and so on. The old-timers knew that their private truths were only partial, and when they met around a cup of coffee, they gossiped about the beginnings and shared their uncertainties and hopes. But, lo and behold, their institutions grew, and they needed large buildings to accommodate all their students. Slowly, before anybody realized it, the buildings became castles, with turrets and drawbridges, and even watchmen in the towers. The castles were very expensive and they needed to justify their existence. Therefore, they demanded ownership of the total truth. . . . But the generation of elders is becoming older. The castles are becoming very expensive to run and, like the English aristocracy, the lords of the manor will soon be opening them only on Sunday for the new genera-tion of tourists. Those who come to my castle will not find me there. (p. 662)

In what follows, I have attempted to synthesize what I regard as some of the most use-ful of the ideas of the several therapists referred to. I begin first with a family systems perspective on the diagnosis of family dysfunction. This is followed by sections on how to conduct the initial interview, family therapy techniques, legal and ethical questions, and research.

Diagnosis Of Family Dysfunction

Tolstoy said in the opening line of *Anna Karenina*, "All happy families resemble one another, but each unhappy family is unhappy in its own way." Family therapists tend to reverse this position, believing that good family functioning is based in diversity, but family dysfunction is due to narrowness and rigidity. Haley (1987) goes so far as to argue that therapies that have a picture of "ideal" functioning are in fact limiting, in that they impose "a narrow ideology, thus, preventing the diversity that human beings naturally display. To put the matter simply, if the goal of therapy is to introduce more complexity, then imposing on clients psychological explanation of their own and other people's behavior is antitherapeutic" (p. 233).

When a system's orientation is applied to psychological problems, the diagnosis of the difficulty is very different from that presented in the *Diagnostic and Statistical Manual of Mental Disorders-IV-TR* (American Psychiatric Association, 2000). Rather than focusing on the internal state of the individual, the family systems approach looks for pathology in the interactions between people who have significance for each other.

Rather than adopting a linear model of causality, the family systems approach perceives causality as circular or recursive. It's not that a child is rebellious because his or her father is too authoritarian, or that the father is authoritarian because the child is rebellious, but that both are caught up in a chronic repetitive sequence of behavior: the "game without end."

Rather than focusing on the way people think or feel, the family systems therapist tends to focus on what they do. The purpose of family therapy is not insight, but behavior change. Within the broad commonality of the systems orientation, each of the major family therapists has emphasized different aspects of human functioning as the source of symptomatic behavior. The following sections provide a compilation of the thinking of a number of family therapists regarding symptomatic behavior.

Family Life Cycle

Family dysfunction is often the result of a failure to accomplish the developmental tasks demanded by the family life cycle (Table 18.3). The fullest conceptualization of a stage approach to family development is generally attributed to Carter and McGoldrick (2005), although the concept dates back to the 1950s (Gerson, 1995). Since Carter and McGoldrick, most of the major family therapists have acknowledged the significance of family life cycle changes as a major source of stress and disequilibrium for the family. Inherent in the life cycle concept is the idea that there are certain developmental tasks that must be accomplished during periods of transition from one stage to another. Successful movement to the next development stage requires changes in the roles and structure of the family. If the family is unable to accommodate the need for change, stress and symptomatology occur.

The demand for change is a normal part of family development. It is not these normal difficulties that create the problem, but rather the chronic mishandling of them. It is the attempted solution that is the problem. Denying the need for change, treating a normal developmental change as if it were a problem, and striving for perfection are all likely to result in family distress. In general, the reaction of a dysfunctional family to a demand for change is met by doing "more of the same." For example, a girl becomes a teenager and exerts more autonomy, parents become concerned for her safety and morality, they introduce or increase their control over her behavior, the girl resents their attempt to control her autonomy and rebels, the parents increase their control, and so forth (Gerson, 1995; Micucci, 1998). In a family with young children, a problem might arise when the grandparents have difficulty in giving up their parental role with their own children, thus interfering with the discipline of their new grandchildren.

The problems associated with family life cycle changes are exacerbated in remarried families because an individual's development is out of synchronization with the developmental stage of his or her family. For example, a newly remarried family is focused on issues of inclusion and forming a viable entity; if that family contains an adolescent, he or she is focused on issues of separation and individuation.

Fusion in the Nuclear Family and/or the Family of Origin

Bowen (1994) conceived a scale of differentiation of self from 0 to 100. At the low end of the scale, people are fused or enmeshed with their families to the extent that they are unable to think or act independently. Their lives are ruled by emotional reactivity. According to Bowen, people diagnosed as schizophrenic would be extremely fused.

TABLE 18.3   Stages of the Family Life Cycle

Family Life Cycle Stage	Emotional Process of Transition: Key Principles	Second-Order Changes in Family Status Required to Proceed Developmentally
1. Leaving home: single young adults	Accepting emotional and financial responsibility for self	a. Differentiation of self in relation to family of origin b. Development of intimate peer relationships c. Establishment of self in respect to work and financial independence
2. The joining of families through marriage: the new couple	Commitment to new system	a. Formation of marital system b. Realignment of relationships with extended families and friends to include spouse
3. Families with young children	Accepting new members into the system	a. Adjusting marital system to make space for children b. Joining in child-rearing, financial, and household tasks c. Realignment of relationships with extended family to include parenting and grandparenting roles
4. Families with adolescents	Increasing flexibility of family boundaries to permit children's independence and grandparents' frailties	a. Shifting of parent/child relationships to permit adolescent to move in and out of system b. Refocus on midlife marital and career issues c. Beginning shift toward caring for older generation
5. Launching children and moving on	Accepting a multitude of exits from and entries into the family system	a. Renegotiation of marital system as a dyad b. Development of adult-to-adult relationships between grown children and their parents c. Realignment of relationships to include in-laws and grandchildren d. Dealing with disabilities and death of parents (grandparents)
6. Families in later life	Accepting the shifting of generational roles	a. Maintaining own and/or couple functioning and interests in face of physiologic decline: exploration of new familial and social role options b. Support for a more central role for middle generation

(continued)

c. Making room in the system for the wisdom and experience of the elderly, supporting the older generation without overfunctioning for them
d. Dealing with loss of spouse, siblings, and other peers and preparation for death

Source: From Carter, Betty & Monica Mc Goldrick (Eds.). *The Expanded Family Life Cycle: The Individual, Family, And Social Perspectives*, 3e. Published by Allyn and Bacon, Boston, MA. Copyright © 2005 by Pearson Education. Reprinted by permission of the publisher.

At the upper end of the scale, people have achieved emotional separation from their families, are able to act autonomously, and can choose to be rational in emotionally charged situations. The individual's level of differentiation is closely related to the differentiation of his or her parents, and the process is transgenerational in nature. People with low levels of differentiation (fusion) are particularly reactive to environmental stressors and when under stress are likely to resolve it by (a) withdrawal, (b) conflict, (c) dysfunction of one spouse, or (d) triangulation of a child that results in dysfunction. When the last occurs, that child, who is caught in the tug of war between the parents, will be even less differentiated than the parents. This is the basis of the intergenerational transmission of dysfunction (Bowen, 1991, 1994).

Boundary Problems

According to Minuchin, family boundaries are created by implicit rules that govern who talks to whom about what (Minuchin, Colapinto, & Minuchin, 2006; Minuchin & Fishman, 1990). When no rules exist, everyone is privy to everyone else's thoughts and feelings. Thus, family boundaries become diffuse, and individuals become enmeshed (fused). When the rules are too strict and communication breaks down, the boundary is said to be rigid and the individuals disengaged. The preferred state is to have clear rules that allow for both individuation and togetherness. The similarity of this concept to Bowen's idea of differentiation of self is obvious, but Minuchin has developed it to refer to both extrafamilial boundaries and intrafamilial boundaries that separate subsystems (i.e., holons).

Family dysfunction can occur because the family is either disengaged from or enmeshed with the external environment. This is frequently a problem with remarried families, where rules regarding contact with ex-spouses may be either rigid or lacking. Dysfunction can also occur when internal subsystems of the family are enmeshed or disengaged. The classic dysfunction in our culture is the mother who is enmeshed with a child (i.e., cross-generational coalition) and the father who is disengaged from both.

Dysfunctional Sequences

Haley (1987) believes family dysfunction is often caused by behavioral sequences that are rigid, repetitive, and functionally autonomous. He describes such a sequence as follows:

1. One parent, usually the mother, is in an intense relationship with the child. By *intense* is meant a relationship that is both positive and negative and where the responses of each person are exaggeratedly important. The mother attempts to deal with the child with a mixture of affection and exasperation.
2. The child's symptomatic behavior becomes more extreme.
3. The mother, or the child, calls on the father for assistance in resolving their difficulty.
4. The father steps in to take charge and deal with the child.
5. Mother reacts against father, insisting that he is not dealing with the situation properly. Mother can react with an attack or with a threat to break off the relationship with father.
6. Father withdraws, giving up the attempt to disengage mother and child.
7. Mother and child deal with each other in a mixture of affection and exasperation until they reach a point where they are at an impasse. (pp. 121–122)

Such patterns can repeat ad infinitum unless some new behavior is introduced into the sequence. It perhaps needs to be pointed out that the dysfunctional behavior should not be "blamed" on any of the individuals; all are equally involved, and each could change the sequence by introducing a new incompatible element. Unfortunately, the family members are not usually aware of the complete sequence and in any case punctuate the sequence in such a way as to hold themselves blameless.

Hierarchy Problems

Haley (1987) and Minuchin (Minuchin & Nichols, 1993) both stress the importance of hierarchy problems in family dysfunction. Problems can occur when the hierarchy is absent, ambiguous, or culturally inappropriate; that is, when no one is in charge, when it is unclear who is in charge, or when the person wielding the power is not sanctioned by cultural mores. Dysfunction may also be due to coalitions that cut across generational boundaries. An example is when a father and child collude to avoid what they feel are the mother's overly rigid rules. Another common example is a family where there is marital conflict, and both parents try to enlist the children on their side of the argument.

Communication Problems

Virginia Satir (1983) placed special emphasis on the ways that people in a family communicate as a source of dysfunction. Communication may be inadequate owing to lack of clarity (e.g., information is deleted: "People get me down." Which people? How do they do that?). Communication can also be confusing because of a lack of topic continuity. This occurs when people are not really listening and their responses to the other become non sequiturs. When people are unwilling to reveal themselves or commit themselves to a statement or request, communication falters (e.g., "I don't suppose you would like to go to my mother's with me?" rather than "I would like you to go with me to my mother's.").

Sometimes communication is problematic because it is incongruent; either the nonverbal behavior or vocal tone communicates a message that contradicts the verbal content. Such incongruency is often the basis for irony and humor, but when it is unintentional and the message is not clarified, the receiver does not know how to respond. In the extreme case, this is the classic "double bind," described by Bateson, Jackson, Haley, and Weakland (1956). Satir (1983) describes this, and the effect that such incongruent communication can have on a child:

> How do mates unconsciously induce a child to behave in such a way that he eventually gets identified as a "patient?" . . . What conditions must be present for a child to experience the pressures associated with a double bind?
>
> **a.** First, the child must be exposed to double-level messages repeatedly and over a long period.
> **b.** Second, these must come from persons who have survival significance for him. . . .
> **c.** Third, perhaps most important of all, he must be conditioned . . . from an early age not to ask, "Did you mean that or that?" but must accept his parents conflicting messages in all their impossibility. He must be faced with the hopeless task of translating them into a single way of behaving. (pp. 45–46)

Low Self-Esteem

Satir (1983) also posits low self-esteem as the basis of much family difficulty. She describes a process similar to Bowen's (1994) intergenerational transmission process to reveal how low self-esteem not only affects the individuals and couples but also is "inherited" by their children. Description of the entire process is beyond the scope of this chapter. The essential elements include low self-esteem in both marital partners, intolerance of each other's differences, and efforts to improve their sense of self-esteem through their children. If the parents don't agree on how the children should behave, the children are confronted with the impossible task of pleasing both parents (another type of double-bind). Because they cannot please both parents, the children develop low self-esteem and may become symptomatic.

Conflict Over Which Family of Origin to Model

Whitaker says, "We assume that dysfunction is related to the struggle over whose family of origin this new family is going to model itself after. One way to view etiology asserts there is no such thing as a marriage; it is merely two scapegoats sent out by families to perpetuate themselves" (Whitaker & Keith, 1981, p. 196). Young people who come from a common cultural background may be less likely to experience this problem, but in our multicultural society, the appropriate behaviors for "wife" or "husband" are often unclear or represent role conflicts. When a child enters the picture before these roles are synchronized, the new roles of "mother" and "father" further complicate the picture. Often the young couple find themselves acting just like their parents, although they are reluctant to admit it.

Cultural Competence in Marriage and Family Therapy

The International Association for Marriage and Family Counselors ethical code (2005) highlights the need for marriage and family therapists to practice in a culturally competent manner. In the first section of this code can be found the following statement:

> Professional counselors realize their perspectives influence the conceptualization of problems, identification of clients, and implementation of possible solutions. Couple and family counselors examine personal biases and values. They actively attempt to understand and serve couples and families from diverse cultural backgrounds. (p. 3)

Taylor, Gambourg, Rivera, and Laureano (2006) stated that being a culturally competent marriage and family therapist involves more than the ability to repeat checklists of generalized norms for particular cultures. In their study on cultural competence in marriage and family therapists, these four researchers noted that cultural competence is derived from a therapist being aware of his or her own assumptions about a client's cultural narratives. They saw this awareness as the fundamental building block of cultural competence. They stated:

> Cultural competence is not a global, measurable phenomenon but a socially constructed notion created by the therapeutic relationship that is influenced by the social locations of the therapist and clients which vary case by case. Family therapy . . . will become culturally competent as the therapist and client constantly strive to gain mutual understanding through the countless interactions that take place within the therapy session. (p. 444)

In other words, Taylor et al. (2006) emphasized the particular over the general and the applied over the theoretical in describing cultural competence in marriage and family therapists. Thus, a marriage and family therapist operating unaware of his or her own cultural assumptions is unable to engage, from the start, any client in a profitable therapeutic relationship.

Narrow Rigid Beliefs and Self-Percepts

In a sense, this brings us full circle. To the extent that one's beliefs are narrow and unchanging, adaptation to the demands of a changing environment or the developmental demands of the family life cycle will be difficult. Milton Erickson held "that individuals with a symptom were constricted by their own certainties, their own rules, whether these rules guided their belief system, their perceptions of self, their patterns of physiological response or relational habits, or their own ideas of contingency (i.e., if A, then B)" (Ritterman, 1986, p. 37). The symptom per se is not the problem but instead is "a metaphorical expression of a problem and attempt at resolution . . . the underlying problem is understood to be inflexibly patterned behavior resulting from internal and/or interactional rules that proscribe available choices and prevent the resolution of developmentally routine or unusual life dilemmas" (Ritterman, 1986, p. 36).

When an individual or a family is unable to resolve a difficulty, it is assumed that the conscious mind is imposing a narrow, restrictive mind-set that does not allow the creative recovery of the resources necessary to solve the problem. From this point of view, the conscious, rational mind must be diverted to allow the creative potential of the unconscious to function. This is done through hypnosis or the use of indirect methods such as metaphor.

The Initial Interview

To gain a better understanding of how family therapists work, let us look at how the initial interview is conducted. The following description owes a great deal to Jay Haley (1987) but also incorporates ideas from other therapists.

Presession Planning

Whenever possible, the therapist should determine in advance who will attend the session and have at least a general idea of the nature of the presenting problems. Whitaker and Bumberry (1988) call this the "battle for structure" and place great emphasis on the importance of the therapist determining who will attend the first session. It is their belief that if the therapist does not have control at this stage, therapeutic leverage is lost, and the family is less likely to be helped. This may entail a presession telephone call or the use of an intake form. On the basis of the data derived from this initial contact, a presession plan should be developed that will include the counselor's hypotheses about the underlying basis of the presenting problem, areas of inquiry that must be addressed to reject or confirm the hypotheses, and a general plan for the session.

The Joining Stage

The most important task of the initial interview is to join with the family, accommodating to their affective tone, tempo, language, and family structure. This is done through mimesis (Walsh & McGraw, 2002). Mimesis is a therapeutic skill "used by the therapist to join with the family and become like family members in the manner or content of their communications" (Sauber, L'Abate, Weeks, & Buchanan, 1993, p. 255). Foreman and Cava (1993) advocate matching the family's style even to the extent of matching breathing, body movements, and representational system predicates (visual, auditory, kinesthetic). Care needs to be taken, however, that this matching does not cross the line into parody.

Tracking is another joining technique and consists of little more than Rogers-like "uh-huhs," reflection of content, and asking for clarification. During this time, the therapist should avoid comment or interpretation (Haley, 1987).

A third aspect of joining is maintenance. This aspect of joining refers to the therapist sensing the family's structure and acting in such a way as to be included within it (Minuchin & Nichols, 1993). If Dad acts as the "central switchboard" in this family, the therapist accommodates to that and contacts other members through him.

During the joining stage, the therapist should not allow the introduction of material related to the family problem. Only after some social contact has been made with every family member should the next stage begin (Haley, 1987). Joining, of course, is not finished at the end of this stage but must be of concern throughout the therapy.

More structured approaches to joining include the use of family chronologies and genograms (McGoldrick, Gerson, & Shellenberger, 1999). Blanton (2005) shares valuable information on joining with Christian families. Both McGoldrick, Giordano, and Garcia-Preto (2005) and Minuchin, Colapinto, and Minuchin (2006) present a wealth of information on joining with economically and/or ethnically diverse families.

The Problem Statement Stage

When significant contact has been made with all family members in the social or joining stage, the therapist introduces the problem stage. During the joining stage, the therapist has learned something of the family structure and hierarchy and uses this information to decide to whom the first question should be directed. Haley (1987) recommends that "the adult who seems less involved with the problem be spoken to first, and the person with the most power to bring the family back be treated with the most concern and respect" (p. 22). He also says that, in general, it is unwise to begin with the identified patient (IP).

Don't attempt to force a mute member to speak. This member is often the IP who has lots of practice in resisting adult coercion. Instead, ask another family member, "What would Johnny say if he chose to talk?" This can be repeated in a round robin if necessary, and in most instances, the mute member will feel the need to defend herself or himself or clarify her or his real feelings.

The second decision the therapist must make is how the problem question should be framed. Obviously, the question can be as vague as "What brings you here today?" or as specific as "What is the problem for which you are seeking help?" It can also be framed to elicit etiologic information or be future-focused on the kinds of changes that are desired. I generally prefer ambiguity and a focus on the future: "When this therapy is successful, how will your family be different?"

When everyone has had an opportunity to express what they see as the "pain in the family" (Satir, 1983), the therapist can begin to flesh out the details to clarify the function that the problem serves in the family. The following series of questions may prove helpful:

1. Who has the problem?
2. Where else have you sought help and how did it work for you? What has been tried, by whom, and for how long? Is there anything you have tried that you feel could have been done more?

3. Why is the symptom a problem? Does anyone in the family not consider the symptom a problem? Who in the family is most upset by the problem?
4. How often does it occur? When? Where? Who reacts to it? In what way? What happens just before it occurs? What happens next?
5. When did the symptom begin? Why did you come in now?
6. How do you account for the problem?
7. Do the parents agree or disagree about the problem, its cause, and the best solution?
8. What would happen if the symptom got better or worse?
9. What do you hope will happen as the result of coming here? What is your ideal goal? What would you settle for? How optimistic are you about improvement? What do you want to see the identified patient doing 2 weeks from now that would show progress? (Bergman, 1985)

The Interaction Stage

When the problem has been reasonably clarified or when it has become clear that the family is not in agreement regarding the nature of the problem, it is time for the therapist to introduce the interaction stage. During the earlier two stages, the therapist has maintained his or her centrality in the communication network, speaking in turn to each of the family members and blocking interruptions and attempts at dialogue between family members. This procedure tends to reduce tension and provide order and relatively clear communication, and it establishes the therapist's power and leadership in the therapeutic process. The focus in the problem phase has been on clarifying how the family views the problem. In the interaction stage, the therapist's focus will be on determining the patterns of interaction that sustain the problem. To get this information, the therapist asks the family to "dance" in his or her presence (Kershaw, 1992).

This occurs most easily and naturally when the family is not in agreement about the problem. When this is true, the therapist can encourage them to discuss their differences and try to reach agreement. During this phase, it is crucial that the therapist abdicate the center of the communication network. All attempts to communicate with the therapist should be referred back to a family member. The therapist does not, however, completely abandon the leadership position; instead, the role changes to being the director of the family drama, introducing a third party when two seem to reach an impasse, or asking family members to change their seating patterns to facilitate new encounters (Grove & Haley, 1993; Minuchin & Nichols, 1993).

If family members are in agreement regarding the problem that brings them to therapy (usually focusing on one person as the cause of the difficulty), then they can be asked to perform the problem. "When Johnny doesn't take out the garbage, what happens? Who is first to notice? Show me how it works." To get the family to act rather than talk about the problem, the therapist has to get to his or her feet, help the family to build an appropriate stage set (in fantasy), and set the scene into action.

Interactions that are developed from the idiosyncratic information presented by the family are most likely to reveal the information needed to understand the problem. Unfortunately, some families are so uncommunicative that the therapist is unable to elicit enough information to stage an appropriate interaction. When this occurs, it is well to have a few preplanned interaction situations available. One that is often useful, particularly in families with young children, is to ask the family to enact a day in their lives. Establish who sleeps where, move them into the appropriate places, and then have the alarm go off. If it is to be successful, the therapist will need to coach this interaction by slowing it down and focusing on the most simple, concrete details of family life. In a large family, who has access to the bathroom at what time is often a major source of conflict. Care must also be taken to ensure that all family members become involved. Other generic interactions might be to plan a family vacation together or decide how to spend a free Saturday. Or using building blocks or crayon and paper, have the family draw their living quarters and discuss who spends the most time with whom in what part of the house.

The purpose of the interaction stage is to determine the family hierarchy, reveal any stable coalitions, locate diffuse or rigid boundaries between family subsystems, and it is hoped, reveal the chronically repeating interactional sequence that sustains the problem behavior. When this information has been obtained, the therapist is in a position to develop the interventions that will lead to beneficial change.

In-Session Conference

When the therapist is working with an observing team or even working alone, it is useful at this point to leave the family and take a few minutes to think about what has been observed in order to abstract from the concrete interactions the patterns that need correction. When working with an observing team, the observers are often more able to perceive these patterns than the therapist who is immersed in the hypnotic pull of the family dance. Moran et al. (1995) contains an excellent description of the use of such a team. The purpose of the in-session conference is to assess the accuracy of the presession hypotheses and to reformulate them in light of the new data gathered during the session. When this has been done, it is possible to design directives (homework) that will begin to change the family's dysfunctional interactions. In some instances, the appropriate homework is not clear, but it is my contention that some homework should still be assigned. Family therapy, or any kind of therapy for that matter, is unlikely to succeed if the therapy is encapsulated in the therapeutic hour. The therapist needs to make an assignment that will establish an ongoing process that keeps the therapy salient throughout the week. When the therapist makes a homework assignment without being sure of its relevance, it is comforting to keep Jeff Zeig's dictum in mind. Zeig, who is an Ericksonian hypnotherapist, says his approach to therapy is "ready-shoot-aim" (personal communication, 1988). In other words, if you wait until you are sure of your interventions, therapy will be a long, drawn-out process. If you go with your hunches and learn from the results, you will probably hit the bull's-eye much sooner.

Goal-Setting Stage

As Haley (1987) has said, "If therapy is to end properly, it must begin properly—by negotiating a solvable problem and discovering the social situation that makes the problem necessary" (p. 8). The purpose of the goal-setting stage is to reach agreement with the family on a solvable problem and to initiate a process that will alter the social situation in such a way that the problem is no longer necessary. It is essential that the problem to be solved be stated in behavioral terms so that one will know when it has been solved. It is equally essential that the problem be one that the therapist believes is capable of solution. Often the process of operationalizing the complaint will be sufficient to produce a solvable problem. When a "rebellious child" problem is operationalized to "staying out after curfew," we have a specific concern to focus on. However, some problems—and this would include most of the categories of the *DSM-IV-TR* (2000)—are not capable of solution. With ambiguous problems, the therapist must reframe the problem in such a way that it can be solved, and in such a way that the family will accept it. This is not an easy task that sometimes taxes the therapist's creative resources. A notable example would be a case in which Haley reframed a case of schizophrenia as "pseudo-schizophrenia" and then went on to help the family specify how the IP's behavior might be improved. It cannot be emphasized enough that the problem to be solved must be stated in behavioral terms (i.e., never negotiate to "improve communication," "raise self-esteem," or "make our family more cohesive").

When agreement has been reached regarding the problem, the therapist should assign homework that will have face validity with regard to the problem but also address the underlying structural or sequential changes that are necessary. In the case of "pseudo-schizophrenia" mentioned previously, one might assume that the family is obsessively monitoring the patient, watching for abnormal behavior. An assignment that would utilize the obsessive nature of the family (i.e., pacing) and still institute a change would be to ask the family to keep an elaborate baseline measure of the "normal" behavior of the patient and bring it to the next session.

In a family with a daughter who is not keeping an assigned curfew, it might appear that the rebelliousness is being secretly (and perhaps unconsciously) reinforced by the father. An intervention might be to put him in charge of the daughter's behavior for a week, asking him during the session to negotiate with his daughter the expectations and consequences of noncompliance.

Initial sessions, particularly with large families, often cannot be conducted within the usual 50-minute hour. If it is not possible to schedule a longer session, it is likely that it will take more than one session to establish the therapeutic contract. When this is true, one should still attempt to give some kind of homework assignment that will increase the power of the therapy. When in doubt, asking family members to each keep a baseline of the behavior that they see as problematic is a good first step.

Ending Stage

The therapist should end the session by setting a second appointment and specifying who should be present. The family should not be asked if they want to return; this should be assumed unless someone indicates otherwise.

Postsession

When working with a team, there should be a post session debriefing to give an opportunity to share various perceptions of the family and the response to the interventions.

When working alone, it is essential to record your impressions of the presenting problem, the family structure, hypotheses regarding needed changes, and, most important, the homework that was assigned. The latter should be recorded verbatim, if possible, to check on the family compliance.

Family Therapy Techniques

In the preceding section, the focus was on the process of conducting the initial interview. In this section, I focus on the techniques utilized by the therapist throughout the therapy. The techniques offered here are derived from several therapeutic points of view.

Circular Questioning

Following Bateson's dictum that "information is a difference; difference is a relationship (or a change in the relationship)," the Milan group developed a technique they refer to as circular questioning (Walsh & McGraw, 2002). The "circular" referred to here is epistemological; their questions are intended to uncover the complementarity of family relationships that make the presenting symptom necessary for family homeostasis. Each member of the family is invited to tell how he or she sees the relationship between two other family members, between two different periods, or any other difference likely to be significant to the family. For example:

1. In terms of family relationships: "Tell us how you see the relationship between your sister and your mother."
2. In terms of specific interactive behaviors: "When your father gets mad at Bill, what does your mother do?"
3. In terms of differences in behavior: "Who gets most upset when Jimmy wets the bed, your father or your mother?"
4. In terms of ranking by various members of the family of a behavior or interaction: "Who is closest to your grandmother? Who is next, and next?"
5. In terms of change in the relationship before and after a precise event: "Did you and your sister fight more or less before your mother remarried?"
6. In terms of differences in respect to hypothetical circumstances: "If one of you kids should have to stay home, not get married, who would be best for your mother? Your father?" (Fleuridas, Nelson, & Rosenthal, 1986)

Perhaps it should be mentioned here, parenthetically, that this procedure would be anathema to some other therapists, including Virginia Satir, who specifically proscribes "gossiping" and "mind-reading." However, the Milan group has demonstrated that often more can be obtained by asking a person what he or she thinks about others than by asking questions that are more personal. When this is done in the family context, where all can hear and respond, the result is quite different than it would be in an interview with an individual.

Reframing

Haley (1987) says, "It cannot be emphasized enough that the problem the therapist settles on must be a problem which the family wants changed but which is put in a form that makes it solvable" (p. 38). While some problems presented by families lend themselves readily to therapeutic intervention, frequently the therapist must reframe the problem. Reframing may include the following:

1. Operationalizing—casting the problem in observable, behavioral terms. The problem of "a child who is driving us crazy" is reframed by specifying the particular behaviors that are problematic and asking the parents to keep a record of their frequency.
2. Emphasizing complementarity—describing the problem in an interactional context, rather than as the property of one member of the family. A father who is depressed is asked, "Who makes you depressed?"
3. Denominalizing—removing a reified diagnostic label and replacing it with a behavior that can be consciously controlled. Anorexia might be reframed as "a girl who refuses to eat."
4. Positive connotation—describing the symptomatic behavior as positively motivated in the service of the family system. A defiant, delinquent boy is described as particularly sensitive to family conflict and his behavior as a sacrificial act designed to keep the parents from divorce.

Giving Directives

Giving directives refers to creating or selecting an intervention that will attack the hypothesized basis of the presenting problem. According to Haley (1987), giving directives has several purposes:

> . . . the main goal of therapy is to get people to behave differently and so to have different subjective experiences. Directives are a way of making those changes happen. . . . directives are used to intensify the relationship with the therapist. By telling people what to do, the therapist gets involved in the action . . . directives are used to gather information. When a therapist tells people what to do, the ways they respond give information about them and about how they will respond to the changes wanted. Whether they do what the therapist asks, do not do it, forget to do it, or try and fail, the therapist has information she would not otherwise have. (p. 56)

Directives can be categorized as either compliance- or defiance-oriented. Compliance-oriented directives are offered to families who may be expected to carry out the assignment as given. When the therapist wants the family to carry out the directive, the following should be considered:

1. The directive should be framed in such a way as to use the language and imagery of the family and be focused on solving the problem presented by the family.
2. Avoid asking the family not to do something; ask them to do something different.

3. Ask everyone to do something.
4. Be extremely concrete and repetitive (unless you have reason to be otherwise).
5. Arrange for concrete, specific feedback.
6. Practice the homework during the session, or at least ask the family to tell you in their own words what the assignment includes.
7. Use antisabotage techniques: brainstorm reasons why they might not be able to comply; suggest probable problems that might interfere with compliance; discuss how they can overcome the problems.

Compliance-oriented directives can be either straightforward or paradoxical; the main idea is that you want them to be carried out. An example of a straightforward directive would be to ask Dad to be in charge of the discipline, and ask Mom to keep a record of problem behaviors and report them for his consideration. An example of a compliance-oriented paradoxical directive would be to prescribe the symptom to occur at a special time and place.

The following are some examples of compliance-oriented directives:

1. Caring days: Ask a hostile couple to act as if they care for each other by daily performing five minor behaviors requested by his or her spouse (LeCroy, Carrol, Nelson-Becker, & Sturlaugson, 1989).
2. Role reversal: Ask a disengaged husband to give his enmeshed wife a vacation from responsibility for the children. He is to be responsible for meting out discipline; she may consult with him but is not to be in charge.
3. Safe practice: Ask a man who is afraid of job interviews to apply for jobs that he would not take if they were offered.
4. Surprise: Ask a couple who are hostile and out of touch with each other to plan a surprise that will please the other but would be so out of character that the other could never guess what it would be. Each should attempt to guess what the other will do and make a written record of his or her guesses.
5. Symptom prescription: Ask a single mother with two boys who are disrespectful to their mother and constantly fighting to hold a daily wrestling match where she is the referee and will enforce fair fighting; boys are to agree to reserve their fighting to these bouts. Mother is to insist on "the bouts" even if the boys are unwilling.

Defiance-oriented directives are offered to families who are assumed to be resistant. The intention is to have the family defy the therapist in such a way as to eliminate the problem behavior. Defiance-oriented directives are always paradoxical. They should be used only by therapists who have considerable supervised experience with the use of such directives; they should never be used if there is a risk the family would be harmed if the directive were followed rather than defied. When the therapist wants the family to defy the directives, the following should be considered:

1. Do this only with families that have demonstrated their resistance.
2. Use this only after you have joined the family sufficiently to make noncompliance a significant issue. Your relationship to the family should be clearly defined as one of bringing about change.

3. The problem to be solved should be clearly defined and agreed on.
4. The rationale for the directive must utilize the family language and imagery and provide an acceptable rationale for the directive. Haley (1987) says that designing paradoxical directives is easy; you simply observe how the family members are behaving and ask them to continue. How you make the directive appear reasonable and how you react to changes that occur are the hard parts.
5. Give the directive and ask for a report.
6. When the family reports that they did not carry out the homework, condemn the noncompliance and be puzzled and surprised by the symptom reduction. Don't take credit for the change!
7. Repeat the directive and warn against relapse.

The following are some examples of defiance-oriented directives:

1. Positive connotation. Reframe the problem behavior in positive terms and indicate that it would be dangerous for the family to change.
2. Symptom increase. Recommend that the problem behavior be increased in order to get a better understanding of it.
3. Restraining. Recommend that the family slow down in its attempts to solve the problem.
4. Symptom retention. Advise the family to retain a certain percentage of the problem in order to remember how awful it was.
5. Predict relapse of a symptom that has been brought under control.

Ordeals

Ordeals are offered to families who are highly motivated to change but can't seem to accomplish their purpose. An ordeal is a behavior that is more obnoxious, frustrating, and time-consuming than the symptomatic behavior. The family must agree to perform the ordeal whenever the symptom occurs. Haley (1993b) noted that to be successful, the ordeal should contain the following elements:

1. The problem must be clearly defined.
2. The person must be committed to getting over the problem.
3. An ordeal must be selected with the client's collaboration: "the ordeal should be voluntary by the person and good for the person experiencing it, but not necessarily for the person imposing it . . . to inadvertently cause a person to suffer is one thing; to arrange it deliberately is quite another" (Haley, 1984, p. 13).
4. The directive must be given with a rationale.
5. The ordeal must continue until the problem is solved.
6. The ordeal is in a social context. The therapist must be prepared to assist in the systemic reorganization that the elimination of the symptom will require.

An example of an ordeal might be a bulimic woman with a stingy husband. The woman has been bingeing and forcing herself to vomit for years. Her husband becomes aware of the symptom, and they come to therapy. After establishing a relationship with them and ensuring the couple's commitment to solving the problem, the therapist might offer the following ordeal. When the wife feels she can no longer avoid a binge, she and her husband should go to the store and buy all the foods that the wife prefers to binge on, spending at least $25.00. They are then to return home, and together they are to unwrap all of the food and stuff it down the garbage disposal. This is to continue until the wife no longer feels the need to binge.

Jay Haley developed the concept of ordeal therapy as the result of his experience with Milton Erickson. He presents some of Erickson's cases that use the ordeal in *Uncommon Therapy: The Psychiatric Techniques of Milton H. Erickson, M.D.* (Haley, 1993c); his further development of the concept is presented in his books: *Conversations with Milton H. Erikson, MD: Volume II Changing Couples* (Haley, 1985), and *Jay Haley on Milton H. Erickson* (Haley, 1993b).

Rituals

Rituals can be used in therapy to help an individual or family move from one status or state to another. Rituals are particularly helpful in closing off past anger and guilt. The following examples illustrate their use:

> *Closing off the past.* A couple who couldn't resist fighting over wrongs done by the other in the past were asked to write down all their complaints, put them in a box, wrap them carefully, and bury them outside the therapist's window. They were told that the past was buried there, and if they wanted to fight over it, they would have to come to the therapist's office. (Coppersmith, 1985)
>
> *Rites of passage.* A gentile couple was having difficulty dealing with their 13-year-old son. They were overinvolved and too restrictive; he was increasingly rebellious. They were asked to plan a "Christian bar mitzvah" to symbolize his coming of age.

Ambiguous Assignments

Assignments that are mysterious and apparently unrelated to the presenting problem can be helpful in encouraging a family to find its own solution to its problems. Although what is to be done should be clear, the purpose for doing it should be completely obscure, at least to the clients. The purpose of the assignment is to depotentiate conscious, linear thinking about the problem and allow creativity in reframing to take place. Milton Erickson often asked people to climb Squaw Peak. The peak, located in north Phoenix near his home, offered a considerable, but not unreasonable, challenge and provided plenty of time to think about why the task was assigned (Lankton, 1988).

Another example would be a task a therapist assigned to a 30-year-old son who was having trouble leaving home: "I'd like you to go to the store and buy a goldfish and everything you will need to take care of it." Interestingly, he defied the directive and instead bought a Christmas cactus because "it will be easier to take with me when I leave after the holidays."

Assigning Directives

When a directive has been determined, the therapist must also decide how to present it to the family in a way that it will be accepted (or, in the case of paradox, rejected). Allow plenty of time to seed the intervention, assign it, clarify it, and practice it. Couch the task in the family's language, and tie task completion to the presenting problem. Whenever possible, dramatize the assignment by delaying the actual presentation as you ruminate on whether the family is ready for it. The extreme of this dramatization is the "devil's pact," where the assignment is delayed for several sessions and offered only after the family has agreed to comply without knowing what the assignment will be.

Haley (1993a) decries the fact that most clinical training does not include developing skill in assigning directives and hence that most clinicians must learn it on their own. He indicates most of his own skill in this area was learned from Milton Erickson (Haley, 1993b).

Collecting the Homework

A cardinal rule of this sort of therapy is to be sure to collect the homework and to take either compliance or noncompliance very seriously. If the homework is ignored or not given sufficient attention, it signals very clearly to the family that compliance is not necessary. The reaction (or nonreaction) of the family to the assignment allows one to aim more carefully on the second attempt. When family members have carried out the task, congratulate them and encourage them to process the experience. Do not explain why the assignment was given or interpret the outcome.

When the family has only partially complied or did not carry out the task, it is often best for the therapist to take the blame for the noncompliance. This assumption of blame indicates to the family that either (a) the assignment was not sufficiently concrete and specific enough for this family to understand or (b) the therapist has miscalculated and the family was not ready for such a task at this time. In either case, to demonstrate its capacity for understanding or its readiness for change, the family will be motivated to complete the next task that is assigned (Haley, 1987).

These techniques are, of course, only a brief introduction to the procedures used by various family therapists. Unfortunately, space does not allow a more complete discussion. I am particularly conscious of having omitted the in-session techniques of Virginia Satir (1983) and Carl Whitaker (Connell, Whitaker, Garfield, & Connell, 1990) and the coaching techniques associated with the transgenerational work of Murray Bowen (Kerr & Bowen, 1988). Useful sources for family therapy techniques are the *Procedures in Marriage and Family Therapy* (Brock & Barnard, 1999), *101 Interventions in Family Therapy* (Nelson & Trepper, 1993), and *101 More Interventions in Family Therapy* (Nelson & Trepper, 1998).

Professional Issues

Specialization or Profession?

At present there exists a strong debate as to whether family therapy is a professional specialization or a distinct profession (Gladding, Remley, & Huber, 2006). Members of a number of different professions (i.e., psychiatry, nursing, psychology, counseling, and social work) practice family therapy as a professional specialization. In addition, there are mental health practitioners who practice family therapy exclusively and view this work as distinct from the activity of other professions. These practitioners go by the title of marriage and family therapist (MFTs). Who is going to win this debate? Gladding et al. (2006) suggested that this debate most likely will be resolved as a "both-and." That is, *both* MFTs and other mental health professionals will practice family therapy, *and* marriage and family therapy will be viewed as a distinct profession.

Professional Associations

A number of professional associations serve mental health practitioners who work with families. The professional association for MFTs is the American Association for Marriage and Family Therapy (AAMFT). Founded in 1942, the goal of this 24,000-member organization is the promotion of marriage and family therapy as a distinct mental health discipline (American Association for Marriage and Family Therapy, 2007a).

    The professional home for counselors is the American Counseling Association (ACA). Since 1986, the ACA has maintained a division for those members whose professional practice involves family therapy. This division is the International Association of Marriage and Family Counselors (IAMFC). The IAMFC's goals include:

1. Educate the public regarding marriage and family counseling.
2. Promote skill development in systems theory, couple counseling, and family counseling.
3. Promote standards in marriage and family counseling.
4. Maintain ethical standards of practice through revision of the IAMFC ethical code.
5. Provide direction and leadership to universities to increase the number of CACREP-accredited marriage and family training programs.
6. Promote public policy and legislation for marriage and family counseling.
7. Monitor public policy and legislation on issues affecting couples and families.
8. Promote research and knowledge in marriage and family counseling.
9. Expand the research and knowledge base on the efficacy of couple and family counseling.
10. Promote awareness of multiculturalism and diversity in marriage and family counseling.
11. Provide professional development opportunities related to diverse family structures.
12. Promote public awareness of diverse family structures. (International Association of Marriage and Family Counselors, 2007)

Currently, the IAMFC has approximately 8,000 members. Other organizations with a family therapy focus include the American Family Therapy Academy (AFTA), Division 43 of the American Psychological Association (APA), and the Family Therapy Section of the National Council on Family Relations (NCFR).

Licensure/Certification

Currently, 49 states have enacted certification or licensure laws for mental health professionals who practice family therapy (American Association for Marriage and Family Therapy, 2007b). A growing trend is state-to-state licensure reciprocity and licensure uniformity (Gladding, 2006). At the federal level, regulations recognizing family therapy as a "core" mental health profession were set forth in the early 1990s (Shields, Wynne, McDaniel, & Gawinski, 1994). National certification as a marriage and family therapist is available to professional counselors through the National Academy for Certified Family Therapists (NACFT).

Program Accreditation

Two organizations accredit programs that train persons to practice family therapy. The Commission on Accreditation of Marriage and Family Therapy Education (COAMFTE) accredits programs that prepare MFTs. COAMFTE accreditation covers both degree-granting programs and postgraduate training institutes. Currently, 98 programs possess COAMFTE accreditation (Commission on Accreditation of Marriage and Family Therapy Education, 2007).

The other accrediting body is the Council for Accreditation of Counseling and Related Educational Programs (CACREP). This organization accredits programs that prepare persons to serve as professional counselors with the following specializations: (a) school counseling, (b) mental health counseling, (c) community agency counseling, (d) student affairs, and (e) marriage and family therapy. CACREP accredits only degree-granting programs. Currently, there are 35 CACREP-accredited marriage and family therapy programs (Council for Accreditation of Counseling and Related Educational Programs, 2007).

Ethical and Legal Issues

The ethical codes of the AAMFT (2001), ACA (2005), and APA (1992) are applicable to the practice of family therapy, but the IAMFC code (2005) is perhaps the most relevant to professional counselors practicing family therapy. Chapter 4 presents the legal and ethical issues related to counseling. However, when one assumes a family systems orientation, some special issues arise. Common issues that are especially problematic for the family therapist include:

Responsibility—Who is the client? Is it possible to serve all members of a family even handedly? Can you define the family system or the relationship as the client? Does insisting on seeing the whole family before treatment can begin deny treatment to those who are motivated? Is it ethical to coerce reluctant members into therapy?

Confidentiality—Is the promise of confidentiality given to the family as a unit, or does it apply to individual family members? What should be done about information obtained from an individual prior to the involvement of other family members? Can you offer confidentiality to children seen in a family therapy context? If family members are seen separately during family therapy, should they be promised confidentiality? Does privileged communication exist for a family? Will a written agreement not to subpoena hold up legally? Can one member of the family waive privileged communication for all?

Therapist control—Is it appropriate for the therapist to increase the family stress in order to bring about change? Should the therapist use indirect (hypnotic, metaphoric) or paradoxical procedures that bypass conscious processes? Is the use of such techniques a violation of the concept of informed consent? In dealing with "inappropriate hierarchies," may the therapist impose his or her own values on the family? Is family therapy antithetical to the feminist perspective?

Informed consent—Who should consent to treatment? What needs to be disclosed? How can a therapist utilize defiance-oriented directives or paradox and provide full disclosure?

Third-party payments—Is it ethical for a family therapist working within a systems perspective to assign a diagnostic label to an individual to obtain payment? Is not such labeling antithetical to a systems therapist's core beliefs? (Adapted from Becvar & Becvar, 2005; Gladding et al., 2006; Margolin, 1982; Patten, Barnett, & Houlihan, 1991)

The current context does not allow space for resolution of these issues; in fact, several of them cannot be readily resolved. The counselor who is interested in working within a family therapy perspective should, however, be aware of these issues and be prepared to grapple with them.

Research In Family Therapy

Background

The history of family therapy research is filled with contradictions. On one hand, this specialization/profession emerged from research projects such as Bateson's work on schizophrenia (Bateson et al., 1956). On the other hand, empirical research has been largely ignored in family therapy (Diamond, Serrano, Dickey, & Sonis, 1996; Gladding, 2006; Lebow & Gurman, 1995; Shields et al., 1994). In a major review of family therapy research, Lebow and Gurman (1995) noted:

> In reviewing the research base of couple and family therapy, one faces a basic dilemma. Traditional empirical research has not been the foundation for the development of these modes of practice, nor has it been the fabric of much of this work. . . . Alternative modes of investigation such as inductive reasoning, clinical observation, and

deconstruction have dominated in the development of methods and treatment models. Some couple and family therapists have even been reluctant to acknowledge that empirical research has an important role. At one discouraging point, now fortunately past, there was considerable debate about whether traditional research had any relevant role in the development of family therapy. (p. 29)

In the past decade, the growth of empirical research in family therapy has been remarkable. Now mental health practitioners, health insurers, and the public at large can compare and contrast family therapy with other types of interventions.

In terms of family therapy research, three questions that any future professional counselor should address are:

1. Does family therapy work?
2. What are the professional practice patterns of family therapists?
3. How does one access family therapy research in order to enhance one's professional practice?

Each of these questions is addressed separately.

Does Family Therapy Work?

Research that examines whether an intervention works is known as *outcome* research. In family therapy, a dearth of outcome research left this question unanswered until the late 1980s. Only at that time had a sufficient number of studies been published to allow researchers to conduct meta-analyses of the family therapy research literature. Meta-analysis is a research technique by which multiple individual studies can be grouped together to empirically analyze the overall effectiveness of a particular intervention approach. Hazelrigg, Cooper, and Borduin (1987) conducted the first meta-analysis of family therapy outcome research. In their meta-analysis of 20 studies, they found that family therapy had a positive effect on clients when compared with either no treatment or an alternative treatment. Subsequent meta-analyses have confirmed that family therapy is indeed an efficacious mental health treatment approach (Shadish & Baldwin, 2003).

In addition to knowledge concerning the overall effectiveness of family therapy, strong evidence exists in the research literature concerning the effectiveness of this type of therapy with a wide range of problems. Table 18.4 lists a variety of issues where treatment by family therapy has been proven efficacious. Overall, it is known that families treated with family-based interventions improved more than at least 67% of families treated with alternative treatments or no treatment (Diamond et al., 1996).

What Are the Professional Practice Patterns of Family Therapists?

Within the mental health service provider community, there is a prejudice that family therapists do nothing more than "interminable marriage counseling for trivial

TABLE 18.4   Research Support for Efficacious Treatment

Issue
Adolescent drug abuse
Agoraphobia
Alcoholism
Anxiety
Conduct/oppositional disorders
Delinquency
Depression
Eating disorders
Parenting skills
Pediatric psychopathy
Schizophrenia

Source: Based on research reported in Alexander & Barton (1995), Diamond et al. (1996), Kazdin (2005), Lebow & Gurman (1995), and Shadish & Baldwin (2003).

problems" (Simmons & Doherty, 1995, p. 5). Surprisingly, little research on the practice patterns of family therapists has been conducted. Thus, research evidence that could challenge this prejudice has not existed until recently. The groundbreaking studies on this topic were conducted by the research team of Bill Doherty and Deborah Simmons.

Doherty and Simmons (1996) studied the professional practice patterns of a random sample of MFTs drawn from 15 states. The practice variables they examined included (a) caseload, (b) presenting problem, (c) diagnosis, and (d) length of treatment. They found that MFTs, on average, had 24 clients in their active caseload and completed 20 client contact hours per week. The clients served by the MFTs presented a multitude of problems at the commencement of treatment. These problems included (a) depression (44%), (b) marital problems (30%), (c) anxiety (21%), and (d) parent–child problems (13%). Adjustment Disorder was the modal diagnostic category (25%). Other prevalent diagnostic categories included Depressive Disorder (23%) and Anxiety Disorders (14%). The median number of sessions per client was 12. Interestingly, almost half (49.4%) of the treatment provided by the national sample of *marriage and family* therapists was individual counseling. Doherty and Simmons's research studies suggest that family therapists *do* serve clients with serious problems.

The AAMFTE studied the pay and work patterns of MFTs (American Association for Marriage and Family Therapy, 2002). Table 18.5 shows the results of this study broken out by working setting (i.e., private practice, agency, and private practice–agency combination). The study also reported that doctoral level MFTs averaged $65,772 per year and master's level MFTs averaged $49,017 per year.

Simmons and Doherty (1998) also studied whether the practice patterns of MFTs differed in reference to training background. They examined whether clinical members of the AAMFT from four disciplinary groups (i.e., counseling, marriage and

TABLE 18.5   MFT Work and Pay Patterns

Work Setting	Annual Average Salary	Average Hours Per Week Providing Therapy	Average Hours Worked Per Week
Private practice	$58,787	28	26.1
Agency	$46,850	37.8	27.8
Both private practice and agency	$55,710	36.4	27.6

family therapy, social work, psychology) differed in terms of clinical practice or client satisfaction. Simmons and Doherty found that "results showed highly similar practice patterns and client outcomes across all four disciplinary groups" (p. 321).

How Does One Access Family Therapy Research in Order to Enhance One's Professional Practice?

The vast majority of family therapy research can be found in professional journals. Both the IAMFC and the AAMFT sponsor such journals and send them to their members: *The Family Journal* (IAMFC) and the *Journal of Marital and Family Therapy* (AAMFT). Easy access to research is one of the major benefits of membership in a professional association. Other family therapy journals include *American Journal of Family Therapy, Australian & New Zealand Journal of Family Therapy, Contemporary Family Therapy: An International Journal, Journal of Feminist Family Therapy*, and *Journal of Family Therapy*.

Summary

This chapter has attempted to introduce the reader to the contextual thinking that is the essence of family therapy. I have tried to illustrate this perspective through descriptions of family therapy diagnosis, interviewing, and treatment. In family therapy, diagnosis focuses on interpersonal rather than intrapersonal dysfunction. Sound family therapy interviewing follows a distinct eight-stage process beginning with presession planning and ending with postsession debriefing. Family therapy treatment is rich with powerful techniques, including circular questioning and ordeal prescription.

In addition to diagnosis, interviewing, and treatment, professional issues of concern to family therapists were addressed: licensure, training, professional development, and ethics. Finally, the evidence for the efficacy of family therapy was reviewed. It is my hope that this brief introduction to the concepts and techniques of family therapy will whet the reader's appetite for further exploration. If that should prove to be the case, the following Web sites relating to the chapter topics, as well as the references marked with an asterisk (*), are good starting points.

USEFUL WEB SITES

American Association for Marriage and Family Therapy
http://www.aamft.org

American Family Therapy Academy
http://www.afta.org

American Psychological Association, Family Psychology Division
http://www.apa.org/divisions/div43

National Council on Family Relations
http://www.ncfr.org

International Association for Marriage and Family Counselors
http://www.iamfc.com

REFERENCES

Ackerman, N. W. (1958). *The psychodynamics of family life*. New York: Basic Books.

Alexander, J., & Barton, C. (1995). Family therapy research. In R. H. Mikesell, D. Lusterman, & S. H. McDaniel (Eds.), *Integrating family therapy* (pp. 91–112). Washington, DC: APA.

American Association for Marriage and Family Therapy. (2001). *AAMFT code of ethics*. Washington, DC: Author.

American Association for Marriage and Family Therapy. (2002). *What MFTs get paid*. Retrieved June 1, 2007, from http://www.aamft.org/resources/Career_PracticeInformation/MFTSalaries.asp

American Association for Marriage and Family Therapy. (2007a). *About the American Association for Marriage and Family Therapy*. Retrieved June 1, 2007, from http://www.aamft.org/about/Aboutaamft.asp

American Association for Marriage and Family Therapy. (2007b). *Directory of MFT licensure and certification boards*. Retrieved June 1, 2007, from http://www.aamft.org/resources/Online_Directories/boardcontacts.asp

American Counseling Association. (2005). *Code of ethics*. Alexandria, VA: Author.

American Psychiatric Association. (2000). *Diagnostic and statistical manual of mental disorders* (4th ed., text revision). Washington, DC: Author.

American Psychological Association. (1992). *Ethical principles of psychologists and code of conduct*. Washington, DC: Author.

Bateson, G., Jackson, D. D., Haley, J., & Weakland, J. (1956). Toward a theory of schizophrenia. *Behavioral Science, 1*, 251–264.

Becvar, D. S., & Becvar, R. J. (2005). *Family therapy: A systematic integration*. Boston: Allyn & Bacon.

Bergman, J. (1985). *Fishing for barracuda*. New York: W. W. Norton.

Blanton, P. G. (2005). How to talk to Christian clients about their spiritual lives: Insights from postmodern family therapy. *Pastoral Psychology, 54*, 93–101.

Bowen, M. (1991). Alcoholism as viewed through family systems theory and family psychotherapy. *Family Dynamics of Addiction Quarterly, 1*, 94–102.

*Bowen, M. (1994). *Family therapy in clinical practice*. New York: Aronson.

*Brock, G. W., & Barnard, C. P. (1999). *Procedures in marriage and family therapy*. Boston: Allyn & Bacon.

Carter, B., & McGoldrick, M. (2005). *The expanded family life cycle: Individual, family, and social perspectives* (3rd ed.). Needham Heights, MA: Allyn & Bacon.

Commission on Accreditation of Marriage and Family Therapy Education. (2007). *Directory of MFT training programs*. Retrieved June 1, 2007, from http://www.aamft.org/cgi-shl/twserver.exe?run:COALIST

Connell, G. M., Whitaker, C., Garfield, R., & Connell, L. (1990). The process of in-therapy consultation: A symbolic-experiential perspective. *Journal of Strategic and Systemic Therapies, 9*, 32–38.

Coppersmith, E. (1985). We've got a secret. In A. Gurman (Ed.), *Casebook of marital therapy* (pp. 369–386). New York: Guilford.

Council for Accreditation of Counseling and Related Educational Programs. (2007). *Directory of accredited programs.* Retrieved June 1, 2007, from http://www.cacrep.org/directory-current.html

Diamond, G. S., Serrano, A. C., Dickey, M., & Sonis, W. A. (1996). Current status of family-based outcome and process research. *Journal of the American Academy of Child and Psychiatry, 35,* 6–16.

Doherty, W. J., & Simmons, D. S. (1996). Clinical practice patterns of marriage and family therapists: A national survey of therapists and their clients. *Journal of Marital and Family Therapy, 22,* 9–25.

Fleuridas, C., Nelson, T., & Rosenthal, D. (1986). The evolution of circular questions: Training family therapists. *Journal of Marital and Family Therapy, 12,* 113–127.

Foreman, B. D., & Cava, E. (1993). Neuro-linguistic programming in one-person family therapy. In T. S. Nelson & T. S. Trepper (Eds.), *101 interventions in family therapy* (pp. 50–54). New York: Haworth Press.

Gerson, R. (1995). The family life cycle: Phases, stages and crises. In R. H. Mikesell, D. Lusterman, & S. H. McDaniel (Eds.), *Integrating family therapy* (pp. 91–112). Washington, DC: APA.

Gladding, S. T. (2006). *Family Therapy: History, theory, and practice* (4th ed). Upper Saddle River, NJ: Prentice-Hall.

Gladding, S. T., Remley, T. P., & Huber, C. H. (2006). *Ethical, legal, and professional issues in the practice of marriage and family therapy* (4th ed). New York: Prentice Hall.

Grove, D. R., & Haley, J. (1993). *Conversations on therapy.* New York: W. W. Norton.

Haley, J. (1984). *Ordeal therapy.* San Francisco: Jossey-Bass.

Haley, J. (1985). *Conversations with Milton H. Erikson, MD: Volume II, Changing Couples.* New York: Triangle Press.

*Haley, J. (1987). *Problem solving therapy* (2nd ed.). San Francisco: Jossey-Bass.

Haley, Jay. (1993a). How to be a therapy supervisor without knowing how to change anyone. *Journal of Systemic Therapies, 12,* 41–52.

Haley, J. (1993b). *Jay Haley on Milton H. Erickson.* New York: Brunner/Mazel.

Haley, J. (1993c). *Uncommon therapy: The psychiatric techniques of Milton H. Erickson, M.D.* New York: W. W. Norton.

Hazelrigg, M. D., Cooper, H. M., & Borduin, C. M. (1987). Evaluating the effectiveness of family therapies: An integrative review and analysis. *Psychological Bulletin, 101,* 428–442.

International Association of Marriage and Family Counselors. (2005). *Ethical code for the International Association of Marriage and Family Counselors.* Retrieved June 1, 2007, from http://www.iamfc.com/ethical_codes.html

International Association of Marriage and Family Counselors. (2007). *Strategic plan.* Retrieved June 1, 2007, from http://www.iamfc.com/strategic_plan.html

*Kazdin, A. E. (2005). *Parent management training: Treatment for oppositional, aggressive, and antisocial behavior in children and adolescents.* New York: Oxford University Press.

*Kerr, M., & Bowen, M. (1988). *Family evaluation.* New York: W. W. Norton.

Kershaw, C. J. (1992). *The couple's hypnotic dance.* New York: Brunner/Mazel.

Lankton, C. (1988). Task assignments: Logical and otherwise. In J. Zeig & S. Lankton (Eds.), *Developing Ericksonian therapy* (pp. 257–279). New York: Brunner/ Mazel.

Lebow, J. L., & Gurman, A. S. (1995). Research assessing couple and family therapy. *Annual Review of Psychology, 46,* 27–57.

LeCroy, C. W., Carrol, P., Nelson-Becker, H., & Sturlaugson, P. (1989). An experimental evaluation of the Caring Days technique for marital enrichment. *Family Relations, 38,* 15–18.

Margolin, G. (1982). Ethical and legal considerations in marital and family therapy. *American Psychologist, 37,* 788–801.

McGoldrick, M., Giordano, J. & Garcia-Preto, N. (2005). *Ethnicity and family therapy.* New York: Guilford.

McGoldrick, M., Gerson, R., & Shellenberger, S. (1999). *Genograms: Assessment and intervention.* New York: W. W. Norton.

Micucci, J. A. (1998). *The adolescent in family therapy.* New York: Guilford.

Minuchin, P., Colapinto, J., & Minuchin, S. (2006). *Working with families of the poor* (2nd ed). New York: Guilford.

Minuchin, S. (1982). Reflections on boundaries. *American Journal of Orthopsychiatry, 52*, 655–663.

˙Minuchin, S., & Fishman, C. (1990). *Family therapy techniques.* Cambridge, MA: Harvard University Press.

Minuchin, S., Montalvo, B., Gurney, B., Rosman, B., & Schumer, F. (1967). *Families of the slums.* New York: Basic Books.

Minuchin, S., & Nichols, M. P. (1993). *Family healing.* New York: The Free Press.

Minuchin, S., Rosman, B., & Baker, L. (1978). *Psychosomatic families.* Cambridge, MA: Harvard University Press.

Moran, A., Brownlee, K., Gallant, P., Meyers, L., Farmer, F., & Taylor, S. (1995). The effectiveness of reflecting team supervision: A client's experience of receiving feedback from a distance. *Family Therapy, 22,* 31–47.

˙Nelson, T. S., & Trepper, T. S. (Eds.). (1993). *101 interventions in family therapy.* New York: Haworth Press.

˙Nelson, T. S., & Trepper, T. S. (Eds). (1998). *101 more interventions in family therapy.* New York: Haworth Press.

Patten, C., Barnett, T., & Houlihan, D. (1991). Ethics in marital and family therapy: A review of the literature. *Professional Psychology: Research and Practice, 22,* 171–175.

Ritterman, M. (1986). Exploring relationships between Ericksonian hypnotherapy and family therapy. In S. de Shazer & R. Kral (Eds.), *Indirect approaches in therapy* (pp. 35–47). Rockville, MD: Aspen Publications.

Satir, V. (1964). *Conjoint family therapy.* Palo Alto, CA: Science & Behavior Books.

˙Satir, V. (1983). *Conjoint family therapy* (3rd ed.). Palo Alto, CA. Science & Behavior Books.

Sauber, S. R., L'Abate, L., Weeks, G. R., & Buchanan, W. L. (1993). *The dictionary of family psychology and family therapy* (2nd ed.). Newbury Park, CA: Sage.

Shadish, W. R., & Baldwin, S. A. (2003). Meta-analysis of MFT interventions. *Journal of Marital & Family Therapy, 29,* 547–570.

Shields, C. G., Wynne, L. C., McDaniel, S. H., & Gawinski, B. A. (1994). The marginalization of family therapy: A historical and continuing problem. *Journal of Marital and Family Therapy, 20,* 117–138.

Sieburg, E. (1985). *Family communication.* New York: Gardner Press.

Simmons, D. S., & Doherty, W. J. (1995). Defining who we are and what we do: Clinical practice patterns of marriage and family therapists in Minnesota. *Journal of Marital and Family Therapy, 21,* 3–16.

Simmons, D. S., & Doherty, W. J. (1998). Defining who we are and what we do: Clinical practice patterns of marriage and family therapists in Minnesota. *Journal of Marital and Family Therapy, 24,* 321–336.

Stanton, D. (1988). The lobster quadrille: Issues and dilemmas for family therapy research. In L. Wynne (Ed.), *The state of the art in family therapy research: Controversies and recommendations* (pp. 5–32). New York: Family Process Press.

Taylor, B. A., Gambourg, M. B., Rivera, M., & Laureano, D. (2006). Constructing cultural competence: Perspectives of family therapists working with Latino families. *The American Journal of Family Therapy, 34,* 429–445.

Walsh, W. M., & McGraw, J. A. (2002). *Essentials of family therapy.* Denver, CO: Love Publishing.

˙Whitaker, C., & Bumberry, W. (1988). *Dancing with the family: A symbolic-experiential approach.* New York: Brunner/Mazel.

Whitaker, C., & Keith, D. (1981). Symbolic-experiential family therapy. In A. Gurman & D. Kniskern (Eds.), *Handbook of family therapy* (pp. 187–225). New York: Brunner/Mazel.

Whitaker, C., & Malone, T. (1953). *The roots of psychotherapy.* New York: Blakiston.

Wynne, L. (1988). An overview of the state of the art. In L. Wynne (Ed.), *The state of the art in family therapy research: Controversies and recommendations* (pp. 249–266). New York: Family Process Press.

19 Counseling Lesbian, Gay, Bisexual, Transgender, and Questioning Clients

JEANNIE FALKNER PHD, LCSW, LMFT
Delta State University

DONNA STARKEY, PHD, LPC
Delta State University

Most counselors will work with sexual minority clients. To provide effective counseling services, beginning counselors need to be equipped with basic knowledge, skills, and values that reflect an informed understanding of sexual orientation and the complex issues that sexual minority clients face throughout their life span. This chapter will provide you with an overview of the concept of sexual orientation on a continuum of sexual identity, together with the language used in communicating one's sexual orientation. Contemporary developmental concepts, including the nurture versus nature etiology of sexual minority orientation, are examined. The impact of external forces, which create psychosocial distress, as well as internal conflicts common among clients, is discussed to provide a contextual component common among LGBTQ clients in an effort to allow you a glimpse into their worldview.

Affirmative counselor practices, counselor self-awareness, and counselor ethics with this population are presented as practical guidelines for empirically based strategies with the LGBTQ population. Two models of sexual identity development are highlighted to emphasize a life span perspective, in addition to an examination of traditional theoretical modalities that may be appropriate when counseling LGBTQ individuals, partners, and families. Next, issues frequently presented for counseling and suggested counselor responses are offered as guidelines for the beginning counselor. Finally, a discussion of counselor issues and helpful Web sites complete the chapter.

Overview

Most people view themselves as having a clearly defined sexual orientation. "I'm straight" or "I'm gay" statements assume that there are narrowly defined categories of sexual identity. The reality is that sexual orientation occurs on a continuum from exclusively homosexual to exclusively heterosexual. Because more than 90% of Americans consider themselves to be exclusively heterosexual (Kinsey, Pomeroy, & Martin, 2003), they make up the majority voice. However, conservative estimates indicate there are about 15 million people of sexual minority status in this country (Survey Says, 2005). Counselors are often given opportunities to assist people in the midst of their understanding of sexual identity, as well as address issues and concerns relative to modern life as a sexual minority. Whether they know it or not, all counselors are likely to have clients who are sexual minorities. The goal of this chapter is to introduce you to working with this client population, which may or may not resemble your own sexual identity.

Let's begin by considering what it means to be homosexual. Many heterosexual, or straight, individuals view homosexuality as sexual contact between members of the same sex. This is not a full representation of sexual minority status, but it is the most common perception. Being a sexual minority means to identify with and have a primary erotic, social, emotional, and psychological interest in the same sex, and to self-identify as such.

Terms

Many terms are used in discussing sexual minority status. It is important to view most of these terms as descriptors rather than labels. Our language affords us words that help us communicate clearly, but these words are not reflective of a person's total identity. Some are more accepted than others. For example, the word *homosexual* is typically used by the heterosexual or sexual majority population and may be perceived as demeaning or marginalizing of the many aspects of the culture. The word *homosexual* is often correlated with the word *gay*, which began as a way for homosexuals to speak in code as they talked about their intimate relationships (Crooks & Baur, 2005). Current language incorporates a broad meaning of the word *gay*, which is often used to include men and women who are sexual minorities, as well as social and political movements, for example, the gay rights movement or a gay political initiative (Crooks & Baur, 2005). The word *lesbian* has a clearer meaning in our language and is used exclusively to define a homosexual woman.

As previously mentioned, sexual orientation exists on a continuum. Some of us are exclusively homosexual, and others are exclusively heterosexual. Those who identify as bisexual feel attraction to persons of the same sex and the opposite sex. Relatively few people identify as exclusively homosexual and may have periods where they identify as bisexual or heterosexual. Because sexual identity is based on attraction, interests, and self-identification, it is best viewed across a life span of development rather than as a fixed point or constant in the person's life. Although acting on attraction, interests, and self-identification certainly provides a behavioral checkpoint for a person, behavior alone is not sufficient to meet criteria for being gay, lesbian, or bisexual. Think of it this way: If a person knows that he is primarily attracted to men, identifies with the social and emotional concerns of gay males, has both an interpersonal and erotic interest in the same sex, but never has a physical encounter with a male, does that make him any less gay? No. If he knows it to be true and self-identifies as such, he is gay. Conversely, someone who identifies interpersonally and sexually with an attraction to the opposite sex, but has a physical encounter with someone of the same sex, may not be homosexual or bisexual. If that behavior was not indicative of a preferred attraction and self-identification, then the person is not gay, lesbian, or bisexual. You can see how critical it is to help others understand their identity process if they come into counseling with sexual identity concerns. Notice that the definition is not based on behavior. It is not merely behavior that identifies us; it is so much more.

Transgender persons are those who transgress societal norms that define sexual identity. This term encompasses a range of identities and behaviors including transsexual, cross dressers, intersexed individuals, androgynous persons, and drag kings and queens. A more recent addition to the culture is the term *questioning*. Questioning individuals are beginning to explore their sexual understanding. There are many words that describe the continuum of sexual identity. To simplify the discussion of this chapter, we will use the acronym LGBTQ to refer to those persons who are best described as lesbian, gay, bisexual, transgendered, or questioning. Such terminology follows the established language of the Association for Lesbian, Gay, Bisexual & Transgender Issues in Counseling (ALGBTIC), a division of the American Counseling Association (ACA). More negative or derogatory words are also part of our modern language. *Dyke*, *queer*, and *faggot* are some terms that are generally offensive, especially when used by the sexual majority population. However, members of sexual minorities often use these same words with humor and good-natured intent.

So who is LGBTQ? Seminal research by Kinsey and colleagues found that 13%–37% of the population has had at least one significant sexual experience with a member of the same gender (Kinsey et al., 2003). Up to 10% of the population is estimated to consider themselves to be gay or lesbian, with approximately 3% self-identifying as bisexual (Diamond, 1993). Clearly, what is important in these figures is the perspective that counselors will work with LGBTQ clients. The question becomes whether they will be allowed to know that by clients who are concerned about the counselor's acceptance of their sexual minority status.

Why Are People LGBTQ?

We have been discussing the components of sexual identity. Later in this chapter we will cover more exhaustively the primary sexual identity development models. At this point, it seems important to discuss the nature versus nurture debate regarding homosexuality. You may already have an opinion as to whether a person's sexual orientation is by choice or by chance. It may be helpful for beginning counselors to ask themselves: What is my opinion based on? Do I have values from my family of origin that helped mold that opinion? What roles do religion and science play in my belief? How have my experiences as a sexual minority or with persons who are homosexual shaped my view?

Developmental Concept. Many people believe that being a sexual minority is the result of life experiences. One popular opinion is that a negative heterosexual, or "normal," sexual experience has the ability to turn a straight person into an LGBTQ. This opinion carries with it the implication that if that person had a corrective heterosexual experience, the sexual orientation would automatically change. Although the research continues to support that many sexual minority adults have had opposite-gender sexual experiences (Rosario, Schrimshaw, Hunter, & Braun, 2006), the research does not support this rationale for the development of sexual identity. Another opinion is that the young LGBTQ was enticed into the fold by an adult who practiced a minority sexual orientation, as if somehow young people could be molded into becoming LGBTQ against their will. Again, the research does not provide evidence to justify that stance.

You have probably been introduced to Freud's work in psychoanalytic theory and encountered his position on homosexuality. Freud believed that part of our normal sexual development included a homoerotic phase. During this time, he posited, if a male was close to his mother and had a poor relationship with his father, he might become gay. Similarly, young females who became fixated on the penis, which you may have heard described as penis envy, might become a lesbian as the result of this phase. Research does not support the attachment to one parent over another as a phenomenon that can be singled out as precipitating sexual minority status in adulthood.

Can You Choose Your Sexual Identity?   Finally, there is the concept of choice. Because self-identification is a critical factor in sexual identity, one's opinion about one's sexuality matters. Men are more likely to identify as gay or straight. Women are more likely to say they base their relationships on the person rather than the gender. Some people are able to be with either sex and ultimately choose to be with the same sex because of increased satisfaction in that relationship.

Biological Issues.   The nature side of the nature versus nurture debate addresses biological differences. In other words, is it possible that sexual minorities are born this way? Many LGBTQs would argue strongly, "Of course, it is biologically based; who would choose to be marginalized in our society as a sexual minority?" Scientific evidence points to clear biochemical and structural differences between homosexual and heterosexual men. Brain differences are evident post mortem, which still leaves open the possibility that those changes occurred across the life span rather than being present from birth. A strong link exists between being LGBTQ as an adult and some elements of gender nonconformity in childhood (Skidmore, Linsemeier, & Bailey, 2006). More gay and lesbian men and women did not fit traditional masculine and feminine roles in childhood than was the case with their heterosexual counterparts. More LGBTQs than heterosexuals believe it to be the way one is at birth. Imagine how your own values will impact your work with clients of differing sexual orientations across the continuum.

Role of Religion

What about religion? Many religions eschew the existence of homosexuality. From a North American Judeo-Christian standpoint, homosexuality is generally viewed as counter to religious ideals. One factor in the development of this view is that the traditional role of sexual activity from a Judea-Christian perspective is for the purpose of reproduction, not pleasure. As such, there is little room for sexual activities that do not allow for procreation. However, different belief systems currently exist within the Judeo-Christian culture, with some denominations being more open to homosexuality as a valid sexual identity. Recent changes, including the ordination of a gay bishop in the Episcopal Church in 2003, are evidence of growing acceptance of sexual minority status even within Christian doctrine.

Cultural Perspectives

There are differences in perception of being LGBTQ across cultures. Cuban, Mexican, and other Latin cultures may view gay men as an affront to the concept of machismo. Other countries are more supportive of sexual minorities and have enacted laws to protect their civil rights. The double minority of being LGBTQ combined with ethnicity creates tremendous difficulty. In effect, these individuals learn to live in three distinct communities: the LGBTQ community, the ethnic minority community, and the larger society. At least one study confirms that African American gays and lesbians experience multiple stigmatized social statuses, resulting in greater depression rates (Cochran & Mays, 1994).

Oppressed Society

The divergent beliefs about the origins of homosexuality have resulted in sexual minorities being classified as disordered or deviant in our culture. LGBTQs have been oppressed for decades, including the period after World War II when these individuals were actively portrayed as perverts and threats to the American society, not unlike the Communists (Carroll, 2005). Schools feared that LGBTQs would be hired as teachers, churches were resistant to accepting them as members, and the medical community explored numerous cures for homosexuality that would seem ludicrous by today's standards, such as castration and lobotomies. However, the emergence of individuals and groups willing to advocate for the rights of LGBTQs began to create change. In 1973, the American Psychiatric Association removed homosexuality from its *Diagnostic and Statistical Manual of Mental Disorders*. This move sent the strong message that being a sexual minority was not indicative of a psychological disorder. In 1995, the American Counseling Association officially recognized what is now known as the Association of Lesbian, Gay, Bisexual & Transgender Issues in Counseling (ALGBTIC). This organization promotes the rights and responsibilities of LGBTQ counselors and their clients and serves as a voice for sexual minorities within ACA.

Homophobia and Hate Crimes

The LGBTQ community continues to face difficulties despite these reforms. A major factor in living as a sexual minority is the role of societal and individual homophobia. *Homophobia* means any antihomosexual attitude or irrational fear of sexual minorities (Crooks & Baur, 2005). Homophobia is also present in an internalized form in sexual identity development, as discussed later in this chapter. Any beliefs, actions, or statements that marginalize or stigmatize persons who are not heterosexual are forms of homophobia. It is a form of prejudice, not unlike racism, and is unfortunately commonly encountered by the LGBTQ population. Homophobia occurs at the individual, local, and national levels. A long-time U.S. Senator and former Senate majority leader hailing from Mississippi, the home state of the authors of this chapter, once compared homosexuality to kleptomania or alcoholism. Unfortunately, because of his personal beliefs, he took a strong stance in opposing workplace discrimination laws to protect LGBTQ persons. Members of the LGBTQ population routinely encounter homophobia ranging from the national scorn of political leaders to smaller but no less significant acts of harassment. College students who are openly LGBTQ may find their dorm room door covered in derogatory terms. Workplace and housing discrimination frequently occurs. Some LGBTQs fear for their lives in places that are not accepting of their sexual orientation. Of critical concern are hate crimes.

In the United States, 20–25% of lesbians and gays report having been victims of hate crimes (Herek, Cogan, & Gillis, 1999). Hate crimes can be assault, robbery, or even murder and are the extreme behavioral counterparts to the verbal insults and harassment experienced so frequently by LGBTQs. Fortunately, in 1990 the United States enacted the Hate Crimes Statistics Act to fund the tracking and documentation of hate crimes. This type of legislation has the potential to reduce the prevalence of such acts against LGBTQs. A classic example of a hate crime due to sexual orientation was the case of Matthew Sheppard, a Wyoming college student brutally beaten to death in 1998. Statistics prior to 2005 reveal that U.S. hate crimes this extreme have mostly been perpetrated by males. Although some theorize that these crimes are caused by a hatred of homosexuals, the majority of the perpetrators of these crimes indicate that they are more likely to have committed them to assert their own masculinity, which they believe has been threatened by the presence of homosexuals (Maurer, 1999, as cited in Crooks & Baur, 2005). There is some evidence that hate crimes are perpetrated by those trying to sublimate their own feelings of homosexuality. Classic research by Kantor (1998, as cited in Crooks & Baur, 2005) shows that although homophobic men denied feeling sexually aroused by explicit gay videos, measures of physical arousal indicated otherwise. This discrepancy probably creates discord in the homophobic male capable of acting out violently via hate crimes.

Ethics of Working With the LGBTQ Population

The 2005 ACA *Code of Ethics* guides counselors in their provision of counseling services. The code specifically addresses issues of diversity and counselor values. When counseling clients of sexual minority status, counselors must examine their own personal values, opinions, and biases. This examination occurs regardless of the sexual identity of the counselor. Code A.5.a specifically states that counselors must have an awareness of their own values and biases and must not impose them onto their clients (ACA, 2005). Additionally, clients have a right to fair and nondiscriminatory treatment that takes their personal culture into account. Later we will discuss the challenges faced by counselors working with the LGBTQ population.

Reparative or Conversion Therapy

A significant ethical issue currently discussed in the literature is the idea of reparative or conversion therapy, which is aimed at changing a client's homosexual orientation to heterosexual. The belief is that the client's LGBTQ identity is wrong, abnormal, or indicative of pathology and thus must be altered for the client to be mentally healthy. Given the previously discussed removal of homosexuality from the *DSM*, it is clear that conversion therapy is in opposition to the position of the American Psychiatric Association. Additionally, the American Counseling Association passed a resolution in 1999 stating that conversion therapy is not a "cure" for LGBTQ clients and is an unproved method in opposition to mental health standards.

Conversion therapy tends to come from a Christian perspective. Despite some evidence of limited behavioral change for clients seeking out such treatment, there is no research indicating its effectiveness in changing sexual orientation (Forstein, 2001). Further, research supports the idea that reparative or conversion methods can be harmful to those who participate in the process (Whitman, Glosoff, Kocet, & Tarvydas, 2006). Consequently, ACA has interpreted its own code of ethics in light of the realities that such practices exist and found that it is not ethical for counselors to offer such services because they are unproven, potentially damaging, and outside the scope of training offered or acknowledged by ACA (Whitman et al., 2006).

Boundary Issues

An additional ethical consideration relates to boundary issues and dual relationships as addressed in the ACA *Code of Ethics*. Multiple relationships between counselors and their clients occur when a relationship exists outside the counseling milieu. Imagine being an LGBTQ counselor who specializes in working with LGBTQ clients. Such a specialty is not uncommon as LGBTQ clients are often more comfortable with counselors of sexual minority status. However, the LGBTQ community is often a relatively small subculture, with LGBTQ persons often going to the same restaurants, bars, athletic clubs, and churches. The counselor might find it difficult to participate in LGBTQ activities without encountering clients. It would be unreasonable to expect these counselors to restrict their social lives to avoid such circumstantial encounters (Remley & Herlihy, 2007). Realistically, LGBTQ counselors must develop strategies to manage and minimize client contact within the LGBTQ community. We suggest the counselor examine the potential risks to both client and counselor, including the nature of the counseling and the frequency of potential client–counselor contact. An open discussion of these risks and appropriate behaviors in each setting, along with written informed consent, is advised. Regular supervision can further protect the interests of both counselor and client.

Ethics of Counselor Training

The ACA *Code of Ethics* (2005) outlines a number of responsibilities for counselor educators who are training students in graduate programs of counseling. Specifically, such programs and their faculty members are required to infuse multicultural diversity throughout the curriculum. Teaching LGBTQ identity development models provides beginning counselors with a foundation to appreciate the inherent concerns in a broad client population. Although such concepts may be included in sexuality counseling or in a social and cultural course, most training programs remain deficient in their preparation of students to counsel sexual minorities (Matthews, 2005).

Nevertheless, counselor education programs should "serve as models of affirmative counseling with gay, lesbian and bisexual clients" (Matthews, 2005, p. 177). For example, you will be exposed to a variety of client types in your program, and there will be emphasis placed on age, gender, race, and ethnicity. Progressive training programs also include sexual minority populations in considering what truly constitutes a diverse client population. Most important, counselor education programs that foster an atmosphere of openness in dialogue about LGBTQ concerns and actively promote teaching concepts relevant to this population provide counselors in training with the richest educational experiences (Matthews, 2005). Your class has already begun this process by using this text and exposing you to sexual identity development models, presenting client concerns, and effective interventions for the LGBTQ population.

Sexual Identity Development

Counselors working with LGBTQ clients have an obligation to understand the process of sexual identity development. This process is likened to a "coming out to the self." A number of theories and models exist, and we will highlight a few to provide you with a broad understanding of a complex process. Following a general overview of sexual identity development phases, we will cover the Cass model, as well as the McCarn and Fassinger model. Note that although developmental in nature, these models are not tied to specific chronological ages. Individuals begin this process at different points along the life span. Many are first confronted with sexual identity issues in adolescence, but others may not begin the process until adulthood. It is important to individualize the models to fit the client.

General Stages

The sexual majority population is often unaware of the process of sexual identity development. Coming out, or disclosing one's sexual minority status, may be the only element of this process that heterosexuals experience. Realistically, coming out is only one part of the overall sexual identity development process. In general, there is an initial step of self-acknowledgment, in which the person realizes a difference in sexual attitudes, beliefs, desires, and perhaps behaviors than the heterosexual world espouses. Self-acknowledgment begins a complex process of self-acceptance, in which the LGBTQ person must battle internalized homophobia and confusion over being LGBTQ. There is often a fear of losing significant relationships, such as those with parents, other family, and close friends. LGBTQ individuals may presume that heterosexuals will not accept their sexual status and thus hide their sexual orientation from important people in their lives.

Disclosure comes only after some measure of self-acceptance and is most closely linked with coming out. Knowing you are LGBTQ and feeling unable to disclose it is a terrifying experience. It may be that you like to sing, that you are in college, or that you are Southern. Now imagine being unable to share that fact about yourself with others and working actively to hide it. That is similar to what it feels like to be closeted as a LGBTQ. The risk of exposure, of disclosing sexual orientation, can be tremendous.

Disclosure for the LGBTQ population rarely comes without some consequence. Disclosure tends to occur in stages: first to those expected to be most accepting, such as other LGBTQs and friends that the person views as safe. Families are often the last to be told. Parents, the majority of whom are heterosexual, may wonder where they went wrong. The fear of family and friends' reactions can keep a LGBTQ person closeted for years or for a lifetime.

Cass Model

The 1979 Cass (1984) model identified six developmental phases in the sexual identity process: (a) identity confusion, (b) identity comparison, (c) identity tolerance, (d) identity acceptance, (e) identity pride, and (f) identity synthesis. The Cass model assumes the person begins with a previously accepted, culturally appropriate, heterosexual identity. In the identity confusion stage, this perceived reality is challenged for the first time. After that, the individual begins to accept the possibility that they may be LGBTQ during the identity comparison stage. Upon this realization, identity tolerance begins, and the person seeks out other LGBTQs but does not make any public disclosures about orientation. In fact, the person is quite secretive during this phase of exploration and may even live a double life while bridging the gap between being straight and being gay. The fourth stage, identity acceptance, is marked by an identity acceptance and selective disclosure of that acceptance. With these disclosures comes a period of identity pride, during which individuals are more vocal about their sexual orientation and may participate socially and politically in the larger LGBTQ culture. Characteristic of this stage is also a tendency to reject traditional heterosexual values in an effort to solidify the LGBTQ identity. Finally, the LGBTQ individual lands in identity synthesis, during which time sexual identity takes its place as only one part of the person's larger identity.

McCarn and Fassinger Model

Additional perspectives relative to lesbian identity development can enhance the counselor's understanding of working with the LGBTQ client. McCarn and Fassinger (1996) proposed their model of lesbian identity formation to address what they saw as deficits in the more generic sexual identity development models and "to be broadly inclusive of the diverse paths one may take to comfortable, integrated lesbianism" (pp. 520–521). This model views lesbian identity formation through the simultaneous lenses of individual sexual identity and the larger group membership identity of being a lesbian by taking both internal and external perspectives. McCarn and Fassinger posit that the process occurs over the four phases of Awareness, Exploration, Deepening Commitment, and Internalization/Synthesis. In Awareness, the individual feels different and notices in the larger community that there are others who have nonheterosexual orientations. During Exploration, the woman notes her erotic feelings and preferences toward other women and begins to explore externally her feelings about the LGBTQ society. A greater self-understanding occurs during the internal part of the Deepening Commitment phase, with a growing awareness of the external consequences of being lesbian, such as marginalization and oppression. Finally, in the Internalization/Synthesis phase, the lesbian begins to develop an overall identity as a woman that includes her sexual identity, as well as reformulating her identity as a member of minority group. The authors of this model recognize that women may develop a clearer self-identity internally prior to reaching such a sense with the larger world. However, the ultimate result of this process is a woman who feels a sense of safety, security, and self-love in her lesbian identity across contexts.

Understanding the role of sexual identity development is critical to effective counseling of LGBTQ clients. Sexual identity development is complex and burdened by the reality of homophobia (McCarn & Fassinger, 1996). Although a counselor cannot assume that the client's presenting concerns will be predicated on sexual identity, it is impossible to consider counseling someone of LGBTQ status without understanding the process of LGBTQ identity formation. The informed and empathic helper is more easily able to enter into the worldview of a diverse client population. Appreciating sexual identity developmental milestones facilitates this understanding. Again, it is presumptive to assume that the presenting concern will center around sexual identity, but equally presumptive to assume that LGBTQ clients have experienced no negative consequences as their sexual identity has emerged.

Counseling the LGBTQ Client

Sexual minorities utilize mental health services at a higher rate than the general population, with an estimated 25%–65% of the lesbian and gay population seeking therapy at some time (Burckell & Goldfried, 2006; Twist, Murphy, Green, & Palmanteer, 2006). To prepare to work with sexual minorities, we again recommend that you begin by examining your own potential covert and overt biases and prejudices, because counselors are likely to be the product of "a society strong in its stance against homosexuality, rendering them vulnerable to the heterosexist attitudes and behaviors present in the environments in which they are immersed," (Savage, Harley, & Nowak, 2005, p. 132).

Many counselors report the classic, and often well intentioned, "I treat everyone the same" attitude, which is frequently an attempt to present themselves as nondiscriminatory. In fact, some research indicates that avoidance behaviors toward sexual minority clients by counselors are not because of antigay beliefs, but because of social anxiety due to fear of offending an LGBTQ individual (Mohr, 2002). Nevertheless, counselors must strive to become aware of the complexities of membership in a sexual minority and go beyond a naive "acceptance" of sexual orientation to a proactive stance that values the individual's sexual orientation. Many LGBTQ clients will prescreen counselors to determine their attitude toward sexual minority clients. To this end, counselors are expected to be affirming in their beliefs and practices with LGBTQ clients and their culture.

LGBTQ-Affirming Counseling

Some simple counselor practices that can reflect LGBTQ-affirming attitudes include adapting paperwork to allow clients the opportunity to indicate they are LGBTQ and to accurately describe the nature of their intimate relationships beyond the basic limiting categories of "married," "single," or "divorced" (Matthews, Selvidge, & Fisher, 2005). The addition of relationship categories such as "partner" or "life partner" may allow a more complete expression of the client's significant relationships. Counselors are also encouraged to offer outreach programs and to provide books and other literature specific to LBGTQ clients, such as *The Advocate*, in the waiting area and counseling offices. An awareness and understanding of the gay subculture, with resources from community centers, churches, bookstores, and support groups for LGBTQ clients, can communicate that the counselor is available to provide a safe and nurturing environment essential for establishing a trusting relationship between counselor and client.

Research posits that counselors who are viewed most competent by LGBTQ clients are those who "were capable of understanding the gay community, who disclosed experiences of working with the gay community, who normalized homosexuality, and who allowed clients to thoroughly explore their sexuality and relationships" (Burckell & Goldfried, 2006, p. 33). In contrast, when a counselor is reluctant or tentative in asking questions about the individual's sexual identity, assumes heterosexuality, or uses heterosexually biased language and traditions, they are viewed as less helpful, regardless of the individual's presenting issue.

In summary, familiarity with the following areas is recommended when counseling sexual minority clients: attitudes about homosexuality and specific sexual acts, awareness of stigmatization and oppression, familiarity with LGBTQ lifestyles, and knowledge about developmental stages of sexual orientation, issues of coming out, and the meaning of a sexual minority identity (Perry & Barry, 1998; Spitalnick & McNair, 2005; Twist et al., 2006).

Presenting Issues in Counseling

The concerns and problems that bring the LBGTQ client to counseling are as unique and complex as each individual. Anxiety, depression, relationship problems, parenting issues, financial stresses, substance abuse, and sexually compulsive behaviors are just a few of the problems affecting the emotional health of both heterosexual and sexual minority clients. As pointed out earlier in this chapter, the LBGTQ client may or may not be entering counseling to address the issue of sexual orientation, and careful attention to the client's personal concerns during the beginning phase of counseling will help to assure that the counselor does not stereotype the client by assuming sexual identity concerns as primary to the counseling milieu. However, most sexual minority clients face common social, political, and legal realities that make up the context of the client's experiences (Spitalnick & McNair, 2005). As a way to integrate an LGBTQ worldview into the counseling context with the presenting concern, Fassinger and Richie (1997) suggest the counselor consider sexual orientation as a culturally specific variable within the broader spectrum of presenting issues.

Coming Out

The coming out process is not linear and, like all identity development, is a continuum of integrated experiences with the potential for growth. Many LGBTQ persons seek counseling for help in addressing both the personal and societal issues associated with the recognition of membership in a sexual minority group. It is important for you to recognize that awareness of one's sexual orientation can occur at any age. As discussed in the Cass identity model, coming out indicates a major shift in one's personal identity, and for many clients it is the most important event in their lives (Pope et al., 2004). Some sexual minority clients recognize that they are "different" and are confused by their attraction to the same sex during adolescence; others come to the realization that they are gay or lesbian after being married and having children with someone of the opposite sex. Obviously, the chronological age and circumstances of the client dictate the counselor's course of action.

During the coming out stage, the recognition that one's sexual orientation is juxtaposed to that which is culturally accepted can result in an overwhelming sense of fear and isolation. Many LGBTQ clients present with issues of depression, anxiety, isolation, and numerous psychosocial concerns without initially revealing their sexual orientation to the counselor for fear of rejection.

Coming Out as an Adolescent.   Romantic relationships and dating are a key developmental task during adolescence, and most LGBTQ individuals realize their same-sex attractions during this developmental period. However, the opportunity for dating someone of the same sex is seldom an option for the LGBTQ teen. In fact, the stigma attached to same-sex desire is most pronounced at this developmental stage (D'Augelli, 1996; Waldner & Magruder, 1999). Imagine that you are a teen attracted to someone of your same sex. How would you handle selecting a date to the prom? What would be the risks if you followed your desires, and what would you lose if you did not? The risks either way are very real. Some believe that LGBTQ teens are at disproportionate risk for suicide and depression (Hartstein, 1996; Saulnier, 1998), but DeAngelis (2002) found little difference in suicide rate between LGBTQ and heterosexual youth. Nevertheless, the LGBTQ adolescent is at very high risk for harassment, violence, and hate crimes that may require medical attention (Blake, Ledsky, Lehman & Goodenow, 2001; Russell, Franz, & Driscoll, 2001). To avoid these risks, many LGBTQ teens report dating members of the opposite sex and capitulating to peer pressures to engage in heterosexual experiences to mask their homosexuality (Savin-Williams, 1994).

Peer and family responses can vary widely. Imagine telling your family that you believe you might be gay or lesbian. The counselor has an obligation to help the

LGBTQ client carefully assess the risks involved if they seriously consider disclosing their sexual orientation to others. The client's expected reactions and responses can be discussed, as some clients may have unrealistic expectations. It is helpful for the counselor to explore any hesitation by the client and to assist the client in anticipating possible outcomes. A negative experience with sexual orientation disclosure can result in further feelings of rejection and stigmatization that may exacerbate the psychological distresses and associated risk-related behaviors (Lemoire & Chen, 2005).

Many LGBTQ adolescents choose not to tell their parents. Many LGBTQ clients do not disclose their sexual identity to their parents until well into adulthood, if at all. However, some adolescents' parents discover their child's emerging sexual identity by reading their journals or personal notes. The first reaction by parents is often to seek help for the child to "fix" the teen's sexual orientation. Thus, the adolescent's disclosure and coming out process is played out in the realm of family counseling, requiring counselor sensitivity for all the parties involved. In families where previous conflicts are evident, the LGBTQ teen's motivation for disclosure may represent a negative vehicle for hostile acting out. When this happens, the LGBTQ teen may be scapegoated and sexual orientation blamed for the family's conflicts. When possible, disclosure should be used productively and as a bridge to increase family intimacy, rather than as a weapon to further alienate family members.

If the client's family and peers are not able to affirm and support the LGBTQ client, the counselor can help the client consider how chosen support and friend networks can become, in effect, their new family of origin. During the initial crisis, the counselor may need to temporarily assume the parent role, as parents who are in need of emotional support themselves are frequently unable to provide support for their child. When conflicts cannot be resolved, the clash over the teen's sexual identity puts the adolescent at risk for depression, anxiety, and peer rejection. Sometimes the teen is kicked out or runs away and becomes homeless as a result of the family's rejection (Savin-Williams, 1994).

Case Study

Steve is a 16-year-old junior in high school who comes to counseling reporting anxiety and sleeplessness. He says that he is often afraid to fall asleep and listens to the radio, sometimes all night. He bites his fingernails to the quick. He reports that when he does fall asleep, he has dreams that make him feel like he is going crazy. His dreams are mostly about being chased or having someone break into his room.

Steve lives with his mother, stepfather, and two half-brothers in a rural town in the Southern United States. Steve's father died from suicide 2 years after his mother and father were divorced because of his father's mental health problems. Steve's mother worries because Steve and his stepfather do not get along. Steve has a good relationship with his two younger half-brothers. Steve's extended family consists of fraternal grandparents and an uncle who is a successful openly gay business person. His uncle visits often and phones regularly. Once Steve mentioned that he didn't want to be like his uncle because "he's weird."

Steve says he has difficulty with peers at school and indicated that people at his school were "jerks." He says he does have several close friends who share his view of the "jerks." He does not share any significant dating experiences or relationships, but reports one of the girls in his group of friends thinks she might be "gay." They attend the school dances and activities together.

Steve never made any other reference to his sexual orientation; instead, he continued to focus on fears of "going crazy." As Steve began to discuss his fears, the counselor suspects that Steve is gay and in the sexual confusion/identity stage of development. The counselor determined that other than a diagnosis of anxiety, there are no other mental illness symptoms present. The counselor decided to work with Steve, reassuring him that he was not "crazy" and teaching him methods for addressing his anxiety.

Questions for discussion:

1. What are you initial thoughts and assumptions regarding Steve and his family?
2. Would you initiate a discussion with Steve about sexual orientation at this stage of counseling?
3. Do you think that sexual orientation concerns may have played a role in his father's mental health issues that resulted in suicide?
4. Would you suggest a family session?
5. Who would you include in the family session?
6. What risks would you foresee for Steve if he acknowledges that he might be gay?

The Role of the School Counselor.   It is encouraging that counselor education programs provide a venue that directs school counselors to examine personal beliefs and to become knowledgeable about LGBTQ student issues. However, this training does not always translate into more proactive measures to create a safe environment for LBGTQ students and their families.

Weiler (2003) suggests that LBGTQ students are most vulnerable in middle and high school. School counselors and principals "should examine their school climate and ensure that students are taught positive, nonbiased behavior" in an effort to provide a safe and open climate for all students' growth and development (Weiler, 2003, p. 11). Several steps to provide a more supportive school atmosphere for the LGBTQ student are suggested:

- Establish a policy that forbids jokes, slurs, or comments the degrade sexual minorities
- Provide education and awareness sessions for teachers and administration
- Use film, video, and library resources that present LGBTQ persons in a positive light
- Place LBGTQ literature and resources in the counselor's office and bulletin boards
- Establish support groups for those students exploring sexual orientation

Coming Out in Adulthood.   Some LGBTQ persons deny their sexual orientation for many years. When individuals are faced with the realization that they are gay, lesbian, or bisexual, they may seek to experiment with same-sex relationships without coming out to their spouse, children, or parents. The counselor can help clients seek a balance between the need for self-disclosure and self-protective coping skills, especially regarding employment risks, potential divorce proceedings, rejection or acceptance by children, and legal issues such as custody and visitation of minor children. Some marriages will end in divorce; some spouses will choose to remain married and reevaluate the terms of the marriage. Bisexual clients often choose a heterosexual relationship because they enjoy the benefits of a traditional family.

Referrals to support groups for both the spouse and the children can give family members a time to become informed and adjust as they adapt to having a sexual-minority spouse or parent. Special attention must be paid to coming out in families from cultures with traditional or punitive attitudes toward homosexuality. For example, the intensity of homophobia is much stronger in Asian cultures. Clients who are members in multiple minority groups face tremendous hardship and challenges. Lesbian women of color face at least three virulent forms of discrimination: sexism, heterosexism, and racism (Pope et al., 2004). Clients who are members of multiple minority groups need help to retain desired positive cultural influences while minimizing any negative cultural representations.

Coming out at any age can be an act of courage with a desire for honesty and recognition despite worries of rejection, anger, disappointment, shame, and possible physical and psychological rejection. Coming out is associated with better overall mental health, as self-acceptance is at the root of living an authentic life.

Parenting Issues

The actual numbers of LGBTQ families in the United States is difficult to determine, as many of these families fear discrimination, rejection, and legal implications. It has been estimated that between 2 and 14 million children are living with LBGTQ parents, and this appears to be an increasing trend (Lambert, 2005; Tasker, 2005). Lesbian and gay parents face common and unique challenges compared with heterosexual parents.

Unfounded fears that LGBTQ parents are incapable of rearing "healthy" children permeate traditional family institutions. Contrary to the view that LGBTQ parents are unfit for parenthood, some research suggests the opposite. In fact, research demonstrates that LGBTQ parents demonstrate numerous positive parenting skills. For example, LGBTQ parents have children who exhibit a more mature social consciousness than children reared by heterosexual parents (Negy & McKinney, 2006). In addition, LGBTQ parents adopt a child-centered approach and have partners who are highly committed to maintaining family integrity (Lynch, 2000; Tasker, 2005).

Gay fathers, when compared with heterosexual fathers, do not differ in their intimacy or involvement with their children and show higher levels of warmth and responsiveness combined with positive controls and limit-setting (Lambert, 2005; Tasker, 2005). Both lesbian mothers and gay fathers exhibited more reasoning strategies when disciplining their children (Tasker, 2005). Contrary to previous assumptions that the sexual orientation of the parents would propagate problems for the children, Kurdek (2004) found that the offspring of LGBTQ parents were as personally and socially successful as the children of heterosexual parents.

Yet, institutionalized prejudice continues to prevent LGBTQ parents from adopting or fostering children. Even when gay and lesbian adults show an interest and willingness to foster and adopt, public agencies continue to resist welcoming LGBTQ parents, in spite of a well-documented shortage of foster homes (Downs & James, 2006; Tyebjee, 2003). Counselors who work with LGBTQ families are advised to review the prevailing laws and attitudes of the courts in their particular geographical region and be prepared to advocate for clients when necessary.

Relationship Issues

Gay and lesbian relationships are both similar to and different from heterosexual relationships. A major difference is society's sanctioning of heterosexual relationships through marriage and the institutional denial of legal and civil rights for same-sex couples. Unlike their heterosexual counterparts, sexual minority couples face broad-ranging institutional discrimination. The ability to share insurance and pension benefits, to care for ill partners, to be recognized as rightful inheritors, and to be granted child custody is driven by marital status, which in most states is denied to same sex couples.

Gay and lesbian couples seek therapy for a variety of reasons, including sexual problems, struggles to seek a balance between intimacy and autonomy, conflicts around financial matters, and power issues (Cove & Boyle, 2002; Forstein, 1994). Both LGBTQ and heterosexual couples desire both attachment and autonomy in their relationships (Spiklnick & McNair, 2005). However, LGBTQ relationships face greater psychosocial stressors and must deal with the societal stigma that prevents many sexual minority couples from being open about their relationships. Common problems, such as internalized homophobia, can generate negative outlooks for finding and maintaining long-term relationships (Downey & Friedman, 1995).

Another major difference between heterosexual and LGBTQ relationships is the influence of sex role behaviors. Sex role behaviors relating to task assignment, such as yardwork and bill paying, are traditionally assigned as male or female duties. Task assignments for the LGBTQ couple tend to be less rigid and allow for more flexible and creative division of labor (Lesser & Pope, 2007; Spitalnick & McNair, 2005).

This same flexibility in determining household responsibilities can also be a source of stress. Same-sex couples report fewer role models, which may leave the same-sex couple needing the help of the counselor to negotiate conflicts regarding money, housework, and child-rearing responsibilities (MacDonald, 1998). Open and non-gender-biased feedback can help the same-sex couple successfully negotiate areas of potential conflict and divide household tasks equitably, based on individual choice rather than traditional gender role assignment.

When counseling a sexual minority couple, the counselor must be knowledgeable and comfortable in discussing sexual behavior patterns, concerns, and potential sexual disorders. Same-sex couples may want to negotiate sexual exclusivity within a range of options generally accepted within the LGBTQ community but contrary to conservative monogamous models. In addition, significant differences have been found between gay and lesbian sexual expectations and practices.

Cove and Boyle (2002) found that the rate of cohabitation and sexual exclusivity is lower in gay couples than in lesbian and heterosexual couples. Reported rates of monogamy put monogamy for gay men at 48% to 63% (Spitalnick & McNair, 2005). Gay couples are generally more sexually active and tend to maintain greater autonomy than lesbian or heterosexual couples (Martell & Prince, 2005). This may be attributed to sex-role socialization, which teaches men to separate sex and love, to be sexually active, to be independent, and to have difficulty in expressing emotions, all of which may inhibit the development of intimacy (Perry & Barry, 1998; Spitalnick & McNair, 2005). You will want to explore the gay couple's satisfaction with their level of intimacy and exclusivity with an open and nonjudgmental attitude, which may prove to be a challenge for the counselor who has a traditional view of "healthy" relationships based on monogamy. Sexual relationships outside the primary relationship are not always considered an affair. The context of the couple's relationship will determine the effect such an activity will have on the couple (Martell & Prince, 2005). Although some heterosexual and lesbian couples agree to nonmonogamous relationships, the acceptance of sexual activity outside a committed relationship is more relevant to gay couples (Martell & Prince, 2005).

Cove and Boyle (2002) report several concerns in the sexual relationships of gay men. They are likely to report negative psychological states during or after sexual encounters, which may reflect an internalized negative sexual identity. Gay men report a wider variety of sexual behaviors and rank their importance differently from heterosexual men. There is less emphasis on penetration, and they are more likely to report difficulties associated with masturbation and oral sex (Cove & Boyle, 2002).

The informed counselor will be aware that most of the traditional assessments and interventions for sexual concerns assume a female partner, focus on penis–vagina intercourse, and may not be appropriate for assessing sexual concerns in LGBTQ couples. The counselor should seek to incorporate a model of sexual function and dysfunction for gay couples separate from those behaviors and concerns reported by heterosexual males (Spitalnick & McNair, 2005).

The beginning counselor also needs a working knowledge of intimacy and sexual behaviors common for lesbian couples. Research reports that lesbian couples have strong sexual desire and high levels of sexual activity early in the relationship, followed by a decline in sexual activity within the first few years of the relationship (Nichols, 1995, as cited in Spitalnick & McNair, 2005). Most lesbian couples value monogamy, romantic love, and emotional intimacy more than do gay couples (Downey & Friedman, 1995) and report more nongenital sexual behavior, such as hugging, cuddling, and kissing, than either gay or heterosexual couples (James & Murphy, 1998). It is not unusual for lesbians to remain friends with ex-partners after becoming involved with a new partner (Clunis & Green, 2000).

In spite of the apparent emotional closeness and tenderness expressed by lesbian couples, more than half of these lesbian partners desired more sexual contact (Downey & Friedman, 1995). To address sexual desire issues in lesbian couples, MacDonald (1998) suggests that counselors employ techniques that aim to facilitate greater sexual intimacy. Addressing the cultural taboo of the female as sexual instigator may allow the cultural context of gender-associated sexual behavior to be addressed openly. Spitalnick and McNair (2005) suggest that informed and supportive counseling may aid the lesbian couple in creating a satisfying relationship that mirrors each partner's sexual desires and expectations.

Domestic Violence

Domestic violence is a major social and health problem in the United States and is prevalent in the LGBTQ community. Although Walker (2000) reports a strong pattern of the incidence of domestic violence and high incidence of abuse in the family of origin, this does not hold true for the families of origin of same-sex partners who experience domestic violence. This may indicate that same-sex partners experience domestic violence more as a result of external societal pressures rather than from exposure to previous violent family behaviors.

Domestic violence between same-sex partners has largely been avoided by governments, law enforcement, and society (Peterman & Dixon, 2003). Isolation, embarrassment, and fears have prevented same-sex partners from seeking help outside their communities. The stereotype that women are not abusive or violent continues to keep lesbian partner abuse largely ignored (Walker, 2000). In addition to the threat of physical violence, lesbian relationships have an increased risk of psychological abuse, including the threat of exposure of their partner's sexual preference to friends, family, community, church, or employer (Peterman & Dixon, 2003).

The lack of support groups, shelters, and treatment programs devoted to the issue of domestic violence among LBGTQ clients further intensifies the problem. Some support groups reportedly will not allow gay men to attend meetings due to the volatility among heterosexual participants already in the groups (Friess, 1997, as cited in Peterman & Dixon, 2003). When there is suspicion of abuse, counselors need to be sensitive to the issues that keep same-sex partners from seeking help. Advocacy for domestic violence programs that are sensitive to the complexities of same-sex relationships is imperative.

Substance Abuse and Addiction

Counselors have long considered the LGBTQ population at risk for alcohol and drug abuse and addiction. Hughes and Eliason (2002) report that although actual levels of abuse and addiction have declined, the risk continues within the LGBTQ population. Substance abuse may be related to conflicts around sexual orientation, with drinking or using drugs providing access to forbidden desires, as well as serving as a coping mechanism for handling the psychological fallout of membership as a sexual minority (Cheng, 2003; Matthews, Lorah, & Fenton, 2006). To compound the risk of substance abuse and addiction, the gay bar is one of the most accessible routes to explore sexual identity in the LGBTQ community.

Alarmingly, many addiction counselors lack information and training with the LGBTQ community and display negative or ambivalent attitudes toward sexual minority clients. They also frequently fail to address sexual orientation issues and are reluctant to refer LGBTQ clients to others who have specialized training (Eliason, 2000; Matthews et al., 2005).

Matthews et al. (2006) highlight several important factors for counselors to keep in mind when working with LGBTQ persons with substance abuse or addiction concerns. First, the counselor ought to make a conscientious effort to directly address sexual orientation rather than waiting for the clients to raise the issue. The LGBTQ client faces a double dose of shame: internalized shame of sexual orientation and the shame associated with addiction. The counselor can reduce the shame and anxiety by normalizing a client's status as a sexual minority so that the substance abuse may be directly addressed. This may even be more critical when counseling occurs in residential or group settings. Some LGBTQ clients report they first observed how minorities were treated in recovery programs before deciding whether to be open with their sexual identity. "When it was clear that bias and prejudice would not be tolerated in a facility, participants felt safer with respect to their sexual orientation," (Matthews et al., 2006, p. 125). Clients need the counselor to help them find a balance between knowing when it is important to be honest in revealing and exploring their sexual orientation and when they should necessarily be cautious. Fortunately, many urban areas offer gay- and lesbian-specific Alcoholics Anonymous and Narcotics Anonymous meetings that may help the LGBTQ in recovery bridge this gap.

Sexual Addiction and Compulsive Sexual Behavior

An often overlooked concern is sexual addiction and compulsive sexual behaviors, which affect both the heterosexual and LGBTQ populations. Sexual addiction can be defined as any sexually related, compulsive behavior that interferes with normal living and causes severe stress in relationships. When working with the LGBTQ sexually compulsive client, the counselor will need a clear view of how being a sexual minority has affected the client's life. Obtaining a thorough sexual history within the context of the client's sexual identity can "help differentiate between the highly sexually active client and the client who is sexually compulsive" (Perry & Barry, 1998, p. 121). Many times the coming out process, regardless of the client's chronological age, includes a period of high sexual activity and general recklessness, which resembles the behavior of the stereotypical college freshman. Both counselor and client must understand that sexual orientation is not the cause of risk-related behavior but may represent an externalization of the hatred and oppression directed toward the client. This period can last from several months to several years. Nevertheless, clients exhibiting this sort of developmental behavior may need assessment for sexual compulsivity.

Religion and Spirituality

Just as mental health professionals have recognized the importance of inquiring about other aspects of culture, they should also inquire about spiritual beliefs and deeply held convictions that enable our clients to make meaning of their lives. Careful inquiry into the meaning associated with religion and spiritual expression is useful to understand the role of religion in the life of the LGBTQ client. Many gays and lesbians continue to be affiliated with the religious group where they were raised. Others choose to attend services at interdenominational churches whose ministry is directly focused on the

LGBTQ population. Conflicts arise when the beliefs of their religious denomination conflict with their sexual orientation. Some LGBTQ clients who have been turned away from church view "religion" with misgiving. Many have been denied marriage rights, while others have been denied ordination or leadership positions within their religious group.

Nevertheless, the depth to which religious identity can be paramount in the psyche cannot be underestimated (Haldeman, 2004). Miranti (1996) notes that "the spiritual and/or religious dimensions inherent in each individual could possibly be the most salient cultural identity" (p. 117). The task of the counselor is to help the client resolve internal conflicts about sexuality and religion and incorporate these potentially incongruent aspects of identity into a synthesized whole. The counselor must maintain a facilitative stance and be particularly vigilant that personal values do not negate the clients' experience of religion or sexuality.

The vast majority of those seeking sexual orientation change therapies do so because of an internal conflict about sexuality and religion (Tozer & Hayes, 2004). We have previously discussed the ethical concerns about conversion therapies. Shidlo and Schroeder (2002) report that the majority of those who undergo conversion therapies experience the treatment as harmful, and participants report associated risks including depression, anxiety, and self-destructive behaviors. Also, a number of distortions and misleading information about same-sex normative life experiences were found to be part of the rationale for conversion therapy (Shidlo & Schroeder, 2002). Nevertheless, Haldeman (2004) warns, "The potential loss of family, community, belief system and core identity is so great, that for some who choose conversion therapy, attempting to change or managing sexual orientation is a steep price, but one they choose to pay" (p. 694).

It is clear that dissonance between sexual and spiritual orientation frequently raises dilemmas for which there are no simple answers. The counselor and client must work carefully, guided by counselor ethics and empirically sound interventions, in the best interests of all concerned.

HIV/AIDS

There have been dramatic advances in the medical treatment of persons with HIV/AIDS. Although HIV/AIDS is no longer considered a "gay person's" disease, the lingering stigma continues to be a barrier to adequate health care resources. People with HIV/AIDS are living longer and often require demanding medical regimens, strict compliance, and complex medical management (Britton, 2000). Clients with HIV/AIDS are dealing with frequent losses and unpredictability in career, partner relationships, their ability to parent minor children, and health status while facing the inevitability of an imminent death. Often HIV-positive clients reexperience the initial shame of belonging to a sexual minority and attempt to keep their diagnosis secret for fear of further rejection by family, friends, and society.

The counselor working with HIV/AIDS clients must walk a fine line between offering hope and remaining present if the client resorts to noncompliance as a way to gain control over their lives. Models that deal with grief and loss can be useful but may prove too one-dimensional. Strategies that provide a strength-based approach, which focuses on helping clients in attaining productive and satisfying lives in spite of their disease, can prove useful. A positive focus on the client's patterns of coping and life skills may increase preventative and medical compliance strategies.

The impact of working with the HIV/AIDS population cannot be denied and can leave the counselor feeling ineffective and disheartened. Yet, we must continue to respect and honor clients as they face incredible odds. Supportive supervision is imperative to help counselors avoid distancing themselves from the client or becoming overly optimistic as they provide a safe place for clients to face the challenges of life with HIV/AIDS.

Career Issues

LGBTQ clients are faced with many decisions relating to the intersection of their employment and their sexual identity. Discrimination against individuals on the basis of their race, ethnic origin, gender, disability, religion, political affiliation, or sexual orientation is, unfortunately, a fact of American society. Counselors who acknowledge potential employment discrimination and address career issues with the sexual minority client provide advantageous groundwork for career exploration (Pope et al., 2004).

An understanding of how individuals construct their own career paths and are influenced by external events can be particularly relevant to understanding career exploration for LGBTQ adolescents (Savickas, 2005). Due to social oppression, sexual minority youth may not be able to negotiate career development at the same time they are beginning to recognize and understand their sexual identity. Counselors can assess where LGBTQ adolescents are placing the majority of their psychological energy and attend to the most salient areas first. A primary focus on sexual identity, however, may prevent the allocation of resources to career development (Schmidt & Nilsson, 2006). Thus, LGBTQ youth may be coping with career tasks at a slower pace and will probably address career development at a later developmental stage.

Counselors must be sensitive to workplace sexual discrimination issues and provide support for the sexual minority client. For example, counselors might help clients prepare for prevalent workplace bias and reduce interview anxiety by role-playing with clients and asking and responding to typical on-the-job questions like "Are you married?" and "How many children do you have?" Counselors can help clients network with other LGBTQ individuals who have integrated open sexual orientation and work into a positive, mentally healthy, and well-integrated life. By career shadowing and networking LGBTQ clients can expand their career options.

Although some national corporations now include sexual orientation in their nondiscrimination personnel policies, many LGBTQ employees continue to experience discrimination at work. In fact, LGBTQ clients often avoid careers that involve working with children or applying for advantageous positions in conservative corporations that discourage sexual minority participation. Even when the corporation provides partner benefits such as health and life insurance, conflicts may arise as partners decide how to present themselves at business social functions. Coming out in the work arena will require considerable contemplation, and relationship issues emerge when partners disagree on the amount of openness each desires.

In summary, the counselor should help the LGBTQ individual network to build strong social support networks and seek the presence of LGBTQ career role models (Schmidt & Nilsson 2006). Because covert counselor bias can affect the LGBTQ client's career development and employment choices, counselors who do not feel adequately prepared to provide LGBTQ-affirming career practices should consider a referral to someone who has experience and resources with sexual minorities (Pope et al., 2004; Pope & Tarvydas, 2002).

Counseling Strategies with LGBTQs

We have already discussed the importance of counselor self-awareness and the necessity of incorporating LGBTQ-affirming practices into your counseling practice. We have presented two models of sexual identity development, which will be important to help you match your counseling strategies with your client's level of identity formation over the life span. Obviously, counseling will look dramatically different for a 45-year-old lesbian who is in McCarn and Fassinger's internalization/synthesis stage and whose partner has been diagnosed with cancer from counseling an angry adolescent who has just announced to his family at Thanksgiving dinner that he is gay.

The next step in providing effective counseling for the LGBTQ population is to review counseling theories and frameworks that may or may not be appropriate for counseling sexual minority clients. Currently, practitioners have few resources that delineate specific therapeutic techniques or conceptual approaches for working with sexual minority clients. We remind counselors that all counseling theories, strategies, and interventions are developed within a cultural context, many of which are at odds with the life experience of LGBTQ clients. Traditional theories of counseling cannot simply be superimposed onto the LGBTQ frame of reference without careful consideration.

Family and Systemic Counseling

Theories of family counseling can be biased in the very definition of *family*. What image comes to your mind when a church or school announces "family night"? An assumption of a traditional heterosexual family system can dissuade sexual minority clients from identifying their relationships in the context of their unique family system. Notice that "family" may consist of same-sex individuals who have children, a bisexual person and heterosexual partner who present themselves as a heterosexual couple, or a single LGBTQ person and close and supportive friends. The counselor cannot rely on templates of family or relationships or life stages drawn from a heterosexual population. Instead, the counselor must be able to work without some of the assumptions embodied in traditional family theory.

Other systemic strategies can also be especially useful in working with LGBTQ clients because they are based in the assumption of context as a defining factor. Narrative therapy, redecision therapy, and other brief and solution-focused therapies are included under the "systemic" approaches. Systemic counseling strategies that examine the relationships between people in families, peers, cultures, and societies would naturally encompass the larger social context, which can either enhance or diminish the life experience of the LGBTQ client. By placing significance on the interchange between the individual, and the systems that influence their lives, the client is able to examine the intricate interplay between external systems and a client's internal experiences. Systemic-based strategies seem well placed as a "socially conscious" framework for counseling sexual minority clients (Malley, 2002).

Person-Centered and Existential Counseling

Person-centered and existential counseling strategies are useful when working with the LGBTQ individual for a number of reasons. Unconditional positive regard, congruence, and empathy on the part of the counselor can provide a safe and accepting frame of reference for the sexual minority who is struggling with coming out issues to communicate openly and honestly about her or his sexual orientation. Counselor congruence and genuineness offers the individual an important sense of hope and allows the client to self-disclose at client's own pace. The process can play a facilitative and constructive role in helping the LGBTQ client overcome psychological distresses and reduce internalized homophobia. This nondirective approach allows the counselor to adopt the "client's perceptual field to gain insight into the individual's unique process" (Lemoire & Chen, 2005, p. 149). Provision of a safe and supportive experience can lead to client-generated insights that promote positive learning experiences and acceptance.

A limitation of person-centered counseling with sexual minority clients is that nondirective strategies do not always give the needed guidance and direction as individuals explore their sexual orientation. A more directive approach in providing "explicit identity validation (reassurance), guided risk assessment regarding possible disclosure, and exposure to positive sexual minority communities" is suggested (Lemoire & Chen, 2005, p. 146). Thus, the counselor can help the client to "seek to predict, articulate, and normalize common experiences in developing and managing a stigmatized identity" (Horowitz & Newcomb, 2002, p. 3).

Couples Counseling

The perceptive counselor must approach traditional models of couples counseling with caution; most assume a heterosexual monogamous sexual orientation. We have previously mentioned many of the similarities and differences between heterosexual couples and LGBTQ couples. These should be kept in mind as you determine which approach appears best suited for your clients.

One approach that has been applied effectively to same-sex couples is integrative behavioral couples therapy (IBCT) (Martell & Land, 2002). Counselors who utilize IBCT techniques "attempt to balance change techniques with acceptance and tolerance techniques" (Martell & Prince, 2005, p. 1431). Problem-solving strategies and reframing is utilized to improve communication skills. For example, when the couple is monogamous, an identified affair might be reframed as symptomatic of "distancing and polarization" or "an attempt to rediscover passion in a relationship whose sexual quality has diminished" (Martell & Prince, 2005, p. 1432). As in all counseling, the counselor's nonjudgmental stance will allow the couple to explore positive solutions, regardless of the presenting issue. Counselors must strive to understand the tenets of the relationship, the meanings associated with the relationship, the goals and desires of the couple, and the larger social pressures within which the relationship exists.

Social Empowerment Strategies

For the counselor who finds that a sociopolitical perspective is appropriate for the needs of the sexual minority client, a social empowerment framework may be helpful. This may be particularly relevant to clients who are in the acceptance stage of sexual identity and seeking to be more vocal about sexual minority identity in the larger political arena. As marginalized persons, LGBTQ persons are frequently overwhelmed by a sense of powerlessness (Savage et al., 2005). The social empowerment model (SEM) is based on conflict theory that assumes society consists of separate groups that have advantages of power and control in relation to social, psychological, political, and economic systems (Zimmerman, 1990, as cited in Savage et al., 2005). A focus on empowerment is a potential conceptual cornerstone for marginalized groups who face discrimination and are denied the rights and resources of the society in which they live. Empowerment is an ongoing process that involves extensive reflection on issues of power and control.

Counselors can offer strategies for sexual minority groups "to circumvent discrimination, scapegoating, and inequities that undermine the development and maintenance of a healthy self-concept" (Savage et al., 2005, p. 131). Empowerment counseling emphasizes that rather than remain powerless and feel helpless, everyone has the ability to shape events within his or her life. The desirable goal of empowerment counseling is enhanced self-advocacy. Collaboration between counselor and client, as they work together toward common goals, models a power-sharing process. Resiliency and self-efficacy are promoted as clients take action on issues that resonate with their personal agendas for change. The final stages of self-empowerment strategies involve the actualization of these newly constructed beliefs into behaviors and actions to positively affect society.

Counselor Issues

As you have read this chapter, we wonder if you have had any thoughts about your own issues in working with LGBTQ clients. If you are of sexual minority status and are in a graduate program to become a counselor, have you considered how you will effectively work with other LGBTQs, heterosexual clients, or homophobic clients? If you are part of the sexual majority population, what attitudes, opinions, beliefs, and biases do you bring to the counseling dynamic?

Of primary importance is the fact that if counselors have not fully addressed these concerns, they may not be given the privilege of knowing an LGBTQ's sexual orientation. Although counselors may be influenced by progressive LGBTQ affirmative stances, they are also subject to societal and cultural norms. Thus the most challenging counselor for a client who is a sexual minority is likely to be the one who believes they are LGBTQ-affirmative but remain influenced by heterosexist norms. Discerning this counselor's stance is much more difficult for the client than identifying abject homophobia, which can then allow the client to make an informed decision about services (Matthews, 2005).

A primary goal of counseling is to create an environment that affords the client the safety to disclose concerns to the counselor. If that safety is not present, disclosure does not occur. The literature suggests that clients tend to disclose more under conditions of greater psychological distress (Stiles, Shuster, & Harrigan, 1992). Thus, the counselor may be privy to the client's sexual minority status for this reason only. Counselors who are aware of their own attitudes, opinions, beliefs, and biases are in a better position to receive and integrate this piece of information while making treatment determinations that best fit the client.

Summary

Counselors are in an ideal position to provide effective counseling for the LGBTQ client, as well as challenge the discriminatory practices faced by many sexual minorities. Recognition of the position of sexual minorities within a hostile society is just a beginning. Counselors and counselor educators must join with our lesbian, gay, bisexual, transgender, and questioning clients to move from a heterocentric worldview to one that celebrates diversity and is inclusive of all of its members. The following Web sites provide additional information relating to the chapter topics.

USEFUL WEB SITES

Association for Lesbian, Gay, Bisexual & Transgender Issues in Counseling
http://www.algbtic.org

The Renaissance Transgender Association
http://www.ren.org

Gay and Lesbian Alcoholic Recovery and Support
http://www.gayalcoholics.com

Parents, Families, and Friends of Lesbians and Gays
http://www.pflag.org

The Association of Welcoming and Affirming Baptists
http://www.wabaptists.org

Episcopal: Integrity:
http://www.integrityusa.org

Jewish: Mosaic:
http://www.jewishmosiac.org/

Lutherans Concerned:
http://www.lcna.org

Mormon: Affirmation:
http://www.affirmation.org/

More Light Presbyterians:
http://www.mlp.org/

Roman Catholic: Dignity USA:
http://www.dignityusa.org/

United Church of Christ: Open and Affirming:
http://www.ucc.org/lgbt/ona.html

United Methodist: Affirmation:
http://www.umaffirm.org/

REFERENCES

American Counseling Association. (2005). *Code of ethics.* Alexandria, VA: Author.

Blake, S. M., Ledsky, R., Lehman, T., & Goodenow, C. (2001). Preventing sexual risk behaviors among gay, lesbian, and bisexual adolescents: The benefits of gay-sensitive HIV instruction in schools. *American Journal of Public Health, 91,* 940–946.

Britton, P. (2000). Staying on the roller coaster with clients: Implications of the new HIV/AIDS medical treatments of counselling. *Journal of Mental Health Counseling, 22*(1), 85–91.

Burckell, L. A., & Goldfried, M. R. (2006). Therapist qualities preferred by sexual minority individuals. *Psychotherapy: Theory Research, Practice, Training, 43*(1), 32–49.

Carroll, J. L. (2005). *Sexuality now: Embracing diversity.* Belmont, CA: Thompson.

Cass, V. C. (1984). Homosexulity identity formation: Testing a theoretical model. *Journal of Sex Research, 20*(2), 143–167.

Cheng, Z. (2003). Issues and standards in counseling lesbians and gay men with substance abuse concerns. *Journal of Mental Health Counseling, 25,* 323–336.

Clunis, D. M., & Green, G. D. (2000). *Lesbian couples: A guide to creating healthy relationships.* Seattle: Seal.

Cochran S. D., & Mays, V. M. (1994) Depressive distress among homosexually active African American men and women. *American Journal of Psychiatry, 151*(4), 524–529.

Cove, J., & Boyle, M. (2002). Gay men's self-defined sexual problems, perceived causes and factors in remission. *Sexual Relationship Therapy, 17,* 137–147.

Crooks, R., & Baur, K. (2005). *Our sexuality* (9th ed). Belmont, CA: Thomson/Wadsworth.

D'Augelli, A. R. (1996). Lesbian, gay, and bisexual development during adolescence and early adulthood. In R. P. Cabaj & T. S. Stein (Eds.), *Textbook of homosexuality and mental health* (pp. 267–288). Washington, DC: American Psychiatric Press.

DeAngelis, T. (2002). New data on lesbian, gay, and bisexual mental health. *APA Monitor, 33,* 46–47.

Diamond, M. (1993). Homosexuality and bisexuality in different populations. *Archives of Sexual Behavior, 22,* 291–310.

Downey, J., & Friedman, R. (1995). Internalized homophobia in lesbian relationships. *Journal of the American Academy of Psychoanalysis, 23,* 435–447.

Downs, C. A., & James, S. E. (2006). Gay, lesbian, and bisexual foster parents: Strengths and challenges for the child welfare system. *Child Welfare, 85*(2), 281–298.

Eliason, M. J. (2000). Substance abuse counselors' attitudes regarding lesbian, gay, bisexual, transgender clients. *Journal of Substance Abuse, 12,* 311–328.

Fassinger, R., & Richie, B. (1997). Sex matters: Gender and sexual orientation in training for multicultural counseling competency. In D. Pope-Davis & H. Coleman (Eds.), *Multicultural counseling competencies: Assessment, education and training, and supervision* (pp. 83–110). Thousand Oaks, CA: Sage.

Forstein, M. (1994). Psychotherapy with gay male couples: Loving in the time of AIDS. In S. Caldwell & R. Burnham (Eds.), *Therapists on the front line: Psychotherapy with gay men in the age of AIDS* (pp. 293–315). Washington, DC: American Psychological Association.

Forstein, M. (2001). Overview of ethical and research issues in sexual orientation therapy. *Journal of Gay and Lesbian Psychotherapy, 5*(3–4), 167–179.

Haldeman, D. (2004). When sexual and religious orientation collide: Considerations in working with conflicted same-sex attracted males. *The Counseling Psychologist, 32,* 691–715.

Hartstein, N. B. (1996). Suicide risk in lesbian, gay and bisexual youth. In R. P. Cabaj & T. S. Stein (Eds.), *Textbook of homosexuality and mental health* (pp. 819–837). Washington, DC: American Psychiatric Press.

Herek, G. M., Cogan, J. C., & Gillis, J. (1999). Psychological sequale of hate-crime victimization among lesbian, gay, and bisexual adults. *Journal of Consulting and Clinical Psychology, 67*(6), 945–951.

Horowitz, J. L., & Newcomb, M. D. (2002). A multidimensional approach to homosexual identity. *Journal of Homosexuality, 42*(2), 1–20.

Hughes, T. L., & Eliason, M. (2002). Substance use and abuse in lesbian, gay, bisexual, and transgender populations. *Journal of Primary Prevention, 22,* 263–298.

James, S., & Murphy, B. (1998). Gay and lesbian relationships in a changing social context. In C. Patterson & A. D'Augelli (Eds.), *Lesbian, gay, and bisexual identities in families: Psychological perspectives* (pp. 99–121). London: Oxford University Press.

Kinsey, A. C., Pomeroy, W. R., & Martin, C. E. (2003). Sexual behavior in the human male. *American Journal of Public Health, 93*(6), 894–898.

Kurdek, L. A. (2004). Are gay and lesbian cohabiting couples really different from heterosexual married couples? *Journal of Marriage & Family, 66*(4), 880–900.

Lambert, S. (2005). Gay and lesbian families: What we know and where to go from here. *The Family Journal: Counseling and Therapy for Couples and Families, 13,* 43–51.

Lemoire, S., & Chen, C. P. (2005). Applying person-centered counseling to sexual minority adolescents. *Journal of Counseling & Development, 83,* 146–154.

Lesser, J. G., & Pope, D. S. (2007). *Human behavior and the social environment: Theory and practice.* Boston: Pearson.

Lynch, J. M. (2000). Considerations of family structure and gender composition: The lesbian and gay stepfamily. *Journal of Homosexuality, 40,* 81–95.

MacDonald, B. (1998). Issues in therapy with gay and lesbian couples. *Journal of Sex & Marital Therapy, 24,* 165–190.

Malley, M. (2002). Systemic therapy with lesbian and gay clients: A truly social approach to psychological practice. *Journal of Community & Applied Social Psychology, 12,* 237–241.

Martell, C. R., & Land, T. E., (2002). Cognitive-behavioral therapy with gay and lesbian couples. In F. W. Kaslow & T. Patterson (Ed.). *Comprehensive handbook of psychotherapy: Vol. 2. Cognitive-behavioral approaches* (pp. 451–468). New York: Wiley

Martell, C. R., & Prince, S. E. (2005). Treating infidelity in same-sex couples. *JCPL/In Session, 61*(11), 1429–1438.

Matthews, C. R. (2005). Infusing lesbian, gay, and bisexual issues into counselor education. *Journal of Humanistic Counseling, Education and Development, 44,* 168–184.

Matthews, C. R., Lorah, P., & Fenton, J. (2006). Treatment experiences of gays and lesbians in recovery from addiction: A qualitative inquiry. *Journal of Mental Health Counseling, 28*(2), 110–132.

Matthews, C. R., Selvidge, M. M. D., & Fisher, K. (2005). Addictions counselors' attitudes and behaviors toward gay, lesbian, and bisexual clients. *Journal of Counseling & Development, 83,* 57–65.

McCarn, S. R., & Fassinger, R. R. (1996). Revisioning sexual minority identity formation: A new model of lesbian identity and its implications. *Counseling Psychologist, 24*(3), 508–534.

Miranti, J. (1996). The spiritual/religious dimension of counseling: A multicultural perspective. In P. Pedersen & D. Locke (Eds.), *Cultural and diversity issues in counseling* (pp. 117–120). Greensboro: University of North Carolina Press.

Mohr, J. J. (2002). Heterosexual identity and heterosexual therapist: An identity perspective on sexual orientation dynamics in psychotherapy. *The Counseling Psychologist, 30,* 532–566.

Negy, C., & McKinney, C. (2006). Application of feminist therapy: Promoting resiliency among lesbian and gay families. *Journal of Feminist Family Therapy, 18*(1–2), 67–83.

Perry, M. J., & Barry, J. F. (1998). The gay male client in sex addiction treatment. *Sexual Addiction & Compulsivity, 5,* 119–131.

Peterman, L., & Dixon, C. (2003). Domestic violence between same-sex partners: Implications for counseling. *Journal of Counseling & Development, 81*(1), 40–54.

Pope, M., Barret, B., Symanski, D. M., Chung, Y. B., Singaravelu, H., McLean, R., et al. (2004). Culturally appropriate career counseling with gay and lesbian clients. *The Career Development Quarterly, 53,* 158–176.

Pope, M., & Tarvydas, V. M. (2002). Career counseling. In R. R. Cottone & V. M. Tarvydas (Eds.), Ethical and professional issues in counseling (2nd ed., pp. 289–331). Upper Saddle River, NJ: Merrill/Prentice Hall.

Remley, T., & Herlihy, B. (2007) *Ethical, legal, and professional issues in counseling* (2nd ed., updated). Upper Saddle River, NJ: Pearson.

Rosario, M., Schrimshaw, E. W., Hunter, J., & Braun, L. (2006). Sexual identity development among lesbian, gay, and bisexual youths: Consistency and change over time. *The Journal of Sex Research, 43*(1), 46–58.

Russell, S. T., Franz, B. T., & Driscoll, A. K. (2001). Same-sex romantic attraction and experience of violence in adolescence. *American Journal of Public Health, 91,* 903–906.

Saulnier, C. F. (1998). Prevalence of suicide attempts and suicidal ideation among lesbian and gay youth. In L. M. Sloan & N. S. Gustavsson (Eds.), *Violence and social injustice against lesbian, gay and bisexual people* (pp. 51–68). New York London: Harrington Park Press.

Savage, T. A., Harley, D. A., & Nowak, T. M. (2005). Applying social empowerment strategies as tools for self-advocacy in counseling lesbian and gay male clients. *Practice & Theory, 83,* 131–137.

Savickas, M. L. (2005). The theory and practice of career construction. In D. Brown & R. W. Lent (Eds.), *Career development and counseling: Putting theory and research to work* (pp. 42–70). Hoboken, NJ: Wiley.

Savin-Williams, R. C. (1994). Verbal and physical abuse as stressors in the lives of lesbian, gay male, and bisexual youths: Associations with school problems, running away, substance abuse, prostitution, and suicide. *Journal of Consulting and Clinical Psychology, 62,* 261–269.

Schmidt, C. K., & Nilsson, J. E. (2006). The effects of simultaneous developmental processes: Factors relating to the career development of lesbian, gay, and bisexual youth. *The Career Development Quarterly, 55,* 22–37.

Shidlo, A., & Schroeder, M. (2002). Changing sexual orientation: A consumer's report. *Professional Psychology: Research and Practice, 33,* 249–259.

Skidmore, W. C., Linsemeier, J. A. W., & Bailey, J. M. (2006). Gender nonconformity and psychological distress in lesbians and gay men. *Archives of Sexual Behavior, 35*(6), 685–697.

Spitalnick, J. S., & McNair, L. D. (2005). Couples therapy with gay and lesbian clients: An analysis of important clinical issues. *Journal of Sex & Marital Therapy, 31,* 43–56.

Stiles, W. B., Shuster, P. L., & Harrigan, J. A. (1992). Disclosure and anxiety: A test of the fever model. *Journal of Personality and Social Psychology, 63*(6), 980–988.

Survey says. (2005). *Gay & Lesbian Review Worldwide, 12*(1), 17–21.

Tasker, F. (2005). Lesbian mothers, gay fathers, and their children: A review. *Journal of Developmental and Behavioral Pediatrics, 26,* 224–240.

Tozer, E. E., & Hayes, J. A. (2004). Why do individuals seek conversion therapy? The role of religiosity, internalized homonegativity, and identity development. *The Counseling Psychologist, 32*(5), 716–740.

Twist, M., Murphy, M. J., Green, M., & Palmanteer, D. (2006). Therapists support of gay and lesbian human rights. *Guidance & Counseling, 21*(2), 107–113.

Tyebee, T. (2003). Attitude, interest, and motivation for adoption and foster care. *Child Welfare, 82*(6), 685–706.

Waldner, L. K., & Magruder, B. (1999). Coming out to parents: Perceptions of family relations, perceived resources, and identity expression as predictors of identity disclosure for gay and lesbian adolescents. *Journal of Homosexuality, 37,* 83–100.

Walker, L. E. (2000). *Battered woman syndrome.* New York: Springer.

Weiler, E. M. (2003). Making school safe for sexual minority students. *Principal Leadership, 4*(4), 10–13.

Whitman, J. S., Glosoff, H. L., Kocet, M. M., & Tarvydas, V. (2006). Ethical issues related to conversion or reparative therapy. *Counseling Today, 49*(1), 14–15.

CHAPTER 20

Counseling Clients with Disabilities

MALACHY BISHOP, PhD

University of Kentucky

Introduction

The purpose of this chapter is to explore counseling concepts and interventions associated with working with clients with disabilities. Recent U.S. Census data suggest that approximately 1 in 5 Americans has a disability (Steinmetz, 2004). It may be assumed, therefore, that at least 20% of counseling clients are persons with a disability, and because many people who seek counseling do so for reasons either directly or indirectly related to a disability or chronic illness, it is likely that the percentage is much higher. It is critical, therefore, that all counselors have at least a fundamental understanding of the medical, social, psychological, and personal aspects of disability. The information in this chapter introduces rehabilitation counseling, the counseling profession that specializes in counseling with persons with disabilities, and also provides a knowledge base necessary for all counselors. This chapter is organized into three main sections. In the first section, the definitions and meanings of *disability* and the counseling implications of this complex and multifaceted concept are discussed. Second, the medical, functional, and psychosocial aspects of several specific disabilities are outlined, and related counseling strategies are presented. Finally, a description of rehabilitation counseling and the recommended education and training for counselors who intend to work with clients with disabilities is offered, followed by a discussion of professional certification and membership issues.

Models and Meanings of Disability: Implications for Counseling

The term *disability* represents a complex construct with widely varied meanings and definitions. Although the concept of disability has deep roots in the history of humanity,

I would like to express my appreciation to my coauthors on previous versions of this chapter, published in prior editions of this book: Hanoch Livneh, PhD, CRC, and Elizabeth Wosely-George, PhD, whose knowledgeable and scholarly contributions are reflected in the present version.

the meaning of the term and the general understanding of the construct have evolved and changed throughout this history. Any single definition of disability reflects both the perspective of the person, agency, or group defining it and the purpose for which it is being defined. Contemporary paradigms for conceiving of and defining disability have emerged for a variety of distinct purposes and through a number of different medical, legal, statistical, economic, and sociopolitical perspectives.

Definitions and Models of Disability

The purpose for defining disability guides the definition, and disability may be defined for a variety of purposes. For example, it may be necessary to specifically define disability for programmatic or legal reasons. This may be the case, for example, when the definition has legal ramifications or is associated with services or benefits, and it is necessary to delineate inclusion or exclusion criteria or establish which people are and are not covered by the legislation or eligible for services (Smart, 2001). Alternately, clinical definitions of disability exist for the purpose of communication about medical diagnosis, treatment, prognosis, and identification of shared characteristics for classification. Disability has also been defined by researchers for the purpose of public health surveys and census data collection, as well as for the purpose of exploring social and personal aspects of experience (Smart, 2001).

In each of these cases, different models or perspectives of disability are represented. In the legislative context, for example, a functional or impairment-based definition is generally used. For example, in the Americans with Disabilities Act (ADA, 1990), the term *disability* is defined, in part, as a physical or mental impairment that substantially limits one or more major life activities. This sort of impairment-based or function-based definition is typical in legislation that guides programs that provide medical, vocational, or financial services or benefits. Such functional or impairment-based definitions are conceived as emerging from the medical perspective, or the medical model of disability, in which disability is seen as a medically diagnosable condition that affects an individual's ability to perform certain physical or cognitive functions (Martin, 1999). In this model, the disability is a characteristic that is intrinsic to, or located within, the individual.

At the other end of the spectrum is the social model of disability. Although there are variations of the social model, common among them is the perspective that disability arises from the social, environmental, and attitudinal barriers that prevent persons with disabilities from societal participation and equality. A distinction is frequently made by proponents of this perspective between (a) impairment, or the individual's biological, physical, or mental condition, and (b) disability, or the social, environmental, and economic barriers that the individual experiences (Smart, 2004). From this perspective, disability is seen as located not within the individual but as resulting in the interaction between the individual and the constructed environments in which he or she lives.

The medical and social models of disability, which represent different ends of a conceptual spectrum, are presented here for the purpose of underscoring the complexity of the construct that is the focus of this chapter. Many other perspectives and models of disability exist, the discussion of which is not within the scope of this chapter, but many useful reviews and dicussions are available (see, e.g., Albrecht, 1992; Hahn, 1993; Llewellyn & Hogan, 2000; Smart, 2001, 2004).

The Personal Meaning of Disability

As is clear from the preceding discussion, disability is at once a legal, social, political, economic, and personal construct with a wide range of public and personal meanings. Indeed, given the variety of social, legal, political, economic, educational, vocational, and medical structures and systems with which each individual interacts, it is quite possible that a person may be considered to have a disability within the context of some or all of these systems, and yet not consider himself or herself a person with a disability. Alternately, it is possible for an individual to see himself or herself as a person with a disability, while other persons and external systems do not.

Of primary importance in the counseling context is the perspective of the client, the personal meaning of the disability to the individual. An individual's personal perspective on his or her disability is a complex and multifaceted one, affected by many personal, interpersonal, cultural, and societal issues, many of which will be discussed here. Gaining an understanding of the client as an individual and developing an understanding of his or her unique perspective is critical to effective counseling with persons with disabilities, just as it is in all of counseling's forms and contexts.

An individual's disability can be seen as one of several important parts of the individual's identity and self-concept. It is rarely the part by which an individual defines himself or herself, but many individuals with disabilities view their disability as a valued part of their lives, their experience, and their identity and would not choose to eliminate the disability, even if they could (Smart & Smart, 2006). As a result, if a counselor dismisses or ignores the disability, perhaps out of his or her personal discomfort, a critical part of the client's identity remains unexplored (Smart & Smart, 2006).

Alternately, counselors serving a client with a disability, particularly a visible or more functionally apparent disability, frequently assume either that the individual's disability is the primary reason that they are seeking services or that, regardless of the client's stated purpose for seeking counseling, the disability must necessarily be the counseling focus. In many cases, of course, dealing with disability-related issues such as coping and adapting, education, self-management, self-advocacy, vocational issues, or resource development is indeed the client's purpose in seeking counseling. However, when it is not, the counselor's misplaced focus and overattention to the disability can prevent the development of an effective counseling relationship. Sensitivity, communication, and careful attention to the client's intentions and goals are, therefore, necessary.

Individual Differences in the Experience of Disability

It has been seen that disability is not a unified concept or experience, but one that is experienced by different people in very different ways. It is meaningless, therefore, to make all-encompassing statements concerning people with disabilities and to suggest that there are universally shared experiences or universally effective counseling interventions. Significant differences in the personal experience of living with a disability can be seen to arise as a result of (a) characteristics of the disability (condition or impairment) itself, (b) characteristics of the individual with a disability, and (c) characteristics of the physical and social environments in which the disability is experienced. These differences, which often have important implications for the counseling relationship, are briefly reviewed here.

Several characteristics of the disability have been identified as potentially affecting the individual's experience of disability. These include the age at onset and type of onset of the disability, the visibility, severity, course, prognosis, and functional implications. The age at onset, or age at which a disability develops, may have significant implications for the individual's experience. Whereas research suggests that for persons with congenital disabilities the process of body image and identity development is likely to be similar to that of children without disabilities (Livneh & Antonak, 1997; Wright, 1983), persons who experience later-onset chronic illness or acquired disability may find their sense of self suddenly and dramatically challenged or altered. In addition, a sudden-onset disability associated with significant functional changes, such as may occur because of a motor vehicle accident resulting in a spinal cord injury or brain injury, will be experienced differently and present a different set of psychosocial issues from a disability or chronic illness that develops gradually and may be associated with only minor changes over time. The course of a disability or chronic illness also affects the individual's experience and influences the nature and scope of challenges that may be faced. The course may be stable and essentially unchanging over time, as in the case of many disabilities resulting from injuries; progressive, as may be the case with cancer and other chronic illnesses; or episodic, as in the case of epilepsy or some forms of multiple sclerosis.

Among the many characteristics of the individual that may result in differences in the experience of disability are the individual's personality, interests, goals, values, cultural influences and identities, gender, age, educational background, and prior experiences. Individual differences, for example, in such frequently described personality traits as introversion and extroversion, optimism and pessimism, and self-esteem affect the individual's personal and social experience of disability. In the realm of values, the individual's religious and spiritual beliefs may have a significant influence on how the person perceives the disability and how the individual interacts with others (e.g., Vash, 1981). Gender differences in the response to and experience of disability have frequently been identified (Patterson, DeLaGarza, & Schaller, 2005). The personal and professional implications of the specific functional effects of a disability may, for example, be experienced differently for males and females, though such differences are also mediated by both personal goals and cultural values.

Influencing all of these individual variables are the broader ethnic and cultural influences to which the individual ascribes and with which the individual is associated. Culture has been described as ways to perceive and organize the world, commonly held by a group of people, and passed along interpersonally and intergenerationally

(Hecht, Anderson, & Ribeau, 1989). Considered in this manner, the great variety of such groups to which an individual belongs, including one's age group, gender group, ethnic group or groups, and so on, influence both the individual's perspective on disability and the larger society's perspective of the individual with a disability.

Finally, the social and physical environments in which the individual lives, works, and plays and through which he or she engages in his or her many life roles and tasks influence the experience of disability. This domain of experience considers the physical accessibility of the environment and the availability of modifications and resources for enhancing access; personal relationships with family, loved ones, and friends; and the broader social attitudinal environment of the community and society in which the individual lives.

Application of Counseling Interventions to Specific Groups of Clients with Disabilities

Because a client's personal needs and counseling goals are frequently either directly determined or affected by the nature of the disability, the following seeks to acquaint the reader with the medical and psychosocial issues and counseling interventions applicable to counseling clients with specific disabilities. Although a comprehensive discussion of the medical and psychosocial aspects of the range of disabling conditions is beyond the scope and purpose of this chapter, only several selected conditions are described: cancer, blindness, deafness, spinal cord injury, cardiac illness, epilepsy, traumatic head injury, and psychiatric disorders. Each condition is first considered as related to its impact upon the person's life (functional limitations, psychosocial implications), and then recommendations for counseling and related interventions are provided.

Counseling Clients with Cancer

Impact of Cancer.   Over the life span, cancer will affect between a quarter and half of the individuals in the United States (Orr & Orange, 2002). Cancer continues to be the second leading cause of death in the United States, accounting for 23.1% of all deaths (American Cancer Society, 2007). Cancer is not a single disease entity. There are more than 100 different types of diseases termed cancer (often referred to as malignancy or neoplastic disease). In men, cancers of the prostate, lung, colon and rectum, and urinary bladder are diagnosed most often, whereas in women, cancers of the breast, lung, colon and rectum, and uterine corpus are diagnosed most often (American Cancer Society, 2007). Among females, lung and breast cancers are the chief causes of fatality, and lung and prostate cancers are the most common causes of death among males. Although cancer can strike at any age group, it is more common in older individuals (Falvo, 1999; Freidenbergs & Kaplan, 1999). Among children, leukemia is the most common type of cancer (Bowe, 2000).

Physical Impact.   Because of the variety of cancer types, it is virtually impossible to cogently discuss all the functional limitations associated with the disorder. Hence, only the most prominent physical limitations resulting from the onset of cancer will be delineated. Limitations on activities of daily living (grooming, bathing, dressing, feeding, toiletry) are more commonly associated with cancers affecting the brain, larynx, head and neck, breast, lung, and upper extremities. Ambulation difficulties result more often from cancers of the lower extremities and the brain. Speech and communication are affected by cancers of the brain, the larynx, and the head and neck. Most cancers, with the possible exception of leukemia, lymphoma, and cancers of the lung and spinal cord, have an adverse effect on the person's sexual functioning and cosmesis. Finally, most forms of cancer, as well as many cancer treatments, are, at one point or another, associated with organic pain, feelings of fatigue, and general weakness (Orr & Orange, 2002).

Psychosocial Impact.   Of the diseases that affect humans, perhaps none creates more distress within individuals than cancer. Despite significant advances in the diagnosis and treatment of cancer over the last decade, the diagnosis of cancer is associated with considerable fear and anxiety. Considering that the diagnosis of cancer brings with it an unknown prognosis, prolonged treatment, extended hospitalizations, disruptions in lifestyle, and uncertain prospects for cure, the period following initial diagnosis represents a time of significant stress (Ey, Compas, Epping-Jordan, & Worsham, 1998; Falvo, 2005). Indeed, although much less is known about the long-term effects of stress, the prevalence rate of extreme psychological distress (anxiety, depression, etc.) among individuals first diagnosed with cancer is reported to be between 30% and 60% (Kangas, Henry, & Bryant, 2002), a rate that is approximately 4 to 5 times that found in community samples. This internal state is due to the impact that the disease has on health and life quality, where fundamental beliefs about being a productive member of society, having personal control over one's life events, and prospective future goals are challenged.

Recommendations for Intervention.   Medical treatment of cancer is directed at eradicating the tumor(s) and detected metastatic areas and is accomplished mainly through surgery, radiation therapy, and/or chemotherapy. Additional treatment modalities include immunotherapy (strengthening the individual's own immune system), hormonal therapy (adjuvant hormone treatment to maximize the benefits of chemotherapy), and bone marrow transplantation. Whereas surgery and radiation therapy are relatively straightforward procedures, chemotherapy, because of its generalized effects on many of the body systems, carries with it a host of related side effects (nausea, appetite loss, hair loss, fatigue, weakness). Counselors who work with clients with cancer should thoroughly familiarize themselves with these added problems and their psychosocial and social-familial implications (Falvo, 2005; Freidenbergs & Kaplan, 1999).

Immediately following the diagnosis of cancer, the counselor's main role is to assist the client with cancer to effectively cope with the ensuing anxiety and stress. The counselor should provide the client with accurate and useful information about the disease, its course, and its prognosis, so that irrational fears and misperceptions may be alleviated and realistic hope instilled. Optimism, or the tendency to induce or maintain a positive state of mind, may mitigate the experience of negative emotions so often noted in patients dealing with cancer (Schnoll, Knowles, & Harlow, 2002). Counselors, however, should be cautious in striking a balance between optimism and realism. The prognosis for persons diagnosed with cancer is increasingly brighter with ongoing medical advances, and counselors should help the client maintain a positive outlook yet at the same time help clients prepare to deal realistically with such challenges as may arise in the months and years following diagnosis. Issues of disease recurrence following treatment; the ambiguity surrounding the cause, treatment, and progression of the disease; the effects of treatment and its associated side effects; and the financial burdens of hospital and treatment costs should all be explored early in the coping process (Falvo, 2005; McAleer & Kluge, 1978).

One of the most painful tasks facing the counselor and client is dealing with the issue of death, dying, and the grieving process. With individuals for whom the disease progresses and the certainty of impending death looms larger, counseling sessions should focus on the acceptance of death. Counseling for the acceptance of death should focus on issues such as facing the agony of separation from loved ones, preparation of the family for the separation, and taking pride in one's past accomplishments ("leaving a mark" on this world).

Freidenbergs and Kaplan (1999) recommend a three-pronged approach to counseling cancer patients: (a) educational interventions (such as clarifying the patient's medical condition and teaching about cancer and its side effects), (b) counseling interventions (such as encouraging the patient to vent feelings and offering reassurance and verbal support), and (c) environmental interventions (such as referring the patient for further health services).

Of the various counseling approaches, two that seem to address many of the aforementioned issues are Gestalt and cognitive-behavioral therapy. Gestalt therapy may benefit clients in resolving unfinished life issues that, because of the impending death, may never be resolved (saying farewell to loved ones and, in general, gaining awareness of personal feelings toward death and dying, pain and suffering). Gestalt therapy techniques may also be appropriate for dealing with the issues surrounding perceived or real functional or anatomical losses. Cognitive-behavioral interventions include muscle relaxation techniques, systematic desensitization, thought stopping, and guided imagery. These techniques can reduce the muscle and cognitive tension associated with anxiety, stress, and pain.

Counseling Clients Who Are Blind

Impact of Blindness.   Visual impairment and blindness represent significant health problems in the United States. There are approximately 10 million blind and visually impaired persons in the United States (American Foundation for the Blind, 2007). Further, because the leading causes of vision impairment and blindness are primarily age-related disease, as a significant percentage of the U.S. population ages, the number of Americans at risk for age-related eye disease will increase and, in fact, is expected to double within the next three decades (Prevent Blindness America, 2002). The following represent the major functional limitations associated with blindness.

Physical Impact. The chief problem faced by a person who is blind is associated with mobility limitations. Restricted freedom of movement creates considerable obstacles for persons who are blind. These obstacles can compromise the capacity to live independently in the community and have direct implications for physical independence, economic independence, employment, and social integration (Panek, 2002).

Psychosocial Impact. Psychological adjustment to blindness or visual impairment is affected by a number of factors, including the extent of the visual loss, the age at which the individual becomes visually impaired, and whether sight loss occurs gradually or suddenly (Falvo, 2005; Panek, 2002). Sight loss is frequently associated with depression, fear, and anxiety. The period of greatest emotional stress typically occurs at the onset of vision loss, rather than at the point of complete blindness (Panek, 2002). Further, the level of depression frequently appears to be related to the extent of the visual loss (Livneh & Antonak, 1997).

Blindness has been described as a highly feared condition and is frequently identified as more feared than other disabilities (Rosenthal & Cole, 1999). For many, blindness is associated with losses across a range of life areas, including loss of physical integrity or "wholeness," loss of visual contact with the environment, and loss of an aspect of communication ability (Panek, 2002). Socially, a person who develops visual impairment may become increasingly dependent on the environment, yet the person may not be emotionally prepared to accept this dependence. Hence, interpersonal relations are frequently marked by self-restraint, insecurity, and cautiousness (Falvo, 2005). Future goals and aspirations can be strongly affected, as can relationships with the physical and social worlds. In addition, a person who is blind often faces negative societal attitudes (rejection, social stereotyping, pity, fear, patronization) that further impede his or her integration into the community.

Recommendations for Intervention. The initial and foremost intervention modalities with blind and visually impaired clients include maximization of the use of residual vision and sight substitutes. Important rehabilitation interventions include orientation and mobility training (cane travel and use of a guide dog) and compensatory communication training (large-type printer, special magnifying lenses, Braille use, Braille typewriters, scanners, optical character recognition, Kurzweil reading machine). The acquisition of such knowledge and skills brings about renewed positive self-esteem and a sense of independence and control of the environment (Falvo, 2005; Rosenthal & Cole, 1999).

The following recommendations are noted in the literature concerning the psychosocial adjustment to blindness (Falvo, 1999, 2005; Panek, 2002; Vander Kolk, 1983).

1. Assist the client in viewing disability functionally (emphasize remaining abilities) rather than anatomically (merely in terms of loss of sight).
2. Help the client understand and express the emotional responses (such as anxiety and depression) that follow adventitious blindness, and work toward acceptance.
3. Explore feelings with regard to attitudes held by family and peers.
4. Help the client understand the feelings of family and peers that result from changes associated with the condition.

5. Be understanding and accepting of the client's emotional responses and use of psychological defenses, and offer supportive counseling accordingly.
6. Avoid fostering unnecessary dependence in the client.
7. Help the client adjust his or her self-concept and personal goals so that realistic limits imposed by the disability are not ignored.
8. Teach the client self-care, socialization, assertiveness, and independent living skills.

Person-centered, Gestalt, and behavioral counseling approaches have been identified as being particularly suited for clients who are blind (Ryder, 2003; Vanderkolk, 1983). Person-centered counseling is characterized by active listening, empathizing, reframing or paraphrasing, and congruence, or being genuine in your response to the client. Behavioral therapy emphasizes modeling of adaptive behaviors via the senses of touch and hearing, reinforcement of appropriate behaviors, and rehearsal of newly acquired behaviors and skills. Gestalt stresses acting out feelings and attitudes and role-playing various inner conflicts associated with loss of sight. Counselors must be aware that clients who are blind rely almost exclusively on auditory cues. The long periods of silence that traditionally are judged to be constructive in allowing for reflective thinking may be interpreted by the client as signs of the counselor's lack of interest, distress, or rejection.

Counseling Clients Who Are Deaf

Impact of Deafness.   Approximately 28 million Americans have some form of hearing loss (National Institute on Deafness and Other Communication Disorders [NIDCD], 2007), including more than 2 million persons who are classified as having profound hearing loss (Kerman-Lerner & Hauck, 1999). Two or three of every 1,000 children in the United States are born deaf or hard-of-hearing, and hearing loss affects approximately 17 in 1,000 children under age 18 (NIDCD, 2007). Like blindness and visual impairment, the prevalence of hearing loss increases significantly with age. Approximately 314 of every 1,000 persons over age 65 have hearing loss, and between 40% and 50% of people 75 and older have a hearing loss (NIDCD, 2007). The number of persons with significant hearing disability is expected to increase substantially over the next few decades.

Physical Impact.   Because people who are deaf are restricted in their information intake to primarily visual channels, the primary problem they encounter is communicative. Although fundamentally a social problem, loss of hearing or reduced hearing poses numerous environmental obstacles that might have a direct effect on the person's safety and security. For example, the inability to readily respond to honking horns, police or ambulance sirens, children crying, a yell for help, a phone ringing, or a tree falling could create decidedly life-threatening situations in the lives of people who are deaf.

Psychosocial Impact.   A number of psychological, social, vocational, and emotional factors should be considered when counseling deaf persons. The extent of psychosocial impact depends to some extent on whether the deafness or hearing loss is congenital or acquired. As mentioned, deafness primarily creates a communicative handicap. The impact of deafness extends to include sociocultural deprivation, experiential depreciation, and isolation from family and friends. Persons with congenital deafness may find support and opportunities for social integration in the deaf community, where a common language is shared. Persons who acquire hearing loss later in life may feel more socially isolated, as though they fully belong to neither the deaf community nor the hearing world (Falvo, 2005). As a result, acquired hearing loss is frequently associated with social isolation and feelings of loneliness, frustration, anxiety, and depression (Falvo, 2005; Livneh & Antonak, 1997). Regarding vocational implications, the impact of deafness or hearing loss on employment depends on the type of work, the age at onset (congenital or acquired), and the extent of the hearing loss (Harvey, 2002). Deafness and hearing loss have the potential to affect both ability to perform work tasks and ability to fully participate in the work culture.

Recommendations for Intervention. When surgical (including cochlear implants) or sound amplification methods (use of a hearing aid) fail to improve auditory functioning, treatment of the person who is deaf is focused on compensatory communication skills training. Among the most commonly used training methods are speech (lip) reading, speech therapy (especially for prelingual hearing loss), finger spelling, sign language, and the use of adaptive equipment (teletypewriters, television decoders, telephone aids such as telecommunication devices for the deaf, or TDD). Counselors who work with clients who are deaf should become proficient, yet remain flexible, in the use of these communicative methods (Falvo, 2005; Harvey, 2002). Counselors should also be prepared to communicate through nonverbal mechanisms, such as written materials, and be able to use body language. In addition, the counselor should acquire sufficient knowledge about people who are deaf, their subculture, and the psychosocial, educational, and vocational ramifications of deafness.

The following list presents counseling and communication guidelines for serving clients who are deaf (Bolton, 1976; Harvey, 2002; National Association of the Deaf, 2007):

1. Be aware that deaf people communicate in different ways, depending on the type of deafness or impairment, age at onset, language skills, amount of residual hearing, lip-reading or sign language skills, and familial, cultural, and personality factors. Find out which combination of communication techniques is most effective with each individual. Do not assume that deaf persons know sign language.
2. Involve family members in the counseling process, paying special attention to their attitudes toward the person who is deaf.
3. Adopt a situation-specific and practical counseling approach (emphasize the here and now).
4. Avoid highly verbal and abstract levels of communication, especially when clients have become deaf prelingually.
5. Allow time and be patient, because clients who are deaf will generally require longer periods of time for services.

6. Become more aware of possible fatigue associated with lengthy communication periods.
7. Be aware that, overwhelmingly, deaf and hard-of-hearing people prefer to be called "deaf" or "hard of hearing" as opposed to "hearing impaired." Nearly all organizations of the deaf use the term "deaf and hard of hearing" (National Association of the Deaf, 2007).
8. Ask if a deaf client wants to have an interpreter present during the counseling session. When using an interpreter, address and talk to the client in the first person. If discussing confidential issues in the presence of an interpreter, ensure that the interpreter understands and respects the confidential nature of the material being discussed.

Counseling Clients Who Have Spinal Cord Injuries

Impact of Spinal Cord Injury.   The number of Americans with a spinal cord injury (SCI) is estimated at 200,000. These figures include individuals diagnosed with either paraplegia or quadriplegia. The incidence of spinal cord injury in the United States is approximately 10,000 new injuries per year (Crewe & Krause, 2002). Of these injuries, the majority resulted from motor vehicle crashes (44.5%), followed by falls (18.1%), acts of violence (16.6%), sports injuries (12.7%), and other causes (8.1%) (Heinemann, 1999). Most people with spinal cord injury are male and, at the time of the accident, relatively young (median age, 26 years). The functional limitations attributed to spinal cord injury are summarized here.

Physical Impact.   Impaired mobility is obviously the primary limitation associated with spinal cord injury. However, in addition to restricted ambulation, individuals with spinal cord injury, depending on the degree and severity of their injury, might also be functionally impaired in personal hygiene (for example, grooming and bathing activities), eating and drinking, dressing, toileting, writing, driving an automobile, and especially in men, performing sexually. Further complications may arise from muscle spasticity, contractures (loss of range of motion), pressure sores, pain, cardiopulmonary and genitourinary system infections, and body temperature regulation (Crewe & Krause, 2002; Falvo, 2005).

Psychosocial Impact.   There is tremendous variation among individuals in terms of the psychological and social response to SCI. This variation appears to depend less on the objective status of the injury than on personal, social, and environmental variables, such as personality, age at onset, level of education, cultural and ethnic background, and social support (Crewe & Krause, 2002). Spinal cord injury is associated with sudden and unexpected life changes in many areas, and although there is considerable disagreement about the psychological response to SCI, depression is frequently identified as a common psychological problem (Crewe & Krause, 2002; Livneh & Antonak, 1997).

Changes in body image invoke perceptual distortions that may result in diminished ability to acquire new physical skills and adapt to environmental requirements. Because social, occupational, and financial problems are rather common, disruption of family life and social roles may occur. Possible long-term psychological reactions to the traumatization are passivity, dependency, passive-aggressiveness, frustration, and feelings of social inadequacy and embarrassment (Cull & Hardy, 1975). Increased substance abuse has also been observed among people with spinal cord injury (Crewe & Krause, 2002; Heinemann, 1999). Finally, attitudinal barriers and public misunderstanding may create additional obstacles that impede the person with spinal cord injury from reintegrating into the physical, social, and vocational environments.

Recommendations for Intervention. For the most part, medical interventions for spinal cord injury are (a) surgery (to relieve pressure on the cord), (b) stabilization of the vertebral column, (c) medication (to relieve autonomic disturbances), (d) skin care, (e) bladder and bowel function training, (f) proper dietary control, (g) sexual functioning retraining, and (h) physical and occupational therapy to improve ambulation, mobility, and proper use of extremities (Hu & Cressy, 1992).

Counseling with people who have a spinal cord injury should address problems created by the injury across several domains, including self-concept, acceptance of disability, independent living issues, sexual and marital adjustment, social relationships, and vocational concerns (Crewe & Krause, 2002; Hayes & Potter, 1995; Hu & Cressy, 1992). Issues that frequently concern clients with spinal cord injury are sexual functioning and socialization. Spinal cord injury is likely to affect sexual arousal and function, fertility and pregnancy, and in some cases, care of the newborn. Because of the potential impact on family goals and the close relationship of sexuality and sexual function to self-esteem and personal identity, counseling in this area is essential. Counselors should be prepared to respond to the emotional impact of changes in sexuality and sexual function and be aware that significant advances have been made in recent years in terms of enabling sexual activity (Crewe & Krause, 2002). Counselors should be ready to deal with these and related sexual and marital concerns at any time during the counseling process. Clients may also need to be taught new interpersonal skills (knowing when to refuse unnecessary help or request assistance without feeling inadequate, embarrassed, or guilty).

Other counseling issues to be addressed include coping with the psychological strain associated with loss of independence and needing to rely on others for personal care and daily function; coping with changes in body function, such as occurrences of spasticity, loss of bowel and bladder control, and maintaining skin and muscle health; social isolation; and vocational issues. Substance abuse issues are also important to assess, although they are frequently overlooked by counselors and rehabilitation professionals (Crewe & Krause, 2002; Heinemann, 1999).

Counseling Clients with Cardiac Impairment

Impact of Cardiac Impairment. Cardiovascular diseases are the leading cause of disability and death in the United States. Almost 80 million American adults (one in three) have one or more types of cardiovascular disease; 37.5 million of these are estimated to be age 65 or older (American Heart Association, 2007). The major cardiovascular diseases are (a) hypertensive heart disease (elevated blood pressure); (b) congestive heart failure (the heart's inability to pump sufficient blood to meet the body's requirements),

(c) arteriosclerotic heart disease (buildup of lipid deposits on the inner walls of the arteries, leading to narrowing or blocking of the passages and resulting in a heart attack or coronary thrombosis), (d) heart attack or myocardial infarction (complete occlusion of the coronary artery, resulting in a portion of the heart muscle being deprived of blood supply), (e) rheumatic heart disease (a childhood disease resulting from rheumatic fever that damages the heart muscle and valves), and (f) various congenital heart defects (Falvo, 2005; Rey, 1999).

Physical Impact.   Chief among the functional limitations associated with cardiac impairment are angina pectoris (chest pain), dyspnea (shortness of breath upon exertion), diet restriction, difficulties in tolerating extremes of temperature, and limitations of vocational pursuits (such as restricted walking, climbing, and lifting ability) and avocational pursuits (such as limited ability to engage in various sports activities). The nature and degree of these limitations are linked directly to the severity and duration of the particular impairment involved (Falvo, 2005; Johnson, Getzen, & Alpern, 2002).

Psychosocial Impact.   Individuals affected by cardiac impairments are likely to exhibit reactions of fear and anxiety during the acute illness phase (during and following a heart attack) and long-term depressive reactions. Anxiety and depression are often magnified because of fears of recurrent attacks, forced dependency, other life stresses, sexual dysfunction, marital conflicts, financial worries, returning-to-work issues, and the reduction in preimpairment activities (Falvo, 2005; Johnson et al., 2002; Rey, 1999). In addition, denial of impairment may be present. Denial may take one of the following forms: (a) total denial of being ill or disabled, (b) denial of major incapacitation, (c) minimization of effects of disability, or (d) admission of illness in the past but denial of its present incapacitation. Although denial can represent an adaptive and beneficial response acutely, chronic denial can interfere with medical treatment and efforts to implement behavior modification (Rey, 1999). Other frequent psychological reactions include fear, helplessness, dependency, anger, and frustration (Livneh & Antonak, 1997).

Recommendations for Intervention.   The goals of cardiac rehabilitation are to prolong the patient's life and improve life quality, both psychosocially and vocationally. These goals are accomplished via educating the client on the nature of the impairment and its risk factors, modifying lifestyle (e.g., weight loss; exercise; restricted diet, alcohol, and tobacco consumption), maintaining psychosocial integrity, and sustaining existing vocational abilities (Falvo, 2005; Johnson et al., 2002; Rey, 1999). Medical interventions related to cardiac impairment include (a) surgical procedures (coronary artery bypass grafting, coronary angioplasty, electronic pacemaker implantation, cardiac transplantation), (b) restrictions on existing diet practices (reducing fat intake, restricting salt), (c) building exercise tolerance, (d) avoiding tobacco usage, and (e) medication (such as nitroglycerine, anticoagulants, beta-receptor blockers, calcium channel blockers, diuretics) to manage vessel dilation, chest pain, high blood pressure, heart rate, and so forth (Falvo, 2005; Johnson et al., 2002; Rey, 1999).

Psychosocial management to improve quality of life can be affected by numerous physical, psychological, social, vocational, and financial interventions. Counselors who work with clients with heart disease should construct a comprehensive psychosocial rehabilitation program that incorporates the following elements (Backman, 1989; Rey, 1999).

1. Provide the client with information on the nature of functional limitations linked to heart disease.
2. Train the client in relaxation techniques, such as progressive relaxation and guided imagery, to relieve emotional stress.
3. Encourage the client to ventilate his or her anxieties, concerns, and other negative emotions in a supportive, therapeutic environment.
4. Assist the client in cognitive restructuring, with the goal of modifying irrational and maladaptive emotional reactions and thoughts.
5. Apply behavioral modification procedures to enable the client to acquire appropriate behaviors necessitated by present physical conditions. Clients may be taught new adaptive behaviors through thought stopping of stress-inducing themes, behavioral prescriptions, role-playing exercises, and behavioral rehearsals of new and adaptive behaviors.
6. Pay attention to sexual concerns and misperceptions such as fears about death resulting from sexual activity.
7. Discuss with the client issues related to returning to work. Explore and analyze vocational interests, assets, and limitations, with the goal of achieving successful and functionally appropriate vocational placement.

Counseling Clients with Epilepsy

Impact of Epilepsy.   Epilepsy is one of the most common neurological disorders, with an age-adjusted incidence of between 20 and 70 per 100,000 and a prevalence of 4 to 10 per 1000 worldwide (Jacoby & Baker, 2000). The incidence of epilepsy in the United States is generally agreed to be between 1% and 2% of the population (Livneh & Antonak, 1997). The reported prevalence of active epilepsy in the United States is about 50 per 1000 persons (Thompson & Trimble, 1996). The word *epilepsy* is a generic term, synonymous with convulsive disorder or seizure disorder. These terms refer to a wide variety of seizure conditions rather than a single condition. Epilepsy may develop from a wide variety of causes, including traumatic brain injury, birth trauma, vascular disease, and substance abuse, and a definitive etiology, or cause, is identified in only about a third of all newly diagnosed cases of epilepsy (Hauser, 1997). Approximately 75% of all people with epilepsy developed seizures prior to the age of 21. With appropriate medication, around 60% of those who have epilepsy can become seizure-free, and an additional 15–20% experience a reduction in their seizure frequency (Fraser, 1999).

Physical Impact.   A seizure involves a disruption of the normal electrical activity of the brain; neurons become unstable and fire in an abnormally rapid manner. This excessive electrical discharge results in a seizure, which may be confined to one area and hemisphere of the brain (partial seizure) or may occur throughout the brain in entirety (generalized seizure) (Fraser, Glazer, & Simcoe, 2002). Thus, the specific functional, cognitive, affective, and behavioral impact of epilepsy depends upon the duration and location in the brain of the seizures (Fraser et al., 2002). As a result, "some seizures impair brain functioning slightly, while others result in a complete cessation of normal activities" (Fraser et al., 2002, p. 339). During seizure-free periods, people with epilepsy are fully functioning members of society. Although ability to drive an automobile is usually not affected, differing states' laws require certain seizure-free periods (that may range from 3 to 24 months) before a driving license is issued or reinstated.

Functional limitations often arise as well from the adverse side effects of anticonvulsant medication. These medications, especially when reaching toxic levels, can cause the user to have a wide array of symptoms. Side effects of antiepilepsy medications may include double vision, fatigue, nervousness or agitation, difficulty in concentrating, nausea, dizziness, gum overgrowth, facial hair growth, sexual dysfunction, and occasionally more severe side effects (Baker, Jacoby, Buck, Stalgis, & Monnet, 1997; Fraser et al., 2002). Generally, at least one side effect will be experienced, and Fisher et al. (2000), in a large community-based U.S. study, reported that almost 20% of people reported that the side effects and the cost of antiepilepsy medication were the worst things about having epilepsy.

Psychosocial Impact.   The impact of epilepsy on a person's life is multidimensional and can span a range of functional and psychosocial domains. Along with the potential physical and cognitive problems associated with seizures, epilepsy has been associated with psychological and emotional problems, social isolation, and problems concerning education, employment, family life, and leisure activities (Thompson & Oxley, 1993). The impact and psychosocial consequences of epilepsy cannot always be understood as resulting directly or logically from the occurrence of seizures. In fact, because it is at once a medical diagnosis, a social label, and to some extent, a part of the personal identity, epilepsy "perhaps more than any other disorder, is associated with profound deleterious psychological and sociological consequences that are not directly related to the actual disease process" (Engel, 2000, p. xiii).

The anxiety and stress associated with the anticipation of seizures, the lack of cognitively structured environment for the person with epilepsy, and the perceived discrediting attribute of epilepsy can result in an immensely taxing psychosocial world. Attempts at concealing the condition from friends, employers, and others can lead to further stress and anxiety, which, in turn, can be associated with increased seizures, resentful feelings of embarrassment, shame and guilt, and social isolation. Also, because of the side effects of anticonvulsant medications, people with epilepsy may experience periods of impairment in various mental processes, including memory, attention, problem solving, and judgment (Fraser, 1999), all of which can increase the psychosocial impact.

Recommendation for Intervention.   Medical treatment of epilepsy consists of drug therapy (anticonvulsant medication), vagus nerve stimulation, and in an increasing number of cases, brain surgery. Commonly used anticonvulsant medications, such as carbamazepine (Tegretol), phenytoin (Dilantin), phenobarbital, valproic acid (Depakene), ethosuximide (Zarontin), lamotrigine (Lamictal), topiramate (Topimax), clonazepam

(Klonopin), and primidone (Mysoline), prevent either hypersynchronic neuron discharge or spread of discharge. Surgical intervention generally consists of removal of a portion of the temporal lobe (temporal lobectomy) when seizures are still uncontrollable after medication use (Bowe, 2000; Fraser et al., 2002). The vagus nerve stimulator (VNS) is an implanted device that delivers regular bursts of energy to the brain via the vagus nerve. The VNS appears to have increased effectiveness in seizure reduction over time (Fraser et al., 2002). Also, the ketogenic diet, which features high fat, low carbohydrates, restricted calorie, and no sugar, may be an effective option for children with hard-to-control seizures. Because the diet induces chemical changes in the body, it must be prescribed by a physician and monitored by a physician and a dietician (Epilepsy Foundation, 2007).

General counseling goals include (a) examining the nature of the epileptic seizures and their effect on the client, (b) dispelling the misperceptions held by client and family regarding epilepsy and its functional implications, (c) discussing with client and family ways of coping with the adverse effects of epilepsy, and (d) minimizing the number of areas affected by the existence of epilepsy and assuming responsibility for, and independence in, one's own life. Counselors should encourage clients with epilepsy to become educated about the condition and its management. Denial of epilepsy is not an infrequent occurrence. Because denial is manifested in failure to comply with medication schedules, ignoring requests to avoid alcohol intake, and/or pursuit of hazardous vocational or avocational activities, the counselor must deal with this repudiation of reality.

Counseling Clients with Brain Injury

Impact of Brain Injury.   Traumatic brain injury (TBI) is often referred to as the "silent epidemic." It is a disability that is quite common but does not receive the same level of public and professional attention focused on less frequently occurring disabilities. For example, approximately 1.5 million persons incur a TBI annually (Brain Injury Association of America [BIA], 2006) and 70,000 to 90,000 of those injured live with long-term, functional impairments (National Institutes of Health [NIH], 1999). Traumatic brain injury, as distinguished from other forms of brain damage, occurs when an external force acts on the skull and causes damage to the brain. The external force either penetrates the skull and meninges (i.e., an open-head injury) or causes the brain to bounce back and forth in the skull without penetration (i.e., a closed-head injury) (Cunningham et al., 1999). Motor vehicle accidents represent the most common cause of TBI, followed by falls (NIH, 1999). Other causes of TBI include assaults, machine accidents, handgun use, child abuse, occupational accidents, and sports-related injuries (Cunningham et al., 1999; NIH, 1999).

The NIH (1999) found that TBI most often occurs with men and persons age under 5, 15 to 24, or over 65. TBI is less common for those with college experience and Whites. Sachs (1991) also suggested that persons with TBI often possess histories of learning problems, dangerous work and leisure interests, and treatment for emotional maladjustment. Cunningham et al. (1999) further noted that TBI incidence rates and socioeconomic resources are inversely related.

Physical Impact.   Because TBI results from either direct and localized damage to the brain or more diffuse insult (concussion, brain swelling, intracranial fluid pressure), its physical manifestations are widely varied (Falvo, 2005). Postinjury impacts are dependent on such factors as secondary injury mechanisms (e.g., cellular disturbances and infections; Cunningham et al., 1999) and the specific region of the brain damaged (Lucas & Addeo, 2006). Physical correlates of TBI typically include various perceptual-spatial deficits, such as visual-motor incoordination, visual dysfunction, muscle spasticity, seizures, and aphasia, and TBI might also be associated with headaches, dizziness, lack of energy, and fatigue. These deficits normally affect the ability to read, write, eat, dress, ambulate, and drive (Dixon & Layton, 1999; Schwartz, 2002).

Psychosocial Impact.   Possible cognitive, physical, and psychosocial functional limitations following TBI may impair one's ability to maintain relationships, continue employment, and live independently. Cognitive problems may include problems with memory, attention, concentration, problem solving, visual perception, abstract reasoning, planning, organization, and information-processing skills (NIH, 1999). Common post-TBI physical problems are hemiparesis, muscle spasticity, visual deficits, bowel and bladder dysfunction, and seizures and sensory impairments (Lucas & Addeo, 2006). Frequently experienced psychosocial outcomes include impulsivity, lability, agitation, passivity, dependency, denial, anger, disinhibition, withdrawal, and low self-esteem (Cunningham et al., 1999).

Emotional reactions directly associated with the onset of injury frequently include anxiety, denial, depression, and agitation. Anxiety is manifested through paniclike and catastrophic reactions to the impairment and persistent irritability (Prigatano, 1989). Denial of the disorder is a common reaction among head-injured people and may include minimizing the consequences of the injury, unawareness of injury-related problems, and failure to acknowledge the injury. Depression, which usually sets in following initial acknowledgment of the injury and its consequences, is manifested by low self-regard, feelings of worthlessness, social withdrawal, and generally diminished or blunted affect. Agitation (usually considered a by-product of lower tolerance for frustration) is typified by emotional lability (frequent and easily triggered changes in temperament), anger, irritability, loss of control over emotions, self-centeredness, lack of concern for others' welfare, and impatience (Falvo, 2005; Cunningham et al., 1999).

Among the major struggles persons with TBI face is defining a new life reality. Many persons with TBI compare themselves with their preinjury family, work, and social lives (Prigatano, 1995). Upon realization that life will not be the same, persons with TBI sometimes feel that live is not worth living and may even consider suicide (Baker, Tandy, & Dixon, 2002). Moreover, persons with TBI may abuse drugs and alcohol in an attempt to adjust to their postinjury lives (Rosenthal & Ricker, 2000).

Recommendations for Interventions.   A wide range of interventions are available for helping clients with TBI. Because a substantial number of the TBI survivors manifest behavioral disorders, the goals of most rehabilitation programs have been geared toward decreasing these behavioral disturbances, increasing socially appropriate behaviors, and preparing the individual to enter the community after the acquisition of independent living and, when feasible, educational and vocational skills.

Behaviorally oriented treatment approaches appear to be particularly useful for counseling clients who sustained head injury. Behavioral management, based on operant conditioning principles such as negative reinforcement (to modify or extinguish maladaptive behaviors), positive reinforcement in the form of social praise and tangible rewards (to increase appropriate social behaviors), behavioral shaping (reinforcing approximations of desired responses), and token economies, is often used with TBI clients (Greif & Matarazzo, 1982; McMahon & Fraser, 1988).

Cognitive retraining and cognition remediation are frequently used interventions, based on the principles of cognitive therapy. Using intensive teaching, cognitive retraining, and extensive rehearsal, clients are taught to improve their mental functions and gradually ameliorate their perceptual, verbal, thought-processing, and problem-solving deficits (Ben-Yishay & Diller, 1983). To achieve these targets, counselors adopt a variety of highly structured activities to facilitate learning: memory aids such as written or tape-recorded reminders and diaries, repeated explanations, and multiple examples to gradually instill confidence in the client in her or his ability to cope with the cognitive challenges of everyday life activities, such as problem solving, money management, and time management (Greif & Matarazzo, 1982; Schwartz, 2002).

Two other approaches are family and group counseling. Because TBI can have a profound effect on the family, and because the family has a significant influence on the individual's reaction to the injury, family counseling is an important component of TBI rehabilitation (Falvo, 2005). Group counseling is another beneficial treatment approach to clients with TBI. It offers participants several advantages, notably socialization with persons facing similar problems, expanding one's repertoire of interpersonal behaviors, alleviating isolation and demoralization, learning how others have progressed in overcoming their difficulties, and engaging in supportive, goal-oriented group activities (Cicerone, 1989).

Counseling Clients with Psychiatric Disorders

For the purposes of this chapter, two groups of psychiatric conditions will be discussed: schizophrenia and major depressive disorder. Schizophrenia is one of the most common diagnoses of clients seeking rehabilitation counseling and presents counselors with a number of unique challenges. Depression represents a potentially significantly disabling condition in its own right and is also frequently associated with other disabilities.

Schizophrenia. Schizophrenia represents a heterogeneous group of disorders with certain core clinical features (Hyman, Arana, & Rosenbaum, 1995). Described as the most chronic and disabling of the severe mental disorders, schizophrenia typically develops in the late teens or early 20s. This illness has the potential to curtail career plans, end relationships, and negatively affect not only the people directly affected but also their families and friends. *The Diagnostic and Statistical Manual of Mental Disorders (DSM)*, currently in its fourth edition (text revision; APA, 2000) specifies five major subtypes of schizophrenia: paranoid, disorganized, catatonic, undifferentiated, and residual. The lifetime prevalence rate for schizophrenia in the general population is approximately 1% (Bond, 1999), and approximately 2.4 million Americans are affected by schizophrenia in any given year (NIMH, 2006). Even with available treatment, most people continue to experience symptoms persistently or episodically throughout a large part of their lives. People with schizophrenia attempt suicide much more often than people in the general population. About 10% (especially young adult males) succeed (NIMH, 2007).

Psychosocial Impact of Schizophrenia.   Schizophrenia is known to have two main categories of symptoms, the "positive" symptoms, which are prominent during the active phase of the illness, and the "negative" symptoms, which are prominent during the prodromal and residual phases. Both categories of symptoms have significant psychosocial impact. It is, however, the positive symptoms that typically lead to psychiatric treatment or hospitalization. These positive symptoms reflect an excess or distortion of normal functions and include hallucinations, disorganized speech, and grossly disorganized or catatonic behavior (APA, 2000). The negative symptoms of the illness are equally disabling and include affect flattening, alogia, avolition, anhedonia, withdrawal, social isolation, attentional impairment, and decreased motivation for self-care.

The psychosocial impact of the illness on people with schizophrenia is costly. The behavioral symptoms and significant cognitive deficits impair interpersonal relationships. Common problems in thinking—poor memory, concentration difficulties, distorted or inaccurate perceptions, and difficulty in grasping concepts—become evident in completion of tasks that were easy prior to onset of the disorder. Accompanying this decline are marked impairment in social functioning, vulnerability to stress, and difficulty in coping with normal activities of daily living. It is estimated that persons with schizophrenia account for between a third and half of the U.S. homeless population (Hong, 2002). The incidence of dual diagnosis (i.e., substance dependence) has also been a detrimental factor in the lives of people with schizophrenia (Doughty & Hunt, 1999).

Recommendations for Intervention.   There is currently no cure for schizophrenia, and treatment is aimed at reducing or controlling the symptoms. In the last two decades, there has been a steadily increasing understanding of the biochemical changes associated with schizophrenia, along with identification of changes in the structures that appear to be involved in the development of schizophrenia (Kaplan & Sadock, 1996; NIMH, 2007). It is also known that environmental factors can have an important influence on the development and course of the illness. Current models suggest an individual may have a vulnerability that, when stressful life events occur, leads to the development of symptoms. Stresses may be biological, environmental, or both (Kaplan & Sadock, 1996).

Antipsychotic drugs remain the mainstay treatment for schizophrenia, especially in alleviating the positive symptoms of the illness. Unfortunately, the older antipsychotic medications have noxious extrapyramidal and anticholinergic side effects that contribute to noncompliance with treatment. The extrapyramidal (motor-related) side effects, some of which respond to treatment with antiparkinsonian anticholinergic side effect medications such as trihexyphenidyl (Artane) and benztropine (Cogentin), also have the potential to cause a permanent physically disfiguring condition known as tardive dyskinesia (involuntary stereotypical movements following prolonged dopamine block).

Newer medications, such as clozapine (Clozaril) and risperidone (Risperdal), appear to offer more favorable side effect profiles. Clozapine, originally introduced into the United States in 1990, has been shown to result in few extrapyramidal side effects. People who are prescribed clozapine, however, need to have their blood monitored on a weekly basis, as the side effect of agranulocytosis (depletion of white blood cells) is potentially lethal. Risperidone (Risperdal) which was introduced after clozapine, is devoid of anticholinergic side effects, such as dizziness, blurred vision, urinary retention, and fecal impaction; however, risperidone may produce extrapyramidal side effects at large dosages. Other new antipsychotics on the market also have favorable side effect profiles. These medications include sertindole (Serlect) and olanzapine (Zyprexa), both introduced in 1996, as well as quetiapine fumarate (Seroquel) and aripripazole (Abilitat).

Counseling treatment should be individualized and based on the recognition that each individual experiences the course and impact of schizophrenia in a unique way. Treatment should address both the abilities and the deficits of the individual (Kaplan & Sadock, 1996) and focus on helping clients understand their condition and its impact on social, psychological, and vocational functioning, as well as on helping clients to cope with this impact. Self-management and treatment compliance is an important counseling concern, as individuals with schizophrenia may deny their need for medication or simply stop taking it in response to the frequently significant side effects (Falvo, 2005).

Behavioral approaches, such as social skills training, are aimed at increasing social skills, self-sufficiency, practical living skills, and interpersonal communication skills (Kaplan & Sadock, 1996). The importance of a counseling relationship in which the individual with schizophrenia feels safe has been emphasized, and the ability of the client to form a therapeutic relationship has been identified as an important predictor of treatment outcome (Kaplan & Sadock, 1996).

Major Depressive Disorder.   Depression, also known as major depressive disorder, is a common and costly mental illness that affects approximately 17.6 million Americans each year. Estimates for the cost of depression to the nation in 1990 ranged from $30 billion to $44 billion. Depression also has an astronomical value in lost work, as high as 200 million days each year. By the year 2020, it has been estimated that major depression will be the second most important cause of disability worldwide (Davidson & Meltzer-Brody, 1999). The lifetime risk for major depressive disorder in community samples has varied from 10% to 25% for women and from 5% to 12% for men (APA, 2000).

Psychosocial Impact of Major Depressive Disorder.   The significant psychosocial impact of major depression is suggested by a review of the symptoms of the illness: persistent sad or "empty" mood, loss of interest in pleasurable activities, decreased sexual drive, and increased fatigue. These symptoms often lead to major problems in interpersonal relationships. Very often, the person with depression is misunderstood and blamed for being lazy. On the job, the individual may frequently be tardy or absent, as motivation and energy levels, compounded by feelings of hopelessness, make work seem meaningless. Irritability, lack of interest, and crying spells make coworkers, family, and friends uncomfortable. Insomnia or hypersomnia and a disturbed sleep pattern, coupled with poor memory and concentration difficulties, often affect decision making and general performance at work and at home. Frequent suicidal ideation and attempts put friends and family on edge, further worsening feelings of guilt. In certain cases, the symptoms are accompanied by psychotic features, such as command auditory hallucinations, further increasing the risk for suicide.

Recommendations for Intervention.   Effective pharmacological and psychological treatments for people diagnosed with major depression are available and are frequently used concurrently. Medication includes the traditional tricyclics, heterocyclics, and monoamine oxidase (MAO) inhibitors, which, in addition to causing sedation, weight gain, and orthostatic hypotension, typically have many anticholinergic side effects such as dizziness, blurred vision, constipation, urinary retention, and fecal impaction. The sedation caused by these medications may make it especially difficult to drive or to operate machines on the job. Furthermore, the use of MAO inhibitors calls for strict avoidance of foods containing tyramine, such as aged cheeses, beer, red wines, smoked fish, dry or fermented sausages, caviar, yeast extracts, liver (beef and chicken), and overripe fruit (Diamond, 2002; Kaplan & Sadock, 1996).

Fortunately, the newer antidepressants fluoxetine (Prozac), fluvoxamine (Luvox), sertraline (Zoloft), citalopram (Celexa), and paroxetine (Paxil), known as selective serotonin reuptake inhibitors (SSRIs), lack the anticholinergic side effects and potential cardiotoxicity of the tricyclics. In addition, they are less sedating and do not cause weight gain. In addition to the SSRIs, other new antidepressants have been introduced. They include mirtazapine (Remeron), nefazodone (Serzone), and trazodone (Desyrel) (Diamond, 2002). Venlafaxine (Effexor), an antidepressant introduced into the United States in 1994, inhibits the uptake of the neurotransmitters norepinephrine and serotonin. Bupropion (Wellbutrin), the only antidepressant that works on the dopamine nerve cells, is reported to have fewer anticholinergic side effects than the tricyclics (Diamond, 2002). Electroconvulsive therapy (ECT) is usually reserved for acute disabling episodes of depression and for cases that are refractory to other therapies.

Following are counseling guidelines to be aware of when serving clients with depression (Bishop & Swett, 2000; Livneh & Antonak, 1997):

1. Encourage clients to vent and verbalize feelings of frustration, grief, loss, guilt, self-blame, and shame.
2. Reinforce the client's strengths and assets by rewarding positive self-statements and participation.
3. Set limited, concrete, and short-term goals to assure success in attaining longer term rehabilitation goals.
4. Interrupt and challenge clients' irrational and self-defeating beliefs and statements.

5. Break down problems perceived as unmanageable or overwhelming into smaller, more manageable, and time-bound issues.
6. Reinforce interpersonal contacts, social participation, and the development of social skills.

Training and Qualifications of Counselors Who Work With Clients with Disabilities

Academic Training and Program Accreditation

Academic training of counselors whose interest lies in working with clients with disabilities is accomplished through rehabilitation counselor education (RCE) programs. These training programs are typically graduate (master's level) programs offered by counselor education or counseling psychology departments. The programs normally require 2 years of academic and clinical training to complete on a full-time basis. Delivery of rehabilitation counseling coursework through distance education options, such as web-based courses and video conferencing, is increasingly used by programs around the country.

The curriculum content in most of these training programs has been developed and verified by the Council on Rehabilitation Education (CORE). CORE was established in 1971 as an accreditation body to oversee the academic and clinical training of rehabilitation counselors and promote effective delivery of rehabilitation services to people with disabilities. There are 102 RCE programs currently accredited by CORE. These programs must show evidence of a graduate-level curriculum that provides its trainees with a course of study that includes, but is not limited to, the following knowledge and/or skill areas: (a) history and philosophy of rehabilitation; (b) rehabilitation legislation; (c) organizational structure of the rehabilitation system (public and private, nonprofit, and for-profit service delivery); (d) counseling theories, approaches, and techniques; (e) case management; (f) career development and vocational counseling theories and practices; (g) vocational evaluation, occupational information, job analysis, and work adjustment techniques; (h) job development and placement; (i) medical aspects of disability; (j) psychosocial aspects of disability; (k) knowledge of community resources and services; (l) rehabilitation research and program evaluation; (m) measurement, appraisal, and testing; (n) legal and ethical issues in rehabilitation counseling; (o) human growth and development; (p) social and cultural diversity; (q) independent living; (r) consultation services; (s) service coordination; and (t) special topics in rehabilitation (such as transition from school to work, supported employment, rehabilitation engineering). In addition, rehabilitation counseling trainees are required to participate in supervised practicum and internship experiences totaling a minimum of 600 clock hours in approved rehabilitation sites and under the supervision of a certified rehabilitation counselor.

Certification and Licensure

The Commission on Rehabilitation Counselor Certification (CRCC) is the primary certifying body of rehabilitation counselors in the United States. The main purpose of CRCC is to assure that professionals who practice counseling with clients with disabilities (rehabilitation counseling) meet acceptable standards of professional expertise. In accordance with the knowledge and skill areas required by CORE for program accreditation purposes, CRCC tests rehabilitation applicants on a broad range of content subjects. The duration of the certification is 5 years, at the end of which the certified rehabilitation counselor (CRC) is required to have accumulated a total of 100 approved contact (clock) hours of continuing education to maintain his or her certification.

State-regulated licensure of counselors who work with clients with disabilities is usually accomplished through the enactment of omnibus state legislation that governs the practice of various professional counselor groups (mental health, marriage and family, community, rehabilitation). These state laws regulate individuals in the use of the title ("professional counselor"), as well as the practice of the profession.

Professional Associations

At present, the following national professional organizations offer membership to counselors who seek to specialize in working with clients with disabilities: (a) the American Rehabilitation Counseling Association (ARCA), a division of ACA; (b) the Rehabilitation Counselors and Educators Association (RCEA), a division of the National Rehabilitation Association (NRA); (c) the National Rehabilitation Counseling Association (NRCA); (d) the Rehabilitation Psychology Division (Division 22) of the American Psychological Association (APA); and (e) the National Association of Rehabilitation Professionals in the Private Sector (NARPPS).

ARCA, NRCA, and RCEA are organizations representing professional rehabilitation counselors and others concerned with improving the lives of persons with disabilities (educators, researchers, administrators). These organizations have as their mission the provision of leadership to promote excellence in rehabilitation counseling practice, training, research, consultation, and professional growth. They further emphasize the importance of modifying environmental and attitudinal conditions and barriers so that more opportunities become available to persons with disabilities in employment, education, and community activities. The membership of ARCA, NRCA, and RCEA is composed of rehabilitation counselors, educators, and other practitioners employed in both the public and private sectors (divisions of vocational rehabilitation, commissions for the blind and visually impaired, hospitals and rehabilitation units, mental health centers, rehabilitation workshops, university services for students with disabilities, self-help organizations, and private rehabilitation organizations).

The Rehabilitation Psychology Division of the APA represents members (mainly psychologists) who are interested in the psychosocial consequences of disability and rehabilitation (personal adjustment and growth, coping strategies, social and attitudinal barriers) in order to better serve persons with disabilities. This division is equally interested in the development of high standards and practices for professional psychologists who serve clients with disabilities. Most of the division members are educators, researchers, and practicing psychologists whose clientele is mainly persons with physical, psychiatric, and cognitive impairments.

Finally, NARPPS is an organization whose members are invariably committed to the advancement of rehabilitation practices in the private for-profit rehabilitation sector. Although traditional counseling activities make up only a minor portion of the job tasks performed by private rehabilitation professionals, they nonetheless offer individual and group counseling services to clients as may be required for achievement of sound vocational choice and successful job placement. Members of NARPPS typically are rehabilitation counselors, rehabilitation nurses, vocational evaluators, and job placement specialists.

Summary

The purpose of this chapter was to acquaint the beginning counseling student with (a) the meaning of disability, (b) the impact of various disabling conditions on the client, (c) intervention strategies commonly adopted by counselors who work with clients with disabilities, and (d) the academic programs, their accreditation procedures, certification and licensure considerations, and the professional organizations of counselors who serve clients with disabilities. Counselors who intend to pursue the career of rehabilitation counseling and specialize in working with clients with disabilities may find it advantageous to directly contact these organizations through their Web sites. The following Web sites provide additional information relating to the chapter topics.

USEFUL WEB SITES

The Commission on Rehabilitation Counselor Certification
http://www.crccertification.com/

American Rehabilitation Counseling Association
http://www.arcaweb.org

National Rehabilitation Counseling Association
http://nrca-net.org/

The Council on Rehabilitation Education
http://www.core-rehab.org/

Rehabilitation Psychology Division of the American Psychological Association
http://www.apa.org/divisions/div22/

National Rehabilitation Association
http://www.nationalrehab.org/

National Council on Disability
http://www.ncd.gov/

REFERENCES

Albrecht, G. L. (1992). *The disability business: Rehabilitation in America*. Newbury Park, CA: Sage.
American Cancer Society. (2007). *Cancer facts and figures, 2007*. Retrieved April 15, 2007, from http://www.cancer.org/docroot/PRO/content/PRO_1_1_Cancer_Statistics_2007_Presentation.asp

American Foundation for the Blind. (2007). *Statistics and sources for professionals*. Retrieved April 30, 2007, from http://www.afb.org/info_document_view.asp?documentid=1367

American Heart Association. (2007). *Heart disease and stroke statistics—2007 update*. Dallas, TX: American Heart Association.

American Psychiatric Association. (2000). *Diagnostic and statistical manual of mental disorders* (4th ed., text revision). Washington, DC: Author.

Americans With Disabilities Act of 1990, 42 U.S.C.A. § 12101.

Backman, M. E. (1989). *The psychology of the physically ill patient: A clinician's guide*. New York: Plenum.

Baker, G. A., Jacoby, A., Buck, D., Stalgis, C., & Monnet, D. (1997). Quality of life of people with epilepsy: A European study. *Epilepsia, 38*, 353–62.

Baker, K. A., Tandy, C. C., & Dixon, D. R. (2002). Traumatic brain injury: A social worker primer with implications for practice [Electronic version]. *Journal of Social Work in Disability & Rehabilitation, 1*(4), 25–42.

Ben-Yishay, Y., & Diller, L. (1983). Cognitive deficits. In M. Rosenthal, E. Griffith, M. Bond, & J. Miller (Eds.), *Rehabilitation of the head injured adult* (pp. 167–182). Philadelphia: F. A. Davis.

Bishop, M., & Feist-Price, S. (2002). Quality of life assessment in the rehabilitation counseling relationship: Strategies and measures. *Journal of Applied Rehabilitation Counseling, 33*(1), 35–47.

Bishop, M., & Swett, E. (2000). Depression: A primer for rehabilitation counselors. *Journal of Applied Rehabilitation Counseling, 31*(3), 38–45.

Bolton, B. (Ed.). (1976). *Psychology of deafness for rehabilitation counselors*. Baltimore, MD: University Park Press.

Bond, G. R. (1999). Psychiatric disabilities. In M. G. Eisenberg, R. L. Gleuckauf, & H. H. Zaretsky (Eds.), *Medical aspects of disability: A handbook for the rehabilitation professional* (2nd ed., pp. 412–434). New York: Springer.

Bowe, F. (2000). *Physical, sensory, and health disabilities: An introduction*. Upper Saddle River, NJ: Merrill.

Brain Injury Association of America. (2006). *TBI incidence: A comparison of traumatic brain injury and leading injuries or diseases*. Retrieved on June 10, 2006, from http://www.biausa.org

Cicerone, K. D. (1989). Psychotherapeutic interventions with traumatically brain injured patients. *Rehabilitation Psychology, 34*, 105–114.

Crewe, N. M., & Krause, J. S. (2002). Spinal cord injuries. In M. G. Brodwin, F. Telez, & S. K. Brodwin (Eds.), *Medical, psychosocial and vocational aspects of disability* (2nd ed., pp. 279–292). Athens, GA: Elliott & Fitzpatrick.

Cull, J. G., & Hardy, R. E. (1975). *Counseling strategies with special populations*. Springfield, IL: Charles C. Thomas.

Cunningham, J. M., Chan, F., Jones, J., Kamnetz, B., Stoll, J., & Calabresa, E. J. (1999). Brain injury rehabilitation: A primer for case managers. In F. Chan & M. J. Leahy (Eds.), *Healthcare and disability case management* (pp. 475–526). Lake Zurich, IL: Vocational Consultants Press.

Davidson, J. R., & Meltzer-Brody, S. E. (1999). The underrecognition and undertreatment of depression: What is the breadth and depth of the problem? *Journal of Clinical Psychiatry, 60*(7), 4–9.

Diamond, R. J. (2002). *Instant psychopharmacology: A guide for the nonmedical mental health professional* (2nd ed.). New York: Norton.

Dixon, T. M., & Layton, B. S. (1999). Traumatic brain injury. In M. G. Eisenberg, R. L. Gleuckauf, & H. H. Zaretsky (Eds.), *Medical aspects of disability: A handbook for the rehabilitation professional* (2nd ed., pp. 98–120). New York: Springer.

Doughty, J. D., & Hunt, B. (1999). Counseling clients with dual disorders: Information for rehabilitation counselors. *Journal of Applied Rehabilitation Counseling, 30*(3), 3–10.

Engel, J., Jr. (2000). Foreward. In G. A. Baker & A. Jacoby (Eds.), *Quality of life in epilepsy: Beyond seizure counts in assessment and treatment* (pp. xiii–xiv). London: Harwood Academic Publishers.

Epilepsy Foundation. (2007). *Ketogenic diet*. Retrieved April 3, 2007, from http://www.epilepsyfoundation.org/

Ey, S., Compas, B. E., Epping-Jordan, J. E., & Worsham, N. (1998). Stress responses and psychological adjustment in cancer patients and their spouses. *Journal of Psychosocial Oncology, 16*, 59–77.

Falvo, D. R. (1999). *Medical and psychosocial aspects of chronic illness and disability* (2nd ed.). Gaithersburg, MD: Aspen.

Falvo, D. R. (2005). *Medical and psychosocial aspects of chronic illness and disability* (3nd ed.). Gaithersburg, MD: Aspen.

Fraser, R. T. (1999). Epilepsy. In M. G. Eisenberg, R. L. Gleuckauf, & H. H. Zaretsky (Eds.), *Medical aspects of disability: A handbook for the rehabilitation professional* (2nd ed., pp. 225–244). New York: Springer.

Fraser, R. T., Glazer, E., & Simcoe, B. J. (2002). Epilepsy. In M. G. Brodwin, F. Telez, & S. K. Brodwin (Eds.), *Medical, psychosocial and vocational aspects of disability* (2nd ed., pp. 339–350). Athens, GA: Elliott & Fitzpatrick.

Freidenbergs, I., & Kaplan, E. (1999). Cancers. In M. G. Eisenberg, R. L. Gleuckauf, & H. H. Zaretsky (Eds.), *Medical aspects of disability: A handbook for the rehabilitation professional* (2nd ed., pp. 137–153). New York: Springer.

Greif, E., & Matarazzo, R. G. (1982). *Behavioral approach to rehabilitation.* New York: Springer.

Hahn, H. (1993). The political implications of disability definitions and data. *Journal of Disability Policy Studies, 4,* 41–52.

Harvey, E. (2002). Hearing disabilities. In M. G. Brodwin, F. Telez, & S. K. Brodwin (Eds.), *Medical, psychosocial and vocational aspects of disability* (2nd ed., pp. 143–156). Athens, GA: Elliott & Fitzpatrick.

Hauser, W. A. (1997). Incidence and prevalence. In J. Engel Jr. & T. A. Pedley (Eds.), *Epilepsy: A comprehensive textbook.* Philadelphia: Lippincott-Raven.

Hayes, R. L., & Potter, C. G. (1995). Counseling the client on wheels: A primer for mental health counselors new to spinal cord injury. *Journal of Mental Health Counseling, 17*(1), 18–31.

Hecht, M., Anderson, P., & Ribeau, S. (1989). The cultural dimensions of nonverbal communication. In M. Asante & W. Gudykunst (Eds.), *Handbook of international and intercultural cmmunication* (pp. 163–185). London: Sage.

Heinemann, A. W. (1999). Spinal cord injury. In M. G. Eisenberg, R. L. Gleuckauf, & H. H. Zaretsky (Eds.), *Medical aspects of disability: A handbook for the rehabilitation professional* (2nd ed., pp. 499–527). New York: Springer.

Hong, G. K. (2002). Psychiatric disabilities. In M. G. Brodwin, F. Telez, & S. K. Brodwin (Eds.), *Medical, psychosocial and vocational aspects of disability* (2nd ed., pp. 107–118). Athens, GA: Elliott & Fitzpatrick.

Hu, S. S., & Cressy, J. M. (1992). Paraplegia and quadriplegia. In M. G. Brodwin, F. Telez, & S. K. Brodwin (Eds.), *Medical, psychosocial and vocational aspects of disability* (pp. 369–391). Athens, GA: Elliott & Fitzpatrick.

Hyman, S. E., Arana, G. W., & Rosenbaum, J. F. (1995). *Handbook of psychiatric drug therapy* (3rd ed.). Boston: Little, Brown.

Jacoby, A., & Baker, G. A. (2000). The problem of epilepsy. In G. A. Baker & A. Jacoby (Eds.), *Quality of life in epilepsy* (pp. 1–12). London: Harwood Academic Publishers.

Johnson, J., Getzen, J., & Alpern, H. L. (2002). Cardiovascular disease. In M. G. Brodwin, F. Telez, & S. K. Brodwin (Eds.), *Medical, psychosocial and vocational aspects of disability* (2nd ed., pp. 237–250). Athens, GA: Elliott & Fitzpatrick.

Kangas, M., Henry, J. L., & Bryant, R. A. (2002). Posttraumatic stress disorder following cancer: A conceptual and empirical review. *Clinical Psychology Review, 22,* 499–524.

Kaplan H. I., & Sadock, B. J. (1996). *Concise textbook of clinical psychiatry.* Baltimore, MD: Williams & Wilkins.

Kerman-Lerner, P., & Hauck, K. (1999). Speech, language, hearing and swallowing disorders. In M. G. Eisenberg, R. L. Gleuckauf, & H. H. Zaretsky (Eds.), *Medical aspects of disability: A handbook for the rehabilitation professional* (2nd ed., pp. 245–272). New York: Springer.

Kraus, J. F., & Sorenson, F. B. (1994). Epidemiology. In J. M. Silver, S. C. Yudofsky, & R. E. Hales (Eds.), *Neuropsychiatry of traumatic brain injury* (pp. 3–41). Washington, DC: American Psychiatric Association.

Livneh, H., & Antonak, R. F. (1997). *Psychosocial adaptation to chronic illness and disability.* Gaithersburg, MD: Aspen.

Llewellyn, A., & Hogan, K. (2000). The use and abuse of models of disability. *Disability & Society, 15*(1), 157–165.

Lubkin, I. M. (Ed.). (1998). *Chronic illness: Impact and* intervention (4th ed.). Boston: Jones & Bartlett.

Lucas, J. A., & Addeo, R. (2006). Traumatic brain injury and postconcussion syndrome. In P. Synder, P. D. Nussbaum, & Diana L. Robin (Eds.), *Clinical neuropsychology: A pocket handbook for assessment* (2nd ed., pp. 351–380). Washington, DC: American Psychological Association.

Martin, E. D. (1999). Foundations of the rehabilitation process. In G. L. Gandy, E. D. Martin, & R. E. Hardy (Eds.), *Counseling in the rehabilitation process: Community services for mental and physical disabilities* (2nd ed., pp. 5–31). Springfield, IL: Charles C. Thomas.

McAleer, C. A., & Kluge, C. A. (1978). Counseling needs and approaches for working with a cancer patient. *Rehabilitation Counseling Bulletin, 21,* 238–245.

McMahon, B. T., & Fraser, R. T. (1988). Basic issues and trends in head injury rehabilitation. In S. E. Rubin & N. M. Rubin (Eds.), *Contemporary challenges to the rehabilitation counseling profession* (pp. 197–215). Baltimore, MD: Paul H. Brooks.

Moos, R. H., and Tsu, V. D. (1977). The crisis of physical illness: An overview. In R. H. Moos (Ed.), *Coping with physical illness* (pp. 3–21). New York: Plenum.

National Association of the Deaf. (2007). *What is wrong with the use of these terms: "deaf-mute," "deaf and dumb," or "hearing-impaired"?* Retrieved April 10, 2007, from http://www.nad.org/deafanddumb

National Institute on Deafness and Other Communication Disorders. (2007). *Statistics about hearing disorders, ear infections, and deafness.* Retrieved April 10, 2007, from http://www.nidcd.nih.gov/health/statistics/hearing.asp

National Institute of Mental Health. (2006). *The numbers count: Mental disorders in America.* Retrieved April 10, 2007, from http://www.nimh.nih.gov/publicat/numbers.cfm#Schizophrenia

National Institute of Mental Health. (2007). *Schizophrenia.* Retrieved April 10, 2007, from http://www.nimh.nih.gov/publicat/schizoph.cfm#suicide

National Institutes of Health. (1999). *Report of the NIH consensus development conference on the rehabilitation of persons with traumatic brain injury.* Bethesda, MD: U.S. Department of Health and Human Services.

Orr, L. E., & Orange, L. M. (2002). Cancer. In M. G. Brodwin, F. Telez, & S. K. Brodwin (Eds.), *Medical, psychosocial and vocational aspects of disability* (2nd ed., pp. 171–184). Athens, GA: Elliott & Fitzpatrick.

Panek, W. C. (2002). Visual disabilities. In M. G. Brodwin, F. Telez, & S. K. Brodwin (Eds.), *Medical, psychosocial and vocational aspects of disability* (2nd ed., pp. 157–170). Athens, GA: Elliott & Fitzpatrick.

Parker, R. M., Schaller, J., & Hansmann, S. (2003). Catastrophe, chaos, and complexity models and psychosocial adjustment to disability. *Rehabilitation Counseling Bulletin, 46*(4), 234–241.

Patterson, J. B., DeLaGarza, D., & Schaller, J. (2005). Rehabilitation counseling practice: Considerations and interventions. In R. Parker, E. Szymanski, & J. Patterson (Eds.), *Rehabilitation counseling: Basics and beyond* (4th ed., pp. 155–186). Austin, TX: Pro-Ed.

Prevent Blindness America. (2002). *Vision problems in the U.S.: Prevalence of adult vision impairment and age-related eye disease in America.* Retrieved August 15, 2003, from http://www.nei.nih.gov/eyedata/pdf/VPUS.pdf

Prigatano, G. P. (1989). Bring it up in milieu: Toward effective traumatic brain injury rehabilitation interventions. *Rehabilitation Psychology, 34,* 135–144.

Prigatano, G. P. (1992). Personality disturbances associated with traumatic brain injury. *Journal of Consulting and Clinical Psychology, 60,* 360–368.

Prigatano, G. P. (1995). The problem of lost normality after brain injury. *Journal of Head Trauma Rehabilitation, 10*(3), 87–95.

Rey, M. J. (1999). Cardiovascular disorders. In M. G. Eisenberg, R. L. Gleuckauf, & H. H. Zaretsky (Eds.), *Medical aspects of disability: A handbook for the rehabilitation professional* (2nd ed., pp. 154–184). New York: Springer.

Rosenthal, B. P., & Cole, R. G. (1999). Visual impairments. In M. G. Eisenberg, R. L. Gleuckauf, & H. H. Zaretsky (Eds.), *Medical aspects of disability: A handbook for the rehabilitation professional* (2nd ed., pp. 565–585). New York: Springer.

Rosenthal, M., & Ricker, J. (2000). Traumatic brain injury. In R. G. Frank and T. R. Elliott (Eds.), *Handbook of rehabilitation psychology* (pp. 49–74). Washington, DC: American Psychological Association.

Ryder, B. E. (2003). Counseling theory as a tool for vocational counselors. *Journal of Visual Impairment & Blindness, 97*(3), 149–156.

Sachs, P. R. (1991). *Treating families of brain-injury survivors*. New York: Springer Publishing Company.

Schnoll, R. A., Knowles, J. C., & Harlow, L. (2002). Correlates of adjustment among cancer survivors. *Journal of Psychosocial Oncology, 20*(1), 37–59.

Schwartz, S. H. (2002). Traumatic brain injury. In M. G. Brodwin, F. Telez, & S. K. Brodwin (Eds.), *Medical, psychosocial and vocational aspects of disability* (2nd ed., pp. 363–374). Athens, GA: Elliott & Fitzpatrick.

Smart, J. F. (2001). *Disability, society, and the individual*. Austin, TX: Pro Ed.

Smart, J. F. (2004). Models of disability: The juxtaposition of biology and social construction. In T. F. Riggar & D. R. Maki (Eds.), *Handbook of rehabilitation counseling* (3rd ed., pp. 25–49). New York: Springer.

Smart, J. F., & Smart, D. W. (2006). Models of disability: Implications for the counseling profession. *Journal of Counseling and Development, 84*(1), 29–40.

Steinmetz, E. (2004). *Americans with Disabilities: 2002*. Current Population Reports, P70–107. Washington, DC: U.S. Census Bureau.

Szymanski, E. M. (1999). Disability, job stress, the changing nature of careers, and the career resilience portfolio. *Rehabilitation Counseling Bulletin, 42*, 279–289.

Thomas, K. R., Thoreson, R. W., Parker, R. M., & Butler, A. (1998). Theoretical foundations of the counseling function. In R. M. Parker & E. M. Szymanski (Eds.), *Rehabilitation counseling: Basics and beyond* (3rd ed., pp. 225–268). Austin, TX: Pro Ed.

Thompson P., & Oxley, J. (1993). Social aspects of epilepsy. In J. Laidlaw, A. Richens, & D. Chadwick (Eds.), *A textbook of epilepsy* (4th ed., pp. 661–704). London: Churchill Livingstone.

Thompson, P. J., & Trimble, M. R. (1996). Neuropsychological aspects of epilepsy. In I. Grants & K. M. Evans (Eds.), *Neuropsychological assessment of neuropsychiatric disorders* (2nd ed., pp. 263–288). New York: Oxford University Press, Inc.

Twelfth Institute of Rehabilitation Issues. (1985). *Rehabilitation of the traumatic brain injured*. Menomonie, WI: University of Wisconsin-Stout, Vocational Rehabilitation Institute, Research and Training Center.

Vander Kolk, C. J. (1983). Rehabilitation counseling with the visually impaired. *Journal of Applied Rehabilitation Counseling. 14*(3), 13–19.

Vash, C. (1981). *The psychology of disability*. New York: Springer.

Wright, B. A. (1983). *Physical disability: A psychosocial approach*. New York: Harper & Row.

Wright, S. J., & Kirby, A. (1999). Deconstructing conceptualizations of "adjustment" to chronic illness: A proposed integrative framework. *Journal of Health Psychology 4*(2), 259–272.

INDEX